*An athletics compendium*

# An Athletics Compendium

## An Annotated Guide to the
## UK Literature of Track and Field

*Compiled by*

Tom McNab, Peter Lovesey, Andrew Huxtable

THE BRITISH LIBRARY
2001

First published 2001 by

The British Library
Boston Spa, Wetherby
West Yorkshire LS23 7BQ

ISBN: 0 7123 1104 1

Series Editor: A E Cunningham

Printed in Great Britain

# Acknowledgements

Numerous individuals contributed to this work and its predecessor, *The Guide to British Track and Field Literature 1275-1968*, but there are some whose encouragement, enthusiasm and practical assistance were indispensable. Outstanding among them is Richard Bond, whose suggestions first started arriving over thirty years ago, and who generously put his personal hand-written catalogue at our disposal, and steadily supplied additions. Richard introduced Hamish Thomson to the project, and through him another remarkable catalogue was made available by e-mail. Two collectors nearer home, David Terry and Kevin Kelly, not only opened their homes and awe-inspiring personal libraries to one of the compilers, but fed him lunch as well as information and advice. Dr Greg Moon, the biographer of Albert Hill, was frequently on the phone to suggest new avenues of research. We thank each of these friends and enthusiasts.

We would also like to express our gratitude to the many others who made substantial contributions, among them Bob Adey, Neil Allen, Don Anthony, Melvyn Barnes, Mike Bateman, Geoff Bradley, Joe Brett, John Bromhead, Ian Buchanan, Eric Cowe, John Goulstone, Stan Greenberg, the late David Guiney, Dr Trevor James, John Keddie, Marvin Lachman, Douglas Mack, Peter Matthews, Andy Milroy, Keith Morbey, Wilf Morgan, Colm Murphy, Tony O'Donoghue, Bob Phillips, Roy Profitt, Warren Roe, Jonathan Rosenthall, Ian R. Smith, David Thurlow, Mel Watman, Richard O. Watson and Clive Williams.

Particular thanks are also due to Sir Eddie Kulukundis, Conical of St Albans, and UK Athletics for their kind financial assistance.

Bibliographic facilities become accessible and user-friendly through the work of dedicated individuals. We wish to thank Dr Richard W. Cox (UMIST) and the staff of the British Library at St Pancras and the Sport England Information Unit at Euston for their invaluable assistance over the past few years. Our own local libraries also contributed substantially to the project, and we are grateful to their staff.

The staff of the British Library Bibliographic Service ensured that our quite disparate skills and enthusiasms were co-ordinated to the best possible effect. The tact, expertise and sheer hard work of Arthur Cunningham, Karen Liddle and Cynthia McKinley made this book into a reality. John M. Jenkins, the author of *A Rugby Compendium,* gave practical help at various stages.

In a work of this kind representing many years of research there are inevitably some omissions and errors, try as one might to strive for accuracy. The most unforgivable omissions are the names of individuals who helped. We apologise to everyone who is not mentioned by name.

Tom McNab
Peter Lovesey
Andrew Huxtable

# Contents

*L. Literature & the Visual Arts*

*M. Reference Works*

# How To Use This Book

*An Athletics Compendium* is a bibliography of books on track and field published in the United Kingdom or Republic of Ireland up to the end of the year 2000, and a guide to that literature. Its aim has been that of any bibliography, to bring together for the convenience of reader and researcher the literature of a discrete area of human activity, the better that it may be accessed, understood, and built upon.

To this end, it includes many titles which do not have athletics as their main focus, but which nevertheless contain information difficult or impossible to find elsewhere and the inclusion of which is necessary to provide a rounded and comprehensive coverage. Some categories of material are excluded. Though newspapers contain the minutiae of records, event reports and commentary which is often the very stuff of research, it would be impractical to attempt an index of such material. Equally, though boys' annuals might yield the occasional item of merit or interest, the research effort required to identify them was deemed disproportionate to the likely return. Both categories are thus excluded. Ephemeral material such as programmes, and promotional and souvenir items are likewise excluded, although occasional instances of these categories may be included to make or illustrate a specific point or where it is thought they may be of particular interest to the researcher. The scope of this compilation is limited to published material: unpublished research and public records are not included.

Though reprints are not included, new editions *are* listed. In the case of serial publications such as *Yearbooks*, *Guides*, and *Annuals* the entry gives the year in which the titles started publication and, if known, the year in which publication ceased. Periodicals are included at title level; individual articles are not. Journal literature is invaluable in providing news and up-to-date information on current topics of interest, on research and work-in-progress. It is also often the means by which new topics for study and research are introduced, trends reported and general communication within a discipline or subject area facilitated. Such information dates quickly and, in this electronic age, is inappropriate for inclusion in a printed bibliography, being best accessed through secondary sources of information – specialist indexing and abstracting services, such as *Sport Bibliography*, a database with international coverage produced by the Sport Information Resource Centre (SIRC) in Toronto. Many such services have long been available as online databases, and many are now available as CD-ROMs or through the World Wide Web, where specialist sites and discussion groups are rapidly taking the place of the traditional learned journal.

Such sites represent a completely new type of resource which the development of the Internet has made possible: where information that it would never have been economic to disseminate in printed form, can be made available in a structured way to users, often free or at low cost. The last few years have seen an explosion in the number of web sites offering information on practically every subject in which there is an academic or hobbyist interest. The resources made available by this burgeoning technology are beyond the scope of this compilation, but the reader's attention is drawn to Richard Cox's useful, albeit dated, *The Internet as a Resource for the Sports Historian* (Frodsham: Sports History Publishing, 1995).

In the main, the entries in this bibliography are derived from the holdings of the British Library (the national library of the United Kingdom), but have been considerably enhanced by the compilers' extensive use of other public and private collections. In some instances, however, full bibliographic information has not been available to the compilers. Such entries have been included only where they have been confident that the item actually exists, even though it has not been possible to obtain full details. Further information on these items, and indeed on any omissions or mistakes in this bibliography, will be gratefully received by the compilers and incorporated in any future edition.

As a specialist subject bibliography, *An Athletics Compendium* does not include those general reference sources which are to be found in any major reference library. These are no substitute for a subject's own specialist literature but can sometimes supply hard to find or otherwise unavailable information, for example most titles in the *Victoria History of the Counties of England* series have a chapter on sport which may well include references to athletics. Another example would be professional or other directories which may include elusive biographical information not readily found elsewhere. Equally, general indexing and abstracting services should not be overlooked for the material they might throw up from journals in other disciplines.

For a similar reason, books on sport in general, or which contain only a section or chapter on athletics, are only included if the compilers have judged their athletic content to be of particular significance. There is a vast and ever-growing literature on sport and sport history, which increasingly provides topics for academic study and research. Such research is illuminating whole areas of British social history and what has already appeared has more than proved the worth of such study. However, unless the compilers have felt such items to be particularly relevant to the literature of athletics they have been omitted.

## ✱ *Arrangement & Layout*

The chapter headings used reflect the categories to be found in the literature and it has thus been possible to list most items just once. Where the scope of a work cuts across the boundaries of the chapter headings, the book has been listed in the most relevant chapter and index entries created under all other appropriate headings. In a few cases where it has been judged more helpful to the user, books have been listed in more than one section.

The order in which books have been listed within each chapter is in most cases immediately apparent, and is always the order considered most useful for the reader. For example, biographies are arranged in alphabetical order by the name of the biographee; competitions, such as the Olympics, are arranged chronologically. Elsewhere the usual arrangement is by date of publication. When more than one book has been published in the same year, they are further arranged alphabetically by title.

Within each lettered chapter books are numbered sequentially, e.g. A1, A2 etc. A new sequence of numbers starts with each chapter. In this way every book has a unique reference comprising the chapter letter and the number of the book within the chapter.

The bibliographic information within each record and the format in which the information is given is in accordance with current bibliographic standards. Not all records will contain the same level of information. Some books, for example, do not give their place of publication. In such instances the entry may therefore omit this information.

All records, whether derived from the catalogue of the British Library or elsewhere, have been arranged in a uniform way. Every effort has been made to include all the information necessary to uniquely identify the item in order to facilitate its purchase, or enable users to obtain it on loan from a public or other library.

A typical entry is laid out below.

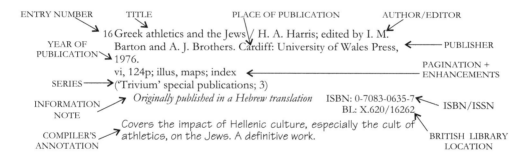

N.B. The location numbers for books held in the British Library refer to books which are not available for loan. They are only available for consultation in the British Library when it is not possible for a reader to consult them elsewhere. Various restrictions may also apply to particular items. Enquiries concerning use of the Library's Reading Rooms should be made in writing to: The British Library, Reader Admission Office, 96 Euston Road, London NW1 2DB.

✱ *Abbreviations used in the Entries*

BL – British Library
D – BL copy destroyed during WW2
ed. – edition
illus – illustrated
ISBN – International Standard Book Number
ISSN – International Standard Serial Number
p – pages
pbk – papreback
rev. – revised
SBN – Standard Book Number
vol. – volume

# The Literature of Athletics

## Overview

Thom's *Pedestrianism* (1813), the first book specifically devoted to athletics, is a rich mixture of biography, history and training manual. It describes the feats of Captain Barclay Allardice, who in 1809 became the first man to walk a thousand miles in a thousand hours. *Pedestrianism* outlines his training methods and provides a comprehensive list of running performances of the eighteenth and early nineteenth centuries.

Captain Barclay's main claim to fame lies in remaining awake at speeds of around three and a half miles per hour, but it is only fair to observe that he ran a mile in four minutes fifty-six seconds and a quarter of a mile in fifty-six seconds, good achievements for the period. But though the Captain's training methods endured in one form or another until well into the twentieth century, they were essentially the conventional wisdom of an earlier period and echoed those previously described in Sir John Sinclair's *The Code of Health and Longevity*, published in 1806.

Thom's performance statistics relate solely to running and provide us with our main understanding of eighteenth century athletics. He observes that the Scot John Todd ran a mile in four minutes ten seconds from Hyde Park Corner to the first milestone in the Uxbridge Road, but makes no comment on the unlikely nature of Todd's feat, or of the achievement of 'Skewball, the Lancashire Shepherd' in running twelve seconds for a hundred and forty yards at Hackney in 1808. Thom's naivety as a chronicler undoubtedly reflects the nature of athletics at the time, of matches run over uncertain distances on turnpike roads or racecourses, with the use of the stopwatch half a century away.

Most of the technical manuals which followed *Pedestrianism* concentrated mainly on endurance running and repeated the Barclay line, with its emphasis on sweating and purging. And though there is occasional mention of field events (often in works on gymnastics), these usually amount to little more than cursory descriptions. Thus, though there was a growth in field event-based rural sports towards the third quarter of the century, these events are not reflected strongly in the technical literature. This is because in the pre-amateur period the public interest lay in running matches with, in the second half of the century, the addition of pedestrian carnivals and a handicap running-based amateur movement.

The first substantial account of amateur athletics is H. F. Wilkinson's *Modern Athletics* (1868). Wilkinson provides a list of amateur and professional records, but, like most subsequent historians, shows little interest in pedestrianism or rural sports. Here I would observe that, as in most of the works of this period, the professional records in field events are incomplete, giving little sense of the rich, highly-competitive nature of Lakeland and Scottish Highland and Border Games. Two decades later, Montague Shearman's monumental *Athletics and Football* (1887) provides an understandably more comprehensive account of amateur athletics' early years, but again, like Wilkinson, he fails to pay much attention to the depth and density of the professional sport. Amateurism ruled.

Almost forgotten, but ranking with Shearman's work, is *The Pedestrian's Record* (1890) by the Lupton brothers, an early attempt to link athletics training with science. They dismiss Barclay's methods as 'calculated to send a man to the grave rather than the cinder path', echoing a general rejection by university-based amateurs of the Captain's regimes. *The Pedestrian's Record* is a work of great vision, in which the Luptons recommend the creation of a 'Jockey Club' of athletics, embracing both amateur and professional codes. Had this been enacted at this early period in the sport's development, then the history of world athletics would have taken a quite different path.

McCombie Smith's *The Athletes and Athletic Sports of Scotland* (1891) takes an understandably more critical view of the amateur movement than either Wilkinson or Shearman and provides us with a rare glimpse of nineteenth century professional Scottish Highland Games. Like the Luptons, McCombie Smith was a radical, making strong recommendations on meet presentation and more accurate measurement and he is rigorous in his assessment of Scottish jumping and throwing performances.

Three other works, Donaldson's *Men of Muscle* (1901), Miller's *Scottish Sports and How to Excel in Them* (1910) and Sutherland's privately published *Scientific Athletics* (1912) reveal the strength of Scottish rural athletics immediately prior to the Great War. Alas, there is no work of similar depth on Lakeland athletics, except possibly Machell's *Some Records of the Annual Grasmere Sports* (1911), which lacks technical content.

The first major work of the twentieth century on the ancient Olympics, Gardiner's *Greek Athletic Sports and Festivals* (1910), was of such quality as to leave little room for later writers. For Gardiner's is a ravishing work, of immense erudition and intelligence, containing a greater range of visual material than most Olympic works which followed it.

Technical works of the last quarter of the nineteenth century reflect the limited nature of competitive athletics in Britain at the time, understandable in that the AAA had existed for less than twenty years, and that the bulk of competition outside of the leading universities consisted of running-based handicap meetings. Not surprisingly, the first substantial technical books came from the United States, where the collegiate competitive structure was beginning to catch up with a strong East Coast club system.

The most impressive of these early works was Mike Murphy's *Athletic Training* (1914). Murphy, who died in 1913, was the inventor of the crouch start, coach to the 1912 United States Olympic team, and father to the Hollywood actor George Murphy. The author of a second book, *Athletics in Theory and Practice* (1913) was the Swede Ernest

Hjertberg, recruited from American collegiate athletics to prepare Sweden for the 1912 Stockholm Olympics. Hjertberg's book was of similar quality to Murphy's, though stronger on field events.

That same pre-war period saw the arrival of F. A. M. Webster's first book, *Olympian Field Events* (1913). Webster lacked at that point the practical experience of either Hjertberg or Murphy, but showed a remarkable early ability to apply scientific rationale to athletics techniques.

A similar attempt to apply scientific discipline to athletics was made by Sam Mussabini, immortalised in the Oscar-winning film *Chariots of Fire*. Mussabini had avidly studied slow-motion film and the photographic sequences of Eadweard Muybridge, in an attempt to analyse athletic movement. Alas, his studies produced only the 'cross arm' action, ludicrous sprinting body-angles and the advocacy of the 'dab' start, a method which had been superseded by Murphy's invention forty years before. Mussabini's advocacy of 'Black Jack', a laxative calculated to stir into violent action the most sluggish of bowels, shows him to be firmly locked in the nineteenth century. A fine coach, his great strength undoubtedly lay in his conditioning of runners and in their psychological preparation, at a time when both areas were poorly developed in the amateur sport.

1913 produced a work quite out of its time: *The Olympic Games and the Duke of Westminster's Appeal for £100,000*, a detailed account of the British Olympic Association's preparations for the 1916 Berlin Olympics. Although only around ten percent of the total sum required was ultimately raised, the BOA nevertheless went about the appointment of national coaches in athletics, swimming and cycling. It is significant that the Amateur Athletic Association (AAA), in appointing the Scots-Canadian W. R. Knox (a Highland Games athlete), realised and accepted the sparseness of technical knowledge within its harrier-based culture. It is also significant that another Highland Games athlete, Sergeant W. Starkey, was later appointed as one of the trainers to the 1924 Paris Olympic team. This is a remarkable work, showing that early in the development of the Olympic movement, British officials had understood and fully accepted its significance, and had realised that sports performance could not in future be left to chance.

The 1920s-40s period saw the rapid evolution of the technical manual, led by F. A. M. Webster. In the United Kingdom, most of these were written by coaches working in universities and public schools, men like Alec Nelson and Guy Butler, or by ex-athletes such as Harold Abrahams and Douglas Lowe. In this period, The Achilles Club pioneered a more specialised kind of technical work, using athletes and coaches. There was, however, no equivalent of the marvellous American Spalding series, which began in the first decade of the century, of which Henry Schulte's *Pole Vault* (1926) and Dink Templeton's *High Jump* (1928) were exceptional.

The 1920s saw the last flutter of the old trainer-coaches, with *The Secret of Athletic Training* (1925) by Harry Andrews and W. S. P. Alexander, and Sam Mussabini's *Running, Walking and Jumping* (1926). Their time was now over, and the Abrahams brothers' *Training for Athletes* (1928) showed the way forward. Alas, English insularity continued to prevail and the Abrahams' book resolutely refused to cover such events as triple jump, pole vault, discus and javelin.

Webster was probably the first writer to reflect the growing interest in women's athletics after the Great War, with *Athletics of To-day for Women* (1930). Here, I would observe that the American Chris Herrick had, earlier, supplied a chapter on athletics in Lucille Hill's *Athletics and Out-door Sports for Women* (1903). The second half of the century saw George Pallett's *Women's Athletics* (1955) and Denis Watts and Lionel Pugh's excellent *Athletics for Women* (1962).

The two great English technical writers of the pre-war period were undoubtedly F. A. M. Webster and Guy Butler. The latter was strongly running-based and pioneered the use of sequence photography. Of the two, Webster was the more eclectic and added to his technical knowledge a profound understanding of the history of amateur athletics. It is a revelation to re-visit the works of Webster, to reflect that for over forty years he toiled without complaint and with little recognition in a sport whose establishment resisted coaching and all that it represented. Hundreds of thousands of words poured from his pen, into a sport strongly based in public schools and universities but weak in Britain's harrier-based clubs. Understandably, many of Webster's technical and training ideas have failed to stand the test of time but it must never be forgotten that in the first half of the century he undoubtedly led the world of athletics coaching. The sport owes him a great debt.

In contrast, Webster's early contemporary, Sam Mussabini, left little behind him for succeeding generations. For Sam was, for all his study of slow-motion photography, firmly rooted in nineteenth century pedestrianism. His main strength lay in his conditioning programmes and in his ability to manage men and bring them to peak condition for major competitions, and this was no small talent. Alas, that talent did not travel in time. The pity is that Mussabini, unlike that other pragmatist, the American Dean Cromwell, was unable to fix his magic upon the printed page. For future generations, Cromwell's *Championship Technique in Track and Field* (1941) is possibly the finest work in English of the first half of the twentieth century.

The immediate pre-war period saw two histories recording the first fifty years of the Amateur Athletic Association (AAA) and the Scottish Amateur Athletic Association (SAAA). Both reveal the essentially conservative nature of both bodies, with little mention of formal planning for future development and even less mention of women's athletics. The AAA history *Fifty Years of Progress, 1880-1930* (1930) reveals the still essentially Oxbridge and public school ethos of athletics at that time, while its Scottish equivalent, *Fifty Years of Athletics* (1933) ignored the rich culture of rural games from which Scottish amateur athletics had been derived.

In 1943, the Scot David Jamieson penned the definitive history of professional running, *Powderhall and Pedestrianism*. This is a wonderful work and the only regret is that Jamieson, who had witnessed such great professionals as Harry Hutchens and A. R. Downer in vibrant action, did not attempt to cover the history of the sport in Europe, the colonies, and the United States. This being said, we have Peter Lovesey's *The Kings of Distance* (1968), the richest writing on professional foot racing that we are likely to encounter. Lovesey's account of Deerfoot and the George-Cummings clashes bring into vivid life an age now as distant from us as Custer and Sitting Bull.

The post-war period saw a radical change in the organisation of British coaching, with the appointment of a dynamic and creative AAA Director of Coaching, G. H. G. Dyson. The AAA Coaching Booklets written by the AAA National Coaches were not the first specialist coaching works in English. As already noted, Spalding had produced in the United States a fine series in the 1910-30 period, books which still make excellent reading.

The AAA booklets did not, however, mean the end of the general manual on track and field athletics, with coaches such as Le Masurier, Watts, Paish and indeed myself producing a prolific flow of material between 1950 and 1990. From the United States came Bresnahan, Tuttle and Cretzmeyer's arid *Track and Field Athletics* (1947), and the still immensely readable *Modern Track and Field* (1953) by Ken Doherty.

The AAA-based manuals initially took a strongly biomechanical line, but I and coaches such as Paish increasingly advocated a more practical, pragmatic approach, and in the 1970s more stress was laid on specialised conditioning and in the phasing of training.

If the fifty year anniversaries of the Amateur Athletic Association and the Scottish Amateur Athletic Association had been low-key works, then the equivalent centenary publications were books of a quite different nature. Lovesey (AAA) and Keddie (SAAA) took approaches which were poles apart, with Keddie taking an event-based approach and Lovesey a direct chronological one. Both resulted in works which, for all the limitations of official accounts, contribute richly to our knowledge of athletics history.

The 1970s witnessed a flood of excellent books on long distance running, driven by the marathon boom in the United States. This was repeated in the UK in the 1980s, the catalyst being the 1981 London Marathon, which stimulated a plethora of works on distance running and with it an increasing focus on its physiology and psychology.

The most popular of these was the American Jim Fixx's *The Complete Book of Running* (1979). Fixx's book is essentially an astute scissors and paste collage rather than a coaching manual and relates to fitness-running rather than to competitive athletics. The period following the first London marathon saw many excellent works on distance running, where Harry Wilson, Denis Watts and Bruce Tulloh were outstanding, but the three great books are unquestionably Fred Wilt's *Run, Run, Run* (strangely, never published in the UK), Peter Coe and Dr David E. Martin's *Better Training for Distance Runners* (1997) and Tim Noakes' monumental *Running Your Best* (1995). The American Wilt was essentially an enthusiastic collator rather than a coach, and the material in *Run, Run, Run*, written by diverse authors, varies considerably in quality. What Wilt's book attempted to do was to move distance running away from 'seat of the pants' coaching to a more rational, scientifically-based approach and this he does excellently. Peter Coe's book could have produced two separate, albeit complementary, works: the first physiologically-based and the second centering on practical coaching. Instead, his partnership with David Martin produced a seamless work of high quality, combining practical knowledge with solid theoretical underpinning. *Better Training for Distance Runners* is immensely readable and will endure for many years as a standard work. Noakes' *Running Your Best* is possibly best described as a compendium and is a rich mine of practice and theory which any athlete and coach can profitably explore. More extensive than the Coe book (in that it goes well beyond middle-distance running), it is a similarly definitive work, a fine mix of theory and practice, and will be an essential source of reference well into the twenty-first century.

The best Olympic histories are undoubtedly Duff Hart-Davis's *Hitler's Games* (1986) and Mandell's *The Nazi Olympics* (1972). Both men apply a clinical historical rigour to their analysis of the 1936 Berlin Olympics and to the Olympic movement, in distinct contrast to much of the Olympic history of the second half of the century.

In 1992 Jennings and Simpson's acid *The Lords of the Rings* appeared, presenting a quite different view of the Olympic movement than previous bland, uncritical, historical accounts. Similarly Turnbull's *Steve Ovett: Portrait of an Athlete* (1982) and Harris's *The Legend of Lovelock* (1965), gave a realistic picture of modern athletics light-years away from the general run of biographies.

As we move into the twenty-first century, there are a few clearly visible patterns in athletics literature. Thus, though the marathon boom has flattened, there still appears to be a strong demand for books on distance running and with it literature on attendant areas such as sports nutrition. We will also undoubtedly see more on such subjects as plyometrics, weight training, and sports psychology.

The demand for comprehensive technical manuals has unquestionably slackened. This may reflect a move away from after-school sport, the provision by governing bodies of more specialised coaching literature and the work of the National Coaching Foundation. And, though much of the literature on sports psychology has been similarly generic, there will probably be more specifically athletic works similar in nature to javelin thrower Steve Backley's *The Winning Mind: a Guide to Achieving Success and Overcoming Failure* (1996).

Though the general athletics book has probably had its day, there is still a need for practical manuals dealing with curricular athletics teaching and the group coaching of young club athletes. Curricular teaching has been paid little attention since my now dated *Modern Schools Athletics* (1966). Similarly, group coaching within clubs has received scant attention, possibly reflecting a declining club population.

What is still signally lacking in the coaching literature is the humane, pragmatic approach taken by the American coach Dean Cromwell in his *Championship Technique in Track and Field* (1941) for, though the present manuals deliver far more knowledge on technique and training than was available to Cromwell, they rarely relate to the athlete as a human being and their practical impact is thereby lessened. And, behind much of the literature, academically correct though it may be, is the assumption that there is a direct correlation 'twixt volume of knowledge in such areas as biomechanics and energy systems, and effective coaching. Thus too much weight has been given in the literature to academic knowledge and too little to the product of practical experience.

Leaving aside the official histories of Keddie and Lovesey, and Mel Watman's fine 1968 work, there is a significant lack of an in-depth warts-and-all history of British athletics, though Downes and Mackay's *Running Scared* (1996) points the way to a more rigorous examination of our recent history. We therefore know little of such issues as the growth pains of British coaching in the Dyson era, the collusion of governing bodies in doping and the breaching of amateur rules, our failure to support an Olympic boycott in 1936, or the death struggles of the British Athletics Federation. Thus, though the economics of publishing make it unlikely, there is a need for a substantial history of British athletics, before many of its twentieth century protagonists depart the field.

Modern Olympic history (particularly the last quarter of the twentieth century) is another area which is ripe for fresh literature, preferably written by authors who have not inhaled the heady vapours of 'Olympism'. So, also, is the socio-political history of international athletics, but all such literature requires the impartiality and rigour of professional historians of the calibre of a Gardiner or a Duff Hart-Davis. Similarly, though biography has always been a type of fiction, I would hope that future athletics biographers would push the envelope to provide a more realistic picture of modern athletics.

## Rural Games

'Pas de documentation, pas d'histoire' best describes the pre-1800 period, Thom's *Pedestrianism* (1813) being our only clear window into the literature of pre-nineteenth century athletics performance. Alas, Thom makes no reference to hurdles or field events and only passing comment on sprints. There is, therefore, little reference in the formal literature to track and field athletics prior to 1800.

This does not, however, mean that the sport did not exist, for it undoubtedly enjoyed particularly vibrant life in rural Ireland, north-west England and the Borders and Highlands of Scotland. That life was, however, a parochial one, of local champions rarely venturing to compete far beyond their homes. Only with the rapid development of the railway system and transatlantic travel in the second half of the century did these champions begin to travel beyond their villages and develop national and even international reputations. In Scotland, this developed within a primitive Highland Games 'Grand Prix' circuit, similar to that which had occurred in the Mediterranean two thousand years before, but without offering comparable incomes.

Shearman, in his monumental *Athletics and Football* (1887), makes only passing reference to rural sports, giving the impression that they had disappeared, superseded by the amateur movement, and shows little understanding of their extent or quality of performance. This is understandable, since Shearman undoubtedly saw athletics as a middle-class movement, bringing 'lesser breeds within the law'. McCombie Smith, in his *The Athletes and Athletic Sports of Scotland* (1891) understandably takes a more robust and perceptive view, and gives us our best picture of the personalities and performances in the Highland Games of the second half of the nineteenth century.

McCombie Smith's work understandably centres on what was an essentially field events culture and on throwing events in particular. He makes it clear that a major problem in making judgements on performance lay in the variable conditions under which Highland Games took place, for this was not a world of take-off boards, flat runways and standard implements. Thus, McCombie Smith has to deal with shots, hammers and ringweights weighing anything from 14lbs to 56lbs, sloping throwing and jumping areas, and 'triple jumps' which could be a hop, step and jump above the Highland Line and two hops and jump below it.

If he is occasionally harsh, then the context outlined above provides adequate explanation, and possibly explains his unwillingness to give full credit even to Donald Dinnie (his brother-in-law), probably the greatest all-round field event athlete of the nineteenth century.

McCombie Smith fails to make more than cursory reference to the rich culture of Scottish Border Games, one as strong as that of the Highland Games until the Great War. These Border Games, like their Highland and Lakeland counterparts, shared, in the May to September period, the 'pedestrian' population with the Highland Games, often on a handicap basis. Unlike the throwing-based Highland Games, the Border Games stressed running and jumping, with standing jumps a particular feature. It is therefore not surprising that it was a Border jumper, William Hogg of Hawick, who may have been the first athlete in the world to break 15 metres in triple jump on level ground (at Alva in 1893) possibly with two hops and a jump. The Border Games did not ignore throwing, but many of their throws, employing standard weights, were 'throws with follow', which made them impossible to compare with Highland performances.

It is possibly for this reason that McCombie Smith gives Border Games such short shrift. Border Games also regularly featured two events specific to them, the six pound shot throw and the 'hitch and kick'. The former was almost certainly a javelin-type throw and a similar event was held (albeit with a much heavier weight) in the Intercalated Olympic Games of 1906. The hitch and kick involved jumping to kick a tambourine or suspended pig's bladder with the take-off foot, and was a standard Border event, never travelling beyond the Highland Line. It re-surfaced, surprisingly, in the New York Highland Games of the 1890s and the great Irish-American high jumper Mike Sweeney still holds the 'record' at nine feet two inches. Indeed, the 1945 Amateur Athletic Union handbook still contained specific rules for the hitch and kick.

The other major Highland Games book is *Men of Muscle* (1901) by the Glasgow journalist William Donaldson. This is not a history, rather a collection of mini-biographies of the 'heavies' of the 1850-1900 period, originally printed as articles in the *Glasgow Evening Times*. It has consequently much more performance detail than McCombie Smith's book, but Donaldson attempts little evaluation of performance or technical comment, and there is only passing reference to running and jumping. *Men of Muscle* does, by inference, paint a picture of a dense, throwing-based, field events culture, and provides a detailed account of the performances of the great Donald Dinnie. It also provides a brief but fascinating glimpse of the Scottish-Canadian John McPherson, a slip of a man who appeared briefly in Scotland in the 1890s to defeat the giants of the Games circuit.

Up till recently, the period between 1900 and 1960 was thought to be almost totally devoid of Highland Games literature. Fortunately, the recent discovery of William Sutherland's privately published *Scientific Athletics* (1912) has provided valuable information on the period between 1900 and the Great War. The core of *Scientific Athletics* consists of unexceptional descriptive and prescriptive material on the events of the Games. Its main focus of interest for athletics historians lies in two other areas.

The first is in a list of the performances of hitherto little-known athletes such as the all-round jumper James Speedie (six feet three inches high jump 1911) and George Murray (twenty-three feet nine inches long jump, 1907). Sutherland's performance lists, though probably far from complete, show a Scottish Games culture at its peak, teeming with jumpers and throwers of high calibre, several capable of winning Olympic medals.

The second element of interest in *Scientific Athletics* is Sutherland's personal training diary, which gives a detailed account of his training from the age of eleven until 1912, when he was twenty years of age. Sutherland, based in the Rogart area of Sutherland, followed as a boy an all-round programme of running, throwing and jumping that would find favour with any modern coach. By the age of twenty, at a bodyweight of only ten stone ten pounds, he had launched the sixteen pound shafted hammer to a massive hundred and twenty feet and the shot to forty-eight feet ten inches. Sutherland's diary is a moving account of a young farm labourer's slow, lonely passage towards athletics success. He appears to have confined most of his competitive life to the remote Rogart area and consequently never competed against A. A. Cameron or the other leading Scottish throwers of the period. There is no record of William Sutherland beyond 1912 and it seems likely that he perished in the Great War.

J. J. Miller's *Scottish Sports and How to Excel in Them* (1908) covers similar ground to *Scientific Athletics*. Like Sutherland's book, it is short on prescriptive advice, but contains in-depth biographical accounts of the Scottish throwers of the 1850-1912 period. Miller's book is significant for its failure to contain a single mention of the great Donald Dinnie, akin to a history of prizefighting without reference to John L. Sullivan.

Fortunately, David Webster and Gordon Dinnie's definitive biography of Dinnie *Donald Dinnie: the First Sporting Superstar* (1999) has recently appeared, and shows Donald Dinnie to be a giant of nineteenth century athletics, and probably the greatest all-round wrestler of his era.

The period from *Scientific Athletics* to the present day has produced several works, but, apart from the Dinnie biography, none of these has added much of substance to our knowledge. Though outside the scope of this guide, an exception is Redmond's *The Highland Games in the United States* which provides our main insight into the development of Scottish Games in the USA. Redmond makes it clear that the Games provided the basis for the American Inter-Collegiate programme, which had its origins in the universities of the East Coast. It is, therefore, hardly surprising that the AAU handbook of 1945 contains detailed rules for such Celtic events as hitch and kick and the 56lb weight throw for height and distance. More surprising is the inclusion of similarly detailed rules for the potato race, the three-legged race, the sack race and a running high jump from a springboard!

By 1920, with a generation of young men lost in foreign fields, the Scottish Border Games were all but dead, English Lakeland Games were fading and even the Highland Games would never return to their former glory. As with pedestrianism, rural sports suffered from the looseness of their organisation, their lack of any central governing body. In 1948, the Edinburgh Scot Tom Young formed the Scottish Games Association, drawing together an almost dead pedestrianism and the surviving Highland, Border and Lakeland Games. The SGA in no way resembled its equivalent amateur organisations, being essentially a loose assembly of local games.

British rural games had, from the mid-nineteenth century, been the province of mainly agricultural workers in field events, to which was added a mix of athletes from mining and steel communities for the running competitions. Shunned by amateur athletics, rural sports possessed no coaching, no clubs, no facilities, no developing national and international competitive structure to stimulate performance. By 1914, trial and error performance development in rural sports had virtually ended and it was only in the period a decade after the Second World War that there was a fitful revival in performance, partly stimulated by amateur training methods and defections from amateur ranks. Alas, the sport suffered from a shrinking base in agricultural and heavy industry, and the competition provided by more active amateur bodies, now supported by Government grants.

Post-World War II performances were therefore for some time almost static. Indeed, had Donald Dinnie or A. A. Cameron returned to compete in a Highland Games of the late 1940s, they would have been able to dominate them just as they had done in their prime.

A paradox in money-based Highland Games is the fact that they were almost invariably sponsored and supported by local lairds who had been nurtured in the public school/university amateur tradition. Had the lairds, in the final quarter of the nineteenth century, insisted on prizes in kind, rather than cash, then the Games would have been amateur and a weak British field events culture might well have been transformed. Such a policy would almost certainly have brought British professional foot-racing to a rapid conclusion.

Our only record of the Lakeland Games of north-west England is Machell's detailed account of the Grasmere Games *Some Records of the Annual Grasmere Sports 1852-1910* (1911). Machell's book is much narrower in scope than the works of either McCombie Smith or Donaldson and gives no general picture of what was undoubtedly a rich Lakeland sports culture. Similarly, no detailed account exists of the even richer Border Games movement or of a dense amateur Irish rural culture.

It is also sad that the last descriptions of the Highland Games lie in the Edwardian period. We have therefore little idea from the literature of the great Scottish 'heavies' Clark, McLennan and Starkey in the 1920-40 period or even of the greatest Scottish all-rounder of all time, Jay Scott, who competed in the 1950s and 1960s.

The entry of the great amateur shot-putter Arthur Rowe in 1964 injected new life into Highland Games and Rowe, quickly absorbing the skills of hammer, caber and ringweight, demolished records that had stood for decades, and provided excellent competition for that great Scottish 'heavy' Bill Anderson. Later, there was a steady flow of ex-amateurs such as Geoff Capes and Doug Edmunds to the Games circuit.

After a century of bitter antagonism to the rural sports which had provided the basis for Scottish amateur athletics, the Scottish Athletic Federation finally abandoned all pretensions to amateurism. Fortunately, the Scottish Games Association continues to administer its own Games and yearly publishes a handbook of records. It is both significant and touching that many of these date back over a hundred years.

It was inevitable that British rural sports, crippled by the losses of the Great War, weakened by a declining agricultural and heavy industry population, and lacking central organisation, should decline rapidly in the twentieth century. Equivalents of the Lakeland Games survived in Kent, the north east and parts of the south west and Wales until the pre-war period and in Yorkshire until the late 1950s. The Border Games had a fitful minor revival in the post-World War II period, then declined to the level of their Lakeland neighbours. Only the Highland Games survived in recognisable form, sustained by tourism and sheer weight of tradition.

In the 1980s, mutations of the Highland Games, spawned from television 'Strong Man' competitions, enjoyed a thankfully-brief vogue. It would, however, be naive to imagine that the Games' 'heavy' events will not continue to suffer some pollution from the movement of steroidal amateur athletes into the Games circuit. This transfer has possibly had its greatest impact in the United States and Canada, where a flourishing Games circuit often features separate competitions for women and junior men.

In Scotland itself, a major problem is proving to be a lack of young throwers with experience of traditional Scottish events and the recent tendency of Games organisers to omit 'light' field events such as pole vault and triple jump. Another concern has been the degree to which Games' conditions should remain unchanged, particularly in events such as pole vault and high jump. Traditionalists have argued, with some justification, that the Games are not conventional athletic meetings and that the 'test' they offer is to compete under primitive, agricultural conditions.

Going into the twenty-first century, it is doubtful if we shall see much addition to the body of literature on our rural sports. The works of McCombie Smith, Machell, Donaldson and Sutherland will remain our window into a world now almost as remote from us as the Cotswold Games of Robert Dover.

## Biography

One of the best sporting biographies of the nineteenth century is *Pedestrianism* by Thom (1813), not because it gives any particular insight into the character of its subject, Captain Barclay Allardice, but because, as already mentioned, it is our only account of the performances of the eighteenth and early nineteenth century. Similarly, biographies of E. C. Bredin (*Running and Training*, 1902) and A. R. Downer (*Running Recollections, and How to Train*, 1908) are of value mainly because of their contribution, albeit limited, to our understanding of nineteenth century pedestrianism.

In the final half of the century, other professional athletes such as W. G. George and Alf Shrubb also produced technical books thinly laced with autobiography. The first half of the twentieth century saw little in the way of biographies of amateurs. A similar work, *Cinder-Path Tales* (1900) by a sprinter, William M. Lindsey, provides us with our only snapshot of American professional athletics.

Biography is the most prolific, but probably the weakest, area of athletics literature. Most biographies are of athletes and usually consist of little more than a list of events and performances, interwoven with innocuous anecdotes. Where administrators such as Avery Brundage and Juan Antonio Samaranch are the subjects, there is often a steep descent into hagiography. Here, David Miller's *Olympic Revolution: the Biography of Juan Antonio Samaranch* (1992) is a classic example, with barely passing reference to His Excellency Samaranch's fascist antecedents.

The best biography of the pre-war period is probably W. R. Loader's *Testament of a Runner* (1960), a vivid account of the author's struggle to break even time for 100 yds in pre-war Oxford University. Rooted in a similar environment and period, Olympic four hundred metre hurdler Robert Tisdall's *The Young Athlete* (1934) is less rich, but provides a clear picture of a world that now seems as distant as that of the ancient Greeks.

In the post-war period, we have Roger Bannister's *First Four Minutes* (1955), probably the best athletics autobiography ever written, and Norman Harris's *The Legend of Lovelock* (1965), a sensitive account of the career of the 1936 Olympics 1500m gold medallist.

American biographies of the highest quality are *Mike Sweeney of the Hill* (Putnam, 1940 – regrettably never published in this country), and *High Above the Olympians* (Bud Spencer, 1960), the story of 'Dink' Templeton. Both are based on the lives of American coaches and it is perhaps a reflection of the importance of the coach in the United States that Sweeney and Templeton have merited such fulsome and substantial biographies.

Of the two works, that on Templeton is the more interesting, relating as it does to an irascible iconoclast, a leader in his field. No one with an interest in the history of coaching in the United States should fail to read *High Above the Olympians*. Templeton spent his life as a university coach, but Mike Sweeney spent forty years at the Hill as a preparatory school coach. World high jump record-holder for seventeen years, he was clearly a magnificent mentor of youth.

Both Sweeney and Templeton were excellent examples of a long-past breed of American coach, men like Knut Rockne, 'Pop' Warner and Dean Cromwell. Bred in American high schools and universities, they had, alas, no equivalent in British sport.

The best biographical account of an administrator is unquestionably Peter Ueberroth's *Made in America* (1986), his description of his work in organising the 1984 Los Angeles Olympic Games. The latter marked a watershed in an Olympic movement blighted by scandal and boycott since the 1972 Munich Olympics. Ueberroth made the Olympic Games for the first time a prized object, sought by governments in every continent. He is ruthless in his assessment of Olympic *blazerati*, and it is perhaps not surprising that no place was ever found for him in the councils of the IOC.

## *The Olympics*

Olympic histories fall into three broad categories. The first comprises accounts of the ancient Games. The revival of the Games in modern times sparked historical studies such as Arthur Lynch's *Religio Athletæ* (1895), and *The Olympic Games, BC 776-AD 1896* (1896). The early twentieth century produced what is probably the definitive book on the ancient Olympics, Norman Gardiner's *Greek Athletic Sports and Festivals* (1910). This is a magnificent work, matched only by Harris's *Greek Athletes and Athletics* (1964).

It is doubtful if Baron Pierre de Coubertin had the work of such historians in mind when he revived the Olympic Games in 1896. If he did, then he ignored the essentially professional nature of the ancient Games, preferring instead to give them a public school/Oxbridge ethos. Many years later, in his *Olympic Memoirs* (1931; English translation 1979), a slim, tantalising work, de Coubertin was to confess that he saw neither virtue nor logic in amateurism and that as early as 1912 he had lost all belief in it:

> To me, sport was a religion, with its church, dogmas, service … but above all a religious feeling and it seemed to me as childish to make all this dependent on whether an athlete had received a five franc coin as automatically to consider the parish verger an unbeliever because he receives a salary for looking after the church.

Alas, by then it was too late. The nations of the world, bedazzled by a British Empire which, like de Coubertin, they believed to be based on public school games and sports and the amateur ethic, had bought into 'Olympism' and there was no way back.

De Coubertin's expressed lack of belief in the amateur ethic is rarely reflected in the second category of Olympic books, the histories of the modern Olympic movement. Written in the main by physical educationists, these works rarely record or reflect de Coubertin's deep reservations about amateurism. Neither do they pay much attention to the way in which the IOC ignored the holes gouged in its amateur code by the Swedes in 1912, American colleges from 1920 onwards, the Nazis in 1936 or the Communist Bloc in the second half of the century.

Such histories also tend to play down the fact that de Coubertin was cold-shouldered by the Greeks in 1896 and the French in 1900. He did not attend the 1904 Olympics, was ignored by the Greeks in their Intercalated Games of 1906, and his 1908 Games (originally planned for Rome) took place only because Britain took over responsibility for them. By 1926, de Coubertin had relinquished control of the IOC and he died in 1937 with a pension from Hitler's government.

There is usually little attention paid to such inconvenient facts in most Olympic histories, or to the drug-tainted nature of much modern Olympic performance. Here, a handful of works written by professional historians or journalists stand out as notable exceptions. Two accounts of the 1936 Olympics, Duff Hart-Davis's *Hitler's Games* (1986) and Mandell's *The Nazi Olympics* (1972) approach the Olympic movement with cool, academic rigour. Both writers conclude that the IOC failed miserably to challenge the Nazi regime on its persecution of Jewish sportsmen and women. They also indict Avery

Brundage for his dishonest report to the United States AAU on the Jewish issue, one which staved off an American Olympic boycott by a mere one and a half votes.

The latter half of the century did, however, see several works on the history of the modern Olympics, the best of these coming from the United States from physical educationists such as John Lucas and John J. MacAloon. Here Wallechinsky's *The Complete Book of the Olympics* (1984) must also be mentioned, for though it would lay no claim to be a comprehensive Olympic history, it is the definitive compilation of results and a rich pudding of Olympic trivia.

The most impressive recent Olympic histories have come from writers outside of sport and relate to the 1936 Olympic Games. Duff Hart-Davis's *Hitler's Games* (1986) and Mandell's *The Nazi Olympics* (1972) have already been mentioned and are works of the highest quality. Similarly, it was an outsider, Peter Ueberroth, who was to provide a significant early insight into the arcane world of the International Olympic Committee, in his *Made in America* (1986). Ueberroth's book is compulsive reading, although it is significant that for all his frankness he makes no mention of his organising committee's attempt to exclude drug testing or of 'lost' positive urine samples in the Los Angeles Games. This apart, most Olympic history has been relatively uncritical, with occasional lapses into hagiography such as David Miller's previously noted biography of Olympic President Juan Antonio Samaranch, *Olympic Revolution* (1992).

Simson and Jennings' *The Lords of the Rings* (1992) could not by any measure be called a hagiography and is a notable contribution to modern Olympic history. If even half of what is contained in *The Lords of the Rings* is true, then the modern Olympic movement, for all its windy rhetoric about 'Olympism', stands discredited. Alas, the main problem with Simson and Jennings' book is not the accuracy of its claims, but the relentless shrillness of its tone. Thus we still await a rigorous, clinical evaluation of the Olympic movement, worthy of such past writers as Duff Hart-Davis and Mandell.

The final, more limited, category, is the Olympic Report. Of these, the 1908 and 1912 Reports stand out as magnificent accounts, not only of the Games themselves, but of the minutiae of their preparations. Here, the 1912 Stockholm Report is most revealing, recording that the Swedes were probably the first nation to formally prepare for the Olympics. In doing so, they drove a coach and horses through amateur regulations by basing their athletes in Stockholm for over three months before the Games. There is no mention of broken-time payments, but no doubt that they were made. This is the first occasion of Olympic authorities turning a blind eye to blatant breaches of the amateur rules to which they expressed such dedication.

The sports historian occasionally comes upon a work which is the athletics equivalent of the Dead Sea Scrolls and, outside of early Olympic Reports, I have recently become aware of two rare treasures. The authorship of *The Olympic Games and the Duke of Westminster's appeal for £100,000: a historical survey of the movement for better organisation in the British preparations for the Berlin Games of 1916, compiled from The Times and official sources* (1913) is uncertain, though Sir Arthur Conan Doyle is a likely suspect. It is an account of the first British attempt to formally prepare for an Olympic Games (Berlin, 1916) and contains the arguments for and against in the columns of *The Times*. This is a work of surpassing excellence and prescience and is required reading for any athletics historian. An earlier work, though narrower in scope, is almost equally absorbing. That is *The Olympic Games of 1908 in London* (1909) by Theodore A. Cook, and represents a robust and splendidly-argued response to American charges of British foul play in the 1908 London Olympics.

## Literature and the Visual Arts

To be brutal, there are few works of high literary merit listed in this section, but there is much of interest; and, more importantly, much that affords insights into little-appreciated areas of the sport and its history. Eminent writers have sometimes used athletics as a theme or background, among them Robert Browning, Wilkie Collins, Arthur Conan Doyle, Walt Whitman, A. E. Housman, Evelyn Waugh, W. H. Auden, Alan Sillitoe, John Cheever, Dannie Abse and Roger McGough. In the visual arts, Rowlandson and Cruikshank depicted early athletics, and sculptors have always derived inspiration from athletes in action, but the richest body of work is in photography, by practitioners as skilled as Tony Duffy, Gerry Cranham, Eamonn McCabe and Chris Smith.

The great advantage of fiction is that it can highlight corners of the sport otherwise overlooked. In the little-known *Man and Wife* (1870), Wilkie Collins gives as vivid a picture of a Victorian athletics meeting as we are likely to find anywhere. Parandowski's *The Olympic Discus* (1939) is a reconstruction of the classical sports of ancient Greece. Peter Lovesey's *Wobble to Death* (1970) is a crime novel set entirely within a Victorian six-day race. My own *Flanagan's Run* (1982) attempts to recapture the flamboyance and eccentricity of the transcontinental races, while *The Fast Men* (1986) does the same for the barnstorming professionals known misleadingly as pedestrians. These novels can supply the immediacy, atmosphere and attitude which is outside the scope of conventional sports histories.

The Olympic Games as a topic for fiction has defeated more writers than it has inspired, but Brian Glanville's *The Olympian* (1969) stands out.

Victorian schoolboy fiction of the style of Talbot Baines Reed and Walter C. Rhoades often featured hare and hounds races and sports day triumphs that show school athletics in its heyday. More rarely, as in *Our Marathon Race* (1910), the girls are put through their paces. The super-hero of the 1940s, the great Wilson, only ever appeared in one book, although his numerous adventures in the *Wizard*, written with a fine blend of fantasy and expertise by Gilbert Dalton, are still remembered with affection by senior citizens. More recent children's fiction, such as Cynthia Voigt's *The Runner* (1986), tends to show running as a journey to self-awareness.

Of all the art forms, poetry best encompasses the rich variety of the sport. There is the pathos of Housman's *To an Athlete Dying Young* (1896) and Henderson's *A. E. Flaxman – Hammer Thrower* (included in F. A. M. Webster's *Great Moments in Athletics*, 1947) the fine evocations of the early Border Games by the Ettrick Shepherd, James Hogg; the heroic achievement of Pheidippides in Browning's poem (1879); the grind of training runs in Cyril Norwood's *Sweats* (1969); a glimpse of greatness in *Fanny Blankers-*

*Koen at Wembley* by Jeff Cloves (1986); and, in case we take it all too seriously, the wicked humour of Roger McGough in his collection *Sporting Relations* (1974).

## The Governing Bodies

The main official histories are those dedicated to the first fifty years of the Amateur Athletic Association and its Scottish counterpart, the SAAA, and to their centenaries. Little other than these official accounts exists in the literature.

We are, therefore, left with these official histories, with their inevitable limitations. For outside of sport, in such areas as politics, there are inevitably two 'histories'. The first is the official account, what Marx calls 'the propaganda of the victors', sometimes little more than hagiography. The second, which usually has to be culled from diverse sources, from such areas as biography and autobiography, anecdote, articles, specialised histories etc., is the stuff of real history. It does not, of course, represent absolute truth, but it almost invariably serves to penetrate the self-justifying curtain of official accounts.

Such histories are uncommon in sport. This is because there is rarely available in the formal literature the volume of unofficial material that exists in more public areas such as politics. Thus, we will never know the details of the discussions within the Amateur Athletic Association which brought W. R. Knox into employment as a national coach in 1913. Sadly, too, we have no knowledge of his few months of work before war broke out in 1914, or why he was not re-appointed subsequent to the Great War. Similarly, most of what occurred in the seminal 1947-62 period in British coaching will never be known, for it has passed with the deaths of protagonists such as Geoffrey Dyson, Harold Abrahams and Jack Crump.

Thus, the history of British athletics is, to some extent, pallid and incomplete. The half-century history of the Amateur Athletic Association, *Fifty Years of Progress, 1880-1930* (1930), is, in the main, a collection of self-congratulatory essays of variable quality about which it is easy, at this distance, to be cynical. The book exudes the ambience of a series of self-indulgent after-dinner speeches by the patricians of an exclusive club, to which members of the lower orders and Fritz and Johnny Frenchman have been grudgingly allowed access. Its Scottish equivalent, *Fifty Years of Athletics 1883-1933*, is dour and unimaginative, giving little hint of the rich Scottish rural athletics culture from which Scottish amateur athletics emerged in the late nineteenth century.

In the former work, the essentially public school/Oxbridge nature of athletics at that time is clear, with full details given of the public schools championships since their inception, but nary a mention of the English Schools AA Championships. There is little mention either of women, though it is observed that in 1924 it had been decided to let them take their own path. In *Fifty Years of Progress*, H. B. Stallard comments:

> In spite of the conflicting opinions … I believe that training and judicious competition will widen a woman's outlook, teach her the value of team sport, and help make her a pleasant companion.

Luckily, the centenary handbooks are of a totally different feather. Peter Lovesey's *The Official Centenary History of the Amateur Athletic Association* (1979) is a brilliant kaleidoscopic account of the first hundred years of the AAA and John Keddie's *Scottish Athletics 1883-1983* (1982), taking a different, event-specific approach, is also outstanding. Alas, being official accounts, there is a predictable, if unintended, sanitisation and there is, therefore, little feeling for the struggles between the administrators and National Coaches in the post-war period, little serious criticism of the hypocrisy of shamateurism, and only limited recognition of the pollution of anabolic steroids in more recent times.

Similarly, the 1979 AAA history, gives little idea of the resistance to change that F. A. M. Webster undoubtedly experienced in the period between the wars, or the desperate struggles of G. H. G. Dyson, as he battled with officials to create a coaching scheme subsequent to the 1948 Olympics. Alas, neither Dyson or even the prolific Webster left behind anything which would enlighten historians on their problems during the periods in which they worked.

Governing body histories have, therefore, much of the flavour of party political broadcasts. Even a scrutiny of national association committee minutes would be unlikely to reveal the cut and thrust of debate which undoubtedly occurred, for this is history which has died in memory.

## *Pedestrianism*

Professional foot-racing is the dark side of the athletics moon. Pedestrianism predates amateur athletics by at least two hundred years, and during its long history has taken four distinct forms: match-racing; challenges involving time or distance; handicap-racing; scratch or handicap races within rural sports, such as Highland or Lakeland Games.

Match-racing began in England in the seventeenth century, reached its peak in the final quarter of the nineteenth century, and ended in the early 1930s. Challenges involving time or distance were almost as common as match-races in the eighteenth century, and sometimes involved triathlon-type 'run a mile, swim a mile, walk a mile' novelty events. By the mid-nineteenth century, these races against time and distance had almost disappeared, and the pages of the sporting press were now thick with match-challenges. Few of these involved athletes of any calibre, and were usually between local runners, with small bets at stake. They frequently centred on public houses and were often competed for on turnpike roads. In the Lancashire area there were often jumping competitions, sometimes involving the use of dumbbells. Indeed, Howard of Chester's 1854 leap of twenty-nine feet seven inches still ranks as the greatest distance ever cleared in a single jump.

Stonehenge's *A Manual of British Rural Sports* (1856) is significant primarily for its inclusion of a complete professional match-race contract. It is detailed, shows clearly that 'starting by consent' was common, and that only if consent proved difficult to secure would a pistol be employed. By the final quarter of the nineteenth century, pistol-starting had, understandably, become standard practice.

By the third quarter of the nineteenth century, a third form of competition had arrived, handicap 'pedestrian carnivals'. These, aided by a burgeoning railway network, now overlapped with an older rural sports tradition, typified by the Scottish and Lakeland Games.

Both match-races and pedestrian carnivals such as those held at Sheffield and Powderhall were fuelled by betting. By the end of the nineteenth century, the latter had a substantial following, particularly in central Scotland and the industrial towns of the North.

In Australia, the sport took a different path, for there no strong rural sports culture had developed. Instead, 'gift' handicap races, often centred round mining communities (similar to British pedestrian carnivals), formed the spine of the professional programme. This was not track and field athletics, for after a brief late-nineteenth century flirtation with events such as high jump and hurdles, the Australians settled for a programme of 'gift' events and occasional match-races. Two Australian works (unpublished in the United Kingdom) *Professional Athletics in Australia* (Percy Mason and Rigby, 1985) and *The Spiked Shoe* (Joe Bull, National Press, 1959) give a good account of the professional sport in Australia, one sometimes plagued by a criminal element. Despite this, Australian professional running has survived in good condition until the end of the twentieth century, primarily because of the integrity of its State governing bodies.

It is often said that British professional foot-racing died of inherent corruption, and it is certainly true that in the late nineteenth century major handicaps such as Sheffield lost the confidence of the public, and that the Hutchens-Gent match-race fiasco of Lillie Bridge in 1887 hastened the decline of professional foot-racing in southern England.

It would, however, be more accurate to say that the sport declined primarily because it failed to form strong, ethical national associations to regulate a betting-based sport. For, though racing had its Jockey Club and soccer its Football Association (organisations embracing both amateur and professional codes) professional foot-racing failed, at its peak, to form a strong professional body, or to be embraced by existing amateur associations.

Another central problem for professional foot-racing was that, even at its zenith, it rarely offered its best athletes anything approaching a good income. Leading runners soon ran out of match-races conducted on a scratch basis and rarely won any of the major handicaps. There were, it is true, occasional 'championship' races, but they had little status and rarely offered big prizes. Such races also exposed the true form of the top professional runner, putting him at the mercy of the handicapper and limiting his competitive options in match-races. The major handicap races, such as Edinburgh's Powderhall Handicap, were more often won by less gifted athletes, men specially prepared by trainers who helped them 'find' yards in the seclusion of remote training quarters.

It is not, therefore, surprising that in the boom years of the early 1860s the impresario George Martin was, even with great runners such as Deerfoot and Jack White ('The Gateshead Clipper') in his stable, forced to trek his tatterdemalion circus of athletes around the country. Similarly, it is not surprising that, a quarter of a century later, W. G.

George, the greatest middle-distance runner of the nineteenth century, had such a short professional career, confined entirely to match-races.

This frugal economic environment made for short-term relationships between professional manager/coaches and ex-amateurs such as George, A. R. Downer and Alf Shrubb. Shrubb was fortunate to extend his professional career on the momentum of the post-1908 Olympics marathon 'boom' which lasted till just before the Great War. This 'Dorando' marathon fever gave professional long distance runners an opportunity to earn good money in the 1908-13 period. Professional races were held all over the world and there were even indoor marathons at the Albert Hall and Madison Square Garden. This short-lived early 'boom' enjoys little documentation in the formal literature; all that remains is the Finn Willi Kolehmainen's 2 hours 29 minutes 13 seconds run at Newark in 1913, a time that was not beaten by amateurs for thirteen years.

By the early 1920s, match-racing was virtually dead and 'carnival' meetings had to compete for audiences with greyhound racing. Professional foot-racing therefore survived in a twilight world of modest handicap events in the industrial areas of Wales, northern England and southern Scotland and in low-prized Highland and Lakeland Games. Only Edinburgh's Powderhall New Year Handicap remained as a major event, always above suspicion, still attracting runners from all over the world.

Fortunately, Powderhall's history is well documented in David Jamieson's fine *Powderhall and Pedestrianism* (1943). Jamieson's seminal work is also the only one to attempt a comprehensive account of professional foot-racing. Here it is less successful, failing to provide much detail on the period before 1850 and nothing of the rich cultures which existed in such areas as Kent, the north east and Wales. Jamieson similarly makes no attempt to describe professional running outside of the United Kingdom. He reveals that 'professional championships' were being held at Hackney Wick as late as 1934. These 'championships' were an odd mix of scratch and handicap running events (with a separate hundred yard dash for professional soccer and rugby league players) and Highland Games throwing events. The 1934 'championships' were held in mid-January and it is some measure of the continuing quality of Scottish professional athletics that William McFarlane took this midwinter 100 yds 'championship' in 9.9 seconds and George Clark the 16lb shot with forty-five feet eight inches. It is likely that several such competitions were held in southern England in the 1900-1940 period. Indeed, the Scot Speedie's record high jump of six feet three inches was achieved at Arsenal FC's Highbury in 1911. Alas, only a rigorous trawl of the newspapers of the time would reveal such events, as there is little in the formal literature.

The best feeling for the atmosphere of nineteenth century foot-racing is expressed in Peter Lovesey's *The Kings of Distance* (1968). Lovesey's enthralling account of the American Indian Deerfoot's time in Britain and of the famous George-Cummings matches provide a vivid glimpse of the seamy subculture of nineteenth century pedestrianism. A. R. Downer's *Running Recollections, and How to Train* (1908) is one of the few personal accounts of the life of a nineteenth century British professional athlete. It is, unfortunately, short on either technical or cultural detail.

American professional foot-racing had, in the nineteenth century, taken a similar route to its British counterpart, via match-races and challenges involving time and distance, but no dense network of rural sports ever developed, though there were Highland Games on Eastern and Western seaboards. By the third quarter of the century, the rapid development of the railway network enabled the best runners to compete in match-races, though the pedestrian carnival never seems to have taken firm root.

Most American handicap and scratch foot-races probably took place in Highland Games. Lindsey's *Cinder-path Tales* (1900) provides a rare, tantalising glimpse of American professional foot-racing, which was ultimately engulfed by the amateur college movement. Similarly, an American work, *Mike Sweeney of the Hill* (Putnam's 1940) draws apart the curtain on the Highland Games of the Eastern seaboard in the final part of the nineteenth century. By the 1920s, American professional athletics had vanished, leaving little in the formal literature.

Jamieson's marvellous *Powderhall and Pedestrianism* takes us to 1943. After that, there is virtually no literature and our only windows on professional athletics are the yearly Scottish Games Association handbooks. The SGA, created just after the Second World War by the Edinburgh-based Tom Young, was a loose assembly of rural games and pedestrian carnivals, an attempt to link a moribund foot-racing culture with a looser, more vibrant Highland Games movement, but was in no way similar in structure to club-based amateur organisations.

Formed in 1976, the International Track Association (ITA) passed virtually unnoticed through the gut of professional athletics. American-based, it attempted an honest professionalisation of track and field athletics, hoping to attract to its ranks athletes from beyond the United States before the public tired of familiar faces doing familiar things. Alas, within two years it had vanished, having failed to add anything fresh or dynamic to the sport. It is unlikely that the ITA organisers knew much of the Australian State organisations, the Scottish Games Association, or of the history of professional athletics. In the end, the ITA turned out to be simply a badly planned, inadequately resourced and ill-conceived venture.

It is, perhaps, not surprising that the second half of the twentieth century has given us so little literature on professional foot-racing, for the sport has pursued a twilight existence since the First World War. Indeed, only the survival of Powderhall has given the sport an occasional prominence. The Scottish sprinter George McNeil's *The Unique Double* (1983), an account of his winning of the Powderhall Sprint and the Australian Stawell 'gift', is our only record of a modern professional foot-racer. It deserves a much wider audience. Brian Lee's *The Great Welsh Sprint: the Story of the Welsh Powderhall Handicap 1903-1934* (1999) is a recent publication.

It is doubtful if a comprehensive history of professional foot-racing will ever be written, simply because so much of it died with the runners and coaches of the nineteenth and early twentieth centuries. Most of its records still lie in the cramped pages of the Scottish Games Association's yearbook. There, the historian will find Harry Hutchens's marvellous thirty seconds for 300 yards in midwinter gloom and the feats of Deerfoot and the six day walkers. Perhaps the fact that so many of these performances of the nineteenth century still rank as 'records' tell us something of the history of professional foot-racing.

## Technical Manuals and Statistics

In theory, the development of the technical manual should run directly parallel with the growth of a sport, in that the more highly developed the sport becomes, the greater the volume and sophistication of its technical material.

By this measure, Greek athletics, which endured for more than a thousand years, should have produced a vast volume of sophisticated technical writing. That it did not may reflect the low level of literacy of Greek coaches but is more likely due to the destruction of the Great Library of Alexandria in the first century AD. This being said, it is perhaps surprising that nothing remains in Roman literature on the rules and techniques of Greek athletics, since they were a feature of many gladiatorial games.

The fragments of the literature which survive tell us little of Greek techniques, rules or training methods. What we do know of the training methods of this mainly pre-Christian period bear marked resemblance to those of the eighteenth and nineteenth centuries. This is perhaps not surprising, since they were based on similar limited, usually erroneous, views of human physiology, reflected in the medical knowledge of the period. What almost certainly developed during the thousand or more years of Greek athletics was a high level of essentially empirical knowledge of training and technique, and with it a profound understanding of competitive psychology. Little of this is reflected in the surviving literature.

The only technical events of the Greek Olympic athletics programme were discus, long jump and javelin, all of which appeared only in the pentathlon. These events must have reached a high level of technical sophistication by the time the Olympics were abandoned in 390 AD, but little record remains either of the detail of their rules or their technical development.

The first modern 'technical' manual is Sinclair's *Results of the Enquiries Regarding Athletic Exercises* (1807). This is a remarkable work, essentially a sub-section of a substantial non-specialist study of health and longevity. Sinclair's book is descriptive rather than prescriptive, the product of responses to a questionnaire which he put to leading trainers of the late eighteenth century. His investigations show that there was, in the early years of the nineteenth century, little difference in the training of horses, fighting cocks, pugilists, greyhounds and runners. All were subjected to the inexorable rigours of sweating, purging and bleeding, a direct reflection of the medical practices of the period. Sinclair was, however, prescient in suggesting that, although the effect of match-based athletic training was temporary, it had health-related value for the non-athlete.

Sinclair's work reveals general agreement on training methods, which related mainly to endurance-based events. It also revealed an early dogmatism in the certainty of tone with which the trainers' views were expressed. Track and field athletics play no part in Sinclair's study, which relates to wager-based match-racing and contests based on time and distance. He describes ancient Greek training. 'Sexual intercourse was strictly prohibited and during the nights plates of lead were worn on the loins, with a view to preventing venereal inclinations.'

Thom's *Pedestrianism* (1813), an account of the competitive history and training methods of Captain Barclay Allardice, is often referred to as the seminal work on nineteenth century training. However, *Pedestrianism*'s training methods merely echo those described in the earlier studies of Sinclair, themselves a reflection of the conventional wisdom of the eighteenth century.

Up to this point, there is no technical content in the literature, which is mainly concerned with endurance conditioning. Barclay's methods, though firmly rejected by amateurs in the second half of the century, lingered well into the twentieth century in many sports and are reflected as late as the 1920s in the writings of Sam Mussabini. His influence can best be ascribed to his personal success as a match-racer and to his training of the pugilist Cribb rather than to any originality or efficacy of method.

There was, in the final quarter of the nineteenth century, a reaction to the training methods of Captain Barclay and the professional trainers who had copied his methods. This came from the university-based amateur movement, and is reflected well in *The Pedestrian's Record* (1890) by the Lupton brothers:

> Severe exercise will not give the body that tone which an athlete should possess,
> unless at the same time due attention is paid to the mode of living.

The Luptons make a strong case for athletics to develop links with the medical profession, in effect creating the discipline of sports science, and stressing the need for gymnastic conditioning for athletes. This is a remarkable work and is required reading for any student of the evolution of training methods.

In the earlier *Modern Athletics* (1868), Wilkinson takes a similar, albeit class-based, line.

> A gentleman, having in all probability been accustomed to a good diet, has
> consequently good blood in his system…. On the other hand, the professional
> 'ped' has probably been leading a loafing, pub house kind of life for some time
> past and living on deleterious 'slops', compared with the Gentleman's nutrient.

Here it is only fair to observe that match-racers were in many ways like prizefighters, in that they prepared for special contests, returning immediately afterwards to their normal mode of living, often centred on public houses.

The rapid development of pedestrianism and Highland Games in the third quarter of the century and the growth of the amateur movement which culminated in the creation of the Amateur Athletic Association in 1880 did little to substantially advance the development of technical works on field events. This is because amateur athletics was primarily a harrier-based culture, and few amateur handicap track and field meetings featured field events. Indeed, events such as triple jump, discus and javelin did not appear in the AAA Championships programme till many years after their appearance in the first Athens Olympics of 1896. This is reflected in the limited technical literature. Where field events *were* developing, in Ireland and in Scottish professional Border and Highland Games, they were doing so within a static rural culture which produced little in the way of technical material. Most of the limited amateur literature on field events was therefore descriptive rather than prescriptive, and offered virtually nothing on training methods.

With the rapid international development of governing bodies in the period immediately following the 1896 Olympics and the speedy growth of the American college system, there was an equally rapid increase in the output of technical books. In this respect, F. A. M. Webster's *Olympian Field Events* (1913) is remarkable, in that it was written by an athlete with limited coaching experience, operating within an athletics culture hostile to field events. In *Olympian Field Events* Webster revealed a remarkable early capacity to analyse technical events of which he must have had only limited practical experience.

In contrast, the American coach Mike Murphy (the inventor of the crouch start) had the advantage of considerable experience in the American East Coast club and collegiate systems and, though he is weak on several field events, his only book *Athletics Training* (Bickers and Son, 1914) reveals his immense knowledge of track athletics. Similarly, the Swede Ernest Hjertberg's *Athletics in Theory and Practice* (1913) reveals a good early understanding of field event techniques.

The works of Webster and Murphy underline the difficulties which all writers of track and field manuals would subsequently face. For athletics is not a sport, rather it is a series of separate sports which happen to occur within the same arena, and thus, though publishers almost invariably request comprehensive coverage, few coaches are ever able to do justice to every event.

Some writers made no attempt to do so. As an example, in Mussabini's *The Complete Athletic Trainer* (1913) he makes it clear that he has no expertise in field events, 'The writer is diffident of touching subjects with which he has so little practical acquaintance'. Mussabini was unquestionably an outstanding coach but *The Complete Athletic Trainer*, like his later *Track and Field Athletics* (1924) and *Running, Walking and Jumping* (1926) reeks of Captain Barclay. Indeed, *Track and Field Athletics* contains a detailed recipe for 'Black Jack', a laxative calculated to shock the most sluggish of bowels into violent motion.

This being said, Mussabini had a coaching record far superior to Webster, taking A. V. Hill to two Olympic golds in 1920 and Harold Abrahams to 100m Olympic victory in 1924, and was without doubt the most successful British coach of the first half of the twentieth century. His thinking is, however, rooted firmly in the nineteenth century and nowhere is this more clearly displayed than in his advocacy of the 'Cross Arm' action in sprinting. Fortunately, early silent 16mm film has survived, showing Harold Abrahams in training in 1923. He is seen miraculously surviving a ludicrous forward lean, using Mussabini's 'cross arm' method. This early instructional film also shows Abrahams in competitive action, running with a conventional posture, using an efficient back and forward arm movement.

Harry Andrews' *Training for Athletics and General Health* (1903) is similarly rooted in the nineteenth century, and is the first coaching manual which openly discusses drugs. Andrews, though he expresses an abhorrence of drugs on health grounds, appears to harbour no ethical objections to them. Indeed, he admits to the employment of strychnine lozenges in training a psychologically-troubled distance runner and indicates that cocaine had already been deployed in athletics. Here we must remember that cocaine was contained in Coca Cola until 1904, and that even heroin was available on prescription in the United States until 1898.

Nowhere is the difference between the 'scientific' approach of early twentieth century writers and the rough and ready empiricism of the nineteenth century 'trainer' more clearly demonstrated than in the works of Mussabini and Webster. *Success in Athletics* (1919) is a remarkable work, marking Webster's continuing attempts to introduce scientific rationale to British athletics coaching, 'Englishmen are slow to overcome their constant fault of trying to "muddle through" in sport or battle'. Alas, even Webster had his eccentricities. 'There are today ... in British East Africa ... fellow-subjects ... capable of jumping with ease 9'0" high, from a slightly raised mound.' Indeed. 'In long jump, the angle of take-off must always be 45°.' Yes, but only if the aim is to jump about 5 metres. *Success in Athletics* is also remarkable in being the first and last athletics manual to show concern for the male testicles: 'in standing long jump, if some support is not worn, the testicles are severely shaken and in the course of time, varioceles may result'.

The late 1920s can be seen as a watershed, the end, in the literature, of the Barclay-type 'trainer'. For, though Mussabini was to study slow-motion film and photographic sequences of Muybridge, these studies produced little in the way of technical development, only the 'cross-arm' action and ludicrous sprinting body angles.

Both F. A. M. Webster and Sam Mussabini were, in their own ways, seekers after truth, the public school-educated Webster and uneducated Mussabini. Because, for all his lack of technical knowledge, for all his reverence for archaic professional training methods, Mussabini had, quite literally, an excellent track record at international level. Webster, for all his science, had none. For all his fecundity (he was the world's most prolific athletics writer in the period 1912-1948), Webster tended to be frugal with personal references, either to himself or to athletes whom he had coached.

In *Coaching and Care of Athletes*, his last technical work, F. A. M. Webster lifts the veil, albeit only partly. He reveals that he had been retired from the army in 1921 because of 75% disability and that he was subsequently coached in javelin by Sam Mussabini in 1923, at the age of forty-five.

> His actual knowledge of javelin-throwing would have been lost on a threepenny-bit. When we started working together ... for two months... Mussabini allowed me one pipe after each meal, had me walking five to ten miles each day...

Webster's account of his year with Mussabini is, strangely, the only record we have of Mussabini in action, albeit in an event with which he was totally unfamiliar. It ended with Webster beating his personal best by about eighteen feet, but failing at the 1924 AAA championships as a result of excessive throwing during a coaching tour.

It is odd that this brief relationship, during which a running coach (Mussabini) instructed a middle-aged field events coach (Webster), constitutes the only personal account which we possess in the formal literature of Mussabini's coaching-skills. Alas, his most famous pupil, Harold Abrahams, left little in his writings describing his time with

Mussabini, which ran parallel to that with Webster and none of Mussabini's other successful athletes, such as William Applegarth and Albert Hill, provide any insight into the man or his thinking.

What Webster's account does reveal is Mussabini's rigorous conditioning methods, geared to professional match-racing, and his ability to absorb technical information from an event which was totally outside his experience: 'What Sam did not know about getting athletes fit was not worth knowing.'

It is sad that Mussabini and Webster's reticence prevents us from knowing much about the character of the two great coaches of the first half of the twentieth century. Webster prefaces his account of his experience with Mussabini thus: 'I wonder if I may be forgiven for relating two incidents in the foregoing connection? I crave indulgence in this respect, since one of the two stories is entirely personal.'

It is probably unfair to make comparisons between the two men for Mussabini coached only runners and, at a time when amateur runners were lightly conditioned, the rigour and severity of his methods were bound to produce success at international level. At this distance, it is probably best to judge Webster as a coach-educator rather than a coach, and his writings were, in their time, probably the most advanced in the world, even if they lacked the benefit of much practical experience at international level. It is probably fanciful to speculate on what use Webster would have made of Mussabini, had he been alive, at his first AAA summer school in 1933. In the event, he looked to the USA and Scandinavia for his technical advice.

The disappearance of the Mussabini-type 'trainer' from the literature does not mean that he no longer existed in British coaching, for clubs and universities continued to employ trainer-type coaches until the late 1950s. Their last hurrah came much later, in the 1970s, when professional coaches, schooled in preparing sprinters for the Powderhall Handicap, made brief, but often successful forays, into amateur athletics. A central feature of their training methods was the 'speed ball' (a punch ball), which stimulated a brief vogue in this type of training in England. Alas, the speed ball did not survive long, and many sports scientists were later to ascribe the success of professionally-trained sprinters to other, less ethical, methods.

The foundations of most athletics techniques, if not training methods, had been firmly established by the third decade of the twentieth century. From then until the immediate post-war period there were modifications, gradual in the main, to techniques already well established, developed by athletes on a trial and error basis and modified by coaches as yet untrained in sports science. Since the Second World War, though sports science has rarely been a creative influence, it has provided a rational basis for the analysis of athletics techniques and training methods.

The technical changes of the pre-war period are difficult to determine from the formal literature. Here, high jump probably provides the best example. The straddle technique (or 'stepover', as it was first described in the 1920s) was not employed in Olympic competition until 1936. It was, however, almost certainly described by the Scottish professional athlete Donald Dinnie as early as the 1870s. Whilst on his first tour of the United States, Dinnie observed that the Scottish-American William Goldie (later Director of Physical Education at Princeton University) dived headfirst over the crossbar. Dinnie was almost certainly describing a primitive 'dive straddle', a technique precluded in amateur athletics until a change of rules in 1938. Similarly, the Scot McCombie Smith describes in 1898 a side-on technique (which was essentially a crude form of 'Western Roll'), a method which the literature describes only a decade later.

The 'Fosbury Flop', essentially a back layout scissors jump, was created by the American Dick Fosbury in 1967, but a fellow American, Clinton Larson, jumped in excess of two metres in the 1920s using a side-on back layout. Only the rules obtaining at that time and the unforgiving nature of the landing areas prevented Larson from taking the next step, the curved run used by 'eastern cut off' jumpers, to turn his back layout into a flop. There was little difference in principle between Larson's technique and that of Fosbury, and Larson's high approach-run speed also anticipated the velocities of the Russian straddle jumpers of the early 1950s.

Full left-foot contact hammer turns have usually been considered to have begun in the late 1920s or early 1930s, but the literature hints that they may have been executed as early as the late nineteenth century. And, though the hitch-kick in long jump is thought to have originated in the 1920s, it almost certainly appeared a decade earlier. Similarly, one of Dean Cromwell's flicker-books of 1938 clearly shows an O'Brien-type throwing position in shot put, over a decade before it was 'invented' by the American Parry O'Brien.

Athletics in the pre-war period was poorly developed. Only in the United States did any depth of coaching culture exist, and even in the USA there was little communication between coaches. The degree of communication was even poorer at international level. Thus, in the high jump sequence of Leni Riefenstahl's film of the 1936 Olympic Games we see frontal back layout (1870s), eastern cut off (1890s), western roll (1910), back layout (1920s), and straddle (late 1920s) all in the same competition. In contrast, in 1972, five years after the 'Fosbury Flop' first appeared, over ninety percent of male international jumpers were using the new technique. This, of course, had little to do with athletics literature, but rather reflected the influence of television.

In Britain, the post-World War I period saw the growth of technical literature from Oxbridge sources, from such writers as Harold Abrahams, Guy Butler, Jack Lovelock and The Achilles Club. Little of their work derived either from theory or from a body of coaching experience, but contained the best of the conventional wisdom of the period. Guy Butler's work was significant in its use of excellent sequence photography, and the Achilles books had the advantage of being written by specialist athletes. The bias of many of these works was towards running and they were aimed at public and grammar schools, rather than the harrier-based club system. The best of these is probably *Athletics* (1938).

No technical work written in Britain in the 1900-50 period can be compared, in its humanity and in its wealth of practical advice, to the American Dean Cromwell's *Championship Technique in Track and Field* (1941). Cromwell's still immensely readable book derives from a quarter of a century of experience within the American collegiate system.

Although he makes no attempt to justify his methods on any scientific basis, *Championship Technique in Track and Field* is rich in practical advice. It is unquestionably the definitive coaching manual of the first half of the twentieth century. Cromwell describes the 1940 Pacific Coast Conference Meet. His team, Southern California, needed to finish fourth in the final event, the 4 x 440 yds relay, to take the title. Alas, Cromwell had only a single specialist quarter miler in Upton, the rest of his team consisting of a jaded mixture of middle-distance runners (Zamperini and Reading) and an unsuccessful 440 yd hurdler (Laret).

> 'Look', I said to Zamperini, 'A nice little lap round the track will get the tension out of your legs and send you home feeling like a million dollars...'
> 'Laret', I said to our puffing low hurdler, 'Anybody who can step over the sticks like you will find striding this flat race just a breeze.'
> 'Reading, the way you sprinted up from nowhere to score a point in that half-mile shows you are full of speed today.' I told our disappointed half-miler.'
> 'And Upton', I said to our disconsolate quarter-miler, 'You're the best 440 man in this meet. It wasn't your fault you got elbowed and pocketed. Now go and show 'em how a champ can run without interference.'
> Cromwell's tatterdemalion squad went on to run themselves ragged to finish in the necessary fourth place winning his Trojans the Conference title. The collection of misfits had run a 3.17 relay... No world record-breaking performance ever made me feel any happier.

The humanity and wisdom of a great coach speaks out from every page of *Championship Technique in Track and Field.* One of Cromwell's favourite sayings was, 'I call all my boys champ, and some of them believe me'. Clearly, over a period of a quarter of a century, a host of great athletes believed him.

The creation in 1947 of the Amateur Athletic Association Coaching Scheme brought with it a totally fresh approach to the technical literature. G. H. G. Dyson, mentored by F. A. M. Webster at the Loughborough School of Sport and Games prior to the Second World War, became Chief Coach to the AAA in 1947, a year before the London Olympics. It says something about the British attitude to coaching at that time that Dyson was allowed to play no part in the preparation of the 1948 British Olympic team. Sadder still, his mentor F. A. M. Webster, then in the last year of a life devoted to athletics, was denied access to his son, the pole vaulter F. R. Webster, at the team's Uxbridge training quarters.

Dyson's first task was to bring into being a body of trained coaches and in the 1947-62 period he almost single-handedly created a British athletics coaching culture. Dyson took forward Webster's work, in creating a scientific rationale for athletic training. He leant heavily towards biomechanics and his definitive work was *The Mechanics of Athletics* (1962), a landmark work, the remarkable product of a brilliant, self-educated man.

Dyson's *Athletics for Schools* (1951) is not, alas, of the same calibre, reflecting his lack of direct experience in schools, and is essentially a watered-down coaching manual. The great pity is that Dyson, an outstanding practical coach, left behind no definitive work on athletics coaching.

Dyson's rational, scientific approach to coaching transformed the athletics literature of the post-war period, bringing to it a new quality of thinking. It also brought with it a devaluation of practical experience, with writers vying with each other to be biomechanically correct, rather than drawing from any strong body of practical knowledge. Pearson's *Athletics* (1963) is a good example of the genre, an uneasy mix of old Oxbridge (A. G. K. Brown on four hundred metre running) and the Dyson (G. F. D. Pearson on shot). A. A. Gold's chapter on high jump provides a good example, a masterpiece of biomechanical/descriptive gobbledegook, of little practical value, calculated more to confuse than to enlighten.

In the 1950s, the key work on distance running was unquestionably *Franz Stampfl on Running* (1955). Stampfl's contribution to Roger Bannister's breaking of the four minute mile barrier in 1954 has never been entirely clear. He became, however, with the publication of *Running*, a major influence upon British middle-distance running in the 1950s.

Stampfl's devotion to the German physiologist Gerschler's interval running methods was absolute, and *Running* could well be called the first progressive resistance book of middle-distance training. Most of the book consists simply of progressively faster sets of repetitions, aimed at the improvement of the cardiovascular system. Other muscular systems tend to receive relatively short shrift, and there is in *Running* little sense of the inevitable ebb and flow of an athlete's development or of athletic psychology. Stampfl was, however, an eclectic coach of world class, as he later showed in his work in Australia in the 1960-80 period.

The seminal works of the 1960s on middle-distance running were unquestionably Percy Cerutty's *Athletics: How to Become a Champion* (1960) and Arthur Lydiard's *Run to the Top* (1962). In both books the personality of the coach strides out from every page. And, though the Australian Cerutty's training methods failed to gain any long-term currency, his 'stotan' philosophy had great impact at the time. In the nineteenth century purgatives had been the purifier, but in Cerutty's world of Portsea sandhills the purifier was pain itself. Cerutty's philosophy had an immediate appeal to the Spartan world of distance running and in the early 1960s runners all over the world sought out sand and sea to test their bodies to the limits. In some ways, with his emphasis on diet and conditioning, Cerutty was an old-style Mussabini-type trainer. Where he differs is in his 'stotan' approach to athletics psychology. For, if coaching is a discipline which admits no limit to human potential, then Percy Cerutty was a coach *par excellence*.

Arthur Lydiard's methods were similarly based on trial and error, this time on the hilly roads of New Zealand, but achieved greater currency and remain the basis of much modern distance training. It has been said that the sports scientist is a man who discovers that something works in practice and returns to his laboratory to discover if it also works in theory. Lydiard's empiricism was later found to be broadly justified in physiological terms by sports scientists, and over the years his methods have been modified and enhanced. This rational scrutiny of the empirical accelerated in the 1980s with the mass marathon movement, and the time from 1980 to the present has probably seen more scientific scrutiny of distance physiology than any previous period.

During the period 1960-80 Wilf Paish and myself were amongst the most prolific British writers in track and field, producing a stream of works derived from an increasing body of practical experience. Until my *Modern Schools Athletics* (1970) the curricular teaching of the sport had been a relatively barren area. Though I attempted to take a realistic view of what could be achieved within the class context *Modern Schools Athletics* was, in the main, unrealistic in many of its technical expectations. The book, a compilation, failed to address the practical realities of teaching large groups of children of varying ability. It is probably at its strongest in the opening chapter on teaching philosophy and in the book's concluding discussion section between the contributors.

Statistical literature was rare until 1951, and the publication of the McWhirter twins' seminal *Get to Your Marks!*. This was followed, in 1964, by Roberto Quercetani's *A World History of Track and Field Athletics*, a rich source of information, though again short on the history of professional athletics. But, though increasingly replete with statistical works, the literature of the last twenty-five years has been in some ways Hamlet without the ghost, in that there is little mention of the drug ingestion which began to corrupt the sport in the period following the 1964 Tokyo Olympics. Indeed, even statistical works showing performance graphs of the post-1964 period, revealing massive, inexplicable jumps in performance, make little mention of illegal pharmaceuticals. Similarly, the statistical works of the late 1980s make little, if any, comment on sudden surges and regression in performance, particularly in women's events where there can now be little confidence in any record from sprints to 10,000m. It is probably true to say that the statistical works of the last quarter of the century are essentially works of fiction. In the technical literature, it is only in the Canadian coach Charlie Francis's book *Speed Trap* (1991) that there is any frank discussion of drugs. Francis will live long in infamy as the coach of the disgraced Ben Johnson, but it is difficult not to feel a twinge of sympathy for him, for the technical content of *Speed Trap* shows him to be intelligent and creative, unquestionably capable of coaching at world level. Francis was merely one of hundreds of coaches throughout the world who colluded directly or indirectly in drug ingestion, but one of the few to be exposed and vilified. This being said, *Speed Trap*, with its descriptions of Francis's athletes arriving at his flat for a beer, a video and an injection, paints a profoundly depressing picture of modern athletics.

Since the end of the Second World War, British technical literature has always strongly reflected its national coaching scheme. Thus, the literature of the 1950s tended to lean towards the biomechanical, reflecting the influence of the AAA chief coach, G. H. G. Dyson. The post-Dyson period was one in which there was no clear technical leadership. Coaches felt free to move away from the restrictions of a biomechanically-biased approach and authors such as Paish and myself attempted to mix science with pragmatism. The 1980s, with Frank Dick as Director of Coaching, moved to a more clinical approach, influenced by Eastern European methodology. The growing body of practical experience of such coaches as Ted King, Peter Coe, Bruce Tulloh, Harry Wilson and athletes such as Steve Backley has made the period leading to the end of the century one in which science and practice are beginning to come into balance. This is particularly true of distance running where the Marathon boom of the 1980s has resulted in a flood of high-quality technical literature. Here Tim Noakes, Peter Coe and David Martin have been prominent with works which provide a rich mix of theory and practice.

Over the years, the AAA/BAAB/BAF event-specific booklets have provided a strong spine of material in the technical area. Of these, *Triple Jump* (McNab,1968), *Javelin Throwing* (Paish, 1967), *Decathlon* (McNab,1971), *Hurdles* (Arnold, 1952), *Triple Jump* (King, 1996), *Shotputting* (Jones, 1987), and *Training Theory* (Dick, 1984) have been seminal works in a series which, though influential, has been variable in quality.

Like most of the works of the period, the booklets have stressed technical development, though there has been a growing emphasis on general and specific physical conditioning. Alas, what has always been lacking in them and in most other technical literature has been any sense of the athlete as a human being, or much material about the ultimate aim of training and conditioning, the competitive arena itself.

What has been lacking most in the technical literature are the clear, unalloyed voices of coach and athlete, speaking directly from practical experience. For coaching, though strongly underpinned by science, is a practical art. Much of the literature does the coaching process a disservice by confining the coach within the disciplines of an essay-based, literary format.

There is, therefore, a gap in the market for technical works which go beyond analytical and narrowly prescriptive accounts, to works in which coaches and athletes discuss the practical issues of athletics training and performance. The latter, the performance arena, is one which particularly deserves attention, being the central aim of all athletics training.

Similarly, the group coaching of young athletes within clubs and the teaching of children in class curriculum time are areas which have been inadequately addressed. These are not technically complex issues, but rather ones which involve the eliciting of technical fundamentals, presentation and organisation. If athletics is to have real meaning and purpose within physical education programmes and to have impact within our clubs, then these are issues which must be addressed, if the technical literature is to progress.

## Conclusion

In athletics literature I would wish for three things. First, that historians would continue to burrow in obscure areas (rural athletics, the dark side of modern Olympic politics, early women's athletics and American professional athletics come immediately to mind), possibly as sections of composite works. Second, that the history of athletics be approached with the same discipline and rigour as that of other areas of society. In the absence of the publication in the formal literature of material on the less popular areas of athletic history, the Internet would seem to offer rich possibilities for the athletics historian. I would also make a strong plea for more attention to be given to oral history. Finally, that our technical manuals would, whilst using strong theoretical underpinning, stress the practical aspects of coaching both in clubs and individual situations, for coaching is, essentially, a practical art.

Some readers may feel that too great an emphasis has been placed on books written in the period prior to the Second World War and, in particular, to those published in the nineteenth and early twentieth centuries. This may, of course, reflect the self-indulgence (and indeed the self-interest) of the compilers and for this we apologise. It is, however, our feeling that post-World War II books are both better known and more readily available to most readers. We feel too that the earlier works may prove to be a greater stimulus to further study and research, and help place both the general and the technical history of athletics in clearer perspective.

I hope that this edition of the *Compendium* will prove to be the catalyst for the production of a wealth of technical and historical studies. I hope, too, that in the words of the essayist Addison, the *Compendium* will 'entertain, edify and instruct'.

Tom McNab
St Albans
Summer 2001

# A. History & Development

## Greek & Roman Athletics

1   Series chronologica Olympiadum, Pythiadum, Isthmiadum, Nemeadum, quibus veteres Græci tempora sua metiebantur / William Lloyd. Oxford: 1700.
folio; index
        BL: 581.k.16

A tabulated listing of the ancient classical games with year-by-year references to champions and games from 776 BC. This is by far the earliest book on the Olympics to be published in the UK and, although the text is in Latin throughout, it is easily comprehensible.

2   Greek athletics, Greek religion, and Greek art at Olympia: an account of ancient usages and modern discoveries; a paper read before the members of the Liverpool Art Club, 4th February 1878 / Sidney Colvin. Liverpool: Printed for private circulation, 1878.
15p; pbk
        BL: YA.1996.a.23752

A short, but interesting, account.

3   Religio athletæ / Alfred Lynch. London: Remington, 1895.
vii, 96p
        BL: 8409.ccc.30

Probably written to coincide with the Olympic revival, it includes chapters on athletes' ideals; athletes' virtue; the Olympic Games; questions of diet; ordinances of the Olympic Games; running; statistics; and, Olympic Games – the National Fete.

4   The Greek Games and their mythology / Clement Gutch. Cambridge: Cambridge University Press, 1900.
vii, 86p; illus
        BL: 4503.bb.47

5   Greek athletic sports and festivals / E. Norman Gardiner. London: Macmillan, 1910.
xxvii, 533p; illus; index
(Handbooks of archaeology and antiquities)
        BL: 2258.a.1/11

This is an exceptional work, covering not only the religious, political and social history of Greek athletics but also (to a lesser degree) that of the Mediterranean sports culture within which it developed. Gardiner also tackles with both energy and intelligence the technical basis of the Greek athletics events and, despite his clear lack of practical experience, draws some sensible conclusions. However, Gardiner's difficulties are clear. His main evidence is literary and artistic and each of these accounts has it limitations, both in its incompleteness and its contradictions. Nowhere is this shown more clearly than in the long jump, where Gardiner shows vase-paintings of standing long jumps with and without weights, single-footed long jumps which look surprisingly static, running with weights and in-flight positions with weights on both hands.

Gardiner includes, as background, accounts of professional jumpers who have used weights but, alas, he does not appear to have seen any of them in action; nor is his account of Howard of Chester's 1854 jump of twenty-nine feet seven inches (made from a boat board) one which is helpful in supporting his view that the Greek long jump was a single leap.

What we lack in the Greek artistic portrayals are sequence-drawings. Thus, many of the jumping and running activities could well be training exercises rather than competitive activity. We have no means of knowing. Certainly, in the surviving photographs of Victorian jumpers using weights, the dumbbells are (unlike in Greek drawings) always seen to be thrown back in flight and, though there is never any sign of a beat-board, it would seem unlikely that objects with both height and depth such as stage coaches could be cleared without their assistance.

Gardiner applies remarkable scholarship to the study of Greek athletics and his account of life in Paleastra and Gymnasium is rich and detailed. If his attempts to analyse athletics techniques raise as many questions as answers, they represent the best that has been placed on record.

6   Greek athletics / F. A. Wright. London: Cape, 1925.
123p; illus
    *Bibliography: p123*        BL: 07912.ee.1

A brief history, followed by chapters on gymnastics, including athletics and military training; physical education; health and bodily exercise; and, Galen's treatise on the small ball. There is a short bibliography.

7    Olympia: its history & remains / E. Norman Gardiner.
Oxford: Clarendon, 1925.

xviii, 316p; illus        BL: 7701.g.29

The story of the recovery of Olympia and of its history.
Again, a seminal work.

8    Greek physical education / Clarence Allen Forbes.
London: Century Education, 1929.

vii, 300p        BL: 12213.f.6(1)

Considerable sections are devoted to athletics in
classical times.

9    Athletics of the ancient world / E. Norman Gardiner.
Oxford: Clarendon, 1930.

x, 246p; illus        BL: 07906.i.29

A shorter and simpler version of *Greek Athletic
Sports and Festivals* (1910), omitting the details and
history of the various athletic festivals of Greece, but
adding chapters on 'The meaning of athletics', 'The
sports of the Ancient East,' 'Athletics and religion,'
'Athletics and art' and 'Athletics and education'. Alas,
despite a quarter of a century of technical
development in athletics, Gardiner adds little of
substance to his technical analysis of twenty years
before. This is nevertheless the definitive work on
Greek athletics and, read together with Harris's later
*Greek Athletes and Athletics* (1964), provides as
much as any historian is ever likely to deliver on Greek
athletics.

10    Greek athletes and athletics / H. A. Harris; introduction
by the Marquess of Exeter. London: Hutchinson, 1964.

244p; illus, maps; indexes        BL: X.410/106

The best description of Greek athletics since E. N.
Gardiner. Harris finds many points of comparison
between the ancient and modern Olympics. He
discusses the various events, outstanding athletes,
the management of a Greek athletic meeting, training
and women in Greek athletics. A marvellous piece of
scholarship.

11    History of ancient Olympic Games / Lynn and Gray
Poole. London: Vision, 1965.

143p; illus; index

*Originally published: New York: Obolensky, 1963*
       BL: X.410/346

12    The ancient Olympic Games / Heinz Schoebel;
translated by Joan Becker. London: Studio Vista, 1966.

163p; illus, maps

*Translation of: Olympia und seine Spiele*    BL: X.415/123

13    Olympia: gods, artists and athletes / Ludwig Drees;
English translation by Gerald Onn. London: Pall Mall,
1968.

193p; illus; index        SBN: 269-67015-7
       BL: X.410/941

Originally published the year before in Germany,
Drees's work is particularly strong on the religious and
political culture of the Games but, like many academic

historians, less strong on the technical nature of
Greek athletics. In discussing the Greek long jump, he
makes no reference to the use of jumping-weights by
English professional jumpers and music hall
performers in the nineteenth and twentieth centuries.
Similarly, he fails to ask why the Greek skamma
(jumping pit) was over fifty feet long, when that
distance may point to multiple jumps within the pit
itself. Particularly notable is his failure to even
mention the *hysplex* (starting gate) described in detail
by Harris four years later. Drees's book is nevertheless
an outstanding work and contains a marvellous
selection of illustrations.

14    Sport in Greece and Rome / H. A. Harris. London:
Thames and Hudson, 1972.

288p; illus; index

(Aspects of Greek and Roman life)

*Bibliography: p275-276*        ISBN: 0-500-40022-9
       BL: X.629/4786

Covers much the same ground as the author's earlier
*Greek Athletes and Athletics*, though some fresh
material is included; both are works of outstanding
merit.

15    Greek athletics / David Buchanan. London: Longman,
1976.

48p; illus, maps; pbk

(Aspects of Greek life)        ISBN: 0-582-20059-8
       BL: X.619/17388

16    Greek athletics and the Jews / H. A. Harris; edited by I.
M. Barton and A. J. Brothers. Cardiff: University of
Wales Press for St David's University College Lampeter,
1976.

vi, 124p; illus, maps; index

('Trivium' special publications; 3)

*Originally published in a Hebrew translation: Tel Aviv: 1972*
       ISBN: 0-7083-0635-7
       BL: X.620/16262

Published posthumously, this book covers the impact
of Hellenic culture, especially the cult of athletics, on
the Jews. A definitive work.

17    Olympic Games in ancient Greece / Shirley Glubok and
Alfred Tamarin. London: Harper and Row, 1976.

116p; illus, 1 map; index
       ISBN: 0-06-022048-1 (cased) • 0-06-022047-3 (pbk)
       BL: X.620/17513

This guide opens with a preliminary discussion of the
Games before devoting a separate section to each
day of the Games. The end of the ancient Games and
the modern Olympics form the concluding sections.

18    The Olympic Games: the first thousand years / M. I.
Finley, H. W. Pleket. London: Chatto and Windus, 1976.

xvii, 138p; illus, maps; index        ISBN: 0-7011-2087-8
       BL: X.622/5202

The authors succeed brilliantly not only in describing
the history of the Games, which were held without a

break from 776 BC to 261 AD at Olympia, but also in provoking the reader into drawing modern parallels and contrasts. The work provides a wealth of detail about the Games, including the participation of juniors and women, the role of trainers, the development of the programme, and the relationship of the Games to politics.

19 The ancient Olympic Games / Judith Swaddling. London: Published for the Trustees of the British Museum by British Museum Publications, 1980.
80p; illus, maps; pbk ISBN: 0-7141-2002-2
BL: X.800/40319

An eminently readable account of the origins and history of the Games practised at Olympia, profusely illustrated with line-drawings, maps and photographs.

☞ Subsequent ed. A32

20 The Olympic Games / Michael Grant; illustrated by John Fraser. Harmondsworth: Kestrel, 1980.
32p; illus, 1 map ISBN: 0-7226-5553-3
BL: X.622/7234

The illustrations are an outstanding feature of this work aimed at the young reader.

21 Sports and games in the ancient world / Věra Olivová; translated by D. Orpington; foreword by W. G. Forrest. London: Orbis, 1984.
207p; illus; index
*Bibliography: p199-203; translated from the Czech*
ISBN: 0-85613-273-X
BL: X.622/21763

The author explores the origins of what has become in modern terminology 'sport', and cites some evidence of athletic activity, particularly running, in the earliest civilisations (Near East and Egypt) of which records exist. Subsequent developments in Greece and in the Roman Empire are described.

22 Sport and recreation in Ancient Greece: a sourcebook with translations / Waldo E. Sweet; foreword by Erich Segal. Oxford: Oxford University Press, 1987.
xiv, 281p; illus, maps; index
ISBN: 0-19-504126-7 (cased) • 0-19-504127-5 (pbk)
BL: YK.1988.b.4862

The first eight chapters offer detailed descriptions of Greek athletics with accompanying questions for students. Each chapter ends with a list of further readings. Of particular interest is the discussion of the various theories which have been put forward for deciding the winner of pentathlon contests. Also includes some fascinating references to walking.

23 Athletes and oracles: the transformation of Olympia and Delphi in the eighth century BC / Catherine Morgan. Cambridge: Cambridge University Press, 1990.
250p; illus, maps; index ISBN: 0-521-37451-0
BL: W.P.11639/46

A prehistory of the Olympic Games which extends Gardiner's *Athletics of the Ancient World*.

24 Arete: Greek sports from ancient sources / edited by Stephen G. Miller. 2nd and expanded ed. Oxford: University of California Press, 1991.
xiii, 227p; illus; index
*Previous ed.: Chicago: Ares, 1979; bibliography: p205*
ISBN: 0-520-07508-0 (cased) • 0-520-07509-9 (pbk)
BL: YC.1991.a.5239

Many topics relating to track and field events are covered, illustrated by short extracts from original texts, such as from Philostratus and Aristotle on the pentathlon (circa 360 BC). The appendix sets out the Olympic and Pythian programmes.

25 Greek and Roman sport: a dictionary of athletes and events from the eighth century BC to the third century AD / David Matz. London: McFarland, 1991.
v, 169p; index ISBN: 0-89950-558-9
BL: YC.1991.a.2627

The athletes listed include charioteers and wrestlers, but also a number of runners, jumpers and throwers.

26 Greek athlete / Fiona Macdonald. London: Macmillan, 1992.
31p; illus; index
ISBN: 0-333-56383-2 (cased) • 0-330-32482-9 (pbk)
BL: YK.1994.b.4207

For children.

27 Ancient Olympics / Richard Tames. Oxford: Heinemann, 1996.
32p; illus, 1 map; index ISBN: 0-431-05943-8
BL: YK.1996.b.13859

For children.

28 The original Olympics / Stewart Ross. Hove: Wayland, 1996.
48p; illus, 1 map; index ISBN: 0-7502-1566-6
BL: YK.1996.b.10704

For children.

29 Sport and society in ancient Greece / Mark Golden. Cambridge: Cambridge University Press, 1998.
xiii, 216p; illus; index
(Key themes in ancient history)
ISBN: 0-521-49698-5 (cased) • 0-521-49790-6 (pbk)
BL: YC.1998.b.4820

30   The ancient Greek Olympics / Richard Woff. London: British Museum, 1999.
32p; illus, 1 map; index      ISBN: 0-7141-2144-4
                       BL: YK.2000.b.2974

     For children.

31   Ancient Olympic Games / Haydn Middleton. Oxford: Heinemann Library, 1999.
32p; illus, map; index      ISBN: 0-431-05918-7
                       BL: YK.2000.b.4192

     For children.

32   The ancient Olympic Games / Judith Swaddling. Rev. and enlarged ed. London: British Museum, 1999.
112p; illus; index; pbk      ISBN: 0-7141-2161-4
                       BL: YC.2000.a.7670

     ☞   Previous ed. A19

## ✳ *Additional References*

33   Festivals, games, and amusements, ancient and modern / Horatio Smith. London: Colburn & Bentley, 1831.
viii, 382p      BL: 7908.aaaa.61

     Includes chapters on the public games of the Grecians and the Olympic Games.

34   The muscles and their story, from the earliest times, including the whole text of Mercurialis, and the opinions of other writers ancient and modern, on mental and bodily development / John W. F. Blundell. London: Chapman & Hall, 1864.
xvi, 304p

     *An adaptation of: Ars gymnastica*      BL: 7420.aa.21
     Has many references to the ancient Olympic Games and athletics in classical times. The text referred to is the 'De Arte Gymnastica'.

35   Themis: a study of the social origins of Greek religion / Jane Ellen Harrison, with an excursus on the ritual forms preserved in Greek tragedy by Professor Gilbert Murray and a chapter on the origin of the Olympic Games by Mr F. M. Cornford. Cambridge: Cambridge University Press, 1912.
xxxii, 559p; illus; index      BL: 4504.bb.41

     ☞   Subsequent ed. A39

36   Vergil's athletic sports; selected from Vergil's Aeneid / edited, with introduction, notes, and vocabulary by S. E. Winbolt. London: George Bell, 1912.
x, 87p; illus, 1 map      BL: 12204.de.12/5

     An educational text in Greek with exercises and dictionary.

37   The renaissance of the Greek ideal / Diana Watts. London: Heinemann, 1914.
185p; illus; index      BL: 7383.l.3

     Includes a discussion of the classical style of discus throwing.

     ☞   Subsequent ed. A38

38   The renaissance of the Greek ideal / Diana Watts. Rev. ed. London: Heinemann, 1922.
x, 144p; illus; index      BL: 7911.h.25

     ☞   Previous ed. A37

39   Themis: a study of the social origins of Greek religion / Jane Ellen Harrison, with an excursus on the ritual forms preserved in Greek tragedy by Gilbert Murray and a chapter on the origin of the Olympic Games by F. M. Cornford. 2nd ed. revised, with preface and supplementary notes. Cambridge: Cambridge University Press, 1927.
xxxvi, 559p; illus; index      BL: 04504.h.46

     ☞   Previous ed. A35

40   Athletics, sports and games / John Murrell. London: Allen and Unwin, 1975.
64p; illus, 1 map; pbk
(Greek and Roman topics; 5)
     *Bibliography: p61-62*      ISBN: 0-04-930006-7
                       BL: X.611/4290

     Though designed as an introductory text for students and covering familiar ground, the author presents clearly the historical development of the four Greek Games before describing in detail the athletics events and the main sites of their performance. The Roman period receives little attention.

41   Aspects of Saxon Irminsul worship and its influence on the ancient Olympic Games / Hans Hubler. Bath: Bath Centre for Classical Studies, 1980.
5 leaves      BL: X.205/1143

42   Athletics and society in ancient Greece: illustrated notes for teachers / Ian Jenkins and Sue Bird. London: British Museum Education Service, 1980.
14p; illus; pbk
(Greek & Roman daily life studies; 3)

43   The Germanic origin of the ancient Olympic Games: with special reference to early octonary and nonary systems / Eric Hillier. London: International Research Publications, 1980.
14p; pbk      BL: X.622/8810

     The author considers the three theories put forward to explain the significance of the four-year cycle of the Olympic Games, and then discusses the existence of nine- and seven-year cycles which operated in north-west Europe. Finally, Hillier deals with the question of why the Olympic and Pythean festivals were altered from octennial to quadrennial in 776 BC and 582 BC respectively.

44 North-west European marriage races and their influence on the Heraean Games at Olympia: the Northern sources of classical Greek athletics (supplement) / J. Goulstone. Bexleyheath: The author, 1980.
5 leaves
    BL: X.520/29274

45 The Northern origin of classical Greek athletics: a study of ritual foot-races in north-west Europe and ancient Greece, with particular reference to the possible Germanic origin of the Olympic Games / R. B. Craven. Bexleyheath: The author, 1980.
6 leaves
    BL: YK.1991.b.9565

46 Athleticism in Athenian art of the late archaic period / M. P. Walsh. Oxford University, 1989. DPhil thesis.

47 Sporting success in ancient Greece and Rome / Audrey Briers. Oxford: Ashmolean Museum, 1994.
48p; illus, 1 map; pbk
(Archaeology, history and classical studies)
*Bibliography: p48*      ISBN: 1-85444-055-1
BL: YK.1996.a.4275

*The booklet is divided into three sections: training, competitions (covering running, jumping, discus, javelin and pentathlon) and chariot racing.*

48 The development of Greek athletics through literature from Homer to the early fourth century BC / J. D. Browne. Trinity College Dublin, 1995. MLitt thesis.

49 Athletes and actors / Anita Ganeri. Oxford: Heinemann, 1997.
32p; illus; index
(All in a day's work)
    ISBN: 0-431-05382-0 (cased) • 0-431-05383-9 (pbk)
BL: LB.31.b.18671

*Children's book about ancient Greece, with chapters on hoplites, Spartans and athletes.*

# British Isles ~ General

50 The boke named the Governour / Sir Thomas Elyot. Londini: T. Berthelet, 1531.
258 folio
*British Library copy imperfect (wanting fol. 85, 86, and 212)*
    BL: G.735

*A guide to principles for living with a chapter (XVI) on 'Sundrye fourmes of exercise necessarye for a gentilman', which describes the merits of running, jumping and throwing. 'Rennyng is bothe a good exercise and a laudable solace. Nedes must rennynge be taken for a laudable exercise sens one of the mooste noble capitaynes of all the Romans took his name from it.' (A reference to Papirius Cursor.) Although not strictly a book on athletics, Elyot's work was sufficiently influential for it to be listed as a significant contribution to the literature of the sport.*

51 Sporting anecdotes: original and select, including characteristic sketches of eminent persons who have appeared on the turf / An Amateur Sportsman [i.e. Pierce Egan]. London: James Cundee for Thomas Hurst, Harris and Wheble, 1804.
vi, 542p; illus
    BL: RB.23.a.18249

*Contains a good account of pedestrianism with details on Captain Barclay, Foster Powell and George Wilson.*

☞ Subsequent ed. A52

52 Sporting anecdotes: a complete panorama of the sporting world: original and select including characteristic sketches of eminent persons who have appeared on the turf / An Amateur Sportsman [i.e. Pierce Egan]. 2nd ed. London: James Cundee, 1807.
xv, 579p
    BL: 7907.de.6

☞ Previous ed. A51; subsequent ed. A53

53 Sporting anecdotes, original and selected / Pierce Egan. New ed., considerably enlarged and improved. London: Sherwood, Jones, 1825.
iv, 592p; illus
    BL: Cup.408.ww.58

☞ Previous ed. A52

54 Manual of British rural sports: comprising shooting, hunting, coursing, fishing, hawking, racing, boating, pedestrianism, and the various rural games and amusements of Great Britain / Stonehenge. London: Routledge, Warne & Routledge, 1856.
xvi, 720p; illus; index
*Stonehenge is a pseudonym for John Henry Walsh*
    BL: 7906.b.1

*Includes a comprehensive section on athletics, with an account of each event, and contains our only example of a professional match-race contract. Amateur and professional records are given from the 1871 editions.*

☞ Subsequent ed. A55; see also: E10

55 Manual of British rural sports: comprising shooting, hunting, coursing, fishing, hawking, racing, boating, pedestrianism, and the various rural games and amusements of Great Britain / Stonehenge. London: Routledge, Warne & Routledge, 1857.
xvi, 720p; illus; index

☞   Previous ed. A54; subsequent ed. A56

56 Manual of British rural sports: comprising shooting, hunting, coursing, fishing, hawking, racing, boating, pedestrianism, and the various rural games and amusements of Great Britain / Stonehenge. London: Routledge, Warne & Routledge, 1857.
xvi, 720p; illus; index

☞   Previous ed. A55; subsequent ed. A57

57 Manual of British rural sports / Stonehenge. 4th ed., entirely revised, with additions. London: Routledge, 1859.
xvi, 720p; illus; index                          BL: 7906.d.1

☞   Previous ed. A56; subsequent ed. A58

58 Manual of British rural sports / Stonehenge. 5th ed., entirely revised with additions. London: Routledge, Warne & Routledge, 1861.
xvi, 720p; illus; index                          BL: 7924.aa.19

☞   Previous ed. A57; subsequent ed. A59

59 Manual of British rural sports / Stonehenge. 6th ed., entirely revised with additions. London: Routledge, Warne & Routledge, 1863.
xvi, 720p; illus; index

☞   Previous ed. A58; subsequent ed. A60

60 British rural sports / Stonehenge. 7th ed., entirely revised with additions. London: Warne, 1867.
xx, 821p; illus; index                          BL: 7906.bb.1

☞   Previous ed. A59; subsequent ed. A62

61 Modern athletics / Henry F. Wilkinson. London: The 'Field' Office, 1868.
120p                                            BL: 7906.aaa.25

Written by a member of London Athletic Club, this is the first historical account of amateur athletics covering the history and progress of athletics and providing a detailed review of every major meeting in the season 1867/8. The technique of the various athletic events is described in detail, and there are accounts of Oxford and Cambridge University athletics and of the history of West London Rowing Club and London AC. Finally, there is a list of amateur and professional records and a section on the feats of Captain Barclay, based on Thom's work. Essential reading.

☞   Subsequent ed. A64

62 British rural sports / Stonehenge. 9th ed., with numerous additions. London: Warne, 1871.
xx, 872p; illus; index
        *8th ed. untraced*                       BL: 7906.bb.2

☞   Previous ed. A60; subsequent ed. A63

63 British rural sports / Stonehenge. 12th ed., re-edited with numerous additions by the 'Field' staff. London: 1875.
640p; illus; index
        *10th and 11th eds untraced*             BL: 7906.cc.2

☞   Previous ed. A62; subsequent ed. A66

64 Modern athletics / Henry F. Wilkinson. 2nd ed. London: The 'Field' Office, 1875.
94p                                             BL: 7905.aaa.34

☞   Previous ed. A61; subsequent ed. A65

65 Modern athletics / Henry F. Wilkinson. 3rd ed. London: The 'Field' Office, 1877.                          BL: D

☞   Previous ed. A64; subsequent ed. A67

66 British rural sports / Stonehenge. 14th ed., re-edited with numerous additions. London: Warne, 1878.
xviii, 964p; illus; index
        *13th ed. untraced*                      BL: 7911.bb.4

☞   Previous ed. A63; subsequent ed. A68

67 Modern athletics / Henry F. Wilkinson. 4th ed. London: The 'Field' Office, 1880.
106p                                            BL: D

☞   Previous ed. A65

68 British rural sports / Stonehenge. 15th ed., with numerous additions. London: Warne, 1881.
966p; illus; index

☞   Previous ed. A66; subsequent ed. A69

69 British rural sports: comprising shooting, hunting, coursing, fishing, hawking, racing, boating and pedestrianism with all rural games and amusements / Stonehenge. 16th ed., re-edited with numerous additions by The Field Staff. London: Warne, 1886.
xviii, 1039p; illus; index                      BL: YA.1993.a.15276

☞   Previous ed. A68

70 Athletics and football / Sir Montague Shearman; with a contribution on paper-chasing by Walter Rye. London: Longmans, 1887.
xxvi, 446p; illus; index
(The Badminton Library of sports and pastimes)
                                                BL: K.T.C.103.a.1/5

Shearman, an eminent judge, athlete and President of the AAA from 1916 to 1929, produced the first major account of athletics. It includes a history of the sport in England, an account of the 1886 AAA Championships, chapters on training, athletic government, the events in detail (with much information about nineteenth century athletes), and an appendix of best performances on record. An article on cross-country running is contributed by Walter Rye. The work is fully illustrated by photographs and photo-engravings. The 1898 and subsequent editions list British and USA records, Amateur Championship winners and Inter-Varsity champions. In addition, Charles Sherrill, pioneer of the crouch start, contributes a chapter on American athletics:

'Mitchell's performance was never eclipsed until M. J. Brooks, a freshman from Rugby, came up to Oxford. Brooks in his first year jumped 5ft 10in at the Inter-Varsity sports, and a few days later eclipsed this by a performance of 5ft 11in at the championship meeting. He was a tall, cleanly built, and rather thin man, with a good deal of strength as well as spring, and his manner of jumping was very striking, although not very graceful when he got over great heights. He took very little run, and in fact almost walked up to the bar, springing straight over it with his legs tucked up high and well in front of him, and invariably looked, when his legs were once over, as if his body would fall crashing on to the bar; but he nearly always managed to jerk his body forward again and to alight upon his toes.... In 1876 Brooks disposed of his own and Glazebrook's record by jumping 6ft at the University sports at Oxford. For so many years it had been considered an impossible feat to jump 6ft that the excitement at the performance was very great, and the Honorary Treasurer of the OUAC, then as now an enthusiastic admirer of "records", threw his hat into the air, oblivious of the fact that the old Marston Ground was covered with puddles, in one of which the hat alighted.'

This is a marvellous work, though Shearman is clearly unaware of the strength of rural sports and pedestrianism, then at their peak in Scotland and Northern England.

☞ Subsequent ed. A73

71 Gymnastics / Rawdon Crawley. London: 1890.

*'Captain Rawdon Crawley' was a pseudonym for George Frederick Pardon*

Despite its title, this is a most interesting book on nineteenth century athletics. Descriptions are given of many professional performances, such as the famous dead-heat in 1865 of Lang and Richards in a mile in 4 mins 17¼ secs. Crawley also highlights the achievements of the great little professional walker, Perkins, who walked the first mile of a three mile race in 1874 in 6 mins 23 secs, finishing in 20 mins 47 secs. Perkins was almost certainly the first athlete to accomplish eight miles in an hour, a feat which he performed several times.

72 Athletics / Harry Hewitt Griffin. London: Bell, 1891.
vi, 119p; illus
(The all England series)      BL: 7908.df.23
*A second edition is thought to have been published in 1893, and a further edition in 1898, but neither have been traced.*

Includes chapters on athletics history (based largely on Wilkinson's 1868 work), on the promotion and management of athletics and on the technique of the various events. Illustrated by photographs. Contributors include: J. Kibblewhite, W. Pollock-Hill, E. H. Pelling, T. Ray and S. Thomas.

'The first AAC Championships were held at Beaufort House on Friday, 23rd March, 1866. The track was a gravel path of about 600 yards to the lap. The sports were (and for thirteen or fourteen years continued to be) arranged to follow the Varsity so as to secure the cream of the "Blue" talent. Thus of sixty-one competitors, thirty-three were from the Universities and Public Schools, four from the Civil Service, seven from the Army, so that outside clubs were poorly represented. The only notable performance was the high jump, wherein T. J. Little and J. H. S. Roupel, both Cambridge, tied at 5ft 9ins – best on record.'

73 Athletics and football / Montague Shearman, with a contribution on paper-chasing by W. Rye and an introduction by Sir Richard Webster, with numerous engravings after Stanley Berkeley and instantaneous photographs by G. Mitchell. 4th ed. London: Longmans, Green, 1894.
xxiv, 464p; illus; index
(The Badminton Library of sports and pastimes)
*2nd and 3rd editions were straight reprints of the 1887 edition*      BL: 7913.pp.1/6a

☞ Previous ed. A70

74 A sporting pilgrimage: riding to hounds, golf, rowing, football, club and university athletics: studies in English sport, past and present / Caspar W. Whitney. London: Osgood, 1894.
xii, 397p; illus      BL: 07905.i.30

An American account of British sport, with a substantial section on athletics. There are many excellent photographs.

'I was amused by the pistol of the Oxford starter, which is a muzzle-loading affair, rivalling the college buildings in antiquity, and when exploded sounded like a high cannon fire-cracker. The men as a rule adopt the standing start. I think I observed only one who started from his hands and knees, and he did not get the advantage (steadiness) that is supposed to belong to that style of getting off the mark.'

75   Athletics / Montague Shearman; with chapters on athletics at school by W. Beach Thomas; athletic sports in America by C. H. Sherrill; a contribution on paper-chasing by W. Rye; and an introduction by Sir Richard Webster; with numerous illustrations by Stanley Berkeley and from photographs. New ed. 1898.
xxvi, 356p; illus; index
(The Badminton Library of sports and pastimes)
                                             BL: 7913.pp.1/6.b

> Despite the edition statement, this is the athletics section of Shearman's *Athletics and Football*, revised and expanded. This edition is particularly valuable in its section on athletics in the USA, though no mention is made of the AAU's early twentieth century attempts to establish formal links with the AAA, as a junior partner.

   ☞  Subsequent ed. A77

76   Athletics of to-day / Harold Graham. London: Ward Lock, 1901.
158p                BL: Mic.A.7509(13) (microfilm copy)

> Contributors are: Alan Hunter, W. H. Workman, R. R. Conway, G. C. Vassall, W. G. Paget-Tomlinson, J. Edwards-Moss, E. L. Gay-Roberts and A. R. Welsh. Chapters are included on each phase of athletics, and on: athletics in London; international athletics; starting, judging and clocking races; and, athletics in the public schools.

77   Athletics / Montague Shearman; with chapters on athletics at school by W. Beach Thomas; athletic sports in America by C. H. Sherrill; a contribution on paper-chasing by W. Rye; and an introduction by Sir Richard Webster; with numerous illustrations by Stanley Berkeley and from photographs. New ed. London: Longman, Green, 1904.
xxvi, 360p; illus; index
(The Badminton Library of sports and pastimes)
                                             BL: 2270.cc.24

   ☞  Previous ed. A75

78   Athletics of to-day: history, development and training / F. A. M. Webster; foreword by Lord Burghley. London: Warne, 1929.
xvi, 368p; illus                   BL: 07911.gg.42

> This is probably the most ambitious of Webster's many works on athletics. He set out here to cover the field that Shearman had pioneered in 1887, with chapters on the history and growth of the sport, on science in athletics and on the history and technique of each event. The events are described in detail and illustrated with photographs of contemporary and earlier athletes. There are firsthand accounts of the early days by such old-timers as Marshall J. Brooks, Walter Rye, C. L. Lockton, J. H. A. Reay and W. Sapte.

79   Fifty years of progress, 1880-1930: the jubilee souvenir of the Amateur Athletic Association / H. F. Pash, hon. editor. London: The Association, 1930.
173p; illus
    *Foreword by Lord Desborough*        BL: X.629/4828

> The jubilee souvenir of the AAA, which has chapters on the formation and early days of the Association, and reviews of important events and decisions. There are separate accounts of athletics in the north, midlands, south, counties, schools and universities. Contributors include Sir Montague Shearman, H. B. Stallard, E. H. Pelling, D. G. A. Lowe, M. C. Nokes, J. W. Turner, A. E. Machin, A. S. Turk, T. W. Higgs, W. M. Barnard, W. W. Alexander and W. W. Webb.

80   British sports and sportsmen: athletic sports, tennis, rackets and other ball games / edited in conjunction with The Sporting Life. London: British Sports & Sportsmen Ltd, 1931?
xiii, 421p; illus                   BL: L.R.255.b.1

> A large and elegant publication with over ninety pages on athletics, including chapters on 'The foundation of British athletic sports', 'A review of athletics', 'The Olympic Games past and present' and 'Some notable personalities'. The outstanding illustrations include a print of the Cotswold Games (1636) and photographs of Lord Burghley, S. J. M. Atkinson, D. G. A. Lowe, Sam Ferris, T. C. Livingstone Learmonth, and various shots of the 1912 Olympic Games.

81   The story of athletics / Marian King; with pictures by Bernard Westmacott. London: Harper, 1931.
156p; illus; index
(City and country)                 BL: 012208.b.2/15

> In his foreword, Grantland Rice asserts that the author 'has covered the ground thoroughly with a variety of types that are certain to prove of great interest to all young readers'. Three chapters, 'How athletics came to us', 'Track' and 'The Olympic Games', cover track and field athletics from an American perspective.

82   The National Cross-Country Union jubilee souvenir 1883-1933 / foreword by E. J. Holt; contributions by J. E. Fowler-Dixon, A. E. Machin, J. H. Hardwick, S. Lambert, Charles Otway and W. T. Rainbow. The Union, 1933.
28p; illus; pbk

   ☞  Also listed at A149

83   Great moments in athletics / F. A. M. Webster. London: Country Life, 1947.
xii, 234p; illus
    *Foreword by Sir William Beach Thomas*   BL: 7913.tt.21

> Taking an event-based approach, Webster recalls outstanding amateur performers, and evokes their triumphant moments with his characteristic enthusiasm. The most memorable character sketch is possibly that of Pat O'Callaghan.

'His arms were straight out, his features set, both feet never off the ground at the same second. This was hammer-throwing perfection. One-two-three-four! Only one man in the world had I ever seen make four turns at such speed, only old Alfred Flaxman at his very best. The spikes of Dr Pat's left boot drove hard into the cinders, his left leg stiffened to form the immovable fulcrum for the throw, his arms swept round from low right to high left and the hammer departed, flying up and out over his left shoulder in a perfect arc. Even the veriest novice among the spectators high up in the back row of the packed stands knew at once that this must be the winning effort.'
This compilation also includes the poem 'A. E. Flaxman – Hammer Thrower Killed in the World War on July 1, 1916', by W. E. B. Henderson, a rare example of one athlete-poet inspired by another.

84 Fifty years of AAA championships / Harold M. Abrahams; forewords by J. A. Williamson and the Marquess of Exeter. London: Carborundum, 1961.
48p

Personal memories of the Championships from 1911 to 1960. There are also tables of best championship performances in this period, winners of championship medals, leading winners and Olympic gold medallists who also won AAA Championships.

85 History of British athletics / Mel Watman; foreword by Lynn Davies. London: Hale, 1968.
256p; illus ISBN: 0-7091-0255-0

Melvyn Watman here produced the successor of *Get to Your Marks!* as a chronicle of British athletics (although the latter work covered world and Commonwealth athletics, too) and thus became the latest historian in the line that began with H. F. Wilkinson exactly a century before. It is by far the most detailed book of its kind, and extends the story of British athletics back in time as well as bringing it up to date. All of the standard events, including walks and relays, are surveyed. This is not, strictly speaking, a history of British athletics, rather a history of British amateur athletics performance, for Watman does not discuss such matters as athletics politics, or competitive and coaching developments. Neither does he deal with the 'professional' roots of amateur athletics and their quality of performance in the pre-World War I period.

86 Athletics sportsgraph / Harold Abrahams; edited by Alan Blackwood. Cheam: Young World Productions for the British Olympic Association, 1972.
92p; illus ISBN: 0-7238-0878-3

Abrahams was the doyen of athletics statisticians from 1925 until his death in 1978. In this work (aimed primarily at a youthful readership), he presented clearly, in a large format, a potted history of track and field for men's and women's events. The graphic design and choice of illustrations are of pioneering importance.

87 Sport in Britain: its origins and development / H. A. Harris. London: Stanley Paul, 1975.
224p; illus; index ISBN: 0-09-124960-0
BL: X.629/10250

One of Professor Harris's earliest memories was watching A. N. S. Jackson, the 1912 Olympic 1500m champion, and this led to 'an enthusiasm of sport over a wide field'. Athletics in Britain is traced to the seventh century Saint Cuthbert. Other chapters cover sport and literature, sport and broadcasting, and the Olympic Games.

88 Athletics in focus / Wilf Paish and Tony Duffy. London: Lepus, 1976.
163p; illus ISBN: 0-860190-10-2
BL: X.622/5485

An experimental and largely successful collaboration between a BAAB national coach and one of the world's leading athletics photographers. A brief comparison of physical characteristics for the various events, based on 1972 Olympic Games data, is followed by sections on competition and the event structure. Each of the events is then discussed in more detail, illustrated by some excellent (mainly) black and white photography. Concluding sections deal with such widely diverse topics as junior athletics, landmarks, political intervention, success and tragedy, nature versus nurture, athletes in training, officialdom, technology in sport, and the competition arena.

89 The official centenary history of the Amateur Athletic Association / Peter Lovesey. Enfield: Guinness Superlatives, 1979.
222p; illus; index
*Bibliography: p207* ISBN: 0-900424-95-8
BL: X.622/7126

Published to mark the foundation of the AAA on 24 April 1880, and dedicated to the memory of Harold Abrahams (1899-1978), this work is an exemplar for future historians of the sport. Starting with unique historical background, the author traces the growth in the influence of the AAA, and covers such topics as rules, facilities, administration and coaching, sponsorship and major personalities. Winners of all AAA Championships (senior, juniors and youths) are given and the book is lavishly illustrated.

90 Athletics: the golden decade / Tony Ward. London: Queen Anne, 1991.
x, 246p; illus; index ISBN: 0-356-19679-8
BL: YK.1991.b.3595

Written from the perspective of an administrator, Ward characterises the 1980s as 'the golden years of British athletics, unprecedented in the century-long history of the sport'.

91   Great moments in British sport / editor, John Lovesey;
     designer, Neil Randon. London: Witherby, 1993.
     192p; illus                                    ISBN: 0-85493-229-1
                                                    BL: YK.1994.b.558

     Most of the accounts included are contemporary.
     Athletes include: Albert Hill, Eric Liddell, Sydney
     Wooderson, Roger Bannister, Christopher Chataway,
     Ann Packer, David Hemery, Mary Peters, Sebastian
     Coe, Daley Thompson, Liz McColgan, Linford Christie,
     and Sally Gunnell.

92   Sport and the making of Britain / Derek Birley.
     Manchester: Manchester University Press, 1993.
     x, 358p; illus; index
     (International studies in the history of sport)
               ISBN: 0-7190-3758-1 (cased) • 0-7190-3759-X (pbk)
                                                    BL: YK.1993.b.14080

     This is the first volume of a trilogy, in which the last
     four chapters take the narrative up to 1888. The
     origins of track and field athletics are traced, and
     their gradual incorporation into the mainstream of
     organised sport is outlined. The formation of the AAC
     (1866) and of the AAA (1880) and the rise of Irish
     field events specialists is noted. The parallel
     development of professional athletics at a number of
     centres in England, and especially Scotland, is
     described.

     ☞  See also: A93; A94

93   Land of sport and glory: sport and British society,
     1887-1910 / Derek Birley. Manchester: Manchester
     University Press, 1995.
     x, 287p; illus; index
     (International studies in the history of sport)
               ISBN: 0-7190-4494-4 (cased) • 0-7190-4495-2 (pbk)
                                                    BL: YC.1995.b.3402

     In this second volume of a trilogy, the author continues
     his account of the formative years of the AAA and of
     the Scottish AAA. Early international contests, such
     as that between London AC and New York AC (1895),
     the Olympic Games (1896), and even the nascent
     British Empire Games (which did not see the light of
     day until 1930), are mentioned. The resistance to the
     inclusion of women's athletics in the Olympic Games
     and the award by the IOC of the 1908 Games to
     London are well covered.

     ☞  See also: A92; A94

94   Playing the game: sport and British society, 1914-1945 /
     Derek Birley. Manchester: Manchester University Press,
     1995.
     x, 342p; index
     (International studies in the history of sport)
               ISBN: 0-7190-4496-0 (cased) • 0-7190-4497-9 (pbk)
                                                    BL: YC.1996.b.2112

     In this final volume of the trilogy, Birley takes his
     account of UK athletics through the most turbulent
     period of twentieth century European history,
     including the pioneering role of the WRAF in women's
     athletics, and its further diffusion in the 1920s

through clubs and universities. The impact of the
Achilles Club in the 1920s and 1930s is highlighted.
The introduction by the AAA of Junior Championships
in 1931 and the formation of the British Amateur
Athletic Board in 1932 are noted. The attempts by the
British Workers' Sports Federation to organise
alternative competitions are referred to, and the
Foreign Office role in the appeasement policy towards
Nazi Germany, as displayed in its attitude towards
British participation in the 1936 Olympic Games, is
made clear.

     ☞  See also: A92; A93

95   Running scared: how athletics lost its innocence / Steven
     Downes and Duncan Mackay. Edinburgh: Mainstream,
     1996.
     224p; illus                                    ISBN: 1-85158-855-8
                                                    BL: YK.1997.b.3326

     The authors set out to show how athletics became
     corrupted in the preceding decade. A perceptive work
     of great quality, covering territory rarely dealt with in
     the literature.

## ✳  *Additional References*

96   The relation of athletic sports to public health / Henry
     Hoole. London: H. Renshaw, 1891.
     40p                                            BL: 07305.e.23(11)

     Includes a brief historical survey of modern athletics.

97   Amateur Athletic Association coming of age dinner
     1901. London: The Association, 1902.
     32p; pbk

     A privately circulated publication of the speeches
     made by Shearman and others on this occasion. Now
     very rare.

98   Character and sportsmanship / Theodore Andrea Cook.
     London: Williams & Norgate, 1927.
     xxvii, 349p; illus                             BL: 010856.d.46

     A wide-ranging survey of sport and its influence on
     national character. Many of the ideas have dated, but
     there are many references to athletics of the period
     1894-1926.

99   Eyes towards Helsinki / Stan Tomlin. London: A.
     Wander, 1949.
     48p; pbk

     Includes United Kingdom 'top ten' lists for both senior
     and junior athletes in 1949.

100  Independent Television's World of Sport 1965 /
     Eamonn Andrews. London: TV World, 1965.
     148p; illus

     A well-illustrated volume with a section on athletics
     largely contributed by Adrian Metcalfe. There are
     articles on Alan Simpson and Anne Smith.

101 Report of the Committee of Enquiry into the development of athletics under the direction of the Amateur Athletic Association and the British Amateur Athletic Board. London: The Association and the Board, 1968.
43p

Chaired by Lord Byers. The mountain laboured and brought forth a mouse. A dim, timid report, few of whose proposals were carried forward.

102 Modern sport: its origin and development through two centuries / John Goulstone. Bexleyheath: The author, 1974.
79p; mimeograph                    BL: X.611/4279

Drawing upon reports in contemporary newspapers and periodicals, the author presents the evolution of a number of sports through the eighteenth and nineteenth centuries. Athletics (pp44-51) is the subject of early statistical treatment, with details of world's best times being published in 1823. Some of the outstanding athletes are mentioned and the origins of hurdling and steeplechasing are traced to their inclusion in a track meeting at Manchester in 1843. The field events featured in programmes during the nineteenth century are described, including the climbing pole vault technique. Other sections deal with arenas, clubs and meetings. Goulstone's booklet offers only eight pages on the history of athletics, mostly drawn from eighteenth and nineteenth century sporting magazines. His methodology offers rich opportunity for the diligent athletics historian, albeit not in the area of comparative performance statistics, particularly in sprints (the stopwatch was invented in the middle of the nineteenth century) and field events (where little statistical evidence exists before 1820). Goulstone surprisingly fails to lay any emphasis on the rich culture of Scottish and Irish games except by mentioning, 'Hammer and shot were common British field events from early times'. Best considered as a series of evocative notes rather than rigorous history, Goulstone covers territory rarely discussed in conventional histories (he offers a particularly good account of the growth of the amateur) and this book is essential reading.

103 Sport and place: a geography of sport in England, Scotland and Wales / John Bale. London: Hurst, 1982.
xvi, 187p; illus, maps; index
*Bibliography: p177-184*          ISBN: 0-905838-65-3
                                   BL: X.629/20094

Bale employs a number of concepts introduced by Rooney in his *A Geography of American Sport: from Cabin Creek to Anaheim* (Reading, MA: Addison Wesley, 1974). After an exemplary introduction, the author presents a range of background material on sports participation in Great Britain. Chapter 9 deals with 'Aspects of athletics', and covers such topics as provision of facilities, patterns of performance (with per capita 'production' of athletes in different event-groups) and Britain's place in the world.

104 The financing of athletics in the United Kingdom: report of a committee appointed by the Chairman of the Sports Council. London: The Sports Council, 1983.
34p; pbk

Chaired by Mr Dick Jeeps, C.B.E.

105 Athletics on the right track. London: Sports Council, 1987.
92p; illus, maps; spiral          ISBN: 0-906577-78-0
                                   BL: BS.387/201

This was the report of a national working party. Intended as a policy document, it presents the results of research carried out in 1982/83, and covers such topics as organisation and administration at national and club level, technical officials, participation, facilities and coaching. The data on tracks and other facilities (indoor and outdoor) relates to 1984.

106 Not another Messiah: an account of the Sports Council 1988-93 / David Pickup. Edinburgh: Pentland, 1996.
ix, 225p; illus; index            ISBN: 1-85821-392-4
                                   BL: YC.1997.b.275

The foreword is by J. Allan Patmore.

107 50 years of Sports Report / introduced by Desmond Lynam; edited by Audrey Adams. London: CollinsWillow, 1997.
224p; illus                       ISBN: 0-00-218806-6
                                   BL: YK.1999.a.4609

108 The history and development of the National Olympian Association (1865-1886) / Ian Stuart Brittain. Leicester University, 1997. MSc thesis.

# Pedestrianism

109 Particulars of the late Mr F. Powell's journey on foot, from London to York, and back again in the year 1772. London: J. Fowler, 1793.

1 folio sheet            BL: 11621.i.11(2)

This appears to be one of the earliest records of a pedestrian performance. For a wager of 20 pounds (or possibly guineas) Powell had to complete the round journey of about 400 miles (this document gives 394 miles, whereas the biographical sketch gives 402 miles) inside six days. Setting out from Hicks's Hall in London about 20 minutes past midnight on 29 November, Powell arrived back at his starting point at 6.30 pm on the following Saturday. The account contains some delightful details:

'At York, he delivered a letter to Mr Clarke, a watchmaker, and then went to the Golden Anchor, where he took a little refreshment, then went to bed for about an hour and a half; after which, at half past five, he set out on his return….'

The report ends with an epitaph on Foster Powell who died on 15 April 1793.

110 Pedestrianism, or, An account of the performances of celebrated pedestrians during the last and present century: with a full narrative of Captain Barclay's public and private matches and an essay on training / Walter Thom. Aberdeen: Brown and Frost, 1813.

286p              BL: 1040.d.23

This is almost certainly the first book on competitive athletics to be written in English. Prompted by the feats of Captain Barclay, the great pedestrian of the early 1800s, it contains a full account of his feats and training methods, which were to influence athletics training for over a century. At an early age Barclay Allardice showed athletics promise by 'walking 6 miles in an hour for 100 guineas on the Croydon Road in 1806'. The feat which gained him greatest fame was the walking of a thousand miles in 1,000 hours on Newmarket Heath in 1809. This was more of a sleep-denying performance than an athletic one, as a calculation will reveal. The wager for the feat was, appropriately, 1,000 guineas. The book also contains 'ranking-lists' of eighteenth century and early nineteenth century performances, which indicate that there was considerable athletic activity at this time.

111 A brief vindication of the legality of the late proceedings against George Wilson, the Blackheath pedestrian / John Laurens Bicknell. London: W. Clarke, 1815.

47p              BL: 515.e.10(6)

In this discussion of the legal implications of Wilson's experiences, Bicknell reviews previous cases concerning pedestrians and examines the law's attitude to footracing over the centuries.

112 Pedestrianism: a correct and minute journal of the time occupied by Mr J. Stokes, of Bristol, during his walk of fifty miles per day for twenty successive days at Saltford, Somerset / J. G. and T. H.; to which is prefixed, a brief memoir of Mr Stokes. Bristol: 1815.

*Authors are Joseph Gilbert and Thomas Howell*
                 BL: T.1090(15)

113 An account of Wm. Pearson the Lancashire pedestrian's running match against time on Newcastle Town Moor, on Monday, July 1, 1822, when he ran 50 miles in 7 hours 50 min. / William Pearson. Newcastle: Marshall, 1822.

1 sheet            BL: L.R.38.c.18(23)

Pearson, described as 'about the middle size of light weight, only about 22 years of age', started his attempt at 1 pm in favourable weather over a measured half-mile stretch of the North Turnpike Road. He wore 'a pair of nankeen pantaloons, a striped shirt, and a handkerchief round his head'. He started with 'a pair of light carpet shoes', but discarded these after about 21 miles, and ran the remaining distance barefoot. Pearson 'ran about 400 yards farther than the limit prescribed to shew that he had done the task completely and without difficulty'. A delightfully detailed description of his refreshment during the run is given, as well as a graphic account of his running action. Reference is also made to his performance a month earlier in running from Newcastle to Durham and back.

114 The book of days: a miscellany of popular antiquities, in connection with the calendar / edited by R. Chambers. London: Chambers, 1863-1864.

2 vols.              BL: 9010.h.9

Volume I includes an account of the running footmen who were the pioneers of the era of pedestrianism, and of Captain Barclay's career, while Volume II includes a section on 'remarkable wagers' which describes various pedestrian feats.

115 Sportascrapiana: cricket and shooting, pedestrian, equestrian, rifle and pistol doings, lion hunting and deer stalking by celebrated sportsmen with hitherto unpublished anecdotes of the nineteenth century, from George IV to the Sweep / edited by Caw (C. A. W.). London: Simpkin, Marshall, 1867.

301p; illus

*Author is C. A. Wheeler; also known as 'Facts in Athletics'*
                 BL: 7905.bb.37

Contains much original material on pedestrianism. Chapter 10 is on 'Training, starting and timing "spirt" runners'. There is an illustration of a spiked running shoe (p213).

'The action of a good "spirt" runner is generally perceptible by his running from the thigh, or say the hip, rather than from the knee. In illustration of the superiority of the former mode, I would cite the contrast between two horses: one with round action cannot get well over the ground; good trotters throw their forelegs out straight, so should a man. A good "spirt" runner should be able to do one hundred yards in ten and a half seconds; a "clinker" can do it in ten, but there are not two men that can do it in less. If you had a man that could do it in ten, you could win £10,000 at Sheffield with him; it is a great place for "fleet of foot", and large sums are gambled on the handicap there every year. There are men that have done it in less time, but as it was only in trials, I take no notice of it.'

☞ Subsequent ed. A116

116 Sportascrapiana: cricket and shooting, pedestrian, equestrian, rifle and pistol doings, lion hunting and deer stalking by celebrated sportsmen with hitherto unpublished anecdotes of the nineteenth century, from George IV to the Sweep / edited by Caw (C. A. W.). 2nd ed. London: Simpkin, Marshall, 1868.

*Author is C. A. Wheeler* BL: 7906.aa.38

☞ Previous ed. A115

117 From Land's End to John of Groats, being an account of his record walk / George H. Allen. London: Fowler, 1905.
xi, 107p BL: 010347.e.2

'Necessity, in the form of Dr Deighton, forced me again to enter the lists. In the spring of 1904, this well-known athlete walked from Land's End to John O'Groats in 24 days 4 hrs. His chief sustenance en route was a much advertised meat-juice ... to prove that flesh-foods generally and meat-juices in particular are utterly unnecessary for such a feat of endurance, now, seemed to be a task it was my duty to perform, in view of my two previous undertakings. My record walk was the result.'
So the book begins. The story ends with Allen covering the distance in close to a week inside the old record. The book has lists of the signatures of people whom Allen met on his way and the full diet of the pedestrian. Though Allen's book is of little literary merit, it gives us a view of athletics in less tense, less sophisticated times and of life in a country uncluttered by traffic, where a pedestrian like Allen could genuinely call the road his own.

118 Hallamshire athletes: growth of football, cricket and kindred sports / J. C. Clegg. 1914.

119 Powderhall and pedestrianism: the history of a famous sports enclosure, 1870-1943 / David A. Jamieson. Edinburgh: W. & A. K. Johnston, 1943.
320p; illus BL: 7916.h.41

Professional athletics is a twilight sport and Jamieson is the only writer in modern times to give it detailed consideration. The book was published during the war and, as a consequence, passed almost unnoticed by the athletics public. It is a painstaking rather than a brilliant book, but contains a wealth of original material. The main theme is the history of the famous Powderhall Stadium, but much information is given on pedestrianism in other parts of Britain. The book is full of great achievements by forgotten athletes. A remarkable work, essential reading for the athletics historian.

120 The Saturday book 11 / edited by Leonard Russell. London: Hutchinson, 1951.
280p; illus BL: ZK.9.a.2805

In the section 'Sport for all seasons' by Olive Cook and Edwin Smith, is reproduced on page 72 an etching of William Gale during his 1877 walk of 1500 miles in 1,000 hours and on page 73 a coloured etching of Captain Robert Barclay (Allardice) during his successful attempt in 1809 on Newmarket Heath to walk 1000 miles in 1,000 successive hours. The caption compares the exploits of Gale and Barclay in some detail.

121 Shanks's pony: a study of walking / Morris Marples. London: Dent, 1959.
192p; illus BL: 7923.o.12

The second chapter, 'Heel and toe' (pp20-29), is concerned with the early pedestrian athletes, among them Captain Barclay, Foster Powell, George Wilson and Abraham Wood.

122 The professionals / Geoffrey Nicholson; photographs by Gerry Cranham. London: Deutsch, 1964.
223p; illus BL: X.449/705

An account of all professional sports in Britain, which includes a chapter on contemporary 'pro' athletics, with good descriptions of the events which led to the Lillie Bridge fire, and of a Powderhall meeting (pp128-43):
'Each week the results of all SGA meetings are sent to his home at Newtongrange where, in file after file, he keeps tabs on 5,000 runners. Even with the aid of this reference system, and with the declarations of their past performances that runners are obliged to make on their entry forms, Young reckons it takes him six weeks to work out the starting positions for the 286 competitors. The 120yds sprint illustrates his method. This he calculated at the New Year on a scratch time of 11.5 secs. He judged only one man, Rickie Dunbar of Edinburgh, to be capable, on known form, of returning this time; Dunbar therefore became back marker. Young had then to award relative marks to the other 139 runners – marks that varied as widely as Davey Walker's one yard to the twenty-six yards, more than a fifth of the total distance, allowed to a man called Clifford from Dumbarton. It needed only one bad under-estimation of a runner's capability to make nonsense of the whole event.'

123 Gold at New Year / John Franklin. Hawick: The author, 1972.

Highlights of the New Year professional meetings in Scotland, with an emphasis on the sprints.

124 Walkers / Miles Jebb. London: Constable, 1986.
xii, 202p; index            ISBN: 0-09-467430-2
                              BL: YK.1986.a.1715

Like the earlier work by Marples, this contains some fascinating material on walkers as athletes, with a chapter devoted specifically to the exploits of such as Foster Powell, Robert Barclay Allardice, Abraham Wood, Richard Manks, William Gale, Edward Payon Weston, John Lees and Ann Sayer.

125 The great Welsh sprint: the story of the Welsh Powderhall Handicap 1903-1934 / Brian Lee. Pontypridd: Gwyn Thomas, 1999.
viii, 87p; illus; pbk

# Women's Athletics

126 Athletics and out-door sports for women, each subject being separately treated by a special writer, with an introduction by Lucille E. Hill. London: Macmillan, 1903.
xvii, 339p; illus             BL: 7912.h.15
*Includes 'Running' by Herbert H. Holton and 'Track athletics' by Christine Terhune Herrick.*

127 Athletics for women and girls: how to be an athlete and why / Sophie C. Eliott-Lynn, with foreword by Lord Desborough and appreciation by R. J. Kentish. London: Robert Scott, 1925.
122p; illus             BL: 7904.de.30

Mrs Eliott-Lynn (later Lady Heath) was a pioneer of women's athletics and the holder of the world high jump record. The book is now chiefly of interest for its many photographs of women athletes of the 1920s.

128 Athletics of to-day for women: history, development and training / F. A. M. Webster; with foreword by the Lord Decies. London: Frederick Warne, 1930.
x, 278p; illus; index        BL: 07906.i.26

Webster wrote the first substantial history of women's athletics with a remarkable perspective considering how new the sport was in Europe. A history and development chapter is followed by chapters on the events, using anecdotal information on the leading athletes of the day. There is an appendix on records.

129 Women's athletics / George Pallett. Dulwich: Normal, 1955.
290p; illus             BL: 7919.e.56

A history of international athletics is followed by sections on the English scene, training and technique, and results and records. Pallett's work is a useful update of Webster's 1930 history. The foreword is by Fanny Blankers-Koen.

130 British women's athletics. Part 1: National / Peter R. Pozzoli. London: Arena, 1965.
84p

Largely statistical, the first part of a planned four volume survey of British women's athletics, including British best performers, top 100 performers in each event, national championships and results and a Ladies Athletic Club directory. In the event only two volumes were published.

131 British women's athletics. Part 2: International 1921-64 / Peter R. Pozzoli. London: Arena, 1965.
123p

Detailed results of all international matches since the Monte Carlo Games of March 1921, followed by a comprehensive index of all international representatives.

132 International women's athletics 1890-1940: a statistical history / compiled by Eric L. Cowe. Bingley: The author, 1985.
159p; pbk             BL: YK.1988.a.3313

The first major statistical study since Pozzoli's, this is wider in scope and more reliable, taking in: all-time best performers and performances lists; evolution of world's best performances; and evolution of national best performances for twenty-seven nations.

133 Grace under pressure: the emergence of women in sport / Adrianne Blue. London: Sidgwick & Jackson, 1987.
xv, 213p; illus; index; pbk
       ISBN: 0-283-99306-5 (cased) • 0-283-99583-1 (pbk)
                        BL: YK.1989.b.2625

Blue describes her book as an informal social history of the emergence of women in sport between 1500 BC and 1992 AD. It is a definitive work. covering social, psychological and physiological aspects of women's development in sport, in which athletics plays an understandably prominent part. Essential reading for the historian of women's athletics.

134 Women and sport / Anne Coates. Hove: Wayland, 1989.
48p; illus; index
ISBN: 1-85210-392-2
BL: YK.1990.b.4586

Athletics features very strongly in this outline history of women's sport from 1840 aimed at a young student readership. Profiles of Mary Peters and Fatima Whitbread are included, as are several archival photographs (from Mary Lines in 1921).

135 Women in sport: issues and controversies / edited by Greta L. Cohen; foreword by Jackie Joyner-Kersee. London: Sage, 1993.
xix, 338p; illus; index
ISBN: 0-8039-4979-0 (cased) • 0-8039-4980-4 (pbk)
BL: YK.1993.b.13155

136 Their day in the sun: women of the 1932 Olympics / Doris H. Pieroth. London: University of Washington Press, 1996.
xii, 186p; illus; index
*Bibliography: p176-179*
ISBN: 0-295-97553-9 (cased) • 0-295-97554-7 (pbk)
BL: 97/03288

Interviews with eleven of the women athletes, swimmers and fencers who represented the USA.

137 From Sophie to Sonia: a history of women's athletics / Noel Henry. Greystones, Co. Wicklow: Noel Henry, 1998.
207p; illus; pbk
ISBN: 0-9532971-0-1
BL: YK.1999.a.9180

138 Early women's athletics: statistics and history / Eric L. Cowe. Bingley: The author, 1999.
vi, 159p; illus; pbk
ISBN: 0-9537030-0-2

An account of British women's athletics before 1921. Includes: all-time lists as at the end of 1920; British women's year lists 1921-1930, including seasonal reviews and results of WAAA Championships (from 1923); Women's Inter-Varsity Athletic Sports 1921-30, including brief biographical notes on selected student athletes; British progression lists to the end of 1930, for both seniors and juniors; results of international matches in Europe 1921-1928. Also included is a concise biography of Sophie Eliott-Lynn and a contribution by John Brant on early Irish women's athletics. This work can, despite some imperfections, be considered as one of the most important to have appeared in the latter half of the twentieth century.

139 'A proper spectacle': women Olympians 1900-1936 / Stephanie Daniels & Anita Tedder; foreword by Paula Radcliffe. Houghton Conquest: ZeNaNA, 2000.
163p; illus; index; pbk
ISBN: 0-9537645-0-8
BL: YK.2000.a.6396

Based on personal memoirs and interviews, this is a valuable record of the women pioneers in the Olympics.

## ✳ *Additional References*

140 'Tripping daintily into the arena': a social history of English women's athletics 1921-1960 / L. Robinson. Warwick University, 1996. PhD thesis.

Seeks to demonstrate that women's athletics was a thriving sport in the early part of the last century, with greater male support than previously supposed.

141 A new dawn rising: an empirical and social study concerning the emergence and development of English women's athletics until 1980 / Gregory P. Moon. Surrey University, 1997. PhD thesis.

# *England ~ General*

142 The Kings Majesties declaration to his subjects, concerning lawfull sports to bee used. Issued by King James, 24 May, 1618. London: 1618.
9p
BL: C.25.f.10

143 Glig-Gamena Angel-Deod, or, The sports and pastimes of the people of England, including the rural and domestic recreations, May games, mummeries, shows, processions, pageants and pompous spectacles, from the earliest period to the present time, illustrated by engravings selected from ancient paintings / Joseph Strutt. London: J. White, 1801.
301p; illus
BL: 7915.k.9

The standard work of reference on the ancient and medieval history of sport in England. 'Rural exercises generally practised' (Book II, chapter II) gives early references to many events of the modern track and field programme. There are also accounts of the Cotswold and Cornish Games. 'Casting of the bar' is frequently mentioned by the romance writers as one part of a hero's education, and a poet of the sixteenth century thinks it highly commendable for kings and princes, by the way of exercise, to throw 'the stone, the barre or the plummet'. After his accession to the throne, Henry VIII, according to Hall and Holinshead, retained 'the casting of the barre' among his favourite amusements. The sledge hammer was also used for the same purpose as the bar and the stone and, among the rustics, if Barclay is correct, an axletree. At the commencement of the seventeenth century these pastimes seem to have lost their relish among the higher classes of the people, and for this reason Peacham, describing a complete gentleman, speaks of throwing the hammer as an exercise proper only for soldiers in camp, or for the amusement of the king's guard, but by no means 'beseeming of nobility'.

   ☞   Subsequent ed. A144

144 Glig-Gamena Angel-Deod, or, The sports and pastimes of the people of England, including the rural and domestic recreations, May games, mummeries, shows, processions, pageants and pompous spectacles, from the earliest period to the present time, illustrated by engravings selected from ancient paintings / Joseph Strutt. 2nd ed. London: White, 1810.
xlix, 357; illus            BL: 7917.dd.15

   ☞   Previous ed. A143; subsequent ed. A145

145 The sports and pastimes of the people of England / Joseph Strutt. A new edition, with a copious index by William Hone. London: William Reeves, 1830.
lxvii, 420, illus; index        BL: 785.i.6

   ☞   Previous ed. A144

146 Ancient customs, sports and pastimes of the English / Jehoshaphat Aspin, with twelve engravings. London: John Harris, 1832.
viii, 256p; illus            BL: 1210.a.4

   Reference is made to javelin throwing during Norman times and discus-throwing, hammer-throwing and running in the reign of Henry II.

   ☞   Subsequent ed. A147

147 Ancient customs, sports and pastimes of the English / Jehoshaphat Aspin. 2nd ed. London: John Harris, 1835.
viii, 256p; illus            BL: 7921.a.62

   ☞   Previous ed. A146

148 Fair play: the games of merrie England / Rudolf Kircher; translated by R. N. Bradley. London: Collins, 1928.
ix, 221p; illus            BL: 07906.e.35

   Originally published as Fair Play: Sport, Spiel und Geist in England (Frankfurt: 1927), the author states that 'The organisation of pure athletics has been carried to

a pitch which is exceptional even for England, resulting in a more thorough general training and bodily fitness. The Amateur Athletic Association governs the athletic world in much the same way as the Bank of England controls the City; it dominates without ruling.' (p37). A separate chapter on athletics (pp81-84) appears in the third part (The sports and their public). 'Compared with the numbers who flock to cricket and football matches, the twenty-five thousand spectators of the greatest English athletic event is modest enough. This is the AAA sports meeting at the famous Stamford Bridge ground. But the attendance comprises the keenest and most expert spectators in the world.' The author concludes by noting the popularity of both cross-country running and race-walking. The black and white photographs are well chosen and finely reproduced; they include two with an athletics theme.

149 The National Cross-Country Union jubilee souvenir 1883-1933 / foreword by E. J. Holt; contributions by J. E. Fowler-Dixon, A. E. Machin, J. H. Hardwick, S. Lambert, Charles Otway and W. T. Rainbow. The Union, 1933.
28p; illus; pbk

   ☞   Also listed at A82

## ✱ *Regions*

150 Norfolk athletes and athletics / Herbert E. Potter. Norwich: Pack, 1904.
80p; illus

   Contains biographies, photographs and exploits of Norfolk athletes including C. G. Wood and Walter Rye. Specialises in the period 1865-85.

151 From turnpike roads to tartan tracks: the history of professional foot racing on Tyneside, 1850-1970 / Frederick Moffatt. Morpeth: The author, 1979.

152 Athletics: development plan October 1982. Leeds: Sports Council, Yorkshire & Humberside, 1982.
24p; pbk

153 Sport and leisure in Victorian Barrow / Bryn Trescatheric. Barrow-in-Furness: Hougenai, 1983.
36p; illus, 2 maps; pbk      ISBN: 0-946522-01-4
                             BL: X.809/56607

   Based on a series of articles which appeared in the North-Western Evening Mail (Summer 1977), this book contains a section on 'athletic all-sorts', including backwards jumping and wheeling a navvy barrow from Barrow to Ulverston inside six hours, as well as the more commonplace footraces and jumping events.

154 A history of sports in Dorking: a compilation of the histories of a variety of the sports which have been practised in Dorking / editor, Celia Newbery. Dorking: The Local History Group, Dorking and Leith Hill District Preservation Society, 1985.
138p; illus; index; pbk                    BL: X.629/27835

*Chris Kohler traces the history of athletics in Dorking, Surrey, from 1888. The most notable member of Dorking St Paul's AC, formed in 1935, was the 1950 European 800m champion, Harold John Parlett.*

155 A very sporting association: the story of the City of Ely Sports 1893-1964 / Roy Stubbings. Ely: Ely Society, 1985.
50p; illus; pbk                        ISBN: 0-903616-09-2
                                       BL: YK.1987.a.683

*The history of the August Bank Holiday sports meeting.*

156 B Georges' running in Devon / John Legge. Exeter: Obelisk, 1987.
48p; illus; pbk                        ISBN: 0-946651-18-3
                                       BL: YK.1988.a.775

*In providing a brief outline of distance running in Devon, the author presents the information in five sections: Town and country races; Club competition; Cross-country championships; Road racing in Devon; Devon relays past and present.*

157 Athletics in the Eastern region. Bedford: Sports Council (Eastern Region) in co-operation with the Southern Counties AA and the governing bodies of athletics in the Eastern Region, 1988.
27p; pbk                                   BL: BS.387/214

158 Athletics: a strategy for sport and recreation in the Northern region. Durham: Northern Council for Sport and Recreation, 1992.
23p; pbk                                BL: DSC-q93/07076

159 A Devon approach to physical education: athletics. Exeter: Devon County Council, 1993.
106p; illus                            ISBN: 1-85522-313-9
                                       BL: DSC-OP-LG/7627

160 On the starting line: a history of athletics in Leicester / Jim Sharlott; foreword by Sebastian Coe including illustrations by George Herringshaw. Leicester: Leicester City Council, 1994.
112p; illus; pbk                       ISBN: 0-901675-25-3
                                       BL: YK.1995.a.2157

*Unusual in its attempt to delineate the history of athletics in one city, it succeeds admirably in pulling together a number of strands: cross-country, race walking, road running, track and field. Other sections deal with schools athletics, clubs and venues, and there are detailed biographies of UK Olympic participants from Leicester.*

161 Focus sport: athletics, North West 1992-1996: a development plan for athletics in the North West. Manchester: North West Council for Sport and Recreation, 1996?
28p; illus, 1 map; pbk                  BL: ZK.9.b.5334

162 Staying the distance: the complete history of distance running in Keighley / Rob Grillo. Keighley: The author, 1999.
150p

✱  *Additional References*

163 The London to Brighton running race / John C. Jewell. London: Road Runners' Club, 1960.
4p; pbk

164 The development of athletics in the Potteries, 1850-1900 / H. P. Mawdsley. Manchester University, 1976. MEd dissertation.

165 Sports and games: history and origins / Brian Jewell. Tunbridge Wells: Midas, 1977.
148p; illus; index                     ISBN: 0-85936-075-X
                                       BL: X.622/5936

*An update to 1900 of Joseph Strutt's seminal work, covering early regional games.*

166 Lakeland sport in the nineteenth century / I. Ward. Liverpool University, 1985. PhD thesis.

167 Everyone's a winner: the history of sport in and around Greater Manchester / Alison Taubman, Pauline Webb and Jenny Wetton. Manchester: Greater Manchester Museum of Science & Industry, 1990.
44p; illus; pbk                        ISBN: 1-870698-60-6

*Prepared for an exhibition organised by the museum, this includes a brief general history of the Olympics and of athletics and other Olympic sports in Manchester.*

# *England ~ Clubs, and County & Regional Associations*

### *Airedale and Spen Valley Athletic Club*

168 ASVAC centenary news, 1880-1980. Airedale: The Club, 1980.
8p; illus
Newspaper format.

### *Aldridge Running Club*

169 Aldridge Running Club: the first five years / Ian Llewellyn & David Smith. Aldridge: The Club, 1993.
16p; illus; pbk

### *Amalgamated Clubs of St. Bartholomew's Hospital*

170 The Amalgamated Clubs of St. Bartholomew's Hospital: year-book of the Abernethian Society and Athletic Clubs, 1893-94. London: The Clubs, 1893.
35p                                              BL: 7689.a.45

### *The Bank of England Sports Club*

171 The house: a history of the Bank of England Sports Club, 1908-1983 / researched and written by A. J. N. Bond & M. O. H. Doughty. Roehampton: The Club, 1984.
402p; illus                            ISBN: 0-9509777-0-5
                                            BL: X.622/24439

### *Bingley Harriers*

172 Bingley Harriers and Athletic Club: the story so far / Mick Watson. Bingley: The Club, 1993.
78p

### *Birchfield Harriers*

173 Birchfield Harriers Club history souvenir programme, 27 July 1929 (1877-1929). Birmingham: The Club, 1929.
80p

174 Birchfield Harriers diamond jubilee souvenir programme, 24 July 1937 (1877-1937) / C. G. Austin. Birmingham: The Club, 1937.
80p
Includes 48 pages on the club's history and statistics.

175 Birchfield Harriers centenary 1877-1977 / Tony Hadley. Birmingham: The Club, 1977.
20p; illus; pbk

176 The history of Birchfield Harriers 1877-1988 / edited by W. O. Alexander & Wilfred Morgan. Birmingham: The Club, 1988.
124p; illus
    *Foreword by Sir Arthur Gold*          ISBN: 0-9514082-0-8
In addition to reports of each season, brief biographies of outstanding personalities, tables of performances in major events, and lists of best performances are included.

### *Birmingham Athletic Club*

177 History of the Birmingham Athletic Club, 1866-98 / E. Lawrence Levy. Birmingham: The Club, 1898.
46p; pbk

178 Birmingham Athletic Club, 1866-1916: pen pictures of a popular past: a jubilee issue / E. Lawrence Levy. Birmingham: The Association, 1916.
72p; illus                                              BL: D
There is a reference copy at Birmingham Central Library.

179 B.A.I.: the Birmingham Athletic Institute remembered / Charles Jenkins, Michele Shoebridge and Patricia Van Zyl; edited by M. Irene Waterman. Studley: Brewin, 1992.
vii, 88p; illus; pbk
    *The title page incorrectly gives the author's forename as 'Michelle'.*          ISBN: 1-858580-06-4
                                            BL: YK.1994.a.2897
The editor was Principal of the BAI Women's Section 1944-75, and the work is based on her thesis 'History of the BAI 1866-1918'.

### *Blackheath Harriers*

180 Blackheath Harriers 1869-1924. Privately published, 1924.
24p; pbk
Probably written by H. J. Dyball, the club secretary.

181 The centenary history of the Blackheath Harriers / D. K. Saunders, A. J. Weeks-Pearson. Hayes: Honorary Secretary of the Harriers, 1971.
248p; illus, map; index
    *Foreword by Sydney Wooderson*          BL: X.622/1462
    ☞   Subsequent ed. A182

182 The centenary history of the Blackheath Harriers / D. K. Saunders, A. J. Weeks-Pearson. Rev. ed. London: The Harriers, 1989.
xx, 267p; illus; map; index
   *Foreword by Sydney Wooderson*

Formed as Peckham AAC in 1869, its base shifted in 1878 and, to reflect this, the name was changed to Blackheath Harriers. Though cross-country formed (and indeed still forms) a strong element in the club's programme, track and, to a lesser extent, field events also attracted support. Among the earliest AAA champions produced by the club was Charles Wood (440yds in 49.8 secs in 1886). The authors emphasise that 'the chief danger of a history written by members ... is inward-looking complacency and resulting inaccuracy', a danger avoided in this richly detailed chronicle.

☞   Previous ed. A181

### Blackpool and Fylde Athletic Club

183 In the beginning… / David Reader. Blackpool: The author, 1996.
39p; illus; pbk

### Bury Athletic Club

184 History of Bury Athletic Club / R. Taylor. Bury: The Club, 1934.

### Cambridge University Athletic Club

185 The Cambridge University Athletic Club: list of rules, holders of challenge cups, old blues, Oxford and Cambridge sports. Cambridge: The Club, 1881-1919.
   *Published at irregular intervals;*
   *continued by: The Cambridge University Athletic Club record book*                    BL: D

☞   See also: A187

186 Fifty years of sport at Oxford, Cambridge, and the great public schools / arranged by Lord Desborough; edited by Arthur C. M. Croome. London: Southwood, 1913-1922.
3 vols.: 332p; 325p; 505p; illus
   *Vols. 1, 2: Oxford and Cambridge; vol. 3: Eton, Harrow and Winchester / edited by R. H. Lyttleton, Arthur Page and Evan B. Noel*
                    BL: L.R.37.a

The first 82 pages of Vol. 1 give results and accounts of every Inter-Varsity meeting from 1864 to 1913, of matches against the American universities and of the beginnings of athletics at Oxford and Cambridge. Croome was an expert hurdler and was credited with having invented the straight-leg pick-up style. Contributors include P. M. Thornton, J. H. Morgan, T. E. Wells, H. C. L. Tindall, G. C. Vassall, W. E. B. Henderson, S. S. Abrahams and P. Stormonth-Darling. Biographies are given of all Blues and there are

numerous photographs. Vol. 2 contains 12 pages on cross-country running and Vol. 3 gives histories of athletics at Eton, Harrow and Winchester, with biographies of the athletes.

☞   Also listed at: A242

187 The Cambridge University Athletic Club record book / F. N. Drake Digby. Cambridge: Metcalfe, 1925-1936?
   *Published at irregular intervals;*
   *continues: The Cambridge University Athletic Club: list of rules, holders of challenge cups, old blues, Oxford and Cambridge sports.*

☞   See also: A185

### Centurions

188 The Centurions: a history / Bob and Ken Watts. London: The Club, 1997.
98p; pbk                    BL: YA.1998.a.6701

A Centurion is an amateur who has walked in competition in Great Britain a hundred miles within twenty-four hours.

### Cheshire Tally-Ho Hare & Hounds

189 History of the Cheshire Tally-Ho Hare and Hounds Club / Henry M. Oxley; with an introduction by E. A. Davies. Manchester: J. Lockwood, 1893.
107p; illus                    BL: YA.1995.a.27266

190 History of the Tally-Ho Hare & Hounds Club: jubilee souvenir booklet / Henry M. Oxley. Manchester: The Club, 1921.

191 History of the Cheshire Tally-Ho Hare & Hounds Club: 80 years of cross-country running / A. M. Hartley & A. M. Crighton; with an introduction by P. Child & C. R. Maguire. Manchester: The Club, 1952.
44p; illus; pbk

### City of Hull Athletic Club

192 City of Hull Athletic Club 1889-1989: (incorporating Hull Harriers) founded 1882 / Robb Robinson. Hull: Local History Archives Unit, Hull College of Further Education, 1989.
20p; illus; pbk
(Local History Archives Unit reprint; no. 16)
                    ISBN: 1-870001-53-2
                    BL: YK.1992.a.3277

### City of London Police Athletic Club

193 City of London Police Athletic Club: 100 years of heroes, 1886-1986 / John Cardwell. London: City of London Police, 1986.
109p; illus

## Coventry Godiva Harriers

194　Athletics in post-war Britain: the history of a leading club, Coventry Godiva Harriers, 1945-1994 / A. P. Drake. Warwick University, 1994. MA thesis.

## Croydon Harriers

195　Croydon Harriers: 1920-1970: a jubilee booklet / edited by Trevor James. Croydon: The Club, 1970.
36p; pbk

196　75 years of Croydon Harriers / Trevor James. Croydon: The Club, 1995.
40p; pbk

## East Grinstead and District Athletic Club

197　East Grinstead and District Athletic Club: history 1978-1997 / John Rogers. Harmsworth: Harmsworth Marketing Services, 1997.
90p

## Elswick Harriers

198　The boys in red: Elswick Harriers, 1889-1989 / Nick Murray. Newcastle upon Tyne: The Club, 1989.
120p; illus; pbk
　　　　ISBN: 0-9514247-0-X (cased) • 0-9514247-1-8 (pbk)

## Essex County Amateur Athletic Association

199　Essex County Amateur Athletic Association: centenary history 1883-1983 / George Havell. London: The Association, 1983.
132p; illus; index; pbk　　　　ISBN: 0-9508732-0-9
　　　　　　　　　　　　　　　BL: X.622/17516

## Gateshead Harriers

200　From dirt track to glory: a story of Gateshead Harriers / Stan Long & Andrew Merrill. Gateshead: The Club, 1978.
56p

## General Electric Company

201　GEC: a brief history: the athletic years / compiled by Basil C. Nielsen. The General Electric Company, 1996.
360p; illus; pbk

## Gosforth Harriers & Athletic Club

202　Gosforth Harriers and A C golden jubilee 1927-1977: 50 years with Gosforth Harriers. Gosforth: The Club, 1977.

## Halesowen Athletic Club

203　Halesowen Cycling and Athletic Club: souvenir brochure. Halesowen: The Club, 1949.
52p; pbk

## Hallamshire Harriers

204　Jubilee of the Hallamshire Harriers 1896-1946. The Club, 1946.
24p; pbk

## Harrow Athletic Club (formerly Old Gaytonians AC)

205　70th anniversary edition – club magazine / Dennis Orme. Harrow: The Club, 1991.
32p; illus
　　　*Special issue of: Old Gaytonians AC magazine, no. 16 (September 1991)*

## Hastings & St. Leonards Cycling and Athletic Club

206　Eighty years awheel: a record of the Hastings and St. Leonards Cycling and Athletic Club from 1876 to 1956 / J. H. Southerden. St. Leonards-on-Sea: A. H. Butler, 1962.
219p; illus　　　　　　　　　　　BL: X.449/1011
　　Mainly about cycling.

## Havant Athletic Club

207　Havant Athletic Club members guide, 1995/6 / edited by Mark A. Cawte. Havant: The Club, 1995.
102p; pbk
　　Contains club history and extensive all-time lists and records.

## Heaton Harriers

208　The Eastenders (Heaton Harriers, 1890-1990): centenary book / William Allen. Heaton: The Club, 1990.
70p; illus; pbk

## Herne Hill Harriers

209　Herne Hill Harriers: a record of sixty years / George Pallett. London: The Club, 1950.
73p; pbk

## Highgate Harriers

210　Fifty years old: Highgate Harriers jubilee souvenir booklet, 1879-1929. London: The Harriers, 1930.
36p; pbk
　　Lists results of Southern Counties cross-country since 1898, Middlesex cross-country, 1922-29 and the London to Brighton relay, 1924-29.

211　Seventy years old: Highgate Harriers, 1879-1949 / Victor Callard. Highgate: The Club, 1949.
24p; pbk

## Horwich RMI Harriers

212 History of Horwich RMI Harriers / Ian E. Campbell. Horwich: The Club, 1987.

## Ilford Athletic Club

213 Ilford Athletic Club silver jubilee: March 1948 / W. H. Mills. Ilford: The Club, 1948.
60p; pbk

214 75th anniversary history of Ilford Athletic Club 1923-1998 / Warren Roe. Hornchurch: The Club, 1998.
192p; illus                    ISBN: 0-9532495-0-6

## Kettering Town Harriers

215 Kettering Town Harriers centenary: 1894-1994. Kettering: The Club, 1994.
20p; pbk

## Leigh Harriers

216 Leigh Harriers and Athletics Club: 50 years of athletics 1909-1959 / compiled by E. Roberts. Leigh: The author, 1960.
36p; illus; pbk

## Liverpool Harriers and Athletic Club

217 Liverpool Harriers and Athletic Club centenary magazine: statistical supplement, 1982 / Michael J. Holmes. Liverpool: The Club, 1982.
35p; pbk

## Liverpool University Athletic Union

218 Liverpool University Athletic Union: the first one hundred years, 1884-1984 / Beryl Furlong. Liverpool: University of Liverpool Guild of Undergraduates, 1984.
122p; pbk                    ISBN: 0-9509895-0-9

## London Schools Athletic Association

219 London Schools Athletic Association 1900 to 1950: a survey of fifty years / C. F. Gosling. London: The Association, 1951.
12p; pbk

## Longwood Harriers Athletic Club

220 Longwood Harriers Athletic Club: diamond jubilee 1888-1948. Longwood: The Club, 1948.

221 Longwood Athletic Club down the years 1888-1988 / J. W. Percy. Longwood: The Club, 1995.
139p

## Lozells Harriers

222 Lozells Harriers diamond jubilee 1899-1949. Birmingham: The Club, 1949.
32p; pbk

223 Lozells Harriers 1899-1959. Birmingham: The Club, 1959.
30p; pbk

## Manchester Athletic Club

224 Manchester Athletic Club: jubilee souvenir 1886-1936 / Fred W. Hatton. Manchester: The Club, 1936.
36p; pbk

225 Manchester Athletic Club: the first hundred years, 1886-1986 / Wilf Richards. Manchester: The Club, 1986.
28p; pbk

## Middlesex County Athletic Association

226 Middlesex County AA: 75 years: a short history of the Association, 1922-1997 / David Terry. London: The Association, 1997.
30p; pbk

## Midland Counties Cross-Country Association

227 100 years of Midland cross-country running, 1879-1979. Tipton: The Association, 1979.
33p; illus; pbk                    BL: X.622/7834

A cross-country race involving 23 runners from Moseley and Birchfield Harriers on 15 March 1879 led to the formation of the Association, with the first championship under MCCCA jurisdiction taking place in 1880. The main developments and setbacks in the history of the Association are outlined, and the many outstanding performers from Walter George to Jack Holden, Basil Heatley, Roy Fowler, Mike Tagg and Ian Stewart are featured.

## Milton Keynes Athletic Club (formerly Wolverton AC)

228 A history of athletics in Wolverton and Milton Keynes 1885-1985 / Brian Graves. Milton Keynes: The Club, 1985.
122p; illus

## Mitcham Athletic Club

229 Mitcham Athletic Club.
2 leaves

A typescript held by Mitcham Library.

### Newham and Essex Beagles Athletic Club

230 A fine spirit: a centenary history of Newham & Essex Beagles Athletic Club, 1887-1987 / Tony Benton; (with a section on race walking by Colin Young). North Weald: The Club, 1987.
48p; illus; pbk                        ISBN: 0-9512316-0-X

### North Eastern Counties Cross Country Association

231 North Eastern Counties Cross Country Association: the first one hundred years / Matt Frazer; research by George Ogle. The author, 1994.
20p; pbk

### North of the Thames Cross Country Association

232 North of the Thames Cross Country Association 1894-1993: a history from its early beginnings to modern times / George Richardson. Loughton: The Association, 1993.
28p; illus; pbk

### North Staffordshire Road Runners' Association

233 North Staffordshire Road Runners' Association: the first twenty years 1974-1994 / George Kay. Stafford: The Club, 1994.

### Northern Counties Athletic Association

234 A short history of the Northern Counties Athletic Association 1879-1979 / E. Illingworth. Leeds: The Club, 1979.
86p; illus                              BL: YL.1987.a.702

### The Northern Cross Country Association

235 The Northern Cross Country Association: a centenary history / Phil Thomas. Prescot: The author, 1982.
38p; illus; pbk                         BL: X.622/14772

    Although Hare and Hounds clubs were a south of England development, competitive cross-country flourished in Lancashire. As the result of an appeal in *Athletic News* (4 October 1882), the NCCA was formed in the following month. On 17 February 1883, 59 runners faced the starter at Manchester Racecourse, New Barns, Salford, to contest the first Northern championship. Thomas traces developments over the succeeding century, quoting copiously from reports in *Athletic News*.

### Nottinghamshire Amateur Athletic Association

236 Nottinghamshire Amateur Athletic Association: souvenir handbook commemorating the twenty-fifth anniversary of the Nottinghamshire Amateur Athletic Association 1926-1951. Mansfield: W. H. Lee, 1951.
81p; illus

### Notts Athletic Club

237 A brief history of Notts AC's cross-country and road running / Fred Allwood, Mary Gash and Keith Picksley. Nottingham: The Club, 1997.

### Old Gaytonians Athletic Club

238 Old Gaytonians Athletic Club diamond jubilee book / edited by Tony Bush. 1980.
64p; pbk

### Oxford University Athletic Club

239 The Oxford University athletic record for 1878 / compiled by Harry T. Eve. Oxford: The University, 1878.                              BL: P.P.2489.xd

240 Inter-university records: full particulars of all competitions between Oxford and Cambridge, 1827-1887 / compiled by C. A. Mudge. London: Wright, 1887.

241 The book of blues: being a record of all matches between the Universities of Oxford and Cambridge in every department of sport / edited by Ogier Rysden. London: F. E. Robinson, 1900-1902.
3 vols.                                         BL: D

242 Fifty years of sport at Oxford, Cambridge, and the great public schools / arranged by the Right Hon. Lord Desborough; edited by Arthur C. M. Croome. London: Southwood, 1913-1922.
3 vols.: 332p; 325p; 505p; illus
    *Vols. 1, 2: Oxford and Cambridge; vol. 3: Eton, Harrow and Winchester / edited by Hon. R. H. Lyttleton, Arthur Page and Evan B. Noel*                BL: L.R.37.a

    The first 82 pages of Vol. 1 give results and accounts of every Inter-Varsity meeting from 1864 to 1913, of matches against the American universities and of the beginnings of athletics at Oxford and Cambridge. Croome was an expert hurdler and was credited with having invented the straight-leg pick-up style. Contributors include: P. M. Thornton, J. H. Morgan, T. E. Wells, H. C. L. Tindall, G. C. Vassall, W. E. B. Henderson, S. S. Abrahams and P. Stormonth-Darling. Biographies are given of all Blues. There are numerous photographs. Vol. 2 contains 12 pages on cross-country running and Vol. 3 gives histories of athletics at Eton, Harrow and Winchester, with biographies of the athletes.

    ☞   Also listed at: A186

243 Oxford versus Cambridge: a record of inter-university contests from 1827-1930 / compiled and arranged by H. M. Abrahams and J. Bruce-Kerr. London: Faber & Faber, 1931.
620p; index
*A 24p supplement was issued in 1932*    BL: 07906.i.56
The most accurate record of Inter-Varsity sport, with a major section on athletics.

## Polytechnic Harriers

244 The Polytechnic Harriers 1883-1933 / Ernest H. L. Clynes; foreword by Sir Kynaston Studd. London: The Harriers, 1933.
56p; pbk
*Limited ed. of 750 copies*

245 From the legend to the living: being the story of the marathon race from its inception in Ancient Greece BC470 and the history of the Poly marathon race from 1909 to its diamond jubilee year 1969 / A. E. H. Winter. London: The author, 1969.
40p; illus; pbk

246 Polytechnic heritage: they made today: a history of the 100 years of the Polytechnic sports clubs and societies / Arthur Winter. London: Polytechnic Harriers, 1976-1980.
4 vols.; illus
*Part 1. 1976 (71p); Part 2: 1903-18. 1997 (57p); Part 3: 1919-29. (69p); Part 4: 1930-65. 1980 (119p)*

247 The Polytechnic Harriers 1933-1983 / David Barrington. London: The Club, 1983.
63p; illus; pbk

248 A short history of a long running race: an illustrated account of one of the world's oldest and most famous marathon races, published to mark the centenary of its organiser, Polytechnic Harriers, 1883-1983. Norwich: Inter-Regional Group, 1983?
8p; illus; pbk

## Ranelagh Harriers

249 The first hundred years of Ranelagh Harriers: founded 1881 / R. Dassett Callis; foreword by Rex O. Lofts. London: The Club, 1980.
xiii, 162p; illus

## Road Runners Club

250 A short history of the Road Runners Club 1952-58 / John C. Jewell. Manchester: Athletic Review, 1958.
4p; pbk

## Rochdale Harriers and Athletic Club

251 Milestones: a history of Rochdale Harriers and Athletic Club 1887-1987 / Joe Salt. Rochdale: The author, 1994.
247p; illus; pbk    ISBN: 0-9524300-0-2

## Rotherham Harriers & Athletics Club

252 Rotherham Harriers & Athletic Club: the history of the club 1887-1979 / E. F. de Roeck. Sheffield: The author, 1981.
80p; illus; pbk    BL: X.629/15659

253 A history of Rotherham Harriers & Athletics Club 1887-1987: and other memorabilia / E. F. de Roeck. Sheffield: The author, 1987.
89p; illus; pbk    BL: YK.1990.a.3087

## Sale Harriers

254 Sale Harriers: 75 years of athletics / Walter Wilson. Sale: The Club, 1986.
158p

## Salford Harriers

255 The Salford Harriers Club: jubilee season 1933-34 / J. H. Hardwick. Salford: The Club, 1934.
40p; pbk

256 Borrowed time: a social history of running: Salford Harriers 1884-1984 / Duncan Scott with Chris Bent. Manchester: The Harriers, 1984.
59p; illus; pbk    ISBN: 0-9509451-0-2
Bent's Master's dissertation (1983) provided the basis of this illuminating study of a club rooted in the harrier tradition.

## Sefton Harriers

257 Sefton Harriers: a centenary history, 1889-1989 / Norman Wilson. Liverpool: The Club, 1989.

## Shaftesbury Harriers

258 Eighty years of Shaftesbury Harriers 1890-1970 / Harold Ashton. Shaftesbury: The Club, 1971.
47p

259 Shaftesbury Barnet Harriers 1890-1990: a short history of an athletic club / Harold Ashton & Glynne Jenkins. Shaftesbury: The Club, 1990.
111p

## Small Heath Harriers

260 Small Heath Harriers: a short history / C. Simpson. Birmingham: The author, 1991.
4p; pbk

## Southern Counties Cross-Country Association

261 Southern Counties Cross-Country Association 1883-1933 / S. Lambert, with a chapter on the war effort by Charles Otway. London: The Association, 1934.
10p; pbk

## Sparkhill Harriers

262 The history of Sparkhill Harriers, 1902-1952 / P. H. B. Holden. Sparkhill: The Club, 1952.

## Stafford Athletic Club (now Cannock & Stafford AC)

263 Stafford Athletic Club history / G. Maddox. Stafford: The Club, 1960.
23p; pbk

## Staffordshire Amateur Athletic Association

264 Staffordshire AAA: the first 50 years / Alan Lindop. Stoke-on-Trent: The author, 1976.

## Surrey Walking Club

265 Unbroken contact: one hundred years of walking with Surrey Walking Club, 1899-1999 / edited by Sandra Brown. Chew Magna: Surrey Walking Club, 1999.
vi, 204p; illus; pbk          ISBN: 0-9537050-0-5
                              BL: YK.2000.a.2254

## Swindon Athletic Club

266 History of Swindon Athletic Club, 1921-1939: part 1 / W. A. Townsend. Swindon: The Club, 1978.
11p; pbk                     BL: X.0705/203(1)

## Thames Hare and Hounds Club

267 The annals of Thames Hare and Hounds 1868 to 1945 / compiled by James Ryan; with, The present generation 1946 to 1968 by Ian H. Fraser; foreword by J. G. Broadbent. London: The Club, 1968.
xiv, 198p; illus             BL: X.449/3579

  This centenary history evokes the spirit of the club's founder, Walter Rye, and his contemporaries, in delightful detail.

☞   Also listed at: L266

## Thames Valley Harriers

268 Thames Valley Harriers jubilee souvenir booklet: a brief record of progress during 50 years, 1887-1937 / 'G. W. P.' London: The Club, 1937.

  The author is George Pluckridge.

269 Thames Valley Harriers 1887-1947: diamond jubilee handbook / Charlie Russell. London: The Harriers, 1947.
40p; pbk

## Universities' Athletic Union

270 50 years of university sport: 1919-1969 / R. F. Kerslake. London?: Universities' Athletic Union, 1969.
32p; pbk                     BL: X.619/10656

  A history of the Union, known from 1919 to 1929 as the Inter-Varsity-Athletic Board of Great Britain and Ireland. Athletics and cross-country are among the sports covered.

## Wakefield District Harriers and Athletic Club

271 Wakefield District Harriers and Athletic Club: the first 100 years / Martin Cunnane. Wakefield: Yorkshire Sport, 1995.
309p illus; pbk              ISBN: 0-9525200-0-1
                              BL: YK.1997.a.2170

## Watford Harriers

272 Watford Harriers / Frank North. London: The author, 1961-
    *Published annually*

## Westbury Harriers

273 Westbury Harriers: the golden years of Pari-Passu, 1924-1984 / Peter J. Griffin. Westbury: The Club, 1984.
84p

274 Westbury Harriers 75th anniversary / Peter J. Griffin. Westbury: The Club, 1999.

## Woodford Green Athletic Club

275 Woodford Green Athletic Club, 1908-1968 / John Hayward. London: The Club, 1970.
127p; illus

## Yorkshire Race Walking Club

276 Yorkshire Race Walking Club: the first seventy years / Geoff Dowling. Leeds?: The Club, 1982.
23p; illus; pbk

# England ~ Schools & Junior

277 Rugby School hare and hounds: big-side runs / R. S. Benson. Rugby: The School, 1877.
35p; pbk

☞ Subsequent ed. A278

278 Rugby School hare and hounds: description of the big-side runs / revised from Robert Seymour Benson's description of 1877, by P. Richardson, with numerous additions. Rugby: A. J. Lawrence, 1883.
35p; pbk

*Cover title: Rugby School bigside runs*     BL: 7923.d.12

☞ Previous ed. A277; subsequent ed. A279

279 Rugby School hare and hounds: description of the big-side runs / revised from Robert Seymour Benson's description of 1877, and P. Richardson's of 1883 by Arthur Llewellyn Danson. Rugby: A. J. Lawrence, 1894.
50p; pbk     BL: D

☞ Previous ed. A278; subsequent ed. A280

280 Rugby School hare and hounds: description of the big-side runs / revised from Robert Seymour Benson's description of 1877, and P. Richardson's of 1883, and of Arthur Llewellyn Danson's of 1894, by A. R. Welsh. Rugby: A. J. Lawrence, 1902.
71p; pbk

Lists the winners and provides maps for each of the courses.

☞ Previous ed. A279

281 Tom Brown's universe: the development of the Victorian public school / J. R. de S. Honey. London: Millington, 1977.
xv, 416p; index

*Bibliography: p408-410*

ISBN: 0-86000-056-7
BL: X.809/43524

A detailed analysis of participation in the Public Schools Athletic Championships organised by the LAC is provided in 'The public-schools community at the end of the Victorian period', with a table showing the representation for the years 1898-1901: 42 schools are listed, shown with a frequency of 1-4. The meeting was 'in decline by 1900', according to the *Public School Magazine*, which appeared from 1898 to 1902. The journal provided for the regular submission of athletics records by schools, thus enabling inter-school comparisons to be made.

282 The Wilson Run: the first hundred years / Norman F. Berry. Sedbergh: Sedbergh School, 1980.
191p; illus; pbk

A profusely illustrated record of the school's annual cross-country race with a short history of similar races in other public schools.

☞ Also listed at: F193

283 The history of the English Schools Athletic Association 1925-1995 / David Young. The Association, 1995.
144p; illus; pbk

284 Rutlish athletics: a brief history from 1899 to the present / Andrew Huxtable. London: Rutlish School, 1995.
52p     ISBN: 0-9526202-0-0

Contains biographical details of 100 individuals, including UK internationals Derek Pugh, Jack Brewer and Ian Matthews.

## ✳ *Additional References*

285 Great public schools / various authors. London: Edward Arnold, 1893.
viii, 344p; illus     BL: 8364.de.34

Contains a detailed and valuable account by Lees Knowles of running at Rugby School.

286 School athletics and boys' races / William Collier. London: Churchill, 1909.
32p; pbk

*Issued by the Medical Officers of Schools Association*

BL: 7305.c.13(6)

A report of a meeting held on 10 March 1909 to discuss whether schoolboys should be allowed to compete in flat and cross-country races of more than one mile in length.

287 Our great public schools: their traditions, customs and games / F. A. M. Webster. London: Ward Lock, 1937.
383p; illus     BL: 8365.e.49

Thirty-six leading schools are included, and their athletics histories and leading personalities are described. Webster himself appears as an alumnus of St Albans. Other outstanding performers cited include F. F. Wolff (Beaumont College), E. F. Housden (King's School, Canterbury), John Thornton (Charterhouse), Jerry Cornes (Cheltenham), R. Salisbury Woods (Dulwich), Thomas Langton-Lockton (Epsom College), Guy Butler (Harrow), Douglas Lowe (Highgate), Arnold Strode Jackson (Malvern), Montague Shearman (Merchant Taylor's), C. B. Fry and Harold Abrahams (Repton), M. J. Brooks (Rugby), H. B. Stallard (Sherborne), R. L. Howland and Robert Tisdall (Shrewsbury) and E. C. Bredin (Wellington).

288 The contribution of schools and universities to the development of organised sport up to 1900 (with special reference to athletics and swimming) / T. M. James. Leicester University, 1977. PhD thesis.

289 The history of the English Schools' Athletic Association, 1925-1980 / D. A. Young. Manchester University, 1981. MEd thesis.

# *Rural Games*

290 The last records of a Cotswold Community: being the Weston Subedge field account book for the final twenty-six years of the famous Cotswold Games, hitherto unpublished, and now edited with a study on the old time sports of Campden and the village community of Weston, by Charles Robert Ashbee. Campden: Essex House, 1904.
lvi, 59p
   *Limited ed. of 75 copies*                          BL: C.99.f.22
   The author, best known for his work as an architect and designer, founded the Guild and School of Handicraft (1888).

291 Some records of the annual Grasmere Sports 1852-1910 / compiled by Hugh W. Machell; the foreword by the Rev. H. D. Rawnsley, profusely illustrated from photographs. Carlisle: Thurnam, 1911.
80p; illus
   *Limited ed. of 250 copies*                         BL: 7911.k.8
   'There was a time when men wrestled for nothing more than a leather belt, when leapers leapt for a pair of gloves, and footracers ran for a handkerchief. Thus it was at the Stone Carrs Meeting in 1787.' Thus begins this record of the Grasmere sports which covers nearly sixty years, with results and reports of each meeting. Even a casual glance through the lists reveals some of the great names of nineteenth century athletics such as Tom Ray the pole-vaulter, the professional triple-jumper Hogg who cleared 49ft 9in in 1893, or Tom Burrows who jumped 48ft 8in in 1888 and later became a world champion at club-swinging. In the 1880s, separate amateur and professional competitions were instituted for a time, and in 1887 the brilliant little American jumper William Byrd Page cleared 6ft 1in for a Games record which still exists.

292 The Grasmere book. Grasmere: Grasmere Games Society, 1953.
   The records of the Grasmere Games are of particular interest to historians of field events since these are the only English professional games where field events have precedence over track.

293 Grasmere sports results 1852-1952. Ambleside: Grasmere Sports Committee, 1953.
24p; illus; pbk

294 A history of Chipping Camden and Captain Robert Dover's Olympick Games / Christopher Whitfield. Windsor: Shakespeare Head, 1958.
xi, 284p                                            BL: 10362.i.1

295 Heigh for Cotswold: a brief account of the Cotswold games. Evesham: Red Apple, 1965.
   *Extract from 'The Book of Days', edited by Robert Chambers (1863/64).*                  BL: Cup.510.aaf.2
   ☞  See also: A297

296 See the conquering hero comes: an illustrated history of the Grasmere Sports Senior Guides' Race / compiled by Michael Miller and Denis Bland. Kendal: The authors, 1973.
40p; illus; pbk
   *Limited edition of 900 copies*                    SBN: 9502986-0-3

297 Heigh for Cotswold!: a history of Robert Dover's Olimpick Games / Francis Burns. Chipping Campden: Robert Dover's Games Society, 1981.
47p; illus, 1 map; pbk                        ISBN: 0-9507487-0-6
                                                    BL: X.629/15986
   Based on the author's 1960 master's thesis, supplemented by subsequent work, this is a lucid account of the Games organised (or possibly revived) in 1612 by Robert Dover in the parish of Weston Subedge, Gloucestershire. As Dr Burns states: 'In their activities the games have been most like the more widely known Lakeland and Highland Games, but Dover's Games have a much longer known history'.
   ☞  See also: A295

298 The midsummer games: elements of cult and custom in traditional English sport / J. Goulstone. Bexleyheath: The author, 1982.
68p; pbk                                            BL: X.950/15212

299 The summer solstice games: a study of early English fertility religion / John Goulstone. Bexleyheath: The author, 1985.
115p; index; pbk                             ISBN: 0-9510556-0-7
                                                    BL: YC.1989.b.2407
   A rich source of accounts of rural games in all parts of Britain and abroad, with references to running,

jumping and throwing from earliest times to the pre-Victorian era.

300 James Hogg and the St Ronan's Border Club / David Groves. Dollar: Mack, 1987.
46p; music; pbk      ISBN: 0-9505416-3-X
BL: YC.1988.a.5419

Hogg founded the St Ronan's Border Games in 1827 and this is a valuable account of the meetings up to 1836; includes some of Hogg's poetry.

## ✱ *Additional References*

301 The scouring of the white horse, or, The long vacation ramble of a London clerk / T. Hughes; illustrated by R. Doyle. Cambridge: 1858.      BL: 12632.d.27

A short work by the author of *Tom Brown's Schooldays* that includes an entertaining description of the Cotswold Games on White Horse Hill, Uffington.

302 Old English sports / Frederick W. Hackwood, with six coloured and thirty-two half-tone plates from old prints. London: Fisher Unwin, 1907.
xvi, 361p; illus      BL: 7904.c.5

Contains an account of Robert Dover's Cotswold Games, and the Wenlock Olympian Society.

303 An edition of Annalia Dubrensia and a history of the Cotswold Games / Francis Burns. Sheffield University, 1960. Master's thesis.

304 Robert Dover and the Cotswold Games / edited by Christopher Whitfield. London: Sotheran, 1962.
xii, 244p; index      BL: 012302.dd.9

The history of the Cotswold Olympick Games together with all the poems of 'Annalia Dubrensia'. The book contains little athletics detail but does show the depth of the roots of English athletics.

305 Grasmere's giants of today / Rex Woods; with line drawings by Gwenllian Woods and photographs by the author. Liss: Spur, 1975.
94p; illus      ISBN: 0-904558-05-3
BL: X.629/10168

A book mainly about wrestling, but with a chapter on fell-racing.

306 The Stonehenge and Silbury Hill games / J. Goulstone. Bexleyheath: The author, 1984.      BL: X.805/6997

# *Services*

307 R.N. and R.M. sports handbook. London: Royal Navy and Royal Marines Sports Control Board, 1930, 1938-1940, 1948.

*The 1948 reprint is in fact a slightly revised edition to cover the years of the Second World War;*
*continued by: Sports and recreations in the Royal Navy*
BL: P.P.2489.fde

☞ See also: A311

308 Games and sports in the Army, 1931. London: War Office, Army Sport Control Board, 1932-
BL: P.P.2489.zcg

Each annual volume presents a brief history of the Army Athletic and Cross Country Association, the rules of the Association, rules of events, officials' duties, lists of officials, entry qualifications, hints on training, and results of team and individual championships.

309 Naval athletics / edited and compiled by M. Cunningham and F. W. Collins. London: R.N. and R.M. Sports Control Board, 1932?
63p; pbk

310 The Royal Air Force athletics and games handbook. London: Royal Air Force Sports Board, 1933-1965?

The early editions include articles by Douglas Lowe, Sam Ferris, Fred Gaby and Jack London.

311 Sports and recreations in the Royal Navy. London: Royal Navy and Royal Marines Sports Control Board, 1948-1950s?

*Continues: R.N. and R.M. sports handbook*
BL: P.P.2489.fdf

☞ See also: A307

312 Royal Navy athletics / Brad McStravick; technical editor Phyl Edwards. London: Royal Navy in association with the British Athletic Federation, 1997?
64p; illus; pbk

# *Scotland ~ General*

313 Fifty years of athletics: an historical record of the
    Scottish Amateur Athletic Association 1883-1933 /
    edited by Kenneth Whitton and David A. Jamieson;
    foreword by Sir Iain Colquhoun of Luss. Edinburgh: The
    Association, 1933.
    160p; illus                                        BL: 7916.b.29

> It is always tempting to criticise past generations for
> their failure to reflect modern attitudes. *Fifty Years
> of Athletics* does, however, show the SAAA to be a
> dour, conservative organisation, contemptuous of the
> rich rural antecedents from which Scottish athletics
> had been derived. It shows an organisation with its
> energies far more focussed upon the protection of the
> amateur code than with the spread of athletics.
> Nowhere is this more obvious than in the Association's
> failure to adopt the full Olympic track and field
> programme, despite the fact that much of that
> programme had been derived from Scottish Highland
> Games. Similarly, its failure to impose quotas on field
> events within the schedules of its open handicap
> meetings crippled the growth of technical events.
> This harrier-based insularity, the sheer lack of
> developmental zeal, not only of the Scots, but of the
> other home nations, can be clearly seen in the records
> of Scottish international matches against England
> and Ireland in the 1893-1932 period for nowhere do the
> European throwing events of javelin and discus appear;
> neither do pole vault or (even against the Irish) that
> essentially Celtic event, triple jump. Similarly, javelin
> and discus did not appear in the Scottish
> championship programme until 1925, or triple jump
> until 1937.
> A study of the results of the Scottish inter-
> scholastic championships is equally interesting. They
> reveal hardly any change in performance levels between
> 1900 and 1933, no evidence of the intervention of
> coaching of any kind.
> *Fifty Years of Athletics* fills in one piece of the jigsaw
> of athletics history in revealing that it was a Scot, D.
> S. Duncan, who broke the tape to declare void the first
> 1908 Olympic 400m final. The second final was the
> only occasion on which an Olympic final was completed
> by a single runner, another Scot, Lieutenant W.
> Halswelle.

314 Scottish athletics 1883-1983: the official centenary
    publication of the Scottish Amateur Athletic Association
    / John W. Keddie. Edinburgh: The Association, 1982.
    x, 264p; illus; index                  ISBN: 0-9508405-0-5

> Keddie provides a rich, detailed account of the
> evolution of Scottish men's athletics in the 1883-
> 1983 period. Like most historians of amateur
> athletics, he gives little weight to its roots in

> nineteenth century rural sports and pedestrianism or
> to the standards achieved there, standards which
> were superior to Scottish amateur athletics up until
> the Great War. He is probably the only athletics
> historian to observe on the paradox of the nation's
> nobility's support for professional Highland Games,
> quoting SAAA Secretary D. S. Duncan in 1923.
> 'Games' committees will never take a step in the right
> direction as long as professionalism in athletic sports
> is encouraged in this country …'. Keddie also provides
> a significant nugget of information relating to the
> British Olympic Association's preparations for the
> 1916 Olympics, observing that five Scottish coaches
> had been appointed in 1914 at a salary of £1 per week
> and two at ten shillings.
> The bulk of Keddie's book is event-based and as with all
> official histories, *Scottish Athletics* is short on
> opinion, but Keddie's work is nevertheless an
> outstanding contribution to athletics history.

315 Runs will take place whatever the weather: the official
    centenary history of the Scottish Cross Country Union
    1890-1990 / Colin A. Shields. Glasgow: The Union,
    1990.
    xvi, 283p; illus                      ISBN: 0-951668-10-2
                                          BL: YK.1992.a.5146

> The first club cross-country race in Scotland was
> organised by Clydesdale Harriers in 1885, and a
> national association formed in 1887. A rival body,
> Scottish Harriers Union, was set up the following year;
> but both bodies were dissolved in 1890 when the SCCU
> was founded. The history of the Union is treated
> decade by decade; national and district championship
> results, an alphabetical listing of SCCU
> representatives in ICCU and IAAF races, principal
> officers of, and clubs affiliated to, the SCCU are given.

## ✻  *Additional References*

316 Alive in the 1900s: with reminiscences of the Scottish
    Council of Physical Recreation / May Brown.
    Edinburgh: Scottish Sports Council, 1979.
    iv, 110p; pbk                         ISBN: 0-906599-22-9
                                          BL: X.619/22206

> Important for its references to the launch of the
> National Coaching Scheme in athletics, from the
> appointment of H. A. L. (Tony) Chapman as National
> Coach for Scotland in 1949, to his resignation
> following the setting up of the Scottish Amateur
> Athletic Joint Coaching Committee, and the revival of
> the SWAAA. The foreword is by Dr H. Stewart
> Mackintosh.

# Scotland ~ Clubs, and County & Regional Associations

## Bellahouston Harriers

317 From long shorts to short longs / Robin Sykes.
Glasgow: Glasgow Sports Consultancy, 1992.
58p; illus
ISBN: 1-870711-05-X

## Clydesdale Harriers

318 Clydesdale Harriers: a centenary history, 1885-1985 /
Brian McAusland. Clydesdale: Ross, 1988.
50p; illus
ISBN: 1-870711-00-9

## Edinburgh Southern Harriers

319 Edinburgh Southern Harriers jubilee year: the story of
the club 1897-1947 / David A. Jamieson. Edinburgh:
The Club, 1947.
7p; pbk

A pamphlet reprinted from the Scots Athlete (Oct/
Nov. 1947).

320 Edinburgh Southern Harriers, the story of the club 1897-
1972 / David A. Jamieson, David G. A. Keddie &
Duncan R. McKechnie. Edinburgh: The Club, 1972.
32p; pbk

321 The Southern way: a history of Scotland's premier
athletic club. Edinburgh: Edinburgh Southern Harriers,
1997.
84p; illus; pbk
Cover title: ESH: the history of Edinburgh Southern
Harriers
BL: YK.1997.a.5900

## Edinburgh University Athletic Club

322 The story of Edinburgh University Athletic Club / edited
by C. M. Usher; foreword by Sir Edward Appleton.
Edinburgh: The Club, 1966.
439p; illus

A comprehensive centenary history covering athletics
and other sports, with a section on women's athletics.

## Garscube Harriers

323 Garscube Harriers: the story 1898-1998 / Colin Shields.
Greenock: The Club, 1998.
18p; illus; pbk

## Glasgow University Athletic Club

324 Glasgow University Athletic Club: the story of the first
hundred years / R. O. MacKenna. Glasgow: The Club,
1981.
128p; illus, 1 map; pbk
ISBN: 0-85261-170-6
BL: X.629/16850

## Glenpark Harriers

325 A short history of Glenpark Harriers / Colin Shields.
Greenock: The Club, 1998.
18p; illus; pbk

## Scottish Amateur Athletic Association

326 Scottish Amateur Athletic Association augmented list of
affiliated clubs. Edinburgh: SAAA, 1885.
Subsequent editions published but untraced

## Teviotdale Harriers

327 First hundred: Teviotdale Harriers Club centenary
1889-1989 / John L. Coltman. Hawick: Teviotdale
Harriers Centenary Committee, 1988.
xiv, 200p; illus; pbk
ISBN: 0-9513562-0-8
BL: YC.1990.a.6961

# Scotland ~ Highland Games

328 A Highland gathering / Edward Lennox Peel, with 31
    illustrations by C. Whymper. London: Longmans, 1885.
    xiv, 185p; illus                                    BL: 7907.bbb.43

329 The athletes and athletic sports of Scotland, including
    bagpipe playing and dancing / William McCombie
    Smith. Paisley: A. Gardner, 1891.
    138p
        *Reissued in 1920 with the title, 'Scottish athletic sports'.*
                    BL: Mic.A.16228(8) (microfilm copy)

    William McCombie Smith was unquestionably a 19th
    century athletics radical, one of the leading minds of
    his period. Contemptuous of the hypocrisies of the
    amateur movement, McCombie Smith was equally
    critical of the organisers of professional Highland
    Games. He was an original thinker, advocating electric
    timekeeping and a cumbrous and impractical method
    of three attempt high jumping involving a series of
    paper(!) crossbars.
    McCombie Smith did not spare the athletes and the
    throwers in particular, claiming that 'no athlete in the
    British Isles can give satisfactory proof ... of having
    putted a 16lb ball or stone 46ft on level ground, with
    the best of three throws'. He is rigorous in his
    assessment of the 'heavies' of the Highland Games.
    'The Athletes and Athletic Sports of Scotland'
    provides us with our clearest account of the rules,
    techniques, performances and competitive conditions
    of the Scottish Highland Games in the final quarter of
    the century, when they were close to their peak. Unlike
    later historians such as James Miller, he is adamant
    that only Donald Dinnie could ever have laid legitimate
    claim to the all-round championship in the throwing
    events.
    This is a marvellous work, far ahead of most amateur
    literature of its period, providing us with a vivid picture
    of the origins of modern athletics.

330 Sports and pastimes of Scotland, historically illustrated /
    Robert Scott Fittis. Paisley: Alexander Gardner, 1891.
    212p                                                BL: 7908.dd.12
    Includes a chapter on the Highland Games.

331 Men of muscle, and the Highland Games of Scotland,
    with brief biographies of the leading athletes of the last
    fifty years, with portraits / Charles Donaldson. Glasgow:
    Carter & Pratt, 1901.
    vi, 133p; illus                                     BL: 7912.df.34

    This is a key book on the Scottish Highland Games. It
    consists of a series of biographies of the greatest
    Scottish athletes of the 1860-1900 period, including
    the magnificent all-rounders, Donald Dinnie and A. A.
    Cameron. Few of the men written of in this book have
    made their way into the ranking lists of modern
    statisticians, but many of them were amongst the
    greatest athletes of the nineteenth century. A work of
    great interest, particularly to the field-events
    historian.

332 Scottish sports and how to excel in them: a handbook
    for beginners / John James Miller, with many
    illustrations. Dundee: John Leng, 1910.
    135p; illus                                         BL: D

    Miller is one of the athletes mentioned in Donaldson's
    earlier work, Men of Muscle, as being responsible for
    the measurement of Hogg's great 49ft 9in triple jump
    at Alva in 1893. Scottish Sports is remarkable in
    that, though it lists in detail the performances of the
    great Scottish 'heavies' of the nineteenth and early
    twentieth centuries, it fails to provide the slightest
    mention of the greatest of them all, Donald Dinnie.

333 Crieff Highland Gathering: a retrospect of fifty years,
    1870-1920 / A. Porteous. Perth: Munro, 1920.

334 The book of the Braemar Gathering. Arbroath: Arbroath
    Herald, 1926?-
        *From 1930 published in Braemar by the Braemar Royal
        Highland Society*                               BL: P.P.2511.sf

    These books, which contain yearly record lists and
    interesting historical articles on the Braemar Games,
    were produced annually as programmes.

335 Highland gatherings: being accounts of the Braemar,
    Northern and Luss Meetings / Iain Colquhoun and
    Hugh W. Machell, with contributions by John
    Macpherson and C. D. McCombe-Smith, and a foreword
    by HRH The Princess Royal, Duchess of Fife. London:
    Heath Cranton, 1927.
    207p; illus; index                                  BL: 10369.d.30

    This book is mainly centred on the Luss Highland
    Games and has little historical or statistical detail on
    the Games in general, but there are some interesting
    stories of Donald Dinnie, the great nineteenth century
    Scottish professional athlete.

336 Aboyne Highland Games: results of principal
    competitions from 1867 to 1927 / edited by W. E. Nicol.
    Aberdeen: The Games Committee, 1928.
    64p; illus

    ☞ Subsequent ed. A338

337 Scottish Highland Games / David Webster; illustrated by
    John Gardner. Glasgow: Collins, 1959.
    160p; illus
    (Greetings booklets)                                BL: W.P.4810/2

    A brief description of the Games, their personalities
    and their history. Contains much of interest for the
    athletics historian, though lacking the detail of
    Donaldson or McCombie Smith.

    ☞ Subsequent ed. A341

338 Aboyne Highland Games, 1929-1960. 5th ed. 1960.
*2nd-4th eds. untraced*

☞ Previous ed. A336

339 A history of the Cowal Highland Gathering / William L.
Inglis. Dunoon: Dunoon Observer & Argyllshire
Standard, 1960.
44p; illus          BL: 7923.d.64

340 History of the Argyllshire Gathering, 1871-1971 /
George Malcolm. Oban: The Oban Times, 1971.
40p; illus; pbk        ISBN: 0-9500681-3-6

341 Scottish Highland Games / David Webster. Edinburgh:
Reprographia, 1973.
413p; illus        SBN: 903065-10-X
         BL: X.800/8863

☞ Previous ed. A337

342 The Games: a guide to Scotland's Highland Games /
Charlie Allan. Gartocharn: Famedram, 1974.
73p; illus, maps

343 Highland Games: the making of the myth / Grant Jarvie.
Edinburgh: Edinburgh University Press, 1991.
ix, 120p; index; pbk
(Edinburgh education and society series)
       ISBN: 0-7486-0244-5
       BL: YK.1991.a.3578

The argument presented displays little understanding
of the Highland Games as part of a rich tapestry of
rural sports reaching into Ireland and Northern
England, or that until 1914 the Scottish Border
Games were of almost equal stature to their Highland
counterparts.

344 The essential guide to the Highland Games / Michael
Brander. Edinburgh: Canongate, 1992.
141p; illus; pbk        ISBN: 0-862413-02-8
       BL: YK.1992.a.6822

A sketch account of the modern Highland Games
movement.

345 The Skye Games: 121st year, 1877-1998 / Isle of Skye
Highland Games Committee. Isle of Skye: West
Highland Publishing Co., 1998.
120p; illus, maps        ISBN: 0-9508790-5-3

## ✱ *Additional References*

346 Scientific athletics / John W. Sutherland. Rogart: The
author, 1912.
176p; illus        BL: D

This is a remarkable work, one of our few glimpses into
the Highland Games of the pre-World War I period when
performances were at their peak. The main aim of the
book is a technical one, but Sutherland has little to
offer beyond general descriptions. The strength of this
work lies in the author's account of his training over
the period of a decade and in his lists of performances
of professional athletes of his period. This latter
includes such great but little-known athletes as
William Speedie (6ft 3in high jump, 47ft 9in triple
jump) and William Murray (23ft 9in long jump) and a
host of other Highland Games throwers and jumpers.
Of equal interest is Sutherland's detailed account of
his daily training in the 1901-1912 period in the remote
area of Rogart in Sutherlandshire. Working initially
with light implements and pursuing an all-round
programme, Sutherland comes up in 1912 (at a weight
of 10st 10lbs) with throws of a 120ft with shafted
hammer and 48ft 10in in 16lb shot – world professional
records.

347 A historical view of Scottish Highland Games until 1900
/ S. A. G. M. Crawford. Birmingham University, 1972.
MA thesis.

348 A sociological analysis of the Scottish Highland Games /
G. Jarvie. Leicester University, 1988. PhD thesis.

# *Wales ~ General*

349 The Welsh AAA history and records to 1955 / D. J. P.
Richards; foreword by Lord Aberdare. Welsh AAA, 1956.
100p; illus

A pioneering history by the former cross-country and
distance runner.

350 Welsh cross country 1996 centenary year =
Canmlwyddiant cymdeithas trawsgwlad Cymru 1896-
1996: souvenir brochure / George Crump, with
contributions from Clive Williams and John Collins;
foreword by Frank Ireland.
36p; illus; pbk

# Wales ~ Clubs

### Neath Harriers

351 Neath Harriers silver jubilee 1986: souvenir booklet /
edited by Alan Currie. Neath: The Club, 1986.
39p; illus; pbk

### Newport Athletic Club

352 Newport Athletic Club, 1875-1975 / W. E. Davies and
others. Newport: Starling, 1974.
184p; illus                                    BL: X.809/19745
   Athletics are covered on pages 171 to 179.

### Roath Harriers

353 Roath [Cardiff] Harriers: a short history of the premier
athletic club in Wales, from its formation in 1882 / V. I.
Pitcher. Cardiff: The Club, 1953.
20p; pbk

### ✲ Additional References

354 Athletic competition in pre-industrial Wales, c.1066-1880
/ Emma Lile. Birmingham University, 1994. MPhil thesis.

# Ireland ~ General

355 The rulebook of the Gaelic Athletic Association. Dublin:
The Association, 1885-
   *Many subsequent editions*
   The 1893 edition includes an article on the Tailteann
   Games and festivals by Dr Douglas Hyde.

356 The Irish athletic record / F. B. Dineen. Dublin: 1906.
   Contains details of Irish, British and American records
   and championships, with an article by P. J. Cusack on
   training.

357 The story of the Gaelic Athletic Association / Thomas
F. O'Sullivan. Dublin: Privately printed, 1916.
xxxx, 200p; illus                                    BL: D
   O'Sullivan gives a good account of the astonishing
   growth of Irish athletics on both sides of the Atlantic.
   There are photographs of M. Cusack (founder),
   M. Davin, P. J. Kelly, F. B. Dineen, P. Davin, J. S. Mitchel,
   P. J. Leahy, M. Sheridan, T. F. Kiely, J. J. Flanagan, M.
   McGrath, P. O'Connor and others.
   '[The Association] has helped not only to develop Irish
   bone and muscle but to foster a spirit of earnest
   nationality in the hearts of the rising generation and it
   has been the means of saving thousands of young
   Irishmen from becoming mere West Britons.'

358 A history of Irish athletics / P. J. Devlin and 'Carbery'.
Dublin: 1924.
   *'Carbery' is a pseudonym for P. D. Mehigan*
   The title listed above is speculative. The co-author,
   'Carbery,' described it as 'a slender work' in preparation
   for the more comprehensive studies of 1943 and 1945.

359 Fifty years of Irish athletics / 'Carbery'. Dublin: Gaelic
Publicity Services, 1943.
127p; illus
   *'Carbery' is a pseudonym for P. D. Mehigan*

360 Seventy years of Irish athletics / 'Carbery'. Dublin:
Carbery, 1945.
119p
   *'Carbery' is a pseudonym for P. D. Mehigan*
   Includes a review of the seasons 1943-4, world and
   Irish records, championship lists and various
   anecdotes of many of the great Irish champions. Peter
   O'Connor contributes an interesting article on the long
   jump. 'Many Irish, English and American newspapers, in
   articles which I have preserved, commented on my
   peculiar style of long jumping, stating that I seemed to
   wriggle or make a second jump midway in the air.... At
   the Olympic Games in Berlin in 1936 I noticed that the
   world famed Jesse Owens gave the same wriggle or lift
   in the air more than midway from the take-off and
   landed forward exactly as I used to.' This may be the
   first record of the hitch-kick or 'hang' technique in long
   jump.

361 Champions of the athletic arena / William Dooley.
Dublin: General Publicity Services, 1946.
104p; illus
   An outstanding book which tells the stories of many
   Irish athletes, from the Davin brothers of the 1870s to
   Bert Healion in the 1940s. The text is rich in detail:
   hundreds of performances are listed and recounted
   with compelling narrative power, unlike most histories.
   Professionals, such as T. M. Malone and G. B. Tincler,
   share the pages with Flanagan, Horgan, O'Connor and

the rest. This rare book achieves the distinction of doing credit to the incomparable personalities about whom it is written.

362 Sixty glorious years of the GAA: a history of national achievement. Dublin: Parkside, 1947.

134p; illus                                              BL: 7918.b.54

Events are described year by year but, so far as athletics is concerned, they are limited to a short notice of outstanding performances.

363 Athletics in Laois / Risteard O'Maclain. Portlaoise: The author, 1956.

364 Irish women's athletics / Peter R. Pozzoli. Enfield: Women's Track and Field World, 1977.

302p; illus, coats of arms; pbk            BL: X.615/1902

The most exhaustive study of women's athletics in one country so far published.

365 Story of the GAA: a history and book of reference for Gaels / Seamus O Ceallaigh; with a foreword by Jack Lynch. Ballinacurra, Limerick: Gaelic Athletic Publications, 1977.

188p; pbk

Includes a chapter on Maurice Davin, the hammer thrower, who was the first President of the GAA.

366 The GAA history / Marcus de Búrca. Dublin: Cumann Lúthcbleas Gael, 1980.

280p; illus                              ISBN: 0-9502722-1-3
                                         BL: YA.1993.a.15737

A general history including athletics, with one of the earliest photographs of a world record, Michael Ryan's 6ft 4½in high jump in 1895.

☞   Subsequent ed. A369

367 Wexford athletics. Enniscorthy: BLE Wexford County Board, 1989.

100p; illus; pbk

368 The politics of Irish athletics, 1850-1990 / Padraig Griffin. Ballinamore, Co. Leitrim: Marathon, 1990.

352p; illus                              ISBN: 0-9513448-0-3

369 The story of the GAA to 1990 / Marcus de Búrca. Dublin: Published for Irish Life Assurance by Wolfhound Press, 1990.

304p; illus; index
(The Irish Life classic collection)      ISBN: 0-86327-274-6
                                         BL: YK.1996.a.9142

☞   Previous ed. A366

370 Looking back: 25 years of BLE in Cork / Colm Murphy. Cork: The author, 1993.

154p; illus; pbk

BLE is 'Bord Luthcleas na Eireann', the Irish governing body officially recognised by the IAAF. This detailed history of athletics in Cork covers the period from 1967 to 1992.

371 Irish women's athletics 1891-1946 / John W. Brant. Hull: The author, 1999.

160p; pbk

# Ireland ~ Clubs, and County & Regional Associations

## Clonliffe Harriers

372 Clonliffe Harriers diamond jubilee souvenir 1886-1946 / Charles F. Rothwell. Dublin: The Club, 1946.

50p; illus; pbk

Includes contributions by T. W. Murphy, Tommy Burton and William Dooley.

373 The Clonliffe Harriers: 75 years of athletic history / foreword by Samuel J. Gray. Dublin: Parkside, 1961.

63p; illus; pbk

Contributions by Billy Morton, Hugh P. Cooney, Charles Rothwell, Dan McAleese and Norman J. McEachren.

## Crusaders

374 Crusaders Athletic Club: 50th anniversary history. Dublin: The Club, 1992.

## Dublin University

375 Dublin University Harriers & Athletic Club: a centenary history 1885-1985 / edited by Alan Gilsenan. Dublin: The Club, 1985.

124p; illus; pbk

## Limerick Gaelic Athletic Association

376 History of the Limerick GAA from earliest times to the present day: Part 1: 1884-1908 / James P. Kelly; foreword by Archbishop Harty. Tralee: The Kerryman, 1937.
224p; illus

Numerous results of Limerick sports meetings, with photographs of a number of well-known athletes.

377 One hundred years of glory: a history of Limerick GAA 1884-1984 / Seamus O Ceallaigh and Sean Murphy. Limerick: Limerick GAA Publications Committee, 1987.
928p; illus

A more substantial work than the 1937 listing, mainly about older sports, but with thirty-four pages on athletics, including some rare photographs.

## Lough Ree Athletic Club

378 Lough Ree AC silver jubilee 1998 / researched and compiled by Lough Ree AC Jubilee Committee; edited by Sean Cahill and Jim Finn. Lanesboro, Co. Longford: Lough Ree AC Jubilee Committee, 1998.
vi, 84p; illus; pbk

## Moyne Athletic Club

379 Moyne Athletic Club (Co. Tipperary): 50 years of athletics (1948-1998) / Paddy Doyle. Moyne, Co. Tipperary: The Club, 1998.
176p; illus

# Ireland ~ Gaelic Games

380 The Aonac Tailteann and the Tailteann Games: their origin, history and ancient associations / T. H. Nally. Dublin: Talbot, 1922.
75p; pbk                        BL: 07707.eee.28

The author refers to the earliest authentic records of the Games as being associated with the death and burial of Queen Tailté, wife of King Eochaidh Mac Erc, who was killed in the battle of Moytura fought in Co. Mayo in 1896 BC. The functions associated with the Aonach, a public national assembly, are described clearly and concisely. The Cuifeach Fuait (Funeral Games) consisted of athletic, gymnastic and equestrian contests of various kinds and the author notes that bye-laws almost identical to those operating at the Aonach were subsequently instituted and enforced later at Olympia, with the essential difference that women were encouraged to attend (unlike the Olympic Games). The Tailteann Games continued to be celebrated as an annual event on the first of August (Lammastide) for many centuries, the last contests occurring in 1169 AD, presided over by the last King of Ireland, Roderick O'Connor. Nally points to the frequent historical references to Greek traders visiting Ireland and suggests that the Hellenic Games probably trace their origin and development to Ireland.

381 The history of the Gaelic games / Ian Prior; illustrated by Helen Averley. Belfast: Appletree, 1997.
76p; illus                        ISBN: 0-86281-663-7

# *Other British Regions*

382 Guernsey athletics 1946-63 / Eric Waldron. St Peter Port: The author, 1964.

383 The history of track and field: Guernsey athletics. Part 1: 1885-1963 / Ramon J. Hollis. Vale: Guernsey Press, 2000. 358p; illus; pbk                 ISBN: 0-9539166-0-X

# *International*

384 Get to your marks!: a short history of world, Commonwealth, European and British athletics / Ross and Norris McWhirter; foreword by Harold Abrahams. London: Nicholas Kaye, 1951.

267p; illus; index                                BL: 7920.f.28

The McWhirter twins spearheaded in Britain the emphasis on statistical data which is a feature of modern athletics writing. This book is a landmark in athletics literature, giving a detailed history of each event for men and women. Each chapter has an appendix listing world, British Empire and United Kingdom best performances to a depth of about 15, for Imperial and metric distances. The text is distinguished by a degree of precision and thoroughness which no athletics historian had achieved before. The section on women's track and field athletics is a particularly novel feature.

385 A supplement to Get to your marks, being a list of qualifying performances for 1951 and newly discovered performances / Ross & Norris McWhirter. London: Nicholas Kaye, 1952.

7p; pbk                                          BL: 7920.f.28a

This supplement brings Get to your Marks! up to 1 January 1952.

386 The history of the International Cross-Country Union, 1903 to 1953: jubilee souvenir / Lawrence N. Richardson. Ambergate: The author, 1954.

170p; illus                                       BL: 7922.b.12

Contributors include E. Hermés (Belgium), F. A. Moran (Eire), J. G. Stubbs, Paul Mericamp (France), F. J. Duffy (Ireland), G. Dallas, R. A. Pritchard and P. Liddington Johns. A well-illustrated account of international cross-country running with descriptions, full results and statistics. This is the first and only history of cross-country running so far produced.

☞   See also: A389

387 All out for the mile: a history of the mile race: 1864-1955 / George W. Smith. London: Forbes Robertson, 1955.

208p; illus                                       BL: 7921.e.120

Includes an Introduction by John Paul Jones and a medical opinion by Dr. J. V. G. A. Durnin; the contributors include Arnold N. S. Jackson, D. A. Jamieson, Ted Meredith, Joe Binks, Marcel Hansenne, Jesse P. Abramson, Robert Harron, Evelyn Montague, Jerry Cornes, Lewis Burton, Sydney Skilton, Guy Butler, Jack Oaten, Erik Rydbeck, Joe Galli, Roy Moor and Norris McWhirter. This account of all the outstanding runs and athletes in this period draws on reports and character-cameos from many experts. Subsequent research has tended to discredit the pattern of progress traced in the early chapters, which ignores the quality of professional runners in the pre-Association period, but the major portion of the book is both absorbing and inspiring.

'Landy had no chance. The decisive blow had been delivered precisely and scientifically; and there was no time left to him to recover and counter-attack. The Englishman, now completely out of danger and beyond his rival's reach, was homing in full flight — as lordly and unconquerable as a lone eagle making for its eyrie in the snow-sprinkled mountains that formed in the background to that memorable scene.'

388 A world history of track and field athletics, 1864-1964 / Roberto L. Quercetani; foreword by Harold M. Abrahams. London: Oxford University Press, 1964.

xxi, 370p; illus                                  BL: X.449/102

The most celebrated statistician of modern times here produces a history which is encyclopedic in its attention to detail and must be considered as the foremost reference book of athletics history. The chapters cover the story of each men's track and field event on the Olympic programme, and the thoroughness of the operation is emphasised by an Index of 1,457 names. Accounts are given of all notable records and championships as well as personal statistics of almost every notable athlete. The accounts of athletics in the thirties and forties are particularly good; the sketches of Nurmi, Hägg and Andersson are gems.

389 International Cross-Country Union 1954-65 / compiled by Lawrence N. Richardson. Ambergate: The author, 1965.

> A supplement to the Jubilee history of the ICCU with comprehensive results covering the period 1954-65, an alphabetical list of all competitors and a section on rules and championship conditions.

☞ See also: A386

390 70 golden years: IAAF, 1912-1982 / edited by Jon V. Wigley; text by Augusto Frasca, Robert Parienté, Roberto Quercetani and John Rodda. London: IAAF, 1982.
152p; illus

> Illustrated history of the Federation with profiles of the four Presidents.

391 International athletics guide 1986-87 / edited by Melvyn Watman. London: Tantivy, 1986.
256p; illus; pbk                          ISBN: 0-900730-33-1

> Reviews the major meetings in 1986, supplemented by admirably detailed surveys of marathons for 1985 and 1986. The editor contributes a section on athletes who have distinguished themselves in other fields, updating Appendix 3 of his *Encyclopædia of Track and Field Athletics*.

☞ See also: M132

392 100 golden moments: IAAF 75 years history of track & field athletics. London: IAAF, 1987.
224p; illus

> Milestones and personalities in the association's history, handsomely illustrated.

393 From LA to New York, from New York to LA / Harry Berry; with a foreword by Peter Gavuzzi. Chorley: The author?, 1990.
173p; illus

> Well-researched history of the trans-Continental races of the 1920s, with copious results.

394 Boston Marathon: the first century of the world's premier running event / Tom Derderian. Centennial race ed. Leeds: Human Kinetics, 1996.
xxvi, 634p; illus, maps; index; pbk    ISBN: 0-88011-479-7
                                        BL: YC.1996.a.2139

> Chapter 1 covers the period from 1897 to 1909; subsequent chapters cover the decades from 1910. The appendices list winners (men from 1897, women from 1966) and runners' affiliations. Though the course is undulating, the start at Hopkinton (463ft) produces an overall downhill effect with the finish at Boston (15ft). In the race results top finishers are given, and, where known, the occupation and longevity of winners. Supplementary information provided includes variation in distances and checkpoint splits for recent races.

395 Empire Games: the British invention of twentieth-century sport / Roger Hutchinson. Edinburgh: Mainstream, 1996.
192p; index                             ISBN: 1-85158-842-6
                                        BL: YK.1997.b.4378

> 'The strange and wonderful story of the birth of modern spectator sports' takes in the ancient Greek games, the Cotswold Games, the codification of sports and the birth of the modern Olympics.

396 Great sporting moments / Chris Ewers, David Harding, Nigel Gross, Karen Hurrell, Dylan Lobo and Jason Tomas; introduction by Ian Cole. Bristol: Dempsey Parr, 1998.
200p; illus; index                      ISBN: 1-84084-029-3
                                        BL: LB.31.b.20034

> The athletes featured are: Thorpe, Owens, Blankers-Koen, Peters, Bannister, Snell, Beamon, Coe, Ovett, Mennea, Thompson, Lewis, Cacho, Baumann, Christie, Kipketer, Bailey and Johnson.

397 World cross country championships, 1999: facts and figures / compiled by David Guiney. Dublin: Adidas Ireland, 1999.
44p; illus, 1 map; pbk

398 Masters track and field: a history / Leonard T. Olson. London: McFarland, 2000.
vi, 314p; illus                         ISBN: 0-7864-0889-8

## ✱ *Australia*

399 The Oxford companion to Australian sport / edited by Wray Vamplew, Katherine Moore, John O'Hara and Richard Cashman; the Australian Society for Sports History with assistance from the Australian Sports Commission. Oxford: Oxford University Press, 1992.
ix, 430p; illus                         ISBN: 0-19-553287-2
                                        BL: YC.1993.b.6167

> Contains several entries of athletics significance, for example: Australian participation in the Olympic Games; Olympic bids by Australian cities; Staging BEG (1938), BECG (1962) and CG (1982); Aborigines in sport; and, Australian Gallery of Sport and Olympic Museum. The appendix lists ABC Sport Australian award winners (from 1951), Australian medallists in the Olympic Games 1896-1992, Australian gold medallists in the Commonwealth Games 1930-1994 and Stawell Gift winners (130yds 1878-1972, 120m 1973 to date). Biographies of over thirty outstanding Australian athletes, coaches and administrators are included.

☞ Subsequent ed. A400

400 The Oxford companion to Australian sport / edited by Wray Vamplew, Katherine Moore, John O'Hara and Richard Cashman. 2nd ed. Oxford: Oxford University Press, 1994.
xiii, 575p; illus        ISBN: 0-19-553568-5
              BL: YK.1995.b.11416

  ☞  Previous ed. A399

## ✱ *Hungary*

401 Hungarian athletics / Gabriel Szabó. London: Athletics Arena, 1966.
28p; pbk

An intensive survey of the sport in Hungary 1875-1965.

402 Hungarian athletics: part two / Gabriel Szabó. London: Athletics Arena, 1967.
34p; pbk

Lists of Hungarian all-time men's best performances decade by decade over ninety years.

## ✱ *Kenya*

403 Sport and the global system: the case of athletics in Kenya / J. M. K. Sang. Keele University, 1994. PhD thesis.

404 Kenyan running: movement culture, geography, and global change / John Bale and Joe Sang. London: Frank Cass, 1996.
xvi, 209p; illus, maps; index
   ISBN: 0-7146-4684-9 (cased) • 0-7146-4218-5 (pbk)
            BL: YK.1997.b.1134

Kenyan athletes made their first entrance on the world stage in 1954. This meticulous work examines the rise of Kenyan middle and long distance runners, whose success is placed in the context of space and time using measures both quantitative and qualitative. The indigenous movement cultures of Kenya and the transitional period between folk-games and modern sport during British colonial rule provide the historical background. The final sections describe recent developments, with track and field and cross-country becoming a global system, the regional per capita production of distance runners, with special reference to altitude, and the paradox of simultaneous development and underdevelopment in Kenyan athletics.

## ✱ *New Zealand*

405 Lap of honour: the great moments of New Zealand athletics / Norman Harris. London: Herbert Jenkins, 1963.
160p; illus         BL: 7926.w.40

## ✱ *Pacific Region*

406 South Pacific athletics handbook / Tony Isaacs. Macclesfield: The author, 1976-1990.

The first attempt to treat statistically one of the more remote areas, there are sections on the performances of South Pacific athletes at major international championships, results of the South Pacific Games, all-time lists of best performances and performances by South Pacific athletes, and an index of outstanding South Pacific athletes. The author was assisted by Yves Pinaud (France).

  ☞  Also listed at: M113

## ✱ *South Africa*

407 South African sports: cricket, football, athletics, cycling, tennis, racing, polo, golf, gymnastics, boxing, shooting etc.: an official handbook / edited by G. A. Parker. London: Sampson Low, Marston, 1897.
xxiv, 234p; illus       BL: P.P.2579.bb

An early compilation with portraits of leading athletes and officials, and chapters on 'South African sports' and 'Athletics and Rhodesian sports'. The championships of 1894-6 are listed in the athletics section.

408 The South African game: sport and racism / Robert Archer and Antoine Bouillon. London: Zed, 1982.
viii, 352p; illus; index
(Africa series)
   *Bibliography: p337-345*
     ISBN: 0-86232-066-6 (cased) • 0-86232-082-8 (pbk)
            BL: X.529/68791

This remains the most complete account of sport in South Africa during the years of white supremacist (apartheid) rule after 1948.

## ✱ *United States*

409 Cinder-path tales / William Lindsey. London: Grant Richards, 1900.
78p
   *An enlarged ed. also published in 1900; first published, Boston: Copeland & Day*
            BL: 012707.i.12

This is a rare and tantalising glimpse into American professional athletics in the nineteenth century. It includes an account of the first meeting between Oxford and Cambridge and Harvard and Yale Universities. Lindsey was a British amateur runner who emigrated to the States and spent the first part of his life there as a 'pro' runner, before settling down as a college athletics coach.
'I learned all the tricks of the trade, gave close finishes always, did an artistic "fainting act" and made myself a subject of regretful, not to say painful, remembrance to a large part of the sporting fraternity.'

Among many anecdotes are those of the Irish hammer thrower who threw a notable distance, but whose hammer was found to be light, 'Faith, I think it must have struck a stone and knocked off a piece', and the Virginian long jumper who suddenly improved from 19ft 6in to beat the world record.

410 The athletic revolution / Jack Scott. London: Collier-Macmillan, 1971.
x, 242p; illus                                    BL: X.619/6660

In the preface, Scott sets out his two main purposes in writing this book as 'to shed some light on the reasons for the turmoil in American athletics while at the same time trying to offer an analysis that might assist those individuals and groups who are struggling to bring about constructive change in the athletic world'.

411 200 years of sport in America: a pageant of a nation at play / Wells Twombly; editors, Jeremy Friedlander, John Wiebusch. London: McGraw-Hill, 1976.
287p; illus                         ISBN: 0-07-065640-1
                                                  BL: X.622/6392

Published to coincide with the US bicentenary, this handsome work has a wide variety of graphic material. It is divided into four parts: The Pastoral Age 1776-1865; The Passionate Age 1866-1919; The Golden Age 1920-1945; The Electronic Age 1946-1976.

412 Sports and freedom: the rise of big-time college athletics / Ronald A. Smith. Oxford: Oxford University Press, 1988.
xiv, 290p; illus; index              ISBN: 0-19-505314-1
                                                  BL: YK.1990.a.407

Though the work deals with the development of sport in US institutions of higher learning during the nineteenth century, the origins are clearly traced to English practice. In pursuing his theme, the author examines four major sports in the first half-century of intercollegiate athletics (rowing, baseball, football, track and field) and specific topics which influenced all the college sports.

## ❋ *USSR*

413 Soviet sport: mirror of Soviet society / Henry W. Morton. London: Collier-Macmillan, 1963.
221p; pbk                                         BL: X.449/57

The author sets out to describe the shifts in CPSU sports policy between 1925 and 1961, the introduction of the GTO awards system, the incentives offered to top performers, the role of sport in USSR foreign policy, the main figures in Soviet sports sociology, the practice of sport in the post-1945 era, and the transition from the Tsarist era of sports administration to the setting up of the USSR Union of Sport Societies and organisations in 1959.

414 Sport in Soviet society: development of sport and physical education in Russia and the USSR / James Riordan. Cambridge: Cambridge University Press, 1977.
ix, 435p; illus; index               ISBN: 0-521-21284-7
                                                  BL: X.629/11316

This remains one of the main works in English on the evolution of sport in Russia and the USSR. The development of athletics is traced from 1886, with the first All-Russia Championships taking place in 1908 and a national association formed in 1911, in preparation for the 1912 Olympic Games. The first national championships, following the 1917 Revolution, were held in 1920 (men) and women followed in 1922. By 1 January 1939, nine unofficial world athletics records had been set by Soviet athletes. The author describes in detail the organisation of Soviet sport after the Second World War, emphasising the importance of the GTO Award Scheme in the attainment of higher standards. Other topics covered are: women's participation relative to men; the role of Spartakiads in domestic competition; the provision of facilities; the coaching structure; professional training; sporting publications; obstacles to mass participation; and the close links between sport and the military.

## ❋ *Additional References*

415 Games of the North American Indians / Robert Stewart Culin. Washington: GPO, 1907.
846p; illus
*Re-issued in facsimile: London: Constable, 1975.*
*ISBN: 0-486-23125-9*
                                                  BL: A.S.911

Published as an appendix to the twenty-fourth annual report of the Bureau of American Ethnology to the Smithsonian Institution, 1902-1903 by W.H. Holmes. Gives details of footraces among Algonquian, Athapascan, Caddoan, Eskimauan, Iroquoian, Muskhogean, Piman, Salishan, Shoshonean, Siouan and Yuman native Americans from 1831 onwards.

416 Aspects of the social history of sport in France, 1870-1914 / R. J. Holt. University of Oxford, 1977. DPhil thesis.

417 Soviet sport: background to the Olympics / James Riordan. Oxford: Blackwell, 1980.
xi, 172p; illus, 1 map; index
           ISBN: 0-631-12201-X (cased) • 0-631-12211-7 (pbk)
                                                  BL: X.629/14449

Published to coincide with the staging of the 1980 Games in Moscow, Riordan surveys the geographical and historical factors affecting sports development in the USSR, before outlining the structure and organisation of Soviet sport, the development of talent, and the professional training of coaches and PE teachers. Specific attention is paid to the important place of women in USSR sport, both as participants and coaches. The primary events of Faina Melnik (discus) and Nadezhda Chizhova (shot) have been transposed, and the illustration on p133 is of Chizhova, not Melnik. Riordan concludes with a brief survey of the involvement of Russia before 1917 and of the USSR after 1917 in the IOC and the increasingly successful participation by the USSR in the Olympic Games from 1952.

418 The emergence of the black athlete in America: American dream or American dilemma? / G. A. Mousinho. Keele University, 1983. PhD thesis.

419 The global sports arena: athletic talent migration in an interdependent world / edited by John Bale and Joseph Maguire. London: Frank Cass, 1994.

xii, 289p; illus, maps; index

*Papers originally presented during a colloquium at Keele University, April 1991*

ISBN: 0-7146-3489-1 (cased) • 0-7146-6116-2 (pbk)
BL: YC.1995.b.5689

The chapter, 'Out of Africa: the "development" of Kenyan athletics, talent migration and the global sports system' by John Bale and Joe Sang is developed at greater length in their book Kenyan running.

420 Sporting colours: sport and politics in South Africa / Mihir Bose. London: Robson, 1994.

xii, 256p; illus; index

ISBN: 0-86051-861-2
BL: YC.1995.a.909

Before tracing its Olympic involvement from 1908 to 1960, Bose highlights the re-admission of South Africa to the Olympic movement in 1992, with the women's 10,000m winner, Ethiopian Derartu Tulu, being accompanied on her lap of honour by runner-up Elana Meyer of South Africa. The author describes the sporting isolation of South Africa over three decades, and, though most of the narrative is devoted to cricket and rugby union, several track and field examples are cited.

421 American Indian sports heritage / Joseph B. Oxendine; with a new afterword by the author. London: University of Nebraska Press, 1995.

xxiii, 334p; illus; index; pbk

*Originally published: Champaign, Ill.: Human Kinetics, 1988*

ISBN: 0-8032-8609-0
BL: YC.1996.a.3539

A number of historical references point to the importance of running in Indian culture: archaeological evidence suggests the construction of specialist running tracks. Betting on athletic contests was a regular practice for both participants and spectators. The establishment of the Carlisle PA school (1879) and the Haskell KS school (1884) for American Indians gave an impetus to the development of track and field programmes. Jim Thorpe, the 1912 Olympic champion, is featured and a dozen other Indian athletes active in the period before 1930 are identified.

This book should be read in tandem with *Indian Running* (Santa Barbara: Capra, 1981), not, alas, published in this country. Both books reveal a rich Indian culture of competitive running.

422 Sport and physical education in China / edited by James Riordan and Robin Jones. London: Spon, in association with ISCPES, 1999.

xviii, 278p; illus, map; index

ISBN: 0-419-24750-5 (cased) • 0-419-22030-5 (pbk)
BL: YC.1999.b.6232

All but one of the contributions refer to track and field or its precursors.

# B. Personalities

## Biographies & Autobiographies

### Akabusi, Kriss

1.   Kriss Akabusi on track / Ted Harrison. Oxford: Lion, 1991.
223p; illus; index       ISBN: 0-7324-0531-9
                                          BL: YK.1991.b.8926

    ☞   Subsequent ed. B2

2.   Kriss Akabusi on track / Ted Harrison. Updated ed. Oxford: Lion, 1995.
246p; illus; pbk       ISBN: 0-7459-3378-5

    ☞   Previous ed. B1

3.   Kriss / Stuart Weir. London: Marshall Pickering, 1996.
viii, 167p; pbk       ISBN: 0-551-03029-1
                                          BL: YK.1996.a.23311

    The author, co-director of an Oxford-based agency, Christians in Sport, follows Harrison's earlier account of Akabusi's track career. Akabusi's active role in Christians in Sport is described.

### Alder, Jim

4.   Marathon and chips: biography of Jim Alder, world record holder / Arthur T. McKenzie. Morpeth: Alder Sports, 1981.
136p; illus
    ISBN: 0-9507604-1-2 (cased) • 0-9507604-0-4 (pbk)
                                        BL: X.629/16692

    The 1966 Commonwealth marathon champion also set a world record for 30,000m in 1964.

### Allardice, Robert Bridges Barclay (Captain Barclay)

5.   Thoughts upon sport: a work dealing shortly with each branch of sport, and showing that as a medium for the circulation of money sport stands unrivalled among the institutions of the kingdom: to which are added memoirs of the Curraghmore Hunt, Punchestown and the Curragh; of Osbaldeston, Ross and Barclay-Allardice; Scott, Dawson, Fordham and Archer: also of the Marquis of Drogheda and Henry W. Briscoe / Harry R. Sargent. London: Photo-Prismatic, 1894.
xvi, 426p; illus       BL: 07905.l.26

    Mainly devoted to hunting and racing, but includes a twelve page account of the career of the pedestrian, Captain Barclay.

### Alston, Rex

6.   Taking the air / Rex Alston; foreword by Lionel Gamlin. London: Stanley Paul, 1951.
264p; illus; index       BL: 10857.bb.38

    This autobiography of the well-known commentator, a sprinter in his Cambridge days, gives a good account of this period as well as an interesting chapter on the Wembley Olympic Games.

### Archer, Jeffrey

7.   Jeffrey Archer: stranger than fiction / Michael Crick. London: Hamish Hamilton, 1995.
xxii, 456p; illus; index       ISBN: 0-241-13360-2
                                        BL: YC.1995.b.5013

    Chapter 8 ('Oxford Blues') deals specifically with the athletics career of Jeffrey Howard Archer (Baron Archer of Weston-super-Mare) at Oxford University. Chapter 4 ('Not that Wellington') mentions his athletic achievement at junior level.

*Astley, John*

8    Fifty years of my life in the world of sport at home and
abroad / John D. Astley. London: Hurst & Blackett,
1894.
2 vols.; illus              BL: 10816.cc.26

Astley gives an absorbing account of his career as a
professional athlete in Britain and in the Crimea and of
his ventures as a promoter of long distance running
events, culminating in his six day races.

*Backley, Steve*

9    The winning mind: a guide to achieving success and
overcoming failure / Steve Backley with Ian Stafford.
London: Aurum, 1996.
168p; illus; index         ISBN: 1-85410-404-7
                      BL: YK.1997.b.3180

A unique view of athletics psychology from Britain's
most successful male javelin thrower. Essential
reading.

*Bannister, Roger*

10    First four minutes / Roger Bannister. London: Putnam,
1955.
224p; illus                 BL: 7921.f.5

A great book by a great athlete. Bannister describes
his development from a gawky junior struggling to get
inside five minutes for the mile to the greatness of
Iffley Road on 6 May 1954.
'We shared a place where no man had yet ventured –
secure for all time, however fast men might run miles in
the future. We had done it where we wanted, how we
wanted, in our first attempt of the year. In the
wonderful joy my pain was forgotten and I wanted to
prolong these precious moments of realisation.'

11    Four minute miler / Robert J. Hoare. London:
Macmillan, 1962.
80p; illus
(The champion library; 1)

An account of Roger Bannister's achievement for
young readers.

12    The four-minute mile / Wyndham Charles; illustrated by
Hookway Cowles. Exeter: Haldon, 1967.
37p; illus
(They reached the top)        BL: X.0449/47
   For children.

*Barclay-Allardice, Robert Bridges  See  Allardice,
Robert Bridges Barclay (Captain Barclay)*

*Barry, John Joe*

13    The Ballincurry Hare / John Joe Barry. Dublin: Athletic
Publications, 1986.
114p; illus; pbk

The Irish middle-distance star of the post-war era
writes a frank and colourful account of his career on
and off the track.

*Bedford, Dave*

14    The Dave Bedford story / as told to James Coote.
Frimley: Penta in association with Avon Tyres, 1971.
66p; illus; pbk         ISBN: 0-903215-00-4
                      BL: X.611/2958

Published at the end of the 1971 season, this biography
of the precocious David Bedford looks back at his
career – three UK records at 10,000m and one each
for the 5,000m and 3000m steeple-chase, sixth
place in the highly competitive 1971 European
Championships 10000m – and expectantly forward to
the 1972 Olympic Games. His relationship with coach
Bob Parker of Shaftesbury Harriers is described and a
substantial section on his beer drinking is included!

*Bell, Kipperr*

15    Kipperr Bell: an American first: 1984 Skol New Year
sprint, Edinburgh, Scotland / Rob Hunter. Aberdeen:
The author, 1984.
110p; illus; spiral bound        BL: X.629/27590

The author, coach to San Diego AA, describes how the
22 year old Bell became a rare American winner of the
114th Powderhall professional sprint. Sections dealing
with coaching for the sprints, handicap races, the
professional track circuits, a brief history of
professional foot racing or pedestrianism, and
professional (SGA) running records are also included.

*Black, Roger*

16    How long's the course?: my autobiography / Roger
Black with Mike Rowbottom. London: Deutsch, 1998.
v, 250p; illus; index        ISBN: 0-233-99207-3
                      BL: YK.1999.b.2506

Britain's most consistently successful 400m
performer opens the account of his athletic career
with a vivid description of his last major race, the 1996
Olympic final. His early career is covered in admirable
detail, including his 1985 European Junior
Championships win, with Black emphasising the
difficult transition for many juniors to the senior
ranks. He discourses on drug use and training regimes
in athletics: the major events from 1986 to 1997,
including physical setbacks, are described. Finally,

Black offers views on issues such as the importance of winning and the administration of British athletics.

☞ Subsequent ed. B17

17 How long's the course?: my autobiography / Roger Black. London: Deutsch, 1999.
298p; illus; index; pbk  ISBN: 0-233-99644-3
BL: YK.2000.a.6135

Contains additional material on Black's plans after failure to be selected for the 1998 European Championships.

☞ Previous ed. B16

### Board, Lillian

18 Lillian / David Emery. London: Hodder and Stoughton, 1971.
191p; illus  ISBN: 0-340-15606-6
BL: X.529/13309

A biography of Lillian Board, Olympic silver medallist at 400m and European 800m champion, by the Daily Mail journalist to whom she was engaged at the time of her tragically early death from cancer at the age of 22.

19 Lillian / David Emery; retold by John Kennett. Glasgow: Blackie, 1973.
90p; illus  ISBN: 0-216-89670-3

### Bowers, Kelvin

20 Closing the distance / Kelvin Bowers. Stoke-on-Trent: Andy Ridler, 1980.
225p; illus, maps; pbk  ISBN: 0-905074-03-3
BL: X.629/17496

Bowers, a sub-4:15.0 miler, visited Percy Cerutty in Australia, and was inspired to run across the world. Some years elapsed before he drew up plans for the 'Stoke to Sydney Marathon', a journey he completed in 75 weeks. Bowers conveys, in some finely crafted prose, the nature of the changing landscapes and people encountered as well as the sustained physical effort involved. The log book shows daily and weekly mileages, cumulative distance, and cities, towns and villages passed through en route.

### Bredin, Edgar

21 Running and training / E. C. Bredin. Northampton: The author, 1902.
xii, 176p  BL: 7912.bb.11

Bredin, who shared the world's record for 440yds, gives an account of his amateur and professional career, and all running events are described and analysed. Much detail is given of the seasons 1893 to 1895. The author also lists an interesting evolution of running records.
'The evening of those '92 championships, very crestfallen, I wandered back to Stamford Bridge (at that time I resided close to the LAC). On entering the then almost deserted grounds, strewn with betting tickets, pieces of programmes, number cards, and other like evidence of a recently held modern athletic meeting, I soon espied old Nat (Nat Perry, Bredin's trainer) seated on a chair near the number board, in a condition decidedly not arrived at by the strictest adherence to temperance principles. In answer to my remark, somewhat hesitatingly put forward, that with better judgement I might have been returned the winner of the quarter mile championship, the veteran blurted out, "Well, you did your running and you got beat; what have you got to grumble at?".'

### Brookes, William Penny

22 British Olympians: William Penny Brookes and the Wenlock Games / Sam Mullins. London: Birmingham Olympic Council in association with the British Olympic Association, 1986.  ISBN: 0-901662-01-1

23 William Penny Brookes and the Olympic connection / Muriel Furbank, Helen Cromarty & Glyn McDonald. Much Wenlock: Wenlock Olympian Society, 1996.
15p; illus; pbk  ISBN: 0-9528683-0-2

Brookes was the visionary who formed an Olympian Society in England as early as 1850, profoundly influencing Pierre de Coubertin who is credited with founding the modern Olympic Games forty-six years later.

### Brown, Richard & Sandra

24 Long, at the top: Richard and Sandra Brown 1982-1993: word-pictures from contemporary writings about two world-class long-distance race walkers & runners / collated by Dudley Harris. 1994?
107p; illus; pbk  BL: YK.1995.b.9001

Includes contributions by twenty-one named writers, including the subjects. Richard and Sandra Brown commenced their long distance careers in 1982 and, after negotiating some 100 mile events, graduated in 1988 to Land's End-John o' Groats. In later seasons, they indulged in a variety of events with distances up to 200km.

### Brundage, Avery

25 The Games must go on: Avery Brundage and the Olympic movement / Allen Guttmann. Guildford: Columbia University Press, 1984.
xiv, 317p; illus; index  ISBN: 0-231-05444-0
BL: X.622/20491

Guttmann takes his title from Avery Brundage's speech on 6 September 1972 in the Munich Olympic Stadium, following the murder of eleven Israeli athletes.

## Buckner, Jack

26  Running the distance: an athlete's year / Jack Buckner.
London: Heinemann Kingswood, 1989.
x, 219p; illus                                    ISBN: 0-434-98135-4
                                                  BL: YK.1990.b.8641

Presented in the form of a diary and written with
considerable humour and insight, the book presents a
rounded picture of life as a full-time athlete.

## Budd, Zola

27  Zola: the official biography / Brian Vine with Zola
Budd. London: Stanley Paul, 1984.
96p; illus; pbk                                   ISBN: 0-09-159271-2
                                                  BL: X.950/38230

This 'official biography' was rushed through the press
almost as fast as Budd's application for UK
citizenship received the approval of Home Secretary
Leon Brittan, and was published even before the 1984
Olympic Games had taken place. The author was the
Daily Mail correspondent deputed to liaise with the
Budd family when the seventeen year old 5000m world
record holder was flown to the UK in March 1984.

28  Zola: the autobiography of Zola Budd / Zola Budd with
Hugh Eley. London: Partridge, 1989.
176p; illus                                       ISBN: 1-85225-089-5
                                                  BL: YC.1990.b.4777

Budd is here presented as a naïve victim, her running
ability being exploited at every turn by those around
her.

## Burghley, Lord, David George Brownlow Cecil

29  Burghley: the life of a great house / Victoria Leatham.
London: Herbert Press, 1992.
240p; illus                                       ISBN: 1-871569-47-8

The writer includes a biographical section about her
father, the 1928 Olympic 400m hurdles champion,
President of the AAA and IAAF, and Chairman of the
British Olympic Association and the Organising
Committee for the 1948 Olympic Games.

## Burn, Rob

30  In the long run: the humorous story of a marathon
runner / Rob Burn. London: Pelham, 1983.
143p; illus, 1 map                                ISBN: 0-7207-1446-X
                                                  BL: X.809/55475

The author, having completed the first London
Marathon in 1981, decided to attempt the New York
Marathon in the same year. Though the pain, and
occasional pleasure, of training is captured, the
humour is somewhat heavy-handed. The author, a
graphic artist, includes three engaging sketches.

## Butcher, G. P.

31  A sporting century 1863-1963: athletics, rugby, cricket /
Anne Pallant. Kingsbridge: The author, 1997.
192p; illus; pbk                                  ISBN: 0-9530189-0-3

The granddaughter of the Victorian athlete, G. P.
Butcher, put together this biography of several
generations of her family. It is noteworthy for the
many reproductions of athletics programmes.

## Campbell, Eddie

32  Eddie Campbell: an appreciation / edited by Lee
Volwerk. Fort William: The author, 1994.

Biography of a fell-runner.

## Capes, Geoff

33  Big shot: an autobiography / Geoff Capes with Neil
Wilson. London: Stanley Paul, 1981.
142p; illus                                       ISBN: 0-09-144970-7

This appeared at the close of the career of the 6ft 6in,
302lb Geoffrey Lewis Capes, who took the UK shot
record from 19.56m to 21.68m.

## Cerutty, Percy

34  Mr Controversial: the story of Percy Wells Cerutty /
Graeme Kelly. London: Stanley Paul, 1964.
168p; illus                                       BL: 010609.a.27

Cerutty, coach to the great Herb Elliott, was a
coaching maverick, a disciple of 'stotan' philosophies
based on the flimsiest of physiological foundations. In
Elliott, he found the perfect vehicle for his theories and
Cerutty fashioned him into an almost unbeatable
running machine.

35  Sport is my life / Percy W. Cerutty. London: Stanley
Paul, 1966.
180p; illus                                       BL: X.449/1678

## Chavasse, Noel Godfrey

36  Chavasse – double VC / Ann Clayton; with a foreword
by the Bishop of Liverpool. London: Leo Cooper, 1992.
261p; illus, maps; index
    *Bibliography: p234-237*                      ISBN: 0-85052-296-X

Devoted mainly to the exceptional war record of the
Oxford Blue and Olympian.

## Chavasse, Noel & Christopher

37  The Chavasse twins / Canon Selwyn Gummer. London:
Hodder & Stoughton, 1963.
255p; illus                                       BL: X.100/57

The frontispiece shows Noel Godfrey and Christopher
Maude Chavasse after being awarded their Blues by
OUAC in 1907. Born in 1884, the identical twins went
up to Trinity College Oxford in 1905, Noel to read

Natural Sciences and Christopher History. They both competed against CUAC in 1907-08 and Christopher also ran in 1906. The diary of the latter's training in the week before the 1907 match is reproduced. Their appearance in the 1908 Olympic Games receives only a cursory mention.

## Christie, Linford

38  Linford Christie: an autobiography / Linford Christie with Tony Ward. London: Stanley Paul, 1989.
iv, 172p; illus; index          ISBN: 0-09-174179-3
                                BL: YK.1990.b.983

Christie's narrative opens with his account of the 1988 Olympic Games 100m final. A reluctance to train assiduously until 1985 (under Ron Roddan) restricted his progress but in 1986 he emerged as one of the world's best sprinters in winning the European 100m title. His clearly unhappy relationship with National Director of Coaching, Frank Dick, forms a recurring motif.

39  Linford Christie / Andrew Ward. London: Hippo, 1993.
48p; illus; pbk
(Sports shots; 5)               ISBN: 0-590-55373-9
                                BL: YK.1994.a.7146

A very small format series designed for young readers.

40  Linford Christie / Duncan Mackay. London: Weidenfeld & Nicolson, 1995.
95p; illus                      ISBN: 0-297-83530-0
                                BL: LB.31.b.12092

The author opens with a vivid account of Christie's first individual world record (200m indoors 20.25) at Lievin in 1995. After backtracking to the European Indoor Championships at Madrid in 1986, when Christie surprisingly won the 200m title, he describes his early life, his introduction to coach Ron Roddan at Thames Valley Harriers, his victory in the 1986 European Championships 100m at Stuttgart, and outstanding moments from his eight subsequent years of competition.

41  To be honest with you / Linford Christie. London: Michael Joseph, 1995.
x, 275p; illus; index           ISBN: 0-7181-4063-X
                                BL: YC.1996.b.8378

This work inevitably covers much the same ground as the 1989 autobiography.

42  My story / Linford Christie. London: Puffin, 1996.
32p; illus; pbk                 ISBN: 0-14-037878-2
                                YK.1996.b.14495

Adapted from 'To Be Honest With You'.

43  A year in the life of Linford Christie / photographs by Jon Nicholson. London: Penguin, 1996.
144p; chiefly illus             ISBN: 0-7181-4064-8
                                BL: LB.31.b.12970

A brilliantly designed book with a minimum of text and excellent photographic coverage. Split into four sections (Winter, Spring, Summer, Autumn), it traces Christie's 1995 season.

44  Linford Christie / Mike Wilson. London: Hodder & Stoughton in association with The Basic Skills Agency, 1997.
28p; illus; pbk                 ISBN: 0-340-67980-8
                                BL: YK.1998.a.361

## Clarke, Ron

45  The unforgiving minute / as told to Alan Trengove; foreword by John Landy. London: Pelham, 1966.
189p; illus                     BL: X.449/2010

The autobiography of the outstanding long distance runner covering his career to the end of 1965.

## Coe, Sebastian

46  Running free / Sebastian Coe with David Miller; foreword by Mary Peters. London: Sidgwick & Jackson, 1981.
174p; illus; index              ISBN: 0-283-98684-0
                                BL: X.629/15632

In common with many other biographies this represented a collaboration between the subject and a professional journalist, and also appeared well before the end of the athlete's career. The high points up to early 1981 are well evoked, as are the rare low points, such as his 1980 Olympic 800m defeat: 'With thirty metres to go I knew I was not going to win. At the finish I just went off the track and the extraordinary thing was that my first reaction was a huge feeling of relief rather than disappointment.'

☞  Subsequent ed. B48

47  The Athletics Weekly file on Sebastian Coe & Steve Ovett / compiled and edited by Mel Watman. Rochester: Athletics Weekly, 1982.
160p; illus; pbk                ISBN: 0-95068102-4
                                BL: X.629/22550

Facsimile reproductions of race reports for the years 1972-1982, together with other material on Coe and Ovett which appeared in the magazine during the period.

☞  Also listed at: B142

48  Running free / Sebastian Coe with David Miller. Rev. and updated. London: Sidgwick & Jackson, 1982.
191p; illus; index; pbk         ISBN: 0-283-98857-6
                                BL: X.808/36655

☞  Previous ed. B46

49 Sebastian Coe / Neil Wilson; illustrated by Peter Jones.
London: Hamilton, 1982.
62p; illus        ISBN: 0-241-10848-9
         BL: X.629/19290

The author traces the career of the 1980 Olympic
1500m champion.

50 Sebastian Coe coming back / David Miller. London:
Sidgwick & Jackson, 1984.
175p; illus; pbk        ISBN: 0-283-99185-2

According to the author's acknowledgements, a
condition of publication was that Coe 'should win a gold
or silver medal in the 1984 Olympic Games'; he did
both. The narrative covers the three-year period from
the close of the 1981 season, taking in the aborted
series of three races with Ovett scheduled for 1982,
the world record 4x800m (with Peter Elliott, Garry
Cook and Steve Cram), the silver medal at 800m in
the European Championships, and his subsequent
withdrawal from further competition with glandular
fever. Possibly the most interesting portions of the
work deal with the coach/father-athlete relationship
and with a discussion of the aerobic-anaerobic
content of 800m running.

51 Sebastian Coe: born to run: the authorized life in
athletics / David Miller; foreword by Steve Ovett.
London: Pavilion, 1992.
232p; illus; index        ISBN: 1-851457-36-4
         BL: YK.1992.b.4793

Miller quotes from his earlier works on Coe and then
represents some other views on his character. The
controversy surrounding his omission from the 1988
Olympic Games team is dealt with thoroughly. Coe
concludes that there has been a neglect by British
governments to consider sport seriously, before giving
his opinions on the respective merits of Birmingham,
Manchester and London as rival candidates to host
the Olympic Games, and the lack of resources devoted
to coaching in the UK.

### Cook, Theodore

52 The sunlit hours: a record of sport and life / Theodore
A. Cook. London: Nisbet, 1925.
xviii, 330p; illus        BL: 07905.k.48

The autobiography of the famous Olympic writer, with
reminiscences of the Games of 1906 and 1908 and,
specifically, of Horine, Abrahams and Nurmi.

### Cram, Steve

53 Steve Cram / Norman Barrett & Mel Watman. London:
Virgin, 1984.
96p; illus; pbk        ISBN: 0-86369-038-6

A concise and competently written account of the
athlete's career up to April 1984.

54 Steve Cram: the making of an athlete / Roger Tames.
London: W.H. Allen, 1984.
210p; illus        ISBN: 0-491-03213-7

This work was the by-product of two Tyne Tees
Television films of Cram, many of the quotations being
taken directly from the recorded programmes. His
1982 victories in the European Championships and
Commonwealth Games are only sketchily described,
but his win over 1500m in the following year at the first
World Championships is recounted in detail. The
epilogue explains starkly the error which Cram made in
the 1984 Olympic Games: 'He believed the 1500
metres final would be a predominantly tactical race
won in a time around 3:38 or 3:39. History seconded
his proposition. Major championships rarely produced
fast races, usually because nobody was prepared to
take up the running in the crucial early stages. Los
Angeles was different... and, in many ways,
marvellously so.'

### Crane, Adrian & Richard

55 Running the Himalayas / Richard and Adrian Crane;
foreword by Lord Hunt of Llanfair Waterdine. London:
New English Library, 1984.
129p; illus, maps        ISBN: 0-450-06082-9
         BL: X.622/21125

The Crane brothers, with some background in
marathon and fell-running, undertook the daunting
task of covering more than 2,000 miles, during which
they climbed 280,000 feet involving 14 peaks above
8,000m over 65 mountain passes, for the charity
Intermediate Technology Development Group. Setting
out on 18 March 1983 from Darjeeling, they arrived in
Rawalpindi on 27 June, having completed the traverse
in 100 days.

### Crump, Jack

56 Running round the world / Jack Crump; foreword by
Harold M. Abrahams. London: Hale, 1966.
256p; illus        BL: X.449/2267

Posthumously published, the autobiography of the
famous administrator ranges over his activities in
athletics from 1925 to 1964, giving an insight into the
numerous problems faced by Britain's team manager
and secretary to the BAAB.

### Cudahy, Mike

57 Wild trails to far horizons: an ultra-distance runner /
Michael Cudahy; illustrated by John Beatty. London:
Unwin Hyman, 1989.
viii, 183p; illus        ISBN: 0-04-440381-X
         BL: YK.1990.b.2006

Jim Perrin suggests, in the foreword, that the text can
be read at several different levels: 'social document,
testament of friendship, sporting chronicle,
topographical companion or transcendental quest'.
Cudahy, who graduated to ultra-distance running via

track events and fell-racing, conveys well, if sometimes in excessively florid style, the effort involved in some very long events: Tan Hill-Cat and Fiddle, Pennine Way, North of England coast-to-coast, Southern Upland's Way, West Highland Way, and High Level Traverse in Scotland.

## Cusack, Michael

58 Michael Cusack and the GAA / Marcus de Búrca.
Dublin: Anvil, 1989.
192p; illus; index; pbk ISBN: 0-947962-49-2
BL: YK.1991.a.11820

Cusack (1847-1906) competed with distinction in throwing events, was the driving force behind the formation of the Gaelic Athletic Association in 1884, and was caricatured by James Joyce in Ulysses and Oliver St John Gogarty in Tumbling in the Hay.

## Cuthbert, Betty

59 Golden girl / as told to Jim Webster; foreword by Sir Wilfrid Kent Hughes. London: Pelham, 1966.
160p; illus BL: X.449/1817

An autobiography of the great Australian sprinter, winner of four Olympic gold medals.

## Davies, Lynn

60 Winner stakes all: Lynn Davies face to face with Peter Williams. London: Pelham, 1970.
156p; illus; index ISBN: 0-7207-0354-9
BL: X.629/2465

The son of a coalminer from Nantymoel in Bridgend, Lynn Davies became the first UK athlete to win an Olympic long jump title (Tokyo, 18 October 1964) with 8.07m. Davies was to continue in competition for three more seasons, retiring after the 1972 Olympic Games. It is a measure of his achievements that his UK record of 8.23 still stood after three decades.

## Davin, Maurice

61 Maurice Davin (1842-1927): first president of the GAA / Séamus O'Riain. Dublin: Geography Publications, 1994.
236p; illus; index ISBN: 0-906602-25-4

Davin set a number of records in the shot and hammer in the 1870s.

## Davin, Pat

62 Recollections of a veteran Irish athlete: the memoirs of Pat Davin, world's all-round athletic champion / Patrick Davin. Dublin: Juverna, 1938.
102p

Based on a series of articles written for the Irish Independent. Davin, from a family of athletes, held the world records for the high jump and long jump in the 1880s. A good account of Irish athletics, including the 'Gaelic Invasion' of America in 1888.

## De Coubertin, Pierre

63 This great symbol: Pierre de Coubertin and the origins of the modern Olympic Games / John J. MacAloon.
London: University of Chicago Press, 1981.
xiv, 359p; illus; index ISBN: 0-226-50000-4
BL: X.622/11280

This is a not entirely accurate work on the moving spirit behind the rebirth of the Olympic Games in the modern era. The author notes in his preface, however, that it 'is an act as much of reconstruction as of narration'.

## Dinnie, Donald

64 Donald Dinnie: the first sporting superstar / David Webster & Gordon Dinnie; edited by Charlie Allan.
Buchan: Ardo, 1999.
158p; illus; index ISBN: 0-9536596-0-7

Donald Dinnie was unquestionably the greatest all-round field events athlete of the nineteenth century. Though essentially a thrower, he was almost certainly the first athlete to clear 6ft 0in in the high jump and was undoubtedly capable of 50ft 0in with the 16lb shot. The book is based mainly on Dinnie's autobiographical articles in Health and Strength Magazine in 1906 so is understandably patchy, but contains some marvellous photographs of the great all-rounder and a remarkable nude sketch. The book also makes it clear that Dinnie was almost certainly the greatest all-round wrestler of his century.

## Downer, Alfred R.

65 Running recollections, and how to train: being an autobiography of Alfred R. Downer and short biographical sketches of E. C. Bredin (with his ideas on training), Len Hurst, Fred Bacon, G. B. Tincler, with method of training in the early part of the present century, and notes on training for boys. London: Gale and Polden, 1908.
150p; illus

*Reissued in facsimile ed. Tarland: Balgownie, 1982.*
*ISBN: 0-946698-00-7* BL: 7912.df

The famous Scottish sprinter gives a full account of his amateur and professional career, and adds biographies of Edgar Bredin and Len Hurst (both of whom contribute training notes), F. E. Bacon and G. B. Tincler. There are photographs of these athletes and of C. A. Bradley, Harry Hutchens, T. F. Keane, C. Harper, 'Treacle' Sanderson, W. Cummings and H. Cullum. Downer's book gives what is possibly the clearest description available of the seedy world of nineteenth century pedestrianism.
'The remainder of the summer I passed in going round the country, running at Scotch Games. These Games are highly diverting.... Imagine a rough stubble field and a "track" staked off thereon about 200yds to the lap, with square corners, and the going like a switchback railway, and you will get a slight idea of

what Scotch Games are like…. The starts are often paced out, and the member of the band who performs on the drum often officiates in the capacity of starter, his instrument taking the part of the pistol …. The best known "peds" as a rule "stand in" with one another, which means they agree to divide among themselves any prize-money the school may win. The poor "locals", as a rule, have to be content with what is left.' Downer, suspended from amateur competition in 1896, was one of the first 'shamateurs', picking up appearance money at the rural handicap meetings which provided the main competitive diet in the Victorian period. The Scottish handicap circuit had its equivalents in England, Wales and Ireland and on the East Coast of the United States, where another great sprinter, A. F. Duffey, was suspended in like manner a decade later. Downer, like many ex-amateurs such as Bredin, W. G. George and Shrubb, found it difficult to make a living in professional athletics, though exceptionally successful in match races. He died of alcoholism in 1912.

### Edwards, Jonathan

66  A time to jump: the authorised biography of Jonathan Edwards / Malcolm Folley. London: HarperCollins, 2000. xi, 260p; illus                        ISBN: 0-00-274031-1
                                                BL: YC.2000.a.8556

Published before his Olympic triple jump victory in Sydney, this absorbing book examines Edwards's long career from 1981 to 1999 showing how he reconciled his strong Christian beliefs with the demands of top-level sport. The athlete adds his own views on 'the Sunday question' in an appendix.

### Elliott, Herb

67  The golden mile: the Herb Elliott story as told to Alan Trengove; foreword by Percy Cerutty. London: Cassell, 1961. xiii, 178p; illus                        BL: 10712.i.32

Elliott's autobiography represents an outstanding contribution to athletics literature. Written in workmanlike and unsentimental prose, the review of Elliott's career provides a convincing and inspiring account of what it means to become the world's finest runner; and the descriptions of Portsea training, the Svengali-cum-Dali presence of Cerutty and the joy of good company provide excellent relief between the narratives of his victories. 'As I mounted the dais to receive my gold medal from Mr. Hugh Weir, of Australia, I found myself doing an emotional somersault. Up to the Games my attitude towards athletics was that it was fundamentally a sport for individuals, not teams. Athletes trained, made sacrifices and pushed their bodies to the limits of endurance for the personal satisfaction they achieved. Like scientists, athletes, I considered, should feel unshackled by national obligations. They ran as individuals, trying to create new standards for the human race; it was immaterial in which country they were born. I had trained for the 1500 metres as an individual and when Mr Weir placed

the medal round my neck my greatest thrill should have been from my triumph as an individual. But when the Australian flag was hoisted and the National Anthem was played the pride that filled my heart was for my country, not myself. The tears welled up and I realised I'd been fooling myself. I am an Australian and I'd been running for my country no matter how strongly cold reason told me I'd been running for myself.'

### Foster, Brendan

68  Brendan Foster / Brendan Foster and Cliff Temple. London: Heinemann, 1978. 220p; illus  ISBN: 0-434-26910-7 (cased) • 0-434-26911-5 (pbk)
                        BL: X.620/17822 • X.611/8158

A detailed biography of the former world record holder for 3000m, it includes extracts from his training diary from 1968 to 1976, and an appendix of his competitions from December 1962 to April 1978.

### Francom, Septimus 'Seppy'

69  Wirral gleanings: including smuggling and 'The Cave', well sinking, three Wirral hills, Wirral's Olympic Marathon runner, injustice in Birkenhead and a wartime fisherman / Greg Dawson. Irby: Dawson, 1998. 53p; illus, maps; pbk          ISBN: 0-9522598-3-4
                                                BL: YK.2000.b.1300

Francom competed in the marathon at the 1912 Stockholm Games. The race was won by Ken McArthur of South Africa, the only British-born runner ever to win the Olympic Marathon.

### Fry, Charles Burgess

70  C. B. Fry: the man and his methods / Arthur W. Myers; with a preface by G. H. R. Dabbs. Bristol: Arrowsmith, 1912. xi, 189p                        BL: 010854.de.31

71  Life worth living: some phases of an Englishman / C. B. Fry. London: Eyre & Spottiswoode, 1939. 423p; illus; index                        BL: 10859.d.5

The autobiography of perhaps the greatest all-round English sportsman. Fry's absorbing story ranges from his schooldays at Repton to his meeting with Hitler in Berlin. Athletics is naturally only one aspect of the story, but his greatest performances are vividly described. 'My housemaster, Mr Forman, was the only coach I ever had in athletics, and that on only one occasion. One afternoon he happened to be crossing the school paddock when I was practising the long jump on the rough turf into an elementary pit. He stopped for a few minutes, told me I did not jump high enough, took off his black mackintosh, and made a heap of it between the take-off and the pit. The mackintosh frightened me into jumping much higher. That was the only piece of coaching I ever remember receiving in athletics in the whole of my career. It is rather interesting that up at Oxford when I jumped over 23ft and did a world's record in the long jump I used to be well over 5 feet in the air in a human ball at the peak of my parabola. No doubt I saw a ghostly mackintosh and remembered Mr Forman's vibrant voice. Nowadays they have invented a new technique called the hitch-kick, with which performers such as Jesse Owens cover some 26 feet.'

72  C. B.: the life of Charles Burgess Fry / Clive Ellis.
London: Dent, 1984.
x, 294p; illus; index      ISBN: 0-460-04654-3
BL: X.950/34764

73  C. B. Fry: an English hero / Iain Wilton. London:
Cohen, 1999.
xiv, 498p; illus; index      ISBN: 1-86066-170-X
BL: YC.2000.a.8818

An account of the great sportsman's life that complements the autobiography with details of his later career as sometime nude model, failed politician, journalist, and head of a sail training school with 'Madame', his formidable wife. Fry's athletic career is covered quite fully in chapters 1-3.

### Gale, William

74  Life and performances of William Gale, the celebrated Cardiff pedestrian / 'Autolycus'; also a few hints on training by W. Gale. London: J. A. Brooks, 1877.
12p      BL: 10803.c.1(5)

This forms a brief account of the life of the diminutive pedestrian (born 21 April 1832) whose career included a short-lived business partnership with George Seward. Gale's career record from 1851 to 1877 is given. Gale contrasts the equally effective modes of progression of walkers Harry Vaughan and Billy Howes.

### George, Walter

75  The '100-up' exercise: a comprehensive description of the 'century' home exercise, together with a sketch of the author's wonderful career, with practical illustrations / W. G. George. London: Ewart, Seymour, 1913.
56p; illus      BL: D

An account of George's method of training at home, including a rare photograph of the start of his famous mile race in 1886 with Cummings. The '100-up' exercise is basically running on the spot and can have contributed little to the performances of the greatest distance runner of the nineteenth century.

### Grace, W. G.

76  W. G. Grace: a biography / W. Methven Brownlee with a treatise on cricket contributed by W. G. Grace.
London: Iliffe, 1887.
166p; illus      BL: 10827.aa.25

The first biography of Grace to be published contains an excellent survey of his athletics career, giving details of his performances between 1866 and 1870, as well as listing his career bests.

### Grey, Tanni

77  Tanni / Ted Harrison. London: CollinsWillow, 1996.
223p; illus; index      ISBN: 0-00-218723-X
BL: YK.1996.b.11096

Carys Davina (Tanni) Grey had, by 1992, become the best known British wheelchair athlete, in which year she won four gold medals in category T3 at the Barcelona Paralympics. Her dominance of the 2000 Olympics suggests another book will need to be written.

### Guiney, David

78  Happy hours. Dublin: PR Books Ireland, 1994.
224p      ISBN: 0-9521698-9-4

By the prolific Irish writer and former AAA shot-put champion.

### Gunnell, Sally

79  Sally Gunnell / Andrew Ward. London: Scholastic, 1993.
48p; illus; pbk
(Sports shots; 6)      ISBN: 0-590-55374-7
BL: YK.1995.a.635

A small format series designed for young readers.

80  Running tall / Sally Gunnell and Christopher Priest.
London: Bloomsbury, 1994.
199p; illus; index      ISBN: 0-7475-1717-7
BL: YK.1995.b.8646

Sally Gunnell is a rare example of an outstanding junior who persevered through to success at senior level. Much of the text is devoted to clear accounts of her training and technique and of the mental aspect of competition. There is also some discussion of her transition from part-time to full-time athlete, the economic basis of athletics, and of drug testing.

81  Sally Gunnell / Jane Coxley. Aylesbury: Ginn, 1995.
32p; illus; index; pbk
(Impact: real lives; set A)      ISBN: 0-602-26555-X
BL: YK.1996.a.15328

Aimed at primary school children, this large print work covers her early life and introduction to athletics, her transition from combined events to 400m hurdles (including her Olympic Games win and world record performance) and her marriage to Jon Bigg.

### Halberg, Murray

82  A clean pair of heels: the Murray Halberg story / as told to Garth Gilmour. London: Herbert Jenkins, 1963.
212p; illus      BL: 10667.t.23

The autobiography of one of New Zealand's greatest long-distance runners, the 1960 Olympic 5000m champion.

## Hampson, Tom

83  One crowded hour / foreword by Eric Parker. London: The Field, 1935.
122p                                              BL: 7916.f.27

> A selection of articles by sportsmen, which includes 'Breaking a world's record' by Tom Hampson, an account of his 800m victory at the 1932 Los Angeles Olympics.

## Hansch, Felice

84  Felice Hansch in sport 1922-1934 / Colin Martin. Glasgow: The author, 1989.
xi, 116p; illus, maps
     ISBN: 0-9514412-1-3 (cased) • 0-9514412-0-5 (leather)
                                         BL: LB.31.a.2400

> This is an unusual work in at least two respects: the subject is the author's Austrian wife, an athlete of modest achievements (8.1 60m, 13.2 100m); and, the design and typography by Heriot-Watt University, Edinburgh.

## Heino, Viljo

85  Viljo Heino 1914-1998: flying Finn – floating Finn / Chris Turner. Walsingham: The author, 1998.
40p; illus; index; pbk

> Within a relatively brief compass, the author expertly places one of the great Finnish long-distance runners in the context of Finnish political and cultural history. Particularly revealing is Heino's sometimes strained relationship with Paavo Nurmi (1897-1973).

## Hemery, David

86  Another hurdle / David Hemery. London: Heinemann, 1976.
viii, 216p; illus; index        ISBN: 0-434-32630-5
                                         BL: X.629/10580

> An extremely valuable work from the 1968 Olympic 400m hurdles champion, in that it describes in detail his training programme from September 1967 to October 1968 and from January 1971 to September 1972, and explains hurdling technique. The appendices cover the administration of athletics in the UK and a complete summary of his career from 1953 to 1972.

## Hewitt, Phil

87  I've started so I'll finish / Phil Hewitt. Braunton: Merlin, 1985.
50p; pbk                        ISBN: 0-86303-236-2
                                         BL: YK.1990.a.2055

> In 1982, at the age of thirty-seven, the author was overweight, smoking forty cigarettes a day, and was 'generally going to seed'. He started running from the end of 1982. This is an account of his training and racing programme in the following two years,

culminating in his completion of the 1984 Wolverhampton Marathon.

## Hewson, Brian

88  Flying feet / as told to Peter Bird. London: Stanley Paul, 1962.
160p; illus                     BL: X.449/233

> The autobiography of one of Britain's finest middle-distance runners, the European 1500m champion in 1958, and winner of six AAA titles at 880yds and the mile.

## Hill, Albert

89  Albert Hill: a proper perspective / Greg Moon. Cheltenham: The author, 1992.
98p; illus; pbk                 BL: YK.1994.a.5699

> Albert George Hill (1889-1969) is still the only British athlete to have won two gold medals in standard individual events at one Olympics and, 'uniquely for a top class performer, became even more successful as a coach'. The author has produced a meticulously researched work, attested by 502 references.

## Hill, Ron

90  The long hard road: an autobiography. Part 1: Nearly to the top / Ron Hill. Hyde: Ron Hill Sports, 1981.
405p; illus ISBN: 0-950788-20-1 (cased) • 0-950788-21-X (pbk)
                    BL: X.0629/584(1) • X.0629/585(1)

91  The long hard road: an autobiography. Part 2: To the peak and beyond / Ron Hill. Hyde: Ron Hill Sports, 1982.
423p; illus  ISBN: 0-950788-22-8 (cased) • 0-950788-23-6 (pbk)
                    BL: X.629/19818 • X.629/19819

> Hill was advised that, for his autobiography to be a commercial success, he would have to shorten his manuscript by half. Fortunately, he decided that this would be impossible, so we have, in two volumes, the most detailed account of any UK athlete's career.

## Hodge, Percy

92  My running career / Percy Hodge. London: All Sports, 1923.
28p; illus; pbk

> The 1920 Olympic steeplechase champion tells his story from his début in Guernsey in 1910 to the end of 1921. A rare, historically important booklet.

## Horan, Frederick

93  From the crack of the pistol: a personal saga / Frederick S. Horan. Dorchester: Longmans, 1955.
277p; illus; index              BL: 4920.k.50

> This is not really an athletics book, but it contains chapters which make it required reading for the athletics historian. These chapters describe university athletics in the 1890s and, particularly, the

great LAC v. New York AC match at Manhattan Field in 1895, when world records tumbled to such 'greats' as Wefers, Sweeney and Kilpatrick. In his race with the latter, Horan became one of the fastest English half-milers of the nineteenth century, running 1:55.4 behind Kilpatrick's world record of 1:53.5. There is also a description of the Yale v. Cambridge meeting of 1895 and a sketch of Horan's son, Forbes's athletics career at Cambridge, 1929-32.

## Horwill, Frank

94  Obsession for running: a lifetime in athletics / Frank Horwill. Kirby Lonsdale: The author, 1991.
101p; illus; pbk

Part biography, part coaching advice from one of Britain's leading authorities on distance running.

## Howell, Denis

95  Made in Birmingham: the memoirs of Denis Howell / Denis Howell. London: Queen Anne Press, 1990.
399p; illus                                ISBN: 0-356-17645-2

Denis Howell is still widely regarded as the best UK Minister for Sport the country has had.

## Hyman, Dorothy

96  Sprint to fame / Dorothy Hyman; edited by Phil Pilley. London: Stanley Paul, 1964.
159p; illus                                     BL: X.449/867

Dorothy Hyman is one of the few women athletes to earn sufficient acclaim to make an autobiography a sound proposition. The book is remarkable for its disarming frankness and its insight into the under-documented world of women's athletics.

## Ibbotson, Derek

97  The Ibbotson story / Mel Watman. London: World Athletic & Sporting Publications, 1958.
47p; illus                                      BL: 7923.e.27

Derek Ibbotson set a world mile record in 1957, the high point in this booklet reviewing his career to that time.

98  Four-minute smiler: the Derek Ibbotson story / as told by Terry O'Connor; foreword by Herb Elliott. London: Stanley Paul, 1960.
175p; illus                                    BL: 010600.d.29

An absorbing, if premature, review of this popular Yorkshire distance runner's career.

## Jackson, Colin

99  Colin Jackson / Elgan Philip Davies; golygwyd gan John Emyr. Aberystwyth: Canolfan Astudiaethau Addysg, 1997.
18p; illus; pbk
*On title page: ALBSU*
ISBN: 1-85644-339-6
BL: YK.1998.a.1789

A biography (in Welsh) of the world record holder at 110m Hurdles, it traces his career from 1983, when he was coached by Malcolm Arnold, to his major championship successes.

## Johnson, Ben

100  Speed trap: inside the biggest scandal in Olympic history / Charlie Francis with Jeff Coplon. London: Grafton, 1991.
306p; illus; index
ISBN: 0-246-13757-6
BL: YK.1993.b.2089

This biography of Ben Johnson constitutes an extended justification of drug use in athletics.
'It is time for the IAAF to promote and sponsor its own open, international research on performance-enhancing drugs.'

101  From hero to zero: the rise and fall of Ben Johnson / Paul Gains. Surbiton: SportsBooks, 2000.
200p; illus                                    ISBN: 1-899807-08-X

## Johnson, Michael

102  Slaying the dragon: how to turn your small steps into great feats / Michael Johnson. London: Piatkus, 1996.
xxi, 232p; illus; pbk
*Foreword by Muhammad Ali*
ISBN: 0-7499-1723-7
BL: YK.1997.b.5060

This is a highly-structured autobiography by the 200m and 400m Olympic champion of 1996. The work is divided into three parts, each of which is further subdivided into three, with alliterative titles. Each of the nine subdivisions contains five training tips and a selection of aphorisms ranging from Aristotle to Milton, from Goethe to Malcolm X. Johnson states in his introduction: 'I have not set out to write about how you can be an Olympic champion or how you can break world records. Those are rarely attainable goals and, honestly, there are probably more worthy ones for most people.'

## Jones, James

103  An account of the greatest feats of pedestrianism that have ever been performed, or, The life of James Jones, the Oxford pedestrian / written by himself. Oxford: 1819.
16p; pbk

## Jones, Lachlan

104 Walk a crooked mile / Greg Jones. London: New Holland, 2000.
320p; pbk          ISBN: 1-86436-640-0

Lachlan Jones, an athlete handicapped by limited vision and cerebral palsy, rose to the top rank of wheelchair racing. Told by his father.

## Jones, Len

105 Age is no distance. Bognor Regis: Felpham, 1988.
105p; illus; pbk        ISBN: 1-870690-7

The story of a veteran marathon runner.

## Keily, Arthur

106 Marathon winner / Arthur Keily. Derby: The author, 1984.
187p; illus; pbk
*Forewords by Ron Hill, George Edwards & Ron Dalton*
BL: X.629/24287

Keily offers some general advice on training and diet, as well as some trenchant views on BAAB administrators and selectors.

## Kiely, Tom

107 Tom Kiely: 'for Tipperary and Ireland' / Bob Withers, research and text; Patrick Holland, editor. Clonmel: Tipperary S.R. County Museum, 1997.
44p; illus; pbk

The Olympic All Round champion of 1904, Kiely also won five AAA titles in the hammer.

## Killanin

108 My Olympic years. London: Secker & Warburg, 1983.
xvii, 238p; illus; index      ISBN: 0-436-23340-1
BL: X.622/16454

Michael Morris, Lord Killanin, was elected to succeed Avery Brundage as IOC President in 1972 and held the post for eight years. He opens his account with the closure of the 1980 Olympic Games in Moscow, pointedly remarking that there are sound practical and moral reasons 'for dissuading politicians from using sport as a means to an end'. Killanin concludes by examining the major issues surrounding the 1980 Games, including his concerted attempts to prevent a mass US-led boycott.
'It was ironic that when Britain was winning Olympic medals in 1924, their troops were trying to put down the rebels in Afghanistan and on the North-West frontier.'
The author considers, in retrospect, that the IOC should have carried out an inquiry after 1980, and is of the opinion that some members should have been expelled.

## Lavan, Sean Thomas

109 Sean Thomas Lavan, 1898-1973: teacher, surgeon, footballer, Olympic athlete. Kiltimagh: Kiltimagh Historical Society, 1996.
23p; illus

Lavan, a 400m/800m specialist, competed for Ireland in the 1924 Olympics.

## Levy, E. Lawrence

110 The autobiography of an athlete / E. Lawrence Levy. Birmingham: Hammond, 1913?
xii, 270p; illus; index      BL: X.629/14601

Levy, editor of The Athlete and an AAA official, was a famous weightlifter. His book contains an illuminating account of the rivalry between Birchfield Harriers and Moseley Harriers. There are also descriptions of the Olympic Games of 1896 and 1908.

## Lewis, Carl

111 Inside track: my professional life in amateur track and field / Carl Lewis with Jeffrey Marx. London: Pelham, 1990.
240p; illus; index      ISBN: 0-7207-1957-7
BL: YK.1991.b.1571

The autobiography of the greatest sprinter-jumper of modern times provides a vivid picture of the life of one of the last great shamateurs.

## Liddell, Eric

112 Eric Liddell: the making of an athlete and the training of a missionary / D. P. Thomson. Glasgow: Eric Liddell Memorial Committee, 1945.
40p; illus; pbk      BL: 10857.a.15

An account of the life of the 1924 Olympic Champion for 400m, based mainly on his own writing and on press reports. Liddell spent twenty years as a missionary in China, the land of his birth, before his death from a brain tumour in a Japanese prison camp in 1945.

113 Scotland's greatest athlete: the Eric Liddell story / D. P. Thomson. Crieff: Research Unit, 1970.
240p; pbk
*Foreword by Sir Arthur E. Porritt*    ISBN: 0-900867-04-3
BL: X.708/6923

The author became acquainted with his subject when they were both students in 1923. This fuller account of his life devotes particular attention to the twenty years of his missionary work in China.

114 Eric H. Liddell, athlete and missionary / D. P. Thomson. Crieff: Research Unit, 1971.
xxx, 230p; illus; index
*Bibliography: pxiii-xiv*      ISBN: 0-900867-07-8
BL: X.200/4812

115 The flying Scotsman / Sally Magnusson. London:
Quartet, 1981.
191p; illus; pbk                                    ISBN: 0-7043-3379-1
                                                            BL: X.629/15426

Magnusson's book is an interesting work, published to
coincide with the release of the Oscar-winning film
'Chariots of Fire'.

116 Eric Liddell: born to run / Peter Watkins; illustrated by
Gavin Rowe. London: MacRae, 1983.
42p; illus                                          ISBN: 0-86203-129-X
                                                            BL: X.808/38900

Large print biography for younger readers based on
the standard D. P. Thomson work.

117 Eric Liddell: God's athlete / Catherine M. Swift.
Basingstoke: Marshall Pickering, 1986.
154p; pbk                                           ISBN: 0-551-01354-0
                                                            BL: YC.1987.a.4628

Liddell's athletic career is recounted for juveniles.

118 Eric Liddell / Sue Shaw. Carlisle: OM, 1993.
28p; illus                                          ISBN: 1-85078-105-2
                                                            BL: YK.1994.a.13776

Aimed at the very young reader.

119 Complete surrender / Julian Wilson; foreword by Sir
David Puttnam. Crowborough: Monarch, 1996.
157p; illus, 1 map; pbk                             ISBN: 1-85424-348-9
                                                            BL: YC.1998.a.1663

Mainly reliant on the accounts of Thomson (misspelt
throughout) and Magnusson, the author of this
biography of Eric Liddell also quotes from some
recently published reminiscences of fellow inmates of
the Weihsien internment camp. In his epilogue, Wilson
refers to the establishment of the Eric Liddell
Foundation which draws together promising athletes
from all over Shandong Province to compete over
400m for the Liddell Cup.

## Lindesay, William

120 Alone on the Great Wall: from the desert to the sea /
William Lindesay. London: Hodder & Stoughton, 1989.
217p; illus; index                                  ISBN: 0-340-50154-5
                                                            BL: YC.1990.b.1008

Lindesay decided his next challenge after negotiating
Hadrian's Wall with his brother, Nicholas, would be the
Great Wall of China. This is a fine account of the run
undertaken by the author in 1987.

## Linsell, Richard

121 The life of Richard Linsell, the Essex cricketer,
pedestrian, and quoit player / by a Friend (Rusticus).
London: The author, 1855.                           BL: 10825.a.57(2)

## Liversidge, Alfred

122 Alfred Liversidge (1836-1921): Swinton's sporting hero /
Giles H. Brearley. Barnsley: Neville-Douglas, 1998.
25p; pbk                                            ISBN: 1-901853-01-2

Liversidge    held    the    professional    half-mile
championship.

## Loader, William

123 Testament of a runner / W. R. Loader. London:
Heinemann, 1960.
170p                                                BL: 7925.bb.32

Testament is probably the best non-technical book
ever written on the subject of sprinting. Loader, 1935
AAA Junior 100yds champion, describes in fine prose
his struggle to break ten seconds for 100yds. This is a
simply marvellous work, essential reading for any lover
of athletics.

## Lovelock, Jack

124 The legend of Lovelock / Norman Harris. London:
Nicholas Kaye, 1965.
180p; illus                                         BL: X.449/944

Harris's tribute to his brilliant but enigmatic
compatriot is in the first rank of athletic biographies.
Through access to Lovelock's private papers and by
methodical research, Harris reveals as much of this
master-runner's make-up as we are ever likely to know.
The text is supported by many extracts from
Lovelock's training diaries which poignantly indicate
the process of physical and psychological
self-examination which brought triumph at the Berlin
Olympics in the 1500m.

## McColgan, Liz

125 Queen of the track: the Liz McColgan story / Adrianne
Blue. London: Witherby, 1992.
192p; illus                                         ISBN: 0-85493-223-2
                                                            BL: YK.1993.b.9184

Fairly representative of the genre, drawing upon
interviews and contemporary press reports. Blue
identifies two issues of particular relevance to women
athletes: the disparity in financial rewards and the
lack of crèche facilities at major meetings.

126 Liz McColgan / Andrew Ward; designed by Ness Wood.
London: Hippo, 1993.
48p; illus; pbk
(Sports shots; 3)                                   ISBN: 0-590-55259-7
                                                            BL: YK.1994.a.10572

A very small format series designed for young readers.

## McCooke, Charlie & Steve

127  The Armoy athletes: a tribute to Steve and Charlie
McCooke / compiled by Robert Hanna; edited by Eull
Dunlop. Ballymena: Mid-Antrim Historical Group, 1990.
60p; illus
      *Foreword by Jimmy Todd*          ISBN: 0-9509265-7-4
                                         BL: YK.1993.b.731

   Steve McCooke competed for Britain in the 1948
   Olympic 10,000m. Many of the reports included
   originally appeared in the Belfast Telegraph.

## MacLaren, Archibald

128  Archibald MacLaren: his work and influence on the
development of physical education, 1850-1884 / D. W.
Taylor. Manchester University, 1980. MEd thesis.

## McNeil, George

129  The unique double / George McNeil. Tranent: The
author, 1983.
      96p; illus                         ISBN: 0-906391-57-1

   McNeil was professional sprint champion of the world,
   winner of both the Powderhall Sprint (1970) and the
   Stawell Gift (1981). His book is the best record in print
   of the life of a professional runner and is required
   reading for any historian of professional athletics.

## McSweeney, Fanahan

130  Living and loving with cancer / Fanahan McSweeney.
Dublin: Quill Print & Design, 1994.
      xii, 251p; illus; pbk            ISBN: 0-9520424-2-8
                                        BL: YK.1996.a.12770

   Irish sprinter Fanahan McSweeney represented
   Ireland in the 400m at the Munich Olympics. In 1986
   he was struck down by spinal cancer and this is his
   personal account of his battle against the disease.

## McWhirter, Ross

131  Ross: the story of a shared life / Norris McWhirter.
London: Churchill, 1976.
      240p; illus; index
      *Foreword by Roger Bannister*      SBN: 902-782-23-1

   As the sub-title makes clear, this account of Ross
   McWhirter, who was assassinated in November 1975,
   is equally the story of his twin, Norris, to that time.
   The brothers were distinguished runners, journalists,
   and authors. They wrote the ground-breaking Get to
   your Marks! and founded the phenomenal Guinness
   Book of Records.

## Maule, Tex

132  Running for life: the odyssey of a heart-attack victim's
jogging back to health. London: Pelham, 1973.
      v, 215p
      *Originally published as: Running scarred. New York:*
      *Saturday Review Press, 1972*      ISBN 0-7207-0689-0
                                          BL: X.329/6431

   The author was for may years a respected
   sportswriter in the USA. Just after his fifty-first
   birthday he had a heart attack. This is the story of his
   recovery, culminating in his completion of the Boston
   Marathon.

## Modahl, Diane

133  The Diane Modahl story: going the distance / Diane
Modahl. London: Hodder & Stoughton, 1995.
      viii, 199p; illus                 ISBN: 0-340-64269-6
                                         BL: YC.1996.b.6301

   As a member of Sale Harriers, Diane Edwards rapidly
   became an outstanding 800m specialist. The result of
   a random drug test taken on 18 June 1994 in Lisbon
   was communicated over two months later as Modahl
   was about to defend her Commonwealth title in
   Canada. The sample, which showed an abnormally high
   ratio of testosterone : epitestosterone, resulted in a
   ban of two years. Her subsequent appeal and
   strenuous attempts to clear her name are recounted,
   the scientific evidence being presented with admirable
   clarity.

      ☞   Subsequent ed. B134

134  The Diane Modahl story: going the distance / Diane
Modahl. Rev. ed. London: Hodder & Stoughton, 1996.
      viii, 261p; illus; pbk            ISBN: 0-340-64282-3
                                         BL: YK.1997.a.2668

      ☞   Previous ed. B133

## Moorcroft, Dave

135  Running commentary: an autobiography / Dave
Moorcroft & Cliff Temple. London: Stanley Paul, 1984.
      156p; illus                       ISBN: 0-09-155200-1
                                         BL: X.950/35536

   Moorcroft opens his account with some reflections
   several hours after running 5000m in 13:00.41 in Oslo
   on 7 July 1982: 'Breaking a world record was what I
   always dreamed about, and yet when it came it had
   taken me by surprise. ... Athletics is not only about
   records, though. It is about winning races, or at least
   getting the best out of yourself.'

## Morgan, Griffith (Guto Nyth-bran)

136 Guto Nyth-bran / William Glanffrwd Thomas. Aberdar: Pugh & Rowlands, 1913.
  BL: X708/1721

   *Biography (in Welsh) of the eighteenth century distance runner who was the inspiration for the annual New Year Nos Galan races.*

## Nankeville, Bill

137 The miracle of the mile / Bill Nankeville; foreword by Gordon Pirie. London: Stanley Paul, 1956.
   160p; illus; index
  BL: 7922.c.40

   *In the post-war era, Nankeville won the AAA mile title four times and set a British 1500m record finishing third in the 1950 European Championships.*

## Naylor, Joss

138 Joss Naylor: fell runner extraordinary / Ken Ledword. The author, 1975.

139 Joss Naylor MBE was here: the complete traverse of all summits listed in the seven 'Lakeland' guides written by Alfred Wainwright; 214 tops visited in seven days: a personal account by Joss Naylor MBE / Joss Naylor. 2nd ed. The author, 1992.
   28p; illus; pbk
   *1st edition untraced*

## Newton, Arthur

140 Running in three continents / Arthur F. H. Newton. London: Witherby, 1940.
   187p
   *Foreword by Joe Binks*
  BL: 2408.b.19

   *Accounts of Newton's races in England, South Africa, Canada and the USA. Includes a good account of the TransAmerica races of 1928 and 1929 and a portrait of coach J. P. Nicholson. After starting serious running at the age of forty, he became the most prolific record-breaker in ultra-running of his time.*

## Noel-Baker, Lord, Philip J.

141 Man of sport, man of peace: collected speeches and essays of Philip Noel-Baker, Olympic statesman 1889-1982 / Don Anthony. London: Sports Editions, 1991.
   175p; illus
  ISBN: 0-9517802-0-4
   *Foreword by Sir Arthur Gold and J. A. Samaranch*

   *As P. J. Baker, the subject ran the 800/1500m double at the Olympic Games of 1912 and 1920, winning a silver medal in the latter year. He was awarded the 1959 Nobel Prize for Peace in recognition of his achievements in the cause of disarmament. A seven page biography is followed by annotated speeches and essays.*

## Ovett, Steve

142 The Athletics Weekly file on Sebastian Coe & Steve Ovett / compiled and edited by Mel Watman. Rochester: Athletics Weekly, 1982.
   160p; illus; pbk
  ISBN: 0-95068102-4
  BL: X.629/22550

   *Facsimile reproductions of race reports for the years 1972-1982, together with other material on Coe and Ovett which appeared in the magazine during the period.*

   ☞   Also listed at: B47

143 Steve Ovett: portrait of an athlete / Simon Turnbull. London: W.H. Allen, 1982.
   174p; illus
  ISBN: 0-491-02697-8
  BL: X.629/20835

   *The author states explicitly that Ovett declined an invitation to collaborate on this work, so there is considerable reliance on previously published interviews. Turnbull has nevertheless succeeded in producing a fair portrait of the phenomenally-gifted Ovett.*

144 Ovett: an autobiography / Steve Ovett with John Rodda. London: Willow, 1984.
   viii, 216p; illus; index
  ISBN: 0-00-218119-3
  BL: X.950/37406

   *Ovett pointedly refers in his preface to the earlier work by Turnbull. In co-operating with John Rodda (The Guardian), Ovett has inevitably produced an account with greater immediacy. His reaction to losing the 1980 Olympic 1500m is characteristically blunt, and he reflects on his disappointing fourth place in the 1983 World Championships 1500m. Ovett comments critically on such matters as administration, selection, sponsorship and drug testing. He minimises his comparative failure at the 1984 Olympic Games through illness. Having finished eighth (and last) over 800m, Ovett dropped out after 1150m in the 1500m final: 'I am left forever with the un-answered question: If I had gone on, would the pain have subsided; in the last home straight of the 1984 Olympic 1500 meters final, would there have been three men in Great Britain vests coming down the straight for the medals, as I had always believed and hoped?'*

## Owens, Jesse

145 Jesse Owens: an American life / William J. Baker. London: Collier Macmillan, 1986.
   xii, 289p; illus; index
  ISBN: 0-02-901780-7
  BL: YK.1987.b.2061

   *'An athlete becomes a national hero only when his personality, achievements, and image fulfil a cultural need beyond the athletic arena. Jesse Owens was a rare individual whose importance transcended athleticism.' This is Baker's epitaph for James Cleveland Owens, whose rise to international pre-eminence in 1935 and 1936 is charted. Baker*

subjects much of Owens's anecdotal evidence to a sceptical gaze, but this remains a largely sympathetic account of a great athlete's life.

146 Jesse Owens: Olympic star / Patricia and Fredrick McKissack; illustrated by Michael David Biegel. Aldershot: Enslow, 1992.
32p; illus; index
(Great African Americans)               ISBN: 0-89490-312-8
                                        BL: YK.1993.a.13206

This large print biography is designed for very young readers.

## Pascoe, Alan

147 Pascoe: the story of an athlete / Alan Pascoe with Alan Hubbard. London: Stanley Paul, 1979.
120p; illus                              ISBN: 0-091349-80-X
                                         BL: X.620/19045

Published at the conclusion of his active athletics career, the biography opens with a detailed account of the planning required for a major championship over 400m hurdles, including the vital mental preparation. There is an excellent photo sequence of his hurdling technique and a list of career highlights, including his Commonwealth and European victories.

## Peters, Jim

148 In the long run / as told by J. H. Peters and his coach 'Johnny' Johnston to Joseph Edmundson; foreword by Philip Noel-Baker. London: Cassell, 1955.
viii, 216p; illus                        BL: 7922.ee.1
The life story of the great marathon runner from 1918 to his retirement after the Vancouver race in 1954.

## Peters, Mary

149 Mary P: autobiography / Mary Peters with Ian Wooldridge. London: Stanley Paul, 1974.
xii, 156p; illus; index                  ISBN: 0-09-122280-X
                                         BL: X.629/6254

An inspiring account of the 1972 Olympic pentathlon champion's career, with particular emphasis on her coach Robert (Buster) McShane. Although she had an exceptionally long career (including 49 pentathlon competitions), only the briefest details are given in the appendix.

## Pickard, Mark

150 Evidence of a misspent youth: an autobiography of a maverick long distance runner / Mark Pickard. London?: The author, 1995.
iii, 220p; illus; pbk                    BL: YK.1995.a.9016
Born in 1960, the author achieved early success, setting most of his best marks at the age of 21, including a UK best of 163m 249yds in 24 hrs. He suffered from osteomyelitis and a number of injuries which prevented further improvements.

## Pirie, Gordon

151 Running wild / Gordon Pirie. London: W.H. Allen, 1961.
224p; illus                              BL: X.449/893

Pirie was the first modern British runner to adopt a professional attitude to distance running. Lacking sports science support though, he pursued an eccentric, essentially trial and error approach, emulating the rigorous programmes of the Czech Emil Zátopek. It was also his misfortune to live in an era in which this committed approach would bring him into conflict with essentially laissez faire British administrators. This is heavily reflected in Running Wild, to the detriment of full accounts of some of his finest races. This story of one of Britain's finest athletes is essential reading for the historian of distance running.

152 The impossible hero: a life of Gordon Pirie / Dick Booth. London: Corsica Press, 1999.
viii, 286p; illus; index                 ISBN: 0-9536671-0-3
                                         BL: YC.1999.b.9562

Few sports biographies cover the entire life of their subject. Drawing on numerous recollections from friends and fellow athletes, this is the extraordinary story of the man who profoundly influenced distance running in Britain and set many records in the process. The later chapters show how Pirie's extreme determination to go his own way in life, as in athletics, was both a strength and a handicap.

## Powell, Foster

153 A short sketch of the life of Mr F. Powell, the great pedestrian who departed this life April 15, 1793 in the 59th year of his age. London: R.H. Westley, 1793.
11p; illus; pbk
   *Library copy includes ms. notes by R. W.*   BL: T.1091(3)

The preamble by the editor describes Powell 'as without partiality the greatest Pedestrian ever known in England, and singularised himself as such for upwards of thirty years'. Born in Horsforth, near Leeds, in 1734, he became articled to an attorney in the Temple in 1762. His first recorded pedestrian exploit occurred in 1764, when he covered 50 miles on the Bath road inside 7 hours. Forays over long distances in Switzerland and France followed, before the first of his four London to York back trips took place in 1773. Subsequent successful attempts were made in 1788, 1790 and 1792, the last taking a record 5 days 15¼ hours. In 1787 he covered the 112 miles return journey from Canterbury to London inside 24 hours. Details of some other of his feats are given and his physical attributes are described: 'His person was tall and thin, about five feet nine inches high, very strong downwards, well calculated for walking, and of rather sallow complexion.' His death at about 4am on 15 April 1793 was 'much regretted by those who had the pleasure of his acquaintance'. He was interred in the burial ground of St. Faith at St. Paul's on 22 April 1793.

## Rand, Mary

154 Mary Mary (an autobiography) / Mary Rand; foreword
by Ron Pickering. London: Hodder & Stoughton, 1969.
158p; illus                                          ISBN: 0-340-10527-5
                                                     BL: X.449/4011

The autobiography of the first British woman athlete
to win an Olympic title in track and field (long jump at
Tokyo on 14 October 1964, with a world record of
6.76m).

## Richards, Bob

155 The heart of a champion / Bob Richards. London: Peter
Davies, 1962.
137p; illus                                          BL: X.449/880

An analysis of inspiration in athletics by the famous
'Vaulting Vicar', Olympic pole vault champion in 1952.

## Riefenstahl, Leni

156 The sieve of time: the memoirs of Leni Riefenstahl.
London: Quartet, 1992.
669p; illus; index
    *Translation of: Memoiren*                       ISBN: 0-7043-7021-2
                                                     BL: YC.1992.b.4231

Helene Bertha Amalie Riefenstahl (born 1902)
commenced work on these memoirs at the age of
eighty and completed them five years later. Her 1936
film Olympia is unquestionably the greatest of all
sports documentary films and The Sieve of Time
includes a detailed account of its making.

157 A portrait of Leni Riefenstahl / Audrey Salkeld. London:
Cape, 1996.
viii, 256p; illus
    *Bibliography: p297-302; filmography: p303-304*
                                                     ISBN: 0-224-02480-9
                                                     BL: YC.1996.b.5056

The making of Olympia is covered and Salkeld
discusses the attempts made by scholars such as
Graham and Infield to unravel conflicting evidence. The
editing of the film and the efforts by Riefenstahl to
recover the material after 1945 are discussed.
Subsequent events surrounding the screening of the
film are mentioned. Roy Fowler, Chairman of the
History Project of BECTU, suggests than an analogy
can be made between Riefenstahl and the great
Russian film maker Sergei Eisenstein.

## Rowe, Arthur

158 Champion in revolt / Arthur Rowe. London: Stanley
Paul, 1963.
160p; illus                                          BL: 10712.e.27

A characteristically forthright autobiography from
the British, Commonwealth and European shot putt
champion.

## Rye, Walter

159 An autobiography of an ancient athlete and antiquary /
Walter Rye. Norwich: Privately printed, 1916.
v, 226p; illus                                       BL: 010855.b.5

Rye's work is in diary-form. He was one of the most
famous of early athletes, a founder member of the
AAA and secretary of London AC. Rye gives a good
account of athletics in the 1860s, including much
detail about Mincing Lane AC and London AC and
about the AAC v. AAA controversy.
'The AAC... was being mismanaged by J. G. Chambers
of Cambridge.... He was a strange character who tried
to combine aristocratic sport with running the
"Amateur Athletic Club" for his own benefit at Lillie
Bridge, and a little shop for the sale of "Welsh produce"
in Arthur Street, Chelsea, in which his trainer, Harry
Andrews, acted as his salesman and manager. His
best athletic performance to my mind was running
second to his great friend "Friday" Thornton
(afterwards MP for Battersea) in a West London RC
half-mile handicap.' Contains a bibliography of Rye's
works.

160 The recreations of a Norfolk antiquary / Walter Rye.
Holt, Rounce & Wortley, 1920.                        BL: W.P.6089

Includes extracts from an unpublished novel, The
Cromer Steeplechase by the pioneering athlete and
journalist.

161 Walter Rye, 1843-1929 / Peter Rye. Dereham: Larks,
1996.
13p; coat of arms; pbk
(Pocket biographies; 10)
    *Cover title: Walter Rye, athlete and antiquary*
                                                     ISBN: 0-948400-42-0
                                                     BL: YK.1996.a.19791

## Ryun, Jim

162 The Jim Ryun story / Cordner Nelson; photos by Rich
Clarkson. London: Pelham, 1968.
272p; illus                                          BL: X.449/2957

A profusely illustrated interim account of the career
of the most precocious miler in history, written when
he was still not twenty years of age.

## Samaranch, Juan Antonio

163 Olympic revolution: the biography of Juan Antonio
Samaranch / David Miller. London: Pavilion, 1992.
266p; illus; index
    *Foreword by King Juan Carlos I of Spain*
                                                     ISBN: 1-85145-768-2
                                                     BL: YC.1993.b.8764

A surprisingly uncritical biography of the seventh IOC
President. The work contains many athletics
references.

☞  Subsequent ed. B164

164 Olympic revolution: the Olympic biography of Juan
Antonio Samaranch / David Miller. Rev. ed. London:
Pavilion, 1994.
284p; illus; index; pbk                    ISBN: 1-85793-403-2
                                           BL: YC.1995.b.3101

The revised edition contains additional material
referring to the selection of Sydney for the Summer
Games of 2000 and the re-election of Samaranch for
a further term.

☞   Previous ed. B163

## Sanderson, Tessa

165 Tessa: my life in athletics / with Leon Hickman.
London: Willow, 1986.
181p; illus                                ISBN: 0-00-218211-4
                                           BL: YC.1986.a.4222

The career record is considerably more detailed than
those normally found in biographies. Tessa was the
Olympic javelin champion (1984) and one of Britain's
most durable athletes.

## Sharples, Madge

166 'Marathon Madge' / Madge Sharples. Hyde: MRG, 1989.
vi, 127p; illus; pbk                       ISBN: 0-951457-50-0
                                           BL: YK.1991.a.9249

The first London Marathon, held on 29 March 1981,
threw up one of the most enduring 'characters' in
Madge Sharples. Then aged 64, she had started
running only in 1978, but by 1989 had completed 47
marathon races.

## Sheridan, Martin

167 The Martin Sheridan story / researchers: Bernadine
Malee, Patrick Bolton; editing committee: Anne Mulroy
and others. Bohola, Co. Mayo: 1998?
xvi, 114p; illus, map; pbk

Biography of the Irish-born US policeman who won five
Olympic gold medals, three silver and a bronze in
throwing and jumping events in the Games of 1904,
1906 and 1908.

## Snell, Peter

168 No bugles, no drums / Peter Snell and Garth Gilmour.
London: Hodder & Stoughton, 1965.
240p; illus                                BL: X.449/1798

An account of the life of the 1964 Olympic 800m and
1500m gold medal winner. Snell, under the tutelage of
coach Arthur Lydiard, revolutionised world middle
distance training in the 1960s.

## Stephen, Leslie

169 The life and letters of Leslie Stephen / Frederic William
Maitland. London: Duckworth, 1906.
viii, 510p                                 BL: 2408.g.1

This book is included for its short, but historically
significant, references to athletics at Cambridge in
the late 1850s. Stephen, who was best known as critic,
editor of the Dictionary of National Biography, and
father of Virginia Woolf, was a fine athlete and, as a
junior tutor, won the University mile and two miles in
1860. He was one of the principal forces behind the
foundation of the Oxford and Cambridge Sports, in
1864: 'Then with the development of athletic sports, in
the more technical sense of the term, Stephen had
much to do. I have not investigated the antiquities of
this subject and must give what I am told with some
reserve. "I almost think," says one of his pupils, "that
Leslie Stephen might have claimed to be the founder of
athletic sports. It was in Harry Hughes's large room
that they began and received their impetus from the
energy of Stephen. The sports were at first very
primitive and rough, even condescending to foolish and
absurd antics. Then, I think, something was done on
Parker's Piece, and then Fenner's ground was the
scene, with Stephen winning the two miles race."'

## Tarrant, John

170 The ghost runner: the autobiography of John Tarrant
(1932-1975) / edited by Mel Watman; foreword by
Christopher W. Brasher. Rochester: Athletics Weekly,
1979.
viii, 120p; illus; pbk                     ISBN: 0-9506810-0-8

Having received a mere £17 for taking part in eight
unlicensed boxing bouts before reaching the age of
twenty, Tarrant was prevented thereafter from
competing internationally as a runner, though he was
reinstated as an 'amateur' for domestic athletics
competition. This posthumously published autobiography recounts in moving detail his struggle
against the athletics establishment and an even more
desperate one against stomach cancer.

## Taylor, Philip

171 Judith's run / Philip Taylor. Blackburn: The author,
1994.

The story of a Bob Graham Round run undertaken
after the author's close friend, Judith, had died.

## Thompson, Daley

172 One is my lucky number / Daley Thompson; with
photographs by Jorge Lewinski and Eamonn McCabe.
London: Allen, 1980.
100p; illus; pbk                           ISBN: 0-491-02820-2
                                           BL: X.622/7254

Aimed at the younger reader, this was the first
biography of the future multiple world record breaker

to be published. Extremely well illustrated in both colour and half tone by Jorge Lewinski and Eamonn McCabe; the former contributes an interesting essay on his equipment and techniques.

173 Daley Thompson / Cliff Temple; illustrated by Stephen Gulbis. London: Hamish Hamilton, 1983.
63p; illus
(Profiles)                    ISBN: 0-241-10932-9
                             BL: X.629/20746

One of a series of profiles of outstanding UK athletes. The author traces the career of the 1980 Olympic decathlon champion.

174 Daley Thompson: the subject is winning / Skip Rozin. London: Stanley Paul, 1983.
198p; illus; index           ISBN: 0-09-151360-X

In common with several other athletics biographies, this was produced well before the end of the subject's career; in Thompson's case, his last decathlon competition was in 1988, and his last (though not necessarily final) appearance in UK lists came six years later. Nonetheless, it remains a most valuable biographical source on Thompson's early life, giving important insights into the motivation which led him to dominate the world decathlon scene for almost a decade.

175 Daley Thompson / Norman Barrett & Melvyn Watman. London: Virgin, 1984.
96p; illus; pbk              ISBN: 0-86369-039-4

A companion volume to that on Steve Cram, it covers Thompson's career up to April 1984.

176 Daley: the last ten years / Daley Thompson with Neil Wilson; photographs by Steve Powell. London: Willow, 1986.
127p; illus                  ISBN: 0-00-218229-7
                             BL: YC.1986.b.3112

Each of the seasons 1975-84 is allocated a chapter; a brief description of one of the ten decathlon events is placed after each of the annual reviews. The colour photography is an outstanding feature of this work.

### Thornton, Percy

177 Some things we have remembered: Samuel Thornton, Admiral, 1797-1859, Percy Melville Thornton, 1841-1911 / Percy Melville Thornton. London: Longmans, 1912.
xi, 337p; illus; index       BL: 010827.h.34

The autobiography of the first English half-mile champion. Contains a good account of athletics in the 1860s and features a photograph of Thornton in his running kit.

### Tulloh, Bruce

178 Four million footsteps / Bruce Tulloh. London: Pelham, 1970.
175p; illus                  ISBN: 0-7207-0406-5
                             BL: X.629/2609

The 1962 European 5000m champion retired from international competition in 1967 and set himself the challenge of running across the USA from west to east. This is his vivid account of the record-breaking Los Angeles to New York crossing (2,876 miles) in 64 days, 21 hrs, 50 mins.

### Ueberroth, Peter

179 Made in America: his own story / Peter Ueberroth with Richard Levin and Amy Quinn. London: Kingswood, 1986.
355p; illus, 2 maps; index
   *Originally published: New York: Morrow, 1985*
                             ISBN: 0-434-98091-9
                             BL: YK.1987.b.2190

A marvellous account of Ueberroth's experiences in organising the 1984 Los Angeles Olympic Games. Ueberroth transformed Olympic economics by savaging the expenses of Olympic blazerati and more importantly by securing the costs of capital facilities by the use of commercial sponsors.

### Walthen, David Anthony

180 The big walk / A Walker. London: Prentice-Hall International, 1961.
x, 198p; illus
   *Author is a pseudonym for David Anthony Walthen*
                             BL: 10196.tt.38

In 1960, the snowbound north of Scotland witnessed the greatest gathering of eccentrics since Peter the Hermit's Crusade. The occasion was the Butlin Land's End to John O'Groat's Race. For months afterwards, hospitals of the Northern Line were littered with the human debris of Butlin's extravaganza. The story of this race makes interesting reading, though the informal style makes it occasionally tedious.

### Watson, Robert Patrick

181 Memoirs of Robert Patrick Watson: a journalist's experience of mixed society / Robert Patrick Watson. London: Smith, Ainslie, 1899.
513p                         BL: 010881.ee.22

Anecdotal and opinionated, these memoirs of a journalist, who also acted as a referee for pedestrian events, have many references to the sport. Some of the most valuable stories, however, are of swimming and pugilism. Watson was a swimmer (from 1870) and briefly a sprinter (10.5 secs for 100yds).

### Wharton, Arthur

182 The first black footballer, Arthur Wharton, 1865-1930: an absence of memory / Phil Vasili. London: Frank Cass, 1998.
xxviii, 217p; illus, 1 map; index
(Sport in the global society)
ISBN: 0-7146-4903-1 (cased) • 0-7146-4459-5 (pbk)
BL: YC.1998.b.6287

Wharton, born in Accra, was the first sprinter to achieve 10.0 secs. for 100yds in Championship conditions when he won the AAA title in 1886. He also won a Sheffield Handicap as a professional and had a long career in football as a goalkeeper.

### Whitbread, Fatima

183 Fatima: the autobiography of Fatima Whitbread / with Adrianne Blue. London: Pelham, 1988.
195p; illus
ISBN: 0-7207-1856-2
BL: YK.1989.b.3123

In 1986, Fatima Whitbread set a world javelin record in the qualifying round of the European Championships, which she won. She won the world title in 1987 and an Olympic silver medal the following year. Less than two years after this book was published, repeated injuries forced her to retire from athletics. A remarkably frank account of a troubled childhood takes this beyond most sports autobiographies.

### Wilson, George

184 Memoirs of the life and exploits of G. Wilson the celebrated pedestrian / George Wilson. London: Dean and Munday, 1815?
30p
BL: 12331.d.37(4)

In 1813, Wilson, a fifty year old long-distance walker, set out to walk 1,000 miles in 20 days. He begins his book: 'I had no connection with the tumblers, rope-dancers, fire-eaters, conjurers, pony-racers, sutlers, gin-sellers, gingerbread merchants, ballad-singers or other purveyors of amusement or luxury who crowded Blackheath for a whole fortnight.' For Wilson was stopped by police before completing his feat and charged with causing a public disturbance. His book is little concerned with athletics, but is a chronicle of unremitting woe with termagent wife, debtors' prison and 'bailiffs' bom at the door', a part of everyday life for the unfortunate Wilson. He records that whilst in debtors' prison he walked 50 miles in 12 hours in a small yard 11 yards by 8 yards, making 10,300 turns! One suspects that the book was written in an attempt to recoup some of his losses after his unsuccessful wager and subsequent court case.

185 A sketch of the life of George Wilson the Blackheath Pedestrian who undertook to walk one thousand miles in twenty days, but was interrupted by a warrant from certain magistrates of the district on the morning of the sixteenth day, after having completed 750 miles / written by himself. London: Privately published, 1815.
84p
BL: 613.k.20(3)

A further and more detailed publication by the unfortunate pedestrian. His experiences inspired two satirical poems: 'The quizzical quorum, or, The fortunes and misfortunes of the Black Beaks of Blackheath' and 'The bench in an uproar!!, or, Chop-fallen magistrate'.

### Wilson, Harry

186 Running dialogue: a coach's story / Harry Wilson with Angela Patmore; with a foreword by Steve Ovett. London: Stanley Paul, 1982.
xi, 230p; illus
ISBN: 0-09-147740-9
BL: X.809/54431

An account of the coaching life of one of Britain's greatest distance coaches of the modern era.

### Wilson, Peter

187 The man they couldn't gag / Peter Wilson. London: Hutchinson, 1977.
387p; illus; index
ISBN: 0-09-128930-0
BL: X.620/17124

Wilson, who spent most of his journalistic career on the Daily Mirror, claims that of his three favourite sports – boxing, lawn tennis and athletics – the last was 'more riddled with hypocrisy than almost any other sport'. He aims some of his most trenchant criticism at the AAA for its treatment of chief coach Geoffrey Dyson. Wilson welcomed the recommendations of the Wolfenden Committee on Sport and the setting up of the Sports Council.

### Wooderson, Sydney

188 Sydney Wooderson and some of his great rivals / Guy Butler. London: Vail, 1948.
39p; illus; pbk
BL: 7917.de.88

The story of Wooderson's sixteen year running career, with an analysis of his greatest races, notably world records for 880yds and 1 mile, European Championships for 1500m and 5000m, and the famous post-war duels with Hägg and Andersson.

189 Sydney Wooderson: forgotten champion / David Thurlow. London: British Sports Association for the Disabled, 1989.
56p; illus

Lavishly illustrated in black and white, this biography was published on the occasion of Wooderson's 75th birthday. His career, from junior record of 4:29.8 for the mile in 1933 to his final appearance in the 1949

National Cross-Country, is covered. Includes details of his training, both before and after 1946 (when he moved up to 5000m).

190 A gentle cyclone: the running career of Sydney Wooderson / written and compiled by Michael Sheridan. Congresbury: The author, 1998.

44p; illus; pbk                                   ISBN: 0-9536597-0-4

This short work forms a useful complement to the 1989 study by Thurlow, as it contains a very detailed record of Wooderson's running career, stretching from a 4¾ miles cross-country in 1929 to a one mile relay leg in 1969. Sir Roger Bannister, commenting on the years that Wooderson had lost due to army service in the 1939-45 period, generously observed that but for this hiatus, Wooderson would have been the first runner to beat four minutes for the mile.

## Woods, Rex

191 Cambridge doctor / Rex Salisbury Woods; preface by the Marquess of Exeter. London: Hale, 1962.

224p; illus; index                                    BL: 10713.i.8

The autobiography of one of England's outstanding shot putters and coaches with many athletic reminiscences and photographs of Cambridge athletes ranging over forty years.
'As senior graduate on the Committee (of CUAC), I did my utmost to build up the membership, standards, traditions, posters and press publicity, and all the amenities of a live social club with its roaring fire, teas and magazines, and ample baths and hot water for its growing membership. I loved the men; I coached all our shot-putters between the wars; and I regarded Fenner's as my baby. However, it is still a joy to be invited to officiate at our major meetings at Cambridge and at the University Sports at the White City where I am bound to meet many friends among old Blues.'

## Zaharias, Babe Didrikson

192 This life I've led: my autobiography / Babe Didrikson Zaharias as told to Harry Paxton. London: Hale, 1956.

xiii, 242p; illus; index
   *Originally published in the US*                  BL: 10892.ee.2

The story of one of the world's greatest women athletes, the star of the 1932 Olympic Games. Zaharias was world-class in hurdles, high jump and javelin, and became the greatest woman golfer of her era.

## Zamperini, Louis

193 Devil at my heels: the story of Louis Zamperini / L. Zamperini with Helen Itria. London: Peter Davies, 1956.

204p; illus                                           BL: 10892.aa.39

The life story of a famous American miler of the 1930s. Of particular interest is an account of Zamperini's time as a prisoner of war of the Japanese, when he was forced to race against a prison guard.

## Zátopek, Emil

194 Emil Zátopek in photographs / František Kozík; with a preface by Emil Zátopek and an epilogue by his physician. London: Collet's Holdings, 1955.

194p; illus

A notable pictorial record of an athlete who was almost as remarkable a photographic subject as he was a runner. His physician writes on 'Zátopek from a medical point of view' and Kozík sketches his career up to the close of 1953.

195 Zátopek, the marathon victor: a reportage on the world's greatest long-distance runner / František Kozík. London: Collet's Holdings, 1955.

216p

A detailed account of the great athlete's career up to the close of 1953.

# Collective Biographies

196 Famous footballers and athletes / edited by C. W. Alcock and R. Hill. London: 1895-1896.

4 parts                                   BL: Mic.A.9439(1)7912.k.3

197 Famous athletes. Manchester: R. Scott, 1908.

10p; illus; pbk

Includes AAA Championship results for 1908, but mainly shows photographs including New York marathon, Salford Harriers, Broughton Harriers and E. R. Voight, Olympic champion.

198 Famous athletes. Manchester: R. Scott, 1909.

16p; illus; pbk

Photos include Ireland v. Scotland teams, H. A. Wilson, Emilio Lunghi, Emil Voight and Bobby Kerr of Canada.

199 Aspirants to AAA and Empire titles: pen pictures of famous athletes, track and field event season 1934 / compiled by 'Irrepressible'. Croydon: Croydon Times, 1934.
28p

*Author is Sydney F. Skilton*                 BL: 10824.aa.29

A small card-cover booklet that previews the 1934 season, containing biographical details on 62 male athletes, 59 of them from the UK.

200 The Graces, E. M., W. G. & G. F. / A. G. Powell & S. Canynge Caple. King's Lynn: Cricket Book Society, 1948.
160p; illus                                   BL: 7919.c.20

In this portrait of the three Grace brothers, prominence is given to the occasion in 1866 when W. G., having scored 224 not out in a total of 521 for England v. Surrey, was given permission to miss the third day in order to compete in, and win, the 440yds hurdles at the National Olympian Games. Some descriptions of a meeting in which E. M. and W. G. competed are given, and quotations from the Western Daily Press provide evidence of poor organisation and haphazard handicapping. The seasons 1867-69 in athletics by W. G. are covered.

201 The world's all sports who's who for 1950 / compiled by H. K. Turner; foreword by HRH the Duke of Edinburgh. Hove: Wex, 1950.
380p                                          BL: 7920.ee.36

Contains biographical profiles of nearly 250 athletes and administrators.

202 British athletes 1951 / N. D. McWhirter and F. W. Blackmore; foreword by Lord Burghley. London: Athletic and Sporting Publications, 1951.
50p; illus; pbk                               BL: 7917.d.58

Includes an article by Jack Crump on 1952 Olympic prospects. There are also photographs and biographical sketches of over 200 of the outstanding British athletes of the period.

203 Sportsman's who's who / Raymond Glendenning and Robert Bateman. London: Museum Press, 1957.
256p                                          BL: 7923.h.38

204 British athletics 1962 / Peter G. Bird. Mitcham: Micron, 1962.
64p; illus

Biographies of fifty British athletes and a preview of the European and Commonwealth Games. Well illustrated with photos by Gerry Cranham.

205 Young Olympic champions / Steve Gelman. London: Scholastic, 1964.
176p; illus; pbk

Includes Didrikson, Mathias, Rudolph, O'Brien and Brumel.

206 Ireland's Olympic heroes / David Guiney. Dublin: Philip Roderick, 1965.
107p

Pen-portraits of Irish Olympic sportsmen since 1896, including many athletes.

207 The lonely breed / Ron Clarke and Norman Harris. London: Pelham, 1967.
187p; illus; index                            BL: X.449/2781

Twenty-one distance runners are introduced in this survey of the period 1886 to 1966, the criterion for inclusion being as much 'the man' as the name, so that Arthur Lydiard, Neville Scott and Edwin Flack appear in company with Nurmi, Lovelock, Kuts and Zátopek.

208 The kings of distance: a study of five great runners / Peter Lovesey; foreword by Harold M. Abrahams. London: Eyre and Spottiswoode, 1968.
197p; illus

An account of the careers of Deerfoot, W. G. George, Alfred Shrubb, Paavo Nurmi and Emil Zátopek. 'By the happiest accident they achieved distinction at neat intervals of about twenty years, which afforded me an opportunity of comparing the conditions in which they lived, trained and competed.' There are appendices on: the evolution of distance running; the progress of distance running in Britain; the training programmes of George and Shrubb; the 100-up exercise (W. G. George's own account); and, lists tracing the evolution of distance running records by all athletes, amateur and professional, for the events from 1 mile to 1 hour. Of particular interest is Lovesey's account of the American Indian Deerfoot's time in Britain, and the match-race series between W. G. George and the Scottish professional William Cummings.

209 Out in front / George Gretton. London: Pelham, 1968.
157p; illus; index

A study of distance competition from its earliest origins to the present day, by a former Oxford University runner.

210 Running blind: the story of Bert Smith and John Stratford and how they ran the marathon / Ralph King. London: Hodder and Stoughton, 1968.
192p

The inspiring story of two blind New Zealand athletes.

211 The sporting Irish / Leo Bowes. Dublin: Mac, 1970.
96p; pbk

Several articles and biographies on athletics.

212 Track and field: the great ones / Cordner Nelson. London: Pelham, 1970.
224p; illus; index              ISBN: 0-7207-0352-2
                                BL: X.629/2648

The author was co-founder (with his brother Bert) and editor of the US magazine Track & Field News in 1948. This collection of biographies is split into two parts: detailed accounts of the careers of Nurmi, Owens,

Warmerdam, Dillard, Zátopek, Mathias, O'Brien, Rafer Johnson, Glenn Davis, Oerter, Elliott, Brumel and Snell, plus rather brief data on 179 others. It should be noted that only male athletes are included!

213 The ten greatest races / Derrick Young; foreword by Christopher J. Chataway. London: Gemini, 1972.
126p; pbk  ISBN: 0-450-01324-3

The author confines his selection to post-1945 events, and none at a distance of less than 1500m. Young is, of course, reliant on other sources for races which he did not witness, and these are cited. Few would argue with the author's final choices, even though one is unashamedly included for its Scottish connection; the ten athletes selected are Ian Stewart, Emil Zátopek, Sydney Wooderson, Roger Bannister, Jim Peters, Chris Chataway, Herb Elliott, Abebe Bikila, Ron Clarke and Jim Ryun. The concluding chapter provides results and intermediate times for all races described.

214 Athletics champions / John L. Foster; illustrated by David Astin. London: Nelson, 1974.
80p; illus; pbk  ISBN: 0-17-432114-7

215 Great moments in the Olympics / Graeme Wright. London: Queen Anne, 1976. ISBN: 0-362-00277-0

☞ Subsequent ed. B220

216 Kings of sport / Steve Douglas; text illustrations by Ken Kirkland. London: Piccolo Pan, 1976.
95p; illus; pbk  ISBN: 0-330-24480-9
  BL: X.619/16965

Aimed at children. Features twenty famous sportsmen, including Roger Bannister, Herb Elliott, Vladimir Kuts and Jesse Owens.

217 Kraft Olympic athletics handbook / compiled and edited by Peter Matthews assisted by Dave Terry (Olympic section) and Harold Abrahams, Andrew Huxtable & Bob Sparks; assistant editor, Tim Lynch-Staunton for the National Union of Track Statisticians. London: Kraft Foods Ltd, 1976.
96p

Contents include details of Britain's Olympic participants (athletes who placed in the first six in the Games from 1896 to 1936, and all competitors from 1948 to 1972), biographical details of Britain's Olympic medallists, UK all-time lists to the end of 1975.

218 The best of Wooldridge / Ian Wooldridge. London: Everest, 1978.
192p; illus  ISBN: 0-905018-73-7
  BL: X.620/18125

These pieces appeared originally in the Daily Mail; those on athletics include interviews with Tommie Smith, John Akii-Bua and Dwight Stones.

219 Lakeland profiles / Rex Woods. Grasmere: Ashecliffe, 1978.

Includes chapters on several Lakeland runners, including Jos Naylor.

220 Olympics greats / Graeme Wright. Rev. and updated ed. London: Macdonald and Jane's, 1980.
159p; illus  ISBN: 0-362-00500-1
  BL: X.629/12893

A revised and updated version of Great Moments in the Olympics (1976), the work contains competently written articles, with some literary and historical allusions, of which two-thirds are on athletics: Pietri, Thorpe, Nurmi, Didrikson, Owens, Blankers-Koen, Zátopek, Brasher, Bikila, Snell, Rand, Davies, Peters and Viren.

☞ Previous ed. B215

221 Black sportsmen / Ernest Cashmore; foreword by Garth Crooks. London: Routledge & Kegan Paul, 1982.
xiv, 226p; illus; index; pbk
 *Bibliography: p213-220* ISBN: 0-7100-9054-4
  BL: X.629/18614

The author, a Research Fellow in the Department of Sociology and Social History at the University of Aston, Birmingham, examines the rise of black athletes, mainly in the UK, but with some reference to the USA, drawing upon interviews with both elite performers and novices. He concludes on this, perhaps slightly ambivalent, note:
'Sport conceals deep, structured inequalities and, for all the positive benefits it yields, it remains a source of hope and ambition for blacks only as long as those inequalities remain.'

222 Classic moments of athletics / Charles Landon. Ashbourne: Moorland, 1982.
141p; illus; index  ISBN: 0-86190-053-7
  BL: X.622/15390

This is a collection of competent accounts of mainly twentieth century athletes. Of 33 chapters, over one third deal primarily or solely with UK athletes, and only four discuss women at any length (Didrikson, Blankers-Koen, Rand, Peters). Field events are under-represented and no sources are given.

223 The golden milers / Norman Giller. London: Pelham, 1982.
93p; illus; index  ISBN: 0-7207-1402-8
  BL: X.622/14355

In a large format, primarily pictorial work, the period from the late nineteenth century to the mid-twentieth century (George to Hägg) is dealt with before biographical details are presented for Bannister, Landy, Ibbotson, Elliott, Snell, Jazy, Ryun, Bayi, Walker, Coe and Ovett. Women are dismissed in a single column.

224 Marathon kings / Norman Giller. London: Pelham, 1983.
96p; illus; index; pbk                    ISBN: 0-7207-1453-2
                                          BL: X.622/16030

In addition to profiles of Louis, Pietri, Kolehmainen, Ferris, Zátopek, Peters, Bikila, Clayton, Shorter, Cierpinski, Salazar, de Castella, and Waitz, supplementary details of their contemporaries appear. The winners of Olympic, European, Commonwealth and AAA titles are included, as is a record progression.

225 Brendan Foster's Olympic heroes, 1896-1984: past Olympic champions and the favourites for LA '84 / Brendan Foster and Norman Giller. London: Harrap, 1984.
141p; illus; pbk                          ISBN: 0-245-54200-0
                                          BL: X.622/19322

Part I contains biographical details of 33 leading contenders for 1984 titles, with photography by All Sport Photographic; Part II is an A-Z guide to the great Olympic champions, including 124 track and field athletes.

226 The Olympians: a quest for gold: triumphs, heroes and legends / Sebastian Coe with Nicholas Mason. London: Pavilion, 1984.
145p; illus; index                        ISBN: 0-907516-44-0

☞ Subsequent ed. B232

227 The Sony Tape guide to who's who in the 1984 Olympics / edited by David Emery; foreword by Brendan Foster. London: Pelham, 1984.
192p; illus; pbk                          ISBN: 0-7207-1519-9

Of the 240 athletes whose detailed biographies are included, all those from so-called Communist countries, except China and Romania, failed to appear at Los Angeles.

228 Great sporting eccentrics / David Randall. London: W.H. Allen, 1985.
192p; illus
     *Bibliography: p187-192*
          ISBN: 0-491-03004-5 (cased) • 0-86379-140-9 (pbk)
          BL: YC.1986.b.1808 • YK.1987.b.4531

Many of the most bizarre stories in athletics history are told in this biographical format.

229 On the right track: contemporary Christians in sport / John D. Searle. Basingstoke: Marshall Pickering, 1987.
191p; pbk                                 ISBN: 0-551-01424-5
                                          BL: YK.1987.a.7153

Includes chapters on Brian Adams, Olympic walker, and Carl Lewis, Olympic gold medallist.

230 The fastest men on earth / Neil Duncanson. London: Collins, 1988.
192p; illus                               ISBN: 0-00-218313-7
                                          BL: YK.1988.b.5503

Published to coincide with a television series, this is a collection of biographies of the Olympic 100m champions from Tom Burke in 1896 to Carl Lewis in 1984. In this sense, the title is somewhat misleading because, of the twenty sprinters described, only ten ever held the world 100m record. The introductory section 'From professional to amateur' is of particular interest.

231 My great Britons / Emlyn Hughes. London: Partridge, 1988.
195p; illus                               ISBN: 1-85225-023-2
                                          BL: YK.1989.b.3365

David Coleman and Sebastian Coe appear in this collection of seventeen tape-recorded interviews.

232 The Olympians: a quest for gold: triumphs, heroes and legends / Sebastian Coe with Nicholas Mason. 2nd ed. London: Pavilion, 1988.

☞ Previous ed. B226 ; subsequent ed. B247

233 Who's who in British athletics / Peter Matthews. Runcorn: Archive in association with Express Newspapers, 1990.
128p; illus; pbk                          ISBN: 0-948946-73-3

Contains detailed biographies of 173 male and 125 female athletes.

234 British Olympians: a hundred years of gold medallists / Ian Buchanan. Enfield: Guinness, 1991.
191p; illus; index                        ISBN: 0-85112-952-8
                                          BL: YK.1991.b.6397

Includes biographical details of 67 track and field gold medallists (including tug-of-war), together with brief data (full name, date/s of birth/death, event/s) of all British track and field participants from 1896 to 1988.

235 The fifty finest athletes of the 20th century: a worldwide reference / Robert J. Condon. London: McFarland, 1991.
viii, 152p; illus; index                  ISBN: 0-89950-374-8
                                          BL: YC.1991.b.3203

236 Great women athletes of the 20th century / Robert J. Condon. London: McFarland, 1991.
ix, 180p; illus; index                    ISBN: 0-89950-555-4
                                          BL: YC.1992.b.1231

After an introduction surveying the development of women's sport from ancient times to the present day, the author applies his subjective judgement in selecting the top five, among them Didrikson-Zaharias and Joyner-Kersee. In a group labelled 'pioneers', Helen Stephens is included. Biographical details and half-tone illustrations of a further 35 other great women athletes are presented.

237 Black American women in Olympic track and field: a complete illustrated reference / Michael D. Davis. London: McFarland, 1992.
xviii, 170p; illus; index ISBN: 0-89950-692-5
 BL: YC.1992.b.4111

From 1932, when Louise Stokes and Tidye Pickett were selected but did not compete, to 1988, when Florence Griffith-Joyner and Jackie Joyner-Kersee won five gold medals between them, the contribution of black US athletes is documented, with biographical details of all athletes selected (whether or not they competed).

238 The International Jewish Sports Hall of Fame. SPI Books, 1992.
 ☞ Subsequent ed. B254

239 Irish marathon legends / Noel Henry; with an introduction by John Treacy. Dublin?: Irish Runner, 1992.
86p; illus; pbk ISBN: 0-9520424-0-1

240 Irish Olympians / Lindie Naughton and Johnny Watterson. Dublin: Blackwater, 1992.
viii, 280p; illus; pbk ISBN: 0-86121-461-7

A detailed history of Ireland's Olympians over the past century, from John Pius Boland to Michael Carruth.

241 More than winning: interviews with great athletes / Alastair Aitken; foreword by Peter Hildreth. Lewes: Temple House, 1992.
284p; illus; pbk ISBN: 0-86332-741-9
 BL: YK.1993.a.4684

Brief biographical details of 42 athletes, of which only four (Board, Manning, Szewinska and Flintoff) are women, and only three (Lusis, Davies and Oerter) were primarily field event exponents, are followed by selected extracts from tape-recorded interviews carried out from 1961 onwards. Some cover a long time-span (1970-89 for Don Quarrie) and supplementary comments are provided for such topics as beginning athletics, qualities that make a star, the English national cross-country championship, and some athletic philosophy.

242 Tales of gold / Neil Duncanson and Patrick Collins. London: Queen Anne, 1992.
207p; illus; index; pbk ISBN: 0-356-20784-6
 BL: YK.1994.b.2149

Brief biographies of Britain's Olympic gold medallists are presented; half-tone illustrations are included.

243 Olympic champions in Manchester / James W. Bancroft. Manchester: Aim High, 1993.
52p; illus; pbk ISBN: 1-872619-05-3
 BL: YK.1994.a.4238

Olympic medallists in track and field athletics with a Manchester connection are featured: Tysoe, Voigt, Owen, Lowe, Roberts, and Shirley Strong. A chronological roll of British Olympic champions and a list of Britain's twenty most successful Olympians are appended.

244 Chasing gold: sportswomen of Ireland / Yvonne Judge. Dublin: Wolfhound, 1995.
158p; illus; pbk ISBN: 0-86327-447-1

Includes chapters on Catherina McKiernan and Sonia O'Sullivan.

245 Great African-American athletes / Taylor Oughton. London: Constable, 1996.
46p; illus; pbk
(Dover coloring book) ISBN: 0-486-29319-X
 BL: YK.1997.b.5257

Brief biographical details of Evelyn Ashford, Valerie Brisco-Hooks, Florence Griffith-Joyner, Rafer Johnson, Jackie Joyner-Kersee, Carl Lewis, Edwin Moses, Jesse Owens and Wilma Rudolph appear, with 'ready-to-color' action illustrations.

246 The greatest: who is Britain's top sports star? / Daley Thompson, Stewart Binns and Tom Lewis. London: Boxtree in association with Channel Four Television, 1996.
256p; illus; pbk ISBN: 0-7522-1048-3
 BL: YK.1996.b.15681

Published to coincide with a television series, this work attempts to answer the question posed in the title by using a scoring system based on five major criteria. Of the 101 biographies included, 19 are of athletes.

247 The Olympians: a century of gold / Sebastian Coe with Nicholas Mason. Rev. and updated ed. London: Pavilion, 1996.
126p; illus; index; pbk ISBN: 1-85793-890-9
 BL: YK.1996.b.15572

A prologue leads into 11 chapters, each with an individual athlete linked to a theme: Lovelock, Nurmi, Owens, Blankers-Koen, Zátopek, Elliott, Oerter, Bikila, Don Thompson, Clarke, Daley Thompson. A postscript is optimistic about the future of the Games.

 ☞ Previous ed. B232

248 The road to glory: portrait of Britain's paralympians / Richard & Fiona Bailey. London: Quiller, 1996.
118p; illus ISBN: 1-899163-27-1

249 Running with the legends / Michael Sandrock. Leeds: Human Kinetics, 1996.
xvi, 575p; illus; index ISBN: 0-87322-493-0

250 Track and field record holders: profiles of the men and women who set world, Olympic and American marks, 1946 through 1995 / David Baldwin. London: McFarland, 1996.
vi, 338p; index ISBN: 0-78640249-0
 BL: YK.1997.b.832

In addition to limiting the period covered to the previous fifty years, only events on the 1992 Olympic Games programme (excluding walks and relays) are considered, and only biographical details of athletes who broke, but did not equal, world records are included. This is an unreliable work: errors of fact and spelling are numerous; venues are generally omitted; and field event performances are given only in the Imperial (US) system.

251 Barnsley's sporting heroes / Annie Storey. Barnsley: Wharncliffe, 1997.
224p; illus; pbk
ISBN: 1-871647-36-3
BL: YK.2001.a.9015

Includes profiles of Dorothy Hyman and John Mayock.

252 Great African Americans in the Olympics / Shaun Hunter. Oxford: Crabtree, 1997.
64p; illus; index
(Outstanding African Americans)
ISBN: 0-86505-809-1 (cased) • 0-86505-823-7 (pbk)

253 Great sporting eccentrics: weird and wonderful characters from the world of sport / Geoff Tibballs. London: Robson, 1997.
ix, 245p
ISBN: 1-86105-122-0
BL: YK.1999.b.1525

From naked running in Lancashire (1824) to backward running across America (1984), many obscure stories are listed in the athletics section.

254 Jewish sports legends: the International Jewish Sports Hall of Fame / Joseph Siegman. 2nd ed. London: Brassey's, 1997.
xxii, 222p; illus
ISBN: 1-574-88128-0
BL: YK.1998.b.7228

Includes brief biographies of 13 Jewish track and field stars and a list of Jewish Olympic medallists.

☞ Previous ed. B238; subsequent ed. B261

255 Scotland's sporting heroes / compiled by Robert Jeffrey and Ian Watson. Edinburgh: Canongate, 1997.
128p; illus
ISBN: 0-86241-732-5
BL: YK.1999.b.4316

Essentially a photographic compilation. Twenty-one male athletes (including three professionals) and two female athletes are included.

256 The book of British sporting heroes / compiled by James Huntington-Whiteley; introduction by Richard Holt. London: National Portrait Gallery, 1998.
239p; illus; pbk
*Published to accompany the exhibition British Sporting Heroes at the National Portrait Gallery from 16 October 1998 to 24 January 1999*
ISBN: 1-85514-249-X
BL: YK.1998.b.9274

This lavishly produced work contains images of 27 outstanding track and field athletes (or pedestrians), two prominent disabled athletes and two cricketers who also had outstanding, if relatively short, athletics careers in the nineteenth century. Each entry gives a thumbnail sketch of the individual's personality, biographical information and details of their greatest sporting achievements. The illustrations pre-dating

the advent of photography are of especial interest: an 1809 aquatint of Captain Barclay, a 1788 engraving of Foster Powell, and an 1815 hand-coloured engraving of George Wilson.

☞ Also listed at: L373

257 Head to head: uncovering the psychology of sporting success; interviews by Geoffrey Beattie. London: Gollancz, 1998.
288p; pbk
ISBN: 0-575-06358-0
BL: YK.1998.a.4793

Of the interview transcripts derived from a BBC Radio 5 Live series, three are devoted to track and field subjects: Liz McColgan, Kelly Holmes and Jonathan Edwards. The first and third were broadcast in December 1995 and the second in January 1997.

258 Sporting doubles: a gallery of great sportsmen who represented their country at more than one sport / Jeremy Malies; foreword by Lord Cowdrey. London: Robson, 1998.
xiii, 197p; illus
ISBN: 1-86105-230-8
BL: YK.1999.b.6249

Includes chapters on Eric Liddell, C. B. Fry and Mildred Didrikson Zaharias.

259 Fifty legends of British sport / C. D. Edwards; with illustrations by Clive Wakfer. Penzance: United Writers, 1999.
300p; illus
ISBN: 1-85200-081-3
BL: YK.1999.a.10361

Twelve track and field athletes are featured: Bannister, Board, Coe, Cram, Davies, Hemery, Ovett, Peters, Rand, Sanderson, Thompson and Whitbread.

260 Who's who in world athletics / edited by Mel Watman. Stanmore: Athletics International, 1999-
*Published annually*

Covers nearly 2500 athletes. Includes a concise history of the World Championships.

261 Jewish sports legends: the International Jewish Sports Hall of Fame / Joseph Siegman. 3rd ed. London: Brassey's, 2000.
xxii, 222p; illus; pbk
ISBN: 1-574-88128-0
BL: YK.1998.b.7228

Includes a list of Jewish Olympic medallists and brief biographies of Jewish track and field stars including Kerri Strug, Marv Levy, Daniel Mendoza, and Ike Berger.

☞ Previous ed. B254

262 Who's who of UK & GB international athletes 1896-1939 / Ian Buchanan. London: National Union of Track Statisticians, 2000.
168p; illus; pbk

Career summaries and statistics of 484 British male athletes who took part in 38 international meetings in the years up to 1939.

## ✱ *Additional References*

263 Our national sports and pastimes. London: Harrison, 1862.

> *Published in parts*

A series of booklets based on engravings first made for the Illustrated Sporting News, and containing portraits and biographical accounts of many pedestrian athletes, including Deerfoot, William Lang, John Levett (distance runners) and William Musgrave (pole-vaulter).

264 Sports and pastimes: men I have met / Joseph Stoddart. Manchester: J. Heywood, 1889.

> 2 vols.                    BL: Mic.A.17299(3) (microfilm copy)

Contains biographical sketches of a number of athletes.

265 The Courage book of sporting heroes 1884-1984 / compiled & edited by Chris Rhys. London: Stanley Paul, 1984.

> 221p; illus                    ISBN: 0-09-15362-0-0

A well-designed and generally well-researched volume containing details of 107 outstanding sportsmen and women; of these twelve are first and foremost athletes (Bannister, Coe, Elliott, Hemery, Lewis, Moses, Oerter, Ovett, Owens, Szewinska, Thompson and Zátopek), plus C. B. Fry whose main claim to fame was as a cricketer.

266 The contenders / Richard Dale and Colin Cameron. London: Boxtree, 1994.

> 160p; illus                    ISBN: 0-7522-0948-5
>                                 BL: YK.1995.b.6207

Produced to tie in with a BBC series, it presents visually and in interviews, athletes Richard Nerurkar, Martin Steele, Matthew Yates, Yvonne Murray, Sally Gunnell, Linford Christie, Mike Edwards, Colin Jackson, Steve Backley, Kelly Holmes and Darren Campbell. It is designed to show the impact of science and technology on training, touching on both physiology and psychology. Biographical details of the main contenders (Murray, Christie, Jackson and Backley) are given. Rob de Castella, Director of the AIS, describes the strategy for developing sporting talent in Australia.

267 West Norwood Cemetery's sportsmen / Bob Flanagan; with line drawings by Don Bianco. London: Local History Publications for the Friends of West Norwood Cemetery, 1995.

> 77p; illus; pbk                ISBN: 1-873520-09-3
>                                 BL: YK.1996.a.7337

Opened in 1837, West Norwood (formerly South Metropolitan) Cemetery contains the graves of several important sportsmen and administrators, including those of Arthur Daniel (1841-1873), winner of 120yds hurdles for Cambridge at the inaugural varsity sports in 1864; Arthur Conquest (1875-1945), winner of AAA pole vault in 1912; Sir Richard E. Webster, later Viscount Alverstone (1842-1915), noted miler and first AAA President; Sir William Brass, created 1st Baron Chattisham of Clitheroe (1886-1945), who ran 100yds for CUAC v. OUAC in 1905 and 1907.

# C. International Competitions

## The Modern Olympic Games & World Championships

### ✱ Histories

1   The Olympic Games, B.C. 776–A.D. 1896. London:
Grevel, 1896.
2 vols.: 1. The Olympic Games in ancient times / Sp. P.
Lambros and N. G. Polites with prologue by T.
Philemon; translated from the Greek by C. A.; 2. The
Olympic Games in 1896 / P. de Coubertin, T. J.
Philemon, N. G. Politis and C. Anninos; English
translation by A. v. K.        BL: 7905.k.20

> A book of great importance to students of the Olympic
> Games. The first volume is largely concerned with the
> ancient Games, the second with the plans and ideals
> of de Coubertin and his supporters. A French edition
> was also published.

2   The cruise of The Branwen: being a short history of the
modern revival of the Olympic Games with an account
of the English fencing team in Athens in MCMVI / Sir
Theodore Andrea Cook. London: Privately published,
1908.
xviii, 165p; illus        BL: 7917.bb.12

> Published prior to the 1908 Games, the book is
> particularly valuable for its account of the rarely
> discussed intercalated Olympics of 1906.

3   Official hand-book of the Olympic Games / edited by
Alex Devine. London: Hudson & Kearns, 1908.
164p; illus

> *Spine title: Olympic Games, London 1908*

> Contains articles: 'On throwing the discus' by G. S.
> Robertson and 'The ancient Olympic Games' by P.
> Gardner.

4   The Olympic Games: being a short history of the
Olympic movement from 1896 up to the present day,
together with an account of the Games of Athens in
1906, and of the organisation of the Olympic Games of
London in 1908 / Sir Theodore Andrea Cook. London:
Constable, 1908.
xxiv, 232p; illus        BL: 7907.ff.57

> Produced prior to the 1908 Games, with programme,
> and lists of the British, South African and United
> States teams, together with much of the material
> that appeared in The Cruise of The Branwen.

5   International sport: a short history of the Olympic
movement from 1896 to the present day, containing the
account of a visit to Athens in 1906, and of the Olympic
Games of 1908 in London, together with the code of
rules for twenty different forms of sport and numerous
illustrations / Sir Theodore Andrea Cook. London:
Constable, 1909.
xxiv, 255p; illus        BL: 07906.de.38

> Cook provides a clue to the origins of the 26mile
> 385yd marathon distance (often attributed to the
> withdrawal of the start in Windsor Great Park for the
> benefit of the royal children) by observing (on Dorando
> Pietri) – 'The 385 yards of cinder path now between
> him and the finish proved harder than all the 26 miles
> which had preceded them.' The 1908 Olympic Report
> lists the distance as exactly 26 miles, with no reason
> given for this particular distance. The likelihood is
> therefore that the distance was measured from
> Windsor Great Park to the entry to the White City
> Stadium, rather than to the finish on the track. Thus
> was history made.
> A reissue of The Cruise of The Branwen, together with
> an account of the 1908 Games. There are many
> excellent photographs of the Games of 1906 and
> 1908. There is a first-class chapter on the perennial
> 'amateur' problem.

6   The Olympic Games and the Duke of Westminster's
    appeal for £100,000: a historical survey of the movement
    for better organization in the British preparations for the
    Berlin Games of 1916, compiled from The Times and
    official sources. London: J. P. Bland, 1913.

    44p                    BL: Mic.A.11037(16) (microfilm copy)

    *This is a work of exceptional significance, being a
    detailed account of British preparations for the 1916
    Berlin Olympics. In 1913, the British Olympic
    Association, unhappy with the results of the 1912
    Stockholm Olympics, sought £100,000 by public
    subscription to prepare a team for the 1916 Berlin
    Games and to fund future Olympic preparation
    programmes. In the event, they raised only a tenth of
    that amount and as a result the Scottish-Canadian
    Highland Games all-rounder W. R. Knox was appointed
    as AAA chief coach in 1914. Knox's appointment was
    terminated by the onset of World War I and no record
    of his work remains.*
    *The book is significant for its account of the
    arguments in the columns of The Times on the
    advisability of Olympic preparations, and is required
    reading for the sports historian. It reveals a deeply
    rooted xenophobia.*

7   The evolution of the Olympic Games, 1829 B.C.-1914
    A.D. / F. A. M. Webster. London: Heath, Cranton &
    Ouseley, 1914.

    xi, 288p; illus; index

    *Preface by Arthur Conan Doyle*          BL: 07906.eee.34

    *Intended as an introduction to the ill-fated VIth
    Olympiad at Berlin in 1916, the book deals with
    athletics from the earliest times. A short account is
    given of the birth of modern athletics and the
    formation of the AAA. Each of the modern Olympic
    festivals is described and full results are given. There
    are photographs of the various stadia and a print of
    the mile race at the Inter-Varsity sports of 1865.*

8   Olympic cavalcade / F. A. M. Webster; foreword by Sir
    Harold Bowden. London: Hutchinson, 1948.

    243p; illus                              BL: 7919.bb.12

    *One of the prolific Webster's last books, this is possibly
    the only one in which he expresses any strong opinion
    on the administration of British athletics and on its
    attitude to coaching. He observes that both the
    Germans (with Kraenzlein) and the Swedes (with
    Hjertberg) had appointed professional Olympic
    coaches as early as the 1910-1916 period: 'Great
    Britain lost a great chance by not taking on Hjertberg
    when he was willing to come to us, and not making
    better use of the late Sam Mussabini ...'.*
    *Nowhere in his previous writings – Webster had written
    over thirty books and innumerable articles and
    pamphlets – is there more than a hint of the
    resistance, the sheer bloody-minded obduracy which
    the British athletics establishment must have
    presented to him in his advocacy in the 1912-1948
    period of his coaching life. Yet here, in the final year of
    his life, Webster opens out at last, 'There is neither
    time or scope in my philosophy for the unpaid*

*amateurs ... interfering in the management and
training or the final selection of a nation's Olympic
team.' Webster's protégé, the visionary AAA Chief
Coach G. H. G. Dyson, appointed in 1947, was to battle
with these 'unpaid amateurs' over the next fifteen
years, as were many great coaches who followed him.*

9   Olympic story: the definitive story of the Olympic
    Games from their revival in 1896, illustrated, with an
    appendix of results and records / edited by Ernest A.
    Bland; foreword by J. Sigfrid Edström. London: Rockliff,
    1948.

    xiii, 252p; illus                        BL: 7918.bb.40

    *Contributors include Fred Dartnell, Ben Bennison and
    H. J. Oaten. The book was re-issued later in the same
    year with the results of the 1948 events.*

10  The story of the Olympic Games / Ralph D. Binfield.
    London: Oxford University Press, 1948.

    184p; illus                              BL: 7917.f.7

11  Olympics old and new / W. M. Hugill, reprinted from
    The Phoenix. 1949.

    9p; pbk                                  BL: 7919.ee.32

    *This essay considers the connection between the
    ancient and modern Olympic Games, quoting both
    advocates and critics of the modern revival, including
    Philip J. Baker (1912). Special mention is made of the
    introduction of Olympic competitions in architecture,
    painting, music, sculpture and literature.*

12  Olympic odyssey: the Olympic story as told by the stars
    themselves from 1896 to 1956 / compiled and edited by
    Stan Tomlin; foreword by Lord Burghley. Croydon:
    Modern Athlete on behalf of Bovril, 1956.

    96p; illus                               BL: 7923.aaa.4

    *Contributors: Sir G. Stuart Robertson, Emil
    Breitkreutz (USA), Arnold Strode-Jackson, Albert G.
    Hill, Guy Butler, Tommy Hampson, Bobby Tisdall,
    Harold Whitlock, Fanny Blankers-Koen and Dorothy
    Tyler. Notable for rare first hand accounts of the early
    Olympics.*

13  Highlights of the Olympics from ancient times to the
    present / John Durant. London: Arco, 1961.

    160p; illus; index                       BL: X.449/1003

    *A somewhat disjointed account of the heroes and
    heroines of the Games, in which the author tends to
    embellish the stories for dramatic effect. Some rare
    and striking photographs redeem the text.*

14  The marathon / John Hopkins. London: Stanley Paul,
    1966.

    111p; illus                              BL: X.449/1830

    *An account of the Olympic marathons since 1896,
    with an appendix which includes results of the various
    international marathon championships.*

15   ATFS Olympic handbook / Donald Harry Potts and Roberto Luigi Quercetani. London: Arena, 1968.
122p

> The most detailed and authoritative history of Olympic athletics 1896-1964.

16   The book of the Olympic Games / Robert M. C. Bateman. London: Stanley Paul, 1968.
xi, 112p; illus     ISBN: 0-09-086180-9
         BL: X.449/2971

> A brief survey of the modern Olympic Games, with by far the greatest emphasis on athletics. All twelve photographs of track and field winners are from the 1964 Games.

17   The 'YZ' book of the Olympics / James Coote. Bromley: The author, 1968.
112p

18   The Olympic Games / John Walsh. 2nd ed. revised by Frank Litsky. London: Watts, 1971.
56p; illus; index
(A first book)
*Originally published: New York: Watts, 1963*
      ISBN: 0-85166-204-8
      BL: X.629/4267

> A conventionally simplified view of the modern revival of the Olympic Games is presented, together with descriptions of some outstanding competitors and moments, and details of record performances in track and field.

19   The Dunlop book of the Olympics / David Guiney. Lavenham: Eastland, 1972.
135p     ISBN: 0-903214-01-6
      BL: X.629/4411

> A collection of 368 short pieces on the Olympic Games from 1896 to 1968 (including the intercalated celebration of 1906), with many on track and field. The author represented Ireland in the 1948 Olympic Games shot putt (his best of 49ft 10in was set in 1953).

☞   Subsequent ed. C24

20   History of the Olympics in pictures / James Coote. London: Tom Stacey, 1972.
152p; chiefly illus     ISBN: 0-85468-205-8

> Coote's book contains a plethora of rarely seen photographs of early Olympic Games.

☞   Subsequent ed. C21

21   History of the Olympics in pictures / James Coote. 2nd updated ed. London: Tom Stacey, 1972.
160p; chiefly illus     ISBN: 0-85468-193-0

☞   Previous ed. C20

22   Olympic Games / Wolfgang Girardi. London: Collins, 1972.
128p; illus, maps; index
(International library)     ISBN: 0-00-100129-9

23   The Olympics 1896-1972: in support of the British Olympic Appeal / Ross McWhirter; edited by Peter Hildreth. London?: Scott International and David Mappin (Promotions), 1972.
95p
*Sponsored by Esso*
      BL: YA.1995.b.4842

> Brief accounts of each celebration of the summer Games. Includes reproductions of some commemorative Olympic postage stamps, an Olympic quiz, and a section on the technical aspects of the Games.

24   The Dunlop book of the Olympics / David Guiney. Rev. ed. Lavenham: Eastland, 1975.
152p     ISBN: 0-903214-07-5
      BL: X.629/10137

> This revised edition includes 37 items on the 1972 Games.

☞   Previous ed. C19

25   The history of the Olympics / edited by Martin Tyler. London: Marshall Cavendish, 1975.
152p; illus
*Some of this material has previously appeared in the partwork 'The Game'*
    ISBN: 0-85685-126-4 (cased) • 0-85685-155-8 (pbk)
      BL: X.622/5340

> A large format, mainly pictorial, history of the modern Olympic Games.

26   Africa at the Olympics / Ramadhan Ali. London: Africa Books, 1976.
162p; illus; pbk     ISBN: 0-903274-07-8
      BL: X.611/7355

> A number of political issues in which African countries became closely involved, such as the isolation of South Africa and Rhodesia, are discussed. Developments in Africa after the 1972 Olympic Games, the emergence of outstanding middle- and long-distance runners in East Africa, the South African Multi-Racial Games (1973), and a preview of the 1976 Olympic Games follow. Statistical data includes the results of the 1965 and 1973 All Africa Games.

27   Fun and games: the amazing story of the Olympics / G. L. Newsum. Gloucester: British Publishing Co. for the National Star Centre for Disabled Youth, 1976.
21p; illus; pbk     ISBN: 0-7140-1574-1
      BL: X.619/17020

28  Incredible Olympic feats / Jim Benagh. London: McGraw-Hill, 1976.
xii, 178p; illus; pbk                ISBN: 0-07-004426-0
                                     BL: X.619/17358

The significant personalities of the Games from 1896 to 1972 and their achievements are described briefly; there is a heavy emphasis on US performers.

29  An Olympic feasibility study / prepared for a working party of representatives of Edinburgh District Council by the Scottish Development Advisory Group. Edinburgh: The Group, 1976.
249p; illus, maps, plans

30  The Olympic Games / Bruce Tulloh. London: Heinemann Educational, 1976.
viii, 72p; illus; pbk
(Heinemann guided readers, upper levels; 5)
                                     ISBN: 0-435-27027-3
                                     BL: X.619/15399

☞  Also listed at: L337

31  The Olympic Games: 80 years of people, events and records / edited by Lord Killanin and John Rodda. London: Barrie and Jenkins, 1976.
272p; illus; index                   ISBN: 0-214-20091-4
                                     BL: X.625/513

Assisted by 48 contributors, the editors succeed admirably in their aim of producing 'the most comprehensive work on the Olympic Games in the English language'. After an extended history of the IOC, there follow brief surveys of the ancient and modern Games, descriptions of sports on the Olympic programme, the background to the Olympics, a Who's Who in the Olympic Games (including sixty outstanding track and field athletes), a listing of medallists in all sports, rules of the IOC, and a list of NOCs.

☞  Subsequent ed. C34

32  Olympics: questions & answers on the major events / Alan Gibbon and Tom McNab. London: Lepus, 1976.
128p; illus; pbk                     ISBN: 0-86019-024-2
                                     BL: X.619/15420

The work, in which athletics is one of seven sports covered, aims to answer both historical and technical questions relating to the Olympic Games events.

33  The Pye story of the Olympic Games / edited by Phil Soar & Martin Tyler. London: Cavendish, 1976.
103p; illus

34  The Olympic Games / edited by Lord Killanin and John Rodda. Rev. ed. London: Macdonald and Jane's, 1979.
319p; illus; index                   ISBN: 0-354-08561-1
                                     BL: X.620/18904

☞  Previous ed. C31; subsequent ed. C208

35  The 1980 book of the Olympics: the Games since 1896: a pictorial record / James Coote. London: Webb, 1980.
129p; illus                          ISBN: 0-86189-008-6

A chapter is devoted to each of the modern Olympics from Athens in 1896 to a preview of the Lake Placid & Moscow Olympics in 1980.

36  The Games: a complete news history / compiled and edited by Marshall Brant. London: Proteus, 1980.
ii, 271p; illus
         ISBN: 0-906071-29-1 (cased) • 0-906071-19-4 (pbk)

The Games as portrayed in English language newspaper clippings.

37  The modern Olympic Games / John Lucas. London: Yoseloff, 1980.
242p; illus; index                   ISBN: 0-498-02447-4
                                     BL: X.622/8245

The author has attempted both a straight narrative history of the modern Games and a critical evaluation of suggestions for reform of the Olympic Movement. Particular attention is focused on the IOC Presidents, Avery Brundage and Lord Killanin. The author advances ten suggested reforms of the IOC. The work lacks a bibliography, the black and white illustrations are poorly reproduced, and many errors occur in the spellings of proper names.

38  The Olympic Games / Nigel Baguley. London: Harrap, 1980.
48p; illus; pbk
(The reporters series)               ISBN: 0-245-53572-1
                                     BL: X.629/15722

39  The Olympic Games ancient and modern. London: British Olympic Association, 1981.
76p; illus

Authors include R. W. Palmer, R. W. Cox, A. H. Jackson, P. G. Kuntz, P. W. Sutcliffe and D. W. Masterson.

40  The Olympic Games: Athens 1896 to Los Angeles 1984 / Peter Arnold. London: Optimum, 1983.
255p; illus                          ISBN: 0-603-03068-8

A well-illustrated photographic record of the modern Olympics.

41  The complete book of the Olympics / David Wallechinsky. Harmondsworth: Penguin, 1984.
xxvi, 628p; illus; pbk               ISBN: 0-14-006632-2
                                     BL: X.622/19325

Wallechinsky's book makes no claim to being a history of the Olympics. It is a rich, results-based chronological account of the modern Olympics.

☞  Subsequent ed. C47

42  The Olympics / Lokesh Sharma; edited by M. J. Akbar; designed by Sunil Sil. London: Sangam (distributor), 1984.
171p; illus; index
(Wills book of excellence)          ISBN: 0-86131-52-1
                                    BL: YK.1990.b.7748

*Following an introduction by Ashwini Kumar, Sharma surveys Olympic history from ancient Greece to the modern revival. Athletes featured include the handful of Indian athletes who performed with distinction: Pritchard, Rebello, Milkha Singh, Gurbachan Singh, Sriram Singh, and P. T. Usha.*

43  Olympics: the games in question / John Rodda and Steven Bierley. London: Channel Four Television, 1984.
32p; illus; pbk          BL: X.622/24700

44  The Olympic bid. Birmingham: Birmingham City Council Olympic Committee, 1986.
3 vols.          BL: DSC-OP-LG/4407/8/9
*Vol. 1: The city strategy and answers to the IOC questionnaire. Vol. 2: Games arrangements and answers to the IF questionnaires. Vol. 3: Media arrangements and answers to the media questionnaires*

45  The British Olympic Association and the Olympic Games. London: The Association, 1987.
39p; illus

46  The Olympics / Peter Tatlow. Hove: Wayland, 1987.
32p; illus; index
(Topics)          ISBN: 1-85210-286-1
                  BL: YK.1987.b.5861

47  The complete book of the Olympics / David Wallechinsky. New ed. Harmondsworth: Penguin, 1988.
xxix, 680p; illus          ISBN: 0-14-010771-1
                           BL: X.622/19325

*Full of engaging detail.*

☞  Previous ed. C41; subsequent ed. C57

48  Faster, higher, further: women's triumphs and disasters at the Olympics / Adrianne Blue. London: Virago, 1988.
ix, 182p; illus; index; pbk
*Bibliography: p177-178*          ISBN: 0-86068-648-5
                                  BL: YK.1989.b.3607

*Gives an overview of the subject then centres upon particular themes and incidents. Several track and field athletes are mentioned: Didrikson, Joyner-Kersee and Drechsler (ch.2), Blankers-Koen, Kristiansen, Brisco-Hooks, Decker-Slaney and Szewinska (ch.4), Sanderson, Whitbread and Felke (ch.8), Budd and Decker-Slaney (ch. 9), Zátopkova and Packer (ch.10), Benoit, Mota, Waitz and Kristiansen (ch.11). Issues of topical importance, such as drug abuse and sex tests, are discussed and a list of Olympic records is appended.*

49  The Olympic fun book / Sally Tagholm; illustrated by Kate Shannon. London: Scholastic, 1988.
48p; illus; pbk          ISBN: 0-590-70911-9
*For children.*

50  The Olympic Games / text by Angela Lucas; illustrations by Jane Pirie. Reading: Young Library, 1988.
24p; illus
(Acorns)          ISBN: 0-946003-89-0
                  BL: YK.1990.a.3341

*Designed for very young readers, facing pages present ten short, large-print texts and beautifully executed colour illustrations, ranging from 4th century BC Olympia to 1984 Los Angeles.*

51  The Manchester Olympic bid, 1996. London: MICP, 1989.
63p; illus          BL: LB.31.b.5513

52  The Olympic Games / William S. Jarrett. Oxford: Facts on File, 1990.
vi, 94p; illus; index
(Timetables of sports history)          ISBN: 0-8160-1921-5
                                        BL: YK.1993.b.8059

*Medallists and very brief event descriptions are given for 1896-1988 celebrations; the work is marred by several inaccuracies.*

53  Silver, gold, bronze / David Guiney. Dublin: Sportsworld, 1990.
135p; illus; pbk
*The story of Irish medal winners at the Games.*

54  The Special Olympics / Graham Bartlett. Leicester: Leicestershire Adult Basic Education Service, 1990.
8p; pbk          ISBN: 1-872617-35-2
                 BL: YK.1992.a.9437

55  The Olympic Games dossier / Stephen Rabley. London: Macmillan, 1991.
32p; illus; pbk          ISBN: 0-333-53666-5
                         BL: YK.1992.b.774

56  The Olympics / Neil Duncanson. London: Wayland, 1991.
48p; illus; index
          ISBN: 1-85210-325-6 (cased) • 0-7502-0242-4 (pbk)
                                        BL: YK.1991.b.6451

57  The complete book of the Olympics / David Wallechinsky. London: Aurum, 1992.
xxviii, 763p; illus; index; pbk          ISBN: 1-85410-199-4
                                         BL: YK.1992.b.4621

☞  Previous ed. C47; subsequent ed. C69

58    The Olympic Games / Mark Eaton. Walton-on-Thames: Nelson, 1992.
64p; illus; pbk
(Nelson English readers library; level 2)
         ISBN: 0-17-556279-2
         BL: YK.1993.a.13719

*One of a series, highlights of the modern track and field events form the centre-piece of this guide.*

59    The Olympics factbook: a spectator's guide to the winter and summer games / Martin Connors, Diane L. Dupuis, Brad Morgan. London: Visible Ink, 1992.
xxvi, 613p; illus; pbk
         ISBN: 0-8103-9417-0
         BL: YK.1993.a.1293

*Track and field is covered, with summaries of medallists presented in order from 1896 to 1988, brief texts on the Games, and an article on 'The Olympics on [US] television'. Time magazine standard of fact checking was not achieved: for example, Fanny Blankers-Koen is referred to as 'the German world record holder in the long jump'.*

60    The viewers' guide to Olympic Games / David Guiney. Dublin: Mars, 1992.
32p; pbk

61    Special Olympics: United Kingdom, Sheffield 1993: Volunteer Training Programme – an evaluation / Karen Dunn, Len Spriggs. Sheffield: Sheffield Hallam University Health Research Institute, 1993.
82p; pbk
(Health Research Institute report no. 3)
         ISBN: 0-86339-594-5
         BL: DSC-7766.0955(3)

62    World athletic championships / David Guiney. Dublin: Mars, 1993.
83p; illus; pbk

63    Historical dictionary of the Olympic movement / Ian Buchanan and Bill Mallon. London: Scarecrow, 1995.
lxxv, 247p; illus
(Historical dictionaries of religions, philosophies and movements; no.7)
         ISBN: 0-8108-3062-0
         BL: YC.1996.a.866

*The work is divided into four parts: Chronology of the Olympic Movement; The Olympic Games and Olympic Winter Games; Introduction to the Olympic Games; Dictionary of the Olympic Movement. The foreword is by Jon Woronoff.*

64    Minds, bodies and souls: an A to Z of the British Olympic heritage network / Don Anthony. London: British Olympic Association, 1995.
44p; illus; pbk

*The first volume of a trilogy documenting the history of British Olympism uses an alphabetical structure to*

list significant names and events. A chronology, short bibliography and list of sports museums are appended.

☞   See also: C91, C92

65    The Olympic spirit: from ancient Greece to modern times / Norman Barrett. Hove: Wayland, 1995.
48p; illus
         ISBN: 0-7502-1613-1

*For children of 10 and over, this features the summer, winter and disabled Olympics.*

66    The Olympic spirit: 100 years of the games / Susan Wels. International ed. CollinsPublishers, 1995.
180p; illus, map; index; illus
         ISBN: 0-00-649054-9
         BL: LB.31.a.6995

67    Robert Crowther's pop-up Olympics: amazing facts and record breakers / Robert Crowther. London: Walker, 1995.
12p; chiefly illus
         ISBN: 0-7445-6188-4
         BL: YK.1999.b.7035

*For children.*

68    Chronicle of the Olympics, 1896-1996 / edited by Christina Banker. London: Dorling Kindersley, 1996.
312p; illus; index
         ISBN: 0-7513-3013-2
         BL: YK.1997.b.2081

*Contents include: medallists 1896-1992; brief history from Greece to the founding of the modern Games; biographical details of all IOC Presidents; reproductions of Olympic posters; descriptions of each Summer and Winter Games; preview of 1996 Games; photographs of outstanding performers. Primarily a visual history.*

☞   Subsequent ed. C86

69    The complete book of the Olympics / David Wallechinsky. London: Aurum, 1996.
800p; illus; index; pbk
         ISBN: 1-85410-400-4

☞   Previous ed. C57; subsequent ed. C98

70    The Daily Telegraph gold medal legends: the Olympic Games, 100 years in pictures / written and edited by Duncan Mackay. London: The Telegraph, 1996.
94p; illus; pbk
         BL: YK.1996.b.15660

*Part I features some outstanding winners, Part II concentrates on the so-called 'Golden Brits', and Part III, entitled 'Tears and Jeers,' recalls incidents such as Lentauw (1904), Pietri (1908), Poland 4 x 100m women (1964), Bedford and Ryun (1972), Decker, Budd and Andersen-Schiess (1984), Johnson (1988), Redmond and Devers (1992).*

71    Field / Tony Ward. Oxford: Heinemann, 1996.
32p; illus; index
(Olympic library)
         ISBN: 0-431-05945-4 (cased) • 0-431-05944-6 (pbk)
         BL: YK.1997.b.6588

*Children's information book about the Olympics.*

72  Flaming Olympics / Michael Coleman; illustrated by
Aidan Potts. London: Hippo, 1996.
160p; illus; pbk
(The knowledge)                    ISBN: 0-590-13753-0
   For children.

   ☞   Subsequent ed. C99

73  Good reasons: 100 years of Olympic marathon races /
Michael Sheridan. Congresbury: The author, 1996.
246p; illus; index; pbk        ISBN: 0-9528192-0-1
                               BL: YK.1996.a.20279

   This is a somewhat more ambitious attempt than the
   Phillips-Gynn work, with a much longer introduction
   and more detailed race reports, which are generally
   more compelling in their descriptive power.

74  Historical dictionary of the modern Olympic movement
/ edited by John E. Findling and Kimberly D. Pelle.
London: Greenwood, 1996.
xl, 460p; illus; index         ISBN: 0-313-28477-6
                               BL: YC.1996.b.3625

   Includes an introduction by John A. Daly and prologue
   by Robert K. Barney. References to track and field
   occur, generally either in the context of programme
   changes (such as the introduction or elimination of
   women's events) or in decisions by the IAAF (such as
   the expulsion of South Africa in 1976).

75  An Irish Olympic Games?: a discussion document /
prepared by The Dublin International Sports Council.
Dublin: The Council, 1996.
28p; illus; pbk

76  Medal aur / golygwyd gan Nicole Carmichael;
ysgrifennwyd gan Philippa Perry; addaswyd i'r Gymraeg
gan Esyllt Penri. [Wales]: Gwasg Addysgol Cymru, 1996.
31p; illus; pbk                ISBN: 1-89986900-X
                               BL: YK.1997.b.4986

   Primarily a pictorial work aimed at the younger reader,
   it contains a brief history of the Olympic Games,
   profiles of some all-time greats, and a section on the
   Paralympics. Included is a photograph captioned
   Fanny Blankers-Koen; it is, in fact, of the English
   runner Pat Lowe.

   ☞   See also: C80

77  Modern Olympics / Richard Tames. Oxford:
Heinemann, 1996.
32p; illus; index
(Olympic library)              ISBN: 0-431-05941-1
                               BL: YK.1996.b.13860

   For children.

78  The modern Olympics: a struggle for revival / David C.
Young. London: Johns Hopkins University Press, 1996.
xv, 252p; index                ISBN: 0-8018-5374-5
                               BL: YC.2000.a.9377

   The author, an avid track and field fan, and Classics
   Professor at the University of Florida, argues that the
   various revivals of the Olympic Games from 1833 to
   1896 were interconnected. Young identifies the
   progenitors of the modern Olympic Games as
   Panagiotis Soutsos and Dr William Penny Brookes.
   Young quotes from Guttmann, Mandell and MacAloon
   on the period that shaped De Coubertin's thinking, and
   stresses that the original ideas for the revival of the
   Olympic Games stemmed from Brookes.

79  The Olympic Games / David Guiney. Dublin:
Sportsworld, 1996.
222p; illus                    ISBN: 1-900110-03-2

80  Olympic gold / edited by Nicole Carmichael; written by
Philippa Perry. London: Two-Can in association with
Watts, 1996.
31p; illus; pbk
(Young Telegraph)              ISBN: 1-85434-357-2

   ☞   See also: C76

81  Olympic track & field athletics guide / Mel Watman.
Stanmore: Athletics International in association with
Shooting Star Media, 1996.
280p; illus; pbk               ISBN: 0-9528011-0-8
                               BL: YK.1996.a.17407

   The first part gives concise descriptions of the
   1896-1992 track and field events with summarised
   results of finals. The second part includes potted
   biographies of more than 2,000 athletes, many of
   whom were considered possible contenders for
   selection in 1996.

   ☞   Subsequent ed. C100

82  100 years of the Olympic marathon / compiled by the
National Union of Track Statisticians; editors, Bob
Phillips & Roger Gynn. London: National Union of
Track Statisticians, 1996.
152p; illus; pbk
(A track stats special)        ISBN: 1-874538-16-6
                               BL: YK.1997.a.5310

   After some introductory remarks on the precursors of
   the modern marathon, detailed accounts of all
   Olympic Games races from 1896 to 1992 are given,
   together with full results and profiles of all winners.

83  Report of the Interdepartmental Group established to
examine the feasibility of Ireland making a bid to host
the Special Olympics World Games in 2003 / Office of
the Tánaiste. Dublin: Stationery Office, 1996.
28p; pbk
(Catalogue lists; Y/47)
   *Chairperson: Cyril Freaney*    ISBN: 0-7076-3814-3
                               BL: CSA.127/1078

84  Track / Tony Ward. Oxford: Heinemann, 1996.
32p; illus; index
(Olympic library)              ISBN: 0-431-05947-0
                               BL: YK.1997.b.6590

   Children's information book about the Olympics.

85  Olympic marathon: a centennial history of the Games'
    most storied race / Charlie Lovett. London: Praeger,
    1997.
    xiii, 176p; illus; index                   ISBN: 0-275-95771-3
                                               BL: YK.1997.b.6065

    The legend of the marathon is treated in a prologue
    before each of the twenty-four men's races – including
    the intercalated Games of 1906 – and four women's
    races in the Games of the modern era are described. A
    brief account is given of the fight to establish the
    women's race. A number of inaccuracies have crept in
    — Foster Powell did not complete a 402-mile round
    trip at age sixty (he died in his 59th year), and the
    White City Stadium was not destroyed by the bombs
    of the Luftwaffe (54,000 spectators were there on 6
    August 1945 to see the mile race between Andersson
    and Wooderson).

86  Chronicle of the Olympics. New ed. London: Dorling
    Kindersley, 1998.
    330p; illus; index                         ISBN: 0-7513-0542-1
                                               BL: YK.1998.b.4523

    ☞  Previous ed. C68

87  Stoke Mandeville road to the Paralympics: fifty years of
    history / Joan Scruton. Brill: Peterhouse, 1998.
    xiv, 370p; illus                           ISBN: 0-946312-10-9
                                               BL: YK.1998.b.6102

    Largely an account of the pioneer Professor Sir Ludwig
    Guttmann (1899-1980) in promoting sport for the
    disabled by someone crucially involved in the various
    organisations established in the field. A number of
    important competitions and significant performances
    are mentioned, and a photograph of the earliest
    outstanding paraplegic javelin thrower, Dick
    Thompson, is included.

88  Crises at the Olympics / Haydn Middleton. Oxford:
    Heinemann Library, 1999.
    32p; illus; index
    (The Olympics)                             ISBN: 0-431-05921-7
                                               BL: YK.2000.b.3391

    For children.

89  Great Olympic moments / Haydn Middleton. Oxford:
    Heinemann Library, 1999.
    32p; illus
    (The Olympics)                             ISBN: 0-431-05920-9
    For children.

90  The history of the Olympics / Nigel Blundell & Duncan
    Mackay. London: Parkgate, 1999.
    512p; illus                                ISBN: 1-902616-61-8
                                               BL: LB.31.c.11180

91  Minds, bodies and souls: an archaeology of the Olympic
    heritage network / Don Anthony. London: British
    Olympic Association, 1999.
    127p; illus; pbk

    The second volume of this trilogy sets out 'an
    uncovering of what has been buried', with emphasis on
    the pre-history of British Olympic history, up to and
    including the first Games of 1896.

    ☞  See also: C64, C92

92  Minds, bodies and souls: an anthology of the Olympic
    heritage network / Don Anthony. London: British
    Olympic Association, 1999.
    172p; illus

    Volume three of the trilogy adds a selection of articles
    by other writers intended 'to give some muscle to the
    flesh'. It features William Penny Brookes and the
    National Olympian Association; the Cotswold
    Olympics; the Liverpool Olympics; the German
    Gymnastic Society; the National Physical Recreation
    Society; Lord Desborough; Courcy Laffan; and an
    overview of the British Olympic Association, 1904-
    1996.

    ☞  See also: C64, C91

93  The modern Olympic Games / Haydn Middleton.
    Oxford: Heinemann Library, 1999.
    32p; illus
    (The Olympics)
                ISBN: 0-431-05919-5 (cased) • 0-431-05924-1 (pbk)
    For children.

94  Olympic games / Chris Oxlade & David Ballheimer.
    London: Dorling Kindersley, 1999.
    60p; illus; index
    (Eyewitness guides)
        *Alternative title: Olympics*         ISBN: 0-7513-6192-5
                                               BL: YK.1999.b.9325

    A well-produced, mainly photographic, conspectus of
    the subject.

95  The Olympics / John Escott. Oxford: Ginn, 1999.
    48p; illus; index; pbk
    (Impact non-fiction)                       ISBN: 0-435-21233-8
                                               BL: YK.1999.a.4543

    Educational reading book for children aged 11 to 14.

96  Athletics, field: pole vault, long jump, hammer, javelin &
    lots, lots more / Jason Page. Tonbridge: Ticktock, 2000.
    32p; illus
    (Ziggy's Olympic book)                     ISBN: 1-86007-151-1
    A children's book.

97  Athletics, track: 100 metres, 200 metres, relays, hurdles &
    lots, lots more / Jason Page. Tonbridge: Ticktock, 2000.
    32p; illus
    (Ziggy's Olympic book)                     ISBN: 1-86007-150-3
    For children.

98   The complete book of the Olympics / David
     Wallechinsky. London: Aurum, 2000.
     880p; illus; index; pbk                    ISBN: 1-85410-692-9
                                                    BL: YK.2001.a.1731

     ☞   Previous ed. C69

99   Flaming Olympics: new edition for Sydney 2000 /
     Michael Coleman; illustrated by Aidan Potts. New ed.
     London: Hippo, 2000.
     160p; illus; pbk
     (The knowledge)                            ISBN: 0-439-01365-8
                                                    BL: YK.2001.a.378

     For children.

     ☞   Previous ed. C72

100  History of Olympic track and field athletics / Mel
     Watman. Stanmore: Athletics International, 2000.
     184p

     A revised and updated version of his Olympic Track &
     Field Athletics Guide.

     ☞   Previous ed. C81

101  The Olympic marathon: the history and drama of sport's
     most challenging event / David E. Martin and Roger W.
     H. Gynn; foreword by Bill Mallon. Leeds: Human
     Kinetics, 2000.
     xvi, 511p; illus, maps; index; pbk      ISBN: 0-88011-969-1

     This authoritative account of the event describes
     each race from 1896 to 1996, with sketch maps of the
     courses and full statistical data.

102  The 100 greatest moments at the Olympics / Mark
     Crossland and Mike Wood; foreword by Daley
     Thompson. London: Generation, 2000.
     112p; illus; pbk                           ISBN: 1-903009-37-5

103  1000 years of the Olympic Games: treasures of Ancient
     Greece / essays by Terence Measham, Elissabet Spathari
     and Paul Donnelly. Aldershot: Lund Humphries, 2000.
     144p; illus; pbk                           ISBN: 1-86317-079-0

     Prepared to accompany an exhibition of material lent
     by the Hellenic Ministry of Culture to the Powerhouse
     Museum, Sydney.

104  What they don't tell you about the Olympics / Bob
     Fowke. London: Hodder Children's, 2000.
     126p; illus; pbk                           ISBN: 0-340-73611-9

     Children's book of odd and humorous anecdotes.

105  Whitaker's Olympic almanack: an encyclopaedia of the
     Olympic Games / Stan Greenberg. London: Stationery
     Office, 2000.
     vi, 271p; illus; pbk                       ISBN: 0-11-702250-0

     A collection of Olympic facts and statistics, records
     and anecdotes from the ancient games to the
     present.

✱   *Additional References*

106  Special Olympics: the competitive aspect – a study of
     Irish participants / C. Morgan. University College
     Dublin, 1988. MA thesis.

# Politics

107  The politics of the Olympic Games / Richard Espy.
     London: University of California Press, 1979.
     xii, 212p; index                           ISBN: 0-520-03777-4
                                                    BL: X.629/12714

     The author asserts, 'the main problem for any
     organization lies in the conflict between its
     organizational patterns of behavior and its stated
     purpose for existence, that is, in the maintenance of
     the organization as opposed to its stated ideal', and
     cites the case of James Gilkes (Guyana), who applied
     to compete in 1976 under the Olympic banner after his
     NOC had decided to boycott the Games, along with
     most African countries. The IOC turned down his
     request.

     ☞   Subsequent ed. C109

108  Munich, Montreal and Moscow: a political tale of three
     Olympic cities / Ernie Trory. Hove: Crabtree, 1980.
     96p; illus; pbk                            BL: X.809/55156

     Comprises articles completed shortly after the
     conclusion of each of the Olympic Games held in 1972,
     1976 and 1980.

109  The politics of the Olympic Games: with an epilogue
     1976-1980 / Richard Espy. London: University of
     California Press, 1981.
     xi, 238p; index; pbk                       ISBN: 0-520-04395-2
                                                    BL: X.629/25133

     Espy's epilogue provides a post-mortem on the 1980
     US-led boycott: 'The real impact of the boycott was to
     show, perhaps better than any other event could have,
     the popularity of the Games and the importance
     attached by governments, business interests and the
     public to participation in them.' He identifies three

major issues for 1984 and beyond: South Africa, China and the effect of the US boycott. An appendix outlines the structure of the IOC and the Olympic system.

☞    Previous ed. C107

110  Five ring circus: money, power and politics at the Olympic Games / edited by Alan Tomlinson and Garry Whannel. London: Pluto, 1984.
x, 116p; pbk                                  ISBN: 0-86104-769-9
                                                        BL: X.629/23139

This rigorous radical-left critique of the Olympic Games consists of eight essays by different contributors. Athletics receives some specific treatment in almost all the chapters, and particularly in that by Jennifer Hargreaves, 'Women and the Olympic phenomenon'.

111  The political Olympics: Moscow, Afghanistan, and the 1980 US boycott / Derick L. Hulme, Jr. London: Praeger, 1990.
xi, 179p; index                              ISBN: 0-275-93466-7
                                                        BL: YC.1991.b.3469

The author identifies four separate techniques employed in the international arena – conventional diplomacy, private persons, support for an alternate event, and governmental pressure on the IOC – and considers the political and economic effects of the boycott on both the USA and the USSR, as well as its effects on the actual competitions and on the Olympic Movement.

112  Future of the Olympic Games / John A. Lucas. Leeds: Human Kinetics, 1992.
248p; pbk                                    ISBN 0-88011-699-4

113  The lords of the rings: power, money and drugs in the modern Olympics / Vyv Simson and Andrew Jennings. London: Simon & Schuster, 1992.
xi, 289p; illus; index                       ISBN: 0-671-71122-9
                                                        BL: YC.1993.b.1915

A devastating criticism of the Olympic movement, using all the skills of investigative journalist. A landmark publication in Olympic history.

114  Olympic politics / Christopher R. Hill. Manchester: Manchester University Press, 1992.
xv, 266p; illus; index                       ISBN: 0-7190-3542-2
                                                        BL: YC.1992.a.2003

☞    Subsequent ed. C116

115  The new lords of the rings: Olympic corruption and how to buy gold medals / Andrew Jennings. London: Simon & Schuster, 1996.
viii, 360p; illus; pbk                        ISBN: 0-671-85571-9

An even more iconoclastic work than The Lords of the Rings and a significant contribution to modern Olympic history.

116  Olympic politics: Athens to Atlanta, 1896-1996 / Christopher R. Hill. 2nd ed. Manchester: Manchester University Press, 1996.
xv, 283p; index
                ISBN: 0-7190-4450-2 (cased) • 0-7190-4451-0 (pbk)
                                                        BL: YC.1996.a.2950

☞    Previous ed. C114

117  Power, politics and the Olympic Games / Alfred Erich Senn. Leeds: Human Kinetics, 1999.
xx, 315p; illus; index; pbk                  ISBN: 0-88011-958-6
                                                        BL: YC.2000.a.2352

118  The great Olympic swindle: when the world wanted its Games back / Andrew Jennings. London: Simon & Schuster, 2000.
390p; illus                                   ISBN: 0-684-86677-3

119  The Olympic Games: a social science perspective / Kristine Toohey and A. J. Veal. Wallingford: CABI, 2000.
ix, 276p; illus; index                       ISBN: 0-85199-342-7
                                                        BL: YC.2000.a.6

120  The Olympics at the millennium: power, politics, and the Games / edited by Kay Schaffer and Sidonie Smith. London: Rutgers University Press, 2000.
xi, 318p; illus; index; pbk
                ISBN: 0-8135-2819-4 (cased) • 0-8135-2820-8 (pbk)
                                                        BL: YC.2000.a.11811

✱   *Additional References*

121  Olympism and nationalism with special reference to the Barcelona Olympic Games / J. Hargreaves. Swindon: Economic and Social Research Council (ESRC), 1993.
41p                                          BL: DSC-3739.0605(R000233970)

# Individual Olympic Competitions

## ✱ 1896 – Athens

122 The first modern Olympics / Richard D. Mandell.
London: University of California Press, 1976.
xiv, 194p; illus; index          ISBN: 0-520-02983-6
                                  BL: X.629/10691

As an extended preamble to his account of the 1896
Games, the author provides a brief history of the
Olympic Games in antiquity, considers proposals for
their revival, and looks at the seminal role of Pierre de
Coubertin in their rebirth. Descriptions of the athletics
events are somewhat sketchy, and more accurate
results (including spellings of proper names) remained
to be published by Mallon (C123).

123 The 1896 Olympic Games: results for all competitors in
all events, with commentary / Bill Mallon and Ture
Widlund. London: McFarland, 1998.
xvi, 152p; index
(Results of the early modern Olympics; 1)
                                  ISBN: 0-7864-0379-9
                                  BL: YC.1999.b.3302

The first in a series which seeks to provide the
definitive version of the results. Includes articles by
Charles Waldstein, Pierre de Coubertin, Miss Maynard
Butler, Thomas P. Curtis, Rufus Richardson and
George Stuart Robertson. Robertson's 'Greek Ode'
also appears in translation.

## ✱ 1900 – Paris

124 The 1900 Olympic Games: results for all competitors in
all events, with commentary / Bill Mallon. London:
McFarland, 1998.
xvi, 335p; index
(Results of the early modern Olympics; 2)
                                  ISBN: 0-7864-0378-0
                                  BL: YC.1999.b.3296

## ✱ 1904 – St Louis

125 The 1904 Olympic Games: results for all competitors in
all events, with commentary / Bill Mallon. London:
McFarland, 1999.
xvi, 271p; index
(Results of the early modern Olympics; 3)
                                  ISBN: 0-7864-0550-3
                                  BL: YC.1999.b.3686

## ✱ 1906 – Athens

126 The 1906 Olympic Games: results for all competitors in
all events, with commentary / Bill Mallon. London:
McFarland, 1999.
xviii, 232p; index
(Results of the early modern Olympics; 4)
                                  ISBN: 0-7864-0551-1
                                  BL: YC.1999.b.3687

## ✱ 1908 – London

127 The Olympic Games of London, 1908: a complete
record with photographs of the winners. London:
Sporting Life, 1908.
236p; illus

128 Programme and general regulations for the Olympic
Games. London: British Olympic Association, 1908.
3 parts                           BL: 7904.dd.18

129 The rules of sport: being the international code of rules
for all competitions in the Olympic Games / British
Olympic Association. London: Constable, 1908.
vii, 180p          BL: Mic.12569(3) (microfilm copy)

130 The Fourth Olympiad: being the official report of the
Olympic Games of 1908 celebrated in London / drawn
up by Theodore Andrea Cook. London: British Olympic
Association, 1909.
794p; illus                        BL: 7904.d.7

This is a detailed and substantial work, revealing that
the White City was built at a cost of £40,000, and
providing a detailed account of Olympic athletic
events. Of particular interest is the account of the
Olympic 400m, where the Scot Lt. William Wyndham
Halswelle ran in the 'final' on his own, subsequent to
the withdrawal (because of an earlier infringement) of
the other three American finalists. Equally interesting
is a detailed account of the 'Dorando' marathon,
indicating that the event was originally scheduled for
exactly twenty-six miles. No mention is made of moving
the Windsor Great Park start-line to accommodate
the royal family, or to add an extra 385 yards in order
that the finish could take place in front of the Royal
Box.

131 The Olympic Games of 1908 in London: a reply to
certain criticisms / edited by Theodore A. Cook.
London: British Olympic Association, 1909.
60p

An acid, crisply-argued rebuttal of American charges
of British foul play in the 1908 London Olympics. A
model of cool, sustained invective.

132 The 1908 Olympic Games: results for all competitors in all events, with commentary / Bill Mallon and Ian Buchanan. London: McFarland, 2000.
xx, 516p; illus, maps; index
(Results of the early modern Olympics; 5)
ISBN: 0-7864-0598-8
BL: YC.2000.b.1010

## ✳ *1912 – Stockholm*

133 Official report of the Olympic Games of 1912 in Stockholm. London: British Olympic Council, 1912.
20p; pbk
A softcover pamphlet that reports on the British performance in the Games. Besides reporting on each sport and listing all medal winners, it gives the members of the IOC and the BOC.

## ✳ *1924 – Paris*

134 The official report of the VIIIth Olympiad, Paris, 1924 / F. G. L. Fairlie. London: British Olympic Association, 1925.
xxiii, 335p; illus
BL: 07911.g.56

## ✳ *1928 – Amsterdam*

135 The official report of the IXth Olympiad, Amsterdam, 1928 / edited by Harold M. Abrahams. London: British Olympic Association, 1929.
xvi, 328p; illus
BL: 7911.h.41

## ✳ *1932 – Los Angeles*

136 The official report of the Xth Olympiad, Los Angeles, 1932 / edited by Captain F. A. M. Webster. London: British Olympic Association, 1933.
xii, 151p; illus
BL: Mic.A.11293(1) (microfilm copy)

## ✳ *1936 – Berlin*

137 The official report of the XIth Olympiad Berlin, 1936 / edited by Harold M. Abrahams. London: British Olympic Association, 1937.
xi, 254p; illus
BL: 07908.g.21

138 The Nazi Olympics / Richard D. Mandell. London: Souvenir, 1972.
xv, 316p; illus, 1 map; index
*Originally published: New York: Macmillan, 1971*
ISBN: 0-285-62043-6
BL: X.629/4437
A study of the 1936 Olympic Games covering events at both Garmisch-Partenkirchen and Berlin, and concentrating on the organisational and political aspects. The author argues convincingly that the connections between the ancient and modern Games are tenuous. An exceptional work.

139 Hitler's Games: the 1936 Olympics / Duff Hart-Davis. London: Century, 1986.
256p; illus; index
ISBN: 0-7126-1202-5
BL: YC.1986.a.1658
The author argues strongly that the nature of the National Socialist regime was sufficiently well known to have justified the boycott of the 1936 Olympic Games in Garmisch-Partenkirchen and Berlin by non-totalitarian countries and presents an impressive selection of evidence. The strong criticism by members of the British athletics team of its organisation is encapsulated by Godfrey Brown.

## ✳ *1948 – London*

140 The 1948 London Olympic Games: programme, Olympic, world's and British records, and useful visitor's guide to London / S. Evelyn Thomas. London: The author, 1948.
95p; illus, maps
BL: 7918.bb.22

141 1948 Olympic guide and programme / edited by L. D. Court and A. G. Ross. Brighton: Gloucester and MEG, 1948.
48p; pbk
*Variant title: Olympic Games guide, 1948 & programme*
BL: 7916.e.70

142 The Athletic Review souvenir of the XIVth Olympic Games, London, 1948 / W. Richards and W. Clark. Manchester: Athletic Review, 1948.
52p; illus
BL: 7917.d.38

143 British Olympic Association official report of the London Olympic Games, July 29-August 14 1948 / edited by Cecil Bear. London: World Sports, 1948.
112p; illus; pbk
BL: 7917.d.28
Includes messages from J. Sigfrid Edström and Viscount Portal, and contributions on athletics by Harold Abrahams, Jack Crump, Evan A. Hunter and Philip Noel-Baker.

144 Daily Telegraph guide to the Olympic Games & London / foreword by Jack Crump. London: Daily Telegraph, 1948.
32p; illus, maps; pbk

145 The XIV Olympiad: an illustrated record / written and compiled by Desmond Laing. London: The author, 1948.
99p; illus
BL: 7919.ee.10
A record of the various bodies and organisations who made the Games a success.

146 XIVth Olympiad, London, 1948: general regulations and programme. London: Organising Committee for the XIVth Olympiad, 1948.
580p
*Secretary of the Committee was Lt. Col. T. P. M. Bevan*

147  The glory of the Games: world, Olympic and European records / F. A. M. Webster. London: A. Wander, 1948.
48p; illus

Contains record lists and winners of all Olympic track and field events.

148  Olympiad 1948 / H. J. Oaten; forewords by Lord Burghley and Jack Crump. London: Findon, 1948.
112p; illus

Contains Olympic records and results to 1936, and a programme of the 1948 Games.

149  Olympic Games athletic pictorial souvenir / P. W. Green. London: Langdon, 1948.
64p; illus

A pictorial souvenir, with biographies, history and prospects. Contributors include Lord Burghley, E. H. L. Clynes, H. E. D. O'Neill, F. W. Blackmore, James Audsley and Jack Crump.

150  The Olympic Games: complete guide: souvenir copy / E. J. Miles and Dai Owen. London: E. J. Miles, 1948.
20p; pbk                                BL: 7917.de.86

151  Olympic Games, London 1948: official souvenir. London: Futura, 1948.
176p; illus

152  Olympics cavalcade and who's who of 1948 / A. J. Wallis; foreword by Lord Aberdare. London: Background, 1948.
80p; illus; pbk                         BL: 7917.de.112

Contains articles on Jesse Owens, Harold Abrahams, Sydney Wooderson, Eric Liddell, Jack Lovelock, Lord Burghley and Bob Tisdall, and brief biographies of 40 athletes active in 1948.

153  The official report of the Organising Committee for the XIV Olympiad. London: The Committee, 1951.
580p; illus                             BL: 7920.d.28

## ✱ 1952 – Helsinki

154  British Olympic Association official report of the XVth Olympic Games, Helsinki, July 19-August 3, 1952 / edited by Cecil Bear. London: World Sports, 1952.
114p; illus; pbk                        BL: 7917.d.53

Includes contributions by Harold Abrahams, Willy Meisl, Jack Crump and K. S. Duncan.

155  XVth Olympiad Helsinki 1952 Olympic Games / Harold M. Abrahams and Jack C. G. Crump; foreword by Lord Burghley. London: Naldrett, 1952.
56p

All events are described by experts, and there are details of past records and a day-to-day programme of the 1952 Games.

156  Helsinki: the XV Olympiad / Stan Tomlin. London: A. Wander, 1952.

157  Official report on Ireland's participation, XVth Olympiad, Helsinki, July-August, 1952. Dublin: Olympic Council of Ireland, 1952.
24p; illus; pbk                         BL: P.P.1860.ca.

158  Our Olympic athletes in action: story of the Olympic Games; British athletes, their records and prospects; the Helsinki Stadium; the 1952 Olympic programme. London: Associated Newspapers, 1952.
63p; illus; pbk                         BL: 7921.bb.22

A booklet produced to raise funds for the Games, which includes an article by Jack Crump ('Youth deserves this reward'), a history of the Games and prospects for each event, with many photographs.

159  Personal diary and guide to the XV Olympiad / Stan Tomlin. London: News Chronicle, 1952.
48p; pbk

160  The world in my diary: from Melbourne to Helsinki for the Olympic Games / Norman Banks. London: Heinemann, 1953.
xv, 258p; illus                         BL: 010028.m.25

## ✱ 1956 – Melbourne

161  Official report on Ireland's participation in the XVIth Olympic Games, 1956. Dublin: Olympic Council of Ireland, 1952.
28p; illus; pbk                         BL: P.P.1860.ca.

162  1956 Olympic Games in story, pictures, records / edited by Roy Scott. London: Flagstaff, 1956.
48p; illus; pbk                         BL: 7923.bb.30

163  The Olympics / Henry Anthony Pawson. London: Newman Neame Take Home Books, 1956.
15p; illus; pbk                         BL: 7923.h.10

A booklet produced before the 1956 Games which surveys Britain's prospects and analyses the factors which produce success. The illustrations include two photographs of the 1908 Games.

164  Official report of the Olympic Games, XVIth Olympiad, Melbourne, November 22-December 8, 1956 / edited by Cecil Bear. London: World Sports, 1957.
112p; illus; pbk                        BL: 7922.h.13

Includes contributions by K. S. Duncan, Harold Abrahams, Willy Meisl and Jack Crump.

165  Across the world for sport: an Olympic odyssey / Joseph J. Walsh; foreword by Lord Killanin. Waterford: Munster Express, 1958.
232p; illus                             BL: 7923.n.18

Since the work records the author's journey to Melbourne in 1956 for the Olympic Games, some of the narrative is devoted to the 1500m victory of his compatriot, Ronald Delany: 'Like the cultured, clear-headed, modest personality that he is, he exhibited beyond the broad smile that lit up his countenance at the tape, no other outward signs of exaltation'.

## ✱ *1960 — Rome*

166 1960 Olympic Games in story, pictures, records / edited by R. Scott. London: Flagstaff, 1960.
48p; illus; pbk
BL: 7925.f.37

A miscellany of over twenty articles ranging from the general (traditions, ideals, terms) to the specific (programme, venues, qualifying standards).

167 British Olympic Association official report of the Olympic Games, XVIIth Olympiad, Rome, August 25 - September 11, 1960 / edited by Phil Pilley. London: World Sports, 1960.
112p; illus; pbk
BL: 7925.de.5

Includes contributions by K. S. Duncan, Harold Abrahams and Willy Meisl.

168 Olympic diary: Rome 1960 / Neil Allen. London: Nicholas Kaye, 1960.
111p; illus
*Foreword by John Disley*
BL: 7925.f.27

A day-by-day account of the Games, with a list of medal winners appended.

169 Olympic Games, 1960: Squaw Valley, Rome / edited by Harald Lechenperg; translated by Benjamin B. Lacy. London: Yoseloff, 1960.
379p; illus
*Foreword by Avery Brundage*
BL: 7925.de.27

170 The road to Rome / Chris Brasher, Peter Radford, Arthur Rowe, Roger Bannister, Sydney Wooderson, Mike Rawson, Michael Ellis, Neil Allen, Derek Johnson, Brian Hewson, Mary Bignall (sic), Norris McWhirter, Peter Hildreth, Derek Ibbotson, Diane Leather, Harold Abrahams, Jack Barlow, Gordon Pirie, Sandy Duncan, Larry Montague, Chris Chataway, Fred Norris, Geoffrey Dyson, John Disley; edited by Chris Brasher. London: Kimber, 1960.
160p; illus
BL: 7925.c.53

Produced by the International Athletes' Club, with recollections of training and races by members of the British Olympic track and field team.

171 XVII Olympiad, Rome 1960 / presented by Harold Abrahams; foreword by Roger Bannister. London: Cassell, 1960.
276p; illus; index; pbk
BL: 7925.e.15

Contributors include: Avery Brundage (USA), William Björneman (Sweden), Douglas Lowe, Duncan McNaughton (Canada), Robert Tisdall (Ireland), Jesse Owens, (USA), Fanny Blankers-Koen (Netherlands),

Emil Zátopek (Czechoslovakia) and Vladimir Kuts (USSR). A series of articles provide the background for the 1960 Olympics, and Harold Abrahams himself writes a brief history of the Games. The remainder of the book comprises a detailed record of all previous Games, a large section of photographs and a good index.

## ✱ *1964 — Tokyo*

172 1964 Olympic Games, Tokyo: October 10-24. London: Flagstaff, 1964.
48p; illus; pbk
*Cover title: The 1964 Olympic Games in story, pictures and records: complete souvenir-handbook and guide*
BL: X.449/263

173 1964 Olympics / Neil Allen. London: Newman Neame Take Home Books, 1964.
15p; illus
BL: X.449/140

A brief outline of the ancient and modern Olympic Games by The Times' athletics correspondent.

174 Tokyo 1964: a diary of the XVIIIth Olympiad / Christopher Brasher. London: Stanley Paul, 1964.
xii, 124p; illus
BL: X.449/747

An account of the Games which brought such success to Britain, by the 1956 Steeplechase Champion. The text is based on a series of articles which were written for the Observer. The appendix gives the full results of the Games.

175 Athletics Arena official Olympics report / Charles Elliott and Tom McNab. London: Athletics Arena, 1965.
32p; illus

A separate publication of the reports which first appeared in Athletics Arena.

176 The British Olympic Association official report of the Olympic Games 1964: XVIIIth Olympiad, Tokyo, October 10-October 24, [and], IXth Winter Olympic Games, Innsbruck, January 29-February 9 / edited by Doug Gardner. London: World Sports, 1965.
104p; illus; pbk
BL: X.441/265

177 Olympic diary: Tokyo 1964 / Neil Allen. London: Nicholas Kaye, 1965.
vii, 115p; illus
*Foreword by Ann Packer*
BL: X.449/1050

A day-by-day account of the Games, with a list of medal winners appended.

178 Olympic Games, 1964, Innsbruck, Tokyo / edited by Harald Lechenperg; translated by Bert Koetter. London: Yoseloff, 1965.
380p; illus
BL: X.441/391

## ✱ *1968 – Mexico*

179 Mexico 1968: a diary of the XIXth Olympiad /
Christopher Brasher. London: Stanley Paul, 1968.
142p; illus                                      SBN: 09-096830-1
                                                 BL: X.449/3450

180 Olympic Games, Mexico City, 1968: the British
Commonwealth Olympic story / Stan Tomlin; with a
foreword by A. Wander. St Albans: A. Wander, 1968.
56p; illus; pbk

181 Olympic report, 1968: Mexico & Grenoble / James
Coote. London: Hale, 1968.
224p; illus                                 ISBN: 0-7091-0615-7
                                            BL: X.449/3406

182 Athletics Arena official Olympic report / edited by
Charles Elliott. London: Athletics Arena, 1969.
92p

   Contains the most complete reports on the 1968
   Olympic track and field events (though the full set of
   fully automatic times did not appear until the article
   by Bob Sparks in ATFS Bulletin 1/84).

183 Official report of the Olympic Games 1968: XIXth
Olympiad, Mexico City, October 12-27; [and], Xth
Winter Olympics, Grenoble, February 6-18 / edited by
Bob Phillips; art editor, Brian Dobbs. London: 'World
Sports', 1969.
104p; illus; pbk                            ISBN: 0-900315-00-8
                                            BL: X.441/1155

## ✱ *1972 – Munich*

184 Olympic Games, Munich, 1972: a guide / Tom McNab.
Leicester: Knight, 1971.
159p; illus; pbk                            ISBN: 0-340-15063-7
                                            BL: X.619/5386

   A succinct and eminently readable guide to the 1972
   track and field programme.

185 Athletics Arena International official Olympic report:
complete results and reports of the track and field
events, 31st August to 10th September 1972 / edited and
produced by Charles Elliott; compiled by Bob Sparks;
photography by Tony Duffy. London: Arena, 1972.
63p; illus; pbk                             ISBN: 0-902175-27-0

   Contains the most complete reports on the 1972
   Olympic track and field events.

186 Munich '72 / Christopher Brasher. London: Stanley Paul,
1972.
152p; illus                                 ISBN: 0-09-114360-8
                                            BL: X.629/4983

   This is the third (and last) Olympic diary by the 1956
   gold medallist. Brasher writes mainly on the track and
   field events in his usual pungent style, treating such
   topics as: the resurgence of Finnish middle and long

distance running; the comparative failures of Bedford,
Hemery, Hill and Jenkins; the doubtful value of altitude
training immediately before major competitions; and
the widespread use of anabolic steroids by throwers.
He criticises the IOC for its inconsistent application of
its own rules, calls for an end to the use of computers
in seeding heats, and recommends a more even
distribution of events over the period of the track and
field programme.

187 The Olympics / Ron Pickering and Norman Harris;
edited for the Sunday Times by Nicholas Mason;
designed by Gilvrie Misstear; women's events prepared
by Gordon Smith. London: Times Newspapers, 1972.
96p; illus; pbk
   *Cover title: The Sunday Times book of the Olympics*
                                            ISBN: 0-7230-0072-7
                                            BL: X.611/3321

   This is, in fact, a guide only to the athletics programme
   of the 1972 Olympic Games. Whilst clearly aimed at
   the layperson, it presents a clear historical survey of
   each event, followed by an assessment of the leading
   contender/s. Notable for its outstanding graphic
   design.

188 The Olympics 1972 / James Coote & John Goodbody.
London: Hale, 1972.
198p; illus                                 ISBN: 0-7091-3804-0
                                            BL: X.629/4932

   Coote was the author of the athletics section. The
   accounts of most events are brief, with the sole
   exception of the pentathlon. Goodbody contributes
   articles on the murder of Israeli team members and on
   Avery Brundage. Results and medal tables are
   included.

189 Olympics 72 Munich: the official British Olympic
Association preview of the XXth Olympiad / edited by
Desmond Marwood. London: Illustrated London News
& Sketch, 1972.
76p; illus; pbk

190 Official report of the Olympic Games 1972: XXth
Olympiad, Munich, August 26-September 11; XIth
Winter Olympics, Sapporo, February 3-13 / British
Olympic Association; edited by Doug Gardner. London:
Sportsworld, 1973.
96p; illus; pbk                             ISBN: 0-900315-05-9

191 Official report of the XXth Olympiad and the Olympic
Games at Munich and Kiel / Olympic Council of
Ireland. Dublin: The Council, 1974.
63p; illus; pbk                             ISBN: 0-9503425-0-5

   The official report of Ireland's participation in the
   Olympic Games.

192 The XX Olympiad: Munich 1972, Innsbruck 1976 /
George G. Daniels. London?: Firefly, 1996.
176p; illus, maps; index
(The Olympic century; v.18)
*Bibliography: p172-173*

## ✳ *1976 – Montreal*

193 Olympic Games, 1976: a guide / Tom McNab; drawings
by Christine McNab. Leicester: Knight, 1975.
160p; illus; pbk
ISBN: 0-340-19164-3
BL: X.619/15213

Though aimed primarily at a juvenile readership,
McNab's concise guide to the Olympic Games track
and field events (he was a BAAB National Coach
1963-77) makes many original and sharply critical
points. Divided into five sections (Olympic history;
Analysis of Olympic results; 1976 – a viewer's guide;
Olympic record progression; 1972 medal winners) the
work employs in the third section a question and
answer format which works very successfully. In the
first section, the most striking paragraph appears on
p62 –
'No Official Olympics were held in 1944. However, behind
barbed wire, in the concentration camp at Gross Born,
Polish officers celebrated the Games on the 13-15
August. On 30th July they produced a series of
special Olympic stamps and on 14th August at the
close of the Games they produced three separate
series. In all 17,580 Olympic stamps were issued. No
records of performance at the Gross Born Games
remain. I am, however, convinced that these Games
were as Olympic as any held before or since.'

194 Full colour preview of the Montreal Games: Olympics 76
/ edited by Peter Dunk. London: Queen Anne, 1976.
48p; illus; pbk

Various authors, including Melvyn Watman and James
Coote.

195 Olympic handbook / Ron Pickering; photography by
Tony Duffy. London: Macmillan, 1976.
126p; illus, 1 map; pbk
ISBN: 0-333-19397-0
BL: X.619/16676

A rather general guide, with sections devoted to
twelve sports in addition to athletics. For each event,
or group of events, a brief introduction is followed by
the full 1972 result and a 1975 world ranking.

196 Olympic report '76 / editor James Coote. London:
Kemp, 1976.
x, 222p; illus
ISBN: 0-905255-03-8
BL: X.629/11270

As in 1972, Coote was responsible for the athletics
section.

197 Official British Olympic Association report Olympic
Games 1976 / edited by Neil Wilson. London: West
Nally, 1977.
80p; illus

198 Official report of Ireland's participation in the XXIst
Olympiad, Montreal, 1976 / Olympic Council of Ireland.
Dublin: Gemini, 1977.
52p; illus; pbk
BL: X.615/1910

## ✳ *1980 – Moscow*

199 The 1980 Olympics handbook: a guide to the Moscow
Olympics and a history of the Games / Norman Giller.
London: Arthur Barker, 1980.
208p; illus; index
ISBN: 0-213-16754-9 (cased) • 0-213-16755-7 (pbk)
BL: X.629/13183

200 The 1980 Olympics: track and field / Matti Hannus;
photography by Mark Shearman. Croydon: Sports
Market, 1980.
224p; illus
ISBN: 0-9507256-0-9

ATFS member and journalist Matti Hannus of Finland
and outstanding British photographer Mark
Shearman combined to produce a comprehensive
record of the Moscow events. Detailed results and
commentaries are well integrated with illustrations (in
both black & white and colour) and punctuated with
Press comments, detailed biographies of the winners,
topical comments, and responses to a thirteen-point
questionnaire by six statisticians.

201 The ITV book of the Olympics / James Coote and
others. London: Independent Television Books, 1980.
144p; illus, 1 map
ISBN: 0-900727-70-5 (cased) • 0-900727-69-1 (pbk)
BL: X.620/19185

The work was published before the boycott of the 1980
Games was declared, so the preview assumed the
participation of leading athletes from the USA and
West Germany. A popular version of Games history is
presented, illustrated by line drawings.

202 Moscow '80 Olympic special / written and edited by
Peter Bills. Manchester: World International, 1980.
63p; illus
ISBN: 0-7235-658-3-X

203 Official handbook of Great Britain's Olympic team,
XXII Olympic Games, Moscow, 1980. London: British
Olympic Association, 1980.
121p; pbk

204 Official report of Ireland's participation in the XXII
Olympic Games, Moscow, 1980 / Olympic Council of
Ireland. Dublin: The Council, 1980.

205 Olympics 1980 / Norman Barrett; designed and
illustrated by David Nash. London: Piper, 1980.
48p; illus; index; pbk          ISBN: 0-330-25979-2
                                 BL: X.611/9242

   A Piccolo book for children.

206 The Games war: a Moscow journal / Christopher
Booker. London: Faber, 1981.
236p; illus, 1 map; index
       ISBN: 0-571-11755-4 (cased) • 0-571-11763-5 (pbk)
                                 BL: X.629/15594

   Sent to cover the 1980 Olympic Games by the Daily
   Mail, the author (a non-sports journalist and first
   editor of Private Eye) presents a lucid account of the
   choice of Moscow by the IOC, the invasion of
   Afghanistan by Soviet troops in 1979, and the boycott
   of the 1980 Games. Booker's Olympic narrative covers
   the period from 16 July to 4 August and he devotes a
   significant part of his report to athletics.

207 Sport: official British Olympic Association report of the
1980 Games. London: Epic, 1981.
107p; illus; pbk                 BL: DSC-d87/17620

   Includes Roy Moor on athletics.

## ✱ *1984 – Los Angeles*

208 The Olympic Games 1984 / edited by Lord Killanin and
John Rodda. 3rd ed. London: Willow, 1983.
344p; illus; index
       ISBN: 0-00-218062-6 (cased) • 0-00-218063-4 (pbk)
                                 BL: X.622/18069

   ☞  Previous ed. C34

209 British challenge at the 1984 Olympics / paintings by
Kevin Whitney with a text by Brian Glanville. London:
Muller, 1984.
119p; illus
       *Includes 24p supplement: Records and achievements*
                                 ISBN: 0-584-11103-7

   This is a rather curious mix of graphic work,
   photography and text. Whitney was appointed BOA
   Official Artist in 1983; he is represented here by 32
   works, of which 21 are oil on canvas, 9 watercolours
   and 2 drawings. Seven athletes are depicted.

   ☞  Also listed at: L370

210 Olympic Games 1984 / Tom McNab. Sevenoaks:
Knight, 1984.
240p; illus, 1 map; pbk          ISBN: 0-340-33345-6
                                 BL: YK.1991.a.546

211 Olympics 84 / Bill Tancred; designed and illustrated by
Chris Reed; photographs by George Herringshaw.
Loughborough: Ladybird, 1984.
57p; illus                       ISBN: 0-7214-0821-4
                                 BL: X.629/23121

   The venues and dates of the Summer Games from
   1896 to 1980 are given, together with a brief guide to
   athletics events, 1980 winners and Olympic records.

212 Olympics 1984 / edited by Martin Tyler. London: Philips
International BV, 1984.
144p; illus

213 Olympics '84: the British challenge / text by Paul Wade;
photographs by Tom Duffy; foreword by Duncan
Goodhew. Poole: Blandford, 1984.
96p; illus, 1 map; index; pbk    ISBN: 0-7137-1449-2
                                 BL: X.622/22351

214 Playfair Olympics 1984 Los Angeles / edited by David
Emery, Stan Greenberg and Ian Morrison. London:
Queen Anne, 1984.
192p; pbk                        ISBN: 0-356-10336-6
                                 BL: X.629/23122

   Track and field data includes a section on decathlon
   and heptathlon with scoring tables, medallists from
   1948, finalists in 1980, current Olympic and World
   records, and top ten world lists for 1983.

215 British Olympic Association Olympic Games 1984
official report / edited by Mike Blake. London: British
Olympic Association, 1985.
132p; illus

216 Olympic glory: the official British Olympic Association
report of the Olympic and Olympic Winter Games /
Caroline Searle, consultant editor; foreword by HRH
The Princess Royal. Sevenoaks: Crier, 1985.
225p; illus

## ✱ *1988 – Seoul*

217 The 1988 Seoul Olympics / J. Horne, P. Taylor, T.
Taylor, G. Whannel. Stoke-on-Trent: North
Staffordshire Polytechnic, Dept. of Sociology, 1988.
48p; pbk
(Occasional paper; 5)            BL: DSC-6219.190(5)

   Proceedings of a day school held at North
   Staffordshire Polytechnic in February 1988.

218 The British Olympic Association guide and team handbook: Seoul, 1988 / edited by Caroline Searle. London: The Association, 1988.
240p; illus; pbk

219 Champions all: the 3M book of the 1988 Olympic Games. London: Petersen in conjunction with Option One, 1988.
160p; illus; index      BL: YK.1989.b.2597

A guide to the Seoul Games, with athletics contributions by Cliff Temple and Mel Watman. World records and winners at the 1987 World Championships are included.

220 Desmond Lynam's 1988 Olympics: the complete guide to the summer games in Seoul. London: Sidgwick & Jackson, 1988.
231p; illus; pbk      ISBN: 0-283-99592-0
BL: YK.1989.b.4404

The athletics section includes records, brief descriptions of each event, past medallists, stars and a miscellany.

221 Olympics 1988. London: Dennis Oneshots, 1988.
29p; unbound      BL: YK.1990.b.4043

222 Olympics 88 / Chris Reed. Loughborough: Ladybird, 1988.
59p; illus      ISBN: 0-7214-1085-5

223 Scotch Videocassettes book of the Olympic Games / edited by Nicholas Keith. London: Petersen, 1988.
124p; illus; pbk      BL: YK.1989.a.3153

Previews of the athletics events at the 1988 Games are given, together with a list of winners at the 1987 World Championships.

224 Seoul '88: the official book of the Games of the XXIVth Olympiad: harmony and progress. London: Collins, 1988.
221p; illus      ISBN: 0-00-215176-6
BL: LB.31.b.236

Presented in the form of daily reports, the work is essentially pictorial, with colour photography by All Sport; the text and captions are by David Miller. Athletics coverage is extensive and a list of medallists is included.

225 The British Olympic Association official Olympic Games report: 1988 Calgary, Seoul / edited by Caroline Searle; foreword by HRH The Princess Royal. London: The Association, 1989.
248p; illus

226 Calgary and Seoul: Games of the XXIV Olympiad / Ernie Trory. Hove: Crabtree, 1989.
84p; pbk      BL: YC.1990.a.5739

The author traces the staging of the 1988 Seoul Games from 1980, when the city's bid was received by

the IOC four days after the official closing date, through its award of the Games in 1981, to the 1984 report agreeing to talks with North Korea about the latter's proposal to send a joint team to Los Angeles and to the 1988 Games.

227 Seoul diary / David Guiney. Dublin: Sportsworld, 1989.
61p; illus; pbk

A diary kept by the veteran Irish athlete and journalist. A list of winners in all events is appended.

228 The Seoul Olympics: the inside story / Park Seh-Jik. London: Bellew, 1991.
xiv, 177p
*Foreword by Juan Antonio Samaranch*
ISBN: 0-947792-96-1
BL: YK.1993.b.11561

Though dealing primarily with the political dimension of the 1988 Games this work also touches on the organisational aspects of the track and field programme – the scheduling of events to meet the demands of US television and the direction of the doping control centre by Dr Pak Chong-se.

229 Global television and the politics of the Seoul Olympics / James F. Larson, Heung-Soo Park. Oxford: Westview, 1993.
xxi, 281p; illus; index
(Politics in Asia and the Pacific: interdisciplinary perspectives)
ISBN: 0-8133-1693-6 (cased) • 0-8133-1694-4 (pbk)
BL: YC.1994.b.4495

## ✱ *1992 – Barcelona*

230 Olympics '92: will you be there? / compiled by Ann Griffiths and David Minton; introduction by Daley Thompson. London: Blackie, 1984.
96p; illus; index
ISBN: 0-216-91607-0 (cased) • 0-216-91608-9 (pbk)
BL: X.629/23113

231 All round guide to the 1992 Olympics / Alastair Yeomans. London: Boxtree, 1992.
64p; illus; pbk      ISBN: 1-85283-674-1
BL: YK.1994.a.513

The sections included are: The story of the Olympics; Star profiles; Quizzes; Total trivia; and, World records.

232 Official report of participation in the XXV Olympiad Barcelona, Spain 1992 / Olympic Council of Ireland. Dublin: The Council, 1992.
64p; illus; pbk

233 Olympic Games: Barcelona 92. Basingstoke: Mosaik, 1992.
205p; illus      ISBN: 3-576-80005-0
YK.1993.b.834

The athletics reports carry a strong emphasis on UK performers. The results section lists only the first six in each event.

234 Olympic glory / edited by Sally Chew. London: British Olympic Association, 1992.

235 Olympics 92 / edited and compiled by Ben M. Baglio; designed and illustrated by Chris Reed and Gavin Young. Loughborough: Ladybird, 1992.
59p; illus     ISBN: 0-7214-1486-9
BL: YK.1992.a.4556

Designed as a short guide to the 1992 summer Olympic Games in Barcelona, the athletics section lists 1988 winners and, where differing, the Olympic record, brief descriptions of rules and equipment for each event. World records are also shown.

236 Olympics '92 special: your essential guide to track and field events / Laurence Anthony. London: Grandreams Ltd, 1992.
48p; illus; pbk     ISBN: 0-86227-958-5

237 Olympic results, Barcelona 1992: a complete compilation of results from the games of the XXV Olympiad / Brad Alan Lewis, Gabriella Goldstein. London: Garland, 1993.
xxxiv, 611p
(Garland reference library of the humanities; v.1752)
ISBN: 0-815303-33-5
BL: YK.1993.b.14716

Track and field results are not fully documented, for example anemometer readings have been omitted. Some events receive brief comments, but many of these refer only to US participants.

## ✱ *1996 – Atlanta*

238 The centennial Olympic Games: Atlanta 1996 / Norman Barrett. London: Aurum, 1996.
80p; illus; pbk     ISBN: 1-85410-416-0
BL: YK.1998.b.3715

Contains four main sections: 1996 Olympic Games; Events; History 1896-1992; Records, other notable facts and feats, summary of games.

239 The IOC official Olympic companion: the complete guide to the games edited by Caroline Searle and Bryn Vaile. Atlanta edition. London: Brassey's, 1996.
400p; illus; pbk     ISBN: 1-85753-128-0

Contributors include Neil Wilson on 'Those magical moments'; Iain Macleod on 'World forces and the Olympic Games'; Richard Eaton on 'Women and the Olympic Games'; Michele Verdier on 'The Olympic Games and the media'; Bert Roughton Jr on 'Atlanta: a personal view'; and Ian Chadband on 'The athletics prospects'. The preface is by Juan Antonio Samaranch.

240 The official British Olympic team handbook / edited by Peter Nichols. Brighton: Wyeth, 1996.
282p; illus; pbk
*Cover title: Atlanta '96*     ISBN: 0-9524044-2-7

241 Olympics '96. Loughborough: Ladybird, 1996.
53p; illus, maps     ISBN: 0-7214-1826-0
For children.

242 Olympics '96 / Neil Morris. London: Puffin, 1996.
80p; illus; pbk     ISBN: 0-14-038091-4
BL: YK.1996.b.9904

The athletics section contains lists of 1992 winners and Olympic records, details of technical matters, quizzes, and profiles of stars.

243 Olympics 96: the official Eurosport guide to Atlanta / edited by Dominic Hart; foreword by Juan Antonio Samaranch. Richmond: Fox, 1996.
148p; illus

In addition to an A-Z guide to the sports (track p54-62, field p66-74), features appear on Carl Lewis, Haile Gebrselassie and Jonathan Edwards, British medal prospects, Eurosport and satellite technology, Olympic controversies, the Paralympics, and plans for Sydney 2000.

## ✱ *2000 – Sydney*

244 Manchester 2000: economic benefits and opportunities of the Olympic Games. London: KPMG Management Consulting, 1993.
75p; pbk     BL: DSC-q96/18036

245 The Sydney 2000 Olympic Games / written and compiled by Meredith Costain. London: Ladybird, 1996.
64p; illus, 1 map     ISBN: 0-7214-2178-4
For children.

246 The BBC guide to the Olympics 2000 / Dan Waddell. London: BBC, 2000.
252p; illus; pbk
*Alternative title: The Olympics 2000*
ISBN: 0-563-55171-2

247 Official Sydney Olympic guidebook / M. Mundell and L. Filleul. London: Lonely Planet, 2000.
252p; pbk

248 Olympics 2000 pocket guide / Bruce Smith with Mark Webb. London: CollinsWillow, 2000.
224p; pbk     ISBN: 0-00-218921-6
BL: YK.2001.a.5165

# *Olympic Records*

249 Track and field Olympic records / compiled by Harold
M. Abrahams; foreword by Philip J. Noel-Baker.
London: Playfair, 1948.

168p; index                                      BL: 7917.f.5

Lists the first six in each event from 1896 to 1936,
including events later discontinued. Also a general
review of the Games and ranking lists, event by event.
Comprehensively indexed.

250 The Olympic Games book: the complete record of all
Olympic track and field events, 1896-1956 / Harold
Abrahams; foreword by HRH the Duke of Edinburgh.
London: Barrie, 1956.

224p; illus; index                             BL: 7922.ee.13

Lists the first six in every event.

251 Guinness book of Olympic records: complete roll of
Olympic medal winners (1896-1960) for the 20 sports to
be competed in the 1964 games and all other essential
information / edited by Norris D. McWhirter and A.
Ross McWhirter; associate editors Stan Greenberg and
Bob Phillips. London: Oak Tree, 1964.

158p; illus                                     BL: X.449/210

Contains a complete roll of Gold, Silver and Bronze
Medal Winners 1896-1960 and a full schedule for the
Tokyo Olympic Games.

252 Guinness book of Olympic records: complete roll of
Olympic medal winners (1896-1964) for the 19 sports to
be competed in the 1968 games and all other essential
information including details of the winter Olympics
(1924-1964) / edited by Norris D. McWhirter and A.
Ross McWhirter. London: Bantam, 1967.

174p; illus                                     BL: X.449/210

253 Guinness book of Olympic records: complete roll of
Olympic medal winners (1896-1968) for the 22 sports to
be competed in the 1972 games, and all other essential
information / edited by Norris D. McWhirter and A.
Ross McWhirter with others. Harmondsworth: Penguin,
1972.

203p; illus; pbk                           ISBN: 0-14-003526-5

254 The Guinness book of Olympic records: complete roll of
Olympic medal winners (1896-1972, including 1906) for
the 28 sports (7 winter and 21 summer) to be contested
in the 1976 celebrations and other useful information /
edited by Norris D. McWhirter and the late A. Ross
McWhirter; associate editors Suzi M. Biggar, Stan
Greenberg. Harmondsworth: Penguin, 1976.

256p; illus; pbk                          ISBN: 0-14-004146-X
                                               BL: X.619/16810

255 The Guinness book of Olympic records: complete roll of
Olympic medal winners (1896-1976, including 1906) for
the 28 sports (7 winter and 21 summer) to be contested
in the 1980 celebrations and other useful information /
edited by Norris D. McWhirter and the late A. Ross
McWhirter; associate editor Stan Greenberg.
Harmondsworth: Penguin, 1980.

x, 278p; illus; pbk                       ISBN: 0-14-004765-4
                                               BL: X.629/12944

256 The Guinness book of sporting facts / Stan Greenberg.
Enfield: Guinness Superlatives, 1982.

192p; illus                               ISBN: 0-85112-252-3

The athletics section provides a selection of data; the
more unusual are progressive world records or bests
at 1 mile and marathon, barriers in track and field,
oldest and youngest, miscellaneous facts on running
and jumping.

257 The Guinness book of Olympics facts and feats / Stan
Greenberg. Enfield: Guinness Superlatives, 1983.

256p; illus; index

        ISBN: 0-85112-273-6 (cased) • 0-85112-293-0 (pbk)
                                               BL: X.622/18493

In addition to summaries of the summer and winter
games from 1896 to 1980 and of each sport with
details of medallists, there are sections on the
Olympic oath, the Olympic flame, merit awards,
stamps, doubles across sport, artistic competitions
and superlatives.

☞   Subsequent ed. C261

258 Olympic Games: the records / Stan Greenberg. Enfield:
Guinness, 1987.

176p; illus; index

        ISBN: 0-8511-2897-1 (cased) • 0-8511-2896-3 (pbk)
                                            BL: YK.1987.b.7118

Descriptions of both the Games and the individual
sports are included. Profiles of Nurmi, Owens, Viren,
Coe, Daley Thompson, Brisco-Hooks and Carl Lewis
appear. The track and field section covers tug-of-war
and medallists are listed.

259 The Olympic Games: complete track and field results
1896-1988 / Barry J. Hugman and Peter Arnold.
London: Arena, 1988.

384p; illus                               ISBN: 1-85443025-4
                                            BL: YK.1989.b.4687

This work draws heavily on the three-volume history by
Ekkehard zur Megede and on the volumes by Bill Mallon
covering the first four celebrations (including the
intercalated Games). Detailed event-by-event reports
for all Games, plus brief biographies of outstanding
participants, are followed by listings of all competitors
with round-by-round progressions for each track event
and qualifying and finals for field events.

260 The Olympic record book / Bill Mallon. London: Garland, 1988.
xv, 522p
(Garland reference library of social science; v.437)
ISBN: 0-8240-2948-8
BL: YK.1988.a.4203

*An arid presentation of Olympic records in almost every conceivable category: overall, summer, winter, by sport, by nations, and by Games.*

261 The Guinness Olympics fact book / Stan Greenberg. Rev. and updated ed. Enfield: Guinness, 1991.
256p; illus; index; pbk
ISBN: 0-8511-2956-0
BL: YK.1991.b.5908

☞   Previous ed. C257; subsequent ed. C263

262 Olympic facts and figures / David Guiney. Dublin: International Olympic Committee, 1992.
44p; pbk

263 The Guinness book of Olympic facts and feats: Stan Greenberg. Enfield: Guinness Publishing, 1996.
256p; illus; index; pbk
ISBN: 0-85112-639-1

☞   Previous ed. C261

# European Championships & Commonwealth Games

264 Results of the third European Championships held at Oslo: August 22-25 1946. London: Programme Publications, 1946.
52p; illus

265 Vth British Empire and Commonwealth Games: Vancouver, 1954; report by the British Empire and Commonwealth Games, Council for England. The Council, 1954?
41p; illus; pbk
BL: YA.1999.a.2813

266 British Empire and Commonwealth Games, Wales 1958: a diary of events including articles on sport in Wales. Cardiff: Dyma Gymru, 1958.
103p; illus

*Includes 'The Story of Athletics in Wales' by B. W. Mulrennan.*

267 Empire Games athletics / Stan Tomlin. Croydon: Modern Athletic Publications, 1958.
64p; pbk

268 The official history of the VIth British Empire and Commonwealth Games, 1958 / compiled and edited by C. E. Newham, with J. D. B. Williams, and Eileen M. Richards. Cardiff: The Organising Committee, 1958.
507p; illus
BL: 7924.c.16

269 The 'Western Mail' Empire Games book: complete record of track and field events, 1930-1954 / edited by H. M. Abrahams; foreword by Sir Arthur E. Porritt. Cardiff: Western Mail & Echo, 1958.
143p; illus
BL: 7923.p.31

*A complete record of track and field events 1930-54. Includes articles by Harold Abrahams, Tommy Hampson, Jim Alford, Jack Oaten and Roger Bannister.*

270 Constitution of the British Empire and Commonwealth Games. London: British Empire and Commonwealth Games Federation, 1964.

☞   Subsequent ed. C274

271 The 1966 Guinness book of British Empire & Commonwealth Games records / edited by Norris & Ross McWhirter. London: Guinness Superlatives, 1966.
80p; illus; pbk

*Includes a programme of events as an insert* BL: X.449/2299

Lists all the gold, silver and bronze medal winners for all sports from 1930; for athletics, the fourth, fifth and sixth placings are also given.

272 The Commonwealth Games book / Stan Tomlin. St Albans: Tomlin for A. Wander, 1966.
32p; pbk

273 Notes on the organisation of the British Commonwealth Games. London: British Commonwealth Games Federation, 1967.
62p; pbk
*Further editions 1976, 1980*

274 Constitution of the British Commonwealth Games. London: British Commonwealth Games Federation, 1969.
48p; pbk

*Includes the Games song, 'The race is run ...' with words by Sir Alan Herbert.*

☞   Previous ed. C270

275 The Guinness book of British Empire & Commonwealth Games records: being a record and analysis of the results of all 9 sports in all eight celebrations of these games (1930-1966), with programme details for 1970 / edited by Norris & Ross McWhirter. London: Guinness Superlatives, 1970.
88p; pbk        ISBN: 0-900424-52-4

276 IXth British Commonwealth Games: Edinburgh – Scotland 1970: report by the Commonwealth Games Council for England. London: The Council, 1971.
47p; pbk

277 The official history of the IXth British Commonwealth Games: Edinburgh, Scotland, 16-25 July 1970 / compiled and edited by William Carmichael and M. McIntyre Hood. Edinburgh: Organising Committee of the IXth British Commonwealth Games, 1971.
408p; illus       ISBN: 0-903089-00-9
                   BL: X.622/950

278 Commonwealth athletics statistics / Stan Greenberg, Paul Jenes, Lionel Peters and Peter Matthews. London: National Union of Track Statisticians, 1986.
160p; pbk       ISBN: 0-904612-10-4

*Contains deep Commonwealth all-time lists to the end of 1985, progressive Commonwealth records, Commonwealth junior records, and Commonwealth Games results 1930-1982.*

279 Guide to the Commonwealth Games / Desmond Lynam. London: BBC Publications, 1986.
128p; illus; pbk      ISBN: 0-563-20496-6
                    BL: YK.1987.a.5968

*Much of the statistical work and some of the narrative was produced by Chris Rhys and Ian Morrison. A brief history of the Games is followed by an athletics section which includes records, brief descriptions of events, past medallists and famous competitors. Details of BBC coverage are given, together with profiles of the commentators Ron Pickering, David Coleman, Stuart Storey and Brendan Foster.*

280 The official Commonwealth Games book / conceived and directed by the Commonwealth Games Consortium; general editor, Peter Matthews; assistant editor, Stan Greenberg. Preston: Opax, 1986.
233p; illus       ISBN: 0-9511020-0-1

*The main features include: a brief history of the Games from 1930 to 1982, a preview of the 1986 events, and reminiscences of Mary Peters, Ron Hill, Lynn Davies and Ron Clarke.*

281 The royal wedding and XIIIth Commonwealth Games: the commemorative book, 1986. London: Macdonald Orbis, 1986.
48p; illus       ISBN: 0-356-14069-5

282 Unfriendly games, boycotted and broke: the inside story of the 1986 Commonwealth Games / Derek Bateman and Derek Douglas. Edinburgh: Mainstream and Glasgow Herald, 1986.
vi, 127p; pbk       ISBN: 1-85158-059-X
                   BL: YK.1990.b.3400

283 Commonwealth Games. London: Harrington Kilbride, 1990-             BL: ZK.9.b.3743

284 The Commonwealth Games: the first 60 years 1930-1990 / Cleve Dheensaw. Harpenden: Queen Anne, 1994.
197p; pbk       ISBN: 1-85291-546-3

285 Commonwealth Games, Kuala Lumpur 1998: official report / edited by Caroline Searle and David Burke. London: Commonwealth Games Council for England, 1999.
24p; illus; pbk      BL: YA.1999.b.1325

*The 1998 results are not published in full and the England team list contains no personal data. Tables of medals by country (1998, total and by sport, and all time total) are given.*

286 Honour of empire, glory of sport: the history of athletics at the Commonwealth Games / Bob Phillips; foreword by David Moorcroft. Manchester: Parrs Wood, 2000.
xvi, 272p; illus      ISBN: 1-903158-09-5
                   BL: YC.2000.a.12684

*Much new material is included about the origin and development of the Games, as well as vivid accounts of the major events and comprehensive results.*

# *Asian Games*

287 Sangam book of Asian Games / Ranjit Bhatia; foreword by J. B. Holt. London: Sangam, 1982.
104p; illus, 1 map; pbk      ISBN: 0-86131-372-0

# D. Coaching

*This chapter includes advisory and tuition guides as well as general 'how to' books, and general fitness books designed for athletes. Books to do with the coaching of specific events are listed under that event.*

## Coaching for Adults

1 Coaching and care of athletes / F. A. M. Webster. London: Harrap, 1938.
447p; illus; index                    BL: 07908.g.41
  *Possibly the best of all Webster's books on coaching. A work which still has much of value to present-day readers.*

2 Athletics for women / D. L. Pugh and D. C. V. Watts; foreword by Miss M. T. Crabbe. London: Stanley Paul, 1962.
134p; illus                        BL: X.449/989
  *The standard book of the period on athletics for women, by two of Britain's National Coaches.*

3 Problem athletes and how to handle them / Bruce C. Ogilvie and Thomas A. Tutko. London: Pelham, 1966.
195p; illus                        BL: X.449/2057
  *A seminal work of sports psychology.*

4 Athletics, track events. London: Training and Education Associates Ltd, 1975.
82p; illus; pbk
(National Westminster Bank sport coaching series)
                              ISBN: 0-85961-000-4

5 Coaching track and field / William J. Bowerman; edited by William H. Freeman; photographs by Toni Nett. London: Houghton Mifflin, 1975.
xi, 394p; illus; index
  *Published in the United States: 1974*   ISBN: 0-395-17834-7
                              BL: X.620/16180
  ☞ Subsequent ed. D10

6 Assistant club coach award: coaching theory manual / edited by Malcolm Arnold. 5th ed. Birmingham: British Athletic Federation, 1981.
1 looseleaf vol.; illus, 1 map
  *Updated by looseleaf amendments; previous eds untraced*
                              ISBN: 0-85134-124-1
                              BL: YK.1995.b.8499

7 Putting it across / Frank W. Dick. 3rd ed. Birmingham: British Athletic Federation, 1982.
24p; illus; pbk                    ISBN: 0-85134-115-2
  ☞ Subsequent ed. D8

8 Putting it across / Frank W. Dick. 3rd ed. Birmingham: British Athletic Federation, 1987.
24p; illus; pbk                    ISBN: 0-85134-115-2
  ☞ Previous ed. D7; subsequent ed. D11

9 Club coach award: coaching theory manual. 4th ed. Birmingham: British Athletic Federation, 1991.
1 looseleaf vol.; illus
  *Updated by looseleaf amendments; earlier editions untraced*
                              ISBN: 0-85134-125-X
                              BL: YK.1995.b.14011
  ☞ Subsequent ed. D12

10 High-performance training for track and field / William J. Bowerman, William H. Freeman. 2nd ed. Leeds: Leisure Press, 1991.
xiii, 243p; illus                  ISBN: 0-88011-390-1
  ☞ Previous ed. D5

11 Putting it across / Frank W. Dick. New ed. Birmingham: British Athletic Federation, 1993.
24p; illus; pbk                    ISBN: 0-85134-115-2
                              BL: YK.1993.a.12122
  ☞ Previous ed. D8

12  Club coach award: coaching theory manual. 5th ed.
Birmingham: British Athletic Federation, 1994.
1 looseleaf vol.; illus        ISBN: 0-85134-125-X
                           BL: YK.1995.b.14011

☞  Previous ed. D9

13  Fundamentals of track and field / Gerry Carr. 2nd ed.
Leeds: Human Kinetics, 1999.
xvii, 284p; illus; pbk
   *Previously published: Champaign, USA: Leisure Press,*
*1991*                 ISBN: 0-7360-0008-9
                         BL: YK.2000.b.1435

This book by the former Olympic athlete (discus and shot) and veteran coach Gerry Carr is aimed at instructors working with beginners and novices.

# Coaching for Beginners & Juniors

14  Physical training, games and athletics in elementary
schools: a text-book for training college students / Mabel
B. Davies. London: Allen & Unwin, 1927.
288p; illus; index     BL: Mic.A.10483/2(8) (microfilm copy)

☞  Subsequent ed. D16

15  Teaching and training athletes / F. A. M. Webster.
London: A. Wander, for Ovaltine, 1928?
74p

☞  Subsequent edition: D19

16  Physical training, games and athletics in schools: a
textbook for training college students / Mabel B. Davies.
2nd ed. London: Allen & Unwin, 1930.
296p; illus; index       BL: 07912.ee.71

☞  Previous ed. D14; subsequent ed. D17

17  Physical training, games and athletics in schools: a
textbook for training college students / Mabel B. Davies.
3rd ed. London: Allen & Unwin, 1933.
318p; illus; index       BL: 7916.c.37

☞  Previous ed. D16; subsequent ed. D18

18  Physical training, games and athletics in schools: a
textbook for training college students / Mabel B. Davies.
4th ed. London: Allen & Unwin, 1936.
320p; illus; index       BL: 07908.e.4

☞  Previous ed. D17; subsequent ed. D22

19  Teaching and training athletes / F. A. M. Webster.
London: A. Wander, 1936?
94p

☞  Previous ed. D15

20  Lessons in athletics / F. A. M. Webster. London: A.
Wander, 1938.
96p

21  A new approach to athletics: a practical guide for
teachers, coaches, and 'keep-fit' leaders / Stanley Wilson.
London: Allen & Unwin, 1939.
135p; illus             BL: 7911.eee.41

22  Physical training, games and athletics in schools: a
textbook for training college students / Mabel B. Davies.
5th ed. London: Allen & Unwin, 1941.
352p                  BL: 7917.aa.8

☞  Previous ed. D18; subsequent ed. D29

23  Athletics teaching and training / F. A. M. Webster;
foreword by Rex Salisbury Woods. London: Pitman,
1948.
xiv, 241p; illus; index      BL: 7919.cc.44

Possibly Webster's least successful book. His drill-like teaching methods, with their endless progressive practices, were out of touch with post-war educational thinking. He outlines a discus teaching-plan in which the athlete is not actually allowed to throw the missile for almost two months. The section on the pole vault is typical of the book:
'Now then — pole-planting and right knee raising with one step forward — go! Class, rest! Now I want each man, retaining the pole in his left hand, to turn about to the right, and, trailing the pole, to step off with his left foot and take six paces.
About turn! March! Left, right, left, right, halt! To your left, about turn!
Poles in the carry position, ready!'

24  Athletics / edited by Harold Abrahams and Jack Crump; foreword by Lord Aberdare. London: Naldrett, 1951.
180p; illus                                      BL: 7919.f.11

*Contributors are T. Hampson, H. H. Whitlock, C. B. Holmes, S. A. Tomlin, G. J. Pallett, D. K. Gardner, Sir A. Abrahams, F. R. Gaby, H. A. L. Chapman, P. W. Green, A. A. Gold and F. Stampfl. A work similar in nature to the Achilles series, aimed at the young athlete.*

☞  Subsequent ed. D27

25  Athletics for schools / Geoffrey H. G. Dyson and Joseph Edmundson; foreword by Lord Burghley. London: University of London Press, 1951.
320p; illus                                      BL: 7385.aa.38

*Though technically sound, this book looks backward into the 1930s rather than forward to the 1960s in terms of its educational approach. The teaching methods advocated are probably too formal to commend themselves to many modern educationalists.*

26  Fundamentals of track and field coaching / Richard I. Miller. London: McGraw-Hill, 1952.
viii, 271p; illus; index          BL: X.620/7582(9)

*Includes a detailed bibliography. This book is primarily directed towards the coaching of the younger athlete, and is based on experience in American universities.*

27  Athletics / edited by Harold Abrahams and Jack Crump; foreword by Lord Aberdare. Rev. ed. London: Naldrett, 1954.
180p; illus                              BL: 7921.e.107

*One of the last dying gasps of the British athletics establishment, a comprehensive manual on coaching by authors who had never been coaches.*

☞  Previous ed. D24

28  How I teach better athletics / John Le Masurier. London: Muller, 1955.
96p; illus
(Play better books)                  BL: W.P.C.566/3

*A short book for beginners, covering all events clearly and concisely.*
*'People sometimes say that athletics is not a sport which develops team spirit. That is nonsense. Anyone who has followed inter-school and inter-club athletic matches will appreciate the tremendous spirit in any team worth its salt: and in the final stage of a closely fought relay race, the tension can be terrific. Athletics develops not only team spirit. It develops something which is almost as important – individuality.'*

29  Physical education, games and athletics for training colleges / Mabel B. Davies. Completely rev. ed. London: Allen & Unwin, 1955.
360p; illus                                    BL: 7922.n.14

☞  Previous ed. D22; subsequent ed. D31

30  Coaching high school: track and field / G. Luke. London: Nicholas Kaye, 1959.
xii, 228p; illus                               BL: 7924.d.6

31  Physical education, games and athletics for training colleges / Mabel B. Davies. 9th ed. London: Allen & Unwin, 1959.
292p; illus
*7th and 8th eds. untraced*            BL: 7922.c.52

☞  Previous ed. D29; subsequent ed. D33

32  Coaching for track-and-field athletics / Victor C. Sealy; foreword by Geoffrey Dyson. London: Museum Press, 1963.
112p; illus                                     BL: 7926.m.9

*This pocket-sized coaching book covers all events and is directed mainly towards schools.*

33  Physical education, games and athletics for training colleges / Mabel B. Davies. 10th ed. revised by Barbara Churcher. London: Allen & Unwin, 1963.
274p; illus                                     BL: 7926.t.37

☞  Previous ed. D31; subsequent ed. D36

34  Schoolgirl athletics: a textbook for colleges of education and schools / Peggy J. Woodeson & Denis C. V. Watts. London: Stanley Paul, 1966.
139p; illus                                    BL: X.449/1872

☞  Subsequent ed. D37

35  Teaching athletics in school and club / Dorothy Tyler; drawings by Jon Ellis. London: Arena, 1967.
23p; illus; pbk                               BL: X.619/9609

36  Physical education for teaching / Barbara Churcher, based on the original work of Mabel B. Davies. 11th ed. London: Allen & Unwin, 1971.
168p; illus                         SBN: 04-371013-1
                                            BL: X.629/3282

☞  Previous ed. D33

37  Schoolgirl athletics: a textbook for colleges of education and schools / Peggy J. Woodeson and Denis C. V. Watts. 2nd ed. London: Stanley Paul, 1973.
142p; illus                        ISBN: 0-09-115500-2
                                            BL: X.629/5471

☞  Previous ed. D34

38  How to teach track events: a guide for class teachers in schools and coaches in athletic clubs / Denis Watts & Harry Wilson. London: British Amateur Athletic Board, 1977.
23p; illus; pbk                            BL: X.619/18239

☞  Subsequent ed. D42

39   Athletics: a handbook for teachers / David Couling.
     London: Hale, 1980.
     167p; illus; index                           ISBN: 0-7091-7543-4
                                                   BL: X.629/15179

40   But first: basic work for coaches and teachers of
     beginner athletes / prepared by Frank W. Dick. London:
     British Amateur Athletic Board, 1982.
     88p; illus; pbk                              ISBN: 0-85134-066-0
                                                  BL: YK.1995.b.3046

     Essentially a scissors and paste collage of mainly
     East German ideas, But First offers many sound
     basic drills.

     ☞  Subsequent ed. D41

41   But first: basic work for coaches and teachers of
     beginner athletes / prepared by Frank W. Dick. London:
     British Amateur Athletic Board, 1983.
     88p; illus; pbk

     ☞  Previous ed. D40; subsequent ed. D44

42   How to teach track events: a guide for class teachers and
     coaches in athletics clubs / Malcolm Arnold. London:
     British Amateur Athletic Board, 1983.
     32p; illus; pbk                              ISBN: 0-85134-069-5
                                                  BL: X.629/20906

     ☞  Previous ed. D38; subsequent ed. D45

43   Teaching athletics 8-13: guidelines for the non-specialist
     / David A. Evans. London: Hodder and Stoughton,
     1984.
     ix, 117p; illus; index; pbk                  ISBN: 0-340-34712-0
                                                  BL: X.629/24112

     Evans's work is the best recent attempt to cover
     athletics for the primary school child.

44   But first: basic work for coaches and teachers of
     beginner athletes / prepared by Frank W. Dick. London:
     British Amateur Athletic Board, 1987.
     93p; illus; pbk                              ISBN: 0-85134-066-0
                                                  BL: YK.1989.b.4169

     ☞  Previous ed. D40; subsequent ed. D47

45   How to teach track events: a guide for class teachers and
     coaches in athletics clubs / Malcolm Arnold. London:
     British Amateur Athletic Board, 1987.
     32p; illus; pbk                              ISBN: 0-85134-085-7

     ☞  Previous ed. D42; subsequent ed. D48

46   The Athletics Congress's track and field coaching manual
     / the Athletics Congress's development committees with
     Vern Gambetta, editor. 2nd ed. Leeds: Leisure Press,
     1989.
     x, 227p; illus
         *1st ed. untraced*                       ISBN: 0-88011-332-4

47   But first: basic work for coaches and teachers of
     beginner athletes / prepared by Frank W. Dick. London:
     British Amateur Athletic Board, 1990.
     93p; illus; pbk                              ISBN: 0-85134-066-0
                                                  BL: YK.1991.b.7535

     ☞  Previous ed. D44; subsequent ed. D50

48   How to teach track events: a guide for class teachers in
     schools and coaches in athletics clubs / Malcolm Arnold.
     Birmingham: British Athletic Federation, 1992.
     35p; illus; pbk                              ISBN: 0-85134-111-X
                                                  BL: YK.1993.a.9892

     ☞  Previous ed. D45

49   Youth coach award: coaching theory manual / compiled
     by Brad McStravick. Birmingham: British Athletic
     Federation, 1992.
     1 looseleaf vol.; illus                      ISBN: 0-85134-113-6
                                                  BL: DSC-q94/09457

50   But first: basic work for coaches and teachers of
     beginner athletes / prepared by Frank W. Dick. [5th ed.].
     London: British Amateur Athletic Board, 1994.
     93p; illus; pbk                              ISBN: 0-85134-066-0
                                                  BL: YK.1995.b.3046

     ☞  Previous ed. D47

51   Coaching the young athlete. Birmingham: British Athletic
     Federation, 1994.

52   Coaching young athletes / BAF national coaches; edited
     by Carl Johnson. Birmingham: British Athletic
     Federation, 1996.
     152p; illus; pbk                             ISBN: 0-85134-134-9
                                                  BL: YK.1996.b.8388

# E. Training

## Training for Adults

1   A collection of papers on the subject of athletic exercises / Sir John Sinclair. London: E. Blackader, 1806.

102p                      BL: 7919.c.47

The articles include Sinclair's 'Observations on the training of pugilists, wrestlers, jockeys and others who give themselves up to athletic exercises, with some queries for discovering the principles thereof, and the process of training running horses, etc. with a view of ascertaining whether the same can furnish any hints serviceable to the human species'. Sinclair's is a work dedicated to the student of general health, rather than sport. It does, however, show that the training methods later attributed to Captain Barclay Allardice were essentially the conventional wisdom of the eighteenth century. Sinclair presciently concludes that athletic training methods, 'though temporary in effect, have much to offer the average man'.

2   Result of the inquiries, regarding athletic exercises, recently made by Sir John Sinclair. Edinburgh: Privately published, 1807.

24p; pbk                    BL: B.734(4)

A separate publication of the section relating to athletics in the appendix of The Code of Health and Longevity.
'With a view of clearing the stomach, and getting rid of all superfluities, either of blood or anything else, and also to promote good digestion afterwards, medicines are given when the training is commenced. They begin with an emetic, and in about two days afterwards give them a dose of glauber salts, from one to two ounces; and, missing about two days, another dose, and then a third. It is supposed that one emetic and three doses of physic will clear any man of all the noxious matter he may have had in his stomach and intestines. In training for running, only one dose of salts at the beginning is necessary, and if it is not found to answer, another dose, in a proper quantity is administered. The celebrated trainer for running, John Smith, generally gave them an emetic, also, after they had been in training with him for some time; and if they were of a plethoric habit, he required them to lose eight ounces of blood from the arm.'

Sinclair's work shows that the training of athletes had been firmly established by the eighteenth century, and that it closely followed the training of horses, fighting cocks and greyhounds. Because it was lodged within a substantial work devoted to health and longevity, its accounts of athletics training principles have tended to be ignored. As a result, Barclay's methods, essentially the same, were treated as definitive and original and lasted in one form or another into the twentieth century. Significantly, Sinclair concludes that, though athletic training methods are ephemeral, they have much to offer the non-athlete, and in this he is an early advocate of health-related exercise.

☞   See also J2

3   British manly exercises: in which rowing and sailing are now first described, and riding and driving are for the first time given in a work of this kind … / Donald Walker. London: T. Hurst, 1834.

xvi, 269p; illus               BL: C.59.g.12

A famous book of exercises which includes running, walking and jumping, with some illustrations. Includes the statement: 'a quarter of a mile in one minute is good running; and a mile in four minutes at four starts is excellent. The mile was perhaps never run in four minutes, but it has been done in four minutes and a half.' Manly Exercises is also interesting for its reiteration of Captain Barclay's training methods, which by the mid-nineteenth century had become standard training procedure:
'The patient is then purged by drastic medicines; he is sweated by walking under a load of clothes, and by lying between feather beds; and his limbs are roughly rubbed. His diet is beef or mutton; his drink strong ale. He is gradually inured to exercise, by repeated trials in walking and running.'

☞   Subsequent ed. E4

4   British manly exercises: in which rowing and sailing are now first described, and riding and driving are for the first time given in a work of this kind … / Donald Walker. 2nd ed. London: T. Hurst, 1834.
xix, 291p, xiii; illus

☞  Previous ed. E3; subsequent ed. E5

5   British manly exercises: in which rowing and sailing are now first described, and riding and driving are for the first time given in a work of this kind … / Donald Walker. 3rd ed. London: T. Hurst, 1835.
xvi, 269p; illus

☞  Previous ed. E4; subsequent ed. E8

6   Peter Parley's book of gymnastics, being his legacy, to promote the health and long life of his young English friends / Peter Parley. London: Darton & Clark, 1840.
136p; illus
(Child's library)
*'Peter Parley' is a pseudonym for Samuel Clark*
BL: 1606/1679

Probably originally published in USA. Includes sections on running and field events.

7   Training, pedestrianism and wrestling. London: W. M. Clark, 1840?
64p
BL: 7908.a.104

8   Walker's manly exercises containing rowing, sailing, riding, and driving to which are now added, for the first time, racing, hunting and shooting / Donald Walker. 6th ed., the whole carefully rev. by 'Craven'. London: Orr, 1840.
viii, 264p; illus
*4th and 5th eds. untraced; 'Craven' is a pseudonym for John William Carleton*
BL: RB.23.a.2486

☞  Previous ed. E5; subsequent ed. E9

9   Walker's manly exercises containing rowing, sailing, riding, and driving to which are now added, for the first time, racing, hunting and shooting / Donald Walker. 8th ed., the whole carefully rev. by 'Craven'. London: Orr, 1847.
xvi, 269p; illus
*7th ed. Untraced; 'Craven' is a pseudonym for John William Carleton*

☞  Previous ed. E8; subsequent ed. E11

10   The training of man for pedestrian exercises / 'Stonehenge'. London: 1855.
*Stonehenge is a pseudonym for John Henry Walsh*

Walsh was one of the most prolific writers of the era. This book had the reputation of being the first book devoted solely to advice on athletics. Much of the work was reproduced in the first edition of Manual of British Rural Sports (1856) of which Walsh was editor.

☞  See also: A54

11   Walker's manly exercises containing rowing, sailing, riding, and driving to which are now added, for the first time, racing, hunting and shooting / Donald Walker. 9th ed., the whole carefully rev. by 'Craven'. London: H. G. Bohn, 1855.
xii, 266p; illus
*'Craven' is a pseudonym for John William Carleton*

☞  Previous ed. E9; subsequent ed. E13

12   Hints upon training / Charles Westhall. London: 1860?
*Author is Charles Hall*

The first of several books by this famous professional athlete.

☞  Subsequent ed. E14

13   Walker's manly exercises containing rowing, sailing, riding, and driving to which are now added, for the first time, racing, hunting and shooting / Donald Walker. 10th ed., the whole carefully rev. by 'Craven'. London: H. G. Bohn, 1860.
xii, 264p, illus
*'Craven' is a pseudonym for John William Carleton*

☞  Previous ed. E11

14   The modern method of training for running, walking, rowing and boxing, including hints on exercise diet, clothing / Charles Westhall. London: Beeton, 1863.
*Author is Charles Hall*
BL: Mic.A.7490(9) (microfilm copy)

A revised and enlarged edition of Hints Upon Training.

☞  Previous ed. E12; subsequent ed. E32

15   Athletic sports and manly exercises / 'S', J. G. Wood and others. London: Routledge, 1864.
477p
*'S' refers to 'Stonehenge', the pseudonym of John H. Walsh*
BL: 7906.a.3

Pages 432-477 are on pedestrianism. Some idea of amateur standards is given by Walsh, who states that 440yds had been run in a minute, 880yds in 2 mins (downhill) and 2¼ mins (flat), 1 mile in 4½ to 5 mins, 2 miles in 'rather less than 10 mins', 4 miles in 20½ mins, and in the long jump '22ft is said to have been done'.

16   Pedestrianism: health and general training / 'S'. London: Warne, 1866.
*'S' refers to 'Stonehenge', pseudonym for John Henry Walsh*
BL: 7913.aa.19(10)

17   Training, in theory and practice / Archibald Maclaren. London: Macmillan, 1866.
vi, 202p; illus
BL: 7907.f.13

An illustrated book by one of the most respected physical educationalists of the era. Maclaren supervised the Oxford Gymnasium, and his ideas influenced university athletes in the dawn of the modern athletic era.

☞  Subsequent ed. E26

18  Gymnasts and gymnastics / John H. Howard. London: Longmans Green, 1867.
299p; illus

Includes a significant chapter on jumping and pole-leaping with rare illustrations of jumping stands.

☞  Subsequent ed. E20

19  A handbook of gymnastics and athletics / E. G. Ravenstein and John Hulley. London: Trübner, 1867.
viii, 408p; illus                              BL: 7907.d.2

Includes the rules of athletics and sketches of runners, jumpers, pole-vaulters and throwers, and a diagram of a javelin of the time.

20  Gymnasts and gymnastics / John H. Howard. 2nd ed., rev. and enlarged. London: 1868.
BL: Mic.A.7851(1) (microfilm copy)

☞  Previous ed. E18

21  Training for pedestrianism / Charles Westhall. London: Ward, Lock, 1868?
*Author is Charles Hall*

22  A system of physical education, theoretical and practical / Archibald Maclaren, with illustrations drawn on wood from life by A. Macdonald and engraved by J. D. Cooper. Oxford: Clarendon, 1869.
518p; illus                              BL: 12205.n.12

Includes a list of amateur and professional records.

23  Athletica: a condensed manual of the practical theory of several branches of athletics / J. R. H. and J. C. C. Maidstone: 1871.
*Authors are James Ridgway Hakewill and John Charles Crawford?*                BL: Mic.A.7567(9) (microfilm copy)

24  Modern out-door amusements. London: Warne, 1871.
viii, 182p                              BL: 7905.aa.6

Pages 55-92 are on athletics and include advice on training and a list of records.

25  Good condition: a guide to athletic training for amateurs or professionals / Charles J. Michôd. London: Hardwick, 1874.                BL: Mic.A.10814(9) (microfilm copy)

Michôd was well-known as a steeplechaser.

26  Training, in theory and practice / Archibald Maclaren. 2nd and enlarged ed. London: Macmillan, 1874.
BL: 7904.aa.1

☞  Previous ed. E17

27  A few practical hints to amateurs on training for walking, running and other athletic sports / Harry Andrews. London: Austin, 1876.
44p                                        BL: D

Advice by a famous trainer of the nineteenth century who had run in the 'Deerfoot troupe' of the 1860s. The chapters cover running, walking, strict training, long distance running and walking, Deerfoot and the English champions, pedestrian notes, amateur notes, remarkable performances and sporting memoranda.

28  The athlete's guide / N. L. Jackson and H. M. Oliver. London: 'Pastime', 1882.

A second edition, though untraced, is thought to have been edited by Jackson and E. H. Godbold. A third and possibly a fourth edition are thought to have been published. Jackson, a famous sporting journalist, was a distance and cross-country runner in the years 1866-68. He was best known as the founder of Corinthian FC. Oliver was editor of the Midland Athlete, and 1879 steeplechase champion.

29  A new handbook on training for athletic exercises / William E. Morden. London: E. Seale, 1887.
58p; illus        BL: Mic.A.10943(16) (microfilm copy)

30  The science and art of training: a handbook for athletes / Henry Hoole. London: Trübner, 1888.
xiii, 124p                              BL: 7908.e.19

☞  Subsequent ed. E35

31  The training instructor for aquatics, pedestrians, swimming, athletics, bicycling, etc. London: Sportsman Offices, 1889.
100p                                      BL: 7906.a.67

A book designed to replace Practical Hints on Training (1879). The preface acknowledges the influence of American and Australian methods but the advice still includes purging, cold baths, an avoidance of butter, sugar and cheese, and a sponge bath of whisky and water before a race!

32  The modern method of training for running, walking, rowing and boxing / Charles Hall. New ed.; revised by E. T. Sachs with an appendix. London: Ward Lock, 1890.
160p; illus        BL: Mic.A.7496(1) (microfilm copy)

A new edition, thoroughly revised and brought up to date by Sachs.

☞  Previous ed. E14

33  The 'Pastime' athletic handbook / N. L. Jackson. London: 'Pastime', 1890s?

34  The complete training guide for amateur and professional athletes. London: Street-Smith, 1891.
64p

Advice on how to train for walking, running and rowing, and how to preserve and improve strength.

35 The science and art of training: a handbook for athletes / Henry Hoole. 2nd ed. London: H. Cox, 1891.
xiii, 124p                                  BL: Mic.A.7795(12) (microfilm copy)

☞ Previous ed. E30; subsequent ed. E36

36 The science and art of training: a handbook for athletes / Henry Hoole. 3rd ed. London: H. Cox, 1895.
xv, 124p                                    BL: Mic.A.7795(13) (microfilm copy)

☞ Previous ed. E35

37 Athletic sports / D. A. Sargent, H. J. Whigham, R. D. Wrenn, P. G. Hubert, Jr., M. Merington, J. W. Roosevelt, D. Osborne, E. S. Martin. London: Kegan Paul, 1898.
xiii, 318p
(The out of door library)                                       BL: 7912.dd.22/2

Advice on the training and technique necessary for athletic events.

38 The young sportsman / edited by Alfred E. T. Watson with numerous illustrations. London: Lawrence & Bullen, 1900.
viii, 663p; illus
*The greater part reprinted from The Encyclopedia of Sport*
BL: 07905.l.18

Includes a detailed section on athletics by Montague Shearman, with sections contributed by Harold Wade (cross-country and steeplechase), C. L. Lockton (hurdles), R. Williams (high jump and pole jump), C. B. Fry (long jump) and G. S. Robertson (hammer and weight).

39 Athletics / Sir William Beach Thomas. London: Ward, Lock, 1901.
356p; illus
(The Isthmian Library series. 1896)                             BL: 07905.g

Contributors: C. N. Jackson, Rev. J. H. Gray, H. A. Munro, A. C. M. Croome, W. M. Fletcher (USA), R. R. Conway and G. S. Robertson. A comprehensive guide to all the athletic events then in vogue, with a notable chapter on cross-country running: 'The ruin of athletics has been the establishment of the theory that the game is not good enough in itself without a substantial bribe. If once this foolish expenditure were banished, there is every reason to think that little meetings would become more instead of less frequent.' Beach Thomas highlights an early problem of amateur athletics: scratch athletic events invariably produced the same winners and most rural meetings copied the professionals and held handicap events to encourage the less-gifted. Initially, these rural meetings were confined by the AAA to offering cups or plaques, a policy which, not surprisingly, proved unpopular. Then, prizes were offered on which a brass plate (detailing the victor's name) could be fixed. This rule naturally limited the range of prizes, and was withdrawn, to be replaced with one in which prizes of little intrinsic value were offered. This proved to be more acceptable, but athletes often sold their prizes or had them replaced at the shop at which they had been bought. The idea of winning a desirable prize proved to be a bridge too far for the amateur authorities and the replacement or selling of a prize was deemed to render an athlete a 'professional'.

40 The training of the body for games, athletics, gymnastics, and other forms of exercise, and for health, growth, and development / F. A. Schmidt and Eustace H. Miles; a translation of F. A. Schmidt's 'Unser Körper', with alterations and additions by Eustace H. Miles. London: Swan Sonnenschein, 1901.
xxiv, 520p; illus
*Reissued in 1904*                                          BL: 7908.h.16

A scholarly analysis of athletic events, with many diagrams and photographs including one of R. S. Garrett, the first modern Olympic discus champion. Pages 344-356 are on walking, pages 380-431 on running and races.

41 Training for athletics and general health / Harry Andrews. London: Pearson, 1904.
122p; index                                                          BL: D

Advice by a famous expert on training methods, with chapters on all running events. An interesting section on the use of drugs, including cocaine and strychnine. This was a different individual from the writer of A Few Practical Hints (1876).

☞ Subsequent ed. E45

42 Codebook of gymnastic exercises / Ludwig Puritz. London: Kegan, Paul, Trench and Trübner, 1905.
287p; illus
*Translation of: Manuel de gymnastique. Hanover: 1883*

A book widely used as a textbook of gymnastics in this country. It has chapters on jumping, pole-vaulting and throwing and is illustrated with woodcuts.

43 Practical track and field athletics / John Graham and Ellery H. Clark. London: Nutt, 1905.
111p; illus                                               BL: 7912.f.26

A notable account of the new methods of training adopted with such success in the USA. Clark was the first Olympic high jump champion.

44 Training for athletics: a comprehensive manual dealing with all branches of sport. London: Health and Strength, 1908.
114p; illus                                               BL: 7911.df.34

The writers include W. G. George, Alf Shrubb, J. Higgins (on jumping), and A. T. Yeoumans (on walking). Higgins contributes what is possibly the only written material on jumping with weights, which was an activity based mainly in the Lancashire area in the second half of the nineteenth century – Howard of Chester cleared 29ft 7in from a boat board in 1854. Jumping with weights had been pursued primarily in wager-based match-events. Later it had moved to the stage and occasionally to the circus, but by World War One it had vanished. Alas, Higgins' account does little to enlighten us on events which now seem as far from us as the medieval tournament.

45   Training for athletics and general health / Harry Andrews. London: Pearson, 1911.

     ☞   Previous ed. E41

46   Athletics / E. H. Ryle, with thirty-two action photographs. London: Eveleigh Nash, 1912.
229p; illus
(The national library of sports and pastimes)
                 BL: 7904.df.34/1

Ryle, an ex-President of Cambridge University AC, compiled a notable work which includes articles by Philip J. Baker (miling), G. R. L. Anderson (hurdles), Sidney S. Abrahams (long jump), W. E. B. Henderson (discus, both styles), Henry Leeke (hammer), E. E. Leader (high jump) and Adolphe Abrahams ('the scientific side'). Interesting comparisons are made between Britain and America, and Ryle deplores the inadequacy of British facilities.
'As an instance of the practical interest in sport I might point out that the New York AC possesses a gigantic central club house standing in its own grounds in the city, admirably equipped in every way and which cost nearly 2,000,000 dollars to erect. There is also a "country house" belonging to the same club outside the town, replete with every comfort. Let the English reader compare the inadequate dressing rooms under the stand at Stamford Bridge which is the sole club house that the London AC possesses or is ever likely to possess with these edifices.'
What Ryle omits to mention is that New York AC was not a specialist athletic club but used the word 'athletic' in a more general sense. In 1995, an attempt was made to commemorate the centenary of the 1895 New York AC v London AC meeting, but New York found it impossible to raise a track and field team from its membership.

47   Athletics in theory and practice / Ernest W. Hjertberg; edited by Sidney Solomon Abrahams, with over 70 photographs from life. London: Hutchinson, 1913.
xii, 280p; illus      BL: Mic.A.7691(1) (microfilm copy)

Hjertberg was the coach of Sweden's 1912 Olympic team, and of a number of leading American clubs. This well-illustrated study was inspired by the 1912 Olympic Games. By modern standards much of the advice is either unscientific or inadequate, but the book is exceptional for its chapters on field events, including the unfashionable javelin, discus and triple jump events. The chapter on javelin throwing is contributed by the father of that event, Eric Lemming. 'Of all the forms of athletics that occur on the programmes at American and Continental meetings, it is the pole jump which possesses most interest for the spectators. This is not difficult to understand, for, of necessity, there must be a certain excitement in seeing a person throw himself up in the air to a height of eleven feet and more. In England pole-jumping only requires to be well-performed to be thoroughly appreciated also.'

48   The complete athletic trainer / S. A. Mussabini in collaboration with Charles Ranson. London: Methuen, 1913.
xii, 262p; illus             BL: 2271.c.19

'Sam' Mussabini was undoubtedly one of the great British coaches of the early part of the twentieth century, but the reader of The Complete Athletic Trainer will occasionally find statements which might well have been penned by Captain Barclay over a century before. 'Purgative medicine, which will touch the liver as well as the stomach should be taken at the outset .... A very good old-fashioned recipe known as "Black Jack" will not easily be bettered.' Later, showing a basic Western Roll type of jump, Mussabini notes in a caption: 'more picturesque than effective'. These cobwebs of the nineteenth century should not deter the reader, for this is a fine book, with particularly good chapters on timing and starting (from the official's viewpoint) and marathon running. There are interesting photos of the professional walker, Cummings, and of Ransom, a dual Sheffield Handicap winner. Mussabini ends his book on a note which might well be emulated by less modest modern authors. Apologising for the exclusion of certain field events, he says: 'The writer is, however, diffident of touching subjects with which he has had so little practical acquaintance, and it would not be fair to his readers for him to paraphrase the works of others and advance second-hand opinions.'

49   Athletic training / Michael C. Murphy; edited by Edward R. Bushnell; with an introduction by R. Tait McKenzie. London: Bickers, 1914.
xxxiv, 174p; illus     BL: Mic.A.10911(1) (microfilm copy)

The training advice of the famous American coach who pioneered many techniques, such as the crouch start, which are a feature of modern athletics. This is one of the first great works of the American collegiate system. Murphy, who died before the publication of his book, was the father of the American film actor, George Murphy.

50   Training for the track, field, and road, with some hints on health and fitness / Harry Andrews; edited by E. Elliot Stock. London: Stanley Paul, 1914.
216p; illus; index             BL: 7911.e.7

The trainer of Alf Shrubb and Jack Morton gives his advice on training, with strong emphasis on the use of massage, skipping and diet. Interesting references to the 'drug habit' in American athletics. 'I have also tried strychnine in tabloid form for a bad case of exhaustion, but, finding it of no practical use, fell back upon a cup of hot meat extract. The latter had almost instant effect.'

51   Success in athletics, and how to obtain it / F. A. M. Webster, T. J. Pryce Jenkins, & R. Vivian Mostyn. London: Sidgwick & Jackson, 1919.
xvi, 240p; illus            BL: 07911.eee.13

An early attempt to produce a technical analysis of athletics, in which mathematical principles and formulae are invoked. Of the authors, Webster's name is well known; Dr. Pryce-Jenkins was a rugby international and R. Vivian Mostyn a County Cricketer and 'expert in athletic dynamics'.

52　Training, and how to keep always fit / Charles Walker Cathcart. Edinburgh: Livingstone, 1921.
52p　　　　　　　　　　　　　　　BL: 7383.dd.21

53　Practical athletics and how to train / Alec Nelson. London: Pearson, 1924.
132p; illus; index　　　　　　　　　BL: 7911.dd.39

Nelson was coach to Cambridge University AC. This is one of the finest books on all-round athletics written up to this time. The book is strongest on running but also surprisingly good on such unfashionable events as the triple jump and pole vault.

☞　Subsequent ed. E65

54　Track & field athletics: a book on how to train / S. A. Mussabini. London: Foulsham, 1924.
94p; illus

*Spine title: Field & Track Athletics*　　BL: 12209.ppp.8/18

Reprinted as Modern track and field athletics in 1931 and 1937.

55　Athletics / F. A. M. Webster; illustrated by A. W. Close. London: Allen & Unwin, 1925.
224p; illus
(British sports library)　　　　　　　BL: 07908.e.22/4

56　The secret of athletic training / Harry Andrews and William S. P. Alexander. London: Methuen, 1925.
xi, 152p; illus　　　　　　　　　　　BL: 7904.ee.24

A backward-looking view of athletics training. Only three years later the Abrahams brothers produced a book, Training for Athletes which is years ahead in outlook. This book is mainly devoted to training for running and walking and has an interesting chapter by Joe Binks on marathon-training. Andrews gives high priority to massage (decried in a later chapter by Binks) and includes a rather involved chapter on sprinting style about 'the mechanical sprint style' and 'the modified chop and full stretch stride'. On the credit side, he comes out strongly against the Mussabini cross-arm action and gives a great deal of solid, practical advice.
'The object of massage is to remove poisonous substances from the muscles (and can be employed with most excellent results in the case of Influenza), strengthen the sinews and ligaments, promote growth of bone and muscle, and tone up the nervous system so as to create perfect co-ordination between it and the muscular energy.'

57　Track and field: principles and details of training and practice for each event / Thomas E. Jones. London: Scribner's, 1925.
xiv, 214p　　　　　BL: Mic.A.8210(8) (microfilm copy)

Jones was coach to the University of Wisconsin.

58　Athletics / Harold M. Abrahams; foreword by Sir Montague Shearman. London: Harrap, 1926.
126p; illus
(Masters of sports)　　　　　　　　BL: 7920.aaa.11/7

59　Illustrated text-book of athletics / Carl Silfverstrand and Moritz Rasmussen. London: Athletic Publications, 1926.
190p; illus
*Foreword by H. B. Stallard;*
*translation of: Illustr. laerbog i fri jdraet*　BL: 7906.ccc.39

60　Running, walking and jumping: track and field athletics, a book on how to train / S. A. Mussabini. London: Foulsham, 1926.
94p; illus
(Foulsham's sports library; no. 6)　　BL: X.629/6605(6)

This must have seemed an old-fashioned approach, even in 1926. Mussabini was probably the last of the old-time trainer-coaches and had a highly successful career, specialising mainly in the training of sprinters. The chapters on running are fairly sound, but those on field events are extremely poor. One illustrative high-jump sequence, purportedly of Lewden (France), has the jumper changing his take-off leg several times in mid-sequence − a skill calculated to puzzle the cleverest.

61　Training for athletes / H. M. Abrahams and A. Abrahams in collaboration with Lord Burghley, D. G. A. Lowe, F. R. Gaby, B. Howard Baker and M. C. Nokes. London: G. Bell, 1928.
viii, 189p; illus　　　　　　　　　BL: 07912.ff.23

This book was well ahead of its time in outlook. The general chapters on training are undoubtedly the best written up to this point, and could be followed with profit even today. The athletic sections are given over to specialists (as was the chapter on training, written by Sir A. Abrahams) and represent the best in practical knowledge available at the time. Abrahams, undoubtedly under the influence of the great coach S. A. Mussabini, stresses cadence rather than stride-length in sprinting, a view which modern coaches have rejected. Similarly, his comments on the value of the hitch-kick have since been nullified. M. C. Nokes contributes a chapter on hammer-throwing which is a technical and literary gem. In discussing certain of the field events, the authors reflect the insularity then prevalent in English athletic circles. 'The only events excluded are the hop, step and jump, throwing the discus and javelin and the pole jump. The first-named calls for no special consideration; the discus and javelin cannot be considered to be British events; whilst the pole-jump, although originally an English pastime, now fails to secure any considerable following in this country, and there is not at the present time any exponent in England who is in a position to write with authority.'

62 Athletics / D. G. A. Lowe and A. E. Porritt. London: Longmans, Green, 1929.
x, 371p; illus; index                BL: 07905.l.44
  Includes contributions on throwing events from M. C. Nokes and high jump from C. T. Van Geyzel.

63 Athletics for men / F. A. M. Webster. London: A. Wander, 1929?
64p

64 Modern athletics / G. M. Butler; foreword by P. J. Noel Baker. Cambridge: Cambridge University Press, 1929.
xvi, 152p; illus                BL: 07905.l.46

65 Practical athletics and how to train / Alec Nelson. 2nd ed. London: Pearson, 1930.
126p; illus; index                BL: 07912.ee.62
  ☞  Previous ed. E53

66 Athletics: how to succeed / W. K. Duckett; foreword by Arthur E. Wotton. London: Evans, 1932.
32p; illus; pbk        BL: Mic.A.6745(14) (microfilm copy)
  ☞  Subsequent ed. E81

67 Exercises for athletes / F. A. M. Webster and J. A. Heys. London: Shaw, 1932.
247p; illus                BL: 7384.v.33

68 Modern athletics: how to train for the various events of the track and field programme / Lawson Robertson. London: Scribner's, 1932.
xii, 161p; illus        BL: Mic.A.12569(17) (microfilm copy)
  Coaching advice by one of the most famous of all American college coaches.

69 Athletic training for men and boys: a comprehensive system of training tables for all events / F. A. M. Webster and J. A. Heys. London: Shaw, 1933.
208p; illus

70 Charlie Hart's hints for all athletes and sportsmen / Charlie Hart. London: Hutchinson, 1933.
156p                BL: 7916.c.14
  Advice from the famous veteran ultra-distance runner. It is closer to Mussabini than Webster in outlook.

71 Service athletics: a manual of training especially prepared for the services, public schools and colleges / William S. P. Alexander and Ian E. F. Campbell. London: Crosby Lockwood, 1933.
133p; illus                BL: 7916.b.17

72 Text book of athletic training / Matthew J. Morgan. London: Athletic Publications, 1934.
83p; illus                BL: 7916.df.47

73 Track and field athletics / D. G. A. Lowe. London: Pitman, 1936.
x, 143p; illus
(Games and recreations series)        BL: W.P.11671/1
  A book which was a good guide to the sport in its time. The later editions, though revised, took little account of modern developments and are of limited value to the modern coach.
  ☞  Subsequent ed. E97

74 Training for health and athletics / H. M. Abrahams and Adolphe Abrahams. London: Hutchinson, 1936.
192p; illus                BL: 7391.pp.32

75 How to excel at games and athletics / A. M. Woollaston. London: Press & General Publicity Service, 1937.
80p                BL: 07908.h.54

76 Track and field athletics / G. T. Bresnahan and W. W. Tuttle. London: Kimpton, 1937.
497p; illus                BL: 7915.s.22
  A standard text book in its time, Track and Field Athletics is a dry, descriptive account of the athletics techniques of the period, with little in the way of practical advice on technical training or conditioning. It is interesting to note that Bresnahan submitted the first patent application (U.S. 1,701,206) for starting blocks on 5 February 1927. The blocks were composed of wood.
  ☞  Subsequent ed. E88

77 Why? – the science of athletics / F. A. M. Webster. London: Shaw, 1937.
388p; illus                BL: 7915.r.16
  In one of the best technical books prior to the Second World War, Webster examines the current theories of training and performance. The ideas of the Abrahams brothers, A. V. Hill, R. Tait Mackenzie, R. Salisbury Woods, D. G. A. Lowe, A. E. Porritt, A. F. H. Newton and others are described. Of particular interest is his account of the career of his protégé, Henry Simmons, who high-jumped for Britain in the 1928 Olympic Games while still a schoolboy, using an Eastern cut-off technique.
  ☞  Subsequent ed. E91

78 Athletics / John Hansen; translated by Norah Holtze; with 101 illustrations. London: Methuen, 1938.
ix, 127p; illus
  *Translation of: Athletik. Løb: Spring, Kast*  BL: 07908.h.46

79 Athletics / by Members of the Achilles Club; edited by B. G. D. Rudd; foreword by Lord Burghley. London: Dent, 1938.
xii, 308p; illus; index
(Modern sports)                BL: X.629/6646(6)
  Contributors include: A. Pennington, A. G. K. Brown, T. Hampson, J. E. Lovelock, E. A. Montague,

J. St. L. Thornton, R. M. N. Tisdall, L. T. Bond, R. L. Howland, D. R. Bell, M. C. Nokes, E. A. Hunter, H. M. Abrahams and Sir A. E. Porritt. This was one of the last major technical contributions of a club which had been seminal in the development of athletics in English public schools in the period between the wars. The Achilles Club's intelligent, empirical approach derived from personal experience rather than coaching, was soon to be overtaken by a more scientific approach led by AAA Director of Coaching G. H. G. Dyson.

☞   Subsequent ed. E98

80   Athletics and training / Guy Butler. London: A. & C. Black, 1938.
247p; illus
(Sportsman's library; vol. 26)          BL: W.P.2607/26

Butler's works, though essentially empirical in nature, always reflected the best thinking of British athletics of his period. He was always at his best on running and on the generic aspects of training, but invariably weak on field events, while he was unashamedly reactionary in his attitudes on triple jump: 'The secret of success in this rather queer form of athletics is the correct spacing of hop and step, so as to allow sufficient balance and momentum for the jump .... In this country, apart from a certain amount of enthusiasm in the North, very few athletes take any interest. The Japanese are especially well suited for it physically and they have taken it up with great gusto. I do not imagine it can ever gain much ground in this country.'

81   Athletics: how to succeed / W. K. Duckett. Rev. ed. London: Evans, 1938.
40p; illus; pbk          BL: Mic.A.6745(15) (microfilm copy)

☞   Previous ed. E66; subsequent ed. E94

82   Indoor athletics and winter training, with photographs and diagrams / F. A. M. Webster. London: Harrap, 1938.
213p; illus; index          BL: 07908.g.62

This is what Scots would call 'cauld kail het up' (cold soup heated up) and contains repetition of much of Webster's earlier works. It has little text specifically related to indoor athletics – not surprisingly, for the sport hardly existed in England at that time.

83   Fitness for athletic Eve: some practical hints for training / Mrs Muriel Cornell. London: A. Wander, 1939?
96p; illus
*Introduction by B. M. Turner*

Advice for women by a pioneer hurdler and long jumper, who held the native record for the latter event for twenty-three years.

84   Training for championship athletics / C. Ward Crampton. London: McGraw-Hill, 1939.
xxi, 303p; illus; index
(Whittlesey House sports series)          BL: 7913.r.15

85   Championship technique in track and field: a book for athletes, coaches, and spectators / Dean B. Cromwell in collaboration with Al Wesson. London: McGraw-Hill, 1941.
xii, 312p; illus
(Whittlesey House sports series)          BL: X.620/7713(12)

Without question this is the great coaching book of the first half of the twentieth century, and can be read with advantage even today. It is the product of applied knowledge of over a quarter of a century of coaching in the American university system. What distinguishes Cromwell's work is his humanity, and the book, rich in anecdote, is a jewel in the crown of athletics literature.

☞   Subsequent ed. E93

86   Athletics for women / F. A. M. Webster. London: A. Wander, 1946.
70p; illus

Training advice for women in preparation for the 1948 Olympics. Lists women's world records at February 1946.

87   Commonsense athletics / Arthur F. H. Newton. London: George Berridge, 1947.
75p; illus          BL: 7919.cc.4

Practical, eminently readable advice, entirely about distance running.

88   Track and field athletics / G. T. Bresnahan and W. W. Tuttle. 2nd ed. London: Kimpton, 1947.
498p; illus          BL: 7917.b.51

☞   Previous ed. E76; subsequent ed. E96

89   Athletic training / John Hansen; translated by Norah Holtze; illustrations by Svend Holtze. London: Methuen, 1948.
59p; illus
*Translation of: Atletiktræning*          BL: 7917.bb.40

90   The Oxford pocket book of athletic training / K. S. Duncan; foreword by Jack Lovelock. London: Oxford University Press, 1948.
84p; illus; pbk          BL: 7920.aa.15

☞   Subsequent ed. E106

91   The science of athletics / F. A. M. Webster. Rev. ed. London: Nicholas Kaye, 1948.
333p; illus          BL: 7918.bb.33

☞   Previous ed. E77

92   The way to win on track and field / Jack London; foreword by Joe Binks. London: D.P., 1948.
x, 85p; illus          BL: 7916.e.72

Jack London, from British Guyana, won a silver medal running for Britain in the 1928 Olympic 100m. The book is dated, with little to offer in any events other than the sprints.

93  Championship technique in track and field: a book for
    athletes, coaches, and spectators / Dean B. Cromwell in
    collaboration with Al Wesson. Olympic Games ed.
    London: McGraw-Hill, 1949.
    x, 333p; illus
    (Whittlesey House sports series)         BL: X.620/7713(13)
    Includes a new chapter containing Cromwell's
    observations of the 1948 Olympic Games in London.

    ☞  Previous ed. E85

94  Athletics: how to succeed / W. K. Duckett; foreword by
    Arthur E. Wotton. Rev. ed. London: Evans, 1950.
    48p; illus; pbk
         *Reissued: 1951*                      BL: 7920.l.17

    ☞  Previous ed. E81

95  Sportswoman's manual / edited by Susan Noel. London:
    Hutchinson's Library of Sports and Pastimes, 1950.
    251p; illus                              BL: W.P.1156/16
    Includes an article on women's athletics by Sylvia
    Cheeseman.

96  Track and field athletics / G. T. Bresnahan and W. W.
    Tuttle. 3rd ed. London: Kimpton, 1950.
    500p; illus                              BL: 7919.bb.32

    ☞  Previous ed. E88; subsequent ed. E105

97  Track and field athletics / D. G. A. Lowe. Rev. ed.
    London: Pitman, 1950.
    141p; illus; index
    (Games and recreations series)

    ☞  Previous ed. E73; subsequent ed. E116

98  Athletics / by the Achilles Club; edited by H. A. Meyer;
    foreword by the Rt. Hon. Philip Noel-Baker. Rev. ed.
    London: Dent, 1951.
    xxiv, 360p; illus; index
    (Modern sports)
         *H. A. Meyer is pseudonym for Hugh Merrick*
                                             BL: X.629/6646(9)
    Contributors include K. S. Duncan, Rev. N. D. Stacey,
    A. G. K. Brown, T. Hampson, R. G. Bannister,
    N. D. McWhirter, R. St. G. Harper, Lord Burghley,
    A. W. Selwyn, L. W. Davies, T. D. Anderson, H. E. Askew,
    R. L. Howland, H. Sivertsen, M. C. Nokes, C. J. Reidy,
    A. F. Hignell, E. A. Hunter, H. M. Abrahams, Sir
    A. E. Porritt and B. G. D. Rudd.

    ☞  Previous ed. E79; subsequent ed. E103

99  Fundamentals of track and field athletics / G. E.
    Gauthier and G. E. Hanley. London: Mayflower, 1951.

100 A guide to training / Leonard H. Ward. London:
    Women's Amateur Athletic Association, 1953.
    36p; pbk

101 Modern track and field: promotion, history, methods / J.
    Kenneth Doherty. London: Bailey & Swinfen, 1953.
    458p; illus; index
    (Books on health and sports series)
         *Originally published: New York: Prentice-Hall, 1953*
                                             BL: 7920.c.53
    By the mid 1960s Doherty's book and Bresnahan and
    Tuttle's Track and Field Athletics were the main works
    of reference in athletics in British colleges of physical
    education. Doherty's book is by far the better work,
    containing as a bonus a rich account of the evolution
    of American collegiate athletics since the beginning of
    the century. It is also a significant contribution to our
    knowledge of the technical history of athletics, since
    most technical evolution had been, for the first half of
    the century, American in origin. Doherty, like most
    American college coaches, lacked background in areas
    such as biomechanics and physiology. However, like
    Dean Cromwell, he had for many years coached
    athletes from a rich genetic pool. Doherty's book is
    therefore strong in pragmatic practical advice, and
    represented in many events the best knowledge of the
    period in the English language. This book should be read
    in tandem with Cromwell's earlier Championship
    Technique in Track and Field (E93). Together the books
    provide a vivid picture of American collegiate athletics
    at the middle of the century, at the end of its age of
    innocence.

    ☞  Subsequent ed. E125

102 Athletics / John Hickson Dodd. London: Educational
    Productions, 1955.
    40p; illus; pbk
    (Know the game)                          BL: W.P.3073/26

    ☞  Subsequent ed. E146

103 Athletics / by members of the Achilles Club; edited by
    H. A. Meyer; foreword by the Rt. Hon. Philip Noel-
    Baker. Further rev. ed. London: Dent, 1955.
    x, 375p; illus; index
    (Modern sports)
         *H. A. Meyer is pseudonym for Hugh Merrick*
                                             BL: X.629/6646(10)
    A further, revised edition in which C. J. Chataway and
    C. W. Brasher are contributors.

    ☞  Previous ed. E98; subsequent ed. 107

104 Weight training for athletics / Oscar State. London:
Amateur Athletic Association, 1955.
90p; illus                                              BL: 7922.de.19

The definitive work of its period on weight training.

☞ Subsequent ed. E113

105 Track and field athletics / G. T. Bresnahan and W. W.
Tuttle and Francis X. Cretzmeyer. 4th ed. London:
Kimpton, 1956.
528p; illus                                             BL: 7922.f.30

☞ Previous ed. E96; subsequent ed. E111

106 The Oxford pocket book of athletic training / Sandy
Duncan and Kenneth Bone; forewords by Jack Lovelock
and Roger Bannister. 2nd ed. London: Oxford University
Press, 1957.
xiv, 93p; illus                                         BL: 7923.f.18

☞ Previous ed. E90

107 Modern athletics / by Members of the Achilles Club;
edited by H. A. Meyer. London: Oxford University
Press, 1958.
x, 210p; illus
    *H. A. Meyer is pseudonym for Hugh Merrick*  BL: 7923.n.27
Contributors: W. R. Milligan, D. G. A. Lowe, T. Hampson,
H. M. Abrahams, ?. J. Noel-Baker, R. St. G. Harper,
K. P. Bone, A. G. K. Brown, K. S. Duncan,
R. G. Bannister, C. J. Chataway, C. W. Brasher,
I. H. Boyd, P. B. Hildreth, D. J. N. Johnson,
W. B. L. Palmer, A. R. Malcolm, Sir Arthur E. Porritt,
N. D. McWhirter. Although British athletics coaching,
driven by the AAA coaching scheme, had by this time
progressed to a more clinical, scientific approach,
there was still room for athlete-based books of this
type. The authors of the final edition (E124), sensitive
to the change in the athletic environment, moved to a
more general, less technical, approach.

☞ Subsequent ed. E103; subsequent ed. E124

108 Athletics: a coaching handbook for tropical areas /
Douglas J. T. Millar and John E. Cawley; foreword by
Malvin G. Whitfield. London: Evans, 1960.
128p; illus                                             BL: 7925.l.7

An illustrated handbook which covers the organisation
of athletics in schools, standards, the events in detail,
training and hints to officials.

109 Athletics: how to become a champion: a discursive
textbook / Percy Wells Cerutty; photographs by M. A.
Stratton. London: Stanley Paul, 1960.
190p; illus                                             BL: 7925.bb.19

A fine inspirational work by one of the world's greatest
middle-distance coaches.
'Athleticism, in my view, is not a sport: nor a cult: it is a
way of life. In my day, I have tried many things — and
from all I turned away, eventually, to turn to
athleticism .... It means to me, all activities that are
based in sweat and effort — and are something added

to our normal, ordinary everyday way of life.'
Cerutty, coach to 1960 Olympic 1500m champion,
Herb Elliott, was an eccentric, a coaching maverick
whose technical and physiological theories do not bear
much scrutiny. He was, however, possessed of great
inspirational qualities, and the sands of Portsea
became the testing-ground for some of the greatest
middle-distance runners of the period.

110 Ballet exercises for athletes / devised by Andrew Hardie;
illustrated by Fougasse. London: Issued by the Amateur
Athletic Association in collaboration with the Royal
Academy of Dancing, 1960.
24p; illus
    *Fougasse is a pseudonym for Cyril Kenneth Bird*
                                                        BL: 7926.c.26

As with early books on weight-training, Hardie's book
ignores the specificity of athletic fitness, making the
assumption that the essentially balletic mobility of
dancers would automatically benefit track and field
athletes. This type of exercise gained little credence
during the 1960s.

☞ Subsequent ed. E161

111 Track and field athletics / George T. Bresnahan, W. W.
Tuttle, Francis X. Cretzmeyer. 5th ed. London:
Kimpton, 1960.
538p; illus                                             BL: 7925.b.90

☞ Previous ed. E105; subsequent ed. E126

112 Track and field for coach and athlete / Jesse P.
Mortensen and John Miller Cooper. London:
Prentice-Hall, 1960.
x, 246p; illus                                          BL: 7925.c.31

☞ Subsequent ed. E138

113 Weight training for athletics / Oscar State. London:
Amateur Athletic Association, 1960.
84p; illus                                              BL: 7922.de.19

The definitive work of its period on weight training.

☞ Previous ed. E104

114 Athletics / Peter Bird; foreword by Jack Crump.
London: Foyle, 1961.
94p; illus; index                                       BL: W.P.2940/251

A survey of the sport which gives a brief account of the
events, but little on training. The book is recommended
for its lucid chapters on the structure and facilities of
the sport.

115 Track and field athletics / Hugh A. L. Chapman; edited
and introduced by Harold M. Abrahams. London:
Foulsham, 1961.
96p; illus
(New sports library; no. 10)                            BL: 7923.nn.1/10

Possibly the best pocket-book yet written on
athletics. Pungent and concise.

116 Track and field athletics / D. G. A. Lowe. 2nd (i.e. 3rd) ed. London: Pitman, 1961.
x, 116p; illus; index
(Games and recreations series)     BL: W.P.11671/60

☞ Previous ed. E97

117 Athletics / Peter Hildreth. London: Arco, 1962.
160p; illus; index
(Handybook)     BL: X.449/74

An historical summary of each standard event followed by advice on technique.

118 The mechanics of athletics / Geoffrey H. G. Dyson. London: University of London Press, 1962.
202p; illus; index     BL: 7926.cc.38

Dyson's work is undoubtedly the most authoritative piece of writing on its subject in the English language. Whatever may be written in the future, his book will have an honoured place in the literature.
'With teachers and coaches, however, a knowledge of mechanics is an essential tool with which to distinguish between important and unimportant, correct and incorrect, cause and effect, possible and impossible.'

☞ Subsequent ed. E121

119 Athletics / edited by G. F. D. Pearson; drawings by A. Burgess Sharrocks. Edinburgh: Thomas Nelson, 1963.
402p; illus     BL: 7926.pp.27

Contributors: A. G. K. Brown, A. C. Elder, H. Wilson, P. B. Hildreth, J. I. Disley, D. W. J. Anthony, H. H. Lockwood, K. J. Brookman, Father J. Coulthard, A. A. Gold, K. D. Whaling, G. J. Pallett, G. F. D. Pearson. Possibly the finest fruit of the AAA Coaching Scheme. The book is on a symposium basis, with separate chapters written by AAA senior coaches. The terms of reference and the quality of the chapters vary considerably, but there are particularly strong contributions on middle distance, discus, hammer and javelin. A work for the coach and student of physical education, rather than the enquiring athlete.

120 Athletics – how to win / edited by Peter Hildreth. London: Heinemann, 1963.
ix, 185p; illus     BL: 7926.f.45

Contributors: G. H. G. Dyson, D. J. N. Johnson, D. A. G. Pirie, P. F. Radford, J. D. Wrighton, G. M. Elliott, J. I. Disley, V. C. Matthews, J. A. Savidge, C. W. Brasher, M. J. Ellis.

121 The mechanics of athletics / Geoffrey H. G. Dyson. 2nd ed. London: University of London Press, 1963.
224p; illus; index

☞ Previous ed. E118; subsequent ed. E123

122 What's what in athletics? / Peter Hildreth. London: Newman Neame Take Home Books, 1963.
15p; illus; pbk     BL: 7926.n.5

A basic introduction to the sport, it contains a brief outline of its history, progress in men's records, and descriptions of events.

123 The mechanics of athletics / Geoffrey H. G. Dyson. 3rd ed. London: University of London Press, 1964.
224p; illus; index

☞ Previous ed. E121; subsequent ed. E131

124 Modern athletics / by Members of the Achilles Club; edited by H. A. Meyer. London: Oxford University Press, 1964.
x, 211p; illus
*H. A. Meyer is pseudonym for Hugh Merrick* BL: 7926.w.44

Contributors: Rt. Hon. Lord Milligan, H. M. Abrahams, P. J. Noel-Baker, R. St. G. Harper, K. S. Duncan, K. P. Bone, A. G. K. Brown, R. G. Bannister, C. J. Chataway, H. J. Elliott, P. B. Hildreth, A. P. Metcalfe, A. R. Malcolm, A. R. McWhirter, Sir A. E. Porritt, N. D. McWhirter, and H. A. Meyer (Hugh Merrick). The two editions of Modern Athletics show a distinctly different editorial policy from the Achilles Club's earlier Athletics (1938 etc). Advice on the technique for each event is replaced by 'a collection of essays by a number of the Club's outstanding performers on their experiences of top-flight athletics as affecting their every-day lives; on the trend of things to come and the ever quickening tempo of the athlete's struggle to achieve success; and on the possible solution of some of the many problems confronting British athletes in the future.' This broader scope permits the inclusion of articles on photography and athletics (H. A. Meyer), sports journalism (A. R. McWhirter), the psychological approach (R. G. Bannister) and the future of athletics (H. M. Abrahams). This form of book was a refreshing development in athletics literature, so long monopolised mainly by technical advice and biographies.

☞ Previous ed. E107

125 Modern track and field / John Kenneth Doherty. 2nd ed. London: Bailey & Swinfen, 1964.
xiv, 557p; illus
*Originally published: New York: Prentice-Hall, 1963*
BL: X.449/11

☞ Previous ed. E101

126 Track and field athletics / George T. Bresnahan, W. W. Tuttle, Francis X. Cretzmeyer. 6th ed. London: Kimpton, 1964.
424p; illus     BL: 07926.a.15

☞ Previous ed. E111; subsequent ed. E135

127 Strength training for athletics / Ron Pickering. London: Amateur Athletic Association, 1965.
72p; illus; pbk
(Instructional booklet)                    BL: X.449/1579

  Pickering brings greater specificity to the use of weights in athletics, in what was the definitive work of its period.

  ☞  Subsequent ed. E133

128 Athletics for student and coach / Ian Ward and Denis Watts. London: Pelham, 1967.
176p; illus                                BL: X.449/2688

  A work written 'primarily for the club coach and the student in college or university'.

  ☞  Subsequent ed. E149

129 Better athletics (with illustrations based on films of Olympic athletics) / A. G. L. Ventre. London: Educational Productions, 1967.
25p; illus; pbk                            BL: X.449/2510

  Largely a book of illustrations.

130 The manual of weight-training / edited by George Kirkley and John Goodbody. London: Stanley Paul, 1967.
x, 161p; illus                             BL: X.449/2360

  Includes 17 pages on weight training for athletics by Ron Pickering.

131 The mechanics of athletics / Geoffrey H. G. Dyson; illustrations by D. R. Dimmock. 4th ed. London: University of London Press, 1967.
224p; illus; index             ISBN: 0-340-08905-9

  ☞  Previous ed. E123; subsequent ed. E139

132 Illustrated guide to Olympic track and field techniques / edited by Tom Ecker and Fred Wilt. London: Faber and Faber, 1968.
256p; illus

  Each Olympic event is illustrated by action-sequence photographs by Toni Nett and John L. Griffith. Commentaries are written by John Disley, Geoff Elliott, Mike Ellis, Dick Ganslen, Geoff Gowan, Peter Hildreth, Fred Housden, Ron Jewkes, Payton Jordan, John Le Masurier, Les Mitchell, Geoffrey Pearson, Ron Pickering, John Powell, Tony Ward, Cornelius Warmerdam and Denis Watts.

133 Strength training for athletics / Ron Pickering. 2nd ed. London: Amateur Athletic Association, 1968.
72p; illus; pbk                            BL: W.P.3877/36

  ☞  Previous ed. E127; subsequent ed. E148

134 Better athletics / John Heaton. London: Kaye & Ward, 1969.
96p; illus                      ISBN: 0-7182-0155-8
                                           BL: X.449/3897

135 Bresnahan and Tuttle's track and field athletics / Francis X. Cretzmeyer, Louis E. Alley, Charles M. Tipton. 7th ed. London: Kimpton, 1969.
ix, 317p; illus                 ISBN: 0-85313-689-0
                                           BL: X.441/1315

  ☞  Previous ed. E126; subsequent ed. E145

136 Champions in the making: quality training for track and field / Payton Jordan, Bud Spencer. London: Pelham, 1969.
vii, 280p; illus; index
  *Originally published: Englewood Cliffs, USA: Prentice-Hall, 1968*                ISBN: 0-7207-0016-7
                                           BL: X.441/1232

  A strong technical manual, though lacking in theoretical basis.

137 Track and field / consultant Don Canham. Folkestone: Bailey & Swinfen, 1970.
128p; chiefly illus
(Athletic Institute series)     ISBN: 0-561-00082-4
                                           BL: X.629/3134

  For beginners, but not necessarily children.

138 Track and field for coach and athlete / John M. Cooper with James Lavery, William Perrin. 2nd ed. Hemel Hempstead: Prentice-Hall, 1970.
xvii, 270p; illus; index        ISBN: 0-13-925750-0

  ☞  Previous ed. E112

139 The mechanics of athletics / Geoffrey H. G. Dyson. 5th ed. London: University of London Press, 1971.
229p; illus; index
  *Bibliography: p222-224*       ISBN: 0-340-08905-9

  ☞  Previous ed. E131; E142

140 Mobility exercises / Peter R. Harper. London: British Amateur Athletic Board, 1972.
63p; illus; pbk
(Instructional booklet)         ISBN: 0-85134-030-X

141 Athletics for the 70's: a training manual / Denis Watts and Antony Ward. London: Barker, 1973.
vii, 225p; illus                ISBN: 0-213-16417-5
                                           BL: X.629/5326

142 The mechanics of athletics / Geoffrey H. G. Dyson. 6th ed. London: University of London Press, 1973.
240p; illus; index              ISBN: 0-340-17442-0
                                           BL: X.629/5603

  ☞  Previous ed. E139; subsequent ed. E151

143 Athletics / compiled by Tony Burrett. London: Macdonald and Jane's, 1974.
63p; illus, maps; index
(Macdonald library of sport)　　　　ISBN: 0-356-04892-6
　　　　　　　　　　　　　　　　　BL: X.622/1885

The work contains a mélange of items: great moments in athletics (Hemery, Meyfarth, Wottle, Beamon and Keino at the Olympic Games), training tactics and technique, how athletics began, track and field, and the Highland Games. Among the topics discussed are the effects of altitude on performance and organisational differences between countries. The end-papers carry colour reproductions of 35 stamps featuring athletics.

144 Modern techniques of track and field / Clarence F. Robinson and others. London: Kimpton, 1974.
viii, 349p; illus; index　　　　　　ISBN: 0-8121-0424-2
　　　　　　　　　　　　　　　　　BL: X.620/7482

145 Track and field athletics / Francis X. Cretzmeyer, Louis E. Alley, Charles M. Tipton. 8th ed. London: Kimpton, 1974.
ix, 329p; illus; index　　　　　　　ISBN: 0-8016-1075-3

　　☞　Previous ed. E135

146 Athletics / Carl T. Johnson. 2nd ed. Wakefield: EP Publishing for the British Amateur Athletic Board, 1975.
41p; illus; pbk
(Know the game)　　　　　　　　　ISBN: 0-7158-0203-8
　　　　　　　　　　　　　　　　　BL: WP.3073/153

　　☞　Previous ed. E102; subsequent ed. E165

147 Learning to be a better athlete: all in colour / contributors John Le Masurier, David R. Kay, Carl T. Johnson; illustrations by 'Prof'. Glasgow: Collins, 1975.
61p; illus　　　　　　　　　　　　ISBN: 0-00-103331-X
　　　　　　　　　　　　　　　　　BL: X.625/148

Large format book for children.

148 Strength training for athletics: instructional booklet / Ron Pickering. New ed. London: British Amateur Athletic Board, 1975.

　　☞　Previous ed. E133; subsequent ed. E155

149 Athletics for student and coach / Ian Ward & Denis Watts. London: Pelham, 1976.
180p; illus　　　　　　　　　　　ISBN: 0-7207-0881-8
　　　　　　　　　　　　　　　　　BL: X.629/10412

　　☞　Previous ed. E128

150 Track and field athletics / Wilf Paish. London: Lepus, 1976.
266p; illus　　　　　　　　　　　ISBN: 0-86019-005-6
　　　　　　　　　　　　　　　　　BL: X.622/5297

The first major work by one of Britain's greatest all-round coaches.

151 The mechanics of athletics / Geoffrey H. G. Dyson. 7th ed. London: Hodder and Stoughton, 1977.
267p; illus; index　　　　　　　　ISBN: 0-340-20034-0
　　　　　　　　　　　　　　　　　BL: X.629/11445

　　☞　Previous ed. E142; subsequent ed. E167

152 Success in athletics / Carl Johnson. London: John Murray, 1977.
96p; illus
(Success sportsbooks)　　　　　　ISBN: 0-7195-3375-9
　　　　　　　　　　　　　　　　　BL: X.629/11299

153 Complete track and field athletics / Robin Sykes. London: Kaye and Ward, 1978.
288p; illus　　　　　　　　　　　ISBN: 0-7182-1185-5
　　　　　　　　　　　　　　　　　BL: X.629/12092

154 Dynamic track and field / Jim Bush with Don Weiskopf. London: Allyn and Bacon, 1978.
xv, 512p; index　　　　　　　　　ISBN: 0-205-06004-8
　　　　　　　　　　　　　　　　　BL: X.620/17801

155 Strength training for athletics: instructional booklet / Frank Dick, Carl Johnson, Wilf Paish. New ed. London: British Amateur Athletic Board, 1978.
illus; pbk

　　☞　Previous ed. E148; subsequent ed. E172

156 Track and field: an administrative approach to the science of coaching / Ralph E. Steben, Sam Bell. Chichester: Wiley, 1978.
xiv, 340p; illus; index　　　　　　ISBN: 0-471-02546-1
　　　　　　　　　　　　　　　　　BL: X.620/17621

157 Enjoying track and field sports / Diagram Group. London: Paddington Press, 1979.
160p; illus; index; pbk　　　　　　ISBN: 0-7092-0152-4
　　　　　　　　　　　　　　　　　BL: X.611/9182

158 The complete book of athletics / Tom McNab. London: Ward Lock, 1980.
208p; illus; index　　　　　　　　ISBN: 0-7063-5927-5
　　　　　　　　　　　　　　　　　BL: X.622/10818

An unusual work, covering the history of athletics and a descriptive/historical/technical account of each event. It is particularly rich in its historical section.

159 Sports training principles / Frank W. Dick. London: Lepus, 1980.
x, 275p; illus; index; pbk　　　　　ISBN: 0-860190-36-6
　　　　　　　　　　　　　　　　　BL: X.629/14391

The definitive work on modern athletics training, bringing together the best of sports training theory.

　　☞　Subsequent ed. E171

160 Athletics fundamentals / Jess Jarver. Newton Abbot:
David & Charles, 1981.
88p; illus
*Originally published: Sydney, Australia: Reed, 1980*
ISBN: 0-7153-8189-X
BL: X.622/12688

161 Ballet exercises for athletes: simple stretching and
suppling routines / Arthur Gold & Andrew Hardie.
London: Charles Elliott, 1983.

☞  Previous ed. E110

162 Athletics / Dave Grosvenor. Cambridge: Cambridge
University Press, 1984.
48p; illus; pbk
(Sport masters)                                    ISBN: 0-521-27145-2
BL: X.622/20574

163 Athletics / Simon Turnbull. Newton Abbot: David &
Charles, 1984.
64p; illus
(Sportsviewers guide)                          ISBN: 0-7153-8534-8
BL: X.629/24154

164 The new Observer's book of athletics / Steve Brennan;
with drawings by Geoff Harrold. London: Warne, 1984.
192p; illus; pbk                                  ISBN: 0-7232-1677-0

165 Track and field athletics / Carl T. Johnson. 3rd ed.:
revised by AAA/BAAB officials. London: A. & C. Black,
1984.
44p; illus, plans; pbk
(Know the game)                                  ISBN: 0-7136-5580-1

☞  Previous ed. E146

166 Athletes in action: the official International Amateur
Athletic Federation book on track and field techniques /
edited by Howard Payne; editorial board, Jim Alford,
Frank Dick, Helmar Hommel; photo-sequences Helmar
Hommel, Howard Payne; additional photographs Tony
Duffy. London: Pelham, 1985.
317p; illus; index
(IAAF development programme book; no. 5)
ISBN: 0-7207-1509-1
BL: X.622/24577

167 Dyson's Mechanics of athletics / Geoffrey H. G. Dyson.
8th ed.; revised by B. D. Woods, P. R. Travers. London:
Hodder and Stoughton, 1986.
x, 258p; illus; index; pbk
ISBN: 0-340-39172-3
BL: YC.1986.a.4732

☞  Previous ed. E151

168 Mobility training / Norman Brook. London: British
Amateur Athletic Board, 1986.
98p; illus; pbk
(Instructional booklet)                         ISBN: 0-85134-079-2
BL: YK.1988.a.3280

169 Wheelchair sports: technique and training in athletics /
Ray Clark; translated by Krishna Ehrenstrale. Cambridge:
Woodhead-Faulkner, 1986.
vii, 112p; illus; index; pbk
*Translation of: Rullstolsidrott*                ISBN: 0-85941-352-7
BL: YK.1987.a.7498

170 Athletes in action / David Hemery. London: Stanley
Paul, 1987.
92p; illus; pbk                                   ISBN: 0-09-166601-5
BL: YK.1987.a.7030

171 Sports training principles / Frank W. Dick. 2nd ed.
London: A. & C. Black, 1989.
288p; illus; index; pbk                          ISBN: 0-7136-5644-1
BL: YK.1990.b.8682

☞  Previous ed. E159; subsequent ed. E174

172 Strength training / Max Jones. Birmingham: British
Amateur Athletic Board, 1990.
86p; illus; pbk                                   ISBN: 0-85134-097-0
BL: YK.1992.a.3404

☞  Previous ed. E155

173 Athletic sports / Diagram Group. London: Franklin
Watts, 1992.
35p; illus; index
(Sports facts)                                    ISBN: 0-7496-0885-4
BL: YK.1992.b.7514

A sound general guide to track and field, cross-
country and road running with sections on major
competitions, world records and discontinued events,
venues of Olympic Games, Commonwealth Games,
World Student Games and World Championships, Hall
of Fame, miscellaneous facts and exercise physiology.

174 Sports training principles / Frank W. Dick. 3rd ed.
London: A. & C. Black, 1997.
ix, 309p; illus; index; pbk                      ISBN: 0-7136-4149-5
BL: YK.1997.b.488

☞  Previous ed. E171

175 Best runs / Joe Henderson. Leeds: Human Kinetics, 1999.
xiv, 239p; illus; index; pbk                     ISBN: 0-88011-896-2
BL: YK.1999.a.9772

✳  *Additional References*

176 A handbook of gymnastics / George Forrest. London:
Routledge, 1858.
*George Forrest is a pseudonym for John George Wood*
BL: Mic.A.7129(10) (microfilm copy)

One of a series entitled 'Routledge's sixpenny
handbooks'. This book was a companion to The
Handbook of Manly Exercises by Stonehenge (1864).
The subject matter included vaulting and jumping. It is
worth observing that several Scottish Border Games
were called 'gymnastic' games.

177 How to train / John Levett. London: Newbold, 1862.

Levett, one of the outstanding professionals of the previous decade, had set a record of 51 mins 45.0 secs. for 10 miles and later retired to Dublin, where he became the leading figure in sporting circles. His book surveys most of the eminent trainers and pedestrians of the day, describes their successes and explains his own methods. 'Thomas Hosspool of Basford, once champion one mile runner, ran one mile at the Copenhagen Grounds, Manchester, in 4 mins 23 secs, defeated by the Great H A [i.e. H A Reed] in a half-mile race for the belt and £50 at Halifax, by 1yd., after an accident at the bottom turn, about 150yds. from the finish. The edge of the race track, which was raised ground, gave way to his foot, just as Tom, as he tells me, was going to tell the Great H A to write home to his friends. This unprecedented half-mile race was run in 1 min. 58 secs. Any man to have beaten either that day would have known they had been running when the race was concluded.'

178 Physical training and how to run, walk and jump / Henry Howard. London: Privately published, 1862.

Howard was a well-known professional athlete, and his book proved very popular.

179 Practical training for the million, or, How to run, walk, jump, box, ride, row, etc. London: Harrison, 1862.
32p; illus

Both editions are particularly interesting for their engravings (the first has 26, the second 50) which include studies of some of the earliest 'amateur' runners in the modern athletic era, including Capt. Patten Saunders who claimed to be the European champion, R. D. Barbor, and J. Macdonald. All the outstanding professionals are also portrayed, and they include Howard the jumper, Levett, Lang, Mills, Brighton and Deerfoot, in various spectacular costumes.

☞ Subsequent ed. E180

180 The complete practical training for the million and guide to the gymnasium. 2nd ed. London: Harrison, 1863.
32p; illus

☞ Previous ed. E179

181 The handbook of manly exercises: comprising boxing, walking, running, leaping, vaulting, etc., with chapters on training for pedestrianism and other purposes / 'Stonehenge', 'Forrest' and others. London: Routledge, Warne & Routledge, 1864.
64p

*Authors are John H. Walsh, John George Wood and others*
BL: 7907.a.50

One of the 'Routledge's sixpenny handbooks'. The text covers training, management, diet and the treatment of accidents occurring in training.

182 Hints on training / John Graham Chambers. London: 1868?

Chambers was a leading figure in the Amateur Athletic Club.

183 Manly exercises, sports and games / by the Champion Players of Old England. London: Dean, 1877.
518p; illus

The sections on walking and running are by Charles Westhall. There are also sections on jumping and pole leaping.

184 Athletic training: prize essays / Robert Vernon Somers-Smith, G. P. Beckley, and A. W. Pollard. London: Simpkin, Marshall, 1882.
48p     BL: Mic.A.15616(11) (microfilm copy)

The essays were submitted for a competition held by London Athletic Club. Somers-Smith, of Oxford University, was a well-known half-miler in the late 1860s.

185 Training simplified: a guide to good health / Robert P. Watson. London: Sands, 1899.
105p

Includes much anecdotal material about nineteenth century athletics.

186 Training / W. G. George. London: Southwood Smith, 1902.
134p; illus
(Athletics and kindred sports; section 2)
*No further volumes in the series were published*
BL: 7907.ff.28

Advice for each event from the great distance runner and contributors, including his brother, A. B. George, on 'American methods' and Hugh W. Innes on walking. A clear picture is given of the training methods of nineteenth century professionals, which had changed little since the days of Captain Barclay, until George's mixture of over- and under-distance work, with periodic time-trials, made a real step towards modern methods.

187 The application of weight training to athletics / Gene Hooks. London: Prentice-Hall International, 1962.
xiii, 254p; illus     BL: 7926.a.17

Covers many sports, including athletics, and includes a bibliography.

188 Skill in sport: the attainment of proficiency / Barbara Naomi Knapp. London: Routledge & Kegan Paul, 1963.
xii, 203p; illus     BL: 7926.k.24

The outstanding British work on the acquisition of physical skills. Of great value to the athletics coach and physical educationalist.

189 Senior coach: coaching theory manual. Birmingham: British Athletic Federation, 1982.
    1 looseleaf vol.; illus; pbk          ISBN: 0-85134-108-X
                                          BL: YK.1995.b.665

    ☞   Subsequent ed. E191

190 Track and field: how champions are made / Peter Batty. London: Evans, 1982.
    32p; illus; index; pbk
    *Originally published: Mahwah, N.J.: Troll Associates, 1975*
                                          ISBN: 0-237-29349-8
                                          BL: X.629/19781

191 Senior coach: coaching theory manual. Birmingham: British Athletic Federation, 1992.
    1 looseleaf vol.; illus          ISBN: 0-85134-108-X
                                     BL: YK.1995.b.665

    Written by the BAF national coaches and edited by Malcolm Arnold.

    ☞   Previous ed. E189

# *Training for Beginners & Juniors*

192 The boy's own book: a complete encyclopædia of all the diversions, athletic, scientific and recreative, of boyhood and youth / William Clarke. London: Vizetelly, Branston, 1828.
    447p                                  BL: 1040.a.4
    A general work, typical of several published about this time, with an interesting section on gymnastic exercises which describes how the widespread popularity of German gymnastics in the first few decades of the century was followed by a rapid decline. The book selects 'exercises which are free from objection', and advises on walking, running, the long leap, the 'high leap with the pole', hop, step and jump and the javelin.

193 The book of sports, athletic exercises, and amusements / William Martin. London: Darton & Clark, 1837?
    238p                                  BL: 1040.a.5
    A book for boys by a schoolmaster.

194 Athletic training for school boys / edited by George W. Orton. London: British Sports Publishing, 1907.
    96p; illus; pbk
    (Spalding's athletic library; no. 16)     BL: 07908.i.14/16
    By the famous Canadian distance runner and 1900 Olympic steeplechase champion. Contains over 40 photographs.

195 A handbook on athletics for the beginner / F. W. H. Nicholas; forewords by R. J. Kentish, R. B. Campbell and R. A. Ray. Aldershot: W. May, 1922.
    xii, 54p
        *Author's name appears incorrectly on the title page as F. H. W. Nicholas*
                                          BL: D
    Written primarily for the army, the text is couched in parade-ground style, but offers the best advice available at the time. The author sprinted for Oxford against Cambridge.

196 Athletics for boys / G. R. Renwick. London: Herbert Jenkins, 1926.
    192p; illus                           BL: 7904.ee.34

197 Athletics for schoolboys / F. A. M. Webster. London: A. Wander, 1928?
    74p

198 How to become an athlete: practical hints for boys and girls. London: Schools Athletic Association, 1928.
    111p; illus; pbk
    Includes articles by H. M. Abrahams, Capt. Evan Hunter, D. G. A Lowe, and Capt. F. A. M. Webster.

199 Improve your athletics: a book for modern girls / A. M. A. Williams. London: University of London Press, 1934.
    xii, 118p; illus                      BL: 7916.eee.8
    After justifying athletics as educationally valuable, the author gives chapters on: the choice of events; running; sprint starts; relay racing; the high jump; the standing long jump; hurdling; and athletic competition. The book is illustrated by photos of leading women athletes.

200 The young athlete / R. M. N. Tisdall in collaboration with Fenn Sherie, with a prefatory note by the Very Rev. C. A. Alington. London: Blackie, 1934.
    160p; illus                           BL: 7916.e.2
    The author begins with the statement, 'I never realised before that athletes could be such fun!' and proceeds to communicate his own love of the sport in a book which must have encouraged many to compete. Tisdall describes his own career and then speaks of the value of training, before describing the technique of preparing for individual events. The chapter on 'The art of hurdling' is understandably the most interesting but perhaps the most inspiring chapter is the final one,

'The Olympic Games,' in which he recounts his victory in the 400m hurdles at Los Angeles in 1932.

'As I stood on my marks I remember realising that I had never before felt so gloriously fit, and I could not believe it was the race over which I had dreamed and schemed for months – the race of my life, in which I was pitted against the greatest hurdlers in the world. Somebody blew a whistle. The starter shouted "Get to your marks!" A deathly silence fell on the huge crowd. I thought I heard a clock strike three somewhere. Noticing Lord Burghley just in front of me, I had the strange feeling for the moment that we must still be at Fenners and that the clock was the old one we used to hear at Cambridge.

"Get set!"

I tautened my muscles and waited. Heavens! Would the starter never fire that gun?

Bang. We were off!'

Tisdall's book is a marvellous evocation of athletics in the pre-war period. It features a wonderful photograph of Tisdall in the Shrewsbury School sports, hurdling using the 'Old English' technique.

201 The young athlete: an athletic handbook for beginners / edited by George Peat; foreword by the Duke of Hamilton. Edinburgh: Scottish Athletic Federation, 1941.
64p; illus; pbk

202 Athletics / Jack Crump. London: Raymond Press for Sporting Record, 1948.
40p; illus; pbk
(Play the game; no. 2)
    *Foreword by Harold M. Abrahams*    BL: W.P.7904/2

203 Athletics. London: National Association of Girls' Clubs and Mixed Clubs, 1952.
7p; pbk

A small booklet which includes tables and a bibliography.

204 In athletics … do it this way: learn your athletics from photographs / Sandy Duncan; with photographs by John Barlee and a foreword by Lord Burghley. London: John Murray, 1952.
96p; illus    BL: 7919.a.33

205 Athletics for boys & girls / Joseph Edmundson and Charles R. E. Burnup; foreword by Geoffrey H. G. Dyson. London: Bell, 1954.
135p; illus    BL: 7921.aaa.55

&#9758;  Subsequent ed. E209

206 Teach yourself athletics / F. N. S. Creek. London: English Universities Press, 1954.
192p; illus
(Teach yourself books)
    BL: W.P.706/150

207 The Olympic approach to athletics / Stan Tomlin. London: A. Wander, 1956.
64p

208 Instructions to young athletes / Robert M. C. Bateman. London: Museum Press, 1957.
124p; illus    BL: 7922.g.19

One of the last works of the Oxbridge culture. Dated and lacking in technical content.

209 Athletics for boys & girls / Joseph Edmundson and Charles R. E. Burnup. Rev. ed. London: Bell, 1961.
136p; illus    BL: 7923.ttt.24

&#9758;  Previous ed. E205; subsequent ed. E214

210 The young athlete's companion: an authoritative guide to training for all track and field events / John I. Disley. London: Souvenir, 1962.
142p; illus    BL: X.449/96

One of the best books for beginners of the period. Disley is at his best with running events and the sections on middle-distance running and the steeplechase are outstanding. 'Success nowadays is due to 10 per cent inspiration and 90 per cent perspiration. Natural ability will get you started but well directed work only will lead you to the rostrum. This work may well have to continue for several years before success comes – training in the winter as well as the summer. Great athletes are planted in the winter, cultivated in the spring and bloom in the summer. The size and perfection of the flower will increase each year as the roots dig down each winter and become strong and mature.'

211 Schoolboy athletics / Percy Wells Cerutty. London: Stanley Paul, 1963.
120p; illus    BL: 7926.f.29

This is essentially a pot-boiler, for Cerutty had no real experience in this area.

212 Tackle athletics this way / Denis C. V. Watts; foreword by Jack C. G. Crump. London: Stanley Paul, 1964.
135p; illus    BL: X.449/177

A guide for young athletes which covers the technical essentials for each event.

&#9758;  Subsequent ed. E225

213 Your book of athletics / Rex Van Rossum. London: Faber & Faber, 1964.
59p; illus
(Your book)    BL: 7926.w.1
Another dying Oxbridge flutter.

214 Athletics for boys and girls / Joseph Edmundson and Charles R. E. Burnup. 3rd ed. London: Bell, 1965.
134p; illus    BL: X.449/1291

&#9758;  Previous ed. E209

215  Track and field for boys / Payton Jordan with Marshall K. McClelland. London: Pelham, 1965.
109p; illus
(Schools library)
*Originally published in the US in 1960*        BL: X.449/1255

216  Athletics / David Lionel Pugh. London: Weidenfeld & Nicolson, 1966.
80p
(The sports for schools series)

217  Track and field fundamentals for girls and women / Frances Wakefield, Dorothy Harkins; with the editorial collaboration of John M. Cooper. Saint Louis: Mosby; distributed in Great Britain by Henry Kimpton, 1966.
x, 263p; illus; index                          BL: X.441/662

☞  Subsequent ed. E222

218  Bovril guide for young athletes / Robbie and Ann Brightwell; foreword by Ron Pickering. London: Bovril, 1967.
8p; pbk
A booklet issued free.

219  Track and field for girls and women / Virginia Parker, Robert Kennedy; illustrated by James Bonner. London: Saunders, 1969.
ii-xii, 115p; illus; pbk            ISBN: 0-7216-7070-9
                                                    BL: X.441/1266

220  Modern schools athletics / edited by Tom McNab. London: University of London Press, 1970.
207p; illus                              SBN: 340-09456-7
                                                    BL: X.620/2214

The definitive book of its period on the subject, Modern Schools Athletics is essentially a series of chapters on the curricular teaching of athletics. Like all books of its kind, it is variable in quality and for the most part operates at too high a technical level. Its best sections are the taped discussions between the author, Wilf Paish, John Anderson and Alan Launder, and the author's opening chapter on basic teaching philosophy.

221  Track and field for college men / Robert E. Kennedy; illustrated by James Bonner. London: Saunders, 1970.
vi, 122p; illus; pbk                ISBN: 0-7216-5384-7
                                                    BL: X.611/2404

222  Track and field fundamentals for girls and women / Frances Wakefield, Dorothy Harkins; with John M. Cooper. 2nd ed. Saint Louis: Mosby; distributed in Great Britain by Henry Kimpton, 1970.
x, 264p; illus; index                 SBN: 8016-5326-6
                                                    BL: X.622/778

☞  Previous ed. E217; subsequent ed. E223

223  Track & field: fundamentals for girls and women / Frances Wakefield, Dorothy Harkins with John M. Cooper. 3rd ed. Saint Louis: Mosby; distributed in Great Britain by Henry Kimpton, 1973.
xvi, 295p; illus; index             ISBN: 0-8016-5327-4
                                                    BL: X.622/1670

☞  Previous ed. E222; subsequent ed. E228

224  Introduction to athletics / Wilf Paish. London: Faber, 1974.
122p; illus                              ISBN: 0-571-10191-7
                                                    BL: X.629/6669

225  Tackle athletics / Denis Watts. London: Stanley Paul, 1974.
168p; illus                              ISBN: 0-09-122240-0
                                                    BL: X.629/6924

☞  Previous ed. E212

226  Athletics for schools / Denis Watts and Bill Marlow. London: Pelham, 1976.
96p; illus                               ISBN: 0-7207-0742-0
                                                    BL: X.629/10966

227  Successful athletics: from beginner to expert in forty lessons / Ron Clarke with Raelene Boyle. London: Pelham, 1976.
80p; illus                               ISBN: 0-7207-0917-2
                                                    BL: X.622/5623

228  Track and field fundamentals for girls and women: Frances Wakefield, Dorothy Harkins, with John M. Cooper. 4th ed. Saint Louis: Mosby; distributed in Great Britain by Henry Kimpton, 1977.
xiii, 284p; illus; index; pbk        ISBN: 0-8016-5328-2
                                                    BL: X.611/7872

☞  Previous ed. E223

229  Track and field / John and Frances Craig. London: Watts, 1979.
64p; illus; index
(A first book)

230  Athletics / words by Gary Paulsen and Roger Barrett; pictures by Heinz Kluetmeier. London: Macdonald Educational, 1980.
32p; illus
(Focus on sport)                        ISBN: 0-356-07162-6
                                                    BL: X.622/8006

A large print guide for very young readers, it covers sprinting, long distance, relay, hurdles, high jump, pole vault, shot, discus and javelin.

231 The Puffin book of athletics / Neil Allen; foreword by
Sebastian Coe. Harmondsworth: Puffin, 1980.
173p; illus; pbk
ISBN: 0-14-031275-7
BL: X.629/12918

The former athletics correspondent of The Times here
presents to young readers a concise guide to the
sport.

232 Your first book of athletics / Guy Drut and Jacques
Piasenta; translated from the French by Ruby McMillan.
London: Angus & Robertson, 1981
46p; illus
*Translation of: L'athletisme*
ISBN: 0-207-95895-5
BL: X.622/9677

233 Athletics: for young beginners: track and field athletics –
fundamental techniques and training procedures / Jess
Jarver. London: Batsford, 1982.
80p; illus; index; pbk
(Competitive sports series)
ISBN: 0-7134-3547-X
BL: X.629/17447

234 Athletics / Moira Gallagher for British Sports
Association for the Disabled. Alton: M.G. Books, 1983?
61p; illus; pbk
(Sport & leisure for the disabled series; no. 2)
ISBN: 0-907365-06-X
BL: X.629/21218

235 The teenage runner / Bruce Tulloh. Marlborough:
Tulloh & Tulloh, 1984.
130p; illus; pbk
ISBN: 0-9509688-0-3

☞ Subsequent ed. E238

236 All-star Olympic tips / David Scott; illustrated by Bryan
Reading. London: Armada, 1988.
112p; illus; pbk
ISBN: 0-00-693017-4
BL: YK.1988.a.3636

Advice and encouragement for children from Britain's
Olympic athletes.

237 Athletics / Tim Weaver. London: Carnival, 1988.
31p; illus; pbk + sound cassette
(Personal best)
ISBN: 0-00-194708-7
BL: Cup.937/455

Aimed at children. The sound cassette was recorded
by Lynn Davies.

238 The teenage runner / Bruce Tulloh. 2nd ed. London:
Kingswood, 1989.
xiii, 156p; illus; pbk
ISBN: 0-434-98177-X
BL: YK.1992.a.11909

☞ Previous ed. E235

239 Take up athletics / principal contributor: Peter Warden.
Huddersfield: Springfield, 1990.
63p; illus; pbk
(Take up sport)
ISBN: 0-947655-74-3

240 Track and field sports / Donna Bailey. Oxford:
Heinemann, 1991.
32p; illus; index
(My world)
ISBN: 0-431-00330-0
BL: YK.1991.a.10295

241 Fun in athletics (indoor): athletics as a team game for
primary school children / written and illustrated by
George Bunner. Rev. 2nd ed. Cheshire: Sports Hall
Athletics Association, 1994.
56p; illus; pbk
*Alternative title: Fun athletics for primary school children:
resource pack; original 1984 edition untraced*
ISBN: 1-873816-03-0
BL: YK.1995.b.7608

242 Athletics / Tony Ward. Oxford: Heinemann, 1995.
32p; illus; index
(Successful sports)
ISBN: 0-431-07436-4
BL: YK.1995.b.9818

243 The young athlete / Colin Jackson. London: Dorling
Kindersley, 1996.
32p; illus; index; pbk
*Includes an Atlanta Olympic Games 1996 athletic events
wall chart*
ISBN: 0-7513-5370-1
BL: YK.1996.b.16960

244 I could be an athlete / Alan MacDonald. London:
Hamlyn Children's, 1997.
32p; illus
(I could be ...)
ISBN: 0-600-59349-5

245 Athletics / Bernie Blackall. Oxford: Heinemann Library,
1998.
32p; illus; index
(Top sport)
ISBN: 0-431-08499-8
BL: YK.1999.b.2555

246 Athletics / Clive Gifford; illustrated by Bert Jackson.
London: Hodder Children's, 2000.
128p; illus; index; pbk
(Super.activ)
ISBN: 0-340-76468-6
BL: YK.2001.a.1457

✳ *Additional References*

247 Positions wherein those primitive circumstances be
examined, which are necessarie for the training up of
children, either for skill in their booke, or health in their
bodie / Richard Mulcaster. London: T. Vautrollier, 1581.
BL: C.175.l.10

This book by the first Headmaster of Merchant
Taylor's School has chapters on exercises and training
the body, exercise athletical, walking, running, and
leaping.

248 Gymnastics for youth, or, A practical guide to healthful and amusing exercises for the use of schools: an essay towards the necessary improvement of education, chiefly as it relates to the body / J. C. F. Gutsmuths, freely translated from the German by C. G. Salzmann. London: J. Johnson, 1800.

xvi, 433p; illus

*Authorship wrongly attributed to the translator on the title page; translation of: Gymnastik für die Jugend. 1793*

BL: 07905.h.21

A most significant and influential book which determined many of the ideas on which English gymnastics was based. It has much material on running, jumping and throwing, and is illustrated with copper engravings.

249 An elementary course of gymnastic exercises intended to develope and improve the physical powers of man / Peter Heinrich Clias. London: Sherwood, Jones, 1823.

xx, 111p; illus                                    BL: 785.h.13

Clias, from Switzerland, was a pioneer of gymnastics who taught in England. He claimed that his pupils had run 'a mile in four minutes, and afterwards in less'.

☞  Subsequent ed. E250

250 An elementary course of gymnastic exercises with the report made to the Medical Faculty of Paris on the subject, and a new and complete treatise on the art of swimming / Peter Heinrich Clias. 4th ed. London: Sherwood, Gilbert & Piper, 1825.

xviii, 184p; illus

*2nd and 3rd eds. untraced*                     BL: 1570/5556

☞  Previous ed. E249

251 The road to manhood / William Beach Thomas. London: George Allen, 1904.

xi, 224p; illus

(The Young England library)                 BL: 012202.aa.3/6

Published in the Young England Library series as a book for boys, this contains much of interest to historians, such as the reason why the shot and hammer became established in the athletics programme on the insistence of a Scottish professional living in Oxford, and G. S. Robertson's account of the discus used in the 1896 Olympics as a 'sort of girdle-cake of wood, with a brass core, and bound with iron'. The chapter on athletics runs to 27 pages and other references occur throughout.

252 Running, jumping and throwing: athletics for boys and girls! / written and illustrated by Frank Sharpley. London: Nicholas Kaye, 1951.

64p; illus                                         BL: 7920.f.34

A book for beginners, written primarily for boys and girls of school age. The author was a Loughborough student who emigrated and became coach to the New Zealand Empire Games team.

# F. Running

## Running ~ General

1 How to excel on the running path: a practical guide to the routine of training. Rugby: Albert Frost, 1894.
37p; pbk

Includes much on diet and medicine, with heavy promotion of Elliman's embrocation and Brand's essence, who paid for advertising space. The events covered are the sprint, mile and ten miles.

2 Hints on running and race-planning / Thomas Hampson. London: Chatterbox, 1935.
96p                                                                    BL: D

A short work by the Olympic 800m champion. It includes a chapter on the public schools sports by Sydney Wooderson, and notes on the Championships and records.

3 Athletics for health: running theory & practice / J. E. Lovelock. Seven Kings: The author, 1937.
23p; illus; pbk          BL: Mic.A.9404(16) (microfilm copy)

4 Running & runners / Guy Butler. London: Herbert Jenkins, 1938.
175p; illus; index                              BL: 7908.eee.7

An unassuming but well informed textbook which teaches technique through a study of more than a hundred champions, from W. G. George to J. E. Lovelock. 'A. G. K. Brown is an outstanding example of the striding runner. So fast does he cover the ground with his strides that even in a 100yds he is only using an honest-to-goodness sprinting action probably for the first 30 yards of the distance. Thereafter he is striding, not sprinting in the technical sense of the word.
On the other hand, an examination of Sydney Wooderson's action at the end of a race seems to show that he very definitely chops his stride; works his arms and generally breaks into a thorough-going sprint.' Although many of the training ideas have been superseded, Butler's original accounts of outstanding runners are of enduring interest. The book is also notable for its wealth of statistical material which includes furlong times taken during various half-miles,

and lap times taken during some 25 outstanding mile/1500m races. The appendix contains a letter from W. G. George vouching for the authenticity of his training times of 59:29 for 12 miles, 49:29 for 10 miles and 4:10.25 for the mile.

5 The art of pace-judgement: an entirely new angle on training and racing for the runner, whether champion or novice / Guy Butler. London: Vail, 1948.
24p; pbk                                         BL: 7917.de.97

6 Racing and training / Arthur F. H. Newton. London: George Berridge, 1949.
94p; illus
    *Variant title: Races and training*          BL: 7918.aaa.62

7 Running / produced in collaboration with J. H. Dodds [i.e. Dodd]. London: Educational Productions, 1961.
32p; illus; pbk
(Athletic techniques)                             BL: 7926.de.4

8 Run to the top / Arthur Lydiard and Garth Gilmour. London: Herbert Jenkins, 1962.
181p; illus                                       BL: 7923.tt.33

Lydiard gives a clear exposition of training methods which were responsible for the success of Olympic champions Halberg and Snell. Like Cerutty, his outlook is essentially empirical, but his writing does not reach the inspirational level of the Australian coach. Lydiard's methods, though at the time unsupported by much in the way of physiological fact, have since become the basis of much modern distance training.

☞ Subsequent ed. F10

9 Modern training for running / John Kenneth Doherty. London: Prentice-Hall, 1964.
xi, 281p                                          BL: X.441/182

Essentially descriptive rather than prescriptive and lacking much in the way of practical coaching advice or physiological analysis, this is a collation of training methods of the period and is a landmark work.

10   Run to the top / Arthur Lydiard and Garth Gilmour.
     2nd ed. London: Athletics Arena, 1967.
     xiii, 149p; illus                                   BL: X.449/4283

     ☞  Previous ed. F8; subsequent ed. F27

11   Running to win: training and racing for young athletes /
     Brian Mitchell. Newton Abbot: David and Charles, 1976.
     119p; illus; index                    ISBN: 0-7153-6948-2
                                            BL: X.629/10618

12   The complete book of running / James F. Fixx. New
     revised ed. London: Chatto and Windus, 1979.
     xvi, 270p; illus; index
          *Previous ed. New York: Random House, 1977*
                                            ISBN: 0-7011-2392-3
                                            BL: X.629/12573

     Fixx's best-seller was an intelligent collage of the
     conventional wisdom of the period, aimed at the health
     conscious fitness-runner.

13   Jim Fixx's second book of running: the all-new
     companion volume to The complete book of running /
     James F. Fixx. London: Angus & Robertson, 1981.
     xii, 217p; illus; index
          *Originally published: New York: Random House, 1980*
                                            ISBN: 0-207-14496-6
                      BL: X.629/20571 • X.629/23328

14   The AAA runner's guide / foreword by Steve Ovett.
     London: Collins, 1983.
     192p; illus; index; pbk               ISBN: 0-00-411753-0
                                            BL: X.629/20592

     A well-written early response to the running boom
     triggered by the first London marathon in 1981.

     ☞  Subsequent ed. F20

15   International running guide 1983 / edited by Clifford G.
     Temple. London: Tantivy, 1983.
     288p; illus; pbk                      ISBN: 0-900730-16-1

     This was the first in a series of guides (again
     short-lived); as a successor to the annual edited by
     Ron Pickering, it contains many similar features.
     Innovations are sections listing films, video and audio
     tapes, and libraries and museums in Europe including
     the UK, and North America.

16   Running with Lydiard / Arthur Lydiard with Garth
     Gilmour. London: Hodder and Stoughton, 1983.
     209p; illus                           ISBN: 0-340-32362-0
                                            BL: YK.1991.a.11968

     ☞  Subsequent ed. F31

17   Running together / Alison Turnbull. London: Allen &
     Unwin, 1985.
     148p; illus                           ISBN: 0-04-709110-X
                                            BL: YK.1989.b.1419

     Advice for beginning women runners.

18   Lore of running / Tim Noakes. 2nd ed. Oxford: Oxford
     University Press, 1986.
     xvi, 534p; illus; index; pbk
          *Previous ed. Cape Town: Oxford University Press, 1985*
                                            ISBN: 0-19-570421-5
                                            BL: YK.1988.b.1852

     ☞  Subsequent ed. F23

19   Sports Illustrated: track: the running events / Mel Rosen
     and Karen Rosen; photography by Heinz Kluetmeier.
     London: Harper & Row, 1986.
     173p; illus; pbk
     (Perennial library)
              ISBN: 0-06-015523-X (cased) • 0-06-091311-8 (pbk)
                                            BL: YK.1988.b.5475

20   The AAA runner's guide / foreword by Steve Ovett.
     New rev. ed. London: Willow, 1987.
     191p; illus; index; pbk
          *Bibliography: p184*
                                            ISBN: 0-00-218251-3
                                            BL: YK.1987.a.2191

     ☞  Previous ed. F14; subsequent ed. F24

21   Running from A to Z / Cliff Temple. London: Stanley
     Paul, 1987.
     160p; illus; index                    ISBN: 0-091664-10-1
                                            BL: YK.1987.b.5654

22   Improve your running skills / Susan Peach; running
     consultants Norman Brook, Charlie Spedding; illustrated
     by Paul Wilding and others; photographs by David
     Cannon. London: Usborne, 1988.
     48p; illus; index                     ISBN: 0-7460-0166-5
                                            BL: YK.1989.a.2416

23   Lore of running / Tim Noakes; foreword by George
     Sheehan. 3rd ed. Leeds: Human Kinetics, 1991.
     xxviii, 804p; illus; index
              ISBN: 0-88011-437-1 (cased) • 0-88011-438-X (pbk)
                                            BL: DSC-94/25085

     ☞  Previous ed. F18

24   The runner's guide. New and completely rev. ed.
     London: CollinsWillow, 1994.
     192p; illus; index, pbk               ISBN: 0-00-218462-1
                                            BL: YK.1994.a.8953

     ☞  Previous ed. F20

25   Running fast and injury free / Gordon Pirie; edited by
     John S. Gilbody. Hook: The editor, 1996.
     60p; illus; pbk

26   The handbook of running / Nick Troop and Steven
     Seaton. London: Pelham, 1997.
     vii, 148p; illus; index
          *Foreword by Sebastian Coe*       ISBN: 0-7207-2064-8
                                            BL: YK.1998.b.33

27  Running to the top / Arthur Lydiard & Garth Gilmour. Oxford: Meyer & Meyer Sports, 1997.
220p; illus; pbk                    ISBN: 3-89124-440-1

☞  Previous ed. F10

28  The complete guide to endurance training / Jon Ackland. London: A. & C. Black, 1999.
viii, 280p; illus; index; pbk       ISBN: 0-7136-5017-6
                                    BL: YK.1999.a.1244

29  How well are you running: (age graded club standards) / Roy Edward Marchant. Wymondham: The author, 1999.
50p; pbk                            ISBN: 0-9536994-0-4

30  The art of running with the Alexander technique / Malcolm Balls & Andrew Shields. London: Ashgrove, 2000.
143p; illus; pbk

31  Running with Lydiard / Arthur Lydiard and Garth Gilmour. Oxford: Meyer & Meyer Sport, 2000.
208p; illus; pbk                    ISBN: 1-84126-026-6

☞  Previous ed. F16

✳  *Additional References*

32  The runner's diary 1979 / edited by David Emery. London: C. H. Enterprises, 1978.
66p; illus; pbk

Includes articles by Cliff Temple, Brendan Foster, John Disley, and others.

33  Bruce Tulloh's running diary and log. Cambridge: Tulloh & Good, 1983-
*Published annually*                BL: ZC.9.a.70

34  The runner's diary / written, designed and printed by Christopher Brennan; drawings by Dutch. Topsham: The author, 1984?        BL: YK.1987.a.519

35  The complete book of running for women: everything you need to know about training, nutrition, injury prevention, motivation, racing and much, much more / Claire Kowalchik. London: Pocket Books, 1999.
xiii, 442p; index; pbk              ISBN: 0-671-01703-9
                                    BL: YK.2001.a.6729

# Track Events ~ General

36  Athletic sports: I. Track events / F. A. M. Webster. London: Frederick Warne, 1929.
64p; illus; pbk
(Warne's recreation books)          BL: X.629/6699(21)

37  Track events: technique, strategy and training / Don Canham; edited by Harold M. Abrahams; designed and illustrated by Tyler Micoleau. London: Herbert Jenkins, 1953.
111p; illus
*Originally published as: Track techniques illustrated: New York: Barnes, 1952*        BL: 7921.de.67

38  The spectator's handbook: an aid to the appreciation of athletics, boxing, cricket, association and rugby football and lawn tennis / J. B. Pick. London: Phoenix Sports, 1956.
144p; illus                         BL: 7922.ee.23

39  Track events / Peter Hildreth. Harmondsworth: Penguin, 1964.
124p; illus
(Improve your athletics; vol. 1)    BL: W.P.4003/110

The latest ideas on track technique, stated in clear concise terms.

40  Track events / Rex Van Rossum. London: Faber & Faber, 1964.
126p; illus
(Popular books)                     BL: W.P.388/30

The author's method, in this book for beginners, is to describe world-class races over the past twenty years, and to draw technical and tactical lessons from them. The chapter on training, in which the author draws on his own experience, is particularly good.

41  Track athletics / Bill Marlow and Denis Watts. London: Pelham, 1970.
109p; illus                         ISBN: 0-7207-0293-3
                                    BL: X.629/2574

42  Athletics – track events / Tom McNab; photographs by Mark Shearman, line drawings by Christine McNab. Leicester: Brockhampton, 1972.
88p; illus
(Illustrated teach yourself)        ISBN: 0-340-15065-3

One of the best books on the basics of track events.

43  Better athletics – track (with jumping) / John Heaton. London: Kaye & Ward, 1973.
96p; illus                          ISBN: 0-7182-0495-6
                                    BL: X.629/6109

Aimed at the younger reader.

44 Athletics, track events / R. Jones. London: Nelson, 1974.
48p; illus; index; pbk
(Sports for the Caribbean; book 3)   ISBN: 0-17-566154-5

45 Learning to be a better athlete / John Le Masurier,
David E. Kay, Carl T. Johnson. Glasgow: Collins, 1975.
61p; illus   ISBN: 0-00-10331-X
BL: X.625/148

46 Track athletics / Nick Whitehead. Wakefield: EP, 1976.
108p; illus   ISBN: 0-7158-0586-X
BL: X.629/11437

47 Athletics, track events / John Le Masurier and Denis
Watts. London: Pelham, 1977.
61p; illus   ISBN: 0-7207-0970-9
BL: X.622/6124

48 Athletics, track events / John Le Masurier and Denis
Watts. London: Black, 1980.
96p; illus; index   ISBN: 0-7136-2001-3
BL: X.629/13485

49 Successful track athletics / Tom McNab. London:
published in collaboration with World of Sport by Letts,
1982.
95p; illus; index; pbk   ISBN: 0-85097-417-8
BL: X.629/18307

50 Track athletics / Jim Alford. London: Batsford
Academic and Educational, 1984.
64p; illus; index
(Competitive sports series)   ISBN: 0-7134-4312-X
BL: X.622/19660

51 Track athletics / The Diagram Group. Harlow:
Longman, 1984.
48p; illus; pbk   ISBN: 0-582-39272-1
BL: X.629/24705

52 Athletics in action, track / David Hemery. London:
Stanley Paul, 1987.
92p; illus; pbk
(Sport in action)   ISBN: 0-09-166601-5
BL: YK.1987.a.7030

Hemery uses to good effect the 'flicker book'
mechanism deployed by the American coach Dean
Cromwell in 1938. An excellent basic primer,
particularly good on running and hurdling.

53 Track athletics / Nick Dean. Hove: Wayland, 1988.
64p; illus; index
(World of sport)   ISBN: 1-85210-317-5
BL: YK.1988.b.5441

54 Skilful track athletics / Nick Whitehead. London: A. &
C. Black, 1990.
96p; illus; index; pbk   ISBN: 0-7136-5759-6
BL: YK.1990.b.7227

55 Track athletics / Carl Johnson. London: A. & C. Black,
1991.
32p; illus; pbk; index
(Know the game)
*Produced in collaboration with the British Amateur Athletic
Board*   ISBN: 0-7136-3409-X
BL: YK.1991.a.11484

☞   Subsequent ed. F57

56 Track athletics / Robert Sandelson. London: Wayland,
1991.
48p; illus; index
(Olympic sports)
ISBN: 0-7502-0080-4 (cased); 0-7502-0294-7 (pbk)
BL: YK.1991.b.5314

57 Track athletics / Carl Johnson. New ed. London: A. &
C. Black, 1994.
48p; illus; index; pbk
(Know the game)
*Produced in collaboration with the British Athletic Federation*
ISBN: 0-7136-3683-1
BL: YK.1995.a.793

☞   Previous ed. F55; subsequent ed. F59

58 Track athletics / Bruce Tulloh. London: Blandford,
1994.
79p; illus; index; pbk
(Play the game)   ISBN: 0-7137-2403-X
BL: YK.1995.a.192

59 Track athletics / Carl Johnson. 2nd ed. London: A. & C.
Black, 2000.
48p; illus; index; pbk
(Know the game)
*Original text by Carl Johnson. Revisions by Graham Knight;
produced in collaboration with UK Athletics*
ISBN: 0-7136-5391-4
BL: YK.2000.a.12959

☞   Previous ed. F57

# *Sprinting, Hurdling & Relay Racing*

60　How to run 100 yards / J. W. Morton. London: British
Sports Publishing, 1906.
44p; illus; pbk
(Spalding's athletic library; no. 9)　　　BL: 07908.i.14/9
　Morton of South London Harriers recorded 9.8 secs.
on several occasions, and was one of the best
sprinters of the period.

61　How to sprint / Arthur F. Duffey. London: British
Sports Publishing, 1906.
47p; illus; pbk
(Spalding's athletic library; no. 8)
　　　BL: Mic.A.6745(17) (microfilm copy)
　In 1902 Duffey had become the first man to run
100yds in 9.6 secs. He was AAA Champion for four
successive years, and was banned by the American
Athletic Union for professionalism following a series of
exposé-type articles in McFaddon's Physical Culture
Magazine.

62　Text book on sprinting / R. E. Walker. London: Health
& Strength, 1910.
73p; illus　　　BL: 7911.df.26
　After a distinguished amateur career (1908 Olympic
100m champion) Walker became a professional, but
never reached the same heights, mainly because of the
high standard of professional sprinting, with
Australians Postle and Donaldson dominating the
period. Although the book is mainly instructional, its
most interesting feature is its list of professional
records, which includes a 5¼ secs 50yds. by H. M.
Johnson in New York in 1884 and a 6.0 secs 60yds. by
Arthur Postle in 1906 in Australia. Equally interesting
is a 9¾ secs mark by F. S. Hewitt in 1870 in Melbourne.
Since Hewitt was credited with a 1:53.5 880yds in
1871, he may have been the world's first sprinter-type
half-miler.

　☞　Subsequent ed. F67

63　How to sprint / A. Atkins. London: British Sports
Publishing, 1915?
47p; illus; pbk
(Spalding's athletic library; no. 8)　　　BL: 07908.i.14/8

64　Hurdling and steeplechasing / F. A. M. Webster.
London: Athletic Publications, 1922.
68p; illus　　　BL: D

　☞　Also listed at: F142

65　Middle distance and relay racing / James E. Meredith.
London: Pearson, 1924.
284p　　　BL: D
　Meredith held the world records for 440yds and
880yds.

　☞　Also listed at: F96

66　Sprinting / Harold M. Abrahams. London: Renwick,
1925.
93p; illus; pbk
(Spalding's athletic library; no. 61)　　　BL: D
　Abrahams was the 1924 Olympic 100m champion.

67　Text book on sprinting / R. E. Walker. Rev. ed. London:
Athletic Publications, 1936.
79p; illus　　　BL: Mic.A.16557(2) (microfilm copy)

　☞　Previous ed. F62

68　Sprint start / Hugh A. L. Chapman. Edinburgh: Athletic
Coaching Committee, Central Council of Physical
Recreation, 1951.
1 folded sheet; illus
(CCPR instructional pamphlet)
　One of a series of pamphlets, each of which consists of
eight diagrams, a page of instruction, and general
training hints on the event.

69　Sprinting / Hugh A. L. Chapman. Edinburgh: Athletic
Coaching Committee, Central Council of Physical
Recreation, 1951.
1 folded sheet; illus
(CCPR instructional pamphlet)

70　Hurdling / J. Le Masurier; foreword by R. St. G. T.
Harper. London: Amateur Athletic Association, 1952.
34p; illus; pbk
(AAA instructional booklet)　　　BL: W.P.3877/5

　☞　Subsequent ed. F74

71　If it's speed you're after / E. McDonald Bailey; foreword
by Philip Noel-Baker. London: Stanley Paul, 1953.
112p; illus　　　BL: 7920.aaa.88
　McDonald Bailey dominated post-war sprinting in
Britain, and this work is partly autobiographical.

72　Sprinting and relay racing / J. W. L. Alford and A. R.
Malcolm. London: Amateur Athletic Association, 1953.
55p; illus; pbk
(AAA instructional booklet)　　　BL: W.P.3877/11
　Includes a foreword by A. G. K. Brown.

　☞　Subsequent ed. F75

73  Franz Stampfl on running: sprint, middle distance and distance events / Franz Stampfl; foreword by Roger Bannister; introduction by Chris Chataway. London: Herbert Jenkins, 1955.
159p; illus; index
*Subsequently reprinted with the cover title 'Running'*
BL: 7918.aaa.70

A fine, lucidly written work which moves from general athletic principles to consideration of the running events in detail. Each chapter has month-by-month training schedules and there is a good concluding chapter on 'The coach's job'. Extracts from Athletics World (N. D. and A. R. McWhirter) enliven the text. 'Guide, philosopher and friend, counsellor and confessor, a prop at times of mental tension, a coach's job is big enough for any man. Indeed it is more than a job, it is a vocation which one follows from the same sort of compulsion that drives some to write, some to paint, and some to build bridges. And when all the shouting is over, when the senior partner in the firm has broken the record, made the head-lines and joined the immortals, the junior partner's reward comes from the satisfaction of a good job well done. Who could ask for more?'
Heavily based on Gerschler's interval-training methods, this book became the definitive middle-distance running manual of its period.

74  Hurdling / J. Le Masurier. 2nd ed. London: Amateur Athletic Association, 1959.
36p; illus; pbk
(Instructional booklet)                    BL: W.P.3877/22
☞  Previous ed. F70; subsequent ed. F78

75  Sprinting and relay racing / J. W. L. Alford. New ed. London: Amateur Athletic Association, 1959.
64p; illus; pbk
(Instructional booklet)                    BL: W.P.3877/25
☞  Previous ed. F72; subsequent ed. F79

76  Sprinting / Mike Agostini. London: Stanley Paul, 1962.
120p; illus                               BL: 7926.s.36
Agostini was the Commonwealth 100yds champion in 1954.

77  Sprints, middle distance and relay running / Robbie Brightwell and Ann Packer. London: Nicholas Kaye, 1965.
144p; illus                               BL: X.449/1706
☞  Also listed at: F107

78  Hurdling / John Le Masurier. 3rd ed. London: Amateur Athletic Association, 1966.
39p; illus; pbk
(Instructional booklet)                    BL: W.P.3877/32
☞  Previous ed. F74; subsequent ed. F82

79  Sprinting and relay racing / Bill Marlow. New ed. London: Amateur Athletic Association, 1966.
45p; illus; pbk
(Instructional booklet)                    BL: W.P.3877/31
☞  Previous ed. F75; subsequent ed. F80

80  Sprinting and relay racing / Bill Marlow. New ed. London: Amateur Athletic Association, 1972.
48p; illus; pbk
(Instructional booklet)                    ISBN: 0-85134-031-8
☞  Previous ed. F79; subsequent ed. F83

81  Track speed: hurdles, sprints & relays / John Le Masurier. London: Stanley Paul, 1972.
94p; illus                               ISBN: 0-09-111470-5

82  Hurdling / Malcolm Arnold. 4th ed. London: Amateur Athletic Association, 1974.
39p; illus; pbk
(Instructional booklet)                    BL: W.P.3877/32
☞  Previous ed. F78; subsequent ed. F89

83  Sprinting and relay racing / Bill Marlow. London: British Amateur Athletic Board, 1977.
39p; illus; pbk
(Instructional book)                       BL: X.619/18198
☞  Previous ed. F80

84  The Allan Wells book of sprinting / Margot Wells. Wakefield: EP, 1983.
96p; illus                               ISBN: 0-7158-0842-7
BL: X.629/21541

85  Sprinting and hurdling / Peter Warden. Marlborough: Crowood, 1986.
109p; illus; index
*An official British Amateur Athletic Board Publication – on cover*                  ISBN: 0-946284-77-6
BL: YK.1987.b.3835

86  Sprints and relays / Frank W. Dick. London: British Amateur Athletic Board, 1987.
90p; illus; pbk                          ISBN: 0-85134-082-2
BL: YK.1987.a.6546
☞  Subsequent ed. F88

87  Speed / Tom McNab; illustrations by David Gifford. Stadbroke: Sackville, 1989.
80p; illus
(Sackville sports clinic)                  ISBN: 0-948615-23-0
BL: YK.1990.a.5306

88  Sprints and relays / Frank W. Dick. New ed. Birmingham: British Amateur Athletic Board, 1991.
90p; illus                               ISBN: 0-85134-104-7
BL: YK.1991.a.12544
☞  Previous ed. F86

89 Hurdling / Malcolm Arnold. 5th ed. Birmingham: British Athletic Federation, 1992.
vii, 72p; illus

           ISBN: 0-85134-107-1
           BL: YK.1992.b.5455

   ☞   Previous ed. F82

90 Sprinter's guide to weight training / Graeme Carey. Leigh-on-Sea: Yellow Hat, 1993.    ISBN: 1-898358-15-X

91 Successful 400 metre running: a yearly training programme designed to fulfil your potential in the toughest track event of them all / Graeme Carey. Leigh-on-Sea: Yellow Hat, 1993.    ISBN: 1-898358-35-4

92 How to teach speed running: sprints, hurdles, relays: a guide for teachers and coaches / Richard Simmons. Birmingham: British Athletic Federation, 1998.
ii, 45p; illus; pbk

           ISBN: 0-85134-147-0
           BL: YK.1998.a.7539

✱ *Additional References*

93 Sports speed / George B. Dintiman, Bob Ward, Tom Tellez; foreword by Leroy Burrell. 2nd ed. Leeds: Human Kinetics, 1997.
xii, 243p; illus; pbk

*Revised edition of: Sport speed. Champaign, Ill: Leisure Press, 1988*    ISBN: 0-88011-607-2

# *Middle & Long Distance Running*

94 Distance and cross-country running / George Orton. London: British Sports Publishing, 1903.
46p

   *Originally published in the USA by Spalding*

   Advice by a famous Canadian distance runner.

   ☞   Also listed at: F147

95 Distance and cross-country running / J. H. Hardwick. London: British Sports Publishing, 1912.
82p; illus; pbk
(Spalding's athletic library; no. 56)    BL: 07908.i.14/56

   A good account of the early history of distance running, with advice on training and rare photographs. The break-down of the One Hour records of Deerfoot, Bacon, Thomas and Shrubb is particularly valuable. One notable fact revealed by the book is that an amateur match between Thomas and Parry in 1889 at Old Trafford drew a crowd of 10,000. The training methods described (though this part of the book is inferior to Shrubb's works) are basically those of Andrews.

   ☞   Also listed at: F150

96 Middle distance and relay racing / James E. Meredith. London: Pearson, 1924.
284p; illus    BL: D

   Meredith held the world records for 440yds and 880yds.

   ☞   Also listed at: F65

97 Running / Arthur F. H. Newton. London: Witherby, 1935.
224p; illus

   *Foreword by W. G. George*    BL: 2270.cc.31

   Essentially practical advice on long distance running given in an easy, informal style. The statistics given as a conclusion cover his training from 1922 to 1935, a total of 102,735 miles at an average of twenty miles per day. Details are also given of world's amateur distance running records on road and track. Newton was one of the great ultra-runners of the twentieth century. Self-taught and with only the haziest idea of physiology, he attempted to apply ultra-distance principles to every running event with often ludicrous results.

98 Middle distance / Hugh A. L. Chapman. Edinburgh: Athletic Coaching Committee, Central Council of Physical Recreation, 1951.
1 folded sheet; illus
(CCPR instructional booklet)

99 Middle distance running and steeplechasing / J. W. L. Alford. London: Amateur Athletic Association, 1951.
44p; illus; pbk
(AAA instructional booklet)    BL: W.P.3877/10

   ☞   Also listed at: F143; subsequent ed. F102

100 Running the half-mile / Leonard H. Ward. London: Women's Amateur Athletic Association, 1955.

   A booklet intended for the 17-19 age group.

101 Modern middle- and long-distance running / Jim Peters,
 'Johnny' Johnston and Joseph Edmundson; foreword by
 Harold M. Abrahams. London: Nicholas Kaye, 1957.
 152p; illus                                    BL: 7923.m.40

 The authors advise that success in running
 presupposes a programme of serious, constructive
 and consistent training and, as evidence, they print
 the detailed schedules of Peters, Landy and Sando.

102 Middle distance running and steeplechasing / J. W. L.
 Alford. 2nd ed. London: Amateur Athletic Association,
 1960.
 67p; illus; pbk
 (Instructional booklet)                  BL: W.P.3877/26

 ☞    Also listed at: F144
      Previous ed. F99; subsequent ed. F106

103 Middle-distance running: the young athlete talks to A. R.
 Mills; illustrated by Calton Younger. London: Phoenix
 Sports, 1961.
 63p; illus
 (Young sportsman series; no. 5)         BL: W.P.16978/5

 An easy to understand format, with a young athlete
 posing questions to Mills, an AAA honorary coach.
 This was undoubtedly the most useful book written for
 the young middle distance runner to this time.

104 Middle-distance running / Percy Wells Cerutty. London:
 Pelham, 1964.
 197p; illus
 (Champions library)                       BL: 7926.t.38

105 Modern distance running / Antony P. Ward; foreword
 by Bruce Tulloh. London: Stanley Paul, 1964.
 160p; illus                              BL: 07926.b.2

 A survey and analysis of distance training methods
 and tactics from earliest times; this is possibly the
 outstanding British work on distance running up to
 this time. An essentially descriptive work.

106 Middle distance running and steeplechasing / J. W. L.
 Alford. 3rd ed. London: Amateur Athletic Association,
 1965.
 67p; illus; pbk
 (Instructional booklet)

 ☞    Also listed at: F145
      Previous ed. F102; subsequent ed. F109

107 Sprints, middle distance and relay running / Robbie
 Brightwell and Ann Packer. London: Nicholas Kaye,
 1965.
 144p; illus                              BL: X.449/1706

 ☞    Also listed at: F77

108 Long distance running / Martin Hyman and Bruce
 Tulloh. London: Amateur Athletic Association, 1966.
 31p; illus; pbk                          BL: X.449/2394

109 Middle distance running / A. P. Ward. 4th ed. London:
 Amateur Athletic Association, 1967.
 56p; illus; pbk
 (Instructional booklet)                  BL: W.P.3877/34

 ☞    Previous ed. F106

110 Tulloh on running / Bruce Tulloh. London: Heinemann,
 1968.
 149p; illus                          ISBN: 0-434-79750-2

 The emphasis in this book by the European 5,000m
 champion of 1962 is on instruction, directed at young
 middle distance runners. There is, however, much
 absorbing autobiographical writing. Training schedules
 are given for all events from 800m to the marathon.

111 Running / Adrian Metcalfe. London: Batsford, 1969.
 127p; illus                            SBN: 7134-0314-4
                                           BL: X.449/3824

 Aimed at the élite athlete.

112 The complete middle distance runner / Denis Watts,
 Harry Wilson & Frank Horwill. London: Stanley Paul,
 1972.
 126p; illus                          ISBN: 0-09-111480-2
                                           BL: X.629/4468

 An outstanding compilation of the best thinking in
 British middle distance running of this period.

 ☞    Subsequent ed. F113

113 The complete middle distance runner / Denis Watts,
 Harry Wilson & Frank Horwill. Rev. ed. London: Stanley
 Paul, 1974.
 126p; illus                             BL: X.629/10176

 ☞    Previous ed. F112; subsequent ed. F116

114 Middle and long distance marathon and steeplechase /
 D. C. V. Watts and Harry Wilson. London: British
 Amateur Athletic Board, 1976.
 78p; illus; pbk
 (Instructional booklets)             ISBN: 0-85134-046-6
                                          BL: X.619/15435

115 Run: the Lydiard way / Arthur Lydiard; with Garth
 Gilmour. London: Hodder and Stoughton, 1978.
 249p; illus; index                   ISBN: 0-340-22462-2
                                          BL: X.629/11906

 Lydiard, now supported in much of his method by
 sports science research, provides the fruit of over two
 decades of work with international athletes.

116 The complete middle distance runner / Denis Watts,
 Harry Wilson & Frank Horwill. Rev. ed. London: Stanley
 Paul, 1982.
 126p; illus; pbk                     ISBN: 0-09-150171-7
                                          BL: X.629/20105

 ☞    Previous ed. F113

117 The competitive runner's handbook / Bob Glover and
Pete Schuder. Harmondsworth: Penguin, 1983.
544p; index; pbk

ISBN: 0-14-046565-0
BL: WP.4003/323

☞ Subsequent ed. F126

118 The complete distance runner / Bruce Tulloh. London:
Panther, 1983.
224p; illus; index; pbk

ISBN: 0-586-05976-8
BL: X.629/22535

*One of the definitive books of its period. Humane and
pragmatic, Tulloh brings together training theory with
a rich experience of distance running, in an
outstanding work.*

119 Running: the IAAF symposium on middle and long
distance events / edited by J. W. L. Alford. London:
International Amateur Athletic Federation, 1983.
80p

120 The competitive edge: mental preparation for distance
running / Richard Elliott. London: Prentice-Hall
International, 1984.
193p; index

ISBN: 0-13-154998-7
BL: YK.1989.a.2790

121 Complete guide to running / Jim Alford and others.
Twickenham: Hamlyn, 1985.
176p; illus; index; pbk

ISBN: 0-600-38521-3
BL: X.622/25494

122 Focus on middle-distance running / written and edited
by John Humphreys and Ron Holman with additional
contributions by Ian Adams and others. London: Black,
1985.
171p; illus; index; pbk

ISBN: 0-7136-2469-8
BL: X.629/26554

123 Running: the women's handbook / Liz Sloan & Ann
Kramer; illustrated by Elaine Anderson; with cartoons by
Jo Nesbitt. London: Pandora, 1985.
xii, 138p; illus; index; pbk
*Bibliography: p133-135*

ISBN: 0-86358-043-2
BL: YK.1987.a.164

124 Bruce Tulloh's running log: the complete runner's
companion / Bruce Tulloh. Wellingborough: Stephens,
1986.
160p; illus; pbk

ISBN: 0-85059-844-3
BL: YC.1986.a.3887

125 Endurance running / Norman Brook. Marlborough:
Crowood, 1987.
128p; illus; index

ISBN: 0-946284-14-8
BL: YK.1987.b.3789

126 The new competitive runner's handbook / Bob Glover
and Pete Schuder. Rev. ed. London: Penguin, 1988.
xii, 628p; illus; index; pbk

ISBN: 0-14-046837-4

☞ Previous ed. F117; subsequent ed. F139

127 Running my way / Harry Wilson. London: Sackville, 1988.
128p; illus; index; pbk
*Bibliography: p120*

ISBN: 0-948615-07-9
BL: YK.1989.b.4441

128 Endurance running events / Norman Brook.
Birmingham: British Athletic Federation, 1992.
116p; illus; index

ISBN: 0-85134-106-3
BL: YK.1992.a.7720

129 Middle distance running: training and competition / Cliff
Temple. London: Stanley Paul, 1992.
151p; illus; index; pbk

ISBN: 0-09-174815-1
BL: YK.1992.a.7162

130 Everyone's guide to distance running / Norrie
Williamson. Oxford: Oxford University Press, 1993.
288p; illus; pbk

ISBN: 0-19-570818-0
BL: YK.1994.a.7640

☞ Subsequent ed. F138

131 Self coached distance runner's handbook / Graeme
Carey. Leigh-on-Sea: Yellow Hat, 1993.

ISBN: 1-898358-00-1

132 Running your best / Tim Noakes, Stephen Granger.
Oxford: Oxford University Press, 1995.
240p; illus; pbk

ISBN: 0-19-570956-X
BL: YK.1995.a.8349

*The definitive work on distance running of the last
quarter of the twentieth century. A fine mixture of
theory and practice.*

133 Running is easy / Bruce Tulloh. London: CollinsWillow,
1996.
192p; illus; index; pbk

ISBN: 0-00-218731-0
BL: YK.1996.a.11227

134 Winning running: successful 800m & 1500m racing and
training / Peter Coe. Marlborough: Crowood, 1996.
128p; illus; index; pbk

ISBN: 1-85223-997-2
BL: YK.1997.b.2707

135 Better training for distance runners / David E. Martin,
Peter N. Coe. 2nd ed. Leeds: Human Kinetics, 1997.
xxvi, 435p; illus; index; pbk
*Previous ed. published as: Training distance runners.
Champaign, US: Leisure, 1991*

ISBN: 0-88011-530-0
BL: YK.1998.b.6174

*One of the definitive works of the period. A rich mix of
theory and pragmatism, in which Coe blends his
practical experience with Martin's sports science
research.*

136 Training for young distance runners / Laurence S.
Greene, Russell R. Pate. Leeds: Human Kinetics, 1997.
xv, 191p; illus; index; pbk

ISBN: 0-87322-406-X
BL: YK.1997.b.3822

137 Daniels' running formula / Jack Daniels. Leeds: Human
    Kinetics, 1998.
    viii, 287p; index; pbk
        ISBN: 0-88011-705-2 (cased) • 0-88011-735-4(pbk)

138 Everyone's guide to distance running / Norrie
    Williamson. 2nd rev. ed. Edinburgh: Mainstream, 1998.
    309p; illus; pbk                    ISBN: 1-840180-65-X

    ☞  Previous ed. F130

139 The competitive runner's handbook: the best-selling
    guide to running 5Ks through marathons / Bob Glover
    and Shelly-Lynn Florence Glover. Rev. ed. London:
    Penguin, 1999.
    xvi, 672p; index; pbk                ISBN: 0-14-046990-7
                                         BL: YK.1999.a.4433

    ☞  Previous ed. F126

140 Improving sports performance in middle and long
    distance running: a scientific approach to race
    preparation / Joanne L. Fallowfield, David M.
    Wilkinson. Chichester: Wiley, 1999.
    xx, 221p; illus; index; pbk          ISBN: 0-471-98437-X
                                         BL: YK.1999.a.8518

## ✻  *Additional References*

141 A selected study of the training methods for middle-
    distance running during the period 1920-1970 with
    particular reference to the mile and 1500m / W. S.
    Renard. Manchester University, 1976. DASE
    dissertation.

# *Steeplechasing*

142 Hurdling and steeplechasing / F. A. M. Webster.
    London: Athletic Publications, 1922.
    68p; illus                           BL: D

    ☞  Also listed at F64

143 Middle distance running and steeplechasing / J. W. L.
    Alford. London: Amateur Athletic Association, 1951.
    44p; illus; pbk
    (AAA instructional booklet)          BL: W.P.3877/10

    ☞  Also listed at: F99; subsequent ed. F144

144 Middle distance running and steeplechasing / J. W. L.
    Alford. 2nd ed. London: Amateur Athletic Association,
    1960.
    67p; illus; pbk
    (Instructional booklet)              BL: W.P.3877/26

    ☞  Also listed at: F102
        Previous ed. F143; subsequent ed. F145

145 Middle distance running and steeplechasing / J. W. L.
    Alford. 3rd ed. London: Amateur Athletic Association,
    1965.

    ☞  Also listed at: F106;  previous ed. F144

146 Introduction to the steeplechase / Graeme Carey.
    Leigh-on-Sea: Yellow Hat, 1993.      ISBN: 1-898358-30-3

# *Marathon, Cross-Country & Road Running*

147 Distance and cross-country running / George Orton.
    London: British Sports Publishing, 1903.
    46p
        *Originally published in the US by Spalding*
    Advice by a famous Canadian distance runner.

    ☞  Also listed at: F94

148 How to become a marathon winner. London: Sporting
    Life, 1908.
    16p; pbk
        A booklet produced after the Olympic Games, in the
        period of enthusiasm for this event arising from the
        Dorando incident.

149 Running and cross-country running / Alfred Shrubb.
London: Health & Strength, 1908.
85p; illus                                    BL: 7920.de.53

*Advice on training by the first notable distance runner to train using recognisably modern methods. The 32 plates include some strangely-posed 'action' photos, and portraits of Shrubb, Harry Andrews, W. G. George, A. Aldridge, Fred Appleby, Arthur Postle, Harry Hutchens and Deerfoot.*

*'The Briton has, I am convinced, a far greater stamina, as has been proved over and over again by our superiority in long distance races .... There are not too many long distance events on the Olympic programme, but those there are should all be annexed by British representatives if only our men will make up their minds to do so. The Marathon race, which we have hitherto allowed to go to one or other of our rivals, should be regarded as a British preserve.'*

*Shrubb, one of the leading 'shamateurs' of the early twentieth century, experienced a new lease of life in the marathon boom which followed the 1908 Olympics. Though marathon was beyond his distance, Shrubb competed successfully in the 1908-13 period, with indoor marathons in Madison Square Garden and the Albert Hall.*

150 Distance and cross-country running / J. H. Hardwick.
London: British Sports Publishing, 1912.
82p; illus; pbk
(Spalding's athletic library; no. 56)     BL: 07908.i.14/56

*A good account of the early history of distance running, with advice on training and rare photographs. The break-down of the One Hour records of Deerfoot, Bacon, Thomas and Shrubb is particularly valuable. One notable fact revealed by the book is that an amateur match between Thomas and Parry in 1889 at Old Trafford drew a crowd of 10,000. The training methods described (though this part of the book is inferior to Shrubb's works) are basically those of Andrews.*

☞   Also listed at: F95

151 Cross-country running / Don Canham; edited by Jack Crump; designed and illustrated by Tyler Micoleau. London: Herbert Jenkins, 1954.
112p; illus
*Originally published in the US as: Cross-country techniques illustrated. New York: Barnes, 1953*     BL: 7919.aa.91

152 The swift runner: racing speed through the ages, including standard points of its foundation breed, the marathon runner / Baroness Wentworth. London: Allen & Unwin, 1957.
146p; illus                                   BL: 7923.l.13

153 Hints on how to organise and manage an 'open' road running race / Ernest Neville. London: Road Runners Club, 1959.
4p; pbk

154 Training for road running / Sam Ferris, John Jewell, Harold Lee. Walton-on-Thames: Road Runners Club, 1965.
40p; illus                                    BL: X.449/1442

155 An introduction to cross-country running and race walking for girls / edited by Cliff Temple; foreword by Rita Ridley. Eastbourne: Women's Cross-Country & Race Walking Association, 1975.
34p; illus; pbk

156 Marathon: the world of the long-distance athlete / Gail Campbell. London: Ward Lock, 1977.
176p; illus, maps; index       ISBN: 0-7061-2551-7
                                BL: X.622/6086

157 Cross country and road running / Cliff Temple. London: Stanley Paul, 1980.
224p; illus; pbk               ISBN: 0-09-141521-7
                                BL: X.629/13432

158 Challenge of the marathon: a runner's guide / Cliff Temple; photography by Mark Shearman. London: Stanley Paul, 1981.
174p; illus; pbk               ISBN: 0-09-146431-5
                                BL: X.629/17015

159 Don't let your first marathon be your last / Brendan Foster. Halifax: Nike International, 1982.

160 The marathon book / Neil Wilson, Andy Etchells, Bruce Tulloh. London: Virgin, 1982.
190p; illus; pbk               ISBN: 0-907080-33-2
                                BL: X.629/18877

☞   Subsequent ed. F164

161 The marathon guide / Don Shelley & Kevin Donovan. Stoke-on-Trent: 1982-
*Title varies*                 BL: YA.1998.a.6298

*The 1982 edition includes the poem 'The roadrunner' by Kevin Donovan.*

162 Focus on the marathon / John Humphreys and Ron Holman. Wakefield: EP, 1983.
160p; illus; index             ISBN: 0-7158-0847-8
                                BL: X.629/21542

163 Joyce Smith's running book / Bryan Smith. London: Muller, 1983.
v, 154p; illus; index; pbk
*Bibliography: p149-150*        ISBN: 0-584-11054-5
                                BL: X.629/20627

164 The marathon book / Neil Wilson, Andy Etchells, Bruce Tulloh; with photographs by Mark Shearman. 2nd ed. London: Virgin, 1983.
192p; illus; pbk               BL: X.629/22739

☞   Previous ed. F160

165  Road racer's guide. London: J. Janikiewicz, 1983-
                                              BL: P.623/1308

166  Target 26: a practical step-by-step guide to running the
     marathon: revised for the '80s / Skip Brown & John
     Graham; with forewords by Dick Beardsley and Nancy
     Ditz. London: Collier Macmillan, 1983.
     xviii, 300p; illus; index; pbk
          *Originally published: New York: Collier Books, 1979*
                                       ISBN: 0-02-028100-5
                                           BL: X.622/20614

167  Guinness book of the marathon / Roger Gynn. Enfield:
     Guinness Superlatives, 1984.
     168p; illus; maps; index
          ISBN: 0-85112-410-0 (cased) • 0-85112-422-4 (pbk)
                                           BL: X.622/20009

     This is the most concise and complete history of the
     event, with an account of its origins, results of major
     championships and international races, biographies of
     twenty leading performers, brief histories of the event
     in several countries of Europe, the Americas, Asia,
     Africa and Oceania, together with much fascinating
     miscellaneous information.

168  Run for your life / Ernest Dudley. Bromley: Columbus,
     1985.
     224p                          ISBN: 0-86287-186-7
                                       BL: X.520/37546
     Once known as the 'Armchair Detective', Dudley
     became a successful veteran marathon runner.

169  How to run a marathon / Tony Benyon and Kevin
     Macey. Sevenoaks: New English Library, 1986.
     120p; illus                   ISBN: 0-450-06151-5
                                       BL: YK.1986.a.1477

170  Mountain Ash and Penrhiwceiber remembered in
     pictures / compiled by Bernard Baldwin. Cowbridge: D.
     Brown, 1986.
     88p; chiefly illus            ISBN: 0-905928-50-4
                                       BL: YV.1990.b.303

     Baldwin was the organiser of the Nos Galen New Year's
     Eve race in Mountain Ash from 1958 onward, and this
     is included in his recollections.

171  Grete Waitz: guide to running / Grete Waitz and Gloria
     Averbuch. London: Stanley Paul, 1987.
     259p; illus; index; pbk
          *Bibliography: p249-251; originally published: New York:*
          *Warner, 1986*                 ISBN: 0-09-172683-2
                                       BL: YK.1988.a.1996

172  A run through Devon's green lanes: a short history of
     cross-country running and road racing in Devon / John
     Legge. Devon: The author, 1987.
     20p; illus

173  Training for ultras / Andy Milroy. Trowbridge: Road
     Runners' Club, 1987.
     65p; pbk

     ☞  Subsequent ed. F179

174  The world of marathons / Sandy Treadwell; foreword by
     Fred Lebow. London: Columbus, 1987.
     189p; illus, maps             ISBN: 0-86287-312-6
                                       BL: YK.1989.b.4028

     Detailed descriptions and course plans of 26 major
     international races are given, together with a brief
     history of each race, including usual weather
     conditions and course records. Tables showing world
     record progression, including splits for Carlos Lopes
     and Ingrid Kristiansen, and the 25 fastest times are
     provided.

175  International ultra training / Andy Milroy. Trowbridge:
     Road Runners' Club, 1989.
     90p; illus; pbk

176  Running your first marathon and half marathon / Bruce
     Tulloh. Wellingborough: Thorsons, 1989.
     64p; illus; pbk               ISBN: 0-7225-1795-5
                                       BL: YK.1990.a.6477

177  Marathon, cross country and road running / Cliff
     Temple. London: Stanley Paul, 1990.
     xiii, 224p; illus; pbk        ISBN: 0-09-174331-1
                                       BL: YK.1990.a.4282

178  The London Marathon / foreword by Lord Snowdon.
     Harpenden: Queen Anne, 1993.
     120p; illus
          *Produced 'with the support of the makers of NutraSweet and*
          *in aid of the Snowdon Award Scheme'*  ISBN: 1-85291-529-3
                                       BL: YK.1995.b.1458

     Patrick Collins contributes a history of the London
     Marathon (pp9-36). The colour frontispiece is a
     portrait by Lord Snowdon of the first race director
     (from 1981), Christopher W. Brasher.

179  Training for ultras / Andy Milroy. 2nd ed. Trowbridge:
     Road Runners' Club, 1993.
     148p; pbk

     ☞  Previous ed. F173

180  Marathon manual / Cathy Shipton with Liz McColgan;
     cartoons by Candy Guard. London: Thorsons, 1997.
     150p; illus; index; pbk
          *Produced 'with co-operation from the British Heart*
          *Foundation'*                 ISBN: 0-7225-3342-X
                                       BL: YK.1997.b.2987

181  Marathon training: the proven 100-day program for
     success / Joe Henderson. Leeds: Human Kinetics, 1997.
     264p; illus; pbk              ISBN: 0-88011-591-2

182 Coaching cross country successfully / Joe Newton, Joe Henderson. Leeds: Human Kinetics, 1998.
144p; illus; pbk
(Coaching successfully)                    ISBN: 0-88011-701-X

183 How to teach endurance running: a guide for teachers and coaches / Phil Banning. Birmingham: British Athletic Federation, 1998.
ii, 42p; illus; pbk                        ISBN: 0-85134-143-8
                                           BL: YK.1999.b.67

184 Road racing for serious runners / Pete Pfitzinger & Scott Douglas. Leeds: Human Kinetics, 1999.
200p; illus; pbk                           ISBN: 0-88011-818-0

185 How to run a marathon / Heather Mull-Stricek. Wilmslow: Sigma Leisure, 2000.
139p; pbk                                  ISBN: 1-85058-746-9
                                           BL: YK.2001.a.788

186 International road running 2000: the complete guide to road running world wide / editor, Duncan Mackay. Surbiton: SportsBooks, 2000.
304p; illus; pbk                           ISBN: 1-899807-06-3

    ☞  Also listed at: M97

187 Marathon running: from beginner to elite / Richard Nerurkar; foreword by Steve Cram. London: A. & C. Black, 2000.
ix, 165p; illus; pbk                       ISBN: 0-7136-5351-5

188 Running tough / Michael Sandrock. Leeds: Human Kinetics, 2000.
xiii, 201p; illus; pbk                     ISBN: 0-7360-2794-7

189 26.2: running the London Marathon / Julie Welch. London: Yellow Jersey, 2000.
223p; illus; pbk                           ISBN: 0-224-05982-3
                                           BL: YK.2000.a.1125

# Mountain and Fell Running

190 The Ben Nevis race: a short history of the famous marathon now run annually up and down Britain's highest mountain / Charles Steel. Fort William: The author, 1956.
40p; pbk                                   BL: 7922.de.28

    ☞  Subsequent ed. F191

191 The Ben Nevis race: a short history of the famous race now run annually up and down Britain's highest mountain / Charles Steel. 2nd ed. Bearsden: The author, 1959.
48p; pbk                                   BL: 7923.g.54

    ☞  Previous ed. F190

192 Ben Nevis races, 1951-60: ten years / Eddie Campbell. Fort William: The author, 1961.

193 The Wilson Run: the first hundred years / Norman F. Berry. Sedbergh: Sedbergh School, 1980.
191p; illus; pbk

    A profusely illustrated record of the school's annual cross-country race with a short history of similar races in other public schools.

    ☞  Also listed at: A282

194 Safety of fell races / Peter O'Neill. Cumberland Fell Runners' Association, 1981.
24p; pbk

195 42 peaks: the story of the Bob Graham Round / Roger Smith. The author, 1982.

196 Everest the easy way / Allan Jones. Wolverhampton: The author, 1983.
53p; illus; unbound                        BL: X.629/22763

197 Studmarks on the summit: a history of amateur fell racing 1861-1983 / Bill Smith. Preston: SKG, 1985.
581p; illus; pbk

198 The Munros in winter: 277 summits in 83 days / Martin Moran; foreword by Hamish Brown. Newton Abbot: David & Charles, 1986.
240p; illus, maps; index                   ISBN: 0-7153-8836-3
                                           BL: YC.1986.b.2411

    ☞  Subsequent ed. F212

199 The Everest Marathon: the highest marathon in the world: an account of the First Everest Marathon in 1987 / edited by Diana Penny Sherpani and Robert Howard; photographs by Robert Howard. Bowness-on-Windermere: Bufo Ventures, 1988.
60p; illus, maps; index; pbk               ISBN: 0-9511230-1-7
                                           BL: YK.1991.b.1812

200 The best of British: fell running champions / Neil Shuttleworth. Broadbottom: The author, 1990.

201 The Everest Marathon: the highest marathon in the world: an account of the Second Everest Marathon in 1989 / edited by Diana Penny Sherpani; photographs by Robert Howard. Bowness-on-Windermere: Bufo Ventures, 1990.
30p; illus, maps; pbk
*Cover title: 1989 Everest Marathon: the world's highest marathon*      ISBN: 0-9511230-2-5
BL: YK.1991.a.5037

202 Running high: the first continuous traverse of the 303 mountains of Great Britain and Ireland / Hugh Symonds with comment and diary extracts from Pauline Symonds, Andrew, Joseph and Amy; foreword by Chris Bonington. Moffat: Lochar, 1991.
255p; illus, maps; index      ISBN: 0-948403-91-8
BL: YK.1991.b.9235

Symonds, who had won the Ben Nevis race in 1985, conceived the idea of tackling all peaks of 3,000 ft and above in the British Isles (277 of which are in Scotland) as a sponsored run for Intermediate Technology.

203 The Everest Marathon: the highest marathon in the world: an account of the Third Everest Marathon in 1991 / edited by Diana Penny Sherpani; photographs by Robert Howard. Bowness-on-Windermere: Bufo Ventures, 1992.
34p; illus, maps; pbk      ISBN: 0-9511230-4-1

204 Himalayan shuffle / Edward Ley-Wilson. Moffat: Lochar, 1992.
240p; illus      ISBN: 1-874027-33-1

205 Mountain navigation for runners / Martin Bagness. Ambleside: Misty Fell, 1993.
55p; illus, maps; pbk      ISBN: 0-9521005-0-9
BL: YK.1994.a.14234

206 Across Scotland on foot: a guide for walkers and hill runners / Ronald Turnbull. Hoddlesden: Grey Stone, 1994.
158p; illus, maps; pbk
*Bibliography: p150-152*      ISBN: 0-9515996-4-X
BL: YK.1995.a.9421

207 The Ben Race: the supreme test of athletic fitness / Hugh Dan MacLennan; foreword by Charles W. S. Steel. Fort William: Ben Nevis Race Association, 1994.
xvi, 218p; illus, maps; pbk      ISBN: 0-9524453-2-8
BL: YK.1995.b.10892

The first timed ascent and descent of Ben Nevis, Britain's highest peak at 4,406ft/1,343m, took place at the end of September 1895. William Swan, a local tobacconist and hairdresser, made the solo round trip in 2:41:00. The first race occurred in 1899 with ten competitors, and the first recorded ascent by a woman came in 1902. No competitions were held during

the period 1910 to 1936, and only six between 1937 and 1950. From 1951 the race has been held annually, with the exception of 1980, when it was cancelled at short notice.

208 The Everest Marathon: the highest marathon in the world: an account of the Fourth Everest Marathon in 1993 / edited by Diana Penny Sherpani; photographs by Robert Howard. Bowness-on-Windermere: Bufo Ventures, 1994.
44p; illus, maps; pbk      ISBN: 0-9511230-5-X

209 The Everest Marathon: the highest marathon in the world: an account of the Fifth Everest Marathon in 1995 / edited by Diana Penny Sherpani. Bowness-on-Windermere: Bufo Ventures, 1996.
34p; illus, maps; pbk      ISBN: 0-9511230-6-8

210 Fell and hill running / Norman Matthews and Dennis Quinlan. Birmingham: British Athletic Federation, 1996.
81p; illus; pbk      ISBN: 0-85134-138-1

211 The last latrine / Richard Grainger. London: Minerva, 1997.
xx, 412p; illus; pbk      ISBN: 1-86106-775-5
BL: YK.1999.a.9553

212 The Munros in winter: 277 summits in 83 days / Martin Moran; foreword by Hamish Brown. New ed. Newton Abbot: David & Charles, 1997.
224p; illus, maps; index      ISBN: 0-7153-0689-8

☞   Previous ed. F198

213 The Everest Marathon: the highest marathon in the world: an account of the Sixth Everest Marathon in 1997 / edited by Diana Penny Sherpani. Bowness-on-Windermere: Bufo Ventures, 1998.
34p; illus, maps; pbk      ISBN: 0-9511230-7-6

214 Macc and the art of long distance walking / Graham Wilson; with illustrations by Gerry Dale. Disley: Millrace, 1998.
152p; illus
*Bibliography: p149-150*      ISBN: 1-90217-301-5
BL: YK.1999.a.5979

215 The Everest Marathon: the highest marathon in the world: an account of the Seventh Everest Marathon in 1999 / edited by Diana Penny Sherpani. Bowness-on-Windermere: Bufo Ventures, 2000.
34p; illus, maps; pbk      ISBN: 0-9511230-8-4

## ✱ *Additional References*

216 Rochdale and the Vale of Whitworth: its moorlands, favourite nooks, green lanes, and scenery-being a companion volume to Old and New Rochdale / William Robertson. Rochdale: The author, 1897.
viii, 396p; illus
> *Also published in facsimile: Littleborough: George Kelsall, 1992. ISBN: 0-946571-21-X • 0-946571-22-8 (leather binding)* BL: YK.1994.a.2535
>
> A key source on old Whitworth races and runners.

217 Twenty years on Ben Nevis: being a brief account of the life, work, and experiences of the observers at the highest meteorological station in the British Isles / William Thomas Kilgour. Paisley: Alexander Gardner, 1905.
154p; illus BL: 010370.e.41
> Includes six pages on the challenge foot-race from the post office at Fort William to the top of Ben Nevis and back, and the race to set an 'authentic competitive record for the climbing of Ben Nevis'.
>
> ☞ Subsequent ed. F218

218 Twenty years on Ben Nevis: being a brief account of the life, work, and experiences of the observers at the highest meteorological station in the British Isles / William Thomas Kilgour. 2nd ed. Paisley: Alexander Gardner, 1906.
168p BL: 010370.e.48
> ☞ Previous ed. F217

219 I bought a mountain / Thomas Firbank. London: Harrap, 1940.
319p BL: 10859.h.17
> Includes a detailed account of the author's traverse of the Welsh Three Thousands in record time.

220 The Three Peaks / Norman Thornber. Clapham: Dalesman, 1949.
30p; illus; pbk
(Dalesman pocket books; no. 7) BL: W.P.1301/7

221 The Three Peaks: introducing Whernside, Ingleborough and Penyghent / W. R. Mitchell, Norman Thornber, Harry Watson & J. N. Frankland. Clapham via Lancaster: Dalesman, 1962.
32p; illus; pbk BL: X.809/564
> Thornber contributes the section on The Three Peaks Walk (pp7-14), tracing its recorded history from July 1887, when two masters from Giggleswick School, J. R. Wynne-Edwards and D. R. Smith, took 14 hours to cover an estimated 27 miles route.

222 A physiological and biochemical profile of the fell runner / D. Simpson. Salford University, 1984. MSc thesis.

223 The Welsh Three Thousands: a guide for walkers and fell runners / Roy Clayton with editorial and historical assistance from Harvey Lloyd; maps and drawings by John Gilham. Hoddlesden: Grey Stone, 1993.
79p; illus, maps; pbk ISBN: 0-9515996-3-1
BL: YK.1994.a.14355

224 The Welsh three thousand foot challenges: a guide for walkers and hill runners / Roy Clayton and Ronald Turnbull; with foreword and history by Harvey Lloyd; maps and sketches by John Gillham. Hoddlesden: Grey Stone, 1997.
128p; illus, maps; pbk ISBN: 0-9515996-6-6
BL: YK.1997.a.4798

225 Lakeland mountain challenges: a guide for walkers and fellrunners / Ronald Turnbull and Roy Clayton; maps, sketches and line drawings by John Gillham. Hoddlesden: Grey Stone, 1999.
159p; illus, maps; pbk ISBN: 0-9515996-8-2

# *Walking*

226 Walking: a practical guide to pedestrianism for athletes and others / Charles Lang Neil with contributions by W. J. Sturgess and W. Griffin. London: C. Arthur Pearson, 1903.
122p; illus BL: 7912.i.21
> Chapters on the science of walking; athletic walking; training; and, records.

227 Walking, and the principles of training / J. P. Sandlands. London: Smith's, 1903.
xvi, 74p BL: 7404.e.25
> The tone of this book, which was prompted by the walking of Dickinson of 600 miles in 10 days under the writer's training, suggests that Sandlands was something of an eccentric. The book has little shape or style and makes difficult reading rambling inconclusively from one subject to another. 'The thought – this must be as much otherwise engaged. It

must not be on the work. The blood follows the thought.
If the thought, therefore, be on the feet, the blood will
be there. This will mean swelling. The thought should be
on the scenery as much as possible.'

228 How to walk: describing the whole art of training
without a trainer / J. Graham and Ellery H. Clark.
London: Evening News, 1904.
60p                                                      BL: 7907.df.40

229 Larner's text book on walking: exercise-pleasure-sport /
George E. Larner. London: Health & Strength, 1909.
76p; illus                                               BL: 7911.df.33

   Larner, who held the world's walking records from one
   to ten miles for many years, gives chapters on walking
   on roads and tracks, on judging, and on a description
   of the walking events in the 1908 Games, both of which
   he won.

230 Race walking: a primer of the sport / Hugh W. Innes.
London: Ewart, Seymour, 1910.
92p; illus          BL: Mic.A.8033(4) (microfilm copy)

   A highly entertaining and idiosyncratic treatment.
   Packed with insights into the characters of
   competitive walking. Numerous illustrations and
   comprehensive record lists.

231 Walking for road and track, with sections on training,
footcare and self-massage / George Cummings. London:
Link House, 1934.
viii, 95p; illus                                         BL: 7916.ee.24

   Cummings was possibly the last of a great line of
   professional walkers. It is, therefore, a pity that so
   much of his book is devoted to training methods which
   seem to have consisted, in the main, of massage.
   Among his outstanding accomplishments were
   100yds in 16½ secs and, at the age of 51, a walk of 8¼
   miles in an hour.

   ☞ Subsequent ed. F232

232 Walking for road and track: with sections on training,
footcare and self-massage / George Cummings. 2nd ed.
London: Link House, 1947.
vi, 87p; illus                                           BL: 7918.aa.132

   ☞ Previous ed. F231

233 Race walking / Harold H. Whitlock. London: Amateur
Athletic Association, 1957.
62p; illus
(Instructional booklet)                          BL: W.P.3877/18

   Includes a foreword by A. H. Pope.

   ☞ Subsequent ed. F235

234 The sport of race walking. Ruislip: Race Walking
Association, 1962.
161p; illus                                              BL: 7923.tt.37

   A well-written and attractively produced volume which
   covers the history of race walking since the days of
   Foster Powell and Barclay Allardice, and gives rules of
   walking and full results of all major events. Line
   drawings of 24 walkers are included.

235 Race walking / Julian Hopkins. 2nd ed. London: British
Amateur Athletic Board, 1976.
50p; illus; pbk
(Instructional book)                        ISBN: 0-85134-050-4
                                                  BL: X.619/16682

   ☞ Previous ed. F233; subsequent ed. F236

236 Race walking / Peter Markham. New ed. Birmingham:
British Amateur Athletic Board, 1989.
40p; illus; pbk                             ISBN: 0-85134-093-8
                                                  BL: YK.1990.a.4446

   ☞ Previous ed. F235

## ✱ *Additional References*

237 Walk! it could change your life: a handbook / John Man.
London: Paddington Press, 1979.
255p; illus; index                          ISBN: 0-7092-0515-5
                                                  BL: X.320/11754

   Includes 'The super walkers' on competitive walking.

# G. Field Events

## Field Events ~ General

1 Olympian field events: their history and practice /
F. A. M. Webster. London: George Newnes, 1913.
128p; illus

    *Introduction by Arthur Conan Doyle*     BL: 7911.ee.2

    Webster's first work shows remarkable early insight
into field events techniques. It gives a full account of
the standard field events with chapters on the 56lb
weight, the standing jumps, hurdling and tug-of-war.
This is the first of Webster's great books. Even at this
early stage he showed his ability to grasp the
essentials of athletic events. The book is particularly
interesting on the historical background to the classic
discus and javelin events.

2 Athletic sports: II. Field events / F. A. M. Webster.
London: Warne, 1929.
64p; illus; pbk
(Warne's recreation books)     BL: X.629/6699(22)

3 The principles of missile games: field athletic sports,
cricket, baseball, lawn tennis, football, bowls, etc. / P. H.
Francis. Liverpool: T. Brackell, 1948.
70p; pbk     BL: 7919.aaa.37

    Covers: putting the shot; throwing the discus, hammer
and weight; the origins of the shot and discus; and, the
long jump, high jump, pole vault and javelin throw.

4 A study of targets in games (tournaments, field athletic
sports, baseball, cricket, football, hockey, golf, lawn
tennis, bowls, etc.) / P. H. Francis. London: Mitre, 1951.
235p; illus; index     BL: 7920.a.46

    The symbology and folklore of targets in games.

5 Field events: technique, strategy and training / Don
Canham; edited and with a foreword by Harold M.
Abrahams; designed and illustrated by Tyler Micoleau.
London: Herbert Jenkins, 1953.
111p; illus     BL: 7920.aaa.84

6 Improve your athletics. Vol. 2: Field events / John Le
Masurier. Harmondsworth: Penguin, 1964.
128p; illus     BL: W.P.4003/111

7 Athletics – field events / Tom McNab; photographs by
Mark Shearman, line drawings by Christine McNab.
Leicester: Brockhampton, 1972.
88p; illus
(Illustrated teach yourself)     ISBN: 0-340-15064-5

    ☞ Subsequent ed. G10

8 Better athletics – field (with cross country and race
walking) / John Heaton. London: Kaye & Ward, 1973.
96p; illus     ISBN: 0-7182-0496-2
                                      BL: X.629/6110

    Aimed at the younger reader.

    ☞ Subsequent ed. G12

9 Athletics, field events / R. Jones. London: Nelson, 1974.
48p; illus; index; pbk
(Sports for the Caribbean; book 4)     ISBN: 0-17-566155-3

10 Athletics – field events / Tom McNab. Leicester:
Knight, 1975.
90p; illus; pbk
(Illustrated teach yourself)     ISBN: 0-340-19379-4
                                      BL: X.619/15119

    ☞ Previous ed. G7

11 Field athletics / Carl Johnson. Wakefield: EP, 1978.
113p; illus
(EP sport series)
         ISBN: 0-7158-0567-3 (cased) • 0-7158-0646-7 (pbk)
                                      BL: X.629/12174

12 Better athletics – field (with cross country and race
walking) / John Heaton. London: Kaye & Ward, 1980.
96p; illus     ISBN: 0-7182-1469-2
                                      BL: X.629/12912

    ☞ Previous ed. G8

13 Athletics – field events / John Le Masurier and Denis Watts. London: Black, 1982.
96p; illus; index
ISBN: 0-7136-2147-8
BL: X629/18232

14 Field athletics / Don Anthony. London: Batsford Academic and Educational, 1982.
64p; illus; index
(Competitive sports series)
ISBN: 0-7134-4281-6
BL: X.622/12609

15 Athletics in action – field / David Hemery. London: Stanley Paul, 1988.
95p; illus; pbk
(Sport in action)
ISBN: 0-09-173568-8
YK.1989.a.3098

16 Field athletics / Adrianne Blue. Hove: Wayland, 1988.
64p; illus; index
(World of sport)
ISBN: 1-85210-316-7
BL: YK.1988.b.5440

17 Skilful field athletics / Carl Johnson. London: Black, 1990.
96p; illus; pbk
ISBN: 0-7136-5769-3
BL: YK.1990.b.3612

18 Field athletics / Carl Johnson. London: Black, 1991.
32p; illus; index; pbk
(Know the game)
*Produced in collaboration with the British Amateur Athletic Board*
ISBN: 0-7136-3408-1
BL: YK.1991.a.11436

☞ Subsequent ed. G21

19 Field athletics / Tim Merrison. London: Wayland, 1991.
48p; illus; index
(Olympic sports)
ISBN: 0-7502-0081-2 (cased) • 0-7502-0295-5 (pbk)
BL: YK.1991.b.5313

20 Guide to weight training for field event athletics / Graeme Carey. Leigh-on-Sea: Yellow Hat, 1993.
1 looseleaf vol.
ISBN: 1-898358-10-9

21 Field athletics / Carl Johnson. New ed. London: A. & C. Black, 1994.
48p; illus; index; pbk
(Know the game)
*Produced in collaboration with the British Athletic Federation*
ISBN: 0-7136-3672-6
BL: YK.1994.a.7270

☞ Previous ed. G18; subsequent ed. G23

22 Field athletics / David Lease. London: Blandford, 1994.
80p; illus; index; pbk
(Play the game)
ISBN: 0-7137-2450-1
BL: YK.1995.a.190

23 Field athletics / Carl Johnson. New ed. updated by John Trower. London: A. & C. Black, 2000.
48p; illus; index; pbk
(Know the game)
ISBN: 0-7136-5390-6
BL: YK.2001.a.94

☞ Previous ed. G21

# Jumping

24 Jumping / F. A. M. Webster. London: Health Promotions, 1922.
100p; illus
(Green cover books; no. 2)
BL: W.P.7176/2

This is one of the cheapest and most poorly-produced of Webster's books but, if the drawings and presentation are deficient, there is still much of interest in the book. Statistics are given on standing jumps, the English records being held by L. H. G. Stafford (long jump 10ft 1in) and W. E. B. Henderson (high jump 4ft 8ins).

25 Jumping / John Hickson Dodd; foreword by A. B. Wignall. London: Educational Productions, 1962.
32p; illus; pbk
(Know the game book)
BL: W.P.3073/57

Dodd was one of Britain's best pre-war high-jumpers and pole-vaulters, clearing 6ft 3¾in and 12ft 6in in 1938. The amateur laws of the pre-war period forced Dodd, as a physical education teacher, into professional athletics. In the immediate post-war period the rules were relaxed, but Dodd was refused re-instatement for the 1948 Olympic Games.

26 Athletics, jumping and vaulting / Denis Watts. London: Pelham, 1976.
62p; illus
ISBN: 0-7207-0919-9
BL: X.622/5620

☞ Also listed at: G61

27 How to teach the jumps: a guide for class teachers / M. Arnold and others; edited by Tom McNab. London: British Amateur Athletic Board, 1977.
36p; illus; pbk
BL: X.619/18322

☞ Subsequent ed. G28

28   How to teach the jumps: a guide for class teachers / Gordon Adams. London: British Amateur Athletic Board, 1981?
38p; illus; pbk           BL: X.529/45982

☞  Previous ed. G27; subsequent ed. G30

29   Jumping / Malcolm Arnold. Marlborough: Crowood, 1986.
102p; illus; index
(Crowood sports books)       ISBN: 0-946284-82-2
                              BL: YK.1987.b.3857

30   How to teach the jumps: a guide for teachers and coaches / David Johnson. New ed. London: British Amateur Athletic Board, 1988.
40p; illus; pbk        ISBN: 0-85134-090-3
                              BL: YK.1989.a.115

☞  Previous ed. G28; subsequent ed. G32

31   Complete book of jumps / Ed Jacoby, Bob Fraley. Leeds: Human Kinetics, 1995.
ix, 147p; illus; index; pbk     ISBN: 0-87322-673-9
                              BL: YK.1995.b.13934

32   How to teach the jumps: a guide for teachers and coaches / David Lease. New ed. Brimingham: British Athletic Federation, 1998.
44p; illus pbk         ISBN: 0-85134-130-6

☞  Previous ed. G30

## ✳ *High Jump*

33   High jumping / G. H. G. Dyson. London: Amateur Athletic Association, 1949.
32p; illus; pbk         BL: W.P.3877/15

☞  Subsequent ed. G34

34   High jumping / G. H. G. Dyson. 2nd ed. London: Amateur Athletic Association, 1950.
32p; illus; pbk
(AAA instructional booklet)     BL: W.P.3877/15

☞  Previous ed. G33; subsequent ed. G36

35   High jumping / Hugh A. L. Chapman. Edinburgh: Athletic Coaching Committee, Central Council of Physical Recreation, 1951.
1 folded sheet; illus
(CCPR instructional booklet)
    The pamphlet teaches the 'western roll' technique.

36   High jumping / G. H. G. Dyson. 3rd ed. London: Amateur Athletic Association, 1953.
32p; illus; pbk
(Instructional booklet)       BL: W.P.3877/14

☞  Previous ed. G34; subsequent ed. G37

37   High jumping / G. H. G. Dyson. 4th ed. London: Amateur Athletic Association, 1957.
40p; illus; pbk
(Instructional booklet)

☞  Previous ed. G36; subsequent ed. Watts G38

38   High jumping. / D. C. V. Watts. 5th ed. London: Amateur Athletic Association, 1964.
32p; illus; pbk
(Instructional booklet)       BL: W.P.3877/29

☞  Previous ed. G37; subsequent ed. G39

39   High jump / D. C. V. Watts. New ed. London: Amateur Athletic Association, 1969.
40p; illus; pbk
(Instructional booklet)       ISBN: 0-85134-005-9

☞  Previous ed. G38; subsequent ed. G40

40   High jump / Frank W. Dick. New ed. London: British Amateur Athletic Board, 1975.
70p; illus; pbk
(Instructional booklet)       ISBN: 0-85134-043-1
                              BL: X.619/15112

☞  Previous ed. G39; subsequent ed. G41

41   High jump / Frank W. Dick. New ed. London: British Amateur Athletic Board, 1980.
90p; illus; pbk
(Instructional book)         BL: X.629/13226

☞  Previous ed. G40; subsequent ed. G42

42   High jump / Frank W. Dick. New ed. Birmingham: British Athletic Federation, 1993.
iv, 72p; illus; pbk        ISBN: 0-85134-112-8
                              BL: YK.1994.b.6878

☞  Previous ed. G41

## ✳ *Long Jump & Triple Jump*

43   The long jump / Denis C. V. Watts. London: Amateur Athletic Association, 1949.
32p; illus; pbk
(AAA instructional booklet)

44   The long jump and the hop, step and jump / Denis Watts. London: Amateur Athletic Association, 1949.
24p; illus; pbk
(Instructional booklet)       BL: W.P.3877/3

☞  Subsequent ed. G45

45   The long jump and the hop, step and jump / Denis Watts. 2nd ed. London: Amateur Athletic Association, 1952.
24p; illus; pbk
(Instructional booklet)       BL: W.P.3877/8

☞  Previous ed. G44; subsequent ed. G46

46  The long jump and the triple jump / D. C. V. Watts. 3rd ed. London: Amateur Athletic Association, 1957.
32p; illus; pbk
(Instructional booklet)                    BL: W.P.3877/19

☞  Previous ed. G45; subsequent ed. G47

47  The long jump and the triple jump / D. C. V. Watts. 4th ed. London: Amateur Athletic Association, 1963.
36p; illus; pbk
(Instructional booklet)                    BL: W.P.3877/28

☞  Previous ed. G46; subsequent ed. G48

48  The long jump / Denis C. V. Watts. 5th ed. London: Amateur Athletic Association, 1968.
31p; illus; pbk
(AAA instructional booklet)                BL: W.P.3877/39

☞  Previous ed. G47; subsequent ed. G50

49  Triple jump / Tom McNab. London: Amateur Athletic Association, 1968.
56p; illus; pbk
(AAA instructional booklet)                BL: W.P.3877/38

This was the first definitive book on the event. The author covers history, teaching method, conditioning and technical development.

☞  Subsequent ed. G51

50  Long jump / David Kay. 6th ed. London: British Amateur Athletic Board, 1976.
47p; illus; pbk
(Instructional book)              ISBN: 0-85134-049-0
                                  BL: X.619/16681

☞  Previous ed. G48; subsequent ed. G53

51  Triple jump / Tom McNab. New ed. London: British Amateur Athletic Board, 1977.
56p; illus; pbk
(Instructional book)                      BL: X.619/17954

A more sophisticated version of the 1968 work, with excellent line illustrations.

☞  Previous ed. G49; subsequent ed. G52

52  The triple jump / Malcolm Arnold. New ed. London: British Amateur Athletic Board, 1986.
42p; illus; pbk                   ISBN: 0-85134-078-4
                                  BL: YK.1986.a.2104

☞  Previous ed. G51; subsequent ed. G55

53  Long jump / Malcolm Arnold. New ed. London: British Amateur Athletic Board, 1987.
57p; illus; pbk                   ISBN: 0-85134-086-5
                                  BL: YK.1988.a.4812

☞  Previous ed. G50; subsequent ed. G54

54  Long jump / Bruce Longden. New ed. Birmingham: British Athletic Federation, 1995.
52p; illus; pbk                   ISBN: 0-85134-127-6
                                  BL: YK.1995.b.14515

☞  Previous ed. G53

55  Triple jump / Ted King. 4th ed. Birmingham: British Athletic Federation, 1996.
v, 59p; illus; pbk                ISBN: 0-85134-132-2
                                  BL: YK.1996.b.8212

The most advanced manual on the event, indeed one of the best of all the AAA/BAAB/BAF publications.

☞  Previous ed. G52

# Pole Vaulting

56  Pole vaulting / Denis Watts; foreword by E. F. Housden. London: Amateur Athletic Association, 1954.
28p; illus; pbk
(AAA instructional booklet)                BL: W.P.3877/7

☞  Subsequent ed. G57

57  Pole vaulting / Denis Watts. Rev. ed. London: Amateur Athletic Association, 1960.
32p; illus; pbk
(Instructional booklet)                    BL: W.P.3877/27

☞  Previous ed. G56; subsequent ed. G58

58  Pole vaulting / Ian Ward. 3rd ed. London: Amateur Athletic Association, 1962.
43p; illus; pbk
(Instructional booklet)                    BL: W.P.3877/27a

☞  Previous ed. G57; subsequent ed. G59

59  Pole vaulting / Ian Ward. 4th ed. London: Amateur Athletic Association, 1966.
43p; illus ; pbk
(Instructional booklet)

☞  Previous ed. G58; subsequent ed. G60

60   Pole vault / Alan Neuff. New ed. London: British
Amateur Athletic Board, 1975.
56p; illus; pbk
(Instructional booklet)      ISBN: 0-85134-045-8
                                 BL: X.619/15312

     ☞   Previous ed. G59; subsequent ed. G62

61   Athletics, jumping and vaulting / Denis Watts. London:
Pelham, 1976.
62p; illus
                         ISBN: 0-7207-0919-9
                              BL: X.622/5620

     ☞   Also listed at: G26

62   Pole vault / Peter Sutcliffe. New ed. Birmingham: British
Amateur Athletic Board, 1991.
100p; illus
(Instructional booklet)      ISBN: 0-85134-100-4
                               BL: YK.1992.a.6820

     ☞   Previous ed. G60

63   A history of the pole vault in the British Isles. Part 1: to
1914 / Harry Berry. Chorley: The author, 1992.
193p; illus

     The most comprehensive history of this event and its
practitioners from earliest times. Includes result lists
from 1839 on.

     ☞   Subsequent ed. G65

64   A history of the pole vault in the British Isles. Part 2:
1919 to 1939 / Harry Berry. Chorley: The author, 1992.
148p; illus

65   A history of the pole vault in the British Isles. Part 1: to
1914 / Harry Berry. Rev. ed. Chorley: The author, 1994.
224p; illus

     ☞   Previous ed. G63

## ✱   *Additional References*

66   Wrestliana, or, The history of the Cumberland &
Westmoreland Wrestling Society in London since the
year 1824 / Walter Armstrong. London: Simpkin,
Marshall, 1870.
xix, 216p                            BL: 7906.aaa.18

     A full account of the transactions of the society with
descriptions of wrestlers and contests and a detailed
list of winners. The events included some early indoor
(from 1864) hurdles and pole vault competitions.

# *Throwing*

67   How to become a weight thrower / James S. Mitchel.
London: British Sports Publishing, 1914.
39p; illus; pbk
(Spalding's athletic library; no. 58)      BL: 07908.i.14/58a

     Advice by the famous Irish-American pioneer of the
hammer throw. Many times AAU Champion in a variety
of heavy events, Mitchel writes well on shot and
hammer, less well on discus. The illustrations include
shots of such 'greats' of the 'heavy' world as
Denis Horgan (shown holding the shot, à la Fuchs,
away from the shoulder) and John Flanagan. An
advertisement of interest is one for an indoor shot,
priced at 28/-.

68   Throwing / F. A. M. Webster. London: Health
Promotions, 1922.
100p; illus
(Green cover books; no. 1)      BL: W.P.7176/1

69   The principles of field athletic sports (putting the shot,
throwing the discus, hammer, and weight) / P. H.
Francis. Liverpool: T. Brackell, 1947.
10p; pbk                            BL: 7919.aaa.9

70   Throwing / John Hickson Dodd. London: Educational
Productions, 1963.
32p; illus; pbk
(Know the game)

71   How to teach the throws: a guide for class teachers / W.
H. C. Paish, C. T. Johnson. London: British Amateur
Athletic Board, 1975.
23p; illus; pbk             ISBN: 0-85134-044-X
                              BL: X.619/15356

     ☞   Subsequent ed. G74

72   Athletics, throwing / Howard Payne assisted by
Rosemary Payne; photography by Howard Payne.
London: Pelham, 1976.
63p; illus                        ISBN: 0-7207-0925-3
                              BL: X.622/5630

73  Athletic throwing / Peter Tancred and Cyril A. Carter.
    London: Faber, 1980.
    126p; illus                              ISBN: 0-571-11479-2
                                                BL: X.629/13614

74  How to teach the throws: a guide for class teachers /
    Carl Johnson. New ed. London: British Amateur Athletic
    Board, 1981.
    32p; illus; pbk                          BL: X.529/41004

    ☞   Previous ed. G71; subsequent ed. G75

75  How to teach the throws: a guide for teachers and
    coaches / Max Jones. New ed. London: British Amateur
    Athletic Board, 1986.
    32p; illus; pbk                          ISBN: 0-85134-081-4
                                                BL: YK.1988.a.2359

    ☞   Previous ed. G74; subsequent ed. G77

76  Throwing / Max Jones. Marlborough: Crowood, 1987.
    128p; illus; index                       ISBN: 0-946284-09-1
                                                BL: YK.1987.b.3836

77  How to teach the throws: a guide for teachers and
    coaches / Carl Johnson. New ed. Birmingham: British
    Athletic Federation, 1993.
    44p; illus; pbk                          ISBN: 0-85134-120-9
                                                BL: YK.1994.a.11165

    ☞   Previous ed. G75; subsequent ed. G78

78  How to teach the throws: a guide for teachers and
    coaches / Carl Johnson. New ed. Birmingham: British
    Athletic Federation, 1998.
    44p; illus; pbk

    ☞   Previous ed. G77

## ✱ *Shot Putting*

79  Shot putting / G. H. G. Dyson; foreword by K. S.
    Duncan. London: Amateur Athletic Association, 1952.
    32p; illus; pbk
    (Instructional booklet)                  BL: W.P.3877/6

    *The product of the work done by Dyson with John
    Savidge, the best British shot-putter in the
    immediate post-war period.*

    ☞   Subsequent ed. G80

80  Shot putting / John Le Masurier. 2nd ed. London:
    Amateur Athletic Association, 1959.
    31p; illus; pbk
    (Instructional booklet)

    ☞   Previous ed. G79; subsequent ed. G81

81  Shot putting / Ron Pickering. 3rd ed. London: Amateur
    Athletic Association, 1968.
    44p; illus
    (AAA instructional booklet)              BL: W.P.3877/37

    ☞   Previous ed. G80; subsequent ed. G82

82  Shot putting / Carl Johnson. New ed. London: British
    Amateur Athletic Board, 1976.
    45p; illus; pbk
    (Instructional booklets)                 ISBN: 0-85134-047-4
                                                BL: X.619/15431

    ☞   Previous ed. G81; subsequent ed. G83

83  Shot putting / Max Jones. 5th ed. London: British
    Amateur Athletic Board, 1987.
    52p; illus; pbk
    (Instructional booklet)                  ISBN: 0-85134-083-0
                                                BL: YK.1988.a.2160

    ☞   Previous ed. G82; subsequent ed. G84

    *One of the best works ever produced on the event.*

84  Shot putting / Max Jones. 6th ed. Birmingham: British
    Athletic Federation, 1995.
    73p; illus; pbk
    (Instructional booklet)                  ISBN: 0-85134-126-8
                                                BL: YK.1995.b.12577

    ☞   Previous ed. G83

## ✱ *Discus Throwing*

85  The discus throw / H. A. L. Chapman. London:
    Amateur Athletic Association, 1950.
    24p; illus; pbk
    (AAA instructional booklet)              BL: W.P.3877/2

    ☞   Subsequent ed. G86

86  Discus throwing / J. Le Masurier. New ed. London:
    Amateur Athletic Association, 1957.
    32p; illus; pbk
    (Instructional booklet)                  BL: W.P.3877/17

    ☞   Previous ed. G85; subsequent ed. G87

87  Discus throwing / John Le Masurier. New ed. London:
    Amateur Athletic Association, 1967.
    40p; illus; pbk
    (Instructional booklet)                  BL: X.619/9733

    ☞   Previous ed. G86; subsequent ed. G88

88  Discus throwing / Wilf Paish. New ed. London: British
    Amateur Athletic Board , 1976.
    40p; illus; pbk
    (Instructional booklet)                  ISBN: 0-85134-052-0
                                                BL: X.619/16797

    ☞   Previous ed. G87; subsequent ed. G89

89  Discus throwing / Max Jones. New ed. London: British
    Amateur Athletic Board, 1985.
    44p; illus; pbk                          ISBN: 0-85134-077-6
                                             BL: YK.1987.a.7297

    ☞  Previous ed. G88; subsequent ed. G90

90  Discus throwing / Max Jones. New ed. Birmingham:
    British Athletic Federation, 1993.
    iv, 52p; illus; pbk                      ISBN: 0-85134-114-4
                                             BL: YK.1993.b.10054

    ☞  Previous ed. G89

## ✳ *Hammer Throwing*

91  Hammer throwing / J. Le Masurier; foreword by D. N. J.
    Cullum. London: Amateur Athletic Association, 1954.
    36p; illus; pbk
    (AAA instructional booklet)
                                             BL: W.P.3877/12

    ☞  Subsequent ed. G92

92  Hammer throwing / J. Le Masurier. New ed. London:
    Amateur Athletic Association, 1959.
    36p; illus; pbk
    (AAA instructional booklet)
                                             BL: W.P.3877/12

    ☞  Previous ed. G91; subsequent ed. G93

93  Hammer throwing / J. Le Masurier. New ed. London:
    Amateur Athletic Association, 1962.
    36p; illus; pbk
    (AAA instructional booklet)
                                             BL: W.P.3877/12

    ☞  Previous ed. G92; subsequent ed. G94

94  Hammer throwing / J. Le Masurier. New ed. London:
    Amateur Athletic Association, 1963.
    36p; illus; pbk
    (AAA instructional booklet)
                                             BL: W.P.3877/12

    ☞  Previous ed. G93; subsequent ed. G95

95  Hammer throwing / J. Le Masurier. New ed. London:
    Amateur Athletic Association, 1966.
    36p; illus; pbk
    (AAA instructional booklet)
                                             BL: W.P.3877/12

    ☞  Previous ed. G94; subsequent ed. G96

96  Hammer throwing / Howard Payne. New ed. London:
    Amateur Athletic Association, 1969.
    147p; illus; pbk
    (Instructional booklet)
                                             BL: W.P.3877/41

    ☞  Previous ed. G95; subsequent ed. G97

97  Hammer throwing / Carl Johnson. New ed. London:
    British Amateur Athletic Board, 1984.
    59p; illus; pbk                          ISBN: 0-85134-073-3
                                             BL: X.629/26860

    ☞  Previous ed. G96; subsequent ed. G99

98  A very peculiar practice: a history of the hammer throw
    in the British Isles 1850 to 1914 / Harry Berry. Chorley:
    The author, 1991.
    104p; illus

    *Includes a chronology of results from 1852 to 1914 and
    top ten rankings from 1881.*

99  Hammer throwing / Alan Bertram. 8th ed. Birmingham:
    British Athletic Federation, 1996.
    iv, 57p; illus; pbk                      ISBN: 0-85134-131-4
                                             BL: YK.1996.a.10687

    *The definitive modern work in English on this event.*

    ☞  Previous ed. G97

## ✳ *Javelin Throwing*

100 The javelin throw / A. R. Malcolm. London: Amateur
    Athletic Association, 1950.
    31p; illus; pbk
    (Instructional booklet)                  BL: W.P.3877/1

    *Includes foreword by F. W. Collins.*

    ☞  Subsequent ed. G101

101 The javelin throw / A. R. Malcolm. 2nd ed. London:
    Amateur Athletic Association, 1952.
    31p; illus; pbk
    (Instructional booklet)                  BL: W.P.3877/30

    ☞  Previous ed. G100; subsequent ed. G102

102 Javelin throwing / David L. Pugh. New ed. London:
    Amateur Athletic Association, 1960.
    31p; illus; pbk
    (Instructional booklet)                  BL: W.P.3877/30

    ☞  Previous ed. G101; subsequent ed. G103

103 Javelin throwing / Wilf Paish. New ed. London:
    Amateur Athletic Association, 1967.
    47p; illus; pbk
    (AAA instructional booklet)              BL: W.P.3877/35

    *Paish's first and definitive book on this event.*

    ☞  Previous ed. G102; subsequent ed. G104

104 Javelin throwing / Wilf Paish. New ed. London: British
    Amateur Athletic Board, 1972.
    48p; illus; pbk
    (Instructional booklet)                  ISBN: 0-85134-035-0

    ☞  Previous ed. G103; subsequent ed. G105

105 Javelin throwing / Wilf Paish. New ed. London: British Amateur Athletic Board, 1980.
48p; illus; pbk
(Instructional book)      BL: X.629/15272

     A more advanced version of the 1967 work, embodying Paish's experience at international level in the ensuing period. Again, a definitive work.

     ☞   Previous ed. G104; subsequent ed. G106

106 Javelin throwing / Carl Johnson. New ed. London: British Amateur Athletic Board, 1987.
76p; illus; pbk      ISBN: 0-85134-088-1
     BL: YK.1989.a.1532

     ☞   Previous ed. G105; subsequent ed. G107

107 Javelin throwing / John Trower. New ed. Edgbaston: UK Athletics, 2000.
iii, 86p; pbk      ISBN: 0-85134-150-0

     ☞   Previous ed. G106

# Combined Events

108 Decathlon / Tom McNab. London: British Amateur Athletic Board, 1971.
71p; illus; pbk
(Instructional booklet)      ISBN: 0-85134-014-8

     The first definitive book on decathlon, this booklet comprehensively covers history, technique and conditioning in a readable and informative manner.

109 Decathlon and pentathlon / Tom McNab. London: British Amateur Athletic Board, 1978.
84p; illus; pbk
(Instructional book)      BL: X.619/18794

110 Combined events / David Lease. Birmingham: British Amateur Athletic Board, 1990.
52p; illus      ISBN: 0-85134-094-6
     BL: YK.1991.a.882

     ☞   Subsequent ed. G111

111 Combined events / David Lease. New ed. Birmingham: British Amateur Athletic Board, 1999.
iv, 59p; illus; pbk      ISBN: 0-85134-148-9
     BL: YK.1999.b.6327

     ☞   Previous ed. G110

# H. Officiating, Organisation & Laws

## Officiating, Organisation & Laws

1   Amateur Athletic Association constitution, objects, and lists of officers and members for 1887 / Amateur Athletic Association. London: The Association, 1887.

The forerunner of the AAA and BAF handbooks. There may have been an earlier publication, as the AAA was founded in 1880.

2   Laws of the Amateur Athletic Association and rules for competition. London: The Association, 1887.
14p; pbk

A separate publication from the above.

3   Rules for competitions under AAA laws. London: Amateur Athletic Association, 1890-
*Issued irregularly*      BL: W.P.12630

4   Sports management / Harry Hewitt Griffin. London: Pitman, 1900.
133p; illus

The book covers various sports, including athletics. It is notable for an article on timing, clocks, clockers and clocking.

☞   Subsequent ed. H5

5   Sports management, including motor gymkhanas, together with a special article on timing, clocks, clockers, and clocking / Harry Hewitt Griffin. London: Putney, 1908.
133p; illus      BL: Mic.A.7476(8) (microfilm copy)

☞   Previous ed. H4; subsequent ed. H7

6   Pedestrianism: proportionate table of starts from scratch / F. B. Taylor. Alnwick: Alnwick & County Gazette, 1910.
1 sheet      BL: 8548.cc.51

7   Sports management, including motor gymkhanas / Harry Hewitt Griffin. London: Putney, 1913.
243p      BL: D

☞   Previous ed. H5

8   Women's Amateur Athletic Association: constitution, laws, rules for competitions. London: The Association, 1923-
*Issued irregularly*
The WAAA was founded in 1922.

9   The organisation and management of athletic meetings / H. F. Pash, C. Otway and J. F. Wadmore. London: Amateur Athletic Association, 1925.
20p      BL: 7904.de.42

Issued free; 5,000 copies of the first edition were issued.

☞   Subsequent ed. H13

10   The Schools Athletic Association: general rules, competition rules and regulations. London: The Association, 1925-
11p; pbk
*Issued irregularly*

11   The advantages of holding athletic meetings under AAA laws. London: Amateur Athletic Association, 1927?

A booklet which was issued free on application.

12   Constitution, laws, rules for athletic meeting and competition. London: Amateur Athletic Association, 1927-      BL: P.P.2489.feb

13   The organisation and management of athletic meetings / H. F. Pash, C. Otway and J. F. Wadmore. 2nd ed. London: Amateur Athletic Association, 1927.
20p      BL: 7904.de.42
*In 1928 the booklet was incorporated with the AAA Official Handbook.*

☞   Previous ed. H9

14  The games master's hand book: how and what to teach /
F. A. M. Webster. London: Shaw, 1934.
192p; illus                                               BL: 7916.ee.4

   *41 pages are devoted to athletics, and are largely
   concerned with the organisation of the sport.*

15  The technique of judging track events / Walter C. Jewell.
London: Amateur Athletic Association, 1950.
20p; illus; pbk                                           BL: 7917.f.24

   ☞  Subsequent ed. H18

16  How to organise and conduct a sports meeting. London:
Amateur Athletic Association, 1951.
42p; illus; pbk                                           BL: X.629/7720

   ☞  Subsequent ed. H21

17  Scoring table for track and field events adopted by the
congress of the International Amateur Athletic
Federation, Brussels, 1950. London: IAAF, 1951.
115p

18  The technique of judging track events / Walter C. Jewell.
2nd ed. London: Amateur Athletic Association, 1954.
40p; illus; pbk                                           BL: 7922.aa.28

   ☞  Previous ed. H15; subsequent ed. H23

19  Scoring table for women's track and field events adopted
by the congress of the International Amateur Athletic
Federation held in Berne, 1954. London: IAAF, 1955.
16p

20  The technique of judging field events / S. E. J. Best.
London: Amateur Athletic Association, 1956.
40p; illus; pbk
(Amateur Athletic Association instructional booklet)
                                                          BL: W.P.3877/13

   ☞  Subsequent ed. H30

21  How to organise and conduct a sports meeting. New ed.
London: Amateur Athletic Association, 1957.
42p; illus; index; pbk                                    BL: X.629/7720

   ☞  Previous ed. H16; subsequent ed. H24

22  The sports organiser's handbook / Henry A. Winckles
and Charles D. Waltham-Weeks; foreword by Lord
Luke. London: Hale, 1957.
256p                                                      BL: 7923.s.6

   *Includes all aspects of organisation, with a medical
   section.*

23  The technique of judging track events / Walter C. Jewell.
3rd ed. London: Amateur Athletic Association, 1958.
48p; illus; pbk                                           BL: 7923.e.20

   ☞  Previous ed. H18; subsequent ed. H31

24  How to organise and conduct a sports meeting. New ed.
London: Amateur Athletic Association, 1960.
40p; illus; pbk                                           BL: X.629/7720

   ☞  Previous ed. H21; subsequent ed. H25

25  How to organise and conduct a sports meeting. New ed.
London: Amateur Athletic Association, 1961.
39p; illus; index; pbk                                    BL: X.629/7720

   ☞  Previous ed. H24; subsequent ed. H28

26  Metric conversion table. Worcester Park: Modern
Athletics Publications, 1962.

   *A pocket-size book containing direct conversions for
   standard field events.*

27  The technique of starting / J. W. Aspland, and,
Timekeeping / H. A. Hathway. London: Amateur
Athletic Association, 1963.
36p; illus; pbk
   *Reissued with amendments 1977*                        BL: 7926.s.42

   ☞  Subsequent ed. H36

28  How to organise and conduct a sports meeting. New ed.
London: Amateur Athletic Association, 1964.
40p; illus; index; pbk                                    BL: X.629/7720

   ☞  Previous ed. H25; subsequent ed. H32

29  Constitution, laws, senior coaches, rules for
competitions. London: Women's Amateur Athletic
Association, 1965.
8, v, 45p                                                 BL: YA.1995.a.7101

30  The technique of judging field events / Victor C. Sealy.
London: Amateur Athletic Association, 1965.
35p; illus; pbk
(Instructional booklet)

   ☞  Previous ed. H20; subsequent ed. H33

31  The technique of judging track events / Victor C. Sealy.
London: Amateur Athletic Association, 1967.
35p; illus; pbk
(Instructional booklet)                                   BL: X.619/9729

   ☞  Previous ed. H23; subsequent ed. H42

32  How to organise and conduct an athletics meeting. New
ed. London: Amateur Athletic Association, 1968.
39p; illus; index; pbk                                    BL: X.629/7720

   ☞  Previous ed. H28

33  How to judge field events / Victor C. Sealy and Cyril
Sinfield. New ed. London: Amateur Athletic Association,
1969.
40p; illus; pbk
(Amateur Athletic Association instructional booklet)
                                                          BL: W.P.3877/13

   ☞  Previous ed. H30; subsequent ed. H41

34 Metric conversion tables / compiled by Bob Sparks and Charles Elliott. Standard ed. London: Arena, 1969.
24p; pbk                                           BL: X.619/10747
*Contains conversion tables for weight, time conversions for running events, distance equivalents, and, wind measurements.*

35 Metric conversion tables / compiled by Bob Sparks and Charles Elliott. Pocket ed. London: Arena, 1969.
16p; pbk                                           BL: X.619/10747a

36 Starting / J. W. Aspland; and, Timekeeping / H. A. Hathway. London: Amateur Athletic Association, 1969.
36p; illus; pbk
☞ Previous ed. H27; subsequent ed. H45

37 The 'Athletics Arena' metric conversion tables / compiled by Bob Sparks. International ed. London: Arena, 1970.
56p; spiral                                        BL: X.619/10903
*Contains six tables for conversions between the imperial and metric systems for field event measurements made according to IAAF rule 145(2).*

38 Scoring table for men's track and field events: incorporating the 1971 intermediate scoring table (electrical timing to 1/100th second) for 100m and 200m and 110m hurdles. London: International Amateur Athletic Federation, 1971?

39 Scoring table for women's track and field events. London: International Amateur Athletic Federation, 1971.

40 Athletics officiating: a practical guide published by Sussex County AAA. Sussex: The Association, 1974.
27p; pbk
*Contributors: M. J. Langmaid, R. D. Webb, H. R. Butchers, G. L. King, J. S. Lauder and A. L. Buchanan.*

41 How to judge field events / Cyril Sinfield. New ed. London: Amateur Athletic Association, 1976.
48p; illus; pbk
(Instructional book)
*Reissued with amendments in 1980*   ISBN: 0-85134-053-9
BL: WP.3877/43
☞ Previous ed. H33; subsequent ed. H50

42 How to judge track events / Dan Davies. New ed. London: Amateur Athletic Association, 1976.
55p; illus; pbk
(Instructional book)
ISBN: 0-85134-051-2
BL: WP.3877/42
☞ Previous ed. H31; subsequent ed. H55

43 Women's Cross Country and Race Walking Association laws and competition rules revised to 1976. Bury: The Association, 1976.
19p

44 Scoring table for men's track and field events. London: International Amateur Athletic Federation, 1977.

45 Starting / J. W. Aspland; and, Timekeeping / H. A. Hathway. London: Amateur Athletic Association, 1977.
36p; illus; pbk                                    BL: X.619/18220
☞ Previous ed. H36

46 Behind the scenes at the athletics meeting / Graham Hart; illustrated by Chris Evans. Cambridge: Dinosaur for Cambridge University Press, 1984.
24p; illus                                         ISBN: 0-521-25847-2
BL: X.990/23558
*A short, well illustrated, guide aimed at the young reader, describing the organisation of an athletics meeting. Crystal Palace, London, is clearly the model.*

47 Torts and sports: legal liability in professional and amateur athletics / Raymond L. Yasser. London: Quorum, 1985.
xii, 163p; index                                   ISBN: 0-89930-092-8
BL: YC.1986.b.3271

48 Starting and marksmanship / Richard Float, Amateur Athletic Association. Marlborough: Crowood, 1987.
64p; illus; pbk                                    ISBN: 1-85223-022-3
BL: YK.1987.a.5856

49 Timekeeping / Alan Tomkins, Amateur Athletic Association. Marlborough: Crowood, 1987.
64p; illus; pbk                                    ISBN: 1-85223-027-4
BL: YK.1987.a.5855

50 The technique of judging field events / Mike Parmiter. New ed. London: Amateur Athletic Association, 1989.
80p; illus; pbk                                    ISBN: 0-85134-091-1
BL: YK.1989.a.5128
☞ Previous ed. H41; subsequent ed. H56

51 Rules for competition. Birmingham: British Athletic Federation, 1990?-
*Published annually*                               BL: ZK.9.a.2765

52 Track and field / Bob Phillips. Chichester: Cherrytree, 1991.
32p; illus; index
(Behind the scenes)                                ISBN: 0-7451-5114-0
BL: YK.1991.b.4961
*One of a series aimed at giving the young reader an insight into the world of top class sport, it presents a general survey of track and field, with sections on training and competition, developments in tracks and equipment, and the lifestyle of an athlete.*

53 Ultra marathon race handbook / edited by Andy Milroy. London: IUA Publications, 1991.
47p; pbk

54 RRC standards scheme: list of accurately measured courses / edited by Stuart Holdsworth. Leicester: Road Runners' Club, 1993.
14p; pbk

55 How to judge track events / David Littlewood. New ed. Birmingham: British Athletic Federation, 1995.
vi, 49p; pbk                    ISBN: 0-85134-129-2
                                BL: YK.1995.b.10128

☞ Previous ed. H42

56 How to judge field events / Mike Parmiter. New ed. Birmingham: British Athletic Federation, 1996.
iv, 52p; illus; pbk             ISBN: 0-85134-139-X
                                BL: YK.1996.a.20947

☞ Previous ed. H50

57 Announcing for track and field athletics: a practical guide. Birmingham: British Athletic Federation, 1997.
12p; pbk

✱ *Additional References*

58 Milocarian Trophy scoring table. London: Milocarian AC, 1946.
32p; pbk

59 A handbook for sports organisers / Joseph Edmundson. London: Evans, 1960.
112p                            BL: 7925.aa.5

Much information relevant to athletics is contained in the chapters on 'The planning and layout of sports facilities' (pp7-25), 'The organisation of a sports day' (pp26-49), 'Organising a cross-country race' (pp50-56), 'The care and maintenance of sport equipment' (pp100-107) and in the list of useful addresses.

60 Official rules of sports and games ... / edited by R. C. Churchill. London: Kaye, 1964-

A volume which first appeared in 1950, but which first included the rules of athletics from this edition.

61 Sport: a guide to governing bodies / compiled by the Information Centre of the Sports Council. London: Sports Council, 1977.
iii, 142p; index; pbk
(Information series; no. 2)     ISBN: 0-900979-45-3
                                BL: BS.387/160

Only details of UK and English governing bodies are included, in the order: general structure and constitution; committee structure; regional structure; officers; membership; coaching awards; proficiency awards; international organisation; events; publications.

# I. Facilities & Equipment

## Facilities & Equipment

1   Sports grounds and buildings: making, management, maintenance and equipment / F. A. M. Webster. London: Pitman, 1940.
xviii, 305p; illus, plans      BL: 7913.w.7

> An exceptionally comprehensive book which collates information from many international sources. There is a place for a modern version of this work.

2   Wembley presents 22 years of sport / Tom Morgan. Wembley: Wembley Empire Stadium, Pool & Sports Arena, 1945.
79p; illus; pbk      BL: 7918.aaa.2

3   Wembley presents 25 years of sport, 1923-1948 / Tom Morgan. Wembley: Wembley Empire Stadium, Pool & Sports Arena, 1948.
103p      BL: 7919.c.18

4   Athletic stadia: layout, construction and maintenance. London: Amateur Athletic Association and National Playing Fields Association, 1957.
56p; pbk

5   Cinder running tracks: a simplified specification. London: Amateur Athletic Association and National Playing Fields Association, 1957.
36p; pbk

6   Sports buildings and playing fields / Richard Sudell and David Tennyson Waters; foreword by Sir George L. Pepler. London: Batsford, 1957.
240p; illus      BL: 7922.h.27

> Includes illustrated material on the layouts of athletics tracks at Hurlingham Park (London), Salford Park (Aston), Maindy Stadium (Cardiff), and Crystal Palace National Sports Centre (London).

7   Notes on the measurement of roads for athletic events / John C. Jewell. London: Road Runners Club, 1961.
17p; pbk

8   Sports ground construction: specifications for playing facilities / R. B. Gooch and John R. Escritt. London: National Playing Fields Association, 1965.
ix, 104p      BL: X.449/2585

> Among the topics of particular relevance to the construction of athletics tracks are gradients, all weather surfaces, track facilities, and field facilities.

  ☞   Subsequent ed. I11

9   Facilities for athletics (track and field) / written under the auspices of a Joint Committee of the National Playing Fields Association and Amateur Athletic Association; drawings by T. L. Cook. London: National Playing Fields Association, 1971.
65p; illus, plans; pbk; index
>    Bibliography: p64      ISBN: 0-900858-52-4
>                    BL: YK.1995.b.12807

  ☞   Subsequent ed. I12

10   Wembley 1923-1973: the official Wembley story / edited by Neil Wilson and others. London: Kelly and Kelly, 1973.
155p; illus; pbk

11   Sports ground construction specifications / R. B. Gooch & J. R. Escritt, for the National Playing Fields Association and Sports Turf Research Institute. London: NPFA, 1975.
x, 126p; illus; index
>    Bibliography: p120-122      ISBN: 0-900858-60-5
>                        BL: X.629/10049

  ☞   Previous ed. I8

12  Facilities for athletics (track and field) / written under the auspices of the Joint Committee of the National Playing Fields Association and the Amateur Athletic Association. 2nd ed. London: National Playing Fields Association, 1980.
91p; illus, plans; index
*Bibliography: p86-87*            ISBN: 0-900858-95-8
                                  BL: X.622/15304

*The main aspects of the subject are covered: planning considerations, management, site selection, track and field events layout, track surfaces, training areas, and guide to equipment requirements.*

☞  Previous ed. I9

13  Glorious Wembley: the official history of Britain's foremost entertainment centre / Howard Bass. Enfield: Guinness Superlatives, 1982.
175p; illus; index                ISBN: 0-85112-237-X
                                  BL: X.622/18669

*Includes a chapter on the 1948 Olympics and a photo of the pre-war indoor championships.*

14  Olympic architecture: building for the summer games / Barclay F. Gordon. Chichester: Wiley, 1983.
xii, 186p; illus; index
     ISBN: 0-471-06069-0 (cased) • 0-471-88281-X (pbk)
                                  BL: X.425/4626

15  The Bridge: the history of Stamford Bridge / Colin Benson. London: Commodore, 1987.
208p; illus; pbk                  ISBN: 0-9509798-1-3

*The famous sports ground began as the headquarters of London AC from 1877 to 1905, and was the main venue of British athletics until 1931.*

16  Usborne book of athletics / Paula Woods; edited by Susan Peach; designed by Chris Scollen; illustrated by Paul Wilding, Guy Smith and Chris Lyon. London: Usborne, 1988.
48p; illus; index                 ISBN: 0-7460-0248-3
                                  BL: YK.1989.b.262

*A spectator's guide to track and field events, with extremely clear presentations of the rules, tactics, techniques, training and equipment for each event.*

17  Arenas: a planning, design and management guide / edited by Andrew Shields and Michael Wright. London: Sports Council, 1989.
xii, 314p; illus
*Foreword by Sebastian Coe*        ISBN: 0-906577-88-8
                                  BL: DSC-GPC/00523

*A comprehensive work on covered stadia.*

18  Sports technology / Neil Duncanson. Hove: Wayland, 1991.
47p; illus, 1 map; index
(Technology in action)
*Bibliography: p45*                ISBN: 0-7502-0131-2
                                  BL: YK.1991.b.8102

*Children's book that includes sports arenas, timing, performance-enhancing drugs, and television.*

19  Manchester 2000 Olympic facilities: environmental profiles: the British Olympic bid – Manchester 2000. London: Department of the Environment, 1993.
109p; illus, plans; spiral        BL: DSC-GPC/02570

20  Athletics – indoor. London: Sports Council, 1994.
24p; illus; pbk
(Guidance notes)                  ISBN: 1-86078-008-3
                                  BL: YK.1995.b.10027

*Covers the planning, design and management of indoor sports hall athletic facilities, training facilities and competition facilities.*

21  Athletics – outdoor. London: Sports Council, 1995.
10p; illus; pbk
(Guidance notes)                  ISBN: 1-86078-007-5
                                  BL: YK.1995.b.9068

*Covers the planning, design and management of outdoor athletics facilities.*

22  The stadium and the city / edited by John Bale and Olof Moen. Keele: Keele University Press, 1995.
347p; illus, maps; index          ISBN: 1-85331-110-3
                                  BL: SPIS796.068

*Based on papers delivered at an international seminar in 1993, fifteen academics from six countries contribute widely diverse chapters. Stadiums with athletics facilities discussed in detail are those in Beijing and Göteborg. The economic impact of an event such as the World Championships is explored. The elements of theatre present at an athletics meeting are noted, and the visual aspects of modern stadium design are considered.*

23  Wembley: the greatest stage: the official history of 75 years at Wembley stadium / Tom Watt & Kevin Palmer. London: Simon & Schuster, 1998.
336p; illus                       ISBN: 0-684-84051-0
                                  BL: YK.2000.b.1070

24 Hysplex: the starting mechanism in ancient stadia: a contribution to ancient Greek technology / Panos Valavanis; translated from the Greek and with an appendix by Stephen G. Miller. London: University of California Press, 1999.
xviii, 183p; illus; index; pbk
(University of California publications: classical studies; v.36)
*Includes summary in Greek; bibliography: pxvii-xviii*
ISBN: 0-520-09829-3
BL: YC.1999.b.6136

A study of the ancient Greek starting-gate.

25 Putney Velodrome and the Velodrome Estate / Pat Heery. London: The author, 1999.
iii, 106p; illus, maps; pbk
ISBN: 0-95335782-0-8
BL: YK.1999.b.4591

History of the track where W. J. Sturgess and J. Butler set world walking records.

## ✱ *Additional References*

26 Wind velocity measurements in athletic stadia, and the effects of winds on sprint performances / D. W. Murrie. Brunel University, 1988. MPhil thesis.

Interesting conclusion that the athletics rule on wind assistance should be withdrawn.

# J. Physiology, Psychology & Fitness

## Physiology, Psychology & Fitness

1  Prospectus of a new work, to be intituled, 'The Code of Health and Longevity' by Sir John Sinclair. London: 1804?

8p                                    BL: 1890.b.3(62)

2  The code of health and longevity, or, A concise view of the principles calculated for the preservation of health, and the attainment of long life / Sir John Sinclair. Edinburgh: Privately published, 1806-1807.

4 vols.                                BL: 41.d.15-18

> In this detailed study, many references are made to athletic sports, both as a form of amusement and as a source of health. Instances are given of the performances of contemporary athletes such as West and Ireland. The appendix includes an account of detailed enquiries into athletic exercises, giving the ideal build of an athlete, optimum ages, time required for training, medicine and diet, exercises, sleep, effects on the body and mind and a defence of the utility of such enquiries.
> 'Running must have been carried, in ancient times, to a very great degree of perfection; but the feats which have been performed in England, in that respect, seem to rival, if not surpass, those even of ancient Greece. Some have run at the rate of ten miles an hour, even in sultry weather; four miles have been run at York in twenty minutes and nineteen seconds. The famous West of Windsor could run forty miles in five hours and a half, which is nearly eight miles an hour; and in eighteen hours, he could have gone over one hundred statute miles. A quarter of a mile has been run in about a second or two under a minute, and the half mile in two minutes; one mile in a quarter of a minute under five; two miles have been done under ten minutes; one hundred yards have been done under ten seconds.'

☞  See also: E2; subsequent ed. J3

3  The code of health and longevity, or, A concise view of the principles calculated for the preservation of health, and the attainment of long life / Sir John Sinclair. 3rd ed., abridged. Edinburgh: Privately published, 1816.

> 2nd ed. not traced

☞  Previous ed. J2; subsequent ed. J4

4  The code of health and longevity, or, A concise view of the principles calculated for the preservation of health, and the attainment of long life / Sir John Sinclair. 4th ed. Edinburgh: Privately published, 1818.

566p, 90p, [9]p; illus          BL: RB.23.b.3391

☞  Previous ed. J3; subsequent ed. J5

5  The code of health and longevity, or, A concise view of the principles calculated for the preservation of health, and the attainment of long life / Sir John Sinclair. 5th ed. London: Sherwood, Gilbert & Piper; Edinburgh: William Tait, 1833.

xx, 430p, 172; illus                BL: a1500/30

☞  Previous ed. J4

6  Handbook: International Health Exhibition of 1884. London: Clowes, 1884.

> Contains: Athletics, or, Physical exercise and recreation / Edmond Warre; Athletics / E. Lyttelton and G. F. Cobb
BL: D

7  The pedestrian's record, to which is added a description of the external human form / James Irvine Lupton and James Money Kyrle Lupton; illustrated with anatomical plates. London: W.H. Allen, 1890.

vi, 224p; illus                        BL: 7908.d.24

> Largely concerned with the physiological aspect of athletics, but also notable for extremely comprehensive lists of amateur and professional British and American records and championship winners. Interesting professional marks include the Scot, Methven's 5ft 11½ins high jump of 1856, and the American Bethune's 100yds in 9.5 secs in 1888. 'While

an athlete is preparing to run, he should train – to develop not only the muscles of the legs, but those of his whole body, and this can be effected in a gym.' Commenting on Capt. Barclay's training methods: 'Such training, if carried into effect, is calculated to send a man to his grave, rather than the cinder path.' The Luptons are originals; creative thinkers on all aspects of athletics and this work is required reading for the athletics historian.

8   Athletics for politicians / Sir Charles Wentworth Dilke, reprinted from the North American Review. London: Athenæum, 1900.
41p
> *Limited ed. of 50 copies*               BL: D

A curiosity piece by the famous politician whose career ended in one of the most celebrated scandals of the century. Dilke's book offers advice on keeping fit by various forms of sport.

9   Athletics – endurance, stamina / H. Light. Manchester: Vegetarian Society, 1906.
6p                       BL: X.329/5473(9)

Lists successes of vegetarian walkers and runners in long distance events such as the Outfitters London to Brighton Walk and the Half Mile Amateur Championship of Scotland.

10   Exercise in education and medicine / Robert Tait Mackenzie. London: Saunders, 1909.
406p; illus                   BL: 7405.h.22

An early work on the relation of athletics to physiological medicine, which contains a number of photographs of athletes.

11   Heart and athletics: clinical researches upon the influence of athletics upon the heart / Felix Deutsch and Emil Kauf; translation by Louis M. Warfield. London: Kimpton, 1927.
187p; index
> *Translation of: Herz und Sport; bibliography: p178-184*
>                           BL: 7404.w.42

Changes in the hearts of track athletes are discussed on pages 64-71.

12   Living machinery: six lectures delivered at the Royal Institution / Archibald V. Hill. London: G. Bell, 1927.
xiv, 256p; illus; index         BL: 7405.pp.28

An outstanding work by one of the first physiologists to study athletic performance. Two of Hill's principal discoveries were the nature of acceleration in sprinting and the physiological justification of even-pace running.

13   Exercise: its functions, varieties and applications / Adolphe Abrahams. London: Heinemann, 1930.
viii, 92p                       BL: 7383.pp.17

14   Keeping fit: home physical exercises / F. A. M. Webster and J. A. Heys. London: Warne, 1931.
vii, 119p; illus

15   Fitness through athletics / Jack E. Lovelock. London: A. Wander, 1938.
> *Produced by Ovaltine*

A booklet produced by the famous New Zealand athlete (John Edward Lovelock).

16   The human machine / Adolphe Abrahams. Harmondsworth: Penguin, 1956.
199p                     BL: 012209.d.4/373

An analysis and description of the human body, and its structure and functions, in terms of inanimate machinery. There are sections on: 'Exercise: its place and functions in modern life'; 'The physiology of exercise'; 'Training in principle and practice'; 'Injuries and disabilities'; 'Records, past, present and future'; and 'Fitness and endurance'. Abrahams was one of the few doctors of his time to show an interest in athletic training, and this book constitutes one of his last contributions to the genre.

17   Notes on the dynamical basis of physical movement / Bernard J. Hopper. Strawberry Hill: St. Mary's College, 1961.
79p
(Strawberry Hill booklets; no. 2)      BL: P.P.7618.hb

The book covers similar ground to that covered by Dyson in *Mechanics of Athletics* (E118) and is an ideal supplement to the study of Dyson's work, though much less lucid.

18   The physique of the Olympic athlete: a study of 137 track and field athletes at the XVIIth Olympic Games, Rome 1960 and a comparison with weight-lifters and wrestlers / J. M. Tanner with the assistance of R. H. Whitehouse and Shirley Jarman; foreword by Sir Arthur E. Porritt. London: Allen & Unwin, 1964.
126p; illus                   BL: X.322/60

A comprehensive study of the physique of 137 Olympic athletes who competed in the Rome Games, reproducing body-build photographs, X-rays and showing the differing sizes, shapes, muscularity and skeletal proportions required for different events. It is worth noting that R. Tait Mackenzie made a pioneer study of athletic physique as early as 1896.

19   Fitness for men / Gordon Pirie. London: Record Books, 1965.
67p; illus
> *With a long-playing gramophone record*   BL: Cup.575.de.7

20 Report of medical research project into effects of altitude in Mexico City in 1965. London: British Olympic Association, 1966.
31p                                BL: Cup.1255.a.41
*The first attempt to investigate the impact of altitude training, prior to the Mexico City Olympics of 1968.*

21 Be fit! or be damned! / Percy Wells Cerutty. London: Pelham, 1967.
174p; illus                        BL: X.449/2385
*Cerutty pursues his 'Stotan' philosophy which harks back to the approach of other notable fitness eccentrics such as the American, Bernard McFadden.*

22 Run for your life: jogging with Arthur Lydiard / Garth Gilmour. London: Minerva, 1967.
126p
*The fitness-running boom did not begin until almost a decade later; Lydiard was well ahead of his time in this early book on running as a means of developing (non-athletic) fitness.*

23 Conditioning for distance running / Jack Daniels, Robert Fitts, George Sheehan. Chichester: Wiley, 1978.
x, 106p; illus; index
(American College of Sports Medicine series)
ISBN: 0-471-19483-2
BL: X.629/11863

24 Dr Sheehan on running / George A. Sheehan. London: Bantam, 1978.
xii, 207p; illus; pbk
*Originally published: Mountain View, Ca.: World Publications, 1975*
ISBN: 0-553-12261-4
BL: X.319/18528

25 Training theory / Frank W. Dick. London: British Amateur Athletics Board, 1978.
84p; illus; pbk              ISBN: 0-85134-058-X
*The definitive work of its period.*

☞ Subsequent ed. J35

26 Diet in sport / Wilf Paish. Wakefield: EP, 1979.
96p; illus; index; pbk       ISBN: 0-7158-0658-0
BL: X.319/19323

☞ Subsequent ed. J37

27 Focus on running: an introduction to human movement / edited by Frank S. Pyke and Geoffrey G. Watson. London: Pelham, 1979.
xii, 178p; illus; index
*Originally published: Sydney: Harper and Row, 1978*
ISBN: 0-7207-1132-0
BL: X.629/12294

28 Playing on their nerves: the sport experiment / Angela Patmore. London: Stanley Paul, 1979.
272p; illus; index           ISBN: 0-09-139510-0
BL: X.629/12755
*Intended as an investigation into élite male sports performers, this work examines such topics as the symbolic nature of sport, sports physiology and psychology, and, most extensively, drug use. Many examples from track and field are cited.*

29 The science of track and field athletics / Howard and Rosemary Payne; foreword by Arthur Gold. London: Pelham, 1981.
384p; illus; index           ISBN: 0-7207-1288-2
BL: X.629/15509

30 Physical structure of Olympic athletes. Part 1: The Montreal Olympic Games anthropological project / volume editor J. E. L. Carter. London: Karger, 1982.
x, 181p; illus; index
(Medicine and sport; v.16)   ISBN: 3-8055-3502-3
BL: DSC-5534.007(16)

31 The runner: energy and endurance / Eric Newsholme & Tony Leech; preface by Sir Roger Bannister. Oxford: Fitness Books, 1983.
vii, 152p; illus; index      ISBN: 0-913115-00-2
BL: YK.1987.a.1018

32 The natural athlete: the athlete's guide to nutrition and fitness plus! / Alan Lewis. London: Century Hutchinson, 1984.
130p                         ISBN: 0-7126-1236-X

33 Physical structure of Olympic athletes. Part 2: Kinanthropometry of Olympic athletes / volume editor J. E. L. Carter. London: Karger, 1984.
245p; illus; index
(Medicine and sport; v.18)   ISBN: 3-8055-3871-5
BL: DSC-5534.0073(18)

34 Physique of female Olympic finalists: standards on age, height and weight of 824 finalists from 47 events / Triloke Khosla, Valerie C. McBroom. Cardiff: Welsh National School of Medicine, 1984.
67p; illus; pbk
*Foreword by Mary Peters*     ISBN: 0-950232-02-5
BL: X.629/25193
*Using age, height and weight data of finalists in the 1972 and 1976 Olympic Games, the authors have computed three derived variables: bulk index, adjusted weight, and body surface area. Table A presents the computations by event, with the mean and standard deviation for each. Table B lists the physical characteristics in ascending order of height and weight (within height).*

35 Training theory / Frank W. Dick. New ed. London: British Amateur Athletic Board, 1984.
84p; illus; pbk
ISBN: 0-85134-058-X
BL: X.629/26859

☞ Previous ed. J25; subsequent ed. J38

36 Diet for runners / Nathan Pritikin. London: Bantam, 1986.
256p; illus; index; pbk
*Originally published: New York: Simon and Schuster, 1985*
ISBN: 0-553-17232-8
BL: YK.1986.a.2164

37 Diet in sport / Wilf Paish. 2nd ed. London: Black, 1989.
96p; illus; index; pbk
ISBN: 0-7136-5739-1
BL: YK.1990.a.923

☞ Previous ed. J26

38 Training theory / Frank Dick. New ed. Birmingham: British Amateur Athletic Board, 1991.
84p; illus; pbk
ISBN: 0-85134-105-5

☞ Previous ed. J35

39 Computerised unit for assessment of sprinters on the track / Bernard Donne, Jim Kilty. Dublin: Cospoir, 1993.
43p; illus; pbk

40 Keep on running: the science of training and performance / Eric Newsholme, Tony Leech, Glenda Duester. Chichester: Wiley, 1994.
xvii, 443p; illus; index
ISBN: 0-471-94313-4 (cased) • 0-471-94314-2 (pbk)
BL: YK.1994.b.11650

Includes training schedules by Bruce Tulloh. Covers the biochemistry, nutrition, physiology and psychology of the sport. An outstanding work.

41 Instant acceleration: living in the fast lane: the cultural identity of speed / Robert R. Sands. London: University Press of America, 1995.
xxv, 124p; illus; index
ISBN: 0-8191-9584-7 (cased) • 0-8191-9585-5 (pbk)
BL: YC.1995.a.2129

The author, describing himself as 'a cultural anthropologist and (white) sprinter', became one of a group of sprinters at the University of Illinois in 1987/88. The book is characterised as 'an attempt to bring together theory and description in a way to appeal to the anthropologist/social scientist and interested lay person'.

42 The winning experience: winning, in sport, in business, in life / Richard Brown. Chelwood: Institute of Human Development, 1996.
180p; illus; pbk
ISBN: 0-9527437-0-2

Advice about the positive approach to life derived from the author's – and his wife Sandra's – record-breaking Land's End to John o' Groats performances.

43 Gold minds: the psychology of winning in sport / Brian Miller; foreword by Kevin Hickey. Marlborough: Crowood, 1997.
158p; illus; index; pbk
ISBN: 1-86126-100-4
BL: YK.1999.b.7721

Brian Miller, the sports psychologist to the British Olympic Association, covers many Olympic sports in this volume, with substantial emphasis on track and field athletes.

44 Running within: a guide to mastering the body-mind-spirit connection for ultimate training and racing / Jerry Lynch, Warren A. Scott. London: Human Kinetics, 1999.
xv, 199p; illus; index; pbk
ISBN: 0-88011-832-6
BL: YK.2000.a.2163

45 Running / edited by John A. Hawley. Oxford: Blackwell Science, 2000.
ix, 96p; illus; index; pbk
(Handbook of sports medicine and science)
ISBN: 0-632-05391-7
BL: YK.2000.a.12366

## ✱  *Additional References*

46 Mexico-68 / Peter Travers and Griffith Pugh. London: Arena, 1968.
4p; pbk
Separate publication of a report on acclimatisation at altitude which first appeared in *Athletics Arena* magazine.

47 Nutrition and athletic performance / Robert N. Singer. London: Arena, 1968.
4p; pbk
Separate publication of an article which first appeared in *Athletics Arena* magazine.

48 A study of forces on the body in athletic activities, with particular reference to jumping / A. J. Smith. Leeds University, 1972. PhD thesis.

49 Some factors affecting the performance of young athletes / R. J. Pickering. Leicester University, 1973. MEd thesis.

50 A biomechanical evaluation of the hurdle clearance techniques of four decathletes / R. M. Bartlett. Alsager: Crewe & Alsager College of Higher Education, Division of Sport, Science & Environmental Studies, 1982.
27p; illus; spiral
BL: X.629/19934

51 A biomechanical evaluation of the javelin throws of eight heptathletes / R. M. Bartlett. Alsager: Crewe & Alsager College of Higher Education, Division of Sport, Science & Environmental Studies, 1982.
38p; illus; spiral
BL: X.629/19938

52 A biomechanical evaluation of the javelin throws of four decathletes / R. M. Bartlett. Alsager: Crewe & Alsager College of Higher Education, Division of Sport, Science & Environmental Studies, 1982.
28p; illus; spiral
BL: X.629/19937

53 A biomechanical evaluation of the long jump take offs of four decathletes / R. M. Bartlett. Alsager: Crewe & Alsager College of Higher Education, Division of Sport, Science & Environmental Studies, 1982.
22p; illus; spiral
BL: X.629/19936

54 A biomechanical evaluation of the long jump take offs of six heptathletes / R. M. Bartlett. Alsager: Crewe & Alsager College of Higher Education, Division of Sport, Science & Environmental Studies, 1982.
27p; illus; spiral
BL: X.629/19939

55 A biomechanical evaluation of the shot putt techniques of four decathletes / R. M. Bartlett. Alsager: Crewe & Alsager College of Higher Education, Division of Sport, Science & Environmental Studies, 1982.
38p; illus; spiral
BL: X.629/19935

56 A preliminary investigation into possible haematological reasons for loss of form in athletes: a research study for the Scottish Sports Council / J. D. Robertson, R. J. Maughan, R. J. L. Davidson. Edinburgh: Scottish Sports Council, 1991.
21p, viii; spiral
(Research report; no. 15)
ISBN: 1-85060-162-3
BL: DSC-7766.064(15)
This study of track and field athletes concluded that the use of routine medical haematological and biochemical tests is relatively ineffective at identifying reasons for loss of form, and that iron deficient anaemia was not a common cause of loss of form in athletes.

57 The nutritional status, and the result of a comprehensive nutrition assessment programme on Irish Olympic athletes, between 1983 and 1988 / M. McCreery. Trinity College Dublin, 1993. PhD thesis.
Confirmation of the critical role of good nutrition and dietary practice in athletic performance.

58 Serum creatine phosphokinase changes in running, football and rugby: an intergroup comparison / Mary Kelly. Dublin: Cospoir, 1993.
23p; illus; pbk

59 A biomechanical and physiological evaluation of combined uphill-downhill sprint running training / Georgos P. Paradisis. Leeds Metropolitan University, 1998. PhD thesis.

60 A biomechanical evaluation of the effect of the stretch shortening cycle in unconstrained and experimentally constrained vertical jumps / Kieran Moran. Ulster University, 1998. PhD thesis.

61 Contributions to performance in dynamic jumps / Mark Arthur King. Loughborough University of Technology, 1998. PhD thesis.

62 A season long investigation of sport achievement motivation in competitive athletes / J. K. Barnes. Bristol University, 1998. PhD thesis.

63 Survival of the fittest: understanding health and peak physical performance / Mike Stroud. London: Cape, 1998.
ix, 213p; illus
*Bibliography: p209-212*
ISBN: 0-224-04485-0
BL: YK.1998.b.4475
The author describes and analyses his experiences in endurance events, drawing much on marathon and ultra-running.

64 Assessment of maximal oxygen uptake in runners: new concepts on an old time / D. M. Wood. Southampton University, 1999. PhD thesis.
BL: DSC-DX204181

65 Biomechanical Research Project, Athens 1997: final report / edited by G.-P. Brüggemann, D. Koszewski, H. Müller. Oxford: Meyer & Meyer Sport, 1999.
175p; illus; pbk
ISBN: 1-84126-009-6
Report on the Biomechanical Research Project at the 6th World Championships in Athletics, Athens 1997, sponsored by the International Athletic Foundation.

66 The kinematics and kinetics of jumping for distance with particular reference to the long and triple jumps / P. Graham-Smith. Liverpool John Moores University, 1999. PhD thesis.

# K. Injuries & Sports Medicine

## Injuries & Sports Medicine

1   Medicina gymnastica, or, A treatise concerning the power of exercise, with respect to the animal economy and the great necessity of it in the cure of several distempers / Francis Fuller. London: Privately published, 1705.
BL: 1038.l.9

*Includes chapters on the power of exercise and the practice of the ancients. One of the first medical books to have a strong athletic bias.*

☞  Subsequent ed. K2

2   Medicina gymnastica, or, A treatise concerning the power of exercise, with respect to the animal economy and the great necessity of it in the cure of several distempers / Francis Fuller. 2nd ed. London: Privately published, 1705.
BL: 1039.l.6

☞  Previous ed. K1; subsequent ed. K3

3   Medicina gymnastica, or, A treatise concerning the power of exercise, with respect to the animal economy and the great necessity of it in the cure of several distempers / Francis Fuller. 3rd ed. London: Privately published, 1707.
BL: 1039.l.7

☞  Previous ed. K2; subsequent ed. K4

4   Medicina gymnastica, or, A treatise concerning the power of exercise, with respect to the animal economy and the great necessity of it in the cure of several distempers / Francis Fuller. 4th ed. London: Robert Knaplock, 1711. 271p
BL: 1568/8208

☞  Previous ed. K3; subsequent ed. K5

5   Medicina gymnastica, or, A treatise concerning the power of exercise, with respect to the animal economy and the great necessity of it in the cure of several distempers / Francis Fuller. 5th ed. London: 1718.
BL: 1039.l.8.

☞  Previous ed. K4; subsequent ed. K6

6   Medicina gymnastica, or, A treatise concerning the power of exercise, with respect to the animal economy and the great necessity of it in the cure of several distempers / Francis Fuller. 6th ed. London: 1728.
BL: 7462.b.57

☞  Previous ed. K5; subsequent ed. K7

7   Medicina gymnastica, or, A treatise concerning the power of exercise, with respect to the animal economy and the great necessity of it in the cure of several distempers / Francis Fuller. 7th ed. London: E. Curll, 1740. xx, 250p
BL: a1509/2065

☞  Previous ed. K6; subsequent ed. K8

8   Medicina gymnastica, or, A treatise concerning the power of exercise, with respect to the animal economy and the great necessity of it in the cure of several distempers. To which is added, Rules for health and long life, Written by an eminent physician [E. Curll?] / Francis Fuller. 9th ed. London: 1777.
*8th ed. untraced*
BL: 41.d.24

☞  Previous ed. K7

9   Oxygen and sparteine in athletics and training: a contribution to the physiology of doping / Oscar Jennings; with five sphygmographic tracings. London: Baillière, 1909.
29p; pbk
BL: 07305.i.40(9)

10   Injuries and sport: a general guide for the practitioner / C. B. Heald. London: Oxford University Press, 1931. xxiv, 543p; illus
(Oxford medical publications)
BL: 20036.a.1(470)

*Almost certainly the first work of its kind published in English, it includes injuries typically occurring in hurdling, javelin throwing, jumping, and running. The research findings of A. V. Hill are cited.*

11  The British encyclopaedia of medical practice / under
the general editorship of Sir Humphry Rolleston.
London: Butterworth, 1936-1941.
13 vols.                                    BL: 7321.ppp.1
    Volume 2 has a section 'Athletics' (pp302-309) by Dr
    Adolphe Abrahams, one of the foremost experts on
    athletics medicine, and Honorary Medical Officer to
    the British Olympic Athletic Team.
    ☞  Subsequent ed. K15

12  Athletic injuries: prevention, diagnosis and treatment /
Augustus Thorndike. London: Kimpton, 1938.
208p; illus; index                          BL: 07481.bb.1
    ☞  Subsequent ed. K13

13  Athletic injuries: prevention, diagnosis and treatment /
Augustus Thorndike. 2nd ed. London: Kimpton, 1942.
216p; illus; index                          BL: 7483.aaa.1
    ☞  Previous ed. K12; subsequent ed. K14

14  Athletic injuries: prevention, diagnosis and treatment /
Augustus Thorndike. 3rd ed. London: Kimpton, 1948.
243p; illus; index                          BL: 7483.aaa.7
    ☞  Previous ed. K13; subsequent ed. K20

15  The British encyclopaedia of medical practice / under
the general editorship of the Rt. Hon. Lord Horder. 2nd
ed. London: Butterworth, 1950-1952.         BL: 2025.b
    W. E. Tucker contributes a new chapter on athletic
    injuries.
    ☞  Previous ed. K11

16  A medical handbook for athletic and football club
trainers / William D. Jarvis foreword by J. P. Curries.
London: Faber & Faber, 1950.
144p; illus                                 BL: 7384.b.44

17  Athletic injuries / P. H. Sharp. London: Athene, 1952.
24p                                         BL: 7483.a.27
    On the homoeopathic treatment of sports injuries.

18  Sports injuries, manual for trainers and coaches /
Donald F. Featherstone; foreword by Rex Salisbury
Woods. London: Nicholas Kaye, 1954.
132p; illus                                 BL: 7484.m.29
    Practical advice for trainers and coaches who may lack
    deep medical knowledge.

19  Sports injuries: prevention and active treatment /
Christopher R. Woodard. London: Max Parrish, 1954.
127p                                        BL: 7484.b.14
    A textbook on 'active treatment', which enables an
    athlete to recover from injuries without losing physical
    condition.

20  Athletic injuries: prevention, diagnosis and treatment /
Augustus Thorndike. 4th ed. London: Kimpton, 1956.
252p; illus; index                          BL: 7442.p.6
    ☞  Previous ed. K14; subsequent ed. K26

21  Circuit training / Ronald E. Morgan and Graham T.
Adamson; forewords by Geoffrey H. G. Dyson and John
H. C. Colson. London: Bell, 1957.
88p; illus                                  BL: 7923.a.6
    Circuit training now forms a part of the general
    conditioning of most athletes. This book explains the
    physiological justification for this type of training and
    contains illustrations and descriptions of the wide
    range of exercises. A seminal work in its period.
    ☞  Subsequent ed. K22

22  Circuit training / Ronald E. Morgan and Graham T.
Adamson. 2nd ed. London: Bell, 1957.
94p; illus                                  BL: X.449/309
    ☞  Previous ed. K21

23  The disabilities and injuries of sport / Adolphe
Abrahams; foreword by Harold M. Abrahams. London:
Elek, 1961.
viii, 95p                                   BL: 7324.e.6

24  Sports injuries and their treatment / John H. C. Colson
and William J. Armour. London: Stanley Paul, 1961.
224p; illus                                 BL: 7326.a.47
    ☞  Subsequent ed. K36

25  Athletic injuries / Elizabeth Mary Page. London: Arco,
1962.
168p; illus
(Handybooks)
    *Cover title: Athletic injuries & their treatment*
                                            BL: X.329/81

26  Athletic injuries: prevention, diagnosis and treatment /
Augustus Thorndike. 5th ed. London: Kimpton, 1962.
259p; illus; index                          BL: X.329/124
    ☞  Previous ed. K20

27  Hints on athletic injuries (with physiotherapy treatments)
/ Cliff Bould. London: Amateur Athletic Association,
1962.
64p; illus                                  BL: X.329/991

28  Sports medicine / edited by John Garrett Pascoe
Williams; foreword by Sir Arthur Porritt. London:
Edward Arnold, 1962.
xi, 420p                                    BL: 7326.tt.15

29  Treatment of injuries to athletes / Donald H.
O'Donoghue. London: Saunders, 1962.
xiii, 649p; illus                           BL: 7326.h.1
    ☞  Subsequent ed. K35

30 Athletic injuries / Lynn O. Litton and Leonard F. Peltier. London: Churchill, 1963.
x, 222p; illus
BL: 07326.p.2

31 Medical care of the athlete / Allan James Ryan. London: McGraw-Hill, 1963.
xii, 343p
BL: 7327.e.23

32 Injury in sport: the physiology, prevention and treatment of injuries associated with sport / edited by J. R. Armstrong and W. E. Tucker; foreword by Sir Adolphe Abrahams. London: Staples, 1964.
xii, 628p; illus
BL: X.320/96

A monumental production by two great orthopaedic surgeons. It is divided into three sections. The first deals with the normal functions of the body in sporting activities; the second deals separately with nineteen major sports, including athletics; and the third section is concerned with treatment.

33 Doping: proceedings of an international seminar organised at the Universities of Ghent & Brussels, May 1964, by the Research Committee of the International Council of Sport and Physical Education, UNESCO / edited by A. de Schaepdryver and M. Hebbelinck. Oxford: Symposium Publications Division, Pergamon, 1965.
xi, 180p; illus
BL: X.320/429

An early seminar in the period immediately preceding the extensive use of anabolic steroids.

34 Medical aspects of sport and physical fitness / John G. P. Williams. Oxford: Pergamon, 1965.
viii, 192p
(Commonwealth and international library; no. 2128)
BL: X.329/1087

An important contribution to the literature of sports medicine.

35 Treatment of injuries to athletes / Don H. O'Donoghue. 2nd ed. London: Saunders, 1970.
xiv, 715p; illus; index
ISBN: 0-7216-6926-3
BL: X.320/2556

☞ Previous ed. K29; subsequent ed. K37

36 Sports injuries and their treatment / John H. C. Colson and William J. Armour. Rev. ed. London: Stanley Paul, 1975.
234p; illus
BL: X.329/10018

☞ Previous ed. K24

37 Treatment of injuries to athletes / Don H. O'Donoghue. 3rd ed. London: Saunders, 1976.
ii-xviii, 834p; illus; index
ISBN: 0-7216-6927-1
BL: SRL

☞ Previous ed. K35; subsequent ed. K41

38 How to prevent and heal running and other sports injuries / Eric Golanty; illustrations by David Wellner. London: Yoseloff, 1979.
135p; illus; index; pbk
*Bibliography: p132*
ISBN: 0-498-02391-5 (cased) • 0-498-02480-6 (pbk)
BL: X.629/13444

39 The runners' repair manual: a complete program for diagnosing and treating your foot, leg and back problems / Murray F. Weisenfeld with Barbara Burr. London: W.H. Allen, 1981.
xvi, 193p; illus; index
*Originally published: New York: St. Martin's Press, 1980*
ISBN: 0-491-02934-9
BL: X.629/15885

40 Sport, culture and ideology / edited by Jennifer Hargreaves. London: Routledge & Kegan Paul, 1982.
ix, 254p; illus; index; pbk
ISBN: 0-7100-9242-3
BL: X.529/52184

Notable for its chapter 'Sport and drugs' (pp197-212) by Martyn Lucking, the 1962 Commonwealth shot putt champion.

41 Treatment of injuries to athletes / Don H. O'Donoghue. 4th ed. London: Saunders, 1984.
714p; illus; index
ISBN: 0-7216-6928-X
BL: SRL

☞ Previous ed. K37

42 Foul play: drug abuse in sports / Tom Donohoe, Neil Johnson. Oxford: Blackwell, 1986.
189p; illus; index
ISBN: 0-631-14844-2
BL: YH.1986.b.293

This work remains the most concise and clear account of drug abuse in sport. The co-authors, both clinical researchers for a major pharmaceutical company, provide a brief historical overview in their introduction, before presenting detailed chapters on stimulants, anabolic steroids, drugs and the female athlete, anti-anxiety drugs, and painkillers. Current trends are examined and speculation as to future trends are presented. The counter-arguments are considered and the most significant cases of drug abuse revealed in 1986 and 1987 are discussed. Three useful appendices and a glossary are included.

43 Drugs in sport / edited by D. R. Mottram. London: Spon, 1988.
xviii, 169p
ISBN: 0-419-13880-3 (cased) • 0-419-13890-0 (pbk)
BL: YK.1989.a.1667 • YK.1989.a.1668

44 Running injuries / Tim Noakes, Stephen Granger. Oxford: Oxford University Press, 1990.
144p; illus; pbk
ISBN: 0-19-570617-X
BL: YK.1992.a.10753

☞ Subsequent ed. K52

45  Winning without drugs: the natural approach to
    competitive sport / David Hemery, Guy Ogden and
    Alan Evans. London: Willow, 1990.
    160p; illus
        *Bibliography: p160*          ISBN: 0-00-218349-8
                                      BL: YK.1990.b.9181

46  Drugs & sport: a comprehensive guide to the responsible
    use of drugs in sport, detailing banned and permitted
    products / edited by Linda Badewitz-Dodd. Chichester:
    Media Medica, 1991.
    146p; pbk
        *Foreword by Arthur Gold*     ISBN: 0-9510119-3-6
        Contents include a chapter on the Sports Council
        Doping Control Unit.

47  Drugs in competitive athletics: proceedings of the First
    International Symposium held on the Islands of Brioni,
    Yugoslavia 29 May-2 June 1988 / edited by James R.
    Shipe, Jr. and John Savory. Oxford: Blackwell Scientific,
    1991.
    v, 139p; illus; index         ISBN: 0-632-03181-6
                                  BL: DSC-4550.2128

48  Physical rehabilitation of the injured athlete / James R.
    Andrews and Gary L Harrelson. London: Saunders,
    1991.
    xii, 547p; illus; index       ISBN: 0-7216-2689-0
                                  BL: DSC-q92/03949

    ☞  Subsequent ed. K54

49  Sports injury handbook: professional advice for amateur
    athletes / Allan M. Levy, Mark L. Fuerst. Chichester:
    John Wiley, 1993.
    xix, 284p; illus; index; pbk  ISBN: 0-471-54737-9
                                  BL: YK.1995.b.7542

50  Running: fitness and injuries: a self-help guide / Vivian
    Grisogono. London: John Murray, 1994.
    xi, 256p; illus; index; pbk   ISBN: 0-7195-5064-5
                                  BL: YK.1994.a.8292

51  Healthy runner's handbook / Lyle J. Micheli with Mark
    Jenkins. Leeds: Human Kinetics, 1996.
    vii, 255p; illus; index; pbk  ISBN: 0-88011-524-6
                                  BL: YK.1996.a.19094

52  Running injuries: how to prevent and overcome them /
    Tim Noakes, Stephen Granger. 2nd ed. Oxford: Oxford
    University Press, 1996.
    176p; illus; index; pbk       ISBN: 0-19-571384-2
                                  BL: YK.1996.a.19977

    ☞  Previous ed. K44

53  Running injuries / edited by Gary N. Guten. London:
    Saunders, 1997.
    xviii, 283p; illus; index     ISBN: 0-7216-6843-7
                                  BL: DSC-q97/23371

54  Physical rehabilitation of the injured athlete / edited by
    James R. Andrews, Gary L. Harrelson, Kevin E. Wilk.
    2nd ed. London: Saunders, 1998.
    x, 693p; illus; index         ISBN: 0-7216-6549-7
                                  BL: DSC-98/07693

    ☞  Previous ed. K48

55  Sudden cardiac death in the athlete / edited by N. A.
    Mark Estes, Deeb N. Salem and Paul J. Wang. London:
    Futura, 1998.
    xvi, 600p; illus; index       ISBN: 0-87993-691-6
                                  BL: DSC-98/23828

56  Arrhythmias and sudden death in athletes / edited by A.
    Bayés de Luna, F. Furlanello and B. J. Maron. London:
    Kluwer Academic, 2000.
    163p; illus; index
    (Developments in cardiovascular medicine; vol. 232)
                                  ISBN: 0-7923-6337-X
                                  BL: GU 67

✱  *Additional References*

57  The aetiology of running injuries / S. L. Rowell.
    Brighton Polytechnic, 1989. PhD thesis.

58  An investigation of the actual and perceived use of
    performance-enhancing drugs in British national
    sprinting from 1960-1990: a research study for the
    Scottish Sports Council / Avril A. M. Blamey.
    Edinburgh: Scottish Sports Council, 1992.
    14p; pbk
    (Research report; no. 28)     ISBN: 1-85060-203-4
                                  BL: DSC-7766.064(28)

59  Rheoli'r camddefnydd o gyffuriau mewn chwaraeon:
    cyngor i athletwyr a hyfforddwyr / Cyngor Chwaraeon
    Cymru. The control of drug abuse in sport: advice to
    athletes and coaches / Sports Council for Wales.
    Caerdydd: The Council, 1998.
    6p; illus; pbk
        *Welsh/English text tête-bêche*

# L. Literature & the Visual Arts

## Adult Fiction

### ✳ Novels

#### Abercrombie, Barbara

1    Run for your life. London: MacDonald, 1984.
249p                                    ISBN: 0-356-10477-X

  Suspense story of a woman novelist who uses marathon running as an inspiration for writing.

#### Ashton, Elizabeth

2    The golden girl. London: Mills and Boon, 1978.
188p; pbk                          ISBN: 0-263-72636-3
                                              BL: H.78/855

  Romantic novel about a woman athlete.

#### Atkinson, Hugh

3    The Games / research and background by Phillip Knightley. London: Cassell, 1967.
442p                                    BL: Nov.11105

  Centred on a British marathon runner, this is 'a purely fictional projection of what could happen to the Olympic movement if politics and money were allowed to erode the spirit in which the Games were originally conceived'.

#### Barling, Tom

4    The Olympic sleeper. London: Eyre Methuen, 1979.
218p                                    ISBN: 0-413-46010-X
                                              BL: Nov.38621

#### Barnes, Linda

5    Dead heat. London: Severn House, 1984.
194p                                    ISBN: 0-7278-1050-2
                                              BL: Nov.52810

  Crime novel involving murder in the Boston Marathon.

#### Bell, Pauline

6    Downhill to death. London: Macmillan, 1994.
201p                                    ISBN: 0-333-63001-7
                                              BL: Nov.1995/169

  Crime novel featuring cross-country and road walking.

#### Booth, Patrick John

7    Sprint from the bell. London: Collins, 1966.
254p                                    BL: Nov.7778

#### Bragg, Melvyn

8    Josh Lawton. London: Secker and Warburg, 1972.
193p                                    ISBN: 0-436-06708-0
                                              BL: Nov.18457

  The main character is a Lakeland fell-runner, though the athletics content is slight.

#### Collins, Wilkie

9    Man and wife: a novel. London: Ellis, 1870.
3 vols.                                 BL: 12628.bb.5

  The master of Victorian melodrama was one of the first novelists to use athletics as a theme. *Man and Wife* describes the fortunes of Geoffrey Delamayn, a champion long distance runner, and is a bitter condemnation of the sport which had been taken up so enthusiastically in England in the mid 1860s. As a social document the novel is important, for it presents fears and superstitions about the dangers of running which were seriously discussed at the time. It also gives a unique description of the atmosphere and scene in a stadium of the period, and its delineation of Perry, the athlete's professional trainer, may well be based on Nat Perry, the most famous English coach of the nineteenth century.

## Crampsey, Robert A.

10  Our country's battles. Belfast: Blackstaff, 1986.
116p      ISBN: 0-85640-357-1 (cased) • 0-85640-358-X (pbk)
BL: YC.1986.a.2869

The story of a freelance reporter covering the 1968 Olympics at Mexico City, with a vivid chapter on Bob Beamon's world record long jump.

## Edmonds, Frances

11  Games. London: Orion, 1996.
viii, 289p      ISBN: 0-7528-0064-7
BL: YC.1996.b.6788

A story of pressure on a British sprinter to use drugs to win the Olympic 100m in the year 2000.

## Evans, I. O.

12  Olympic runner: a story of the great days of Ancient Greece / illustrated by Edward Osmond. London: Hutchinson, 1955.
256p; illus; index      BL: 7922.ee.5

## Ferguson, Peter

13  Monster Clough: a novel. London: Hodder & Stoughton, 1962.
189p      BL: Nov.4200

A convincing account of an athletic career from schooldays to retirement. The height of 'Monster' Clough's achievement is a county championship, but his contests in minor club meetings are related with compelling skill. Unusually, the hero is a field events athlete, initially a long jumper and later a shot putter.

## Fraser, Alison

14  Running wild. Richmond: Mills & Boon, 1996.
188p; pbk
ISBN: 0-263-14808-4 (cased) • 0-263-79575-6 (pbk)
BL: H.96/2587

Romantic story of an athlete who dreamed of winning an Olympic medal.

## Frith, Nigel

15  Olympiad. London: Unwin Paperbacks, 1988.
224p; pbk      ISBN: 0-04-440155-8
BL: H.88/916

Set in the year of the first Olympics, this tells the story of suitor-runners who compete for the hand of Atalanta.

## Garner, Shelley

16  The flame and the vision. London: Frederick Muller, 1962.
254p; illus      BL: Nov.4132

About a pentathlon competitor in the ancient Olympic Games.

## Glanville, Brian

17  The Olympian. London: Secker & Warburg, 1969.
310p      SBN: 436-18105-3
BL: Nov.13876

The narrative traces the progress of a promising 18 year old working-class club quarter-miler.

## Goddard, Kenneth

18  Balefire. London: Corgi, 1983.
337p; pbk
*Originally published: Toronto: Bantam, 1982*
ISBN: 0-552-99062-0
BL: X.950/27460

An Olympic mystery novel.

## Goldman, William

19  Marathon man. London: Macmillan, 1975.
252p
*Originally published: New York: Delacorte Press, 1974*
ISBN: 0-333-18073-9
BL: Nov.22792

Thriller with some athletics references, in which the hero, a jogger, is inspired by Paavo Nurmi and Abebe Bikila.

## Grant, David (pseudonym of David Craig Owen Thomas)

20  Moscow 5000. London: Michael Joseph, 1979.
447p      ISBN: 0-7181-1780-8
BL: Nov.24493

## Graves, Richard

21  The spiritual Quixote, or, The summer's ramble of Mr. Geoffry Wildgoose: a comic romance, in three volumes. London: Dodsley, 1773.
3 vols.
*Published anonymously*      BL: 12614.eee.20

Includes a scene where a preacher makes a fool of himself at the Cotswold Games.

## Haile, Terence

22  The sports stars in danger. Richmond: Stanley Baker, 1952.
96p      BL: 012642.n.222

A crime novel that combines the kidnapping and murder of sportsmen, including athletes.

*Hamer, Malcolm*

23   Predator. London: Little, Brown, 1995.
     476p                                      ISBN: 0-316-87488-4
                                               BL: Nov.1996/889

     Dubious practices at management level in a number of
     sports, touching only briefly on athletics at the
     Olympic Games.

*Hamer, Mike*

24   'Death games': the Olympic bid mystery. Manchester:
     Rosewood, 1995.
     312p; pbk
     (Manchester murder mysteries)
        *Variant title: Olympic hello*        ISBN: 1-898213-05-4
                                               BL: H.96/2462

     Manchester's bid for the Olympics is the theme of this
     crime novel; there are only slight references to
     athletics.

*Hastings, Phyllis*

25   Naked runner. London: Hale, 1987.
     173p                                      ISBN: 0-7090-2888-1
                                               BL: Nov.1987/1473

     In an eighteenth-century setting, a shepherd boy
     becomes a running footman.

*Healy, Jeremiah*

26   Right to die. London: Macmillan, 1991.
     243p                                      ISBN: 0-333-56606-8

     Crime novel in which a private eye enters the Boston
     Marathon.

*Henry, Anne*

27   The glory run. London: Harlequin, 1985.
     253p; pbk                                 ISBN: 0-373-16090-9
                                               BL: H.86/367

     Romantic novel about a Texas State 1500m champion
     who makes a comeback when she falls in love with her
     coach.

*Hill, Reginald*

28   Killing the lawyers. London: Collins Crime, 1997.
     287p
     (A Joe Sixsmith novel)                    ISBN: 0-00-232607-8
                                               BL: Nov.1997/573

     Incorporates a plot about attempts to make a runner
     throw a race.

*Hodges, Jo*

29   The girl with brains in her feet. London: Virago, 1998.
     216p; pbk                                 ISBN: 1-86049-565-6

     The struggles of a black runner. Hodges also wrote the
     screenplay of the film.

*Holt, Tom*

30   Olympiad: an historical novel. London: Little, Brown,
     2000.
     xv, 368p; illus, 1 map                    ISBN: 0-316-85390-9
                                               BL: Nov.2000/597

     A comic historical novel providing a 'reliably false'
     account of the 8th-century BC foundation of the
     Olympic Games.

*Inigo, Martin (pseudonym of Keith Miles)*

31   Stone dead. London: Sphere, 1991.
     244p; pbk                                 ISBN: 0-7474-0204-3
                                               BL: H.91/1562

     The main character is a former Olympic distance
     runner, though the novel is set mainly in the world of
     golf.

32   Touch play. London: Sphere, 1991.
     229p; pbk                                 ISBN: 0-7474-0203-5
                                               BL: H.91/2992

     Second novel featuring the former Olympic distance
     runner, set mainly in the world of tennis.

*Johnson, Gillard*

33   Raphael of the olive. London: Bennett, 1912.
     355p                                      BL: NN.815

     Romantic novel set in 175-164BC, with the Olympic
     Games as background.

*Johnson, William O.*

34   Hammered gold. London: W.H. Allen, 1983.
     267p; pbk
        *Originally published: New York: Pocket Books, 1982*
                                               ISBN: 0-352-31342-0
                                               BL: H.83/1210

     Thriller about a plan to eliminate potential winners at
     the 1984 Olympics.

*Keegan, Alex*

35   Cuckoo. London: Headline, 1994.
     410p                                      ISBN: 0-7472-1107-8
                                               BL: Nov.1994/1957

     First of a series set in Brighton and featuring
     detective athlete Caz Flood.

36  Kingfisher: a Caz Flood mystery. London: Headline, 1995.
    403p                                    ISBN: 0-7472-1326-7
                                                BL: Nov.1995/859

    DC Flood investigates some hit-and-runs and missing persons, including a running rival.

37  Vulture: a Caz Flood mystery. London: Headline, 1995.
    410p                                    ISBN: 0-7472-1200-7
                                                BL: Nov.1995/255

    DC Flood investigates a serial rape case in which the victims all belong to the same jogging group.

38  Razorbill. London: Headline, 1996.
    vii, 408p                               ISBN: 0-7472-1644-4
                                                BL: Nov.1996/310

    DC Flood, undercover as a running coach, investigates the death of a runner in Lanzarote.

## Langley, Bob

39  Fellrunner. Sutton: Severn House, 1996.
    250p                                    ISBN: 0-7278-4889-5
                                                BL: Nov.1996/972

## Lear, Peter (pseudonym of Peter Lovesey)

40  Goldengirl. London: Cassell, 1977.
    377p                                    ISBN: 0-304-29848-4
                                                BL: Nov.35862

    Exploitation of America's star athlete as she prepares for the Moscow Olympics.

## Lester, Paul

41  The Super-Olympics, Banjul 2020 AD. Birmingham: Protean, 1998.
    3p; pbk
        *Story first published in the anthology Time out (New Fiction, 1993)*                          ISBN: 0-948683-30-9
                                                BL: YK.1999.a.8252

## Loader, William R.

42  Staying the distance. London: Cape, 1958.
    222p                                    BL: NNN.11904

    A novel about an average athlete who with exceptional perseverance eventually wins an epic 5000 metre race at White City Stadium. The climax is undeniably reminiscent of the Chataway-Kuts duel: 'The great stadium was rent with noise. It was a mighty paean honouring courage and strength. The vision of two figures was burnt into the brain of every person present. And the figure in the white vest, eyes closed and face deathly pale was crossing the line two feet in front of the figure in the red vest.'

## Lockridge, Ross Franklin, Jr

43  Raintree County. London: Macdonald, 1949.
    1056p                                   BL: 12730.b.19

    Central to the plot of this long novel is the race over 300 yards on 4 July 1859 to determine the fastest runner in Raintree County. An abridged edition was published in 1957 when the film was released.

## Lovesey, Peter

44  Wobble to death. London: Macmillan, 1970.
    190p                                    ISBN: 0-333-11069-2
                                                BL: Nov.15118

    Crime novel centred on a Victorian Six-Day race.

45  Invitation to a dynamite party. London: Macmillan, 1974.
    188p                                    ISBN: 0-333-15656-0
                                                BL: Nov.21007

    Crime novel including a Victorian hammer-throwing competition.

## Lundberg, Knud

46  The Olympic hope: a story from the Olympic Games, 1996 / translated by Eiler Hansen and William Luscombe. London: Stanley Paul, 1958.
    171p
        *Translation of: Dat Olympiske håb*      BL: NNN.11938
    A futuristic novel about the 800m at the 1996 Olympics. This is a remarkable work, which features distance runners undergoing amputation of their arms (!) to improve performance, possibly a prescient metaphor for drug-ingestion in the final quarter of the twentieth century.

## Macgowan, Jonathan (pseudonym of David M. Thurlow)

47  Death at the Games. London: Hale, 1980.
    192p                                    ISBN: 0-7091-8081-0
                                                BL: Nov.40680

    A mystery in which the British marathon champion is murdered on the approach to the stadium.

## McNab, Tom

48  Flanagan's run: a novel. London: Hodder and Stoughton, 1982.
    472p          ISBN: 0-340-24393-7 (cased) • 0-340-27482-4 (pbk)
                                      BL: Nov.46076 • Nov.46077

    An account of a 3000 mile trans-America race in 1931. Widely regarded as the most successful athletics novel of the twentieth century.

49  Rings of sand. London: Hodder and Stoughton, 1984.
    285p          ISBN: 0-340-33162-3 (cased) • 0-340-27826-9 (pbk)
                                      BL: X.950/35319 • X.950/35320

    An account of a professional take-over of the Olympic movement.

50 The fast men. London: Hutchinson, 1986.
288p        ISBN: 0-09-164210-8 (cased) • 0-09-164301-5 (pbk)
BL: YC.1986.a.5938

Possibly the only sports Western ever written, this is an account of professional foot-racing in the American West of the 1870s.

### McNeish, James

51 Lovelock. London: Hodder and Stoughton, 1986.
398p        ISBN: 0-340-36430-0

Fictional treatment of the career of Jack Lovelock, the 1936 Olympic 1500m champion.

### May, Jonathan (pseudonym of Christopher Wood)

52 Confessions from the Olympics. London: Sphere, 1980.
139p; pbk        ISBN: 0-7221-5999-4
BL: H.80/756

Humorous fiction in the 'confessions' series.

### Mayer, Albert I.

53 Olympiad / illustrated by Cleveland J. Woodward. London: Harper, 1938.
ix, 268p; illus        BL: 12718.dd.14

Carefully researched novel set in 464BC, with detailed descriptions of the events of the classical Games.

### Messman, Jon

54 To kill a jogger. London: Hamlyn, 1980.
184p; pbk
*Originally published in USA as: Jogger's moon*
ISBN: 0-600-20049-3

Crime novel about serial killings of joggers in New York city parks.

### Miles, Keith

55 Not for glory, not for gold. London: Century, 1986.
312p
*Based on a screenplay by David Williamson*
ISBN: 0-7126-1271-8 (cased) • 0-7126-1272-6 (pbk)
BL: YK.1986.a.1531 • YC.1986.a.4438

Fictional treatment of Bannister's four minute mile.

### Mitchell, Gladys

56 The longer bodies. London: Gollancz, 1930.
287p        BL: NN.16379

A crime novel with an athletics background.

57 Adders on the heath. London: Michael Joseph, 1963.
240p        BL: Nov.1475

A murder novel with an athletics background.

58 A javelin for Jonah. London: Joseph, 1974.
200p        ISBN: 0-7181-1193-1
BL: Nov.20901

Crime novel in which a javelin and a shot are employed as murder weapons.

### Moffatt, James

59 The marathon murder. London: New English Library, 1972.
124p; pbk

Crime novel written in response to a challenge issued by the BBC Television Late Night Line-up team.

### Molloy, Maura

60 One Tailteann week: a chronicle of the Games in ancient days. Dundalk: Dundalgan, 1930.
66p; illus; pbk        BL: 012603.bb.21

Fictional account of the ancient Games of Ireland.

### Neville, Margot (pseudonym of Margot Goyder & Neville Joske)

61 Murder of Olympia. London: Geoffrey Bles, 1956.
223p        BL: NNN.8937

A crime novel set at the Olympic Games, Melbourne, 1956.

### Owen, John

62 The running footman, or, The sentimental servant. London: Gollancz, 1931.
352p        BL: NN.18375

A novel which takes as its hero one of the running footmen of the eighteenth century.

### Parandowski, Jan

63 The Olympic discus / translated by A. M. Malecka and S. A. Walewski. London: Minerva, 1939.
301p
*Translation of: Dysk Olimpijski*        BL: 12593.l.13

An historical novel of athletes and athletics in ancient Greece.

### Parker, Robert B.

64 Wilderness. London: Deutsch, 1980.
256p        ISBN: 0-233-97276-5

Crime novel featuring a jogger who witnesses murder.

## Patterson, James

65 The Jericho commandment: a novel. Feltham: Hamlyn, 1980.
256p; illus
*Originally published: New York: Crown, 1979*
ISBN: 0-600-20019-1
BL: Nov.40795

A Jewish terrorist group at the 1980 Olympics in Moscow.

## Price, Victor H. J.

66 The other kingdom. London: Heinemann, 1964.
231p
BL: Nov.3253

A novel which describes a Belfast university student's efforts to become a world-class miler.

## Reich, Christopher

67 The runner. London: Headline, 2000.
496p ISBN: 0-7472-7257-3 (cased) • 0-7472-7258-1 (pbk)

A former Olympic sprinter and European Champion is hunted for war crimes committed during his service as an SS officer.

## Ridpath, Michael

68 Free to trade. London: Heinemann, 1995.
344p
ISBN: 0-434-00170-8
BL: YC.1995.b.1381

An Olympic 800 metre bronze medallist becomes a financial trader.

## Roszel, Renee

69 Nobody's fool. London: Silhouette, 1986.
250p; 1 genealogical table; pbk ISBN: 0-373-50452-7
BL: H.87/1075

Romantic novel in which the heroine dares the hero to run against her in the nine-mile Tulsa Run.

## Salisbury, John (pseudonym of David Caute)

70 Moscow gold. London: Futura, 1980.
320p; pbk ISBN: 0-7088-1702-5

A paperback original about the disappearance of Russia's star woman athlete before the 1980 Olympics.

## Staalesen, Gunnar

71 At night all wolves are grey / translated from the Norwegian by David McDuff. London: Quartet, 1986.
214p
*Translation of: I mørket er alle ulver grå*
ISBN: 0-7043-2558-6
BL: Nov.1986/656

Crime novel in which the private eye protagonist and his contact in the police are long distance runners.

## Stanwood, Brooks (pseudonym of Howard Kaminsky & Susan Kaminsky)

72 The glow: a novel. London: Raven, 1980.
297p
*Originally published: New York: McGraw-Hill, 1979*
ISBN: 0-354-04460-5
BL: Nov.39960

Horror novel whose premise is that a group of runners are zombies.

## Stratford, George

73 In the long run: London: Citron, 2000.
226p; pbk ISBN: 0-7544-0126-X

The setting is South Africa, and the Comrades' Marathon.

## Thorne, Guy (pseudonym of Cyril Arthur Edward Ranger Gull)

74 The race before us. London: White, 1910.
vii, 312p BL: 012622.cc.27

The race of the title is a road race from Piraeus to the Acropolis between William Blair, author of 'The philosophy of sport' and world record holder for the mile, and Danilo Christos.

## Travis, Pete

75 The round. Preston: TKI Publications, 1998.
239p

Based around the 24-hour Bob Graham round of forty-two Lakeland peaks.

## Trott, Susan

76 The housewife and the assassin. London: Gollancz, 1979.
264p
ISBN: 0-575-02729-0
BL: Nov.39734

Crime novel featuring a jogger.

## Trow, M. J.

77　Lestrade and the deadly game. London: Constable, 1990.
240p
　　　　　　　　　　　　　　　ISBN: 0-09-469720-5
　　　　　　　　　　　　　　　BL: NOV.1990/1301

　　Humorous crime novel set at the 1908 Olympic Games, including descriptions of Halswelle's 400m and Dorando's marathon.

## Vacha, Robert

78　Moscow 1980. London: Star, 1979.
265p; pbk
　　　　　　　　　　　　　　　ISBN: 0-352-30258-5
　　　　　　　　　　　　　　　BL: X.708/21849

　　Politics and international intrigue in the run-up to the 1980 Olympics.

## Walker, David H.

79　Geordie. London: Collins, 1950.
192p
　　　　　　　　　　　　　　　BL: NNN.874

　　A Highlander, Geordie MacTaggart, eventually wins the Olympic shot. The later film, starring Bill Travers, changed Geordie's event to hammer.

80　Come back, Geordie. London: Collins, 1966.
221p
　　　　　　　　　　　　　　　BL: Nov.8669
　　A weak sequel to 'Geordie'.

## Walsh, Maurice

81　The small dark man. London: W. & R. Chambers, 1929.
304p
　　　　　　　　　　　　　　　BL: NN.16031

　　Set in the Highlands, this novel has ten pages of athletics content.

## Warren, Patricia Nell

82　The front runner. London: Bantam, 1976.
314p; pbk
　　　*Originally published: New York: Morrow, 1974*
　　　　　　　　　　　　　　　ISBN: 0-552-10286-5
　　　　　　　　　　　　　　　BL: H.77/26

　　Harlan Brown narrates the story of how he trained Billy Sive into a bright long distance prospect for the 1976 Montreal Olympics.

## Waugh, Evelyn

83　Decline and fall: an illustrated novelette. London: Chapman & Hall, 1928.
xii, 288p
　　　　　　　　　　　　　　　BL: Cup.407.ff.31
　　Includes the famous account of sports day at Dr Fagan's school.

## Weatherby, William J.

84　Chariots of fire: a true story / based on the screenplay by Colin Welland. London: Granada, 1982.
126p; illus; pbk
　　　　　　　　　　　　　　　ISBN: 0-586-05776-5
　　　　　　　　　　　　　　　BL: H.84/999

　　Based on the Oscar-winning film.

# ✳ Short Stories – Single Author Collections

## Beachcroft, T. O.

85　A young man in a hurry, and other stories. London: Boriswood, 1934.
255p
　　　　　　　　　　　　　　　BL: NN.22503

　　The title story is based on an athlete's life; also contains 'The half-mile'.

## Cheever, John

86　The enormous radio, and other stories. London: Gollancz, 1953.
237p
　　　　　　　　　　　　　　　BL: 12651.i.22

　　The story 'O youth and beauty!' has as its subject a former track star, a hurdler, who cannot come to terms with life after sport.

## Doyle, Arthur Conan

87　The return of Sherlock Holmes. London: Newnes, 1905.
403p
　　　　　　　　　　　　　　　BL: 012631.aa.26

　　In 'The adventure of the three students' Holmes solves a mystery through observation of long-jump details.

## Harraden, Beatrice

88　Untold tales of the past; with drawings by H. R. Millar. Edinburgh: Blackwood, 1897.
viii, 271p
　　　　　　　　　　　　　　　BL: 12626.e.17

　　Includes 'The garland of wild olives' about the Olympic Games in 400BC.

## Horler, Sydney

89　Dying to live, and other stories. London: Hutchinson, 1935.
288p
　　　　　　　　　　　　　　　BL: NN.24072

　　'Good for Geekie', written in 1916, has an athletics theme.

## Morrison, Arthur

90　Martin Hewitt, investigator. London: Ward & Lock, 1894.
324p
　　　　　　　　　　　　　　　BL: 012629.gg.1

　　'The loss of Sammy Throckett', first published in the Strand (March to September 1894) is about a professional sprinter.

*Sillitoe, Alan*

91  The loneliness of the long-distance runner. London:
W.H. Allen, 1959.
176p                                               BL: NNN.13909

A collection of short stories, of which the most
famous describes the thoughts of a borstal boy in the
course of a cross-country run.

*Somerville, E. Œ. & Martin Ross*

92  Some experiences of an Irish RM, with illustrations by Œ
Somerville. London: Longmans, 1899.
viii, 309p; illus                                  BL: 012331.i.7
*Martin Ross is a pseudonym of Violet Florence Martin*

'Occasional licences' includes an entertaining account
of an Irish country sports meeting, with 'hop, step and
leap' and tug-of-war.

*Webster, F. A. M.*

93  Old Ebbie: detective up to date. London: Chapman &
Hall, 1923.
255p                                                BL: NN.8898

Includes 'The double problem'.

✳  *Short Stories – Anthologies*

94  Best sports stories / edited with an introduction by Paul
Edwards. London: Faber, 1966.
223p                                             BL: X.909/7818

Includes extracts from 'Monster Clough', by Peter
Ferguson.

95  Penguin modern stories 10 / edited by Judith Burnley.
Harmondsworth: Penguin, 1972.
157p; pbk                                   ISBN 0-14-003382-3

Includes Brian Glanville's 'Three or four cultures'. Set
during the 1968 Olympic Games in Mexico City, the
story is written from the viewpoint of a British 200m
sprinter, Marion, and describes her passing
involvement with a Uruguayan wrestler, Antonio, as
they are caught up in the brutal suppression of
student protests.

96  The Mystery Guild anthology / edited by John Waite.
London: Constable, 1980.
166p                                     ISBN: 0-09-463950-7
                                            BL: X.989/88508

Includes 'Aristotle and the fatal javelin' by Margaret
Doody, in which the philosopher investigates.

97  Free agents / Max Apple. London. Faber: 1986.
197p
*Originally published: New York: Harper Row, 1984*
                                            ISBN: 0-571-13852-7
                                            BL: Nov.1986/178

In 'Carbo-loading', the main character is a marathon
runner.

98  A twist in the tale / Jeffrey Archer. London: Hodder &
Stoughton, 1988.
192p                                       ISBN: 0-340-40538-4
                                            BL: YC.1988.b.8145

'Christina Rosenthal' is the love/hate story of a Jewish
miler taunted by a girl.

99  Irish sporting short stories / edited by David Marcus.
Belfast: Appletree, 1995.
207p; pbk                                  ISBN: 0-86281-535-5
                                            BL: H.96/2769

'The last season' by Michael Bowler, is on marathon
running.

100 In Kensington gardens once … / H. R. F. Keating;
drawings by Gwen Mandley. Jesmond: Flambard, 1997.
109p; illus; pbk                           ISBN: 1-873226-23-3
                                            BL: YK.1997.b.3246

Includes 'Runners', about a woman intrigued by the
joggers in Kensington Gardens.

✳ *Miscellanies*

101 The sporting life / chosen by Alan C. Jenkins. London:
Blackie, 1974.
298p; illus                                ISBN: 0-216-89789-0
                                            BL: X.989/26584

Includes 'The funeral games', from the Iliad by Homer,
translated by E. V. Rieu and extracts from Samuel
Pepys' Diary with reference to a foot-race in Hyde
Park.

102 Sporting literature: an anthology / chosen by Vernon
Scannell. Oxford: Oxford University Press, 1987.
320p; index                                ISBN: 0-19-212250-9
                                            BL: YC.1987.a.3483

Section XI, 'We run because we must', has extracts of
prose and poetry from Joseph Strutt, William Morris,
C. H. Sorley, Nicarchus, A. E. Housman. F. A. M.
Webster, Evelyn Waugh and Alan Sillitoe.

# Children's & Teenage Fiction

## ✳ *Novels & Storybooks*

### *Adamson, Jean & Gareth Adamson*

103 Topsy and Tim's sports day. Glasgow: Blackie, 1977.
24p; illus
(Topsy and Tim handy books)
ISBN: 0-216-90406-4 (cased) • 0-216-90407-2 (pbk)
For very young readers.

### *Allen, Joy*

104 Sports day for Charlie / illustrated by Michael Charlton.
London. Hamish Hamilton, 1990.
40p; illus
ISBN: 0-241-12904-4
BL: YK.1990.a.6216

### *Avery, Charles Harold*

105 Out of the running: a school story. London: Collins,
1904.
279p
BL: 012803.c.22
The Crottle Cup at Claybrook School is awarded to the
winner of the 'famous ten-mile cross-country run' and
forms most of the narrative from chapters 21-26.

### *Barbour, Ralph Henry*

106 Winning his 'Y': a story of school athletics. London:
Appleton, 1910.
vii, 286p; illus
BL: 012705.bb.32
This, and the Barbour novels below, are set in the USA,
where they were published simultaneously.

107 For Yardley: a story of track and field. London:
Appleton, 1911.
vi, 298p; illus
BL: 012704.dd.6

108 Beaton runs the mile. London: Appleton, 1933.
291p; illus
BL: A.N.1518

### *Barnett, John* (pseudonym of *John Reginald Stagg*)

109 The Skipper of the XI: a story of school life. London:
Blackie, 1915.
225p
BL: 012804.d.14
Includes two chapters on athletics.

### *Barrie, Alexander*

110 Ben goes for gold. London: Blackie, 1991.
118p
ISBN: 0-216-93081-2
BL: YK.1991.a.4659

### *Bateman, Robert*

111 Young runner. London: Constable, 1958.
159p
(Sports fiction series)
BL: W.P.4522/1

### *Batt, Elizabeth*

112 The scarlet runners / illustrated by Daphne Rowles.
London: Lutterworth, 1967.
61p; illus
(Junior gateway series; no. 8)

### *Bee, Dora*

113 Our marathon race / with coloured illustrations by
Arthur Twidle. London: Religious Tract Society, 1910.
320p; illus
BL: 04430.k.23
During the marathon craze that followed Dorando's
famous run, a group of girls organise their own six-mile
'marathon'.

### *Bevan, Marjorie*

114 Five of the Fourth. London: Sampson Low, 1926.
vi, 250p; illus
BL: 12801.i.21
The chapter 'Sports day' features schoolgirl athletics.

### *Bird, Richard* (pseudonym of *Walter Barradell-Smith*)

115 The sporting house: a school story / with illustrations by
T. M. R. Whitwell. London: Humphrey Milford, Oxford
University Press, 1921.
282p; illus
BL: 012802.cc.11
School story featuring a boy athlete.

116 The Ryecroft rivals. London: Blackie, 1923.
256p
BL: 12802.bb.45
School story that opens with a cross-country race.

117 The Wharton medal / illustrated by Frank Insall.
London: Oxford University Press, 1929.
259p; illus
BL: 12812.g.20
School story featuring running.

### *Buckeridge, Anthony*

118 Jennings follows a clue. London: Collins, 1951.
Chapter 16, 'Darbishire runs a race', has the main
athletics content, and other references appear
elsewhere.

## Burrage, A. Harcourt

119 The mysteries of Saddleworth. London: Nelson, 1928.
247p; illus                                      BL: 12811.aaa.13

Story with a cross-country race as its main action.

120 Odds against / with illustrations by Comerford Watson.
London: Evans, 1947.
240p; illus                                      BL: 12830.eee.41

Chapter 21, 'The victor', features an inter-house cross-
country race.

## Butterworth, Nick & Mick Inkpen

121 Sports day. London: Hodder and Stoughton, 1988.
32p; illus                                 ISBN: 0-340-42284-X
BL: LB.31.a.1663

## Carlson, Nancy

122 Loudmouth George and the big race. London: Dent,
1984.
32p; illus
*Originally published: Minneapolis: Carolrhoda, 1983*
ISBN: 0-460-06160-7
BL: X.990/23105

## Cave, Kathryn

123 Running battles / illustrated by Derek Brazell. London:
Viking, 1992.
122p; illus                                ISBN: 0-670-84591-4
BL: YK.1993.a.10658

Lynda's little sister is an Olympic runner in the making,
and male prejudices have to be overcome at the local
club.

## Childs, Rob

124 Sandford on the run. London: Blackie, 1981.
123p                                       ISBN: 0-216-91131-1
BL: X.990/18036

A novel of school athletics, both track and field.

125 The big race / illustrated by Tim Morwood. London:
Young Corgi, 1988.
91p; illus; pbk                            ISBN: 0-552-52461-1
BL: YK.1989.a.2019

Features a cross-country race.

126 Run for it! Aylesbury: Ginn, 1995.
64p; illus; pbk
(New reading 360: level 10; 5)            ISBN: 0-602-26403-0
BL: YK.1995.a.9772

Cross-country theme.

## Christopher, Matt

127 Run, Billy, run. London: Little, Brown, 1980.
145p; pbk                                  ISBN: 0-316-13993-9
BL: H.95/1260

## Cleary, Beverly

128 Strider / illustrated by Paul O. Zelinsky. London:
Hamish Hamilton, 1991.
136p; illus                                ISBN: 0-241-13134-0
BL: Nov.1994/719

Friendship with an abandoned dog inspires a boy to
develop as a personality through athletics.

## Cleaver, Hylton

129 The Harley first XI. London: Humphrey Milford,
Oxford University Press, 1920.
272p; illus                                     BL: 12801.cc.25

Contains several references to the school sports and
a full description of the cross-country race (pp106-
114).

130 Roscoe makes good: a story of Harley / illustrated by H.
M. Brock. London: Humphrey Milford, Oxford
University Press, 1921.
296p; illus                                    BL: 012802.cc.16

Chapter 22 is centred on the mile race in the school
sports.

131 The Harley first XV. London: Humphrey Milford,
Oxford University Press, 1922.
288p; illus                                      BL: 12800.c.47

Has a lengthy description of the school mile race
(pp174-179).

132 On with the motley. London: Mills & Boon, 1922.
310p                                               BL: NN.7827

Contains a number of references to miling at school
level.

133 The ghost of Greyminster. London: Collins, 1933.
288p                                            BL: 20053.bb.23

Chapters 11, 'On the right track', and 25, 'Recompense',
are concerned with the school sports.

134 Lucky break. London: Warne, 1950.
254p; illus
(Crown library series)                          BL: 12833.b.14

Chapters 12 and 13 are concerned with a private
cross-country match for £1,000 in which the breaking
of the hero's pince-nez is central to the drama.

## Culper, Felix

135 Orville and Cuddles go to the Olympics / illustrations by L. Vant. London: Dragon, 1986.
24p; illus; pbk
ISBN: 0-583-31041-9
BL: YK.1987.a.2774

## Davis, Sophie

136 Sports day / illustrated by Trevor Bond. London: Hodder and Stoughton, 1979.
33p; illus; pbk
(Humbert and Woomfa series)
ISBN: 0-340-23896-8
BL: X.990/15129

## Delgado, Alan

137 Mile-a-minute Ernie / illustrated by Colin Wheeler. London: Constable, 1967.
140p; illus
(Out and about books)
BL: 012845.c.5/12

## Delves, Nancy

138 Well played Scotts: a school story for girls. London: Sampson Low, Marston, 1930.
v, 250p; illus
BL: 012809.c.31.

One of the few girls' school stories to feature athletics.

## Dickens, Frank

139 Albert Herbert Hawkins (the naughtiest boy in the world) and the Olympic Games. London: Benn, 1980.
32p; illus
ISBN: 0-510-00084-3
BL: L.49/393

## Edwards, Hazel

140 The pancake Olympics / illustrations by Tony Oliver. London: Arnold, 1981.
67p; illus; pbk
(Young magpie library)
ISBN: 0-7131-0600-X
BL: X.990/17867

## Elrington, H.

141 The Manor School / drawings by Hume Henderson. London: Nelson, 1927.
283p; illus
BL: 12801.ppp.11

Includes accounts of a paperchase and a school sports day.

## Farrar, Frederic W.

142 St. Winifred's, or, The world of school. Edinburgh: 1862.
BL: 12808.bb.43

Includes an early description of a school high jump competition.

## Finnemore, John

143 Teddy Lester's chums / illustrated by Lucien Davis. London: Chambers, 1910.
BL: 012808.aaa.19

School story, with cross-country and hurdling prominent.

## Freeman, R. M.

144 Steady and strong, or, A friend in need: a school story. London: Griffith & Farran, 1891.
379p; illus
BL: 012803.eee.21

School story featuring the mile at an inter-scholastic sports meeting.

## Goodyear, R. A. H.

145 The boys of Castle Cliff School. London: Blackie, 1921.
288p
BL: 012802.bb.36

Chapter 2, 'The junior sports championships', features the school sports day.

146 The sporting Fifth at Ripley's: a public school story. London: Sampson Low, Marston, 1924.
314p; illus
BL: 012802.aa.19

A walking race, steeplechase and sports day are featured in this school story.

147 The boys of ringing rock. London: Ward, Lock, 1925.
256p
BL: 012807.dd.39

Contains a description of the 100 yds race at a school sports.

## Hadath, Gunby

148 Young Hendry. London: Hodder & Stoughton, 1929.
320p
BL: 12812.h.1

School story with athletics reference.

149 The new school at Shropp. London: Oxford University Press, 1930.
283p; illus
BL: 012809.c.22

Includes two chapters on cross-country running.

## Hardcastle, Michael

150 The rival games / illustrated by Trevor Parkin. London: Methuen Children's, 1988.
126p; illus
(A Pied Piper book)
ISBN: 0-416-00382-6
BL: YK.1988.a.4001

A village Olympic meeting features a barefoot high-jumper.

## Hayens, Herbert

151 'Play up, Blues!' / illustrated by Gordon Browne. London: Collins Clear-Type, 1919.
320p; illus        BL: 12813.dd
> Includes chapters on hare and hounds and a school sports day.

152 'Play up, Queens! / illustrated by Gordon Browne. London: Collins' Clear-Type, 1919?
320p; illus        BL: 12813.dd
> Chapter 16 features a half-mile race.

153 'Play up, Greys!' / illustrated by Gordon Browne. London: Collins' Clear-Type, 1922.
318p; illus        BL: 12813.dd
> A cross-country run is featured in chapter 32.

154 'Play up, Royals!' / illustrated by Gordon Browne. London: Collins' Clear-Type, 1925?
318p; illus        BL: 12813.dd
> Chapter 14 features a mile race.

155 'Play up, Swifts!' London: Collins, 1928?
313p; illus
> Includes two chapters, 'A ripping scheme' and 'Barrington's triumph', about an inter-school sports meeting.

156 'Play up, Tigers!' / illustrated by Cyril Holloway. London: Collins' Clear-Type, 1929?
282p; illus        BL: 12813.dd
> Chapter 7 features a hare and hounds race.

157 'Play up, Eagles!' / illustrated by Leslie Otway. London: Collins' Clear-Type, 1930?
284p; illus        BL: 12813.dd
> Chapters 3-5 feature running and a half-mile race.

158 'Play up Kings!' London: Collins' Clear-Type, 1930?
318p; illus        BL: 12813.dd
> Has a chapter on the school champion's defeat in the annual sports.

## Heldmann, Bernard

159 The Belton scholarship: a chapter from the life of George Denton. London: Griffith & Farran, 1882.
viii, 345p; illus        BL: 12810.bb.36
> Chapters 6 and 7 feature a paperchase.

## Heming, Jack

160 Playing for the school. London: Sampson, Low, 1936.
vi, 250p        BL: 20055.c.20
> Includes a chapter 'How Rookwood won the mile' and other running references.

## Hoare, Robert J. *See* Peters, Jim & Robert J. Hoare

## Hughes, Thomas

161 Tom Brown's schooldays / 'An Old Boy'. Cambridge: Macmillan, 1857.
viii, 420p
> A mile run between mile-posts on the road, and Hare and Hounds cross-country illustrate athletics at Rugby School when the modern era of athletics was beginning.

## Huline-Dickens, Frank *See* Dickens, Frank

## Inkpen, Mick *See* Butterworth, Nick & Mick Inkpen

## Isenberg, Barbara & Susan Wolf

162 The adventures of Albert, the running bear / illustrations by Dick Gackenbach. London: Methuen Children's, 1983.
30p; illus        ISBN: 0-416-26870-6
                             BL: X.992/5079

## Magee, Wes

163 Sports day at Scumbagg School / illustrated by Scoular Anderson. London: Orchard, 1996.
64p; illus        ISBN: 1-85213-974-9
                             BL: YK.1996.a.6307

## Murray, William

164 The sports day / illustrated by Jill Corby and Terry Burton. Loughborough: Ladybird, 1990.
48p; illus
(Read with me; 9)        ISBN: 0-7214-1322-6

## Newman, Marjorie W.

165 Jean's great race. London: Every Girl's Paper, 1929.
192p
(Girls' school time stories)        BL: 12839.c.15/4

## Nichols, John Beverley

166 Prelude: a novel. London: Chatto & Windus, 1920.
x, 293p        BL: NN.6026

## Oakden, David

167 The discus thrower: a story of Ancient Greece / illustrated by Edward Blake. Saffron Walden: Anglia Young Books, 1992.
56p; illus; pbk        ISBN: 1-871173-20-5
                             BL: YK.1993.a.13796

### Oliver, Martin

168 The winner's wreath / illustrations by Martin Remphry. London: Watts, 1999.
63p; illus
(Sparks)    ISBN: 0-7496-3368-9 (cased) • 0-7496-3555-X (pbk)

### Parker, Mary Louise

169 Suzette wins her way. London: Sampson Low, Marston, 1947.
v, 246p    BL: 12830.c.22
The chapter 'Sports day' features schoolgirl athletics.

### Peters, Jim & Robert J. Hoare

170 Spiked shoes / illustrated by Harold Beards. London: Cassell, 1959.
vii, 184p; illus    BL: 12840.ee.25
Young adult novel co-written by the marathon star.

### Petersen, Christian

171 Mystery comes to St. Christopher's. London: Sampson Low, Marston, 1937.
256p; illus    BL: 12833.b.18
Includes a chapter featuring cross-country.

### Pullen, Godfrey F.

172 Jerry smashes through. London: Sampson Low, 1936.
vi, 249p    BL: 20055.h.12
School story featuring a competition in a professional race.

### Reed, Talbot Baines

173 Follow my leader, or, The boys of Templeton: a school story / illustrated by W. S. Stacey. London: Cassell, 1885.
vii, 376p    BL: 12811.c.10
Features harriers running at school level, with runs of up to twelve miles (pp 50-56; 73-76; 310-327).

174 Tom, Dick and Harry. London: Religious Tract Society, 1894.
320p    BL: 4429.f.33
School story with a sports day climax.

175 The master of the shell. London: Boy's Own Paper, 1913.
315p    BL: 04430.g.49
Much of the heart of the book (chapters 12-15) is plotted around a school sports meeting.

### Reith, Angela

176 The great Olympics / designed and illustrated by Peter Longden. London: Ark, 1979.
20p; illus; pbk
(Buddy bear books)    ISBN: 0-85421-845-9
BL: X.990/19218

### Rhoades, Walter C.

177 Our fellows at St. Mark's: a school story. Edinburgh: Nimmo, 1891.
253p; illus    BL: 012803.ee.8
The first four chapters tell of events at a school sports day.

178 The last lap: a school story. London: Humphrey Milford, 1923.
288p    BL: 12802.bbb.46

179 The whip hand: a school story. London: Blackie, 1925.
255p    BL: 012807.bbb.30
Includes chapters 'The track', 'The sports' and 'The mile'.

### Richardson, Sheila, D. Whitehouse & G. I. Wilkinson

180 Teenage twelve, book 7: sports day / illustrated by Josephine Crickmay. Glasgow: Gibson, 1966.
16p; illus

### Rogers, Pamela

181 Sports day / illustrated by Janet Duchesne. London: Hamilton, 1972.
48p; illus
(Gazelle books)    ISBN: 0-241-02087-5

### Ross, Stewart

182 Athens is saved!: the first marathon / illustrated by Sue Shields. London: Evans, 1997.
62p; illus
(Coming alive)    ISBN: 0-237-51747-7
Fictional treatment featuring Cimon the Stutterer as the Greek messenger who brings news of the victory.

### Russell, Christopher

183 Geordie racer. London: BBC, 1990.
128p; illus; pbk
(Look and read)    ISBN: 0-563-34770-8
Accompanied a TV series and features the Great North Run.

### Russell, Gary

184 Placebo effect. London: BBC, 1998.
279p; pbk
(Doctor Who)                          ISBN: 0-563-40587-2
                                      BL: H.99/1817

   Doping at the Olympics in a Dr Who adventure.

### Saddler, Allen

185 The relay race / illustrated by Gareth Floyd. London:
Methuen Children's, 1986.
90p; illus, 1 map
(A Pied Piper book)                   ISBN: 0-416-53950-5
                                      BL: YK.1986.a.1383

### Scott, Thomas Henry

186 Wireless Watson. London: Frederick Warne, 1933.
256p                                  BL: 20053.a.17.

   'Wires' Watson is a brilliant runner who always puts his
   wireless experiments before sport.

### Shipton, Paul

187 The ultimate trainers / illustrated by Judy Brown.
Oxford: Oxford University Press, 1996.
55p; illus; pbk                       ISBN: 0-19-916915-2
                                      BL: YK.1997.a.5063

   Based on a pair of magic running shoes.

### Taylor, Jeremy

188 Channel runner. London: Penguin, 1996.
40p; illus; pbk                       ISBN: 0-14-081493-0
                                      BL: YK.1996.a.20452

   Educational text.

### Traynor, Shaun

189 The giants' Olympics / illustrated by Linda Birch.
London: Methuen Children's, 1987.
93p; illus                            ISBN: 0-416-61340-3
                                      BL: YK.1987.a.2312

### Trease, Geoffrey

190 Mission to Marathon / illustrated by Paul Fisher-
Johnson. London: A & C Black, 1997.
88p; illus, 1 map; pbk                ISBN: 0-7136-4671-3
                                      BL: H.97/2487

   Set in Ancient Greece, and with an obvious parallel
   with the original marathon runner, this tells of a boy
   who runs a great distance to warn his family of the
   impending battle.

### Voigt, Cynthia

191 The runner. London: Collins, 1986.
181p
   *Originally published: New York: Atheneum, 1985*
                ISBN: 0-00-195896-8 (cased) • 0-00-195897-6 (pbk)
                                      BL: Nov.55603

   Young adult novel set in the 1960s about a boy fixated
   on cross-country running.

### Waddell, Martin

192 Little frog and the frog Olympics / illustrated by Trevor
Dunton. Harlow: Longman, 1994.
16p; pbk
(The book project: read-on)           ISBN: 0-582-12138-8
                                      BL: YK.1996.a.11088

### Webb, W. S. K. (pseudonym of Gilbert Lawford Dalton)

193 The truth about Wilson. London: Thomson, 1962.
190p
(Red lion library)                    BL: X.907/3743

   Book version of the first series of Wilson stories
   published in the Wizard in 1943-4.

### Webster, Frederick Annesley Michael

194 The boy from the blue: a school story. London: Warne,
1929.
288p                                  BL: 12812.k.18

   In a description of the school inter-house sports there
   are vivid descriptions of the boy hero's high jumping
   and pole vaulting.

195 Carruthers of Colnhurst: a school story. London: Warne,
1933.
287p                                  BL: 012808.i.68

   School novel with strong sports theme, including high
   jumping, hurdles and the Public Schools
   Championships.

196 Millding College: a story of school life. London: Shaw,
1935.
252p                                  BL: 20055.ff.3

   A student from Nashville, USA, joins the school as an
   accomplished athlete and competes in the school
   sports.

197 Chums of Long Dormitory. London: Warne, 1936.
287p                                  BL: 20055.h.18

   Includes an account of a hare and hounds
   cross-country race.

### White, Constance M.

198 Three cheers for Penny. London: Hutchinson, 1953.
224p                                  BL: 12830.f.104

*Wilson, Forrest*

199 Super Gran superstar / illustrated by David McKee.
Harmondsworth: Puffin, 1982.
153p; illus; pbk                          ISBN: 0-14-031484-9
                                          BL: X.990/19111

   Super Gran competes in the British Games at
   Millbank Stadium.

*Wodehouse, P. G.*

200 The pothunters. London: A. & C. Black, 1902.
272p                                      BL: 012641.cc.37

   Wodehouse's first novel, about a schoolboy suspected
   of theft from the sports pavilion; includes chapters on
   the sports and the cross-country race.

201 The head of Kay's / illustrations by T. M. R. Whitwell.
London: A. & C. Black, 1905.
280p; illus                               BL: 012803.d.46

   The final chapter, 'The sports', features athletics.

*Wolf, Susan  See  Isenberg, Barbara & Susan Wolf*

## ✱ *Short Stories – Single Author Collections*

*Avery, Charles Harold*

202 The school's honour, and other stories. London: Sunday
School Union, 1895.
192p                                      BL: 4400.dd.4

   Includes 'A last run'.

*Cate, Dick*

203 On the run. London: Macmillan, 1973.
128p; pbk
(Topliners)                               ISBN: 0-333-14365-5
                                          BL: H.73/507

   Three junior fiction stories, two on running, 'The Cock of
   the North' and 'A split second'.

*Childs, Rob*

204 Tricks on the track, and, Take a run and jump; illustrated
by Beryl Sanders. London: Cambridge University Press,
1991.
48p; illus; pbk                           ISBN: 0-521-40654-4
                                          BL: YK.1991.a.5130

   'Tricks on the Track' is about running, 'Take and run and
   jump' is about a gymnast who turns to the long jump.

*Clark, David (pseudonym of Michael Hardcastle)*

205 Run, illustrated by Richard Kennedy. London: Ernest
Benn, 1973.
32p; illus
(Inner ring sports)
            ISBN: 0-510-07839-7 (cased) • 0-510-07840-0 (pbk)
                                          BL: X.990/8069

   Part fictional/part instruction, the title story is a
   short story about a girl runner.

*Coke, Desmond*

206 The house prefect, illustrated in colour by H. M. Brock.
London: Hodder & Stoughton, 1908.
311p; illus                               BL: 012808.aaa.30

   The title story features a steeplechase.

*Hellard, Susan*

207 Dilly tells the truth: stories of the world's naughtiest
dinosaur / illustrated by Susan Hellard. London:
Piccadilly, 1987.
51p; illus                                ISBN: 0-946826-67-6
                                          BL: YK.1987.a.1085

   'Dilly and the gold medal' has the dinosaur competing
   in the Olympics.

*Jennings, Paul*

208 Unreal!: eight surprising stories. Harmondsworth: Puffin,
1985.
107p; pbk                                 ISBN: 0-14-031965-4
                                          BL: YK.1987.a.1132

   'Wunderpants' is about running.

*Layton, George*

209 The fib, and other stories. London: Longman, 1975.
2 vols.

   Includes 'The mile'.

*Rix, Jamie*

210 Fearsome tales for fiendish kids, illustrated by Ross
Collins. London: Hodder Children's, 1996.
216p; illus                               ISBN: 0-340-66735-4
                                          BL:Nov.1996/1361

*Wodehouse, P. G.*

211 Tales of St. Austin's. London: A. & C. Black, 1903.
282p                                      BL: 012803.aaa.11

   Includes 'Manoeuvres of Charteris' featuring a
   schoolboy miler at a public sports meeting.

## ❋ Short Stories – Anthologies

212 The best book for boys. London: Dean, 1930.
95p; illus                              BL: 012807.e.78
    Includes 'The paper chase' by P. M. Frost.

213 Warne's pleasure book for boys. London: Frederick
Warne, 1930.
188p; illus                             BL: P.P.6754.ack
    Includes 'The big run' by A. W. Seymour.

214 The great book of school stories for boys / edited by
Herbert Strang. London: Oxford University Press, 1932.
146p; illus
    Includes 'Mappin's mile' by Gunby Hadath (22p).

215 The golden budget book for boys. London: Blackie,
1938?
96p; illus                              BL: P.P.6751.bba
    'A fighting finish', by A. W. Seymour, is about a
    talented, but reluctant, athlete.

216 Good sports!: a bag of sports stories / collected by Tony
Bradman; illustrated by Jon Riley. London: Doubleday,
1992.
209p; illus                             ISBN: 0-385-40232-5
                                        BL: YK.1993.a.12117
    Includes 'Fun run' by Robert Leeson and 'Gate crashed'
    by Brian Morse.

# *Poetry*

## ❋ Single Author Collections

### *Abse, Dannie*

217 Tenants of the house: poems, 1951-1956. London:
Hutchinson, 1957.
79p                                     BL: 11659.cc.59
    Includes 'The race'.

### *Ahlberg, Allan*

218 Please Mrs Butler / verses by Allan Ahlberg; pictures by
Fritz Wegner. Harmondsworth: Kestrel, 1983.
93p; illus                              ISBN: 0-7226-5792-7
                                        BL: X.990/23229
    Includes 'If I wasn't me' and 'The runners'. For children.

### *Anonymous*

219 The ancient English romance of Havelok the Dane,
accompanied by the French text, with an introduction,
notes and a glossary, by F. Madden. London: Roxburghe
Club, 1828.                             BL: G.88.(1)
    A poem thought to be composed in the thirteenth
    century (the manuscript is held in the Bodleian)
    containing probably the earliest description in English
    literature of an athletics contest (lines 1004-1058).
    The hero is a champion at putting the stone and wins a
    contest at Lincoln by twelve feet. It is of interest that
    Peter de Langtoft's chronicle, translated by Robert
    Mannyng of Brunne (1338) states: 'men sais in
    Lyncoln Castelle ligges yit a stone that Havelok cast'.
    Etymological    dictionaries    quote    'Havelok'    as
    containing the earliest recorded instance of the verb
    'to putt'.

220 Layamon's Brut, or, Chronicle of Britain; a poetical semi-
Saxon paraphrase of the Brut of Wace. Now first
published … by Sir F. Madden. London: Society of
Antiquaries, 1847.
3 vols.                                 BL: Ac.5665/4
    Modern rendering of an early English (c1200) text
    which makes reference (ii, 344ff) to a sports meeting
    with running, leaping and throwing.

### *Auden, W. H.*

221 Collected poems of W.H. Auden / edited by Edward
Mendelson. London: Faber, 1976.
696p; index                             ISBN: 0-571-10833-4
                                        BL: 2039.g
    Includes 'Runner'.

### *Bacchylides*

222 Complete poems; translated by Robert Fagles; with a
foreword by Maurice Bowra; introduction and notes by
Adam M. Parry. London: Yale University Press, 1998.
123p; illus; pbk
    *Originally published: New Haven: Yale University Press,*
    *1961; translated from the Greek; with new translator's note*
                                        ISBN: 0-300-07552-9
                                        BL: YC.1998.a.4330

## Barakat, Richard

223 Olympiad. Dublin: Clancy, 1992.
36p; pbk                          ISBN: 0-9519267-0-5
                                   BL: YK.1993.a.13357

   Comprises poems: Invocation; Diskobolos; Wrestler;
   Foot race I; Foot race II; Archer; Fencer; Rowers;
   Charioteer; Equestrians; Cretan bullfight; Hurlers;
   Boxers; Javelin throw; Race in armor; Pentathlete;
   Marathon.

## Browning, Robert

224 Dramatic idylls, first series. London: Smith, Elder, 1879.
143p                               BL: 011651.e.112

   A collection of poems which includes 'Pheidippides', the
   story of the Greek runner of Marathon.

## Clare, John

225 The village minstrel, and other poems / John Clare.
London: Taylor & Hessey, 1821.
2 vols.; illus                     BL: 993.b.8

   'The village minstrel', a long poem, includes a rustic
   sports meeting and a smock race.

## Danys (pseudonym of David Nigel Schiff)

226 Runner's high: running and other physical poems.
London: Kierani, 1995.
iv, 28p; illus; pbk                ISBN: 0-9526563-0-2

   Of the eighteen poems in this collection, only one does
   not take athletics as its theme. The allusion to
   'runner's high' is to the 'long distance runner's
   experience of euphoria brought on by production and
   release of endorphins inside the brain'.

## Dunn, Douglas

227 The happier life. London: Faber and Faber, 1972.
72p                                ISBN: 0-571-09931-9
                                   BL: X.989/15217

   Includes 'Runners'.

## Eberhart, Richard

228 Collected poems, 1930-1976: including 43 new poems.
London: Chatto and Windus, 1976.
xvii, 364p                         ISBN: 0-7011-2165-3
                                   BL: X.989/50951

   Includes 'Track'.

## Fidler, Harry

229 The marathon off Dawston Green. Carlisle: Chas.
Thurnam, 1913.
1 sheet                            BL: 1879.c.12(34)

## Gay, John

230 Rural sports: a poem. London: Tonson, 1913.
22p                                BL: 643.1.26(4)

## Gunn, Thom

231 The man with night sweats. London: Faber and Faber,
1992.
88p        ISBN: 0-571-16238-X (cased) • 0-571-16257-6 (pbk)
                                   BL: YK.1994.a.5578

   Includes 'Courtesies of the interregnum', about an
   ageing athlete.

## Hogg, James

232 Queen Hynde: a poem: in six books. London: Longman,
Hurst, Rees, Orme, Brown and Green, 1825.
443p                               BL: 992.l.11

   Epic poem that includes a description of a sixth
   century athletics contest between the Scots and
   their Danish invaders.

## Homer

233 The Iliad and Odyssey of Homer, translated by Pope /
Homer. New ed. London: C. Bathurst, 1783.
4 vols.                            BL: 1607/4322

   Book 23 of the Iliad describes the funeral games of
   Petroclus and Book 8 of the Odyssey describes the
   classical games.

## Housman, A. E.

234 A Shropshire lad. London: Kegan Paul, 1896.
vii, 96p                           BL: C.71.h.19

   Includes 'To an athlete dying young'.

## Johnson, Derek J. N.

235 Athletics is my joy, my one and only love, and other
poems. Gravesend: The author, 1979.
4 unbound leaves                   BL: X.950/18400

   The poet was the Olympic silver medallist at 800m in
   1956.

## Kingscott, K. N.

236 The athlete, and other poems / K. N. Kingscott.
Ilfracombe: Stockwell, 1968.
23p; pbk                           BL: X.907/17107

## McGough, Roger

237 Sporting relations; with illustrations by the author. Expanded and rev. ed. London: Viking, 1996.
vii, 71p; illus                                    ISBN: 0-670-86883-3
                                                   BL: YK.1996.a.22701

*Includes a number of short, humorous poems, including eleven loosely related to athletics featuring a sprinter, low hurdler, cross-country runner, high jumper, triple jumper, shot putter, hammer thrower, javelin thrower and caber tosser.*

## Nichols, Grace

238 Give yourself a hug; illustrated by Kim Harley. London: A. & C. Black, 1994.
64p; illus; index                                  ISBN: 0-7136-4054-5
                                                   BL: YK.1995.a.5209

*Includes 'When my friend Anita runs'. For children.*

## Nonnus, of Panopolis

239 Dionysiaca. With an English translation by W. H. D. Rouse. London: Heinemann, 1940.
3 vols.
(Loeb classical library)                           BL: 2282.d.154

*Book 37 of this epic poem written about AD500, and derivative of Homer, describes the games held at the funeral of Opheltes, including foot race, discus and javelin.*

## Pindar

240 The Olympick odes [I and II] of Pindar, in English meetre, as they were lately found in an original manuscript of those sublime lyrick translators, T. Sternhold, J. Hopkins, and others / translated by Philhomeropindarus, in a style intended to burlesque that of Sternhold and Hopkins's version of the Psalms. London: E. Curll, 1713.
36p                                                BL: 161.k.33

241 Odes of Pindar with several other pieces in prose and verse; translated from the Greek by G. W., to which is prefixed A dissertation on the Olympic Games by Gilbert West. London: Dodsley, 1749.         BL: 74.f.10

*West gives translations of the Olympic, Nemean and Isthmian Odes. His dissertation is a lengthy essay on the history of the Olympic Games which includes the arguments for dating their origin as 776 BC. There is also a translation of Lucian's Of Gymnastic Exercises. 'To recompense the women for their being excluded from the Olympic Games, they also celebrated a festival of their own, instituted, as it is said, in honour of Olympian Juno, by Hippodamia, the wife of Pelops. In this festival the virgins, distributed into three classes, according to their different ages, contended in the foot-race: from which agreeable spectacle, I am willing to hope, for the sake of both sexes, that the men were not excluded'.*

242 Six Olympic odes of Pindar: being those omitted by Mr West, translated into English verse by H. J. Pye. London: White, 1775.
vii, 73p                                           BL: 237.h.16

243 The Olympian and Pythian Odes (the Nemean and Isthmian Odes), with notes, explanatory and critical, introductions, and introductory essays / C. A. M. Fennell. Cambridge: Cambridge University Press, 1879-1883.
2 vols.                                            BL: 11335.ee.4

*This text is noteworthy for the inclusion of an article on the pentathlon as it was organised in classical times.*

## Pindar, Peter

244 The bench in an uproar!!, or, Chop-fallen magistrate: a poem. London: 1816?
*Author is possibly C. F. Lawler*
                                                   BL: C.131.d.5(10)

*A poem occasioned by the proceedings consequent upon the arrest by the Greenwich magistrates of the pedestrian George Wilson.*

## Quintus Smyrnaeus

245 The fall of Troy; with an English translation by Arthur S. Way. Greek & English. London: Heinemann, 1913.
xi, 627p; index
(Loeb classical library)                           BL: 2282.d.15

*Book 4 describes the games for the funeral of Achilles.*

## Richardson, George (pedestrian)

246 The Irish footman's poetry, or, George the Runner against Henry the Walker, in defence of John the Swimmer [i.e. Taylor, the Water Poet]: being a surrejoinde to the rejoinder of the rusty Ironmonger [i.e. H. Walker] who endeavoured to defile the cleare streames of the Water-Poet's helicon. London: 1641.
                                                   BL: 11623.bb.37

## Roberts, George

247 The prospect, or, Rural sports: a poem to which is added, a letter to a young lady in Worcestershire. London: 1754?
22p                                                BL: 11630.e.5(4)

## Rye, Walter

248 Rubbish and nonsense. Norwich: A. Goose, 1887.
160p                                               BL: 012330.k.35

*A miscellaneous collection of prose and poetry that includes the critical verses about J. G. Chambers and his control of the AAC.*

*Scott, Walter*

249 The lady of the lake: a poem. Edinburgh: 1810.
BL: 643.l.12

Canto V includes the burghers' sports at Stirling Castle, when the Douglas wins contests at casting the bar and putting the stone.

*Shewan, Alexander*

250 Homeric Games at an ancient St. Andrews: an epyllium edited from a comparatively modern papyrus and shattered by means of the Higher Criticism. Edinburgh: James Thin, 1911.
xii, 158p     BL: 012314.k.10

A satirical poem in Greek hexameters, with an English prose version.

*Somerville, William*

251 Hobbinol, or, The rural games: a burlesque poem, in blank verse. Dublin: Faulkner, 1740.
vi, 53p     BL: 1509/644

A burlesque poem in blank verse which describes the kind of rural festival which eventually developed into the modern athletics meeting.

*Statius, Publius Papinius*

252 Works; with an English translation by J. H. Mozley. London: Heinemann, 1928.
2 vols.
(Loeb classical library)
*Text in Latin and English on opposite pages*
BL: 2282.d.103

Book VI of the Thebaid has a description of the first Nemean Games, with some of the most detailed of all classical accounts of athletics, including foot racing and the discus throw.

*Virgil*

253 The Æneid of Virgil in English blank verse translated by J. Miller. London: 1863.     BL: 11375.bb.33

Book V describes the funeral games of Anchises, including a foot race.

*Webb, Francis*

254 Francis Webb: collected poems / preface by Herbert Read. London: Angus & Robertson, 1969.
ix, 270p; pbk     ISBN: 0-207-13612-2
BL: X:958/22838

Includes 'This runner'.

*Whitman, Walt*

255 The complete poems of Walt Whitman / edited by Francis Murphy. Harmondsworth: Penguin Education, 1975.
892p; index; pbk     ISBN: 0-14-080811-6
BL: X.908/40133

Includes 'The runner'.

*Wilson, George*

256 The quizzical quorum, or, The fortunes and misfortunes of the Black Beaks of Blackheath: a new ballad. 2nd ed., corrected and enlarged showing how they stopped a poor labouring man, named George Wilson, with a comical warrant, whilst walking upon the King's highway. London: Wm. Hone, 1814?
1 sheet     BL: 806.k.16(50)

Possibly written by Wilson himself.

*Wooldridge, Ian*

257 Thoughts on watching a great hammer thrower: and other poems from the press box. Woking: Surrey Poetry Circle, 1980.
4 unbound leaves     BL: X.950/18364

Contain the poems 'For I'm a jolly jogger', 'Thoughts on watching a great hammer thrower', 'Ode on a runner at Crystal Palace', 'Lines on Brian Hooper' (the pole vaulter), 'The joy of sprinting', and 'Athletics is my joy, my one and only love'.

✱ *Poetry – Anthologies*

258 Annalia Dubrensia: being a collection of verses by various writers upon the yeerly celebration of Mr R. Dover's Olimpick Games upon Cotswold Hills / edited by M. W. London: Matthew Walbancke, 1636.
BL: B.630(1)

The 33 poets who write in honour of the Games include Michael Drayton, Ben Jonson, Sir William Davenant and Thomas Heywood.

259 Poetical miscellanies, consisting of original poems and translations / by the best hands. London: Mr. Steele, 1714.
318p     BL: 1077.l.26

Includes 'The smock race at Finglas', describing an event for women in the annual games outside Dublin.

260 Pastorals, epistles, odes, and other original poems, with translations from Pindar, Anacreon, and Sappho / Ambrose Philips. London: 1748.     BL: 11632.a.28

This collection includes Philips' translation of two of Pindar's Olympic Odes, entitled 'The First Olympionique' and 'The Second Olympionique'.

261 Friendship's offering: a literary album. London: 1829.
BL: P.P.6605

Includes 'The minstrel boy' in which James Hogg (the Ettrick Shepherd), founder of the St Ronan's Border Games, recalls performing at 'the leap, the race or the throw'.

262 Athletic sports / Joseph Mason and John Fraser. In: Prize papers written on various subjects for the Boy's Own Magazine. London: S. O. Beeton, 1864.
BL: 12273.d.5

Contains two poems, both entitled 'Athletic sports' (pp127-153).

263 The poetry of sport / selected and edited by H. Peek, with a chapter on classical allusions to sport by Andrew Lang, and a special preface to the Badminton Library by A. E. T. Watson; illustrated by A. Thorburn, L. Davis, C. E. Brock. London: Longmans, Green, 1896.
xl, 484p; illus
(The Badminton Library of Sports and Pastimes. 1885)
BL: 2270.cc.21

Andrew Lang's essay on classical sport has some references to ancient athletics, and there are extracts from Spenser and Thomas Randolph.

264 Sports and pastimes in English literature / compiled and edited by L. S. Wood and H. L. Burrows. London: Nelson, 1925.
256p
(Teaching of English; no. 61)          BL: 012207.aa.1/44

The following poems on athletic subjects are included: 'Athletic ode' (G. Santayana), 'The athlete' and 'Before the race' (E. C. Lefroy) and 'The song of the ungirt runners' (C. H. Sorley).

265 Anthology of sporting verse / selected, with a preface, by E. B. Osborn. London: Collins, 1930.
288p                                         BL: 11601.k.30

Osborn's introduction has a reference to hammer-throwing (casting of the sledge) in the drama of John Ford (1629). The poetry includes Sir Theodore Cook's 'The Olympic spirit', awarded the silver medal for literature at the 1920 Olympics; and references to athletics by Edmund Spenser in 'Astrophel' (1595) and 'Mother Hubberds tale' (1613).

266 The annals of Thames Hare and Hounds 1868 to 1945 / compiled by James Ryan; with, The present generation 1946 to 1968 by Ian H. Fraser; foreword by J. G. Broadbent. London: The Club, 1968.
xiv, 198p; illus                             BL: X.449/3579

An appendix includes club verses: 'The Thames Hare and Hounds at Roehampton 1871' by Walter Rye; 'The Nightmare' by White and Brown (P. J. Burt?); 'Winchester House, 12th February, 1887' by Little Peter (A. E. Stenning); and, 'Kensit's team v. Askew's team 1943' by E. R. Askew.

☞ Also listed at: A267

267 The Penguin book of South African verse / compiled and introduced by Jack Cope and Uys Krige. London: Penguin, 1968.
331p; pbk

Includes 'The comrades' marathon' by Chris Mann.

268 Forty years on: an anthology of school songs / compiled by Gavin Ewart. London: Sidgwick & Jackson, 1969.
254p; illus                      SBN: 283-98069-9
BL: X.439/1710

Includes 'Down the Hailey Lane', recollecting hare and hounds running, by G. H. Sunderland Lewis (Haileybury); 'Down the hill' by E. E. Bowen (Harrow), on cross-country; and, 'Sweats' by Cyril Norwood (Marlborough), on cross-country training runs.

269 The Greek anthology and other ancient Greek epigrams: a selection in modern verse translations, edited with an introduction by Peter Jay. London: Allen Lane, 1973.
447p; illus, maps; index        ISBN: 0-7139-0344-9
BL: X.989/25669

Includes two short poems by Lucilius translated by Peter Porter, 'A recent earthquake' (on sprinting) and 'Marcus in the armed Hoplites race'; and 'Dedication of a torch' by Krinogoras, translated by Alistair Elliott.

270 The Oxford book of American light verse / chosen and edited by William Harmon. Oxford: Oxford University Press, 1979.
l, 540p; index                   ISBN: 0-19-502509-1
BL: X.989/54135

Includes 'A mighty runner' by Nicarchus, translated by Edwin Arlington Robinson.

271 The poetry of motion: an anthology of sporting verse / edited by Alan Bold. Edinburgh: Mainstream, 1986?
201p; index                      ISBN: 0-906391-70-9
BL: YC.1987.a.2801

Includes 'The runner' by Walt Whitman; 'Elegy on the death of James Fleming' by James Kennedy; 'To an athlete dying young' by A. E. Housman; 'The hundred yards race' by J. K. Stephen; 'I saw a man pursuing the horizon' by Stephen Crane; 'Song of the Ungirt runners' by Charles Hamilton Sorley; 'Highland Games' by Norman McCaig; 'School sports, at the turnstiles' by Iain Crichton Smith; 'High jump poem' and 'Long jump poem' by Stephen Morris; 'Fanny Blankers-Koen at Wembley' by Jeff Cloves; 'The smiler with the knife' by Bill Costley; 'Running sequence' by Susan Wilkins; 'Runners' and 'In ten seconds' by Douglas Dunn; and 'The high jump' (anonymous).

272 Selected poems and songs; edited by David Groves. Edinburgh: Scottish Academic, 1986.
xxxiii, 232p; music
*At head of title: The Association for Scottish Literary Studies*
ISBN: 0-7073-0471-7
BL: YC.1987.a.9676

Includes Hogg's 'The cutting o' my hair' in which the poet recalls winning races at St Boswell's and other local fairs.

273 Sports poems / compiled by John Foster. Oxford: Oxford University Press, 1990.
16p; illus; pbk
(Jackdaws poetry)
ISBN: 0-19-916339-1
BL: YK.1991.a.8268

Includes 'Sports day' by Theresa Heine and 'The fastest runner' by Irene Yates. For children.

274 Does W trouble you?: a book of rhyming poems / edited by Gerard Benson; illustrated by Alison Forsythe. London: Viking, 1994.
159p; illus
ISBN: 0-670-85082-9
BL: YK.1994.a.18024

Includes 'Tidying up' by Simon Pitt, about a boy's thoughts as he puts away athletic gear. For children.

275 Crossing boundaries: an international anthology of women's experiences in sport / Susan J. Bandy, Anne S. Darden, editors. Leeds: Human Kinetics, 1999.
xvi, 311p; illus; pbk
ISBN: 0-7360-0088-7
BL: YC.2000.a.7347

Poems include: 'The sprinters' by Lillian Morrison; 'Women's tug of war at Lough Arrow' by Tess Gallagher; 'Marathoner' by Stephanie Plotin; 'Running' by Leslie Ullman; 'Runner resumes training after an injury' and 'Runner at twilight' by Grace Butcher; 'Red runner' by Diane Wakoski; 'Running with Helena' by Theresa W. Miller; 'Morning athletes' by Marge Piercy; 'Women who run' by Laurel Starkey; 'Running' by Ellen E. Moore; 'Amateur athletic meeting' by Elisabeth Smither; 'The runner' by Erin Moure; 'Muscle like metaphor pulls thin and tough' by Vivian Jokl. Prose includes 'A running girl: fragments of my body history' by Ulla Kosonen; 'Her marathon' by Jenifer Levin; and 'Breaking the speed record' by Cristina Peri Rossi.

276 Poems in the modern vein / edited by Henry Parker. London: Oddball, 2000.
64p; pbk

A general anthology of poems with a sporting theme.

# Plays

## Benfield, Derek

277 Running riot: a farcical comedy in three acts. London: Evans, 1958.
95p; illus
BL: W.P.13182/101

A farce with background music in which husband, fleeing wife, is mistaken for an Olympic runner and involved in a spy plot.

## Bower, Margaret

278 Triad 66: three plays for women. Macclesfield: New Playwrights' Network, 1988?
29, 23, 24p; 1 plan; pbk
*Contents: Pictures at an exhibition; Running past; What is to become of Mama?*
ISBN: 0-86319-138-X
BL: YC.1988.a.13266

'Running past' is a one-act play in which four women are reunited twenty-eight years after winning Olympic gold medals as Britain's sprint relay team.

## Burnand, Sir Francis Cowley

279 Sporting intelligence extraordinary!: a match is arranged to come off at the Royal Olympic Theatre … between the Unknown and the Seneca Indian, Deerfoot: a farce, in one act. London: 1862.
16p; pbk
(Lacy's acting edition; vol. 53, no. 789)
BL: 2304.e.27

First performed at Royal Olympic Theatre, 16 December 1861.

## Erba, Edoardo

280 Marathon / English version by Colin Teevan. London: Oberon, 1999.
60p; pbk
*Translation of: Maratona di New York. Milan: Ricordi, 1994*
ISBN: 1-84002-139-X

Steve and Mark, two runners intending to compete in the New York Marathon, carry on a dialogue whilst training at night. The play was first produced in Italy in 1993, and this English version was staged in London six years later.

### Saroyan, William

281 Sam, the highest jumper of them all, or, The London comedy. London: Faber & Faber, 1961.
96p; illus                                    BL: 11567.h.17

A play, first produced in 1960 at the Theatre Royal, Stratford. Its main character is a jumper who eventually clears 7ft 9in (off-stage).

### Shirley, James

282 Hide Park, a comedie. London: 1637.          BL: 644.c.50

A play in five acts which features a foot-race in which the runners traverse the stage followed by their supporters calling bets and ultimately arguing and drawing swords.

### Toyne, Stanley Mease

283 The race: a play of Marathon. Oxford: Shakespeare Head, 1934.
viii, 67p                                     BL: 011781.i.135

# Essays & Reminiscences

## ✱ Single Author Works

### Allen, Roland

284 All in the day's sport. London: Allen, 1946.
vi, 186p                                      BL: 7918.b.50

The author, a Fleet Street journalist, meets C. B. Fry at the 1936 FA Cup Final (ch.25 'Champagne in the car park'), recording some of the Corinthian's views and achievements. Allen's observations on the 1936 Olympic Games in Berlin are presented (ch.33 'The man who may not have been Hitler').

### Angle, Bernard John

285 My sporting memories. London: R. Holden, 1925.
256p; illus; index                           BL: 07906.e.22

Angle was best known for his involvement in boxing, but there are interesting chapters on the Brighton Road Walks and the Olympic Games. The illustrations include a rare photo of the ultra-walker, William Gale.

### Cleaver, Hylton

286 Sporting rhapsody. London: Hutchinson's Library of Sports & Pastimes, 1951.
223p; illus                                   BL: W.P.1156/22

A journalist on the *Evening Standard*, Cleaver was assigned at short notice to cover the 1936 Olympic Games, and offers some thoughts on their organisation. He discusses the role of the professional in sports coaching, referring to Geoff Dyson as a professor, since his primary role was to coach coaches, rather than athletes.

287 Before I forget. London: Hale, 1961.
190p; illus                                   BL: 10765.d.10

In his final work, Cleaver reflects on the UK performance at the 1952 Olympic Games and provides a nice vignette of Emil Zátopek: 'No runner has ever developed the spectacular to a greater degree than he; no man's personal success has sprung so surely from personality. No coach can possibly have taught Zátopek to run his first lap as if he were exhausted already, yet the fact that he did, made his last lap look superb.'

### Cobbett, Martin

288 Sporting notions of present days and past selected from the 'Referee' / edited by Alice Cobbett. Edinburgh: Sands, 1908.
vii, 366p                                     BL: 7904.bbb.14

Cobbett writes interestingly on W. M. Chinnery and the early days of London AC (pp1-22) and on pedestrianism in the nineteenth century (pp301-20).

### Doust, Dudley

289 Sports beat: headline-makers, then and now / foreword by Harry Carpenter. London: Hodder & Stoughton, 1992.
240p; illus                                   ISBN: 0-340-55900-4
                                              BL: YK.1992.a.7603

A collection of pieces one of which is devoted to 'Mary Peters: The golden girl' –'She still remembers, vividly, those two golden days in 1972 and exactly twenty years later, on September 3, 1992, plans to return to the Olympiastadion in Munich. "It'll be nice", she says. "I'll just go with a few friends. The place will be empty!" ' (from the postscript).

## Doyle, Sir Arthur Conan

290 Letters to the press: the unknown Conan Doyle / compiled with an introduction by John Michael Gibson and Richard Lancelyn Green. London: Secker & Warburg, 1986.
376p; index
ISBN: 0-436-13303-2
BL: YC.1986.a.2938

Contains eleven letters on the subject of the Olympic Games.

## Farrell, John Emmet

291 The universe is mine / John Emmet Farrell. Glasgow: The author, 1993.
92p; illus; pbk
ISBN: 1-870711-10-6
BL: YK.1994.a.16030

Farrell contributed a column 'Running commentary' to the magazine *The Scots Athlete* for many years, and this material forms the basis for much of the work. The closing section deals with the development of veteran athletics from 1970 and the author's successful participation in the World Veterans Championships.

## Gale, Frederick

292 Modern English sports: their use and their abuse. London: Sampson Low, 1885.
xx, 201p
BL: 7906.ccc.15

Includes a chapter on general athletics (pp58-79).

## Graydon, John Allen

293 Never-to-be-forgotten sports thrills. London: Findon, 1946.
64p; illus; pbk
BL: 7917.e.8

Includes 'How Dorando won the marathon', 'A peer becomes world champion' (about Lord Burghley), and 'Mighty atom of the running track' (about Sydney Wooderson).

294 More never-to-be-forgotten sports thrills. London: Findon, 1946.
64p; illus; pbk
BL: 7917.e.17

Includes 'Sydney Wooderson surprises the world' and 'Blind man helped produce Britain's greatest walker' (about Tommy Green of Belgrave Harriers).

## Hoby, Alan

295 One crowded hour. London: Museum Press, 1954.
160p; illus; index
BL: 7919.f.87

The author was a sports journalist on the *Sunday Express*; he writes about Zátopek ('The most agonised face in the world'), Government aid ('Hypocrites' paradise – what is an amateur?'), Bannister ('The master miler'), and Gordon Pirie ('Gordon Pirie: what now?').

## Keating, Frank

296 Bowled over!: a year of sport with Frank Keating. London: Deutsch, 1980.
220p
ISBN: 0-233-97284-6
BL: X.629/15195

Keating's reflections on the 1979 season concentrate principally on the rivalry between Coe and Ovett; the views of John Walker and Alan Pascoe on their respective characters and abilities are quoted.

## Ledbrooke, Archibald W.

297 Great moments in sport / illustrated by Edmund L. Blandford. London: Phoenix House, 1956.
127p; illus
BL: 7921.f.16

Includes chapters on Bannister's mile with Landy, Chataway's athletic career and Dorando's marathon.

## Lennox, William Pitt

298 Pictures of sporting life and character. London: Hurst & Blackett, 1860.
2 vols.: iv, 369p; ix, 339p; illus
BL: 7906.d.11

The first volume refers to pedestrianism and quotes from a report in the *Leamington Spa Courier* of May 1820 on the extraordinary pedestrian feat of a Birmingham woman of seventeen who walked forty miles a day for six successive days. The author contributes some general remarks on training, and notes the pedestrian feat of Yates in 1859, alluding to the earlier performance of Barclay. The second volume has an account of professional athletics at Garratt Lane, Wandsworth, and a reference to the match between the author and Jack Spalding in Hill Street, off Berkeley Square, which netted £60.

299 Fifty years: biographical reminiscences. London: Hurst & Blackett, 1863.
2 vols.: viii, 364p; viii, 364p
BL: 10826.g.6

The first volume contains references to Captain Barclay and other pedestrians; the second volume contains references to the pedestrians Eaton and Crisp and gives a detailed account of the challenge sprint match between the author and Jack Spalding.

300 Sport at home and abroad. London: Hurst & Blackett, 1872.
2 vols.
BL: 7906.de.10

Volume 1 covers sports of London in bygone times; the brief account of training (including mention of the discus), closely follows that of the 1860 work. A repetition of the 1820 report appears with a detailed biography of the pedestrian Foster Powell.

301 Celebrities I have known, with episodes, political, social, sporting and theatrical. London: Hurst & Blackett, 1876-1877.

4 vols. in 2 series                                  BL: 10804.cc.5

A résumé of the career of Captain Robert Barclay Allardice is given in volume 2, including accounts of meetings with him by the author; mention is also made of the pedestrian Thomas Standen.

## Macadam, John

302 The Macadam road. London: Jarrolds, 1955.

192p; illus                                           BL: 7921.e.125

These are the varied reminiscences of a sports writer from Gourock who eventually joined the Daily Express. He recalls his trip to Berlin in 1936 to cover the Olympic Games and his failure to secure an interview with Hitler; characterises Joe Binks as 'the Number 1 Athletics writer, not so hot on the writing but more knowledgeable than the athletes themselves'; and gives an eye-witness account of Bannister's performance at Oxford on 6 May 1954, describing it as his 'finest sporting hour'.

## Mallalieu, Joseph P. W.

303 Sporting days. London: Phoenix Sports, 1955.

190p; illus                                           BL: 7919.bb.52

A collection of articles on sporting events which includes a good account of the Oxford and Cambridge Sports of 1953.

304 Very ordinary sportsman. London: Routledge & Kegan Paul, 1957.

viii, 167p                                            BL: 7923.r.10

Includes a chapter on the Olympic Games, with an account of Dorando's marathon.

## Miller, David

305 Our sporting times / foreword by Will Carling. London: Pavilion, 1996.

288p                                  ISBN: 1-85793-880-1
                                      BL: YK.1996.b.11007

All the contributions in this collection first appeared in The Times; several are pertinent to athletics, covering such topics as Coe's 1500m victory at Los Angeles (1984), the search for Oxbridge's lost élite (1986), the final Olympic appearance of Daley Thompson at Seoul (1988), Boulmerka's win at Barcelona (1992), and – perhaps most interesting of all – an interview with the Corinthian, B. Howard Baker (1892-1987) in 1983.

## O'Connor, Ulick

306 Sport is my lifeline: essays from the Sunday Times / foreword by Norris McWhirter. London: Pelham, 1984.

xviii, 141p; illus; index            ISBN: 0-7207-1522-9
                                     BL: X.629/24180

The author, a biographer, playwright, poet, and sometime barrister, was also a talented athlete (11ft 7¾in pole vault in 1951) and journalist. This collection of his work from The Sunday Times includes six pieces on athletics published in the period 1975-80. 'The other day, a seventy-three-year old man ran a lap round the outside of the Olympian stadium in Los Angeles. He hadn't been able to get in, as the building was locked on a public holiday. Forty-eight years before, Robert Morton Newburgh Tisdall won the Olympic 400m hurdles title there.'

## Seth, Ronald Sydney

307 The first time it happened: fifty memorable occasions in the story of man. London: Odhams, 1965.

352p; illus                                           BL: X.529/2669

Sections on the first modern Olympics (pp248-254) and the first four-minute mile (pp336-342).

## Stafford, Ian

308 Playgrounds of the gods: the fulfilment of a sporting fantasy. Edinburgh: Mainstream, 1999.

255p; illus                          ISBN: 1-84018-222-9

Includes the author's account of training with the Kenyan distance runners, Kiptanui and Komen (pp77-106).

## Stenner, Tom

309 Sport for the million. London: Stanley Paul, 1958.

200p; illus                                           BL: 7923.ff.60

The author was responsible for Greyhound Racing Association publicity for more than sixteen years, and thus came into contact with the organisation of athletics events at the White City in the post World War II period.

## Whitcher, Alec E.

310 Sportsman's club. Brighton: Southern Publishing, 1948.

229p; illus                                           BL: 7920.aaa.28

J. W. Morton, AAA 100 yds champion from 1904 to 1907, contributes the article on athletics, in which he recounts his career and training methods. 'The New York Herald in their issue of 16th October, 1905 … "Champion Sprinter Laughs at Training" … "Englishman Morton smokes and drinks all he likes and then wins. How to become a champion – smoke 30 cigarettes a day; puff down a dozen pipefuls of tobacco; drink a few bottles of beer; do any old thing; don't train. Such is the rule of John W. Morton, England's great sprint champion, now in this country, and who has lost only two races to the hard-trained Yankee athletes …". Of course, much that he didn't say appeared and Jack explains that most of what he did say was but a joke, as the reporter was so persistent – he never dreamed this would be printed.'

## ✱ *Anthologies*

311　Prize essays on physical education / L. O. Pike, Lord W. Lennox, and R. Evans. Liverpool: Liverpool Athletic Society, 1863.　　　BL: Mic.A.9397(2) (microfilm copy)

The Liverpool Athletic Society was one of the first organisations to hold regular open athletics meetings. These essays won prizes at the Society's Olympic Festival in 1863.

312　A new book of sports: reprinted from the 'Saturday Review'. London: R. Bentley, 1885.

iv, 376p　　　　　　　　　　BL: 7908.aaaa.57

A reissue of a series of articles which appeared in the Saturday Review. They include 'Athletic sports' (pp55-64) and 'Athletics in America' (pp280-288).

313　The 'House' on sport / by members of the London Stock Exchange; compiled and edited by W. A. Morgan. London: Gale & Polden, 1898.

xv, 470p; illus　　　　　　　　　BL: 7908.h.10

This book is notable for the chapters of personal reminiscences on athletics by Walter M. Chinnery (the first amateur to beat 4½ minutes for the mile) and on walking by Fred A. Cohen. 'In 1863 some athletic enthusiasts, doing business in and round Mincing Lane, started some meetings for sports, and shortly after formed a club which was called the Mincing Lane Athletic Club. The ground at Bow was generally used for the sports, but after a time they were held at the Old Brompton ground …. Towards the end of 1864 I became Hon. Sec. of the MLAC, which in 1865 changed its name to the London Athletic Club. With the friendly co-operation of Lord Jersey (first president of the LAC), Sir R. E. Webster (now Attorney-General), the late J. G. Chambers, Guy Pym, P. M. Thornton and others, the club became most popular and successful.'

314　Notes on athletics: by members of the Cambridge University Athletic Team, 1922, with 15 illustrations; with a foreword by W. R. Seagrove. Cambridge: Fabb & Tyler, 1922.

60p; illus

(Cambridge Review 'new blue' series; no. 3)

BL: W.P.6930/3

A collection of articles which first appeared weekly in the Cambridge Review during the Lent Term of 1922.

315　The game's afoot!: an anthology of sports, games, & the open air / edited by Bernard Darwin. London: Sidgwick & Jackson, 1926.

xv, 331p　　　　　　　　　　BL: 12298.aaa.7

An anthology of sporting prose, including Samuel Pepys' description of a foot race, and W. Thom on Captain Barclay's 1,000 mile walk (pp249-253).

316　They're off!: a journalistic record of British sports by leading writers of the press / edited by Charles W. Miles; foreword by the Earl of Derby. London: Archer, 1934.

278p; illus　　　　　　　　　　BL: 2271.d.22

Contains a chapter on athletics of 19 pages, by Arthur Hardy, with reminiscences of outstanding athletes.

317　Sunday Pictorial sports parade / edited by George Casey. London: The Sunday Pictorial, 1949.

160p; illus

Includes articles by Gunder Hägg ('Is the four minute mile possible?') and Geoff Dyson ('Faster and faster, higher and higher') and a photo feature on the 1948 Olympic marathon.

318　With the skin of their teeth: memories of great sporting finishes in golf, cricket, rugby and association football, lawn tennis, boxing, athletics, rowing and horse-racing / edited by G. O. Nickalls. London: Country Life, 1951.

168p; illus　　　　　　　　　　BL: 7919.f.35

Contributors include Harold M. Abrahams on athletics (Duncan Robertson's marathons, Dorothy Tyler's high jumping and Syd Atkinson's hurdling).

319　Sports report / edited by Eamonn Andrews and Angus Mackay. London: Heinemann in association with Naldrett, 1954.

200p; illus

*Angus Mackay is pseudonym for Harry Murdoch Mackay*

BL: 7921.b.52

Includes Jack Crump on 'Athletics as the last ditch in amateur sport'.

320　Sports report number two / edited by Eamonn Andrews and Angus Mackay. London: Heinemann in association with Naldrett, 1954.

192p; illus　　　　　　　　　　BL: 7922.bb.2

Includes 'The British approach to sport' by John Arlott, 'Athletics round up 1924-1954' by Harold Abrahams, 'The good fortunes of war' by Peter Wilson, 'Fair cheating' by Bill McGowran, and 'Globe trotting and athletic team managing' by Jack Crump.

321　Peter Dimmock's Sportsview / edited by Paul Fox. London: Thames, 1955.

125p; illus　　　　　　　　　　BL: 7920.d.36

A number of items are included which have an emphasis on athletics: Sports history on film, Britain's Olympic prospects, The four-minute mile, and features on Ken Jones and Gordon Pirie.

322 Peter Dimmock's BBC Sportsview 2 / edited by Paul Fox. London: Thames, 1956.

95p; illus                                        BL: W.P.14364

Features are included on Britain's steeplechase stars, Australian distance runners, Thelma Hopkins, Dorothy Tyler and Alan Thomas.

323 Peter Dimmock's BBC Sportsview 3 / edited by Paul Fox. London: Thames, 1957.

95p; illus                                        BL: W.P.14364

Items on athletics include profiles of John Young, Mike Lindsay, Nick Head and Frank Sando, a comparison of coaches Franz Stampfl and Geoffrey Dyson, and a valedictory piece, 'The last of the amateurs'.

324 Sport / edited by Kenneth Wheeler. London: Hamlyn, 1965.

143p; illus                                       BL: X.441/415

A good, well-illustrated record of many sports. The first 24 pages are on athletics, and include many notable photographs, some in colour.

325 People in sport / Brian Glanville. London: Secker & Warburg, 1967.

255p                                              BL: X.449/2621

Selections from Glanville's writing, principally for *The Sunday Times*. Included are pieces on the Rome and Tokyo Olympics, the Amazons (women in sport), Gordon Pirie and a mythical hypochondriac athlete, Ron Trudge.

326 Today's athlete / edited by Brian Mitchell. London: Pelham, 1970.

175p; illus; index                               SBN: 7207-0426-X
                                                  BL: X.629/2797

Wide-ranging essays from Ranjit Bhatia, David Couling, Brendan Deary, Geoffrey Fenwick, Tom McNab, Brian Mitchell, Jack Scott, Peter Scott, Bruce Tulloh and Tony Ward. Of particular interest is 'The evolution of African athletes' by Fenwick, since it appeared at the point when South Africa became isolated in world sport and other African nations began to make a significant impact.

327 Great sporting headlines / introduced by Ian Wooldridge. London: Collins, 1984.

128p; illus; pbk                                 ISBN: 0-00-217354-9
                                                  BL: L.45/3148

This collection of mainly newspaper material has been culled from several sources and includes many track and field pieces. The earliest item is devoted to Dorando Pietri entering the stadium at the end of the Olympic Marathon (1 August 1908) and the most recent to Zola Budd at the Los Angeles Olympic Games (13 August 1984).

328 Running: the power and glory / compiled by Norman Harris. Haywards Heath: Partridge, 1986.

143p                                              ISBN: 1-85225-009-7
                                                  BL: YA.1995.b.8188

The compiler has selected 27 pieces for this anthology, ranging in subjects over the century up to 1984. Among the authors represented are Peter Lovesey, Grantland Rice, W. R. Loader, W. B. Bennison, E. A. Montague, J. P. Abramson, Michael Melford, Roger Bannister, Cordner Nelson, Larry Montague, John Rodda, John Underwood, Neil Allen, Ron Hill, Cliff Temple, Kenny Moore, David Miller, Mel Watman and Harris himself.

329 Running for clocks and dessert spoons: sporting lives / edited by Ian Clayton. Castleford: Yorkshire Art Circus, 1988.

64p; illus; pbk
(Speaking from experience)                        ISBN: 0-947780-32-7
                                                  BL: YK.1990.a.2299

This collection of reminiscences aims 'to present a glimpse into the everyday aspects of sporting life' in Yorkshire. The athletics section by Gerald Brookman deals with the sport in West Yorkshire from the early 1950s when handicap events were still popular.

330 Moments of greatness, touches of class / edited by Andrew Longmore with contributions by Simon Barnes and others; forewords by Ilie Nastase and Ion Tirac. London: Kingswood, 1991.

x, 310p; illus; pbk                              ISBN: 0-413-65360-9
                                                  BL: YK.1991.a.6314

This collection of articles, sold in aid of the Romanian Orphanage Trust, covers eleven sports; just one relates to athletics. 'A golden afternoon in Stuttgart' is Jack Buckner's compelling description of his 5000m victory at the 1986 European Championships.

331 Sporting sensations: great moments in world sport / Evening Standard sports writers. London: Ward Lock, 1993.

176p; illus; index; pbk                          ISBN: 0-7063-7127-5
                                                  BL: YK.1993.b.8238

Includes athletics by Neil Allen, on George, Halswelle, Liddell, Owens, Bannister, Packer, Beamon, Hemery, Viren, Bayi, Ovett, Coe, Lewis and Griffith-Joyner.

332 The winning edge: outstanding athletic interviews / Alastair Aitken. Lewes: Book Guild, 1998.

viii, 238p; illus; pbk                           ISBN: 1-85776-320-3
                                                  BL: YK.2000.a.4162

333 The ATFS Golden Jubilee book: celebrating the 50-year history of the Association of Track & Field Statisticians / Roberto Quercetani (general editor), Bob Phillips (editor). Glossop: National Union of Track Statisticians, 2000.

180p; illus; pbk

Contributions from thirty-eight members of the Association, including founder-members McWhirter, Quercetani, Potts, and Regli.

# Educational Aids & Reading Books

334 The ancient Olympic Games / J. D. Bentley; illustrated by Dorothy Ralphs. Amersham: Hulton Educational, 1970.
31p; illus
(Round the world histories; no. 18)      ISBN: 0-7175-0052-7
BL: X.709/28021

Fourteen-year old Myron, accompanied by his father, watches the Games at Olympia in 436BC; four years later, having been coached in the intervening period, Myron returns to secure victory in the discus throw.

335 You're on your own / Evan Owen; illustrated by Dan Pearce. London: Evans, 1973.
80p; illus; pbk
(Checkers)      ISBN: 0-237-29008-1

A reader for adolescents with learning difficulties.

336 Running harder / Donald Honig; photographs by Bill Powers; consultants Harold N. Friedman, Corinne Bloomer. London: Watts, 1976.
47p; illus
(Target books)      ISBN: 0-85166-605-1
BL: Cup.1281/402

A story for adults with learning difficulties.

337 The Olympic Games / Bruce Tulloh. London: Heinemann Educational, 1976.
viii, 72p; illus; pbk
(Heinemann guided readers, upper level; 5)
ISBN: 0-435-27027-3
BL: X.619/15399

☞   Also listed at: C30

338 Picture sets and practice packs: visuals and work cards for language development. 1: The Olympics / Brian Abbs, Evelyn Davies, Peter Town. London: Longman, 1976.
1 portfolio; chiefly illus
*Contents: Teacher's booklet, 4 folded sheets, 10 copies each of 4 folders*      ISBN: 0-582-55317-2
BL: Cup.1285/202

339 Sporting events / R. E. Wigglesworth. London: Cassell, 1981.
1 vol.; illus; index; pbk
(Cassell discovery books; no. 4)
*Contents: Wimbledon; The Olympic Games; The TT; The World Cup*      ISBN: 0-304-30274-0
BL: X.629/17459

340 Mathematics in sport 4: the decathlon / Dave Kirkby. Sheffield: Eigen, 1983.
12p; illus; pbk      ISBN: 1-85039-163-7
BL: YC.1986.a.3278

341 Mathematics in sport 6: the marathon / Dave Kirkby. Sheffield: Eigen, 1984.
12p; illus; pbk      ISBN: 1-85039-165-3
BL: X.629/25620

342 Spotlight on the Olympics / Amanda Alvey. London: Cassell, 1984.
vi, 58p; illus; pbk
(Cassell graded readers: Level 4)      ISBN: 0-304-30820-X
BL: X.958/27771

343 Athlete / Henry Pluckrose; illustrated by Martin Salisbury. Oxford: Blackwell Education, 1988.
24p; illus; index; pbk
(Oranges and lemons; Level 4)      ISBN: 0-631-90202-3
BL: YK.1989.a.4533

344 Olympics: Key Stage 1 / Zoë Dawson. Hemel Hempstead: Simon & Schuster Education, 1992.
64p; illus, maps; spiral
(Photocopy masters)      ISBN: 0-7501-0347-7
BL: YK.1995.b.449

345 Olympics: Key Stage 2 / Zoë Dawson. Hemel Hempstead: Simon & Schuster Education, 1992.
64p; illus, maps; spiral
(Photocopy masters)      ISBN: 0-7501-0348-5
BL: YK.1995.b.2056

346 The runner / Amanda Brown. Harlow: Longman, 1993.
38p; illus; pbk
(Longman gems)    ISBN: 0-582-21749-0
BL: H.94/2830

A story written specially for Botswanan and Southern African children.

347 Going for gold! / Andrew Donkin. London: Dorling Kindersley, 1999.
48p; illus, maps; index
(Eyewitness readers; Level 4)    ISBN: 0-7513-6213-1

348 The Olympic Games / Steve Flinders. Oxford: Oxford University Press, 1999.
30p; illus, 1 map; pbk
(Oxford bookworms: factfiles; v3)    ISBN: 0-19-422872-X
BL: YK.2000.a.48

Stage 3 reader for children.

349 Athlete: Ada has asthma / Eleanor Archer. London: Watts, 2000.
24p; illus; index
(Making it!)    ISBN: 0-7496-3669-6
BL: YK.2000.a.7393

A book for young readers showing how a young sprinter with asthma manages her disease.

**✳ *Additional References***

350 Athletics for A level Physical Education AEB (1998 onwards) A level Syllabus / Jan Roscoe, Dennis Roscoe; illustrated by Shirley Doolan. 3rd ed. Widnes: J. Roscoe, 1996.
xviii, 58p (looseleaf); illus
*Bibliography: pxviii*    ISBN: 1-901424-08-1
BL: YK.1997.c.2

351 Athletics for A level Physical Education OCEAC A level Syllabus / Jan Roscoe, Dennis Roscoe; illustrated by Shirley Doolan. Widnes: J. Roscoe, 1996.
73p (looseleaf); illus
*Bibliography: p73*    ISBN: 1-901424-10-3
BL: YK.1997.c.3

# *Religious & Philosophical Tracts*

352 Musings for athletes: twelve brief philosophical essays designed to accompany a quiet hour / Charles Box. London: Simpkin, Marshall, 1888.
iii, 169p; illus    BL: 4400.l.43

353 The ethics of athletics: fraternal words to young men, also adopted for general readers. Stirling: Drummond's Tract Depot, 1890.
31p; pbk
(Athlete series; no. 2)
*Written by Arthur Robert Morrison Finlayson*
BL: 4404.bb.54

354 The runner's Bible / compiled and annotated for the reading of him who runs by Nora Holm. London: Allen & Unwin, 1940.
xv, 158p    BL: 3048.e.15

# *Film & Television*

355 Sports in view / edited by Peter Dimmock. London: Faber, 1964.
189p; illus    BL: X.449/437

*A team of commentators write about their sports in relation to television. The chapter on athletics is contributed by David Coleman.*

356 Games and sets: the changing face of sport on television / Steven Barnett. London: BFI Publishing, 1990.
214p; illus; index
 *Bibliography: p207-208*
  ISBN: 0-85170-267-8 (cased) • 0-85170-268-6 (pbk)
    BL: YK.1990.a.6525

*A perceptive study of the increasingly close link between sport and television, with some acute observations on early developments.*

357 Television in the Olympics / Miquel de Moragas Spà, Nancy K. Rivenburgh, James F. Larson, in cooperation with researchers from 25 countries. London: Libbey, 1995.
xvii, 276p; illus; pbk
 *Bibliography: p267-276*  ISBN: 0-86196-538-8
    BL: YK.1996.b.8094

*Primarily an in-depth investigation of television coverage at the 1992 Barcelona Games, but provides much historical data. The three areas covered by the book are: economic, organisational and technological infrastructures for Olympic television; communicating culture, Olympism and politics in the opening ceremony; and the viewing experience. Athletics coverage receives particularly significant treatment in chapters 6 and 11.*

## ✳ *Additional References*

358 The films of Leni Riefenstahl / David B. Hinton. London: Scarecrow, 1978.
v, 162p; illus; index
 *Bibliography: p152-157*  ISBN: 0-8108-1141-3
    BL: X.989/52859

*The author states in his preface, 'When I met Jesse Owens some time after publication of the first edition, he could hardly restrain his show of affection for Leni Riefenstahl. As a "star" of the film, he knew that "Olympia" is not, as described by one popular movie guidebook, a "glorification of the Nazi state", but an international celebration of athletic competition.' Hinton concludes, 'As one critic has observed, "Olympia" can be seen as a complete reversal, if not a refutation, of what was shown in "Triumph of the Will".'*

☞ Subsequent ed. L361

359 Sport in the movies / Ronald Bergan. London: Proteus, 1982.
160p; illus; index
  ISBN: 0-86276-031-3 (cased) • 0-86276-017-8 (pbk)
    BL: X.622/15933

*Chapter 6 (Olympia!) provides brief synopses of many films devoted mainly or entirely to track and field.*

360 Leni Riefenstahl and Olympia / Cooper C. Graham. London: Scarecrow, 1986.
xi, 323p; illus; index
(Filmmakers; no. 13)
 *Bibliography: p294-310*  ISBN: 0-8108-1896-5
    BL: YC.1988.a.1918

361 The films of Leni Riefenstahl / David B. Hinton; foreword by Anthony Slide. 2nd ed. London: Scarecrow, 1991.
xii, 175p; illus; index
(Filmmakers; no. 29)
 *Filmography: p154-162; bibliography: p163-168*
    ISBN: 0-8108-2505-8
    BL: YC.1993.a.363

☞ Previous ed. L358

362 Olympia / Taylor Downing. London: BFI Publishing, 1992.
96p; illus; pbk
(BFI film classics)
 *Bibliography: p96*  ISBN: 0-85170-341-0
    BL: YC.1993.a.532

*This monograph is devoted to what, over sixty years after its release, is still regarded as the meisterwerk in the field of Olympic cinema, the record of the 1936 Berlin Olympics by Leni Riefenstahl. A brief survey of 'The Olympics on film 1896-1932' is followed by a résumé of Riefenstahl's career before she made Olympia, and details of the film's production and finance.*

363 Sport on film and video: the North American Society for Sport History guide / Judith A. Davidson, editor and compiler and Daryl Alder, compiler. London: Scarecrow, 1993.
194p; index  ISBN: 0-8108-2739-5
    BL: YC.1994.b.2495

*Films included range from general interest to specific historical, sociological and psychological topics in sport, but primarily instructional films and commercial films are excluded. In addition to a guide to using the filmography, four indexes are provided: title, distributor, name and topic.*

# Painting & Sculpture

364 How to draw athletes in action / Arthur Zaidenberg. London: Abelard-Schuman, 1966.

64p; illus                                    BL: aX.421/919

Some advice is offered on appropriate drawing materials. Several examples, made principally with pen and Indian ink, of athletes running, high jumping, long jumping, hurdling, pole vaulting, javelin throwing, shot putting, hammer throwing and discus throwing are presented.

365 Faster, higher, stronger: an exhibition about the Olympic dream / text by Robert Mclean, Sean Wilkinson and Ian O'Riordan. Edinburgh: City of Edinburgh, Dept. of Recreation, 1997.

15p; illus                              ISBN: 0-905072-81-2

Catalogue for an exhibition held at the City Art Centre, Edinburgh in 1997.

## ✳ Additional References

366 Modern athletics and Greek art: notes on the Borghese gladiator and the Apobates relief of the Acropolis / W. M. Ramsay. Oxford: Horace Hart, 1885.

16p; pbk

367 Studies in Greek athletic art / K. T. Frost. Oxford University, 1907. BLit thesis.

368 Illustrations from the XIVth Olympiad Sport in Art Exhibition, London, 1948; held at the Victoria and Albert Museum. London: The Museum, 1952.

48p; illus; pbk                            BL: 7812.ee.20

The criteria which the works submitted had to meet were: by living artists; produced since 1 January 1944; related to sport or games; previously approved by the Olympic Committee of the nation under which the artist claims citizenship. Includes 15 half-tone illustrations relating to athletics.

369 Sporting life: an anthology of British sporting prints / Paul Goldman. London: British Museum Publications, 1983.

126p; illus; index; pbk

*Bibliography: p120-121*          ISBN: 0-7141-0793-X
                                            BL: L.49/2053

Exhibition catalogue. The chapter on 'Athletics and gymnastics' details a number of early prints, including portraits of Captain Barclay and George Wilson, and works by Rowlandson, Collet, Greengrass and Paterson.

370 British challenge at the 1984 Olympics: paintings by Kevin Whitney / with a text by Brian Glanville. London: Muller, 1984.

119p; illus                              ISBN: 0-584-11103-7

☞ Also listed at: C209

371 Harry Holland: the painter & reality / Edward Lucie-Smith. London: Art Books International, 1991.

136p; illus; index                      ISBN: 0-946708-22-3
                                            BL: LB.31.b.6443

An ESAA 440yds winner in 1958, Wright Henry Holland (born 1941) became a prominent figurative painter. One of his works on an athletics theme, 'Fosbury Flop' (1978), is reproduced in this outstanding biography.

372 A dictionary of sporting artists 1650-1990 / Mary Ann Wingfield. Woodbridge: Antique Collectors' Club, 1992.

354p; illus

*Bibliography: p338-340*          ISBN: 1-85149-140-6
                                            BL: YK.1993.b.415

The index of artists by sports includes entries for athletics, Olympic sports and walking/pedestrianism.

373 The book of British sporting heroes / compiled by James Huntington-Whiteley; introduction by Richard Holt. London: National Portrait Gallery, 1998.

239p; illus; pbk                        ISBN: 1-85514-249-X
                                            BL: YK.1998.b.9274

Published to accompany the exhibition 'British Sporting Heroes' at the National Portrait Gallery from 16 October 1998 to 24 January 1999. Features portraits and photo-portraits, with brief biographies, of: Harold Abrahams, Sir Roger Bannister, Captain Barclay, Lillian Board, Lord Burghley, Linford Christie, Sebastian Coe, Lynn Davies, C. B. Fry, W. G. George, Tanni Grey, Sally Gunnell, Chris Hallam, David Hemery, Albert Hill, Eric Liddell, Douglas Lowe, Steve Ovett, Ann Packer, Mary Peters, Gordon Pirie, Foster Powell, Mary Rand, Tessa Sanderson, Daley Thompson, Don Thompson, Allan Wells, Fatima Whitbread, George Wilson, and Sydney Wooderson.

☞ Also listed at: B256

# Photography

374 The sportfolio: portraits and biographies of heroes and heroines of sport & pastime. London: Newnes, 1896.
140p; illus                                    BL: Cup.1253.d.18

*High-quality studio portraits of fifteen athletes, with biographies, among them Bacon, Bradley, Bredin, Crossland, Dixon, Sturgess and Thomas. Also includes good shots of C. B. Fry as a cricketer, and of Catford and Herne Hill tracks.*

375 The human figure in motion: an electrophotographic investigation of consecutive phases of muscular actions / Eadweard Muybridge. London: Chapman & Hall, 1901.
280p; illus                                    BL: Tab.443.b.1

*Muybridge (1830-1904) was a pioneer in the photography of animal and human movement. The series, most of which show consecutive phases of movement simultaneously from two or three viewpoints, includes athletes race walking, starting, running, high and long jumping and putting. Full descriptions of each series are given. Of particular interest to the athletics historian are the sequences on the standing jumps.*

376 Athletes in action / F. A. M. Webster. London: Shaw, 1931.
304p; illus                                    BL: 07912.e.63

*This book of outstanding action photographs was certainly the best of its kind published to that time. There is a fine stroboscopic sequence of Earl Thomson and some equally good single shots of Harold Osborn. Possibly the best photos are of the Australian long jumper Dr Honner performing a 2½ hitch-kick, showing a massive backward rotation of the trunk, and a shot of Charlie Hoff, the Norwegian pole-vaulter of the twenties, showing a clear 'fly-away' finish technique.*

☞ Subsequent ed. L378

377 Girl athletes in action / F. A. M. Webster. London: Shaw, 1934.
208p; illus                                    BL: D

*At this point, British competitive women's athletics had existed for little more than a decade, and Webster's work was therefore well ahead of its time, and liberal in its approach.*

378 Athletes in action / F. A. M. Webster. Rev. ed. London: Shaw, 1941.
318p; illus                                    BL: 7917.a.10

☞ Previous ed. L376

379 Track and field / Tony Duffy; colour photographs by Tony Duffy, All-Sport Limited. Hove: Wayland, 1980.
64p; illus; index                        ISBN: 0-85340-777-0
                                              BL: X.629/14648

380 Great action photography / edited by Bryn Campbell. London: Ebury, 1983.
160p; illus; index                       ISBN: 0-85223-325-6
                                              BL: X.421/25137

*An extensive interview by the editor with each photographer precedes a selection of his best work. Athletics is featured in the portfolios of all eight photographers: Erich Baumann, Tony Duffy, Gerry Cranham, Fred Joch, Neil Leifer, Walter Iooss jr, Chris Smith and Andy Hayt.*

381 Winning women: the changing image of women in sport / photographs by Tony Duffy; text by Paul Wade; additional research by Gordon Richards and Katherine Arnold. London: Queen Anne, 1983.
156p; illus                              ISBN: 0-356-09493-6
                                              BL: X.622/16725

*Contains nineteen photographs of women athletes.*

382 Sports photography / Steve Powell & Tony Duffy in association with Keith Nelson; foreword by Daley Thompson. London: Batsford, 1984.
167p; illus; index                       ISBN: 0-7134-3740-5
                                              BL: X.622/22918

*Based on the experiences of All-Sport photographers, this fine work contains many examples drawn from their coverage of athletics. The decathlon world record holder, Daley Thompson, is featured prominently.*

383 Eamonn McCabe: photographer / with text by Simon Barnes; with foreword by Edward Lucie-Smith. London: Kingswood, 1987.
xxii, 88p; chiefly illus                 ISBN: 0-434-98110-9
                                              BL: LB.31.b.3489

*A sparkling collection of black and white work, split between sport and landscapes. The former include twelve track or field subjects. Barnes describes a shot from the 1984 Olympic 1500m: 'It shows Ovett on the brink of collapse, and an uncanny moment as Cram, cool and almost dainty, turns to look at Ovett with an expression of well-bred disdain on his face, while Ovett crashes onto the line. Ovett looks haggard and desperate: a spent force.'*

384 Sport in focus / Chris Smith; essays by Dudley Doust, Hugh McIlvanney, Brendan Foster, Brough Scott. London: Partridge, 1987.
126p; illus                              ISBN: 1-85225-001-1

*Although only 15 black and white athletics shots are represented in this collection, they are of an exceptionally high order. The introduction is by Sebastian Coe and some text is contributed by Brendan Foster.*

385 Visions of sport: celebrating twenty years of Allsport, the international sports picture agency in association with Crosfield Electronics. London: Pelham, 1988.
158p; chiefly illus      ISBN: 0-7207-1863-5
BL: L.B.37.b.211

Published to mark the twentieth anniversary of the foundation of Allsport Photographic agency in 1968 by Tony Duffy, this volume contains an astonishing selection of work. Short essays are included; those on athletics are by Patrick Collins on Sebastian Coe, Neil Wilson on Daley Thompson, and John Rodda on Bob Beamon.

386 Visions of sport: a celebration of the work of the Allsport photographic agency, the world's finest sports photography / picture editor: Bob Martin; editorial contributors, Nick Edmund & Peter Nichols. Hexham: Kensington West Productions, 1993.
179p; illus      ISBN: 1-871349-32-X
BL: LB.31.b.12235

A new collection of 140 photographs by members of All Sport UK; 20 are athletics subjects. Profiles of Mike Powell, Jackie Joyner-Kersee and Daley Thompson also appear.

387 Sportfolio Allsport / Chris Beeson and Kate Donovan. London: Carlton, 1998.
136p; illus
*Spine title: Sportfolio: visions of Allsport*
ISBN: 1-85868-624-5
BL: LB.31.b.17557

This selection of very striking colour photographs includes nine examples from track and field in the seasons 1995-1997. Prominent are Igor Potapovich, Michael Johnson, Daniel Komen, Michael Powell and Colin Jackson.

388 Gold rush: photographs of Olympic athletes / Jason Bell. Stockport: Dewi Lewis, 2000.
184p; illus      ISBN: 1-899235-33-7

# Humour

389 Athletics through the looking glass / Brian Mitchell; drawings by Tony Sharrad. Tonbridge: Wildlife and Country Photos, 1972.
102p; illus; pbk      ISBN: 0-9500845-1-4

A waspishly humorous collection of pieces on a number of aspects of athletics.

390 Punch on the Olympics / edited by William Davis. London: Punch, 1976.
166p; pbk; illus      ISBN: 0-905076-02-8

Articles and cartoons.

391 Jog-along-happily and the Cindertrack Kid / Stan N. Allen. Thornton Heath: Heath Technical Services, 1983?
51p; illus; pbk      BL: X.950/34386

Much of the material had been published previously in *Veteris* and *Running* (formerly *Jogging*) magazines; twenty-two items are included, many relating to the sport at club level. In 'Marathon and road racing', an apocryphal reference to the Cold War is woven in: 'How about the International marathon that started in West Berlin, was allowed into the Eastern sector between 13 and 19 miles, and then finished back in the West. It seems that they had 150 starters and 852 finishers.'

392 Not the 1984 Olympics: an incomplete guide / Tom Hepburn; illustrations Rod Proud. London: Willow, 1984.
39p; illus; pbk      ISBN: 0-00-218139-8
BL: L.42/3019

The exuberant and colourful illustrations are the main feature of this light-hearted look at the Olympic Games. The author states, correctly: 'Statistics, that insidious *raison d'être* of sport, are virtually absent here.'

393 Confessions of a brain damaged runner / A. Hacker of Milton Keynes; with cartoons, Bi-Ped. Oxford: B. Forster, 1987.
37 leaves; illus; pbk      ISBN: 0-9503382-2-2
BL: YC.1988.b.8867

Author's real name is Bob Forster.

394 Great sporting fiascos / edited by Tony Brett Young; foreword by HRH the Duke of Edinburgh. London: Robson, 1991.
160p; illus      ISBN: 0-86051-768-3
BL: YK.1993.a.7211

Among the brief anecdotes are several with relevance to athletics: 'A right Royal disaster' (1908 Olympic Marathon); 'Thrown by the question' (Bill Toomey); 'Quick off the mark' by Menzies Campbell; 'Im-patient encounter' by Sebastian Coe; 'Stick with the Irish team' by Frank Keating; 'Come on the Caymans' by Gary and Heather Oakes; and 'Two right feet' by Tessa Sanderson.

395 The Oxford book of Australian sporting anecdotes / edited by Richard Cashman, David Headon, Graeme Kinross-Smith. Oxford: Oxford University Press, 1993.
x, 286p; index          ISBN: 0-19-553468-9
                        BL: YK.1994.a.15526

The editors state in their introduction that the collection contains 255 'snapshots', offering 'a kind of kaleidoscopic history of Australian sport, capturing its essential humour, eccentricity, larrikinism, poignancy and heroism'. The anecdotes are arranged chronologically, ranging from ultra-long distance performer William Francis King in the 1840s and the aboriginal sprinters Charles Samuels and Bobby McDonald in the 1880s, to some outstanding performers of the second half of the twentieth century: Marjorie Jackson, Betty Cuthbert, John Landy, Raelene Boyle, Maureen Caird and Ron Clarke.

396 Running shorts / Stan Greenberg; illustrations by David Arthur. Enfield: Guinness, 1993.
128p; illus; index          ISBN: 0-85112-507-7
                            BL: YK.1993.a.14103

A collection of anecdotes, quotes, and facts relating to athletics. It contains, for example, a succinct account of 'Wilson the Wizard'.

397 Great sporting wisdom / compiled by John Scally; cartoons by Richard Jolley. London: CollinsWillow, 1996.
192p; illus; pbk          ISBN: 0-00-218733-7
                          BL: YK.1997.a.1300

Athletic Aberrations (ch.1) is divided into three sections: On the track (22 entries), Field of dreams (12 entries), and Soundbytes (11 entries). One of the older entries is a *Daily Graphic* headline after Fanny Blankers-Koen won Olympic Gold in 1948: 'The world's fastest woman is an expert cook'. The Golden Foot in Mouth Award contains 40 of the compiler's top favourite utterances by David Coleman, most of which are from athletics commentaries.

# *Quotations*

398 Chambers sporting quotations / edited by Simon James. Edinburgh: Chambers, 1990.
250p; index; pbk          ISBN: 0-550-20489-X
                          BL: YK.1991.a.1160

Athletics is covered in: Athletes; Athletics; Decathlon; Discus; Hurdles; Javelin; Marathon; Olympic Games; Pole vault; Records; Running; Triple jump; Tug-of-war; Walking; and, Winning and losing.

399 Sports quotes of the eighties / compiled by Peter Ball, Phil Shaw. London: Mandarin, 1990.
231p; illus; pbk          ISBN: 0-7493-0366-2
                          BL: YK.1990.a.4423

The quotes are arranged chronologically, and athletics is quite well represented. The (perhaps only partially tongue-in-cheek) jibe by Steve Ovett in 1980: 'The decathlon? Nine Mickey Mouse events and a 1500m' was answered (indirectly) in the same year by Daley Thompson: 'When I lost my world record I took it like a man: I only cried for 10 hours.'

400 The sporting word / compiled by Desmond Lynam and David Teasdale; illustrated by Claudio Muñoz. London: BBC Books, 1994.
256p; illus; index pbk          ISBN: 0-563-36971-X
                                BL: YK.1995.a.6585

Athletics is well represented in this very comprehensive selection of quotations. The quotes of 71 athletes, coaches, scientists, administrators and journalists are included.

# Cartoons & Quiz Books

401 The Athletics Arena athletics cartoon book / Jon
Hudson. London: Arena, 1966.
47p; illus; pbk                                    BL: X.419/8138

402 Sports quiz book: hundreds of questions on popular
sports plus eight pages of results and records / compiled
by Michael Shepherd; edited by J. B. Foreman. London:
Collins, 1967.
48p; illus                                         BL: X.441/825

   Six quizzes, each containing 15 questions, cover the
   Olympic Games, the European Championships, the
   British Empire and Commonwealth Games, the AAA
   Championships, and track and field. An appendix lists
   men's and women's world record holders at 31
   December 1966.

403 Asterix at the Olympic Games / Goscinny. Drawings by
Uderzo; translated by Anthea Bell and Derek Hockridge.
Leicester: Brockhampton, 1972.
48p; illus, 1 map
      *Translation of: Astérix aux jeux olympiques.*
      *Neuilly-sur-Seine: Dargaud, 1968*     ISBN: 0-340-15591-4
   Strip cartoon set in 50BC has the little Gaul winning
   the race of 24 stades by default.

404 Sports picture quiz book / John Grafton; with 240
photographs from Photoworld – a division of F.P.G.
London: Constable, 1977.
140p; illus; index; pbk
      *With answers*                           ISBN: 0-486-23404-5
                                                   BL: X.611/7867

   Track and field is one of ten major sports included, with
   photographs which record some of the outstanding
   performers, from Martin Sheridan, Harry Hillman and
   Ray Ewry, to Ralph Boston, Peter Snell and Dwight
   Stones. Each of the captions to 35 photographs
   (numbers 187-221) contains at least one question.

405 The twelve tasks of Asterix: 1, The race / Goscinny.
Drawings by Uderzo. Sevenoaks: Hodder and Stoughton,
1978.
19p; illus; pbk
      *Translation of: Les 12 travaux d'Asterix. Paris: Dargaud,*
      *1976*                                    ISBN: 0-340-22871-7
                                                   BL: X.990/16373

406 The twelve tasks of Asterix: 2, The javelin / Goscinny.
Drawings by Uderzo. Sevenoaks: Hodder and Stoughton,
1978.
19p; illus; pbk
      *Translation of: Les 12 travaux d'Asterix. Paris: Dargaud,*
      *1976*                                    ISBN: 0-340-22884-9
                                                   BL: X.990/16374

407 Sports quiz / Gordon Jeffery. London: Armada, 1979.
124p; illus, 1 map; pbk
      *Fill-in book with answers*               ISBN: 0-00-691571-X
                                                   BL: X.619/19862

   Several of the miscellaneous quizzes include questions
   on track and field, as does one of two quizzes on the
   Olympics; there are four separate quizzes on athletics.

408 The golden rules of athletics / Ian Heath. London:
Corgi, 1985.
47p; illus; pbk                                    ISBN: 0-552-12597-0
                                                   BL: YV.1987.a.1397

409 The Cartoon Aid Olympic book. London: Cartoon Aid,
1988.                                              ISBN: 0-948836-25-3
                                                   BL: YV.1990.b.599

   Cartoons from around the world, many featuring track
   and field subjects.

410 Interesting athletes: a newspaper artist's look at Blacks in
sports / George L. Lee. London: McFarland, 1990.
176p; illus; index; pbk                            ISBN: 0-899504-82-5
                                                   BL: YC.1990.a.5612

   Born in 1906, Lee arrived in Chicago in 1927 and was
   already producing sports drawings. These first
   appeared in the *Chicago American* in 1930. Amongst
   the distinctive line drawings with small boxed captions
   included in this collection are the following track and
   field figures: Jesse Owens, Dehart Hubbard, Wilma
   Rudolph, Harrison Dillard, Eddie Tolan, Rafer Johnson,
   Ralph Metcalfe, Frazier Thompson and Alice
   Coachman.

411 The Independent on Sunday book of sports questions
and answers / edited by Simon O'Hagan and Chris
Maume. London: Boxtree, 1994.
292p; index; pbk                                   ISBN: 0-7522-1610-4
                                                   BL: YK.1995.a.4416

   Topics on athletics include: effort expended in
   marathons, future of record breaking, marathons run
   on tracks, speed achieved by sprinters, and victorious
   pacemakers.

# Stamps, Coins & Medals

412 A philatelic history of the Olympic Games / Ernie
Trory. Brighton: Crabtree, 1956.

iv, 39p; illus
BL: 08236.f.2

The first eight Olympiads (1896-1927) of the modern
era are covered; issues were few in this period. An
appendix lists surcharges, overprints, errata, Olympic
rings and special labels. An aerial photograph of
Shepherds Bush (White City) in 1908 is included.

413 Sports stamps / Carl-Olof Enhagen. London: Stanley
Paul, 1961.

275p; illus
BL: X.519/1106

The work is divided into three parts – Scope and
design; Olympic stamps; Individual sports and their
stamps. Athletics is strongly represented (pp62-98)
with designs grouped by event. The descriptions are
amplified by black and white reproductions. The
appendix has three tables summarising issues (1896-
1960).

414 The encyclopedia of sports stamps / Robert M. C.
Bateman. London: Stanley Paul, 1969.

173p; illus
SBN: 09-096880-8
BL: X.519/6467

Designed for use with Stanley Gibbons catalogues, the
work contains entries by countries, by sports, and by
certain specific major events. Also included are lists
for individual events and subjects such as women in
sport. There are separate entries for 29 track and
field athletes who had then been depicted on stamps.

415 The commemorative coinage of modern sports / Mary
A. Danaher. London: Thomas Yoseloff, 1978.

183p; illus; index
ISBN: 0-4980178-7-7

Covers collecting of coins of Olympic, World and
regional games.

# M. Reference Works

## Directories, Yearbooks & Annual Guides

1 The athlete for … [1866-1871]. / edited by W. P. London: Chapman and Hall, 1867-1870.

> *Author is W. Pilkington; continued by: The athlete almanack; editions for 1867 and 1870 not published*
>
> BL: P.P.2489.fd
>
> A book of the results of all major amateur events in the previous season.
>
> ☞ See also: M2

2 The athlete almanack for [1872] / edited by H. F. Wilkinson. London: 1871-

> *Continues: The athlete for …*   BL: P.P.2489.fd
>
> A record of all athletic sports for the previous year, covering 323 meetings. Results of Oxford and Cambridge meetings and AAC Championships since their inauguration are given.
>
> ☞ See also: M1

3 The Athletic News almanack and diary for 1876 / A. H. Mills. Manchester: Athletic News, 1876.

4 The Athletic News annual for 1877: a work of reference on athletics, rowing, the ring, etc. / compiled by A. H. Mills. Manchester: Athletic News, 1877.

5 The amateur athletic annual for 1879 / compiled and edited by H. C. Powell. Walsall: Simpkin, Marshall, 1879.

> BL: P.P.2489.fe
>
> A most thorough review of a year's athletics, which contains lists of all outstanding performances made in Britain in each event during the season of 1878. There were no other issues.

6 The sporting annual, or, The sportsman's guide and athlete's companion for 1878-79 / R. Watson. London: Etherington, 1879.

148p

> Give details of athletics in 1878, with results of numerous meetings and amateur records (pp5-23). There is also a substantial section on pedestrianism.

7 Athletes' and cyclists' guide and directory for 1889/90 / A. E. Hunnable. London: Simpkin, 1889.

8 Athletic News athletic directory. Manchester: Athletic News Office, 1905-1912?   BL: P.P.2489.feh

> An annual list of all athletic clubs in the United Kingdom, with secretaries' addresses. A list of records and review of the previous season is included.

9 The sporting and athletic register, 1908: including the results for the year 1907 of all the important events in athletics, games and every form of sport in the United Kingdom, together with the records and notable achievements of past years. London: Chapman and Hall, 1908.

643p

> *Reissued in the same year to include the results of the 1908 Olympics*   BL: P.P.2489.zcc

10 Burke's who's who in sport and sporting records, 1922. London: Burke, 1922.

378p

> Includes biographies of ninety-three athletes; and records and results of athletics and pedestrianism.

11 International athletic annual, 1922 / edited by Maurice Loesch. London: Athletic Publications, 1922.

151p

> *Originally published: Geneva: Argus Athlétique, 1922*
>
> BL: P.P.2418.i

The annual gives all national and international records of athletic events and championships (amateur and professional), including women's athletics, where applicable, for USA, Britain, Australia, Canada, South Africa, Sweden, Norway, Denmark, Finland, France, Italy, Belgium, Switzerland, Germany, Austria, Hungary, Czechoslovakia, Luxemburg and Holland. An interesting feature is the inclusion of lists of the best 15 performers in each event in 1921. Unfortunately, this excellent publication does not appear to have been repeated, and the next comparable book was the

*Olympic Handbook* (1948) *of Potts and Quercetani, which led to the publication in Switzerland of the first ATFS International Athletic Annual in 1951.*

12   Young athlete and junior international yearbook 1968. London: Arena, 1968.

*Only one issue published*

All-time and previous year best performers: girls, intermediate and junior; and boys, youth and junior. There is also a record of results, and a world's best junior performers of all time list.

13   British athletics / National Union of Track Statisticians. London: British Amateur Athletic Board, 1969-1973; 1983-

*Between 1974-1982 published as: UK athletics annual*

14   World of athletics [1979] / edited by Ron Pickering; compiled by Mel Watman. London: Macdonald and Jane's, 1979-
239p; illus
*Published annually*                    ISSN: 0143-1617
                                        BL: P.441/429

Biographical details of the 1978 Commonwealth and European champions appear in the first issue, as well as a longer profile of Steve Ovett by Cliff Temple.

15   World sporting records / compiled by David Emery and Stan Greenberg. London: Bodley Head, 1986.
192p; illus, maps
        ISBN: 0-3703-0746-1 (cased) • 0-370-30747-X (pbk)
                                    BL: YK.1987.b.6756

The introduction contains graphics of 100m, 110m hurdles, 100m and marathon progression, percentage differences between men's and women's records, and predictions for the year 2000. The athletics section (pp16-79) presents a selection of events for particular examination.

## ✳ *Additional References*

16   The Sportsman's pocket-book. London: The Sportsman Offices, 1876-1884?                    BL: P.P.2489.na

A review of each previous season's sport, including a section on athletics.

17   The Sporting Chronicle annual. London: Sporting Chronicle, 1877-1939.               BL: P.P.2489.dd

A detailed review of each previous season's sport with substantial sections on athletics and pedestrianism.

18   The Sporting Life companion, containing Sporting Almanack for [1877]- London: Sporting Life Office, 1877-1930.                              BL: P.P.2489.dc

A review of each previous season's sport, including sections on athletics and pedestrianism.

19   The sportsman's year-book: containing a digest of information relating to the origin and present position of British sports / edited by J. K. Angus. London: Cassell, Petter, Calpin, 1879-1880.
        *Only two issues published*        BL: P.P.2489.zc

20   Routledge's sporting annual. London: Routledge, 1882-1883.
        *Only two issues published*        BL: P.P.2489.zd

A summary of the previous year's sport, including athletics.

21   The year's sport: a review of British sports and pastimes for 1885 / edited by Alfred E. T. Watson. London: Longmans Green, 1886.
549p                                    BL: P.P.2489.zcb

The athletics section is a detailed review of all the important meetings in the 1885 season. It is anonymously written, but the writer was probably Mark Beaufoy.

22   The sportsman's year-book / edited by C. S. Colman and A. H. Windsor, with contributions by various hands. London: Lawrence and Bullen, 1899.
        *Only one issue published*        BL: P.P.2489.zdb

23   The sporting annual, illustrated / edited by Arthur Binstead and Gerald Fitzgibbon. London: Treherne, 1903.
        *Only one issue published*        BL: P.P.2489.zde

Contains records of every sport, including athletics.

24   Record of sports. Liverpool: Royal Insurance Company, 1904?-1914?         BL: Mic.A.12320(1) (microfilm copy)

A review of the previous year's sport, with lists of records.

25   The sportsman's year book [1905] / edited by Arthur Wallis Myers. London: Newnes, 1905.
354p                                    BL: P.P.2489.zdg

A review of the previous season's sport, including athletics.

26   Official year book / London Railways Athletic Association (afterwards Railways Athletic Association). London: The Association, 1914-
        *No issues published between 1915-1920*    BL: P.P.2489.zcf

Covers several sports, including athletics.

# *Handbooks*

27 The athletes' directory and handbook for [1892]: an alphabetical list of the principal clubs in the United Kingdom, with secretaries' names / compiled and edited by Albert Saunders. London: Cook, Hammond & Waud, 1892-

  *Published annually* BL: P.P.2489.fda

  Saunders, a member of Ranelagh Harriers, compiled a list of the principal clubs in the UK with secretaries' names, etc. Includes a review of the previous year's athletics and lists of records for the home countries.

28 SAA yearbook. London: Schools Athletic Association, 1926-1934.

  *Continued by: The Schools Athletic Association handbook*

  The SAA, founded in 1925, became the English Schools Athletic Association.

  ☞ See also: M31

29 The official annual handbook. London: Amateur Athletic Association, 1928-1956.

  *Continued by: Amateur Athletic Association handbook*
  BL: P.P.2489.fea

  ☞ See also: M37

30 Metropolitan Police Athletic Association handbook. London: 1935-

31 The Schools Athletic Association handbook. London: SAA, 1935-1938.

  *Continues: SAA yearbook; continued by: English Schools Athletic Association handbook*

  ☞ See also: M28, M39

32 International Amateur Athletic Federation handbook. London: IAAF, 1951-1993.

33 Surrey County Athletic Association handbook [1951] / edited by T. N. Rowe. Waddon: The Association, 1952-

  *Editor and place of publication vary*

34 English Cross-Country Union handbook, 1953-54. London: ECCU, 1953.

  *Continued by: The official handbook and rules of the English Cross-Country Union*

  Contains ECCU and International Cross Country Union rules, championship results from 1876 and lists of affiliated associations, clubs and secretaries.

  ☞ See also: M35

35 The official handbook and rules of the English Cross-Country Union. London: ECCU, 1954-

  *Continues: English Cross-Country Union handbook, 1953-54*

  ☞ See also: M34

36 East London Schools' Athletics Association handbook. London: Pyramid, 1956- BL: P.P.2489.fez

37 Amateur Athletic Association handbook. London: Amateur Athletic Association, 1957-

  *Continues: The official annual handbook; continued by AAA and WAAA handbook including rules for competition*

  ☞ See also: M29, M43

38 IAAF official handbook. London: International Amateur Athletic Association, 1957-

39 English Schools Athletic Association handbook. Bexhill: The Association, 1959-

  *Published annually; place of publication varies*
  BL: P.P.7612.gx

  ☞ See also: M31

40 Southern Counties annual [1961]. London: Southern Counties Amateur Athletic Association, 1961. 64p

41 All-Britain athletics: annual handbook for 1964 / edited by Stan Tomlin. St Albans: The editor, 1965. 68p

  *Only one issue published*

  Record and result lists of all major events, including English, Scottish, Welsh and Irish schools, and cross-country.

42 World athletics handbook 1970 / compiled by Bruce Tulloh; statistics by Andrew Huxtable and others; photographs by Ed Lacey. London: Mayflower, 1970. 188p; illus; pbk ISBN: 0-583-11734-1
  BL: X.619/4239

  The major 1969 indoor and outdoor competitions are described, both domestic and international, with results; brief surveys of the European Cup, European Championships, Olympic Games, and British Empire & Commonwealth Games are given, in each case supported by statistical sections; profiles of 26 Commonwealth stars are provided; and the final section lists records and best performances in ten categories.

43 AAA and WAAA handbook including rules for competition. London: Amateur Athletic Association and Women's Amateur Athletic Association, 1987-

  *Continues: Amateur Athletic Association handbook; continued by: British Athletic Federation handbook*

  A combined book for the two associations.

  ☞ See also: M37, M44

44    British Athletic Federation handbook including rules for competition. Birmingham: British Athletic Federation, 1992-

> *Variant title: BAF handbook; continues: AAA and WAAA handbook including rules for competition*

☞  See also: M43

✱  *Additional References*

45    John Lawrence's handbook of cricket in Ireland, and record of athletic sports, football, &c.: fourteenth number [1878-1879] / compiled and edited by J. T. H. Dublin: The author, 1879.

xii, 227p; illus                             BL: YA.1999.a.5463

> Includes athletics results lists for Dublin University, the Irish Civil Service, the Irish Champion Athletic Club, the North of Ireland Athletic Club and six Irish schools and colleges.

# Statistics & Records ~ UK & General

46    The performances of C. Hall, better known as C. Westhall. Westminster: Blanchard, 1867.

20p                                          BL: 10825.a.59

> A small book which lists all matches made by the famous pedestrian.

47    The athletes' record of performances and handbook / H. Morgan Browne. London: Willetts, 1894.

48p

> *Only one issue published*          BL: P.P.2489.fdb

> Complete details of British clubs and records. There is also a photograph of H. A. Heath (SLH), National CC Champion 1892/3, with biographical details.

48    Sporting and athletic records / Hubert Morgan Browne. London: Methuen, 1897.

xx, 366p             BL: Mic.A.6613(2) (microfilm copy)

> Possibly the most comprehensive compilation of records produced in the nineteenth century. The lists comprise world's, British, American and public schools and various meeting records, and cover all standard and most non-standard events in professional and amateur athletics. Running records are given for every mile up to 623 miles, and walking records for every mile up to 531 miles.

49    Athletic records to date, and containing some important laws and rules for competitions under the constitution of the Amateur Athletic Association / compiled by F. A. M. Webster. London: British Sports Publishing, 1922.

128p; illus

(Spalding's athletic library)                      BL: D

> Includes an essay on the Public Schools Championships, lists of most major championships, and records.

50    AAA championships, 1880-1931 / Harold M. Abrahams and J. Bruce Kerr; foreword by Lord Desborough. London: Amateur Athletic Association, 1932.

84p; index

> *A 2-sheet supplement covering the 1932 Championships was published*

> An accurate result list of every AAA Championships, listing the first three in each event.

51    Athletic records & results [1937] / Harold M. Abrahams and Lawrence N. Richardson. London: Seeley, Service, 1937.

47p                                          BL: 07908.ff.55

> A supplement to *The Lonsdale Book of Sporting Records* (1937).

☞  See also: M52

52    The Lonsdale book of sporting records 1937. London: Seeley, Service, 1937.

457p; illus

(The Lonsdale Library; vol. 25)

> Contents include Harold Abrahams on athletics with records and results of major meetings in 1936; L. N. Richardson on cross-country; and Howard Marshall on the Olympic Games.

☞  See also: M51

53    British athletics record book / compiled by A. Ross McWhirter, Ian Buchanan & Norris D. McWhirter. London: The authors, 1957-1958.          BL: P.P.2489.zcw

> Includes progressive record lists and best performance lists.

54  British athletics [1959] / compiled by the members of the National Union of Track Statisticians. London: British Amateur Athletic Board, 1959-
    *Published annually*          BL: P.P.7612.ft
    This title, currently edited by Rob Whittingham and Peter Matthews, is the statistical Bible for British athletics, containing records lists, merit rankings, and event-by-event performance lists for senior, junior, youth and women performers.

55  British best performances [1958-1963] / Andrew Huxtable. London: National Union of Track Statisticians, 1959-1964.
    *Published annually*          BL: P.P.8001.bu

56  Northern Ireland: report of 1958 season. Ballymena: N. Ireland Association of Track and Field Statisticians, 1959.
16p; pbk

57  Scottish athletics yearbook: lists of Scottish best performers / produced by the Scottish Association of Track Statisticians. Edinburgh: The Association, 1960-1983; 1993-
    Currently edited by Arnold Black, the most recent issue (1999) ran to 256 pages and included deep Scottish lists and results for all age groups, as well as feature articles.

58  The young athlete / Stan Tomlin; compiled by Bob Sparks. London: A. Wander, 1960.
64p
    Contains United Kingdom and World junior all time lists, information about the Schools AA Championships and an article by Derek Johnson.

59  British athletics 1960: junior and youth performances. London: National Union of Track Statisticians, 1961.
26p

60  British best performances of all time / edited by Andrew Huxtable; foreword by Harold M. Abrahams. London: National Union of Track Statisticians, 1961.
86p; pbk
    *Includes a 14 page supplement with additional 1960 performances*          BL: P.P.8001.bt
    ☞  Subsequent ed. M68

61  Encyclopædia of British athletics records / Ian Buchanan. London: Stanley Paul, 1961.
272p; illus
    *Foreword by Harold M. Abrahams*      BL: 7924.bbb.25
    A review with results of all British international matches 1921-1960; a list of all British international representatives since 1908; Olympic, European and Commonwealth Games champions; and lists, to a depth of ten, of United Kingdom best performers as at 31 December 1960.

62  British junior all-time best performers annual / Ian R. Smith. London: Arena, 1963-1964.
    *Continued by: 1965 youth and junior all-time and 1964 British performers annual*
    ☞  See also: M66

63  United Kingdom best performers of all time / compiled by the National Union of Track Statisticians. London: The Union, 1963.
66p; pbk

64  United Kingdom indoor track and field handbook / compiled by Andrew Huxtable & Patrick Mackenzie. London: NUTS, 1964.
38p; pbk          BL: X.449/597
    The first comprehensive record of indoor athletics in Britain, which lists world, European, Commonwealth, UK all-comers and UK national 'records'. The major indoor arenas are described.
    ☞  Subsequent ed. M69

65  United Kingdom junior and intermediate ladies all time and best performers annual / Peter Vincent Martin. London: Arena, 1964-1966.
    *Continued by: Top girls*
    ☞  See also: M70

66  1965 youth and junior all-time and 1964 British performers annual / Ian R. Smith on behalf of the NUTS. London: Arena, 1965.
    *Continues: British junior all-time best performers annual; continued by: Junior and youth all-time and British performers annual*
    An extension of the Junior annual first published in 1963.
    ☞  See also: M62, M67

67  Junior and youth all-time and British performers annual. London: Arena, 1965-
    *Continues: 1965 youth and junior all-time and 1964 British performers annual*
    ☞  See also: M62, M66

68  British best performances of all time / edited by Andrew Huxtable; foreword by Roberto L. Quercetani. 2nd ed. London: National Union of Track Statisticians, 1966.
148p; pbk
    ☞  Previous ed. M60

69  United Kingdom indoor track & field handbook / compiled by Andrew Huxtable and Patrick Mackenzie. 2nd ed. London: NUTS, 1966.
78p          BL: X.449/2263
    ☞  Previous ed. M64; subsequent ed. M73

70   Top girls [1966] / compiled by Peter V. Martin. London: Arena, 1967-

*Continues: United Kingdom junior and intermediate ladies all time and best performers annual*

A statistical compilation of all-time and 1966 junior and intermediate best performances, and 1966 WAAA Junior and Intermediate Championship medallists.

☞   See also: M65

71   UK top teenagers 1967 / Ian R. Smith. London: Arena, 1967.

25p; pbk

Lists the best junior and youth performers (male) of 1966.

72   UK junior all time list / edited by Cliff Temple; compiled by David Cocksedge, Alan Lindop and Peter Martin; foreword by Mike Farrell. London: National Union of Track Statisticians, 1971.

64p

Contains detailed all-time lists for youths, junior men and girls, and UK age records.

73   United Kingdom indoor track and field handbook / edited by Andrew Huxtable. 3rd ed. Birmingham: Midlands Counties AAA, 1971.

52p

☞   Previous ed. M69

74   Welsh athletics [1977]: a statistical survey of the [1976] track and field season / compiled by J. Clive Williams. Cardiff: The author, 1977-1981.

*Continued by: Welsh athletics annual*

By 1981, this annual had increased in size to ninety pages and was illustrated. It was relaunched in 1982.

☞   See also: M77

75   UK junior all time handbook / compiled by the National Union of Track Statisticians. London: BAAB, 1979.

128p; pbk                     ISBN: 0-85134-057-1
                              BL: X.629/16351

Contains detailed all-time lists of junior men and women, UK age records, and results of European Junior Championships 1970-77.

76   British marathon ranking list, 1980 / compiled by John Walsh. Carmarthen: The author, 1981.

49p

77   Welsh athletics annual / edited by Alan Currie. Neath: The editor, 1982-

*Continues, Welsh athletics; editions from 1984 to 1995 edited by Alan and Brenda Currie*

Alan and Brenda Currie took over from Clive Williams. Since 1988, Welsh year lists have been produced by Ken Bennett.

☞   See also: M74

78   Northern Ireland athletics / John Glover and Alan Keys. Belfast: The authors, 1983-

Northern Ireland top tens for men and women, senior and junior, for the previous year.

79   Athletics / Ken Mays. London: Telegraph, 1984.

128p; illus

(Daily Telegraph pocket sports facts)   ISBN: 0-86367-019-9
                                        BL: X.629/26832

80   Track & field athletics: the records / Peter Matthews. Enfield: Guinness Superlatives, 1986.

175p; illus; index; pbk             ISBN: 0-85112-463-1
                                    BL: YC.1986.b.1696

The material, much of it complementing the author's earlier 1982 work, is presented in the following main sections: event-by-event survey, milestones in the history of the sport, features, major championships, and national surveys.

81   The TV viewer's guide to athletics 1986-1987 / edited by Steven Downes and Peter Matthews; foreword by Steve Jones. London: Aurum, 1986?

128p; illus; pbk                    ISBN: 0-948149-38-8

82   Daily Mirror platinum athletics yearbook 1987 / edited by Vic Robbie. London: Mirror Group Newspapers, 1987.

85p

83   ITV athletics yearbook / Randall Northam & Richard Russell. London: Arena, 1988-

84   A statistical history of UK track & field athletics / edited by Andrew Huxtable. London: National Union of Track Statisticians, 1990.

312p; pbk                           ISBN: 0-904612-11-2
                                    BL: YK.1991.a.6211

Contains progressive UK records for all standard events (and some non-standard) in most cases from the nineteenth century; lists of men and women who have represented Great Britain & Northern Ireland (Ireland before 1922) in international matches or championships, both indoors and outdoors; UK all time lists for both men and women, at least 100 deep in standard events, detailed with placing, date and venue.

85   All time list / Liam Hennessy. Dublin: BLE, 1992.

28p; pbk

86   Athletic sports / John Morton. London: Watts, 1992.

(Sports facts)                      ISBN: 0-7496-0585-4

87   South East athletics yearbook / Liz Sissons and others. Chessington: The author, 1992-

Annual statistics for the counties of Berkshire, Essex, Kent, and Surrey.

88  British athletics: statistical review of [1993] / National Union of Track Statisticians. Stockport: Umbra Software, 1993-

89  Bailiwick of Guernsey sporting records / Mike Medhurst. Guernsey: The author, 1996.
304p; pbk
  *Spine title: Guernsey sporting records*    ISBN: 0-952941-20-1
                                              BL: YK.1996.a.23598
  Athletics, cross-country, marathon and walking results and records are given, together with profiles of Robert Elliott, Jay Peet and Percy Hodge. Historical achievements are set within the context of Commonwealth (1970-94), Island (1985-95) and Olympic (1920-96) Games.

90  British athletics yearbook / edited by Phil Minshull. London: Kogan Page, 1996-
  *Published in association with the British Athletic Federation; 1997 issue edited by Duncan Mackay*

91  British all-time lists: as at 31 December 1997 / editor, Martin Rix; assistant editor Rob Whittingham. Stockport: Umbra Software, 1998.
282p; pbk                    ISBN: 1-898258-07-4
                             BL: YK.1999.a.5281
  A minimum of 40 performances and 100 performers are listed for standard events, with shorter lists for non-standard events. Full details are given for each mark, and indexes provide a summary of entries for each athlete. Club affiliations are not provided, and a list of javelin performances made with the 'old' (pre-1986) model has been omitted.

92  British junior athletics handbook 1998 / edited by Lionel Peters. London: World Junior Athletic News, 1998.
                             ISBN: 1-874538-22-0

93  Athletics Weekly 1999 annual review: in association with Athletics International. Peterborough: Descartes, 1999.
71p; illus; pbk

94  400 metres: a statistical survey of British running / Peter Matthews; introduction by David Thurlow. London: National Union of Track Statisticians, 1999.
64p; pbk
(Track stats booklet; no. 1)

95  Javelin: a statistical survey of British throwing / Ian Tempest. London: National Union of Track Statisticians, 1999.
65p; pbk
(Track stats booklet; no. 2)

96  High jump: a statistical survey of British jumping / Ian Tempest. London: National Union of Track Statisticians, 2000.
88p; illus; pbk
(Track stats booklet; no. 3)

97  International road running 2000: the complete guide to road running world wide / editor, Duncan Mackay. Surbiton: SportsBooks Ltd, 2000.
304p; illus; pbk              ISBN: 1-899807-06-3
  ☞   Also listed at: F186

98  Long spikes, short rations: British athletics 1950 / Michael Sheridan; with a foreword by Dorothy Parlett and John Parlett. Congresbury: The author, 2000.
126p; illus; pbk             ISBN: 0-953659-71-2
                             BL: YK.2000.b.4980
  A mainly statistical study of one year, with some background articles.

# *Statistics & Records ~ International*

99 World Sports international athletics annual / compiled by the Association of Track and Field Statisticians. London: World Sports, 1953-1984

> *Editors include Roberto L. Quercetani and Fulvio Regli; continued by: International athletics annual* BL: P.P.2489.fei

This was in fact the third annual to be produced by the ATFS, the 1951 and 1952 editions having been published in Lugano, Switzerland. These first statistical publications of the ATFS (founded in Bruxelles on 26 August 1950) were the standard bearers for a procession of titles. It should not be forgotten that Maurice Loesch had produced an International Athletic Annual as early as 1922 and that lists of best performers were made by H. C. Powell in 1879, but the 1951 publication established unprecedented standards of research, listing, for instance, the world's top thirty men for each event for 1950, followed by the top fifty Europeans, and the thirty best European performances. In subsequent years these lists have grown considerably with no loss of accuracy.

> ☞ See also: M117

100 Progressive World, European and Olympic Games records to 1956. 2nd ed. London: International Amateur Athletic Federation, 1956.
174p

> The first edition was published in Sweden by Bo Ekelund in 1946.

> ☞ Subsequent ed. M112

101 Official list of world, European and Olympic Games records compiled to 9 December 1958. London: International Amateur Athletic Federation, 1959.
34p

102 The Paragon year book of international athletics statistics, 1959 / compiled by Fionnbar Callanan; edited by David Guiney. Dublin: Paragon, 1959?
31p; pbk

103 Sport international / edited by Charles Harvey. London: Sampson Low, Marston, 1960.
416p; illus                                    BL: 7923.w.6

> Thirty pages on athletics, with championship results of many countries, by Norris McWhirter.

104 Distance running records / compiled by Dave Roberts; foreword by John Jewell. Glasgow: The International Athlete, for the Road Runners Club, 1962.
59p; illus; pbk                                BL: X.449/282

> Contains progressive world records from 10 miles to 30,000m, detailed results of all major road races, names of holders of RRC standard certificates and photographs of outstanding road runners.

> ☞ Subsequent ed. M114

105 World's all time best performers: middle and long distances / Ian Reeves Smith. London: The author, 1962.
14p

106 Track and field progressive performance lists / compiled by Stan Greenberg; edited by Stan Tomlin. London: 'Ovaltine', 1964.
116p

> Lists of progressive best performances by world, Olympic, Commonwealth, European and British men and women athletes, including marks not accepted by governing bodies such as the IAAF, but later regarded as authentic.

107 Almanack of sport, 1966 / edited by Charles Harvey. London: Sampson Low, 1965.
624p

> *Only one issue published*                    BL: P.441/11

> Includes a section on athletics by Norris McWhirter, with lists of records and championship winners, a brief history, short biographies of famous athletes, notes on athletic venues and a calendar for 1966.

108 African athletics / Yves Pinaud. London: Arena, 1966-

> Comprises a best performers' list for the previous year and a top ten in each men's event from 1961.

109 Commonwealth statistics / compiled by Stanley Greenberg. London: Arena, 1966-1968.

110 International marathon statistics / compiled by Roger Gynn. London: Arena, 1969-1972.
(Athletics Arena statistical handbooks)        BL: P.441/233

111 British Commonwealth statistics / Stan Greenberg. London: Athletics Arena, 1970.
72p

> Contains Commonwealth all-time lists to the end of 1969 and progressive Commonwealth best performances, for both men's and women's events.

112 Progressive world record lists 1913 to 1970 / J. B. Holt; preface by the Marquess of Exeter; foreword by F. W. Holder. 3rd ed. London: International Amateur Athletic Federation, 1970.
108p; pbk

> *Supplements for 1970 and 1971 also issued*

> ☞ Previous ed. M100

113 South Pacific athletics handbook / Tony Isaacs. Macclesfield: The author, 1976-1990.
> *Continued by: Pacific statistics*

> The first attempt to treat statistically one of the more remote areas, it contains sections on the performances of South Pacific athletes at major international championships, results of the South Pacific Games, all-time lists of best performances and performances by South Pacific athletes, and an index of outstanding South Pacific athletes. The author was assisted by Yves Pinaud (France).

> ☞   Also listed at: A406; see also: M122

114 Distance running progressive bests / compiled by Andy Milroy. 2nd ed. London: Road Runners Club, 1978.
19p
> ☞   Previous ed. M104

115 The long distance record book / compiled by Andy Milroy. Trowbridge: The author, 1981.
57p; illus; index
> The introduction covers the history of what came to be known as ultra running. A comprehensive record and result list for distance and road runs is included.

> ☞   Subsequent ed. M120

116 The Guinness book of track and field athletics facts and feats / Peter Matthews. London: Guinness Superlatives, 1982.
288p; illus; index          ISBN: 0-85112-238-8
                            BL: X.622/13914

> Contains a vast array of data in the entertaining style of the *Guinness Book of Records* under these headings: milestones in athletics history, world records, world athletics, continental athletics, African, American, Asian, Oceania, Europe, and Great Britain.

117 International athletics annual: current world lists, world records, athletes: profiles, major events. London: Sports World, 1985-1986.
2 vols.; illus; index
> *Continues: World Sports international athletic annual; continued by: Athletics*          BL: ZK.9.a.534

> ☞   See also: M99, M118

118 Athletics: the international track and field annual / Association of Track & Field Statisticians. London: Sports World, 1987/8-
> *Continues: International athletics annual*     BL: ZK.9.a.1218

> ☞   See also: M117

119 Athletic world records in the 20th century / Lionel C. F. Blackman; foreword by Primo Nebiolo. Lewes: Book Guild, 1988.
291p; illus
> A workmanlike survey of world record progression since the IAAF was founded in 1912, with some biographies and graphical presentations.

120 The long distance record book / compiled by Andy Milroy. 2nd ed. Trowbridge: The author, 1988.
99p; index
> ☞   Previous ed. M115

121 European junior handbook / edited by Lionel Peters. London: National Union of Track Statisticians, 1989-
> *From 1991 published by World Junior Athletic News; published every two years; 1993 edition published in Spain*
>                            BL: ZK.9.a.6193

122 Pacific statistics / Tony Isaacs. Trowbridge: The author, 1991-
> *Continues: South Pacific athletics handbook*

> ☞   See also: M113

123 Ultra marathon rankings and records / Andy Milroy. Trowbridge: Road Runners' Club, 1996.
38p; pbk

124 World record breakers in track and field athletics / Gerald Lawson. Leeds: Human Kinetics, 1997.
xii, 468p; illus; pbk          ISBN: 0-88011-679-X

125 Athletics 98: the Association of Track & Field Statisticians year book / edited by Peter Matthews. Surbiton: SportsBooks, 1998.
608p; illus; pbk          ISBN: 1-899807-03-9

126 World youth athletics handbook / edited by Lionel Peters. London: World Junior Athletic News, 1999.
> *Continued by: World junior athletics annual*
>                            ISBN: 0-95365591-1

> ☞   See also: M127

127 World junior athletics annual 1999/2000 / edited by Lionel Peters. London: World Junior Athletic News, 2000.
> *Continues: World youth athletics handbook*

> ☞   See also: M126

# Encyclopaedias

**128** The encyclopaedia of athletics / compiled by Melvyn Watman; foreword by Harold Abrahams. London: Hale, 1964.

228p; illus; index                                    BL: X.449/547

*An entertaining and authoritative work of reference by an Athletics Weekly writer who ultimately took over as editor, and wrote The History of British Athletics.*

☞   Subsequent ed. M129

**129** The encyclopaedia of athletics / compiled by Melvyn Watman; foreword by Harold Abrahams. 2nd ed. London: Hale, 1967.

231p; illus                                          BL: X.449/2613

☞   Previous ed. M128; subsequent ed. M130

**130** The encyclopaedia of athletics / compiled by Melvyn Watman; foreword by Harold Abrahams. 3rd ed. London: Hale, 1973.

244p; illus; index                      ISBN: 0-7091-4010-X
                                                      BL: X.629/5795

☞   Previous ed. M129; subsequent ed. M131

**131** Encyclopaedia of athletics / compiled by Mel Watman; foreword by Harold Abrahams. 4th ed. London: Hale, 1977.

240p; illus; index                      ISBN: 0-7091-5443-7
                                                     BL: X.629/11416

☞   Previous ed. M130; subsequent ed. M132

**132** Encyclopædia of track and field athletics / compiled by Mel Watman. 5th ed. London: Hale, 1981.

240p; illus; index                      ISBN: 0-7091-9242-8
                                                     BL: X.629/16585

*The fifth (and, almost certainly, final) edition of the work first published in 1964, updates the material to May 1981.*

☞   Previous ed. M131

**133** Hamlyn encyclopaedia of athletics. Twickenham: Hamlyn, 1985.

208p; illus; index                      ISBN: 0-600-50042-X
                                                    BL: YC.1986.b.194

*This English translation is from a work first published in Italy (1983). Each of the standard track and field events (including relays, but excluding walks and decathlon/heptathlon) are covered. Details on technique, training, profiles of some of the most historically significant performers and IAAF world record progression are given for each event. Many action sequences are included, together with specifications of track layout and equipment, descriptions of timing, measurement and muscle physiology, and diagrams of biomechanical analyses and aerodynamic factors.*

✱   *Additional References*

**134** The encyclopaedia of sport / edited by the Earl of Suffolk and Berkshire, Hedley Peek, and F. G. Aflalo. London: Lawrence & Bullen, 1897-1898.

2 vols.                                               BL: 7904.dd.8

☞   Subsequent ed. M135

**135** The encyclopædia of sport & games / edited by the Earl of Suffolk and Berkshire. New and enlarged ed. with illustrations in colour & black & white. London: Heinemann, 1911.

4 vols.                                               BL: 7920.d.19

☞   Previous ed. M134

**136** Encyclopaedia of sport and sportsmen / edited by Charles Harvey. London: Sampson, Low, 1966.

624p; illus                                          BL: X.449/2361

*Includes a section on athletics by N. D. McWhirter, with AAA Championships results, brief history, and progressive world records.*

# Dictionaries

**137** Track and field athletics: sports dictionary in seven languages / edited by F. Hepp. London: Collet's, 1960.

335p

**138** The Sackville illustrated dictionary of athletics / Tom Knight and Nick Troop. Stradbroke: Sackville, 1988.

160p; illus                             ISBN: 0-948615-12-5
                                                    BL: YK.1990.b.6346

*The history of athletics is dismissed summarily and a list of medallists in the Olympic Games close the work. Sandwiched between are biographies of 316 outstanding performers.*

# Bibliographies & Filmographies

139 Catalogue of the Carnegie historical collection of books on physical education, sport and recreation and health education published before 1946 / compiled by Joan Newiss. Leeds: City of Leeds and Carnegie College of Education Library, 1969.
54p; pbk
  *Reproduced from typewriting*          BL: 2738.a.14
  The collection contains a number of titles on athletics by authors such as Harold M. Abrahams and F. A. M. Webster.

140 The guide to British track and field literature, 1275-1968 / Peter Lovesey and Tom McNab. London: Athletics Arena, 1969.
110p; indexes          ISBN: 0-902175-00-9
                        BL: 2738.g.3
  A pioneering work and the foundation of the current compilation. In addition to bibliographical details of works published in the United Kingdom, annotations are given for many titles. Author and title indexes are included, together with an appendix of foreign literature, and an essay on 'Some trends in the development of British track and field literature'.

141 Author catalogue of the National Centre for Athletics Literature / compiled by John Bromhead. Birmingham: The Library, University of Birmingham, 1972.
18p; pbk          ISBN: 0-902487-04-3
                  BL: X.615/430
  The National Centre for Athletics Literature (NCAL) was started by the initiative of Dr Kenneth W. Humphreys, Librarian at the University of Birmingham, with the support of the National Union of Track Statisticians. For an account of its origin and formation see NUTS Notes (vol. 6, no. 1 and vol. 16, nos. 1, 2).

  ☞ Subsequent ed. M144

142 A complete list of the Dave Roberts papers in the National Centre for Athletics Literature, the Library, the University of Birmingham / compiled by John Bromhead. Birmingham: The Centre, 1976.
ii, 17p; pbk          ISBN: 0-7044-0233-5
                      BL: Cup.1281/471

143 A catalogue of sports films / compiled by the Information Centre of the Sports Council. London: The Council, 1977.
ii, 66p; index; pbk
(Information series; no. 3)          ISBN: 0-900979-54-2
                                     BL: BS.387/102
  16mm films only are included. Most are, therefore, of a short, instructional nature; 24 are listed in the first edition, 45 in the second.

  ☞ Subsequent ed. M147

144 Author catalogue of the National Centre for Athletics Literature / compiled by John Bromhead. 2nd ed. Birmingham: The Centre, 1980.
54p; pbk          ISBN: 0-7044-0389-7
                  BL: X.909/44936

  ☞ Previous ed. M141; subsequent ed. M149

145 Author catalogue of the National Centre for Athletics Literature / compiled by John Bromhead. 2nd ed; supplement no. 1. Birmingham: The Centre, 1981.
16p; pbk          ISBN: 0-7044-0592-X • ISSN: 0262-530X
                  BL: X.629/21200

146 PERDAS: 1950-1980: a list of theses, dissertations and projects on physical education, recreation, dance, athletics and sport, presented at United Kingdom universities / compiled by J. S. Keighley. Lancaster: LISE, 1981.
184p; index; pbk          ISBN: 0-901922-11-0
                          BL: X.629/17215

147 A catalogue of sports films / compiled by the Information Centre. 2nd ed. London: Sports Council, 1983.
v, 64p; illus; index; pbk
(Information series; no. 3)          ISBN: 0-906577-27-6

  ☞ Previous ed. M143

148 Running: a guide to the literature / Bob Wischnia, Marty Post. London: Garland, 1983.
xi, 148p; illus; index          ISBN: 0-8240-9105-1
                                BL: X.629/23953

149 Author catalogue of the National Centre for Athletics Literature / compiled by John Bromhead. New ed. Birmingham: The Centre, 1988.          ISBN: 0-7044-0937-2
  A revised edition of the catalogue of NCAL holdings first published in 1972.

  ☞ Previous ed. M144

150 The Neal-Schuman index to sports figures in collective biographies / compiled by Paulette Bochnig Sharkey. London: Neal-Schuman, 1991.
xiv, 167p
  *Variant title: Index to sports figures in collective biographies*
                          ISBN: 1-55570-055-1
                          BL: YK.1993.b.359
  Designed for easy use by children and young adults, the work is divided into two parts. Part I contains the main entries, whilst Part II has indexes by sport (track and field 101 entries), index to women's sports figures, index to sports figures by country of origin, bibliography and book codes.

151 Bibliography of British athletic club histories: bulletin / compiled by Trevor James. Sutton Coldfield: Distance Learning Ltd in association with Centre for Athletics History, 1997-
  *Published annually*                    ISSN: 1464-8369
                                          BL: 2725.e.3807

## ✱ *Additional References*

152 The sports pages: a critical bibliography of twentieth-century American novels and stories featuring baseball, basketball, football, and other athletic pursuits / Grant Burns. London: Scarecrow, 1987.
  x, 274p; index                    ISBN: 0-8108-1966-X
                                          BL: 2725.d.731

  *Includes an eight-page section on jogging, running and other track events.*

153 Women in sport: a select bibliography / Michele Shoebridge. London: Mansell, 1987.
  xii, 231p; index
  *Foreword by Sue Campbell*         ISBN: 0-7201-1858-1
                                          BL: 2725.d.573

  *Reflecting a heightening interest in women's sport, this pioneering work contains sections devoted to bibliographies, conference proceedings, major subject areas, individual sports, biographies, serials, and organisations. Author and subject indexes are also included.*

154 Information sources in sport and leisure / editor Michele Shoebridge. London: Bowker-Saur, 1992.
  xix, 345p; illus; index
  (Guides to information sources)          ISBN: 0-86291-901-0
                                          BL: YC.1992.a.2344

  *Containing much of relevance to a researcher on track and field athletics. Part I: General overview of sources, statistical sources, government and sport. Part II: Sports science, sports medicine, history of sport, sociology of sport, individual sports. Part III: The Olympic Games, leisure, physical education, physical fitness, coaching. Part IV: European information sources, North American information sources. Appendices: International organisations, acronym list.*

155 A guide to the holdings of sports books in the bookshops of Britain / Rupert Sebastian Cavendish. Bromley: Association of Sports Historians, 1999.
  84p
  (Sporting heritage series; no. 4)

# *Periodicals*

156 The sporting magazine. London: 1793-1870.   BL: Hendon

157 Bell's life in London & sporting news. London: 1822-1886.                               BL: Hendon

158 The field. London: 1856-                   BL: Hendon

159 The sporting life. London: 1859-1999.      BL: Hendon

160 Illustrated sporting news. London: 1862-1865
  *Continued by: Illustrated sporting & theatrical news*
                                               BL: Hendon

  ☞  See also: M162

161 Sporting gazette. London: 1862-1879.
  *Continued by: Country gentleman*            BL: Hendon
  ☞  See also: M170

162 Illustrated sporting & theatrical news. London: 1865-1870.
  *Continues: Illustrated sporting news;*
  *continued by: Illustrated sporting & dramatic news*
                                               BL: Hendon

  ☞  See also: M160, M166

163 Land & water. London: 1866-                BL: Hendon

164 The swimming, rowing, and athletic record. Vol. 1, no. 1-2. London: 1873.
  *Continued as: The swimming record and chronicle of sporting events*
                                               BL: Hendon

  ☞  See also: M165

165 The swimming record and chronicle of sporting events. Vol. 1, no. 3-53. London: 1873-1874.
  *Continues: The swimming, rowing, and athletic record*
                                               BL: Hendon

  ☞  See also: M164

166 Illustrated sporting & dramatic news. London: 1874-1943.
　　　*Continues: Illustrated sporting & theatrical news*
　　　　　　　　　　　　　　　　　　　　　BL: Hendon

　☞　See also: M162

167 Athletic news. Manchester: 1875-1931.　　BL: Hendon

168 The athletic record: a monthly journal exclusively
　　devoted to athletics / edited by Fitz Boyd. No. 1-16.
　　London: 1875-1876.　　　　　　　BL: P.P.2489.zb

169 Ixion: a journal of velocipeding, athletics, and aerostatics.
　　London: 1875-　　　　　　　　　BL: 1866.a.5(1)

170 Country gentleman. 1880-
　　　*Continues: Sporting gazette*　　　　BL: Hendon

　☞　See also: M161

171 Sport. Dublin: 1880-1950.　　　　BL: Hendon

172 The sporting mirror. London: 1881-1884.　BL: Hendon

173 Scottish athletic journal. Glasgow: 1886-1888. BL: Hendon

174 Sport & play. Birmingham: 1886-1895.
　　　*Incorporated into Bicycling news*　　BL: Hendon

　☞　See also: M179

175 Athletic journal. Manchester: 1887-1891.　BL: Hendon

176 The magazine of sport. London?: 1888/89-　BL: Hendon

177 The gymnast: a monthly journal of gymnastics and
　　athletics. London: 1890-1899.　　　BL: Hendon

178 Sporting sketches. London: 1894-1907.　BL: Hendon

179 Bicycling news. Birmingham?: 1895-
　　　*Incorporates: Sport & play*　　　BL: Hendon

　☞　See also: M174

180 Irish athletic & cycling record. Belfast: 1897-1900.
　　　　　　　　　　　　　　　　　　BL: Hendon

181 Pearson's athletic record. London: 1897-1899.
　　　*Continued as: Pastimes*　　　　BL: Hendon

　☞　See also: M182

182 Pastimes. Vol. 3, no. 1-Vol. 4, no. 47 (Feb. 11-Dec. 30).
　　London: 1899.
　　　*Continues: Pearson's athletic record;*
　　　*continued by Pastimes. New series*　BL: Hendon

　☞　See also: M181, M183

183 Pastimes. New series. Vol. 4, no. 48-52 (Jan. 6-Feb. 3).
　　London: 1900.
　　　*Continues: Pastimes*　　　　　BL: Hendon

　☞　See also: M182

184 Sport & play & Wheel life. Birmingham: 1901-1938.
　　　　　　　　　　　　　　　　　　BL: Hendon

185 C. B. Fry's magazine. London: 1904-1913.　BL: Hendon

186 The W.G. athletic weekly. London?: 1904-　BL: Hendon

187 The athlete: an up-to-date periodical of physical culture.
　　Vol. 1, no. 1-10 (June 1905-April 1906). London:
　　1905-1906.
　　　　　　　　　　　　　　　　BL: P.P.1832.gch

188 Irish athletic news. Belfast: 1909-1911.　BL: Hendon

189 The athletic field and swimming world. Vol. 1, no. 1-14
　　(February). London: Health & Strength, 1910.
　　　*Published weekly*　　　　　　BL: Hendon

190 All sports weekly. London?: 1924-1930.　BL: Hendon

191 British Olympic journal. London: British Olympic
　　Association, 1926-
　　　*Possibly continued by: World sports*　BL: P.P.1859.beb

　☞　See also: M195

192 Superman: the national athletic and physical culture
　　monthly. London: Link House, 1930-1935.
　　　*Published monthly; from November 1934 to April 1935 this*
　　　*was the official publication of the AAA*

193 Amateur sport and athletics: official organ of the
　　Amateur Athletic Association and the Scottish AAA.
　　Vol. 1, no. 1-5 (June-October). London: The Association,
　　1935.　　　　　　　　　　　BL: P.P.1832.gat

194 The athlete / edited by F. A. M. Webster. Vol. 1, no. 1-
　　11 (July 1936-June 1937). 1936-1937.
　　　*Continued as: Every sport, incorporating The athlete*
　　　　　　　　　　　　　　　　BL: P.P.1832.gcr

　☞　See also: M197

195 World sports: the official organ of the British Olympic
　　Association. London: 1936-1972.
　　　*Possibly a continuation of British Olympic journal; continued*
　　　*by Sportsworld*　　　　　　BL: P.P.1832.gaz

　☞　See also: M191, M213

196 The British athlete. London: 1937-　　BL: P.P.1832.get

197 Every sport, incorporating The athlete. Vol. 1, no. 1-Vol.
　　2, no. 3. 1937.
　　　*Continues: The athlete*　　　　BL: P.P.1832.gcr

　☞　See also: M194

198 Athletics. Vol. 1, no. 1-Vol. 3, no. 12. London: 1945-
　　1949.
　　　*Continued as: Athletics weekly*　BL: P.P.1832.gdb

　☞　See also: M203

199 The Scots athlete. Glasgow: April 1946-June 1958.
   *Subsequently incorporated in: The international athlete*
                                                          BL: P.P.1832.gdc

   ☞   See also: M207

200 Athletic review: the national magazine for the all-round
   athlete. Manchester: 1947-1959.
   *Vol. 1, no. 1 was issued as the official organ of the Northern
   Counties Athletic Association*          BL: P.P.1832.gdf

201 AAA coaching bulletin. Vol 1, no. 1-5 (Feb.-Dec.).
   London: AAA, 1949.
   *Incorporated in: The athlete*

   ☞   See also: M202

202 The athlete: official publication of the Amateur Athletic
   Association. Vol. 1, no.1-Vol. 3, no. 2 (Spring 1950 -
   Summer 1952). London: The Association, 1950-1952.
   *Published quarterly; incorporates: AAA coaching bulletin;
   continued in part by: The modern athlete*

   ☞   See also: M201, M205

203 Athletics weekly. Vol. 4, no. 1- London: 1950-
   *Continues: Athletics; from 1965 incorporates: Modern
   athletics; from 1969 incorporates: Women's athletics*
                                                          BL: P.P.1832.gdb

   ☞   See also: M198, M212

204 Athletics world. Vol. 1, no. 1-Vol. 3, no. 12. London:
   McWhirter Twins, 1952-1956.
   *Published monthly*

205 The modern athlete: incorporating the official coaching
   bulletin of the Amateur Athletic Association. Vol. 1, no.
   1-Vol. 5, no. 4. St Albans: Sparta, 1953-1957.
   *Published monthly; later issues published: Croydon: Modern
   Athletic Publications; continues in part: The athlete; continued
   as: Modern athletics*

   ☞   See also: M202, M206

206 Modern athletics: official organ of the Association of
   Athletic Coaches. Vol. 1, no. 1-Vol. 7, no. 2. Worcester
   Park: The Association, 1957-1964.
   *Later published: Croydon: Modern Athletic Publications;
   continues: The modern athlete; subsequently incorporated into:
   Athletics weekly*          BL: P.P.1832.gdq

   ☞   See also: M203, M205

207 The international athlete. Glasgow: 1958-
   *Incorporates: The Scots athlete*          BL: P.P.1860.aan

   ☞   See also: M199

208 NUTS notes. Vol. 1, no. 1-Vol. 19, no. 4. London:
   National Union of Track Statisticians, 1959-1981.
   *Published irregualrly; continued by: Track stats*

   ☞   See also: M219

209 World athletics. London: Chatham, July 1961-Sept. 1962.
                                                          BL: P.P.7616.az

210 Athletics arena. Vol 1, no.1-Vol. 8, no. 7. London:
   Arena, 1963-1971.
   *Published monthly*

211 The British athlete. 1963-1965.

212 Women's athletics. Vol. 1, no. 1-Vol. 2, no. 4. 1968-1969.
   *Published monthly;
   subsequently incorporated into: Athletics weekly*

   ☞   See also: M203

213 Sportsworld: official magazine of the British Olympic
   Association. London: August 1972-
   *Continues: World sports*          BL: P.443/149

   ☞   See also: M195

214 Athletic review. Ashton-in-Makerfield: Publicity Print
   Publishing, 1978-1979.
   *Published monthly*

215 Athlete's world. Droitwich: Peterson, 1979-1985.
   *From 1982 incorporates: Athletics monthly;
   continued by: Athletics today*          BL: P.443/403

   ☞   See also: M216, M220

216 Athletics monthly. Brighton: A.C.M. Webb, 1980-1981.
   *Incorporated in: Athlete's world*          BL: P.441/921

   ☞   See also: M215

217 Running. 1980-1993.
   *Published monthly;
   continued by: Runner's world*

   ☞   See also: M225

218 Marathon and distance runner. Droitwich: Peterson,
   1982-1987.
   *Published monthly*          BL: P.443/618

219 Track stats: a quarterly digest of athletics statistics. Vol.
   20, no. 1- London: National Union of Track Statisticians,
   1982-
   *Published quarterly; continues: NUTS notes*

   ☞   See also: M208

220 Athletics today. Droitwich: Peterson, 1985-1993.
   *Published monthly; continues: Athlete's world*
                                                          BL: P.443/608

   ☞   See also: M215

221 Today's runner. Peterborough: EMAP Pursuit, 1985-2000.
   *Published monthly*          ISSN: 0267-162X
                                                          BL: ZC. 9.b.457

222 New studies in athletics. London: IAAF, 1986-
   *Published quarterly*          BL: ZK.9.a.1696

223 Athletics today. Kingston-upon-Thames: Athletics
   Today, 1987-1993.
      *Published weekly*

224 Olympics. London: Redwood, 1992-          BL: ZK.9.b.7432

225 Runner's world. London: Rodale, 1993-
      *Continues: Running*

                                             ISSN: 1350-7745
                                             BL: P. 443/399

   ☞   See also: M217

226 Athletics international. Stanmore: 1994-
      *Published every two weeks*

227 Inside track. Vol. 1, no. 1 - Vol. 1, no. 4. Mortimer:
   Inside Track Magazine, 1998.
      *Published monthly*

# Name Index

# C

# E

Earl of Derby *See* Derby, Edward George Villiers Stanley, 17th Earl of Derby

Earl of Suffolk and Berkshire *See* Howard, Henry Charles, 18th Earl of Suffolk and Berkshire

East Grinstead and District Athletic Club A197

East London Schools' Athletics Association M36

The Eastenders *See* Heaton Harriers

Eaton, Josiah L299

Eaton, Mark C58

Eaton, Richard C239

Eberhart, Richard L228

ECCU *See* English Cross-Country Union

Ecker, Tom E132

Edinburgh Southern Harriers A319-321

Edinburgh University AC A322

Edmonds, Frances L11

Edmund, Nick L386

Edmundson, Joseph B148, D25, E205, E209, E214, F101, H59

Edström, J Sigfrid C9

Edwards, C D B259

Edwards, Diane *See* Modahl, Diane

Edwards, George B106

Edwards, Hazel L140

Edwards, Jonathan B66, B257, C243

Edwards, Mike B266

Edwards, Paul L94

Edwards, Phyl A312

Edwards-Moss, J A76

Egan, Pierce A51-53

Ehrenstrale, Krishna *(translator)* E169

Elder, A C E119

Eley, Hugh B28

Eliott-Lynn, Sophie A127, A138

Elliott, Alistair *(translator)* L269

Elliott, Charles C175, C182, C185, H34-35

Elliott, G M E120, E132

Elliott, Herb B34, B67, B98, B212-213, B216, B223, B247, B265, E124

Elliott, Peter B50

Elliott, Richard F120

Elliott, Robert M89

Ellis, Clive B72

Ellis, Jon *(illustrator)* D35

Ellis, M J C170, E120, E132

Elrington, H L141

Elswick Harriers A198

Ely, George Herbert *See* Strang, Herbert

Elyot, *Sir* Thomas A50

Emery, David B18-19, B227, C214, F32, M15

Emyr, John B99

English Cross-Country Union M34, M35

English Schools Athletic Association A283, A289, M28, M31, M39

Enhagen, Carl-Olof L413

Erba, Edoardo L280

Escott, John C95

Escritt, John R I8, I11

Espy, Richard C107, C109

Essex County Amateur Athletic Association A199

Estes, N A Mark K55

Etchells, Andy F160, F164

The Ettrick Shepherd *See* Hogg, James

Evans, Alan K45

Evans, Chris *(illustrator)* H46

Evans, David A D43

Evans, I O L12

Evans, R L311

Eve, Harry T A239

Ewart, Gavin L268

Ewers, Chris A396

Ewry, Ray L404

Exeter, Marquess of *See* Cecil, David, *Lord Burghley*, 6th Marquess of Exeter

# F

Fagles, Robert *(translator)* L222

Fairlie, F G L C134

Fallowfield, Joanne L F140

Farrar, Frederic W L142

Farrell, John Emmet L291

Farrell, Mike M72

Featherstone, Donald F K18

Felke, Petra C48

Fennell, C A M L244

Fenwick, Geoffrey L326

Ferguson, Peter L13, L94

Ferris, Sam A80, A310, B224, F154

Fidler, Harry L229

Filleul, L C247

Findling, John E C74

Finlayson, Arthur Robert Morrison L353

Finley, M I A18

Finn, Jim A378

Finnemore, John L143

Firbank, Thomas F219

Fisher-Johnson, Paul *(illustrator)* L190

Fittis, Robert Scott A330

Fitts, Robert J23

Fitzgibbon, Gerald M23

Fixx, James F F12-13

Flack, Edwin B207

Flanagan *(fictional)* L48

Flanagan, Bob B267

Flanagan, J J A357, A361, G67

Flaxman, A E A83

Fleming, James L271

Fletcher, W M E39

Flinders, Steve L348

Flintoff-King, Debbie B241

Float, Richard H48

Flood, Caz *(fictional)* L35-38

Floyd, Gareth *(illustrator)* L185

Folley, Malcolm B66

Forbes, Clarence Allen A8

Ford, John L265

Foreman, J B L402

Forrest, George *See* Wood, John George

Forrest, W G A21

Forsythe, Alison *(illustrator)* L274

Foster, Bob L393

Foster, Brendan B68, B225, B227, C279, F32, F159, L384

Foster, John L273

Foster, John L B214

Fougasse *See* Bird, Cyril Kenneth

Fowke, Bob C104

Fowler, Roy A227

Fowler-Dixon, J E A149, L374

Fox, Paul L321-323

Fraley, Bob G31

Francis, Charlie B100

Francis, P H G3-4, G69

Francom, Septimus B69

Frankland, J N F221

Franklin, John A123

Frasca, Augusto A390

Fraser, Alison L14

Fraser, Ian H A267, L266

Fraser, John L262

Fraser, John *(illustrator)* A20

Frazer, Matt A231

Freaney, Cyril C83

Freeman, R M L144

Freeman, William H D5, D10

Friedlander, Jeremy A411

Friedman, Harold N L336

Friends of West Norwood Cemetery B267

Hägg, Gunder  A388, B188, B223, L317

Haile, Terence  L22

Hakewill, James Ridgway  E23

Halberg, Murray  B82

Halesowen Cycling and Athletic Club  A203

Hall, Charles  *See* Westhall, Charles

Hallam, Chris  L373

Hallamshire Harriers  A204

Halswelle, Wyndham  A313, C130, L77, L331

Hamer, Malcolm  L23

Hamer, Mike  L24

Hampson, T  B83, C12, C269, D24, E79, E98, E107, F2

Hanley, G E  E99

Hanna, Robert  B127

Hannus, Matti  C200

Hansch, Felice  B84

Hansen, Eiler  *(translator)*  L46

Hansen, John  E78, E89

Hansenne, Marcel  A387

Hardcastle, Michael  L150, L205

Hardie, Andrew  E110, E161

Harding, David  A396

Hardwick, J H  A149, A255, F95, F150

Hardy, Arthur  L316

Hargreaves, Jennifer  C110, C121, K40

Harkins, Dorothy  E217, E222-223, E228

Harley, Kim  *(illustrator)*  L238

Harmon, William  L270

Harper, C  B65

Harper, Peter R  E140

Harper, R St G  E98, E107, E124, F70

Harraden, Beatrice  L88

Harrelson, Gary L  K48, K54

Harris, Dudley  B24

Harris, H A  A10, A14, A16, A87

Harris, Norman  A405, B124, B207, C187, L328

Harrison, Jane Ellen  A35, A39

Harrison, Ted  B1-2, B77

Harrold, Geoff  *(illustrator)*  E164

Harron, Robert  A387

Harrow AC  A205

Hart, Charlie  E70

Hart, Dominic  C243

Hart, Graham  H46

Hart-Davis, Duff  C139

Hartley, A M  A191

Harty, Archbishop  A376

Harvard University AC  A409

Harvey, Charles  M103, M107, M136

Hastings, Phyllis  L25

Hastings & St Leonards Cycling and Athletic Club  A206

Hathway, H A  H27, H36, H45

Hatton, Fred W  A224

Havant AC  A207

Havell, George  A199

Havelok the Dane  L219

Hawkins, Albert Herbert  *(fictional)*  L139

Hawley, John A  J45

Hayens, Herbert  L151-158

Hayt, Andy  *(photographer)*  L380

Hayward, John  A275

Head, Nick  L323

Headon, David  L395

Heald, C B  K10

Healion, Bert  A361

Healy, Jeremiah  L26

Heath, Ian  L408

Heatley, Basil  A227

Heaton Harriers  A208

Heaton, John  E134, F43, G8, G12

Hebbelinck, M  K33

Heery, Pat  I25

Heine, Theresa  L273

Heino, Viljo  B85

Heldmann, Bernard  L159

Hellard, Susan  *(illustrator)*  L207

Hemery, David  A91, B86, B259, B265, E143, E170, F52, G15, K45, L331, L373

Heming, Jack  L160

Henderson, Hume  *(illustrator)*  L141

Henderson, Joe  L175, F181

Henderson, W E B  A83, A186, A242, E46, G24

Hennessy, Liam  M85

Henoch, Lilli  B254

Henry, Anne  L27

Henry, Noel  A137, B239

Hepburn, Tom  L392

Hepp, F  M137

Herbert, *Sir* Alan  C274

Hermés, E  A386

Herne Hill Harriers  A209

Herrick, Christine Terhune  A126

Herringshaw, George  *(photographer)*  A160, C211

Hewitt, F S  F62

Hewitt, Martin  *(fictional)*  L90

Hewitt, Phil  B87

Hewson, Brian  B88, C170

Heys, J A  E67, E69, J14

Heywood, Thomas  L258

Hickey, Kevin  J43

Hickman, Leon  B165

Higgins, J  E44

Higgs, T W  A79

Highgate Harriers  A210-211

Hignell, A F  E98

Hildreth, Peter  B241, C23, C170, E107, E117, E119, E120, E122, E124, E132, F39

Hill, Albert G  A91, B89, C12, L373

Hill, Archibald V  E77, J12, K10

Hill, Christopher R  C114, C116

Hill, Lucille E  A126

Hill, R B  B196

Hill, Reginald  L28

Hill, Ron  B90-91, B106, C280, L328

Hillier, Eric  A43

Hillman, Harry  L404

Hinton, David B  L358, L361

Hjertberg, Ernest W  E47

Hoare, Robert J  B11, L170

Hoby, Alan  L295

Hockridge, Derek  *(translator)*  L403

Hodge, Percy  B92, M89

Hodges, Jo  L29

Hoff, Charlie  L376

Hogg, James  A300, L261, L232, L272

Hogg, Robert  A291, A332

Holden, Jack  A227

Holden, P H B  A262

Holder, F W  M112

Holdsworth, Stuart  H54

Holland, Harry  *(artist)*  L371

Holland, Patrick  B107

Holland, Wright Henry  *See* Holland, Harry  *(artist)*

Hollis, Ramon J  A383

Holloway, Cyril  *(illustrator)*  L156

Holm, Nora  L354

Holman, Ron  F122, F162

Holmes, C B  D24

Holmes, Kelly  B257, B266

Holmes, Michael J  A217

Holmes, Sherlock  *(fictional)*  L87

Holt, E J  A149

Holt, J B  C287, M112

Holt, Richard J  A416, B256, L373

Holt, Tom  L30

Holton, Herbert H  A126

Holtze, Norah  *(translator)*  E78, E89

Holtze, Svend  *(illustrator)*  E89

Homer  L101, L233

Hommel, Helmar  E166

Hone, William  A145

Honey, J R de S  A281

Honig, Donald  L336

Stratford, George  L73
Stratford, John  B210
Stratton, M A *(photographer)*  E109
Strode-Jackson, Arnold  A87,
    A287, A387, C12
Strong, Shirley  B243
Stroud, Mike  J63
Strug, Kerri  B261
Strutt, Joseph  A143-145, L102
Stubbings, Roy  A155
Stubbs, J G  A386
Studd, *Sir* Kynaston  A244
Sturgess, W J  F226, I25, L374
Sudell, Richard  I6
Super Gran *(fictional)*  L199
Surrey County Athletic
    Association  M33
Surrey Walking Club  A265
Sussex County AAA  H40
Sutcliffe, P W  C39
Sutcliffe, Peter  G62
Sutherland, John W  A346
Swaddling, Judith  A19, A32
Swan, William  F207
Sweeney, Mike  B93
Sweet, Waldo E  A22
Swift, Catherine M  B117
Swindon AC  A266
Sykes, Robin  A317, E153
Symonds, Hugh  F202
Szabó, Gabriel  A401-402
Szewinska, Irena  B241, B254,
    B265, C48

# T

'T H'  *See* Howell, Thomas
Tagg, Mike  A227
Tagholm, Sally  C49
Tait McKenzie, R  *See* McKenzie,
    R Tait
Tally-Ho Hare & Hounds Club
    *See* Cheshire Tally-Ho Hare &
    Hounds
Tamarin, Alfred  A17
Tames, Richard  A27, C77
Tames, Roger  B54
Tancred, Bill  C211
Tancred, Peter  G73
Tanner, J M  J18
Tarrant, John  B170
Tatlow, Peter  C46
Taubman, Alison  A167
Taunyane, Len  C70
Taylor, D W  B128
Taylor, F B  H6
Taylor, Jeremy  L188

Taylor, John  L246
Taylor, P  C217
Taylor, Philip  B171
Taylor, R  A184
Taylor, T  C217
Teasdale, David  L400
Tedder, Anita  A139
Teevan, Colin *(translator)*  L280
Tellez, Tom  F93
Tempest, Ian  M95, M96
Temple, Cliff  B68, B135, B173,
    C219, F15, F21, F32, F129,
    F155, F157-158, F177, L328,
    M14, M72
Terry, David  A226, B217
Teviotdale Harriers  A327
Thames Hare and Hounds Club
    A267
Thames Valley Harriers  A268-269
The Bank of England Sports Club
    A171
The Northern Cross Country
    Association  A235
Thom, W  A110, L315
Thomas, Alan  L322
Thomas, David Craig Owen  L20
Thomas, Phil  A235
Thomas, S Evelyn  C140
Thomas, Sid  A72, F95, F150, L374
Thomas, William Glanffrwd  B136
Thompson, Daley  A91, A396,
    B172-176, B246-247, B259,
    B265, C102, C230, C258, L305,
    L373, L382, L385-386, L399
Thompson, Dick  C87
Thompson, Don  B247, L373
Thompson, Frazier  L410
Thomson, D P  B112-114
Thomson, Earl  L376
Thorburn, A *(illustrator)*  L263
Thornber, Norman  F220-221
Thorndike, Augustus  K12-14,
    K20, K26
Thorne, Guy  L74
Thornton, J St L  A287, E79
Thornton, P M 'Friday'  A186,
    A242, B159, B177
Thorpe, Jim  A396, A421, B220
Throckett, Sammy *(fictional)*  L90
Thurlow, David M  B189, L47, M94
Tibballs, Geoff  B253
Tincler, G B  A361, B65
Tindall, H C L  A186, A242
Tipton, Charles M  E135, E145
Tisdall, Robert  A287, C12, C152,
    C171, E79, E200, L306
Todd, Jimmy  B127

Tolan, Eddie  L410
Tomas, Jason  A396
Tomkins, Alan  H49
Tomlin, Stan  A99, C12, C156, C159, C180,
    C267, C272, D24, E207, M41, M58, M106
Tomlinson, Alan  C110
Toohey, Kristine  C119
Toomey, Bill  L394
Town, Peter  L338
Townsend, W A  A266
Toyne, Stanley Mease  L283
Travers, P R  E167, J46
Travis, Pete  L75
Traynor, Shaun  L189
Treacy, John  B239
Treadwell, Sandy  F174
Trease, Geoffrey  L190
Trengove, Alan  B45, B67
Trescatheric, Bryn  A153
Troop, Nick  F26, M138
Trory, Ernie  C108, C226, L412
Trott, Susan  L76
Trow, M J  L77
Trower, John  G23, G107
Trudge, Ron *(fictional)*  L325
Tucker, W E  K15, K32
Tulloh, Bruce  B178, C30, E235, E238,
    F33, F58, F105, F108, F110, F118, F124,
    F133, F160, F164, F176, J40, L326,
    L337, M42
Tulu, Derartu  A420
Turk, A S  A79
Turnbull, Alison  F17
Turnbull, Ronald  F206, F224-225
Turnbull, Simon  B143, E163
Turner, B M  E83
Turner, Chris  B85
Turner, H K  B201
Turner, J W  A79
Tutko, Thomas A  D3
Tuttle, W W  E76, E88, E96, E105, E111,
    E126
Twidle, Arthur *(illustrator)*  L113
Twombly, Wells  A411
Tyler, Dorothy  C12, D35, L318, L322
Tyler, Martin  C25, C33, C212
Tysoe, Alfred  B243

# U

Uderzo *(illustrator)*  L403, L405-406
Ueberroth, Peter  B179
Ullman, Leslie  L275
Underwood, John  L328
Universities' Athletic Union  A270
Usha, P T  C42
Usher, C M  A322

White and Brown *See* Burt, P J
White, Constance M  L198
Whitehead, Nick  F46, F54
Whitehouse, D  L180
Whitehouse, R H  J18
Whiteley, James Huntingdon- *See* Huntingdon-Whitely, James
Whitfield, Christopher  A294, A304
Whitfield, Malvin G  E108
Whitlock, Harold H  C12, D24, F233
Whitman, Walt  L255, L271
Whitney, Caspar W  A74
Whitney, Kevin *(illustrator)*  C209, L370
Whittingham, Rob  M54, M91
Whitton, Kenneth  A313
Whitwell, T M R *(illustrator)*  L115, L201
Whymper, C *(illustrator)*  A328
Widlund, Ture  C123
Wiebusch, John  A411
Wigglesworth, R E  L339
Wigley, Jon V  A390
Wignall, A B  G25
Wildgoose, Geoffry *(fictional)*  L21
Wilding, Paul *(illustrator)*  F21, I16
Wilk, Kevin E  K54
Wilkins, Susan  L271
Wilkinson, David M  F140
Wilkinson, G I  L180
Wilkinson, Henry F  A61, A64-65, A67, M2
Wilkinson, Sean  L365
Williams, A M A  E199
Williams, Clive  A350, M74, M77
Williams, J D B  C268
Williams, John Garrett Pascoe  K28, K34
Williams, Peter  B60
Williams, R  E38
Williamson, David  L55
Williamson, J A  A84
Williamson, Norrie  F130, F138
Wilson, Forrest  L199
Wilson, George  A51, A111, A121, B184-185, B256, L244, L256, L369, L373
Wilson, Graham  F214
Wilson, H  E119

Wilson, H A  B186, B198, D38, F112-114, F116, F127
Wilson, Julian  B119
Wilson, Mike  B44
Wilson, Neil  B33, B49, B176, C197, C239, F160, F164, I10, L385
Wilson, Norman  A257
Wilson, Peter  B187, L320
Wilson, Stanley  D21
Wilson, Walter  A254
Wilson, William *(fictional)*  L193, L396
Wilt, Fred  E132
Wilton, Iain  B73
Winbolt, S E  A36
Winckles, Henry A  H22
Windsor, A H  M22
Wingfield, Mary Ann  L372
Winter, A E H  A245, A246
Wischnia, Bob  M148
Withers, Bob  B107
Wodehouse, P G  L200-201, L211
Woff, Richard  A30
Wolf, Susan  L162
Wolfenden Committee on Sport  B187
Wolff, F F  A287
Wolverton AC  A228
Women's Amateur Athletic Association  E100, F100, H8, H29, M43
Women's Cross Country and Race Walking Association  F155, H43
Wood, Abraham  A121, 124
Wood, C G  A150, A182
Wood, Christopher  L52
Wood, D M  J64
Wood, John George  E15, E176, 181
Wood, L S  L264
Wood, Mike  C102
Wood, Ness *(designer)*  B126
Woodard, Christopher R  K19
Wooderson, Sydney  A91, A181-182, B188-190, B213, C152, C170, F2, F4, L293-294, L373
Woodeson, Peggy J  D34, D37
Woodford Green AC  A275
Woods, B D  E167

Woods, Gwenllian *(illustrator)*  A305
Woods, Paula  I16
Woods, Rex  A305, B219
Woods, Rex Salisbury  A287, B191, D23, E77, K18
Woodward, Cleveland J *(illustrator)*  L53
Wooldridge, Ian  B149, B218, L257, L327
Woollaston, A M  E75
Workman, W H  A76
Woronoff, Jon  C63
Wottle, Dave  E143
Wotton, Arthur E  E66, E94
Wrenn, R D  E37
Wright, F A  A6
Wright, Graeme  B215, B220
Wright, Michael  I17
Wrighton, J D  E120
Wynne-Edwards, J R  F221

# Y

Yale University AC  A409
Yasser, Raymond L  H47
Yates, Irene  L273
Yates, J  L298
Yates, Matthew  B266
Yeomans, Alastair  C231
Yeoumans, A T  E44
Yorkshire Race Walking Club  A276
Young, Colin  A230
Young, David A  A283, A289
Young, David C  C78
Young, Derrick  B213
Young, Gavin *(illustrator)*  C235
Young, John  L323
Young, Tony Brett  L394
Younger, Calton *(illustrator)*  F103

# Z

Zaharias, Mildred 'Babe' Didrikson *See* Didrikson-Zaharias, Mildred 'Babe'
Zaidenberg, Arthur  L364
Zamperini, Louis  B193
Zátopek, Emil  B151, B194-195, B207-208, B212-213, B220, B224, B247, B265, C171, L287, L295
Zátopkova, Dana  C48
Zelinsky, Paul O *(illustrator)*  L128

# Title Index

# C

# D

# E

Eamonn McCabe L383

Early women's athletics A138

East Grinstead and District Athletic Club A197

East London Schools' Athletics Association handbook M36

The Eastenders (Heaton Harriers, 1890-1990) A208

Eddie Campbell B32

Edinburgh education and society series A343

Edinburgh Southern Harriers jubilee year A319

Edinburgh Southern Harriers, the story of the club 1897-1972 A320

An edition of Annalia Dubrensia and a history of the Cotswold Games A303

Eighty years awheel S206

Eighty years of Shaftesbury Harriers 1890-1970 A258

Elegy on the death of James Fleming L271

An elementary course of gymnastic exercises intended to develope and improve the physical powers of man E249

An elementary course of gymnastic exercises with the report made to the Medical Faculty of Paris on the subject, and a new and complete treatise on the art of swimming E250

The emergence of the black athlete in America A418

Emil Zátopek in photographs B194

Empire Games A395

Empire Games athletics C267

The encyclopaedia of athletics M128-131

Encyclopædia of British athletics records M61

The encyclopaedia of sport M134

The encyclopædia of sport & games M135

Encyclopaedia of sport and sportsmen M136

The encyclopedia of sports stamps L414

Encyclopædia of track and field athletics M132

Endurance running F125

Endurance running events F128

English Cross-Country Union handbook, 1953-54 M34

English Schools Athletic Association handbook M39

Enjoying track and field sports E157

The enormous radio, and other stories L86

EP sport series G11

Equestrians L223

Eric H Liddell B114

Eric Liddell B118

Eric Liddell: born to run B116

Eric Liddell: God's athlete B117

Eric Liddell: the making of an athlete and the training of a missionary B112

ESH A321

The essential guide to the Highland Games A344

Essex County Amateur Athletic Association A199

The ethics of athletics L353

European junior handbook M121

The Everest Marathon F199, F201, F203, F208-209, F213, F215

Everest the easy way F196

Every sport, incorporating The athlete M197

Everyone's a winner A167

Everyone's guide to distance running F130, F138

Evidence of a misspent youth B150

The evolution of the Olympic Games, 1829 BC-1914 AD C7

Exercise J13

Exercise in education and medicine J10

Exercises for athletes E67

Eyes towards Helsinki A99

Eyewitness guides *(series)* C94

Eyewitness readers; Level 4 L347

# F

Facilities for athletics (track and field) I9, I12

Facts in athletics A115

Fair play A148

The fall of Troy L245

Famous athletes B197-198

Famous footballers and athletes B196

Fanny Blankers-Koen at Wembley L271

The fast men L50

Faster, higher, further C48

Faster, higher, stronger L365

The fastest men on earth B230

The fastest runner L273

Fatima B183

Fearsome tales for fiendish kids L210

Felice Hansch in sport 1922-1934 B84

Fell and hill running F210

Fellrunner L39

Fencer L223

Festivals, games, and amusements, ancient and modern A33

A few practical hints to amateurs on training for walking, running and other athletic sports E27

The fib, and other stories L209

The field *(1856)* M158

Field / *Ward* C71

Field & track athletics E54

Field athletics / *Anthony* G14

Field athletics / *Blue* G16

Field athletics / *Johnson* G11, G18, G21, G23

Field athletics / *Lease* G22

Field athletics / *Merrison* G19

Field events G6

Field events: technique, strategy and training G5

The fifty finest athletes of the 20th century B235

Fifty legends of British sport B259

Fifty years L299

Fifty years of AAA championships A84

Fifty years of athletics A313

Fifty years of Irish athletics A359

Fifty years of my life in the world of sport at home and abroad B8

Fifty years of progress, 1880-1930 A79

# G

# H

# I

# N

# O

# P

Soviet sport: mirror of Soviet society  A413
Spalding's athletic library *(series)*  E194, F60-61, F63, F66, F95, G67, M49
Sparks *(series)*  L168
Speaking from experience *(series)*  L329
The Special Olympics  C54
Special Olympics: the competitive aspect – a study of Irish participants  C106
Special Olympics: United Kingdom, Sheffield 1993  C61
The spectator's handbook  F38
Speed  F87
Speed trap  B100
Spiked shoes  L170
The spiritual Quixote  L21
A split second  L203
Sport *(1880)*  M171
Sport / *Wheeler*  L324
Sport: a guide to governing bodies  H61
Sport & leisure for the disabled series  E234
Sport and leisure in Victorian Barrow  A153
Sport and physical education in China  A422
Sport and place  A103
Sport & play *(1886)*  M174
Sport & play *(1901)*  M184
Sport and recreation in Ancient Greece  A22
Sport and society in ancient Greece  A29
Sport and the global system  A403
Sport and the making of Britain  A92
Sport at home and abroad  L300
Sport, culture and ideology  K40
Sport for the million  L309
Sport in action *(series)*  F52, G15
Sport in Britain  A87
Sport in focus  L384
Sport in Greece and Rome  A14
Sport in Soviet society  A414
Sport in the global society *(series)*  B182
Sport in the movies  L359
Sport international  M103
Sport is my life  B35
Sport is my lifeline  L306
Sport masters *(series)*  E162
The sport of race walking  F234
Sport: official British Olympic Association report of the 1980 Games  C207
Sport on film and video  L363
Sportascrapiana  A115-116
The sportfolio  L374
Sportfolio Allsport  L387
Sportfolio: visions of Allsport  L387
Sporting and athletic records  M48
The sporting and athletic register, 1908  M9
Sporting anecdotes  A51-53
The sporting annual  M6
The sporting annual, illustrated  M23
A sporting century 1863-1963  B31
The Sporting Chronicle annual  M17

Sporting colours  A420
Sporting days  L303
Sporting doubles  B258
Sporting events  L339
The sporting Fifth at Ripley's  L146
Sporting gazette  M161
Sporting heritage series  M155
The sporting house  L115
Sporting intelligence extraordinary!  L279
The sporting Irish  B211
The sporting life *(1859)*  M159
The sporting life / *Jenkins*  L101
Sporting life: an anthology of British sporting prints  L369
The Sporting Life companion, containing Sporting Almanack for …  M18
Sporting literature  L102
The sporting magazine  M156
The sporting mirror  M172
Sporting notions of present days and past selected from the 'Referee'  L288
A sporting pilgrimage  A74
Sporting relations  L237
Sporting rhapsody  L286
Sporting sensations  L331
Sporting sketches  M178
Sporting success in ancient Greece and Rome  A47
The sporting word  L400
Sports and freedom  A412
Sports and games  A165
Sports and games in the ancient world  A21
Sports and pastimes  B264
Sports and pastimes in English literature  L264
Sports and pastimes of Scotland, historically illustrated  A330
The sports and pastimes of the people of England  A143-145
Sports and recreations in the Royal Navy  A311
Sports beat  L289
Sports buildings and playing fields  I6
Sports Council guidance notes *(series)*  I20-21
Sports Council Information Centre information series  H61, M143, M147
Sports day / *Butterworth & Inkpen*  L121
Sports day / *Davis*  L136
Sports day / *Heine*  L273
The sports day / *Murray*  L164
Sports day / *Richardson, Whitehouse & Wilkinson*  L180
Sports day / *Rogers*  L181
Sports day at Scumbagg School  L163
Sports day for Charlie  L104
Sports facts *(series)*  E173, M86
Sports fiction series  L111
The sports for schools series  E216
Sports for the Caribbean *(series)*  F44, G9
Sports ground construction  I8
Sports ground construction specifications  I11
Sports grounds and buildings  I1

# U

# V

# W

The W G athletic weekly  M186
W G Grace  B76
Wakefield District Harriers and Athletic Club  A271
Walk! it could change your life  F237
Walk a crooked mile  B104
Walkers  A124
Walker's manly exercises  E8-9, E11, E13
Walking  F226
Walking, and the principles of training  F227
Walking for road and track  F231-232
Walter Rye, 1843-1929  B161
Walter Rye, athlete and antiquary  B161
Warne's pleasure book for boys  L213
Warne's recreation books *(series)*  F36, G2
Watford Harriers  A272
The way to win on track and field  E92
We run because we must  L102
Weight training for athletics  E104, E113
Well played Scotts  L138
The Welsh AAA history and records to 1955  A349
Welsh athletics …  M74
Welsh athletics annual  M77
Welsh cross country 1996 centenary year  A350
The Welsh three thousand foot challenges  F224
The Welsh Three Thousands  F223
Wembley  I23
Wembley 1923-1973  I10
Wembley presents 22 years of sport  I2
Wembley presents 25 years of sport  I3
West Norwood Cemetery's sportsmen  B267
Westbury Harriers  A273
Westbury Harriers 75th anniversary  A274
The 'Western Mail' Empire Games book  C269
Wexford athletics  A367
The Wharton medal  L117
What they don't tell you about the Olympics  C104
What's what in athletics?  E122
Wheel life  M184
Wheelchair sports  E169
When my friend Anita runs  L238
The whip hand  L179
Whitaker's Olympic almanack  C105
Whittlesey House sports series  E84-85, E93
Who's who in British athletics  B233
Who's who in world athletics (annual)  B260
Who's who of UK & GB international athletes 1896-1939  B262
Why? – the science of athletics  E77
Wild trails to far horizons  B57
Wilderness  L64
William Penny Brookes and the Olympic connection  B23
Wills book of excellence *(series)*  C42
The Wilson Run  A282
Winchester House, 12th February, 1887  L266

Wind velocity measurements in athletic stadia, and the effects of winds on sprint performances  I26
Winner stakes all  B60
The winner's wreath  L168
The winning edge  L332
The winning experience  J42
Winning his 'Y'  L106
The winning mind  B9
Winning running  F134
Winning without drugs  K45
Winning women  L381
Wireless Watson  L186
Wirral gleanings  B69
With the skin of their teeth  L318
Wobble to death  L44
Women and sport  A134
Women in sport: a select bibliography  M153
Women in sport: issues and controversies  A135
Women who run  L275
Women's Amateur Athletic Association: constitution, laws, rules for competitions  H8
Women's athletics *(1968)*  M212
Women's athletics / *Pallett*  A129
Women's Cross Country and Race Walking Association laws and competition rules revised to 1976  H43
Women's tug of war at Lough Arrow  L275
Woodford Green Athletic Club, 1908-1968  A275
Works / *Statius*  L252
World athletic championships  C62
World athletics  M209
World athletics handbook 1970  M42
World cross country championships, 1999  A397
A world history of track and field athletics, 1864-1964  A388
The world in my diary  C160
World junior athletics annual 1999/2000  M126
World of athletics …  M14
The world of marathons  F174
The world of school  L142
World of sport *(series)*  F53, G16
World record breakers in track and field athletics  M124
World sporting records  M15
World Sports international athletics annual  M99
World sports: the official organ of the British Olympic Association  M195
World youth athletics handbook  M126
The world's all sports who's who for 1950  B201
World's all time best performers  M105
Wrestler  L223
Wrestliana  G66
Wunderpants  L208

# Y

A year in the life of Linford Christie  B43
The year's sport  M21
Yorkshire Race Walking Club  A276

The young athlete / *Jackson*  E243
The young athlete / *Tisdall & Sherie*  E200
The young athlete / *Tomlin*  M58
The young athlete: an athletic handbook for beginners
  E201
Young athlete and junior international yearbook 1968
  M12
The young athlete's companion  E210
The Young England library *(series)*  E251
Young Hendry  L148
Young magpie library *(series)*  L140
A young man in a hurry, and other stories  L85
Young Olympic champions  B205
Young runner  L111
The young sportsman  E38
Young sportsman series  F103

Young Telegraph *(series)*  C80
Your book *(series)*  E213
Your book of athletics  E213
Your first book of athletics  E232
You're on your own  L335
Youth coach award  D49
The 'YZ' book of the Olympics  C17

# Z

Zátopek, the marathon victor  B195
Ziggy's Olympic book *(series)*  C96-97
Zola: the autobiography of Zola Budd  B28
Zola: the official biography  B27

# Subject Index